THE CHALLENGE OF FISCAL DISPARITIES FOR STATE AND LOCAL GOVERNMENTS

STUDIES IN FISCAL FEDERALISM AND STATE–LOCAL FINANCE

General Editor: Wallace E. Oates, *Professor of Economics, University of Maryland and University Fellow, Resources for the Future, USA*

This important series is designed to make a significant contribution to the development of the principles and practices of state–local finance. It includes both theoretical and empirical work. International in scope, it addresses issues of current and future concern in both East and West and in developed and developing countries.

The main purpose of the series is to create a forum for the publication of high quality work and to show how economic analysis can make a contribution to understanding the role of local finance in fiscal federalism in the late 20th century.

Titles in the series include:

Financing Decentralized Expenditures
An International Comparison of Grants
Edited by Ehtisham Ahmad

The Fiscal Behavior of State and Local Governments
Selected Papers of Harvey S. Rosen
Harvey S. Rosen

Financing Federal Systems
The Selected Essays of Edward M. Gramlich
Edward M. Gramlich

Local Government Tax and Land Use Policies in the United States
Understanding the Links
Helen F. Ladd

Fiscal Federalism and State–Local Finance
The Scandinavian Perspective
Jørn Rattsø

The Challenge of Fiscal Disparities for State and Local Governments
The Selected Essays of Helen F. Ladd
Helen F. Ladd

The Challenge of Fiscal Disparities for State and Local Governments

The Selected Essays of Helen F. Ladd

Helen F. Ladd

Professor of Public Studies and Economics, Duke University, USA

STUDIES IN FISCAL FEDERALISM AND STATE–LOCAL FINANCE

Edward Elgar
Cheltenham, UK • Northampton, MA, USA

© Helen F. Ladd, 1999

All rights reserved. No part of this publication may be reproduced, stored in a retrieval system or transmitted in any form or by any means, electronic, mechanical or photocopying, recording, or otherwise without the prior permission of the publisher.

Published by
Edward Elgar Publishing Limited
Glensanda House
Montpellier Parade
Cheltenham
Glos GL50 1UA
UK

Edward Elgar Publishing, Inc.
6 Market Street
Northampton
Massachusetts 01060
USA

A catalogue record for this book
is available from the British Library

Library of Congress Cataloguing in Publication Data

Ladd, Helen F.
 The challenge of fiscal disparities for state and local
governments : the selected essays / of Helen F. Ladd.
 (Studies in fiscal federalism and state–local
finance)
 Includes bibliographical references.
 1. Local finance—United States. 2. Municipal finance—United
States. I. Title. II. Series.
HJ9141.L33 1999
336′.01473—dc21   98–45784
                                                                CIP

ISBN 1 85898 687 7

Printed and bound in Great Britain by MPG Books Ltd, Bodmin, Cornwall

To Ted, with love

Contents

Acknowledgements ix
Introduction xi

PART I MEASURING LOCAL FISCAL DISPARITIES AND INTERGOVERNMENTAL AID

1. 'Local Education Expenditures, Fiscal Capacity, and the Composition of the Property Tax Base', *National Tax Journal*, **XXVIII** (2), June 1975, 145–58 — 3
2. 'State Aid to Offset Fiscal Disparities Across Communities', with Katharine L. Bradbury, Mark Perrault, Andrew Reschovsky and John Yinger, *National Tax Journal*, **XXXVII** (2), June 1984, 151–70 — 17
3. 'Measuring Disparities in the Fiscal Condition of Local Governments' in *Fiscal Equalization for State and Local Government Finance*, John E. Anderson (ed.), 1994, Greenwood Publishing Group, 21–53, references — 37
4. 'The Case for Equalizing Aid', with John Yinger, *National Tax Journal*, **XLVII** (1), March 1994, 211–24 — 71
5. 'The Determinants of State Assistance to Central Cities', with John Yinger, *National Tax Journal*, **XLII** (4), December 1990, 413–28 — 85
6. 'Which Level of Government Should Assist the Poor?', with Fred C. Doolitle, *National Tax Journal*, **XXXV** (3), September 1982, 323–36 — 101
7. 'The State Aid Decision: Changes in State Aid to Local Governments, 1982–87', *National Tax Journal*, **XLIV** (4, Part 2), December 1991, 477–96 — 115

PART II TAX STRUCTURE AND TAX LIMITATIONS

8. 'State Tax Structure and Multiple Policy Objectives', with William M. Gentry, *National Tax Journal*, **XLVII** (4), December 1994, 747–72 — 137
9. 'Mimicking of Local Tax Burdens Among Neighboring Counties', *Public Finance Quarterly*, **20** (4), October 1992, 450–67 — 163
10. 'Property Tax Revaluation and Tax Levy Growth Revisited', *Journal of Urban Economics*, **30**, 1991, 83–99 — 181
11. 'State Responses to the TRA86 Revenue Windfalls: A New Test of the Flypaper Effect', *Journal of Policy Analysis and Management*, **12** (1), Winter 1993, 82–103 — 198
12. 'An Economic Evaluation of State Limitations on Local Taxing and Spending Powers', *National Tax Journal*, **XXXI** (1), March 1978, 1–18 — 220

13 'Why Voters Support Tax Limitations: Evidence from Massachusetts' Proposition 2½', with Julie Boatright Wilson, *National Tax Journal*, **XXXV** (2), June 1982, 121–48   238
14 'Who Supports Tax Limitations: Evidence from Massachusetts' Proposition 2½', with Julie Boatright Wilson, *Journal of Policy Analysis and Management*, **2** (2), Winter 1983, 256–79   266
15 'The Tax Expenditure Concept After 25 Years' in *Proceedings of the Eighty-Seventh Annual Conference on Taxation*, Columbus, Ohio: National Tax Association, 1995, 50–57   290

PART III TAX POLICY AND LAND USE

16 'Fiscal Impacts of Local Population Growth: A Conceptual and Empirical Analysis', *Regional Science and Urban Economics*, **24**, 1994, 661–86   301
17 'Population Growth, Density and the Costs of Providing Public Services', *Urban Studies*, **29** (2), 1992, 273–95   327
18 'City Taxes and Property Tax Bases', with Katharine L. Bradbury, *National Tax Journal*, **XLI** (4), December 1998, 503–23   350
19 'Spatially Targeted Economic Development Strategies: Do They Work?', *Cityscape: A Journal of Policy Development and Research*, **1** (1), August 1994, 193–218   371

PART IV SCHOOL FINANCE

20 'Statewide Taxation of Nonresidential Property for Education', with Edward W. Harris, *Journal of Education Finance*, **21**, Summer 1995, 103–22   399
21 'How School Districts Respond to Fiscal Constraint' in *Selected Papers in School Finance*, National Center for Education Statistics, 1996, 39–59   419
22 'How and Why Money Matters: An Analysis of Alabama Schools', with Ronald F. Ferguson in *Holding Schools Accountable: Performance-Based Reform in Education*, Helen F. Ladd (ed.), Brookings Institution, 1996, 265–98   440

Name index   475

Acknowledgements

The author and publishers wish to thank the following who have kindly given permission for the use of copyright material.

Academic Press Inc. for article: 'Property Tax Revaluation and Tax Levy Growth Revisited', *Journal of Urban Economics*, **30**, 1991, 83–99.

Brookings Institution for extract: 'How and Why Money Matters: An Analysis of Alabama Schools', with Ronald F. Ferguson in Helen F. Ladd (ed.), *Holding Schools Accountable: Performance-Based Reform in Education*, 1996, 265–98.

Carfax Publishing Ltd. for article: 'Population Growth, Density and the Costs of Providing Public Services', *Urban Studies*, **29** (2), 1992, 273–95.

Elsevier Science Ltd. for article: 'Fiscal Impacts of Local Population Growth: A Conceptual and Empirical Analysis', *Regional Science and Urban Economics*, **24**, 1994, 661–86.

Greenwood Publishing Group for extract: 'Measuring Disparities in the Fiscal Condition of Local Governments' in John E. Anderson (ed.), *Fiscal Equalization for State and Local Government Finance*, 1994, 21–53, references.

John Wiley and Sons Inc. for articles: 'State Responses to the TRA86 Revenue Windfalls: A New Test of the Flypaper Effect', *Journal of Policy Analysis and Management*, **12** (1), Winter 1993, 82–103; 'Who Supports Tax Limitations? Evidence from Massachusetts' Proposition $2^1/_2$', with Julie Boatright Wilson, *Journal of Policy Analysis and Management*, **2** (2), Winter 1983, 256–79.

Journal of Education Finance for article: 'Statewide Taxation of Nonresidential Property for Education', with Edward W. Harris, **21**, Summer 1995, 103–22.

National Center for Education Statistics for article: 'How School Districts Respond to Fiscal Constraint' in *Selected Papers in School Finance*, 1996, 39–59.

National Tax Association for articles: 'Local Education Expenditures, Fiscal Capacity, and the Composition of the Property Tax Base', *National Tax Journal*, **XXVIII** (2), June 1975, 145–58; 'State Aid to Offset Fiscal Disparities Across Communities', with Katharine L. Bradbury, Mark Perrault, Andrew Reschovsky and John Yinger, *National Tax Journal*, **XXXVII** (2), June 1984, 151–70; 'The Case for Equalizing Aid', with John Yinger, *National Tax Journal*, **XLVII** (1), March 1994, 211–24; 'The Determinants of State Assistance to Central Cities', with John Yinger, *National Tax*

Journal, **XLII** (4), December 1990, 413–28; 'Which Level of Government Should Assist the Poor?', with Fred C. Doolittle, *National Tax Journal*, **XXXV** (3), September 1982, 323–36; 'The State Aid Decision: Changes in State Aid to Local Governments, 1982–1987', *National Tax Journal*, **XLIV** (4, Part 2), December 1991, 477–96; 'State Tax Structure and Multiple Policy Objectives', with William M. Gentry, *National Tax Journal*, **XLVII** (4), December 1994, 747–72; 'An Economic Evaluation of State Limitations on Local Taxing and Spending Powers', *National Tax Journal*, **XXXI** (1), March 1978, 1–18; 'Why Voters Support Tax Limitations: Evidence from Massachusetts' Proposition $2^1/_2$', with Julie Boatright Wilson, *National Tax Journal*, **XXXV** (2), June 1982, 121–48; 'City Taxes and Property Tax Bases', with Katherine L. Bradbury, *National Tax Journal*, **XLI** (4), December 1988, 503–23; 'The Tax Expenditure Concept After 25 Years' in *Proceedings of the Eighty-Seventh Annual Conference on Taxation*, 1995, 50–57.

US Department of Housing and Urban Development, Office of Policy Development and Research for article: 'Spatially Targeted Economic Development Strategies: Do They Work?', *Cityscape: A Journal of Policy Development and Research*, **1** (1), August 1994, 193–218.

Public Finance Quarterly for article: 'Mimicking of Local Tax Burdens Among Neighboring Counties', **20** (4), October 1992, 450–67.

Every effort has been made to trace all the copyright holders but if any have been inadvertently overlooked the publishers will be pleased to make the necessary arrangements at the first opportunity.

Introduction

As a graduate student at Harvard in the early 1970s, I had the privilege of working with Richard Musgrave, one of the giants in the field of public finance. He and others at Harvard exposed me to the significant work in the field, most of which focused on taxes and spending at the national level. However, at that time, some productive new work on the taxes and spending of subnational governments was beginning to emerge.

One strand of work was inspired by Charles Tiebout's seminal 1956 article in which he argued that a system of local governments would generate efficient provision of local public services. During the late 1960s and early 1970s, economists at Princeton University and elsewhere were examining the assumptions underlying the Tiebout model, with particular attention to the role of the local property tax. The use by local governments of property taxes rather than the lump sum benefit taxes postulated in the Tiebout model rendered questionable Tiebout's conclusion about efficiency. In 1969, Wallace Oates published the first empirical investigation of the Tiebout mechanism which appeared to indicate that people do indeed vote with their feet, and one of his students, Bruce Hamilton, developed a model in which local zoning could transform the property tax into a benefit tax of the type postulated by Tiebout (Hamilton, 1975).

The second strand was the innovative research by Peter Mieszkowski which would alter how economists viewed the incidence of the property tax. While acknowledging the 'old view' that the property tax was regressive, Mieszkowski drew on the much older views of Harry G. Brown who argued in the 1920s that the property tax was a tax on capital and Arnold Harberger's general equilibrium approach to tax incidence to develop the 'new view' of the property tax (see Mieszkowski, 1972). According to this view, the burden of a nationally uniform property tax would be borne by the owners of capital and hence would generate a progressive burden while differences across districts would still generate a regressive impact through their effects on the prices of housing and other local goods.

The third strand was the modelling of local government expenditures as exemplified by two innovative empirical papers in the *American Economic Review* (Borcherding and Deacon, 1972, and Bergstrom and Goodman, 1973). By adapting the standard model of consumer choice in the private sector to the public sector, these papers justified the use for empirical investigation of the median voter model and demonstrated the potential for productive empirical research in this area. In the policy arena, the importance of better modelling of the local expenditure decision was highlighted by the 1971 Serrano v. Priest Court case in California that challenged the use of the property tax as a revenue source for schools.

As a young economist interested in pursuing applied, policy-oriented research based on a strong conceptual foundation, I found the new work on local governments appealing and full of potential. I launched my professional research career by writing an evaluation of the local property tax for a volume on taxes edited by Richard Musgrave (not included here). My view in 1973, and the one that I maintain to this day, is that the property tax is a far better tax than the public and many economists had at that time acknowledged. In writing that chapter, I came to appreciate one of the major features related to the analysis of local taxes: it is extremely difficult, and often not desirable, to separate the analysis of a local tax from the expenditure side of the budget. That insight served as the basis for my dissertation, *Local Public Expenditures and the Composition of the Property Tax Base* (1974), and for much of my subsequent research.

For the purposes of this volume I have divided my articles into four overlapping categories. The first, which evolved directly from my dissertation research, addresses the concept and measurement of fiscal disparities across local jurisdictions and the design of intergovernmental aid programmes to offset them, themes that I have continued to address in various forms throughout my career. The second category is the design of taxes and tax structures. Included here are articles on the mix of taxes at the state level, the structure of particular taxes, and tax limitation measures. The third category is the interaction between taxes and land use. Articles in this category address both the fiscal effects of rapid population growth and the use of tax subsidies to promote growth in distressed urban areas. The fourth category includes a few of my articles on education finance.

Part I Measuring disparities and designing intergovernmental aid programmes
Local governments differ greatly in their ability to raise local revenue to meet the expenditure demands placed upon them. In my first journal article, Chapter 1 on 'Local Education Expenditures, Fiscal Capacity, and the Composition of the Property Tax Base' (1975), I explored the meaning of a local school district's capacity to raise revenue for local schools. The California school finance decision had drawn attention to the heavy reliance of school districts on local property taxes and to interdistrict disparities in the total property tax base per pupil. Implicit was the view that expenditures are closely linked to the total property tax base and that the breakdown of the base among commercial, residential and industrial property was not consequential. Drawing on the new approaches to modelling local public spending, I set out to show that the composition of the tax base mattered. In particular I focused on the effects of commercial and industrial property on the 'tax price' faced by local voters and hence on their decisions about how much to spend on education. Using data for the 78 communities in the Boston metropolitan area, I estimated a median voter model for education which allowed industrial property (which is geographically more footloose) to have a different effect than commercial property on the ability of local districts to raise revenue for education. The estimates of fiscal capacity derived from this behavioural approach differed in some significant ways from the simpler measure, the per pupil size of the property tax base. In particular, the use of the simpler measure tends to overstate the capacity of districts with a lot of low income households.

Disparities on the revenue side are clearly not the whole picture. A government's ability to meet the expenditure need of its citizens depends not only on its ability to raise revenue but also the magnitude of the pressure it faces on the expenditure side of its budget. Over the next few years, I teamed with various other scholars including John Yinger, Andrew Reschovsky, Katharine Bradbury and Ronald Ferguson to develop conceptually sound approaches for measuring both the revenue-raising capacity and expenditure need of local governments. John Yinger and I used these measures in our evaluation of the fiscal problems of US cities which appeared as *America's Ailing Cities: Fiscal Health and the Design of Urban Policy* (1991), and various combinations of us used them in the design of intergovernmental aid programmes in Massachusetts and Minnesota. In Massachusetts, a few of us worked closely with Governor Dukakis' Task Force on intergovernmental aid in the early 1980s to help the state implement a regression-based approach consistent with our newly developed conceptual framework. This approach is described in Chapter 2 in our 1984 article 'State Aid to Offset Fiscal Disparities Across Communities'. In Minnesota we worked with a legislative special commission to rethink that state's approach to aiding its cities. In contrast to Massachusetts, Minnesota did not implement the approach, but there is little doubt that our report had a significant impact on the nature of subsequent discussions about aid to local governments in that state.

Our preferred approach to measuring the fiscal condition of local governments is conceptually consistent with the economists' model of the local spending decision. Since that decision is made by resident voters, we chose to make the measure of revenue-raising capacity comparable across districts by asking how much revenue each jurisdiction could raise if it imposed a uniform burden (defined as a fixed percentage of resident income) on residents, augmented by the amount that would be 'exported' to nonresidents. Although this approach differs somewhat from my 1975 approach to measuring capacity, it still accounts for the differing contributions of the various components of the property tax base. Our approach differs more significantly from the alternative, more common, approach advocated by the US Advisory Commission on Intergovernmental Relations which started from the assumption of a uniform tax rate. On the expenditure side, we start by estimating an expenditure model which includes as 'cost factors' a variety of characteristics of the jurisdiction that are outside the control of local public officials. Jurisdictions that have above-average values of the cost factors are then deemed to have above-average costs, and hence above-average expenditure need. This approach builds on the distinction between outcomes and intermediate products produced by the public sector as developed most clearly by Bradford, Malt and Oates (1969). The requirement that cost factors be outside the immediate control of local officials is particularly important when the measure is to be used as the basis for giving aid to offset disparities; if local officials can affect the measure, they would have inappropriate incentives to do so in a way to generate additional aid. No such incentives are implicit in our approach.

Not all analysts accept this approach. Others build on the approach developed for states by the US Advisory Commission on Intergovernmental Relations by measuring local capacity as the amount of revenue generated by a representative tax system and by measuring expenditure need as the average spending per capita in each functional area adjusted by factors to account for the workloads faced by each jurisdiction. Chapter 3, 'Measuring Disparities in the Fiscal Condition of Local Governments' (1994), compares and contrasts the different approaches and uses six major studies, including our Minnesota study, to illustrate them.

My attention to the technical problem of measuring local fiscal disparities reflects my normative view that higher levels of government should try to make more equal the ability of lower-level jurisdictions to meet the expenditure needs of their residents.

John Yinger and I spell out the equity arguments for intergovernmental aid in Chapter 4, 'The Case for Equalizing Aid'. The central theme of the paper is that the appropriate design for an equalizing aid programme depends on the equity objective of the donor government. We place equity objectives into two classes: categorical equity, which relates to public sector spending either on specific functions or on all functions, and distributional equity, which is aimed at equalizing the real income of local residents. We then show how aid programmes can be designed to achieve the various objectives. This paper contributes to the literature by highlighting the similarities and differences among aid formulas in a common framework, by incorporating cost considerations (which are equivalent to differences in expenditure need) into the various formulas, and by highlighting the role of capitalization in the discussion of equalizing real incomes.

An additional policy-relevant question that emerged from my research with John Yinger on the changing fiscal condition of large US cities was whether state governments directed intergovernmental assistance to the neediest cities. We addressed this question empirically in Chapter 5, 'The Determinants of State Assistance to Central Cities'. Our innovation was to define state assistance broadly to include both intergovernmental grants and institutional assistance, such as granting a city access to a tax with export potential or state takeover of city service responsibilities. Based on this broad definition, John Yinger and I found that states did in fact target assistance to the neediest cities. In addition we found that states regarded grants and institutional assistance as substitutes, a finding that highlights the importance for research of understanding the institutional arrangements within which state and local governments operate.

The final two papers in Part I were motivated by changes in fiscal federalism proposed or enacted during the Reagan administration. I wrote Chapter 6 with Fred Doolittle, 'Which Level of Government Should Assist the Poor?' (1982) in response to President Reagan's proposal to devolve responsibility for income support programmes to state and local governments, a proposal that was not adopted then but has recently been implemented in modified form by the 1996 reform of welfare. Writing this introduction now in the late 1990s, I find myself wishing that this 1982 paper had had more of an impact on current policy makers in Washington. The article examines in some detail the argument that the financing of redistributive functions such as welfare should be turned over to the states and concludes that in general they should not be. The conclusion is based on a careful consideration of the spatial dimension of concern about the poor and macroeconomic conditions which make the states inappropriate supporters of the safety net during recessions. The paper thus affirms the long-standing view of economists that the federal government should take primary fiscal responsibility for assisting poor people. However, allowing the states to supplement the national programmes may be appropriate; and, in some cases, such as with assistance programmes that provide direct services, it may make sense to have state or local governments administer the programme. It is interesting to note the significant devolution of managerial responsibilities down to the county level currently occurring as part of the 1996 welfare reform act. Given its emphasis on providing job training and job search services for poor people, this devolution of administrative responsibilities makes sense. The problem with the 1996 reform, in my view, is that the shift to block grant financing of welfare left the states to bear too much of the marginal cost of expanding assistance to poor people during downturns in the economy.

As a consequence of federal budget cuts during the early 1980s, the federal government significantly reduced its direct aid to local governments, thereby reversing the trends of the previous 15 years when it had dramatically increased federal aid to cities and had initiated general revenue sharing with local governments. A key policy issue was whether the state governments would offset the cuts in federal aid by providing additional state aid to local jurisdictions. Addressing this question in Chapter 7 forced me to consider why states ever provide aid to their local jurisdictions. To do so, I postulated that state policy makers try to maximize a welfare function that includes direct state services and the level of local services net of taxes as perceived by state policy makers. The innovative part of this model is the introduction of the perceived level of local services, where the perception of state policy makers depends on how the services are financed. For example, state policy makers might place less value on locally provided services financed by the federal government than those financed by the state government. Based on changes in state aid to local governments between 1982 and 1987, the analysis generated the striking result that the state governments had offset many of the cutbacks in federal aid to local communities. Other interesting results were that the elasticity of state aid with respect to own-source resources appears to be less than one and that higher federal aid to states does not induce states to be more generous to their local governments.

Part II Tax structure and tax limitation measures
In the absence of much scholarly attention to how states might determine the most appropriate mix of taxes (other than in the abstract literature on optimal tax theory), the prevailing view within the policy community was that propounded by the US Advisory Commission on Intergovernmental Relations (ACIR). The ACIR argued that state tax structures should be balanced in the sense that, by analogy to a three-legged stool, each state should rely equally on income, sales and property tax revenue. While that view had a lot of superficial appeal (and probably did some good in encouraging some states to expand their use of broad based taxes), I found it conceptually unsatisfying. It was not clear to me why states should aim for a similar mix of taxes given their differing values and differing economies. Hence, in an early policy paper (not included here) I argued that the concept of balance among revenue sources should be replaced by the concept of balance among policy goals and I emphasized the importance of variation in state economies. Subsequently, William Gentry and I formalized this approach by developing it within the context of a portfolio choice model of state tax structure. Our paper, Chapter 8, 'State Tax Structure and Multiple Policy Objectives', provided a viable alternative to the more abstract literature on optimal taxation as a way of providing guidance to states on the appropriate mix of their taxes. One interesting finding to emerge from our analysis was the dominance of income taxes in the optimal portfolios of two very different states, North Carolina and Massachusetts. This similarity notwithstanding, the significant differences in the economies of the two states and in the characteristics of their taxes led to different optimal tax structures and different policy tradeoffs. These findings

argued against the policy prescription that states should have similar tax structures based on equal tax shares.

Another contribution to the small but growing literature on the determination of local taxes is Chapter 9, 'Mimicking of Local Tax Burdens Among Neighboring Counties'. Although not discussed much in the academic literature, tax mimicking is often mentioned by policy makers as a justification for particular tax decisions. For example, local officials might defend a decision to raise the rate of the local sales tax on the grounds that the new rate would not be out of line with those in neighbouring jurisdictions. Data on all large US counties provided a good test of the mimicking hypothesis. The degree of clustering of tax burdens among neighbouring counties within metropolitan areas compared to that among non-neighbouring counties within states, and coefficients on the neighbourhood tax variable in various regression equations provided solid evidence of tax mimicking. In particular, a $1 increase in the taxes in neighbouring counties leads to about a $0.50 increase in taxes in the subject county, a finding that is remarkably consistent with estimates from a cross-state study of mimicking with respect to the income tax (Case, 1993).

I have also examined how the structure of individual taxes affects the behaviour of public officials or taxpayers. For example, in two separate papers, one on Massachusetts and one on North Carolina, I used the natural experiment of district-wide revaluation to examine the extent to which revaluation of property made it possible for local officials to exploit the confusion that arose about the magnitude of tax payments to raise property tax levies by more than they otherwise would. Included here as Chapter 10 is the more recent paper based on North Carolina data: 'Property Tax Revaluation and Tax Levy Growth Revisited'. My finding in both studies of some evidence of discretionary behaviour in the short run implies that the demand-based model of local tax decisions may work best as a long run equilibrium model. With respect to policy, this research supports the conclusion that fiscal institutions matter and provides some basis for formal truth-in-taxation laws or full disclosure laws to tighten the link between voter demand and local budgetary decisions.

I dealt with a related issue and was able to rely on another natural experiment in Chapter 11, 'State Responses to the TRA86 Windfalls: A New Test of the Flypaper Effect'. The relevant institutional fact in this situation was that many state income taxes are definitionally linked to the federal income tax. A simple economic model of state government behaviour would predict states would offset any windfall changes in state revenues associated with changes in the federal tax code by giving them back to taxpayers so as to maintain tax revenues at the desired level. However, an alternative body of literature on how subnational governments respond to intergovernmental grants would predict that states would keep some of the windfall gains because of the 'flypaper effect', which causes funds to stick where they first appear. Analogously, some of the windfall gains that arose because of the the link between federal and state tax bases might stick where they first appeared, that is, in the budgets of state governments. An additional dollar of TRA86 windfalls appears to have led states to retain, on average, about 40 cents – that is, to increase their income tax revenue by 40 cents more than they would have in the absence of the windfalls. Thus, once again, institutional details – in this case in the form of definitional linkages between state and federal tax codes – matter in the sense that they affect fiscal outcomes.

A related line of research relates to limitations on state and local taxes. Such limitations attracted significant public attention with the passage in 1978 of Proposition 13 in California, which rolled back property taxes in that state to 1 per cent of market value. While some may use that event to mark the advent of the limitation movement, interest in state imposed limitations on taxing and spending powers had in fact been growing throughout the 1970s. It was that interest that inspired Chapter 12, my pre-Proposition 13 article 'An Economic Evaluation of State Limitations on Local Taxing and Spending Powers' (1978). My cross sectional empirical analysis of the determinants of willingness to support such controls indicated that states relying heavily on property taxes and those with rapid rates of expenditure growth were more likely than others to impose controls. The puzzle was why such limitations were necessary. According to a standard median voter model view of the world, local voters should be able to induce public officials to provide the desired level of public spending, with no need for outside restraints. My analysis suggested that the economic benefits from controls motivated by the desire to limit local public spending were likely to be slight, while the costs, in terms of distortions in service levels, were potentially significant. With respect to the goal of securing property tax relief, I developed a partial adjustment model as a justification for temporary controls in some cases.

My subsequent work on this topic included an edited volume on tax limitation (*Tax and Expenditure Limitations*, 1981) and a series of articles based on my extensive survey research in Massachusetts in 1980 right after the state's voters passed Proposition $2^1/_2$, which significantly limited the level and growth of property taxes in that state. My detailed analysis of the survey data with sociologist Julie Wilson provided new insights into support for such limitations. Included as Chapters 13 and 14 are two of our papers, one that explains why voters supported the tax limitation measure and a second that investigates which voters supported it.

Particularly challenging in sorting out the motivations of voters was the variation across voters in their expectations about how the state government would respond to the measure to roll back local property taxes. Would the state follow the lead of California two years earlier by providing significant amounts of new aid to local governments despite the fact that Massachusetts, in contrast to California, had no state budget surplus? Or would state officials take a hands-off approach on the grounds that a vote for Proposition $2^1/_2$ was a vote either to reduce local public services or in protest against inefficiency and waste at the local level? We addressed this variation in expectations by including in our survey various questions about what voters believed would happen and modelled voters' behaviour as the result of an interaction between their preferences, perceptions and attitudes on the one hand and their expectations on the other. Emerging from this research were results consistent with research by other analysts in Michigan and California. The main finding was that a vote for Proposition $2^1/_2$ was much more an attempt to obtain lower taxes and more efficient government than to reduce the level of public services. In addition, we concluded that the vote on Massachusetts' Proposition $2^1/_2$ – and by extension the votes to restrain or roll back taxes in other states – should not be interpreted simply as expressions of the narrowly defined self-interest of the voters. Other characteristics, such as sex, race, educational background also influence voting behaviour in significant ways. As a result, with a few important exceptions, support for tax limitation was distributed broadly across almost all demographic subgroups of the population.

The final paper in Part II, Chapter 15, on tax expenditures addresses another key aspect of the structure of particular taxes at all levels of government. This paper is a slightly enhanced version of my Presidential Address to the National Tax Association in 1994. The concept of tax expenditures had been introduced more than 25 years earlier by Stanley Surrey, then a federal tax administrator and Professor of Law at Harvard University, as a means of accounting for those provisions of the tax code that functioned like public expenditures. Until that time, the absence of an accounting mechanism for these components of the tax code meant that, compared to other budgetary elements, they received little attention and scrutiny. Stanley Surrey believed that accounting for tax expenditures would serve as a 'pathway to tax reform', and ultimately lead to their demise. I argued that the tax expenditure concept is extremely useful as a conceptual tool for addressing a major component of government activity. However, contrary to Surrey's hopes and aspirations, most tax expenditures themselves are here to stay. Somewhat ironically, the fact that we have not and will not meet Surrey's goal of eliminating them is what continues to make the tax expenditure concept so important. Given the strong historical, institutional and political pressures to continue using the tax system not just as a revenue-raising device, but also as a policy tool, it is essential to have a way to account for and to scrutinize the special provisions that provide incentives or subsidies to particular activities or groups of individuals.

Part III Interactions between land use and local taxes and spending

During the 1970s and 1980s, many local governments, substate regions and states showed increasing interest in limiting or managing local population growth. Established residents were concerned in part that rapid growth would require greater public spending and higher local taxes. In the late 1980s, I became interested in two interrelated questions: what do we know about the impact of rapid growth on local taxes and spending and how does the density of development affect public sector spending? As I elaborated in Chapter 16, 'Fiscal Impacts of Local Population Growth: A Conceptual and Empirical Analysis', economic theory provides no clear prediction. Some factors push in one direction and others push in the other direction. For example, to the extent that population growth creates a harsher environment for providing public services, it will increase per capita spending. To the extent that communities adjust their spending with a lag, population growth will reduce per capita spending. Hence, empirical work is needed to determine the direction and magnitude of the overall impact and the mechanisms through which the impacts arise.

To answer the empirical question, I constructed a sample of all large counties (representing more than 50 per cent of the US population) for the years 1978 and 1985 (which represent similar points in the economic cycle) to examine how changes in population affected changes in spending in various functional areas and tax burdens. My analysis, which is also reported in Chapter 16, provided empirical support for the fiscal concerns of taxpayer voters in fast-growing areas in that the sum of local spending on current operations plus interest increases at a faster rate than population. I also used this data set to explore the effects of density on spending as reported in Chapter 17,

'Population Growth, Density and the Costs of Providing Public Services' (1992). These papers provide new insights into a variety of issues of concern to policy makers, citizens and planners. For example, I challenged the conventional wisdom that high density development necessarily leads to lower public sector costs than lower density development and I document a U-shaped relationship between the rate of population growth and per capita local public spending.

Of more concern to areas with declining populations are the impact of taxes on the size of the local tax basee, and geographically targeted strategies to promote economic growth. Katharine Bradbury and I examined the impact of taxes in Chapter 18, 'City Taxes and Property Tax Bases' (1988). Using data for 86 large US cities in 1972, 1977 and 1982 and taking full account of the simultaneous determination of tax bases and rates, we found that a 10 per cent increase in a city's property tax rate decreased the property tax base by about 1.5 per cent. Local income taxes and taxes levied by overlying jurisdictions also had negative impacts on the city's property tax base. We concluded that taxes affect local property values more than is typically implied by previous studies.

Chapter 19, 'Spatially Targeted Economic Development Strategies: Do They Work?' critically examines the literature on state-enacted enterprise zones. I begin by distinguishing pure place strategies, which describe the original English version of enterprise zones, from place-based people strategies, which are more descriptive of the US zones, from pure people strategies. Based on a careful review of the literature, I conclude that the enterprise zone strategy is not a cost effective way to increase job opportunities for disadvantaged residents in distressed urban areas.

With the support of the Lincoln Institute of Land Policy in Cambridge, Massachusetts, I had the opportunity to reflect more deeply on the interactions between local tax and land use policies. That work culminated in *Local Government Tax and Land Use Policies in the United States: Understanding the Links* (1998), for which I served as primary author and editor. This book takes the first comprehensive look at how the two most important functions of US local governments – their power to tax and their power to regulate land use – interact with each other. Based on much of my own work and that of other public finance experts, the book reviews and challenges many elements of the conventional wisdom in the fields of urban public finance and planning.

Part IV School finance

Anyone who works on state and local finance is inevitably drawn into issues related to the financing of schools. Having come of age when the early court cases were successfully challenging the constitutional inequities of property tax financing of schools, I have long been interested in such issues. Indeed, education finance was the major policy issue motivating my Ph.D. dissertation in the early 1970s and is currently the focus of much of my current intellectual energy. Two of the papers included here build on my more general work in state and local public finance. Chapter 20 is my paper with Edward W. Harris, 'Statewide Taxation of Nonresidential Property for Education' (1995), which evaluates the substitution of a state-wide tax on business property for the local property tax on business for education in New York State and represents a logical extension of my work on disparities and intergovernmental aid.

It, in turn, replicates an earlier paper (not included here) which was an outgrowth of my thesis and was based on Massachusetts data. Similarly, Chapter 21, 'How School Districts Respond to Fiscal Constraint' (1998) uses as its basic building block the concept of local fiscal condition that emerged from my work on fiscal disparities. The question in this paper is how the composition of school spending and staffing varies in districts facing different fiscal constraints. It turns out that districts respond to fiscal constraint by trying to protect the level of instructional spending, that central administration spending and staffing appear to be a luxury that is more affordable for districts in strong fiscal condition, and that spending on capital outlays is more responsive than other categories to a district's fiscal condition.

The school finance court cases of the 1970s and 1980s focused directly on variation across districts in school funding and its relationship to the property tax wealth of the district. The courts generally accepted the view that there was a clear and direct link between spending on education and educational outcomes. Consequently, during that period, public finance experts typically analysed finance issues without delving too far into broader issues of educational policy. However, the combination of Eric Hanushek's challenge to the view that money matters (1986 and subsequent articles) combined with a new emphasis on educational outcomes, typically as measured by student performance, brought to the fore the link between spending and outcomes. Ronald Ferguson and I address that issue in Chapter 22, 'How and Why Money Matters: An Analysis of Alabama Schools' (1996). Our analysis of the determinants of student test scores in Alabama provides strong support for the hypothesis that measurable school inputs – particularly the quality of teachers as measured by their test scores and their education, and class size – affect student learning. Given our attention to good data, a large sample and a sound specification, we believe that these results are credible and deserve attention.

But, of course, the policy solution to the problem of low-performing schools is not simply to provide more funds. Instead the challenge is to redesign financing systems that provide appropriate incentives for schools to improve. Because this challenge requires a broader knowledge of educational processes, my current interest in education is now taking me outside the traditional field of local public finance and is forcing me to think more about accountability, governance structures and educational processes.

Conclusion

As should be clear from my 25 years of research in the area of state and local taxes and spending, I am firmly committed to policy-driven empirical research. Productive empirical research in this policy area is feasible because of the large variation across local governments in their taxes and spending and because of the external shocks that periodically affect some jurisdictions and not others. The challenge for the empirical researcher is to be continually on the lookout for the types of natural experiments – such as district wide revaluation and federal tax reform – that can shed light on theoretical concepts such as the median voter model for local governments and the 'flypaper' effect in intergovernmental aid. Empirical work is important because the best theories often do not generate clear and unambiguous predictions even about the direction of the outcomes. Also empirical work in this field forces one to appreciate the importance of the institutional details that play such an important role in state and local public finance.

Policy-driven research runs the risk of becoming obsolete. In fact, however, my experience during the past 25 years has been that the policy issues in the state and local arena are never fully resolved and continually reappear, sometimes in different states and sometimes in new guises. Examples include periodic efforts to devolve responsibilities to state and local governments, ongoing discussions of school finance inequities, recurrent efforts to reduce reliance on the local property tax, continual interest in the use of tax abatements as a tool of local economic development, and concerns about fiscal disparities among local jurisdictions. I would like to think that some of my past research reported here can provide some useful models for new research in this area and that it will provide a valuable perspective on some of the historical arguments about ongoing policy issues.

Throughout my professional career, I have benefited greatly from my interactions with various groups of scholars. One was the group of urban public finance economists who were members of Taxation, Resources, and Economic Development (TRED), whose annual conferences on local public finance were sponsored for more than 20 years by the Lincoln Institute of Land Policy. Another was the group of local public finance economists with whom I worked closely during my years as an assistant and associate professor at Harvard. This group included many of my co-authors of the various papers in this volume or of other papers not included here: John Yinger, Katharine Bradbury, Andrew Reschovsky, Howard Bloom, Fred Doolittle, Ronald Ferguson and Julie Boatright Wilson. I cannot imagine a more supportive group of friends and colleagues, and I am extremely grateful to them all. I have also been blessed to live in two states with very different fiscal structures, Massachusetts and North Carolina. I have no doubt that one's view of state and local public finance is influenced in part by the institutions with which one is most familiar. My move to Duke University and North Carolina in 1986 clearly broadened my perspective and has provided a source of new data with which to test some of my older ideas and also to develop some new ones.

One of the most rewarding aspects of research in the field of state and local public finance arises from the great variation across states in their institutional details and the policy issues they face. The increasing interest of countries around the world – particularly the countries of the former Soviet Union and developing countries – in decentralizing their governmental systems will continue to make the study of subnational fiscal issues rewarding and exciting for many years to come.

References

Bergstrom, T.C. and R.P. Goodman (1973), 'Private Demands for Public Goods', *American Economic Review*, **LXIII** (3), June, 280–97.

Borcherding, T.E. and R.T. Deacon (1972), 'The Demand for the Services on Non-Federal Governments', *American Economic Review*, **LXII** (5), December, 891–901.

Bradford, D., R. Malt and W.H. Oates (1969), 'The Rising Cost of Local Public Services: Some Evidence and Reflections', *National Tax Journal*, **22**, June, 185–202.

Case, Anne (1993), 'Interstate Tax Competition After TRA86', *Journal of Policy Analysis and Management*, **12** (1), 136–48.

Hamilton, Bruce W. (1975), 'Zoning and Property Taxation in a System of Local Governments', *Urban Studies*, **12** (2), 105–11.

Hanushek, Eric (1986), 'The Economics of Schooling: Production and Efficiency in Public Schools', *Journal of Economic Literature*, **24**, September, 1141–77.

Ladd, Helen F. (1973), 'The Role of the Property Tax: A Reassessment' in R.A. Musgrave (ed.), *Broad Based Taxes: New Options and Sources*, Baltimore: Johns Hopkins Press, Committee for Economic Development.

Ladd, Helen F. (1974), *Local Public Expenditures and the Composition of the Property Tax Base*, Ph.D. dissertation, Harvard University.

Ladd, Helen F. (1981), *Tax and Expenditure Limitations*, Washington, DC: Urban Institute.

Ladd, Helen F. (1998), *Local Government Tax and Land Use Policies in the United States: Understanding the Links*, Cheltenham, UK, Northampton, MA: Edward Elgar.

Ladd, Helen F. and John Yinger (1991), *America's Ailing Cities: Fiscal Health and the Design of Urban Policy*, Baltimore: Johns Hopkins University Press.

Mieszkowski, Peter (1972), 'The Property Tax: An Excise Tax or a Profits Tax?', *Journal of Public Economics*, **1** (1), April, 73–96.

Oates, Wallace H. (1969), 'The Effects of Property Taxes and Local Public Spending on Property Values: An Empirical Study of Tax Capitalization and the Tiebout Hypothesis', *Journal of Political Economy*, **77**, November/December, 957–71.

Tiebout, Charles M. (1956), 'A Pure Theory of Local Public Expenditures', *Journal of Political Economy*, **64**, October, 416–24.

PART I

MEASURING LOCAL FISCAL DISPARITIES AND INTERGOVERNMENTAL AID

National Tax Journal

VOLUME XXVIII, NO. 2   JUNE 1975

LOCAL EDUCATION EXPENDITURES, FISCAL CAPACITY, AND THE COMPOSITION OF THE PROPERTY TAX BASE

HELEN F. LADD*

ABSTRACT

The education expenditure implications of the composition of the local property tax base are examined in the context of a median voter, individualistic utility maximization expenditure model. On the basis of a 1970 cross section regression analysis of education expenditures in the Boston SMSA, the study concludes that commercial property has a stronger expenditure effect than industrial property. In addition, it is found that the commonly used measure of local fiscal capacity for education, the total property tax base per pupil, compares unfavorably from a distributional point of view with the behavioral concept of fiscal capacity advocated in this study.

A series of recent court decisions concerning local education expenditures has drawn attention to the heavy reliance of school districts on

*Assistant Professor of Economics, Wellesley College. This paper is based on my doctoral dissertation, *Local Public Expenditures and the Composition of the Property Tax Base* (Unpublished Ph.D. dissertation, Harvard University, 1974). I am indebted to my thesis advisor, Richard A. Musgrave, for his invaluable guidance in my dissertation research and for reading an earlier version of this paper. Financial support for the dissertation was provided by a Ford Foundation interdisciplinary grant to Harvard University.

Editor's Note: It is with special pleasure that we publish this paper, based on Professor Ladd's thesis, which was the 1974 winner of the NTA-TIA annual competition for outstanding doctoral dissertations in government finance and taxation.

local property taxes and to interdistrict disparities in the total property tax base per pupil.[1] The assumption underlying the emphasis on intercommunity tax base disparities is that education expenditures are closely linked to the size of the total property tax base and that the breakdown of the base among commercial, residential, and industrial property is not important. This study argues that the composition of the property tax base affects local decisions to provide educational services and that the separate components of the base consequently deserve greater attention in the determination of local fiscal capacity for education.

Section I focuses on the tax price effects of commercial and industrial property in the context of a median voter model of local education expenditures. In section II, regression equations based on the 78 communities in the Boston Standard Metropolitan Statistical Area (SMSA) are presented and analyzed.[2] A behavioral approach to the measurement of local fiscal capacity that is consistent with the median voter expenditure model is discussed in section III. In the final

[1] For a useful survey of the early decisions, see Ferdinand P. Schoettle, "Judicial Requirements for School Finance Reform and Property Tax Redesign: The Rapidly Evolving Case Law," *National Tax Journal*, XXV (September, 1972), pp. 455–72.

[2] In Massachusetts, municipalities have responsibility for most local public services including elementary and secondary education. Hence, communities are the appropriate unit of observation for local education decisions in the Boston SMSA.

section, the estimated expenditure equations are used to derive the fiscal capacity implications of the behavioral model for the communities in the Boston SMSA.

1. *Tax Price Effects of Non-Residential Property*

This section examines how the components of the property tax base affect the local demand for education services in the context of an individualistic utility maximization model adapted to the process of collective choice by a majority rule, median voter assumption. Utility maximization behavior implies that, within a particular community, the education level desired by each resident can be expected to vary with each resident's income or wealth, his share of the cost of public services as determined by the tax structure, and his preferences for education. An assumption of majority rule is used to transform residents' conflicting demands for education into a single community demand function. This assumption about the political process implies that the effective demand of the community is the quantity demanded by the voter desiring the median quantity of the public service.[3]

Let us initially assume that education is the only locally provided public service, that it is financed entirely by a flat rate tax on residential, commercial, and industrial real estate, and that resident voters perceive as their share of the tax burden only the part that falls on them directly in their capacity as homeowners. In line with traditional consumer theory, each resident voter is assumed to desire a level of education services that maximizes his utility subject to his own budget constraint. The budget constraint of the median voter in a particular community can be expressed as:

$$Y_M = P_X X_M + (t+d) H_M$$

where

Y_M = family income of the median voter

P_X = the price of the composite good, non-housing private goods and services

X_M = non-housing private goods and services

t = the community tax rate

d = fraction of the value of the housing stock expended yearly

H_M = the value of the housing stock of the median family.

Hence $d \cdot H_M$ is the annual cost of housing services and $t \cdot H_M$ is the annual cost to the median voter of the publicly provided good, education. Assuming the same level of education services, E, is provided to all families in the community and that the resource cost of education services is P_E, the community tax rate can be expressed as

$$t = \frac{P_E \cdot E \cdot n}{n \cdot H_A + NR}$$

where

P_E = resource cost per unit of education

E = education services per family

n = number of families

H_A = average value of housing stock in the community

NR = the value of non-residential property in the community.

Hence, the perceived tax price of an additional unit of education services

---

[3] It can be shown that as long as preferences are single peaked, the budget preferred by the median voter is the only budget that will win at least a majority of the votes when paired against any other budget. See Duncan Black, "On the Rationale of Group Decision Making," *Journal of Political Economy*, Vol. 56 (February, 1948), pp. 23–34.

[4] Throughout the analysis, education is assumed to be characterized by complete rivalness in consumption. The model can easily be generalized to include the possibility of non-rival consumption. See T. C. Bergstrom and R. P. Goodman, "Private Demands for Public Goods," *American Economic Review*, LXIII, No. 3 (June, 1973) pp. 280–97 and T. E. Borcherding and R. T. Deacon, "The Demand for the Services of Non-Federal Governments," *American Economic Review*, LXII, No. 5 (December, 1972), pp. 891–901.

from the point of view of the median voter is[5]

$$\frac{P_E \cdot n \cdot H_M}{n \cdot H_A + NR}$$

Multiplying and dividing this expression by H_A, yields

$$P_E \cdot RB \cdot H_M/H_A$$

where RB is defined as $(n \cdot H_A)/(n \cdot H_A + NR)$, the residential fraction of the tax base.

Thus, from the point of view of the median voter, the perceived tax price of education services is composed of three components: P_E, the resource cost per unit of education services; RB, the residential fraction of the tax base; and H_M/H_A, a within community housing distribution component. For the purpose of analyzing the expenditure effects of non-residential property the key component is RB. In the context of this simple model, the higher the fraction of non-residential property, the lower the share paid by resident voters and consequently the larger the quantity of education demanded, the precise relationship depending on the magnitude of the price elasticity of demand for education.

To this point, it has been assumed that resident voters perceive as their share of the property tax burden only the part that falls on them directly in their capacity as homeowners. This implies that commercial and industrial property have similar impacts on the tax price and consequently similar impacts on the demand for education services.

More realistically, however, resident voters may perceive that they bear part of the property tax levied on local firms. If resident voters believe, for example, that firms are mobile in response to inter-community fiscal differentials, then higher resident related public expenditures in the current period, and consequently higher tax liabilities for firms, will adversely affect the local commercial and industrial tax base in the future. In this case, part of the property tax levied on firms would be perceived to be shifted to local residents in the form of a reduced future tax base. Alternatively, residents may fear that they will bear the burden of higher business taxes in the form of higher prices for locally consumed private goods and services. This requires that the additionally taxed firms have sufficient market power to increase prices, or at least that residents perceive that firms have such power. In both cases, RB is an underestimate of the tax price of public education as perceived by local residents.

To deal with these possibilities, the tax price term needs to be generalized to RB* as follows:

$$RB^* = 1 - \alpha \cdot C - \beta \cdot I$$

where C and I are the commercial and industrial fractions of the tax base. The parameters α and β represent the fractions of the commercial and industrial property tax *not* shifted onto local residents. For example, if there is no perceived tax shifting onto local residents, α and β are both 1 and we are back to the simple case discussed above in which the tax price is equal to the residential fraction of the tax base. As α and β approach 0, the perceived tax price approaches 1 in spite of the presence of business property.

The two parameters, α and β, need not be equal. If resident voters are concerned about the size of the future tax base, α may well be greater than β. This is based on the view that industrial property, being footloose and not tied to the local market, is more responsive to fiscal factors than is commercial property. On the other hand, if firms shift their property tax burden onto local residents in the form of higher prices, it is likely that β will exceed α, that is, the proportion not shifted is greater for industrial than for commercial firms. The industrial firms, producing for a market larger than the local community, are unlikely to have the market power necessary to

---

[5] The total expenditures on publicly provided education of the median voter are $t \cdot H_M = (P_E \cdot E \cdot n/(n \cdot H_A + NR)) \cdot H_M$. Differentiating this with respect to E yields the tax price expression in the text.

raise prices. Moreover, a smaller proportion of industrial output than of commercial output is bought locally.

Thus, in this generalized model, the precise expenditure effects of commercial and industrial property depend on the parameters α and β and on the price elasticity of demand for education. Since the values of α and β are unknown, they are estimated along with the expenditure equations as a whole in the empirical work discussed in the following section.

2. Regression Analysis

A. The Education Expenditure Model

Cross section education expenditure equations were estimated across communities in the Boston SMSA for the calendar year 1970. The equations are of the following general form:

$$E = f(Y, WR, RB \text{ or } RB^*, LS, SBG, FG, PUP, PRIV, POV, PROF),$$

where

- E = Education expenditures per pupil (includes locally raised tax revenue for education plus state and federal grants for the calendar year 1970).
- Y = Median family income.
- WR = Market value of residential property per pupil.
- RB = Residential fraction of the assessed property tax base.
- RB^* = Generalized tax price term.
- LS = Local tax share calculated from Chapter 70 state aid matching rate ($LS = 1/(1+m_i)$ where m_i is the matching rate in the ith community).
- SBG = Chapter 70 state aid per pupil when non-matching.
- FG = Categorical state and federal grants per pupil.
- PUP = Public school pupils as a fraction of the population.
- $PRIV$ = Private school pupils as a fraction of the population.
- POV = Fraction of families with income below the poverty level.
- $PROF$ = Professional, technical, and kindred workers as a fraction of the population.

This equation is consistent with the individual utility maximization model adapted to the process of collective choice by a majority rule, median voter assumption. In essence, it states that the demand for education in each community is a function of the income and wealth of the relevant local voter, the community tax price of education, intergovernmental aid, and preferences.[6]

Median family income (Y) represents the budget constraint of the median voter. Elsewhere, it has been shown that the use of median family income to represent the income of the median voter in cross sectional analysis can be justified even if the demand for education is not a monotonic function of income as long as income distributions across communities meet certain regularity assumptions.[7]

Residential wealth per pupil (WR) is included as a proxy for the personal wealth or permanent income of local resident voters. It is important to note that in the context of an individualistic utility maximization model of local education expenditures, residential wealth, not the total property wealth of the community, is the correct wealth variable. Non-residential taxable property has a price effect, not a wealth

---

[6] It should be noted that no direct test is made of the underlying median voter model. Such a task would require a detailed analysis of micro voting data, a task beyond the scope of this study. Instead, the model is accepted as a reasonable approximation of reality, particularly in the context of Boston metropolitan area communities, many of which are governed by pure or representative town meetings.

[7] T. C. Bergstrom and R. P. Goodman, "Private Demands for Public Goods," *American Economic Review*, LXII, No. 3 (June, 1963), pp. 380–97. Moreover, as George Peterson has shown, use of median family income in cross section school district studies yields income elasticities of demand for education very similar to those based on individual data from education referenda. See George E. Peterson, "The Demand for Public Schooling: A Study in Voting and Expenditure Theory," (Mimeo), Urban Institute, Washington D.C., 1973.

effect, on the demand for education services.

The residential fraction of the tax base in each community (RB) or its more sophisticated counterpart RB* (discussed above) represents the share of the cost of locally raised revenues perceived to be paid by local residents.[8] As such, RB or RB* comprises one component of the tax price of public education faced by local resident voters. Since the non-residential components of the property tax base exert their major impact through this tax price term, the crucial role of this variable in the analysis should be emphasized.

In Massachusetts, the major state aid to education program (Chapter 70) takes the form of matching grants to local communities where the matching rate relevant to the ith community (m_i) varies by formula inversely with the per pupil property tax base. Hence, from the point of view of local resident voters, the fraction (LS) of an additional dollar of education services to be financed from local tax sources is a second component of the tax price term.[9] Thus, the tax price of education services as perceived by resident voters is the product of the share locally financed (LS) and the proportion of the share perceived to be borne by residents (RB*).[10]

Because of a series of restrictions and limitations on the Massachusetts matching aid program, the matching rate (m) effectively equals zero for about one-half of the communities in the sample. For these communities, the local share component equals unity and the state aid received in the form of Chapter 70 grants is treated as state block grants for education (SBG). All other state and federal aid for education is included in the variable FG. Since these are categorical aid grants, the marginal expenditure impact of an additional dollar of aid in this form is expected to be close to one.

The remaining four variables (PRIV, PUP, POV, and PROF) are included to control for preference differences across communities and are further discussed below.

Except that the tax price variables (RB or RB* and LS) are predicted to appear in multiplicative form, the underlying theory does not imply a particular specification. The choice of the log-log form for estimation is based in part on the reasonable view that intercommunity variations in the tax price, the key variable for this analysis, are likely to have a multiplicative impact on education demand. That is, they are likely to affect demand with constant elasticity rather than with constant marginal impact.

B. *Regression Results*

The distinguishing feature of the three equations presented in Table I is the treatment of the tax price terms, RB or RB* and LS. In equation 1, which is estimated by ordinary least squares, the natural logs of RB and LS are included as separate variables. Equation 2 substitutes the generalized term RB* for RB while equation 3 constrains the expenditure elasticities of RB* and LS to be identical by defining the tax price term as LS·RB*. RB*, it will be recalled, is the share of

---

[8] Since the community demand for education services is assumed to be the demand of the median voter, theory requires the inclusion of the additional tax price term H_M/H_A where H_M represents the housing stock of the median voter and H_A the average housing stock in the community. For a variety of reasons, including Census data limitations, the problem of how to treat renters, and the question of the identity of the median voter, the empirical counterpart to the desired term may be subject to substantial error. Such a term was constructed but showed very little variation across communities and hence was dropped from the estimated equations.

[9] LS is defined as $1/(1+m_i)$ where m_i is the matching rate applicable to the ith community.

[10] It should be noted that there is no resource cost of education services included in the basic equation. This can be partially justified on the assumption that the observations come from a single market area in which the prices of factor inputs are constant across communities. Although this assumption is probably reasonable for capital inputs, it may be less acceptable for labor inputs. While it would be desirable to include an index of teacher salaries as an explanatory variable, difficulties arise in defining an index fully corrected for quality differences. Hence, following earlier studies of local education expenditures, no explicit resource cost variable is included.

the local tax cost perceived to be paid by local voters and is defined essentially as $(1-\alpha \cdot C - \beta \cdot I)$ where α and β represent the fractions of the commercial and industrial property tax payments not shifted to local residents and C and I are the commercial and industrial fractions of the tax base.[11] Unfortunately, the parameters α and β in RB* are unknown and hence must be estimated along with the equation as a whole. This was achieved by searching over plausible values of α and β in equations 2 and 3, and choosing those values that minimized the sum of squared residuals of the equation.

Before turning to the estimates of the tax price elasticity of demand, let us briefly examine the other parameter estimates. Since all variables are in log form, the reported coefficients are elasticities.

The income and residential wealth elasticities are positive as expected, and statistically different from zero. While the point estimates of the income elasticity (.42 to .45) are lower than those reported in other studies, this can be explained by the inclusion in the equation of residential wealth and the fraction of the residential population that is professional, both of which are positively correlated with income across communities and have positive expenditure impacts.

The estimated elasticity of state block grants for education (SBG) is positive and implies a marginal impact at the means of .45, .51, and .57 in the three equations. That is, about 50¢ of each dollar in educational aid is spent on education, the rest leading to increases in other public services or disposable income. The marginal impact of one dollar of additional categorical aid (calculated at mean values) implied by the point estimates of the FG elasticity is about $1.10. This is consistent with the view that these grants are for specialized purposes on which local communities would have spent less than the allotted amount in the absence of aid.

The predicted effect of a higher fraction of public school pupils in relation to the total population is unclear. On the one hand, the higher the proportion of families with school age children, the stronger the positive interest group effect on the effective demand for school spending. In the other direction, if more pupils per capita reflect more pupils per family, then family income per pupil is reduced, implying a negative effect on education expenditures. The estimated coefficient of pupils per capita (PUP) is consistent with this double effect view, being insignificantly different from zero in all three equations. PRIV, the number of private school pupils per capita, is expected to enter with a negative sign since families who opt out of the public school system by sending their children to private schools are likely to exert pressure to contain public school spending. The estimated elasticity is negative, but insignificantly different from zero.[12]

The log of the fraction of families with below poverty line income (POV) is included in the equation because its positive correlation with categorical grants per pupil (FG) and its negative correlation with the residential fraction of the tax base (RB) would result

---

[11] Actually, the precise RB* is slightly more complicated because of the presence of small amounts of vacant land and personalty. In the equations, RB* is specified as $(1-\alpha \cdot C - \beta \cdot I - VL) \cdot X$ where C, I and VL refer to the fractions of real property value accounted for by commercial, industrial, and vacant land respectively, and X is the ratio of realty to the total tax base.

[12] The possibility of simultaneous equations bias with respect to the variable PRIV ought to be noted. If the decision of parents, in a given community, to send children to private schools is determined in part by the level of public spending on education, then the coefficient of PRIV would be biased toward zero and other parameter estimates might be affected as well. This bias has been ignored on the basis of results reported by Eric Toder, "Equalizing Educational Expenditures: A Welfare Analysis of Some Plans for Reform of Spending on Public Education," (Mimeo), 1973. He found no evidence that the level of public spending on schools affected the percentage of children attending private schools. Instead, his results suggest that parents of private school students are motivated more by the characteristics of the other public school students than by the level of resource inputs as measured by education expenditures.

TABLE 1
EDUCATION EXPENDITURES
(All variables in log form, absolute values of t-statistics in parentheses.)

Equation 1: Ordinary least squares

E = .4590 Y + .2392 WR − .3091 RB − .4853 LS + .0301 SBG
   (2.901)   (2.529)   (2.661)   (1.625)   (1.701)

− .0265 PUP − .0179 PRIV + .0775 POV + .1018 PROF − .0567
  (.2566)   (.7812)   (1.650)   (1.519)   (.0345)

R^2 = .65   S.E.E. = .0168

Equation 2: Search over α, β in RB*

E = .4204 Y + .2911 WR − .7230 RB* − .5861 LS + .0344 SBG
   (2.668)   (2.975)   (3.177)   (1.970)   (1.962)

+ .1062 FG + .0133 PUP − .0241 PRIV + .0648 POV + .1058 PROF − .5338
  (4.205)   (.1267)   (1.052)   (1.394)   (1.600)   (.3444)

α = .71, β = .39
R^2 = .67   S.E.E. = .1054

Equation 3: Search over α, β in TP = RB* · LS

E = .4148 Y + .3006 WR − .6529 TP + .0386 SBG + .1057 FG + .0178 PUP
   (2.681)   (3.111)   (3.175)   (3.447)   (4.228)   (.1701)

− .0238 PRIV + .0650 POV + .1039 PROF − .4770
  (1.049)   (1.433)   (1.583)   (.3208)

α = .79, β = .45
R^2 = .67   S.E.E. = .1047

Definition of variables: E = education expenditures per pupil (includes locally raised tax revenue for education plus state and federal grants in aid for the calendar year 1970); Y = median family income; WR = market value of residential property per pupil; RB = residential fraction of the assessed property tax base; LS = local tax price calculated from Chapter 70 matching rate (MP = 1/(1 + m) where m is the matching rate); SBG = Chapter 70 state aid per pupil when non-matching; FG = categorical state and federal grants per pupil; PUP = public school pupils as fraction of total population; PRIV = private school pupils as fraction of total population; POV = fraction of families with income below poverty level; PROF = professional, technical, and kindred workers as fraction of the population; RB* = $(1 - \alpha \cdot C - \beta \cdot I - VL) \cdot X$ (See footnote 11 above); TP = RB* · LS.

Data Sources: The tax base data were provided by the Massachusetts Department of Corporations and Taxation. The residential, commercial, industrial, vacant land, and personalty percentages of the property tax base are estimates made by that department in consultation with local assessors, adjusted for the purposes of this study to treat all rental property as residential. State Tax Commission assessment sales ratios were used to convert the assessed value of residential property to market values. The education aid and pupil data were supplied by the Massachusetts Department of Education. All socioeconomic variables are from United States Bureau of the Census, *Census of Housing: 1970* or *Census of Population: 1970*.

in biased coefficients of those two variables if it were left out. A possible interpretation of the positive elasticity is that communities with an above average fraction of poor families need to spend more on education than other communities to provide a given level of educational output. The final taste variable, the fraction of the resident population comprised of professional or technical workers (PROF), serves the function of controlling for preference differences across communities.

Expenditure Effects of Commercial and Industrial Property

The education expenditure effects of commercial and industrial property depend on the estimated price elasticity of demand and on the parameters α and β. In equation 1, the point estimate of the tax price elasticity is −.31 for RB, the tax base composition component of the tax price, and −.49 for LS, the local share component. The parameters α and β are constrained to be 1 by the definition of RB as the residential fraction of the tax base. The combination of the empirical finding of a higher elasticity estimate for LS (in absolute value terms) and the *a priori* reasoning that RB may be an overestimate of the tax base composition component of the tax price term because of tax shifting considerations suggest that −.31 is an underestimate (in absolute value terms) of the true tax price elasticity of demand.

The substitution of the generalized term RB* in equation 2 allows for the tax price effects of perceived shifting of the non-residential tax base and, hence, is theoretically superior to equation 1. As noted above, the values of the parameters α and β were found by searching over plausible values and choosing those values that minimized the sum of squared residuals. As can be seen in equation 2, $\alpha = .71$, $\beta = .39$, and the point estimate of the RB* elasticity is −.72. Since the difference between the estimated coefficients of RB* and LS is statistically insignificant in equation 2, the equation was reestimated with the coefficients constrained to be identical. This is presented as equation 3. In this case, the estimated value of α is .79, of β, .45, and of the tax price elasticity of demand, −.65.[13]

The finding that, in equations 2 and 3, α and β are less than 1, confirms the view that the residential fraction of the tax base (RB) is an underestimate of the perceived tax base composition component of the tax price. Moreover, the higher value of α implies that commercial property has a larger impact on a community's willingness to provide education services than does industrial property.

The magnitudes of the expenditure elasticities of commercial and industrial property implied by the estimated coefficients are shown in Table II. The estimated expenditure effects of commercial and industrial property are constrained to be identical in equation 1 because of the built in restriction that the two property types affect RB in precisely the same manner. The reported results for equations 2 and 3 in which this restriction is relaxed are to be preferred. The stronger education expenditure effects associated with commercial property (elasticity of .58) than with industrial property (elasticity of .32 or .33) are consistent with the view that resident voters perceive that industrial property is potentially more mobile than commercial property in response to fiscal differentials across communities. Consequently, resident voters seem to be less willing to raise taxes for resident related services paid by industrial firms than by commercial firms.

One final empirical issue related to the composition of the property tax base remains. Potentially, the provision of non-education public services specifically to business firms could induce a reduction in residents' demand for education services. This is based on the view that the public provision of business related services from which residents receive no direct benefit reduces the income available to residents to be spent on all other goods and services, including public education. It should be noted, however, that the provision of business related services may be a cost that residents are willing to pay to receive the benefits of living close to their jobs and retail outlets. As such, it would not exert a depressing effect on the demand for education.[14]

---

[13] To test for the possibility that β is downward biased because it reflects weak preferences for education across communities as well as tax base composition differences, another taste controlling variable, the fraction of the resident population working in manufacturing was included in some of the regressions not reported here. In all cases, this variable was insignificant and had virtually no effect on the other coefficients. Hence, the evidence does not support the view that the low relative value of β is caused by taste differentials across communities.

[14] For a good discussion of the "municipal overburden" hypothesis, of which the discussion in the text is one variant, see Harvey E. Brazer *et al.*, *Fiscal Needs and Resources: A Report to the New York State Commission on the Quality, Cost, and Financing of Elementary and Secondary Education* (Mimeo, November, 1971), Ch. V. The municipal overburden views of that study are summarized in Robert W. Hartman and Robert D. Reischauer, *Reforming School Finance* (Washington, D.C.: The Brookings Institution, 1973), p. 71.

This issue was examined empirically in two ways. First, a proxy variable was included to represent the level of non-school expenditures relating to the presence of business property. This variable was constructed from the business property coefficients of a non-school expenditure equation for the same Boston SMSA communities. Second, total non-school expenditures per pupil were included in the education equation which was then estimated by two stage least squares. In neither case was there any evidence to support the hypothesis of a negative impact on education expenditures of high non-school expenditures. In all variations tested, non-school expenditures entered the education equation with a small *positive* coefficient and a t-statistic well below unity. Hence, on the basis of empirical evidence, it is concluded that all the education expenditure effects of non-residential property operate through the tax price term with the empirical magnitudes as reported in Table II.

3. *Local Fiscal Capacity for Education: A Behavioral Approach*

This section develops a behavioral approach to the measurement of local fiscal capacity available for elementary and secondary education services, drawing upon the individualistic utility maximization expenditure model of the previous two sections. For the present purpose, fiscal capacity is defined as a measure of the ability of communities to finance education services.[15] Two communities will be said to have equal fiscal capacity if, in the absence of taste or preference differentials across communities, they can be expected to provide the same level of education services. Two communities will differ in terms of fiscal capacity to the extent that, again in the absence of taste or preference differentials, they can be expected to provide different levels of education. The implementation of this concept requires the determination of estimated education expenditure levels across communities, holding preference constant, a task

TABLE II

EDUCATION EXPENDITURE RESPONSE TO DIFFERENCES IN COMMERCIAL AND INDUSTRIAL PROPERTY
% Difference in Education Expenditures Caused by 1% Difference in: *

	Commercial Property (C) (expressed as fraction of real property)	Industrial Property (I) (expressed as fraction of real property)
Equation #		
1	.42	.42
2	.58	.32
3	.58	.33

* The expenditure responses were calculated as follows: For each equation, the percentage difference in RB or RB* implied by a 1% difference in C or I was calculated using mean values of RB or RB*. This percentage difference was then multiplied by the estimated elasticity of RB or RB*. Note that 1% differences in C and I do not correspond to equivalent differences in the total tax base.
Source: Calculated from Table I.

suited to the multiple regression analysis of the previous section. In general, fiscal capacity, as defined here, will depend on both income and the components of the property tax base with the weights determined by the regression equation.

The question arises of why one would want to measure fiscal capacity in this manner. The method can only be justified in relation to the purpose for which the fiscal capacity concept is to be used. Consider a policy maker at

[15] For a general discussion of the measurement of fiscal capacity, see Advisory Commission on Intergovernmental Relations, *Measures of State and Local Fiscal Capacity and Tax Effort: A Staff Report* (Washington, D.C.: U.S.G.P.O., October, 1962) and *Measuring the Fiscal Capacity of State and Local Areas* (Washington, D.C.: U.S.G.P.O., March, 1971). For brief summaries of the issues and methodology involved in local fiscal capacity studies, see Harvey E. Brazer *et al, Fiscal Needs and Resources: A Report to the New York Commission on the Quality, Cost and Financing of Elementary and Secondary Education* (Draft, November 1971), Ch. IV and Julius Margolis *et al, Metropolitan Fiscal Disparities: Problems and Policies: A Report to the Metropolitan Council of the Twin Cities Area* (University of Pennsylvania/The Fels Center of Government, 1971), Chs. 3–4.

the metropolitan, state, or federal level who is concerned about variations in locally provided education services associated with communities' ability or willingness to finance those services. While he accepts the notion that local public services should be allowed to vary with preferences, he would like to correct, or at least partially correct, for differences in service levels caused by fiscal inability to generate tax revenue. Hence, he requires a measure of fiscal capacity that specifically reflects the ability and willingness of communities to generate tax revenue for elementary and secondary education.

If all communities were strictly residential and if family income and residential wealth were perfectly correlated across communities, a behavioral approach to fiscal capacity measurement would not be necessary. Consider two residential communities, one with a property tax base per family of $PVAL_1$ and the other $PVAL_2$. If the wealth elasticity of demand for education were equal to 1, then a behavioral measure of relative fiscal capacity based on estimated expenditures would yield the same result as the more traditional measure $PVAL_2/PVAL_1$.

When the wealth elasticity of demand is not equal to one, the behavioral measure differs from the tax base measure. But even here, not much is gained by defining relative fiscal capacity with reference to average behavior, that is with reference to the wealth elasticity of demand. The state policy maker wanting to neutralize residential wealth differentials across communities can, in this case, use the traditional tax base measure of fiscal capacity and at the same time take the wealth elasticity of demand into consideration when determining how the matching aid rate ought to vary in relation to fiscal capacity so defined across communities.[16] Very little would be gained by taking the demand elasticity into consideration when initially determining local fiscal capacity.

The advantages of the behavioral approach appear when the composition of the property tax base varies across communities. The issue here is how to weight the components of the property tax base in determining fiscal capacity. Consider specifically two communities that differ in tax base composition only. It is assumed that they have the same total property tax base per pupil, but that one community (R for residential) has all residential property while the other community (B for balanced) has a combination of residential and nonresidential property. In addition, it is assumed that education is the only locally provided public service, and that the median voters in the two communities have similar preferences.

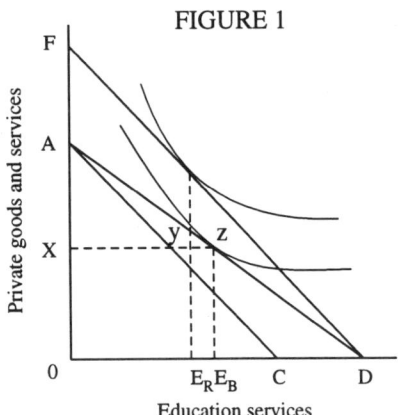

FIGURE 1

Figure 1 portrays the situation graphically on the simplest view of the incidence of the business component of the tax. Specifically, the figure assumes that resident voters in the balanced community perceive as their share of the property tax only the part that they bear directly by statute as homeowners.[17] In addition, the re-

[16] An excellent example of this approach to the determination of state matching aid rates for education can be found in Martin S. Feldstein, "Wealth Neutrality and Local Choice in Public Education," *American Economic Review*, March, 1975, pp. 75–89.

[17] The private goods axis includes all goods not provided by the local public sector including housing services. For graphical convenience, it is assumed that annual housing services and housing values are perfectly correlated with income across communities, an assumption requiring,

source prices of education and private goods are assumed equal to $1 in both communities. Hence, the budget constraint facing the median voter in community B, portrayed by AD, has slope of −RB where RB is the residential fraction of the tax base. As discussed above, RB is the tax price in community B of the publicly provided service, education.[18] For each $1 increase in education expenditures the additional cost to local residents is RB·$1. Note that in the absence of taxable business property, the median voter in this community would have faced the budget constraint AC with slope of −1.

The budget constraint facing the median voter of community R (for residential) is depicted by FD which has a slope of −1, reflecting its strictly residential tax base. FD has been constructed so that the maximum level of public goods (and consequently the total tax base) is the same in the two communities. This requires that total income (OF) and also residential property values be higher in community R than in community B.

As a result of the assumption of similar preferences across communities, indicated in the figure by one set of indifference curves representing the preferences of the median voter in both communities, relative fiscal capacity can be measured by expenditures on public services. As drawn, the balanced community has higher fiscal capacity by $(E_B - E_R)/E_R$ per cent, but no general statement can be made since the result depends on the relative income or wealth and price elasticities of demand for publicly provided services. In comparing the two communities under consideration, it can be shown that the balanced community will have higher expenditures and, therefore, higher fiscal capacity if the negative of the price elasticity of demand is greater than the wealth elas-

ticity of demand.[19] Thus, how differences in equal total tax base communities ought to be treated in terms of fiscal capacity is an empirical question since it turns on the magnitudes of the price and wealth elasticities of demand. What the behavioral approach emphasizes is that since residential and non-residential property affect the budget constraint in different ways, they make differing contributions to the ability and willingness of communities to finance elementary and secondary education.[20]

Generalization of the price term from RB to RB* to account for the possibility of tax shifting does not alter the basic analysis. By relaxing the constraint that the two property types affect the tax price in the same man-

---

[18] Implicit in this presentation is the assumption that all residents are homeowners and that the median voter owns housing equal to the community average.

[19] Consider two communities with the same total property tax base per capita, all of which is residential property in both communities. Assuming similar preferences, both communities would provide the same level of public services. Now let there be an equal expansion in the property tax base per capita in the two communities where in community R the increase is in the value of residential property while in B, the increase is in the value of non-residential property. Assuming the wealth increase in R is equally distributed among residents, the median voter experiences a wealth effect. In B, however, the median voter experiences a price effect with the introduction of the non-residential property. Thus, the condition for equivalent equilibrium level expenditures in the two communities is

$$\eta_{E \cdot P} \cdot \frac{dP}{P} = \eta_{E \cdot W} \cdot \frac{dW}{W}$$

where $\eta_{E \cdot P}$ is the price elasticity of expenditures and $\eta_{E \cdot W}$ is the wealth elasticity. Since the percentage change in price (dP/P) is equal to the negative of the percentage change in wealth (dW/W), the two communities will have equal expenditures only if $\eta_{E \cdot P} = \eta_{E \cdot W}$.

[20] This argument for differential weighting of the components of the property tax base differs from the ACIR representative tax system type argument for differential weighting of tax bases. The issues posed by the presence of several components of a single tax base (single in the sense that within the taxing jurisdiction a uniform rate must apply to the whole base) differ from those posed by the presence of a variety of tax bases all of which can be taxed at different rates within a single jurisdiction.

---

among other things, no capitalization into housing prices of net fiscal advantages across communities. While not necessary to the spirit of the overall argument, the assumption facilitates graphical comparison of communities with different tax base composition.

ner, this generalization allows the relative contributions of commercial and industrial property to differ. As in the simple case, the appropriate fiscal capacity weights for the tax base components are an empirical question, but here they depend on the parameters α and β as well as on the tax price elasticity of demand.

In summary, several points should be noted about this behavioral approach to fiscal capacity measurement. Average preferences play a role in that they determine the wealth and price elasticities of demand for education. Differences in preferences across communities (and hence differences in actual expenditures reflecting preference differences), however, do not enter the analysis.

Second, differences in family income across communities are included as a determinant of differential ability to finance education even though income is not locally taxed. This is justified in terms of the median voter expenditure model in which the income constraint of the individual voter plays a central role.

Finally, the approach focuses on the level and distribution of public services across communities to the exclusion of the tax rate or tax burden side of the analysis. Returning to Figure 1, it can be seen that the school tax rate is higher in community B than in community R since by assumption and construction both have the same total tax base and, as drawn, B has higher public expenditures. Also as drawn, however, the explicit tax burden on the average resident is lower in B since non-residential property bears YZ of the cost of public services per capita leaving only XY to be financed by residents. The point is that the definition of fiscal capacity employed here focuses exclusively on the level of public services and ignores the tax burden side, the justification being the assumption that the policy maker's major concern is that communities not be restricted in their provision of education because of a lack of ability to finance those services.

4. Implications for Fiscal Capacity

The parameter estimates from the preferred equation, equation 3, were applied to the measurement of fiscal capacity available for educational services in the Boston SMSA in two ways. First they were used to derive rough estimates of the expenditure elasticities associated with each type of property. Second, they were employed to calculate a behavioral index of fiscal capacity for education across communities that could be compared to the more commonly used measure, total property tax base per pupil.

A. Elasticities by Property Type

Using the behavioral approach to fiscal capacity measurement developed above, the basis for determining the appropriate relative weights for the components of the property tax base is the comparison of the expenditure effects associated with *equivalent differences* in each tax base component. Equivalent differences are defined to be differences that correspond to equal differences in the total property tax base per pupil.[21] The results for equation 3 are presented in Table III.

TABLE III

EDUCATION EXPENDITURE EFFECTS OF A 1% DIFFERENCE IN THE TOTAL PROPERTY TAX BASE

Type of Property	Expenditure change (in %)
Residential	.38
Commercial	.48
Industrial	.21

Source: Calculated from Table I.

The figures for commercial and industrial property reflect the average expenditure impact of each type of property through the tax price term. The residential property expenditure effect includes three separate effects: a

---

[21] Differences in each type of property equivalent to a one percent difference in the total property tax base per pupil for the 78 community sample are 1.33% for residential property, 10.16% for commercial property, and 13.23% for industrial property.

direct positive effect through the variable WR that picks up the wealth effect of residential property, an indirect negative effect through the tax price term (higher residential property implies a higher tax price, *ceteris paribus*), and an indirect positive effect of residential property through its partial correlation with family income across communities.

The figures in Table III show that the three types of property make differing average contributions to a community's willingness to finance education services, and consequently make different contributions to a community's fiscal capacity. Specifically, if the weight for residential property is taken to be 1, then, on the basis of the Table III figures, the appropriate weights for commercial and industrial property are 1.26 and .55 respectively.

B. *Comparison of a behavioral measure of fiscal capacity to total tax base per pupil*

On the basis of these rough findings, it becomes appropriate to examine in more detail the implications for the measurement of fiscal capacity of differential weighting of the tax base components and of taking income differences into explicit consideration. Accordingly, two separate indices of fiscal capacity have been calculated for the 78 communities in the Boston metropolitan area. The first index PVAL (for property value) shows the relative value of taxable property per public school pupil in each community. Thus, it is an index in which each tax base component is weighted equally, and income is given a weight of zero. The second index has been formed using the preferred equation, in which all variables other than income and tax base variables were set equal to their means for the sample as a whole.[22] Hence, CAP gives a measure of the relative capacity of communities to finance education based on each community's actual income level and tax base composition and on the average sample behavior as measured by the regression equation explaining education expenditures.

One method of comparing PVAL and CAP is to examine the relative rankings implied by the two indices. To the extent that the rankings are similar, the two approaches yield similar conclusions about relative fiscal capacity.[23] Communities for which there is a 10 or more difference in rank using one

TABLE IV

COMPARISON OF INDICES
Communities for which rank by PVAL exceeds rank by CAP by 10 or more positions.

Community	PVAL rank	CAP rank
Beverly	42	24
Boston	30	7
Cambridge	71	53
Everett	74	54
Lynn	52	21
Saugus	48	23
Waltham	62	46
Watertown	58	48
Wilmington	22	11

Communities for which rank by CAP exceeds rank by PVAL by 10 or more positions.

Bedford	39	49
Braintree	35	45
Hingham	27	40
Lexington	28	60
Lynnfield	49	59
Medfield	15	36
Norwell	14	26
Sherborn	54	70
Sudbury	41	66
Topsfield	12	39
Walpole	31	47
Wayland	45	62
Westwood	56	73

Communities are ranked in ascending order for each index. Hence, the higher the rank the greater the relative fiscal capacity.

[22] Specifically, the fiscal capacity for the ith community is anti-log $[.4148\,LY_i + .3006 \cdot LWR_i - .6529\,\text{Log}\,(LS_i(1 - .79C_i - .45I_i - VL_i) \cdot X_i) + .0386L\overline{SBG} + .1057L\overline{FG} + .0178L\overline{PUP} - .0238L\overline{PRIV} + .0650L\overline{POV} + .1039L\overline{PROF} - .4770]$, where L refers to the natural logarithm.

[23] It should be noted that the range of the two indices differs substantially. PVAL varies from a low of .53 to a high of 2.11 and CAP from a low of .77 to 1.52. For both indices 1 represents total fiscal capacity in the Boston SMSA divided by the total number of students. The discussion in the text deals only with the rankings implied by each index and not with the actual indices.

index compared to the other are presented in Table IV. Of the 22 total communities for which this is true in the 78 community sample, the first nine in the table, several of which are large cities, exhibit greater relative fiscal capacity when market value per pupil (PVAL) is the index rather than CAP while the next thirteen show greater relative fiscal capacity for CAP. The finding that 28 per cent of the sample communities have their rankings significantly affected by the particular index used suggests that PVAL does indeed give a distorted picture of the relative ability of communities to provide education services.

The nature of this distortion can be seen by looking at some simple correlation coefficients. Letting RP be the rank of each community when PVAL is used and RC be the rank when CAP is used, the simple correlations of the difference (RP–RC) with five socio-economic and tax composition variables are as follows:

Y	WR	POV	C	I
−.62	.06	.47	.05	.36

where Y is median family income, WR is residential property per pupil, POV is the fraction of families with below poverty level income, C is the commercial property fraction of the assessed realty tax base, and I is the industrial property fraction of the assessed realty tax base. The negative correlation with median family income (Y) and the positive correlation with the fraction of families in poverty (POV) show that PVAL overstates capacity (i.e. RP > RC) in low income communities and in communities in which there is a high incidence of poverty. The very small positive correlation with residential wealth per pupil is the result of a high positive correlation of both RP and RC with WR.[24] It suggests that use of PVAL creates very little systematic distortion in relation to the residential base per pupil. The final two correlation coefficients imply that PVAL overstates fiscal capacity in highly industrialized communities and has little systematic distorting effect in relation to the fraction of the base that is commercial.

In conclusion, there is clear evidence that PVAL gives a distorted picture of relative fiscal capacity, where fiscal capacity is defined in terms of the relative ability of communities to provide education services. If the index is the basis for state or federal aid to local communities, the purpose of which is to reduce disparities in education service levels caused by differing abilities to finance such services, then, as has been shown, the distortions caused by PVAL work to the disadvantage of low income communities.

[24] The correlation is .78 for RP and .75 for RC.

[2]

STATE AID TO OFFSET FISCAL DISPARITIES ACROSS COMMUNITIES[†]

KATHARINE L. BRADBURY,* HELEN F. LADD,** MARK PERRAULT,*** ANDREW RESCHOVSKY**** AND JOHN YINGER*****

ABSTRACT

Both the availability of taxable resources and the costs of producing local services vary widely across jurisdictions. This situation is widely regarded as inequitable, and many state aid programs have been designed to offset the fiscal disadvantages faced by jurisdictions with relatively low resources or relatively high costs. Existing programs, however, account for these fiscal disparities in an ad hoc manner, particularly on the cost side. This paper defines the concept of uncontrollable costs, presents a regression-based method for measuring cost differences, calculates a community's fiscal disadvantage as a function of its costs and resources, and designs state aid programs to offset this fiscal disadvantage. The approach presented here is based on simple concepts and can be implemented with readily available data. It was developed as part of the debate over state aid in Massachusetts where a modified version of the approach has recently been enacted.

ONE of the most dramatic features of the United States system of local governments is that residents of some jurisdictions face significantly higher tax burdens or receive significantly lower levels of public services (or both) than residents of other jurisdictions blessed with more resources or lower costs. This feature raises an important set of equity concerns for policymakers. Even with substantial redistribution of income among individuals, it is likely that lower income people and those who face discrimination in the housing market will live in jurisdictions that have fiscal disadvantages relative to communities inhabited by higher income, more mobile households. The primary purpose of this paper is to use economic analysis to develop improved ways of designing state aid programs to offset these fiscal disadvantages. The paper does not argue the case for fiscal equity, but rather develops a new set of grant formulas that can be used to achieve any degree of fiscal equalization chosen by policymakers.

In a formal sense, fiscal disparities exist when local governments must levy different tax rates to provide the same level of public services. Disparities reflect differences both in the abilities of local governments to raise revenues and in the costs of providing public services. The measurement of disparities in revenue capacity is now fairly well understood, and many existing intergovernmental aid programs have been designed to offset some of these revenue disparities. Differences across communities in the costs of providing public services, however, are less well understood and less often the basis of equalizing aid programs. Consequently, this paper focused on the measurement and use of cost indexes in intergovernmental aid programs.

Much of the research reported here was developed in the context of recent local aid debates in Massachusetts, with the explicit goal of influencing the outcome of those debates. As discussed in Section IV of this paper, Massachusetts recently enacted a new local aid distribution formula that embodies many of the ideas in this paper. The rest of the paper is organized as follows: Section I defines the concept of cost disparities and surveys the use of need or cost measures in existing grant programs. Section II shows how to measure cost disparities and applies the procedure to Massachusetts cities and towns. Section III incorporates cost indexes into in-

*Federal Reserve Bank of Boston.
**Kennedy School of Government, Harvard University.
***Joint Committee on Taxation, Massachusetts Legislature.
****Tufts University.
*****Visiting Professor, University of Michigan.

tergovernmental aid formulas. The paper ends with a brief conclusion.

I. Cost Disparities and Intergovernmental Aid

Cost disparities refer to differences in the cost of providing local public services. These disparities are hard to measure because the production process for local public services is difficult both to describe and to measure. Nevertheless, this paper shows that cost disparities can be described in a systematic way, and measured with readily available techniques. This section carefully defines cost disparities and explains how they have been used and measured in existing intergovernmental aid programs.

Definition of Cost Disparities

Bradford, Malt, and Oates (1969) first made the distinction between public spending and public service or output levels. Public spending refers to the size of the municipal budget, whereas public output refers to the results of public spending, such as fire protection, weekly garbage pick-ups, or public school pupils learning arithmetic. As explained by Bradford, Malt, and Oates, this distinction is important because the level of public output depends not only on public spending, but on a variety of environmental factors in each community.

Furthermore, the cost of providing any given level of public output depends both on factors under the control of government officials and on factors largely outside of their control. For example, local governments can control the number of firefighters assigned to each firehouse, but they cannot control the environmental factors that directly affect the cost of providing any given level of fire protection. These costs will be higher in a community with densely packed frame houses, or with tall buildings, than in a community with brick houses on one-acre lots. To achieve the same level of fire protection (measured, say, by the probability of any resident experiencing a serious loss from fire), the denser community must hire more firefighters and purchase more fire equipment. Similarly in education, more teachers, and often special equipment and materials are necessary to provide education in a community where relatively many children participate in remedial, vocational, or bilingual education programs.

Throughout this paper the term "cost disparities" refers only to cost differences that are outside the control of local officials. Only these uncontrollable cost differences are appropriately offset by equalizing intergovernmental aid programs; policies to offset controllable cost differences would have the undesirable effect of weakening cities' incentives to control costs.[1] These cost disparities produce what some people have referred to as variations in service "needs." A city into which relatively many people commute, for example, is often said to "need" more spending per capita than other cities to provide the same level of public safety services for its residents. That is, a community into which many people commute has higher uncontrollable costs than other cities. By defining a community's needs in terms of the effects of environmental cost factors, we hope to clarify and make more precise the concept of needs. In this way, the focus is on differences in the costs of providing local services rather than controversial value judgments about what each community "needs."

Measures of Costs or Needs in Existing Grant Programs

The most common measure of needs in general-purpose U.S. intergovernmental aid programs is simply population. For example, population serves as the only need measure in the three-factor formula for distributing federal general revenue sharing funds to states. Similarly, it is the standard measure of need included in many state revenue sharing programs. Only a handful of states use more precise measures of needs, such as population density, the number of public housing units, or the number of welfare-eligible school age children, for distributing general-purpose state aid to their local governments (Advisory Commission on Intergovernmental Relations, 1980).

The more narrowly defined are the programmatic goals of an inter-governmental aid program, the more likely is it that needs will be measured by something other than population. Several federal block grants include explicit measures of needs in their distribution formulas. The size of the poverty population and number of overcrowded housing units are included, for example, in the formula for distributing community development block grant funds.[2] Explicit need measures are also included in many of the categorical aid programs that still account for more than 60 percent of federal aid to state and local governments. This fact is not surprising since need-related variables, such as the number of poor children or the presence of hazardous waste sites, are essential components of distribution formulas for programs that must target funds narrowly to meet their programmatic goals.

Formulas for distributing state aid to local school districts provide the most frequent example of attempts to include measures that reflect differential costs per unit of service provided. To compensate local school districts for the extra costs of providing education to "special needs" children, such as those with learning disabilities or those coming from disadvantaged households, several states distribute aid proportionately to "weighted" pupils, where the weights reflect the extra cost of educating these students.[3] So far as we know, however, no state has adopted the regression-based educational cost indexes recently developed by a number of economists (Chambers, 1978, 1980; Wendling, 1981; and Brazer and Anderson, 1975).

Several other countries are ahead of the United States in terms of measuring and integrating comprehensive need or cost factors into general-purpose aid programs designed to equalize fiscal positions. The central governments of the United Kingdom, Australia, and West Germany, for example, all distribute grants to lower level governments partially on the basis of differing costs of providing government services (Advisory Commission on Intergovernmental Relations, 1981). The United Kingdom has experimented with both regression-based and client-group approaches to measuring needs. Until 1979, a "needs equalization" grant to local governments was based on a regression of local government expenditures on various demographic, geographic, and socio-economic variables. Variables with statistically significant regression coefficients were used as indicators of need, and were entered into the grant formula with their coefficients as weights. Because the regression included neither resource nor preference variables, however, critics charged that the coefficients of the included variables were seriously biased. Under the client-group approach introduced in 1980, experts employed by the central government identify various groups of people as being in need of particular local services. The estimated cost per person of providing a standard amount of the service then provides the basis for determining the "expenditure needs" of each local government. This client-group approach has been criticized for giving the central government too much influence over local government spending decisions.[4]

These examples illustrate that most of the attempts to allocate grants to state and local governments on the basis of cost or need differences have been quite *ad hoc*.[5] The next two sections of this paper describe a method of measuring cost disparities and demonstrate how to incorporate this measure into general-purpose grant formulas.

II. Measuring Cost Disparities

Environmental costs are part of the technology of producing local public services. A jurisdiction with high costs cannot produce as much with the same spending as a jurisdiction with low costs. To analyze the impact of environmental costs on the production of local services, we integrate the distinction between expenditures and service levels into a standard model of local voting behavior. This analysis yields a relationship between local expenditures and environmental cost variables that can be estimated and translated into a cost index. This section derives this expenditure equation and develops cost indexes for the cities and towns of Massachusetts.

Environmental Costs and Local Expenditures

A large literature on local expenditure determination, much of which is reviewed by Inman (1979), builds on a model of decision making by a decisive voter, often assumed to be the median voter. In the standard model, the decisive voter's utility depends on the level of local spending. Following Bradford, Malt, and Oates (1969), a more appropriate formulation is for utility to depend on the level of local services. Let Z_d be the decisive voter's consumption of a composite private good (including housing), and S be the level of local services in a jurisdiction, which is the same for all households in the jurisdiction. Then the decisive voter attempts to maximize her utility, which is a function of Z_d and S.

In attempting to maximize her utility, the decisive voter is confronted with two constraints: her own budget constraint and the budget constraint of her jurisdiction. Her income (net of federal and state taxes), Y_d, must be equal to her spending on Z plus her local taxes, assumed here to be all in the form of property taxes. Thus, her own budget constraint is $Y_d = Z_d + tV_d$, where t is the effective property tax rate, V_d is the market value of her property, and the price of Z is assumed to be unity.

The production function for local services shows up in the jurisdiction's budget constraint. The service level, S, is a function of the level of per capita spending, E, and of environmental costs and the costs of inputs, such as employees and equipment. This production function, like any production function, can be inverted to yield a cost function, namely E(S,P,C), which indicates the per capita amount that must be spent to obtain an output level S in a jurisdiction with input costs P and environmental costs C. The jurisdiction's budget constraint limits local per capita expenditures to the per capita amount of government revenues. Let V be the average property value in the jurisdiction and let A be the per capita intergovernmental aid and non-property-tax revenue received by the jurisdiction. Then the jurisdiction's budget constraint is $E(S,P,C) = t\bar{V} + A$.

Thus, the decisive voter's goal is to pick Z_d, S, and t to

Maximize $U_d(Z_d,S)$

Subject to $Y_d = Z_d + tV_d$

$$E(S,P,C) = t\bar{V} + A \qquad (1)$$

The first-order conditions of this problem imply that the decisive voter selects the level of local services at which

$$(\partial U_d/\partial S)/(\partial U_d/\partial Z_d)$$
$$= (\partial E/\partial S)(V_d/\bar{V}). \qquad (2)$$

The left-hand side of this condition is the marginal rate of substitution (MRS) between local public services and the composite private good, which can be interpreted as the amount the decisive voter would pay for another unit of public services. The right-hand side is the marginal production cost of services, which depends on input and environmental costs, multiplied by the decisive voter's tax-price, $V_d/\bar{V}$. In other words, the right-hand side is the decisive voter's own marginal cost of another unit of S, and this condition indicates that the decisive voter picks the level of S at which her own marginal cost is equal to her own marginal benefit.

This simple model identifies the broad categories of variables that influence expenditure determination. The voter's MRS between S and Z_d obviously depends on preferences. Furthermore, the level of S at which this MRS reaches a particular value depends on the decisive voter's consumption of Z and therefore depends on the decisive voter's income and on the fiscal resources available to the jurisdiction. As noted, the marginal production cost of S depends on P and C. These results combine to imply that the level of expenditure is a function of the community's resources, cost variables, and the voter's resources and preferences (labeled D for demand), or

$$E = f(\bar{V}, A, P, C, D). \quad (3)$$

Much work has been done and more remains to be learned about the best functional form for this type of model.[6] Within the context of a state aid debate, however, the benefits of simplicity outweigh the gains from precise specification. Thus, we simply identify key variables in each of the categories in equation (3) and estimate a simple linear relationship between per capita expenditures and these variables. This approach rules out tests of detailed hypotheses about local decision making, but permits the estimation of the impacts on local spending of the variables in these categories.

This simple approach is a practical compromise—not an ideal solution. In particular, it provides better estimates of the impact of environmental cost factors on spending than on local public services. Presumably, voters respond to higher environmental costs just as they would respond to any higher price—by substituting away from local services. For any non-zero price elasticity, a simple linear model will underestimate the impact of environmental costs on local services. Fortunately, estimated price elasticities tend to be very low (about −0.3, see Inman, 1979), but some underestimation remains. This issue is obviously important for the design of policy, and we return to it below.

An Application to Massachusetts

This section describes an expenditure regression for Massachusetts and uses it to calculate cost indexes. The sample for this regression is the 336 cities and towns in Massachusetts with a 1980 population above 500. The dependent variable is total operating expenditure per capita in each city and town in Massachusetts, including school and non-school local expenditure.[7]

As shown in Table 1, virtually all of the explanatory variables in the expenditure regression fall into the categories identified earlier: fiscal resources, cost factors, and demand factors. The property tax is the only major tax that local governments in Massachusetts are allowed to use, so the regressions include a single tax base, namely equalized property value per capita, the official state estimate of the market value of the property in each community. Other resource variables for each community include local non-property-tax revenues and four intergovernmental variables, namely federal categorical aid, federal general revenue sharing, total state aid received by the community, and state aid to regional school districts (allocated to the cities and towns in each district).

Many environmental cost variables can be identified, but some may be difficult to interpret because of their correlation with other expenditure determinants, such as the tax base or voter preferences. Thus, we interpret as environmental cost variables only those variables that unambiguously reflect cost considerations. The regression includes nine explicit cost variables: the number of "weighted" pupils per capita; population density; per capita employment (by place of work) in trade and services, in manufacturing, and in state or federal government; crime rate; percent of the population below the poverty line; age of the housing stock; and the miles of local roads per registered vehicle.

Each of these variables has a strong link to environmental costs. The pupil weights, which are calculated by the Massachusetts Department of Education for use in the Chapter 70 School Aid Program, reflect the fact that some pupils, such as those with learning disabilities, are more expensive to educate than others. Higher population density increases the costs of certain public services such as fire and police protection. The three employment variables reflect the fact that more employment relative to population implies more commuters into a community and hence more congestion and additional demands for street maintenance, sewer and water service, police and fire protection, and traffic control.[8] Higher crime rates directly increase the costs of providing a

Table 1

DESCRIPTION OF THE VARIABLES

Variable	Description	Mean (Standard Deviation)
Dependent		
EXPEND	Total 1980 operating expenditures per capita on school and municipal services (excluding transit assessments)	$752 ($210)
Cost Factors		
DENSITY	1980 population divided by square miles of area	1,279 (2,508)
WFTE	Weighted full-time equivalent pupils per capita in 1980	0.24 (0.04)
CRIME	Number of crimes reported per 1000 inhabitants in 1980	40.64 (23.25)
HOUSAGE	Fraction of 1980 year-round housing units built before 1940.	0.39 (0.16)
GOVER	Number of state and federal government employees per capita in 1980 by place of work	0.05 (0.04)
MANUF	Number of employees in agriculture, forestry, fisheries, mining, construction, manufacturing, and transportation per capita in 1980 by place of work	0.11 (0.13)
TRADE	Number of employees in trade, finance, insurance, real estate, and services per capita in 1980 by place of work	0.13 (0.10)
POVERTY	Percent of population with 1979 income below the poverty level	0.07 (0.04)
MILES	Local road mileage per registered vehicle in 1980	0.01 (0.02)
Resources		
EQV80	Total property tax valuation per capita in 1980 as equalized by the Massachusetts Department of Revenue	$20,213 ($13,781)

Table 1 (continued)

Variable	Description	Mean (Standard Deviation)
Resources (cont.)		
LOCREV	Estimated local receipts (motor vehicle excise fees, special assessments, etc.) per capita in 1980	$82.17 ($59.50)
STAID	State aid (other than regional school aid) paid to the city or town per capita in 1980	$154.88 ($ 67.34)
FEDAID	General revenue sharing entitlements per capita in 1980	$19.96 ($ 8.97)
GRANTS	Total direct federal aid (other than general revenue sharing) per capita in 1980	$35.61 ($81.96)
REGAID	Aid to regional school districts allocated to each member community per capita in 1980	$66.66 ($81.70)
Other		
ELDERLY	Fraction of population age sixty-five and over in 1980	0.12 (0.04)
INCOME	Personal income per capita in 1979	$7,599 ($1,755)
POPRAT	Rate of population change defined as 1980 population divided by 1970 population	1.16 (0.29)
POPRAT2	Rate of population change squared	1.43 (0.93)

Source: Sources include federal publications such as the "1980 Census of Population and Housing" and "Eleventh Period Entitlements," Office of Revenue Sharing, U.S. Department of the Treasury; and local sources such as the Massachusetts Division of Employment Security, the Massachusetts Departments of Education and Public Works, and the Massachusetts Taxpayers' Foundation. For the MANUF and TRADE variables, the number of employees in industry divisions for municipalities with disclosure problems was estimated by taking the percentage of total employment in the city or town equal to the average percentage for municipalities in the same population class for that industry division. For the CRIME variable, population class average rates were used for 98 small towns for which crime rates were not available.

given level of police protection.[9] Higher concentrations of poor people generally result in higher education costs and may also lead to higher public health and recreation costs (but not higher local welfare costs since the state government pays for welfare in Massachusetts). In general, an older housing stock requires increased fire protection costs and, perhaps more important, is likely to indicate that the public infrastructure, including sewers and bridges, is also old and more costly to maintain. And finally, cities and towns with an extensive network of roads have higher snow removal and road maintenance costs.

In addition to resource and cost variables, the regression includes two variables to reflect the voter's resources and preferences for local services and two variables to reflect adjustments to population change. The elderly generally support lower levels of public spending than the population as a whole, so the first demand variable is the proportion of each community's population age 65 and over. The other demand variable is the community's per capita income. Finally, the regressions include the rate of change in community population between 1970 and 1980 and the square of this population change. These variables reflect the fact that expenditures tend to be higher than would otherwise be expected in cities and towns that are experiencing either rapid increases or rapid decreases in population. In both cases, a period of several years may be necessary to adjust public services to the new population level.[10]

Input prices such as municipal wage rates are not included in the regression. On the other hand variation across communities in input prices may reflect the effects of environmental factors outside the control of local officials. For example communities with unfavorable working conditions associated with high density, high crime rates, or large proportions of pupils from disadvantaged households may have to pay above average wages to attract municipal employees. The exclusion of wage rates from the regression equation correctly allows the environmental cost variables to capture the expenditure effects of wage variations of this type. Stated differently, the coefficients of the environmental cost factors measure their two effects on spending: direct effects through the production function and indirect effects through their impacts on wage rates.

On the other hand some of the variation in wage rates may partially reflect discretionary choices by local public officials. To the extent that variations of this type are not correlated with the environmental cost factors (or other variables in the equation), their expenditure impacts will appear in the error term of the regression. Ideally, it would be desirable to include in the regression a price variable that measures these discretionary variations. Such a measure would be both conceptually and empirically difficult to construct, however, especially given the limited data on input prices available at the community level.

The regression results are presented in Table 2. Overall, the regression performs well and many of the coefficients are significantly different from zero. Among the cost variables, density, weighted pupils, and the crime rate are significant at the .01 level. Housing age and trade employment are significant at the .05 level. However, the other four cost variables, government and manufacturing employment, poverty, and road miles, are not statistically significant and their effects on spending are small. In addition, five of the six resource variables and one of the demand variables are highly significant.

To calculate a cost index based on these results, the next step is to predict what each community would have spent if it had average resources, average demand, and average population change, but retained its own values for the cost variables.[11] We carry out this "prediction" by substituting the average values for the resource and other non-cost variables plus the actual values of the cost variables into the estimated regression equation. Thus, variation in these predicted expenditures reflects variation in environmental cost factors alone.

The final step is to translate these predicted expenditures into a cost index by

Table 2

MASSACHUSETTS EXPENDITURE MODEL

Explanatory Variable	Estimated Coefficient	t-Statistic
Costs		
DENSITY	0.0114**	4.04
WFTE	1123**	6.17
CRIME	0.990**	3.33
HOUSAGE	111*	2.05
GOVER	21.6	0.16
MANUF	66.6	1.38
TRADE	160*	2.17
POVERTY	148	0.71
MILES	400	1.01
Resources		
EQV80	.00712**	12.56
LOCREV	1.17**	11.36
STAID	0.430**	3.67
FEDAID	3.24**	4.91
GRANTS	0.037	0.53
REGAID	−0.589**	−6.10
Other		
ELDERLY	−327	−1.77
INCOME	0.0326**	7.18
POPRAT	−130	−1.15
POPRAT2	34.1	1.07

Dependent Variable: EXPEND: Adjusted R^2 = .786; Number of observations = 336.

* Significantly different from zero at the 5 percent level (2-tailed test).

** Significantly different from zero at the 1 percent level (2-tailed test).

dividing each prediction by the mean per capita expenditure for all 351 cities and towns in Massachusetts. The value of this index for a particular community can be interpreted as one plus the proportionate increase in spending in that community that is due to that community's environmental cost factors compared to the average.

The estimated cost index ranges from highs of 1.40 in Boston and 1.34 in Cambridge to a low of 0.70 in the town of Harvard (no connection to the university!). In other words, these estimates suggest that Boston or Cambridge would have to spend 30 to 40 percent more per person to provide the same level of public services as a community with average costs, and they would have to spend about twice as much as towns like Harvard. Several other communities, including Somerville, Lawrence, Lynn, and Springfield, have costs that are at least 15 percent above average, while other communities, including Shrewsbury and Chatham, have costs that are more than 10 percent below average.[12] These figures should be viewed as conservative estimates of the true cost differences; as noted above, they represent better measures of the impact of costs on expenditures than on service levels.

III. Designing State Aid Formulas to Offset Cost and Revenue Disadvantages

Cost indexes can be integrated into state aid formulas in a number of different ways, depending on the objective of the aid program.

Defining the Objectives of State Aid

As noted earlier, equalizing aid programs have been designed in several states and countries to account for the fact that costs are higher and resources lower in some local areas than in others and to partially or fully offset these cost and revenue disadvantages. Jurisdictions with relatively high costs must pay more than lower cost communities to achieve the same level of local services, and jurisdictions with relatively few taxable resources must make a greater sacrifice than wealthier towns to obtain the same revenues. Therefore, we design an equalizing state aid program to meet the following objective:

> To the extent possible within the state aid budget, offset the additional spending that a jurisdiction must undertake to achieve the same level of services as some baseline jurisdiction and offset the additional sacrifice that a jurisdiction must make to raise the same revenue as a baseline jurisdiction.[13]

This objective requires policymakers to specify the baseline jurisdiction which, as discussed below, is a decision about the desired degree of equalization.

This objective is similar to the objective, which is familiar to economists, of compensating jurisdictions for real income losses—in particular for the real income losses they experience because their costs are higher or their resources lower than those of a baseline jurisdiction.[14] Figure 1 illustrates our objective as it relates to the compensation of cost differences. Service level S^* represents the level that would be chosen by a baseline community given its possibility set (denoted by Z_1S_1) among private goods (Z) and local public goods (S), and the preferences of the decisive voter (indicated by indifference curves I_1 and I_2). (The decisive voter's tax price, which is not important for this discussion, is assumed to be unity.) A jurisdiction with the same resources as the baseline jurisdiction but with higher costs would have the possibility set denoted by Z_1S_2 and would choose a service level of S_H. A block grant of $(Z^* - Z_2)$ to the high-cost jurisdiction would compensate that jurisdiction for the extra spending needed to reach the baseline service level, S^*.

In practice, however, our method of estimating cost differences focuses on expenditures—not on service levels. Hence, the high-cost jurisdiction's cost disadvantage relative to the baseline jurisdiction is measured by $(Z^* - Z_H)$. This difference understates the true cost disadvantage, $(Z^* - Z_2)$, whenever the price elasticity of demand is nonzero, or, in terms of the figure, whenever S_H differs from the service level S^* chosen by the baseline community. The amount $(Z^* - Z_H)$ accurately

Figure 1

COMPENSATION FOR COST DISADVANTAGES

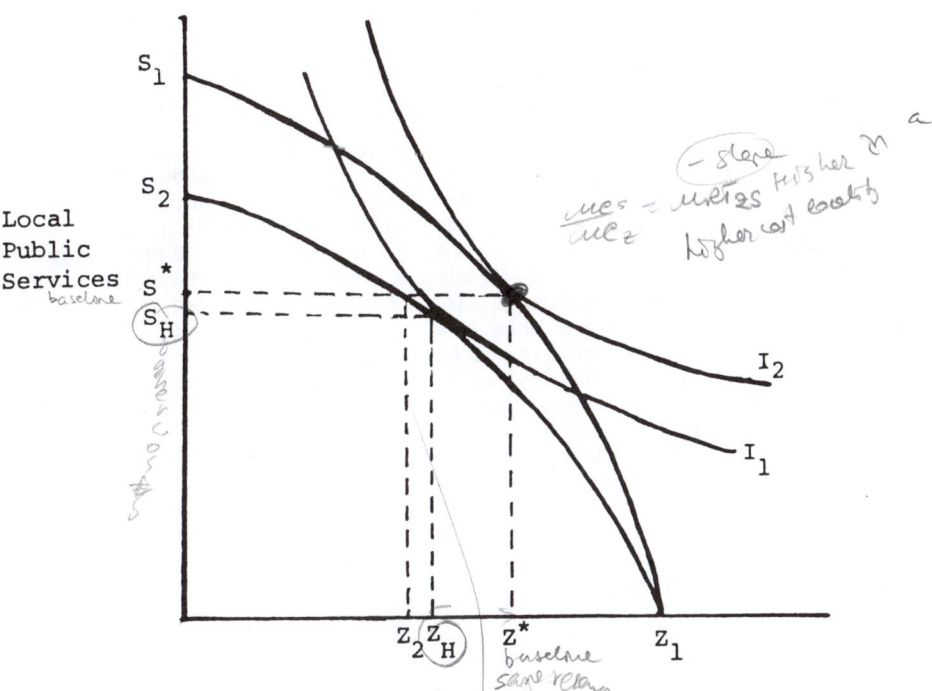

measures the cost-induced extra spending in the high cost jurisdiction; it fails to account, however, for the fact that the jurisdiction has responded to the higher costs by reducing its service level. Consequently, aid based on our calculations understates the amount of aid required for full compensation.

It is instructive to compare our chosen objective with an alternative objective, that of providing sufficient aid to the high cost jurisdiction to induce it to provide the service level available in the baseline jurisdiction. This categorical equity objective derives from the judgment that some categories of public services are so important that all citizens should have access to some minimum level. The amount of block grant aid required to assure that a high-cost jurisdiction would provide the service level available in the baseline jurisdiction, S^*, depends on the community's price and income elasticities of demand. For reasonable values of these elasticities, the aid required to meet this categorical equity objective would be greater than the aid required to meet our objective.[15]

Deriving a State Aid Formula to Offset Fiscal Disadvantages

The overall fiscal position of a city can be summarized by its *need-revenue* gap.[16] This gap does not measure the city's actual budget deficit; instead, it measures the difference between what the city must spend to provide a basic package of local services and its available revenues at a standard level of tax effort. The city's relative fiscal position can then be measured as the difference between its own need revenue gap and the gap in some baseline community. This produces a measure of the city's *fiscal disadvantage* which summarizes the impacts of high costs or low resources or both on the ability of the city to provide a basic package of local services.

The starting point in defining a community's need-revenue gap is its cost index. If the community with average expenditures on local public services spends $\bar{E}$ and C_i is community i's cost index, then $\bar{E}C_i$ approximates what community i would have to spend to obtain the average community's service level. Because high-cost communities are likely to have responded to the higher price for public services implied by above-average costs by consuming fewer services, $\bar{E}C_i$ is a conservative estimate of what it would actually cost community i to obtain the service level enjoyed by the average community.

On the revenue side, the resources available to each community are measured at a standard level of tax effort, to be chosen by state policymakers. Following the Advisory Commission on Intergovernmental Relations (1971), for example, the standard level of tax effort for each tax could be defined as the average local tax rate in the state.[17] If the standard tax rate is $\bar{t}$ and the tax base per capita in community i is B_i, then the revenue available to community i at a standard level of tax effort is ($\bar{t}B_i$). If many taxes are used, the elements of this expression should be interpreted as vectors.

Hence, community i's need-revenue gap, G_i, is

$$G_i = \bar{E}C_i - \bar{t}B_i \quad (4)$$

and its fiscal disadvantage is defined as

$$G_i - G^* = \bar{E}C_i - \bar{t}B_i - G^*$$
$$\text{if } G_i - G^* > 0 \quad (5)$$

where G^* is the gap in the baseline community. If $G_i - G^* < 0$, no fiscal disadvantage exists in community i. Note that G^* must be explicitly chosen by policymakers. For example, if policymakers choose a baseline gap of zero, only those communities with positive need-revenue gaps would be deemed to have fiscal disadvantages and therefore to have a claim on state aid designed to offset such disadvantages. Thus, the policy parameter G^* is the baseline level of the need-revenue gap above which aid will be awarded. For a given state aid budget, a high value for G^* would concentrate aid in the communities with the largest gaps and a low value would spread aid more thinly among a greater number of communities. Thus, the choice of G^* is equivalent to selecting the degree of equalization for the state aid program.

Suppose the state has appropriated M dollars for state aid and has decided to offset the same proportion of the fiscal disadvantage in each community. If A_i is the aid per capita to community i and N_i is the population of community i, then the aid formula must meet the following three conditions:

$$A_i = r[G_i - G^*] \quad (6)$$

$$\sum_i A_i N_i = M \quad (7)$$

$$A_i > 0. \quad (8)$$

The fraction of the gap offset, r, is constant across communities, but is unknown. Substituting (5) and (6) into (7) and solving for r yields the following expression for total aid to community i:

$$A_i N_i = \frac{[(\bar{E}C_i - \bar{t}B_i) - G^*]N_i}{\sum_j [(\bar{E}C_j - \bar{t}B_j) - G^*]N_j} M, \quad (9)$$

where j indicates the set of communities with fiscal disadvantages, that is, with need-revenue gaps greater than the baseline gap G^*.[18] This formula indicates that community i's share of the total aid budget is proportional to its population multiplied by its fiscal disadvantage. Similarly, its per capita aid is proportional to its fiscal disadvantage. Communities with need-revenue gaps less than the baseline would receive no aid under this equalizing program.

What determines r, the fraction of each eligible community's disadvantage that is offset by aid? Solving equations (6) and (9) for r yields:

$$r = M/\sum_{j}[(\bar{E}C_j - \bar{t}B_j) - G^*]N_j \qquad (10)$$

where, as before, the summation includes only those communities with gaps larger than G^*. The fraction of the disadvantage that is offset will be larger, the larger is the budget M. The fraction will also be larger, the higher is the chosen baseline gap G^*, since increasing G^* reduces the number of communities receiving aid. Given M and G^*, greater fiscal disparities across communities within the state, as measured by the size of the need-revenue gaps, leads to a smaller fraction of the fiscal disadvantages being offset. Similarly, the fraction will be smaller if larger population centers have greater per capita disadvantages, on average, than smaller towns. Equation (10) can also be used to calculate the budget required to eliminate fiscal disadvantages. Setting r equal to one and multiplying both sides of (10) by the summation reveals that the required budget is the sum of the population-weighted fiscal disadvantages.

In using this approach to design an equalizing aid program, one must decide how to treat existing state aid. One alternative is to take a *comprehensive* approach that would ignore the distribution of existing aid. The state budget for this approach would be the sum of the total amount appropriated for general-purpose aid programs in the previous year plus any additional funds state policymakers were willing to devote to local aid in the current year. This comprehensive approach has the advantage of accomplishing as much equalization as possible given the total aid budget. It has the disadvantage that implementing it within a single year could require huge aid adjustments that might not be politically acceptable; many communities, for example, might receive substantially less aid with the new comprehensive aid program than the amounts they received the previous year.

The formula for a comprehensive aid program is based on need-revenue gaps that do not count existing general-purpose state aid as available revenues. To use equation (9) as a formula for this type of aid program, at least two other sources of revenue, namely federal revenue sharing aid, and special-purpose (categorical) state aid should be included with $\bar{t}B_i$ in the calculation of each community's gap.[19] Because existing general purpose state aid is excluded from the gap calculations, G_i will be greater than zero for most, if not all, communities.

An alternative approach is to use equation (9) to design a new *incremental* state aid program, that is, a program that would help offset any fiscal disadvantage remaining after accounting for all existing state aid programs. In effect, this approach accepts existing aid programs as given, so that no community would receive less aid than it received the previous year, and accomplishes as much equalization as possible with the funds appropriated for the new aid program. With this approach, existing state aid, as well as federal aid, should be added to standardized local revenue, $\bar{t}B_i$, in calculating the need-revenue gaps. Because all revenue sources are included in the gap calculations, average revenue would be approximately equal to average expenditure, implying that the average of G_i over all communities would be about zero.

Note that the scope of the aid program affects the choice of the policy parameter G^*. To reach the same number of communities, G^* must be considerably larger for a comprehensive state aid program than for an incremental aid program because the average gap is positive, and probably large, for a comprehensive aid program, but zero for an incremental program. In either case, however, higher values for G^* concentrate aid among the communities with the largest gaps.

The role of G^* is illustrated in Figure 2. Once the total budget of the aid program is determined, per capita aid in a community depends only on the need-revenue gap in that community and the baseline gap G^*. Figure 2 portrays three

Figure 2

THREE HYPOTHETICAL INCREMENTAL AID PROGRAMS
TO OFFSET NEED-REVENUE GAPS

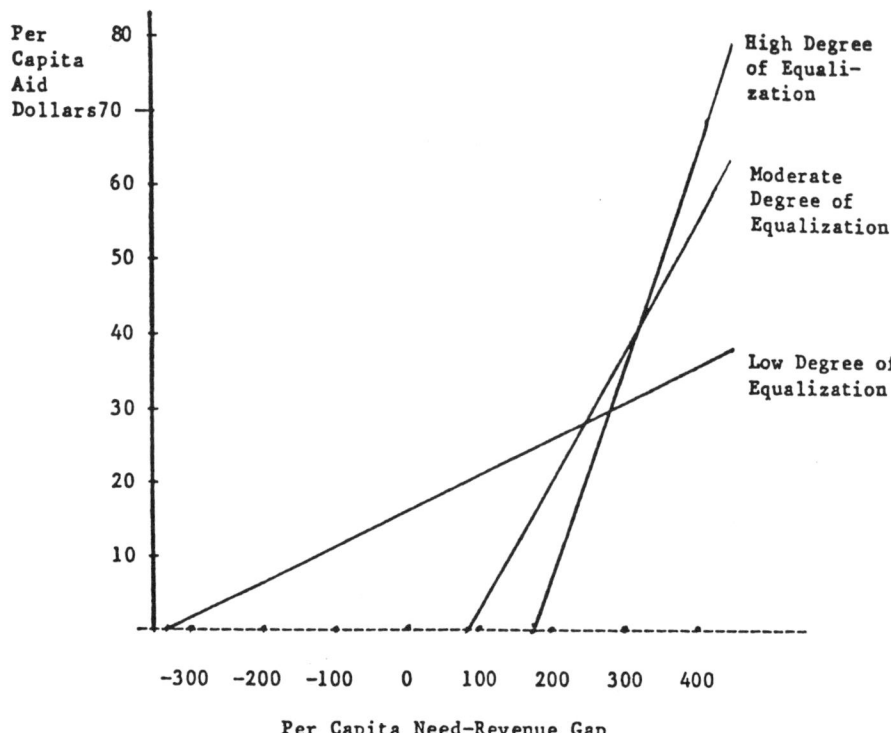

incremental aid programs for cities and towns in Massachusetts, each with a budget of $150 million. The highest value of G* is set so that only one third of the communities receive aid—those with the largest need-revenue gaps; the lowest value of G* is set so that all but 10 percent of the communities receive aid; and the middle value is set so that 50 percent of all communities receive aid. The slopes of the lines in Figure 2 depend on the number of communities at each gap value and on their populations. In fact, the slope of each line is equal to r, which depends, as explained earlier by equation 10, on the population-weighted gaps of all communities receiving aid.

The choice of G* substantially alters the amounts and distribution of aid across communities. The three aid programs illustrated in Figure 2 have the same total budget and the same measured need-revenue gaps for each community; they differ only in G*, the baseline gap above which aid is awarded (shown by each line's intercept on the horizontal axis). In these examples, a community with a zero gap would receive over $15 per capita under the "low-equalization" program, but nothing if either of the other two programs were adopted (although it would obviously continue to receive aid under existing programs). The low equalization program spreads aid over more communities and therefore provides less aid to high gap jurisdictions; a community with a need-revenue gap of $350 would receive over $15 more per capita under the high equalization program than it would receive under the low equalization program.

Any of the three hypothetical aid programs shown in Figure 2 would provide greater average per capita aid to Massachusetts' larger cities than to the state's smaller towns because the cities, on average, have the greatest fiscal disadvantages. The high equalization program, however, would focus considerably more aid on the large cities than would the low equalization program. The average community with population over 50,000 would receive about 50 percent more per capita aid under the high equalization program than under the low equalization program. In contrast, towns with populations below 5,000 would average only a couple of dollars of aid per capita under the high equalization programs, but about seven times more under the low equalization program. Small towns receive very little aid under a program with high equalization because most of their need-revenue gaps are smaller than that program's baseline G*.

Deriving a State Aid Formula to Offset Only Cost Disadvantages

Several states already have aid programs that partially offset revenue disparities. Policymakers in these states may therefore want to focus any additional aid resources on offsetting cost disadvantages. This section briefly summarizes how cost indexes can be incorporated into an aid formula to accomodate this narrower goal.

Community i's per capita cost disadvantage is what it must pay for a standard bundle of services in excess of what a community with average costs must pay, or $(\check{E}C_i - \check{E}C)$. Since $\check{C} = 1$ by definition, community i's cost disadvantage is $(\check{E}C_i - \check{E})$. Alternatively, policymakers may not want to use the average community as a baseline. If C* is the cost index of the baseline community, then the cost disadvantage of community i is $(\check{E}C_i - \check{E}C^*)$. If policymakers want aid to be proportional to this cost disadvantage, then $A_i = r'(\check{E}C_i - \check{E}C^*)$. Combining this expression with equations (7) and (8) yields the following aid formula to offset cost disadvantages alone:

$$A_iN_i = \frac{(C_i - C^*)N_i}{\sum_k (C_k - C^*)N_k} M \qquad (11)$$

where k indicates the set of communities with positive cost disadvantages. Thus, community i's share of the aid budget is proportional to its population multiplied by the difference between its cost index and the baseline cost index selected by policymakers.

Updating of Cost Indexes used in Aid Formulas

The use of cost indexes (such as those calculated in this paper) in state aid formulas raises one final issue, namely, when and how the indexes should be updated as the characteristics of cities and towns change over time. This issue raises two questions: when to update the regression and when to update the cost indexes. Because the impact of cost factors on spending is unlikely to change very fast, the regressions need not be updated very often. On the other hand, values of cost variables for individual communities may change rapidly over time. The cost index could be updated using the original regression estimates by collecting the most recent data on the cost variables and substituting these new data into the cost index calculations. Concern about obsolete information should be tempered by the fact that only changes in the *relative* positions of individual communities, not across-the-board increases or decreases in individual variables, require a change in the cost index.

IV. Implementation in Massachusetts

Unlike many research projects, this one was undertaken with the explicit goal of encouraging state policymakers in Massachusetts to develop a new and innovative way to distribute state aid to local governments. Massachusetts was ripe for a new approach. The 1980 voter-initiated tax limitation measure, commonly known as Proposition 2 1/2, severely restricted the capacity of local governments to raise taxes for local public services. Although state aid increased in the following years, the state government distributed the additional money in an *ad hoc* manner using a different approach each year. With the election in 1982 of a new governor committed to increasing state aid and to making such aid more predictable, the state seemed receptive to a new approach to local aid. The new administration encouraged the development of new approaches by holding weekly task force meetings of interested groups during the winter of 1983 and the fall of 1984. The active participation of two of the current authors in these task force meetings provided an ideal forum for the discussion and development of the approach described in this paper.

The outcome of this process plus additional work by legislative staff members was a program to distribute additional local aid in fiscal year 1985 that strongly resembles the approach outlined in this paper. In particular, the program relies on a regression-based cost index and distributes incremental aid in proportion to each community's fiscal disadvantage. Massachusetts has thus become the first state in the country to implement a general revenue sharing program that incorporates regression-based estimates of the differing costs of providing local public services.

Three aspects of the aid program that was actually enacted highlight some of the issues associated with the implementation of an aid program of this type. First, the actual program is based on a revised and smaller number of cost factors than the approach described above. Some of the cost factors that were statistically insignificant in our analysis (namely, two of the employment variables and the poverty variable) or that proved controversial (namely, the crime rate) were dropped  as cost factors. At the same time, one new factor was added, the number of subsidized family housing units per community, even though it was not statistically significant. The final set of factors represented a consensus among interested parties. Various political considerations played a larger role than statistical significance in the final determination of which variables to include. Road miles per vehicle, for example, was included despite its statistical insignificance to please the rural communities, while subsidizing housing was included to help some of the larger urban communities.

Second, a number of changes were made in the measurement of fiscal resources. One, for example, was the inclusion of "excess" free cash, defined to be a community's free cash in excess of 10 percent of its previous year's tax levy. State policymakers apparently viewed excess free cash as a potential revenue source that local communities could reasonably be expected to draw on before receiving additional state aid. One controversial issue was whether to use the somewhat outdated state estimates of equalized property valuation, or whether to use more recent measures of full and fair cash value that more accurately represented current property values in communities that had recently revalued their property. In this and in other discretionary decisions, state policymakers opted for the choice that would be most beneficial to the state's largest cities, in this case the use of the equalized valuations.

Third, and most important, two key decisions were made that tended to make the aid less equalizing. Both decisions led to the distribution of less aid to communities with large fiscal disadvantages in order to distribute the available aid resources to a greater number of communities. First, about 20 percent of the additional aid was withheld from the equalizing pot to be distributed on a straight $5 per capita basis. This assured that all communities (even those with zero or negative gaps) would share in the distribution of the new local aid for FY 1985. Fifty-six of the state's 351 cities and towns received only this minimum per capita aid.

Figure 3

DISTRIBUTION OF FISCAL YEAR 1985 STATE AID TO MASSACHUSETTS CITIES AND TOWNS

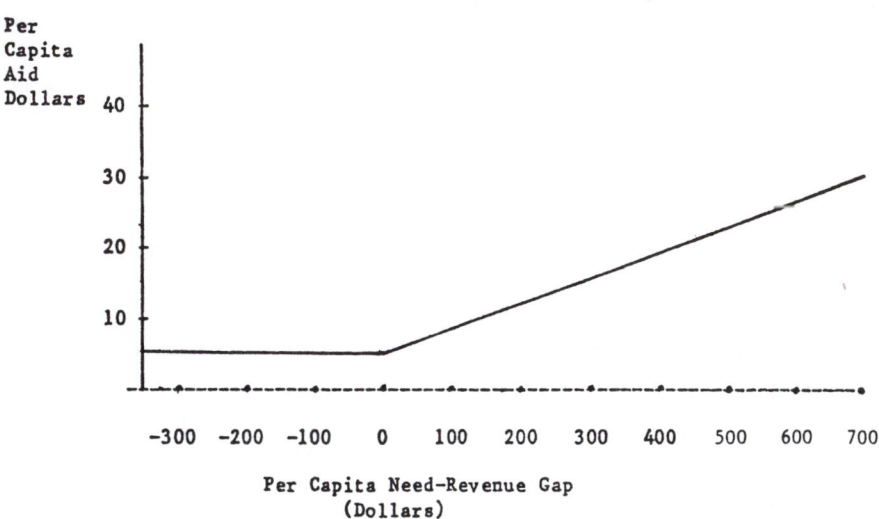

Second, the baseline gap was set equal to zero, instead of some higher number, so that most communities receive equalizing aid. Figure 3 illustrates the pattern of the FY 1985 allocation of new aid among communities. All communities receive at least $5 per capita, with the neediest community receiving $47. This range is somewhat misleading, however, since only 9 communities receive more than $30 per capita. Over one-half of the state's cities and towns receive between $15 and $25 per capita, but most of the largest cities (over 50,000 population) receive over $25 per capita. Among places that receive only the minimum $5 per capita grant (no additional equalizing aid) are many wealthy suburban towns and resort communities.

The differences between the aid program enacted for fiscal year 1985 and the hypothetical programs described in Section III can be seen by comparing Figures 2 and 3. Although the two figures are not exactly comparable,[20] high gap communities clearly receive less aid under the enacted program than under any of the hypothetical programs. This low degree of equalization occurs because the $5 minimum reduces the grant resources available for filling need revenue gaps above the baseline, and the zero baseline gap distributes aid to more communities than the baseline gaps in the hypothetical moderate and high equalization programs.

V. Conclusion

Disparities in the costs of providing local public services arise because economic, social, and demographic factors beyond the control of local governments make it more expensive to provide any given level of public services in some communities than in others. This paper shows how these cost differences can be measured and incorporated into local aid distribution formulas. Cost differences are measured here with a multivariate regression model grounded in the economic theory of local government decision making. Regression analysis is a powerful tool for this purpose since it separates expenditure impacts of uncontrollable cost factors from those of resource and preference variables. Although it underestimates the true impact of cost factors on service levels, this regression-based approach to the measurement of cost or need differences is superior to the largely ad hoc measures found in existing grant-in-aid programs. These uncontrollable cost differences are used to define a city's need-revenue gap and its fiscal disadvantage relative to a baseline community. An aid program designed to offset fiscal disadvantages would provide aid in proportion to the size of communities' need-revenue gaps relative to the gap of some baseline community.

Massachusetts' recent decision to incorporate regression-based estimates of costs into a fiscal year 1985 local aid distribution formula demonstrates the feasibility of the approach developed here. At the same time, the Massachusetts experience shows that the adoption of a need-revenue approach does not by itself guarantee a substantial reduction in fiscal disparities, especially in the short run. The state will distribute approximately $2.3 billion in aid to local governments in FY 1985, much of which is not distributed in an equalizing way. Only approximately $110 million in additional aid for 1985 will be distributed according to a formula that explicitly accounts for cost and revenue disparities. Given this incremental approach to offsetting fiscal disadvantages, substantial equalization will occur only gradually over time and requires that new state funds be appropriated each year and that they continue to be targetted to the communities with the largest need-revenue gaps.

FOOTNOTES

[1] The findings and conclusions of this paper do not necessarily reflect the official views of any of these institutions.

[1] See Le Grand (1975) for a discussion of the importance of this distinction between uncontrollable and controllable costs in the design of intergovernmental aid programs.

[2] Gonzalez (1980) provides a list of the exact formulas used in a number of major federal grant programs.

[3] For example, in Massachusetts each student in a bilingual program receives a weight of 1.4, low-income students a weight of 1.2, students in special education programs a weight of 4, and regular day students a weight of 1.

[4] Le Grand (1982) provides a more detailed discussion of the use of these two approaches in the United Kingdom.

[5] In addition, studies measuring the extent to which existing aid programs target funds to fiscally needy communities also use relatively ad hoc measures of fiscal need. See, for example, Peggy Cuciti (1978) who uses as a need measure an index that includes factors such as density, housing age, crime and unemployment rates, and poverty.

[6] The simple formulation in equation (3) abstracts from the extensive literature on the tax price of local public services. (See, for example, Helen F. Ladd, 1975.) According to that literature, $\hat{V}$ would enter the equation only as part of the tax price term. To test hypotheses about the price elasticity of demand, correct specification of the tax price term would be required; for current purposes, the more general specification suffices and is preferable on the grounds that it is easier to explain and more consistent with common perceptions about the role of the property tax base.

The simple model could also be extended in a variety of other ways. For example, the decisive voter's decision about housing consumption can be made explicit. This extension is important whenever assessed values are flexible so that decisions about housing consumption influence property tax payments. Matching grants can be considered in addition to block grants. Political factors also can be introduced. For example, one could assume that the wage rate of public employees, which is included in P in the cost function for local services, is endogenous. In this case, the decisive voter selects P subject to its impact on costs and to the supply of public employees. These and other extensions alter the functional form of (3) and may introduce simultaneity or new variables, but they do not alter the general formulation: the level of local expenditures is always a function of community resources, costs, and demand factors. (See Inman, 1979 and Yinger, 1983).

[7] Total expenditure includes regional school district expenditures allocated to member cities and towns, but excludes capital spending financed through bonds, spending from most federal funds other than revenue sharing, and transit assessments. These assessments are levied on the cities and towns in Massachusetts to pay for public transit, but they bear little relationship to service levels actually received, especially in the Boston area. Because they are outside local control and because they are not closely related to service levels, these assessments do not belong in a model of local expenditure determination. They are, however, added back to predicted expenditures to calculate the cost index.

[8] More employment also leads to more resources, but this effect is accounted for by the property tax base variable.

[9] Since more police activity can reduce the crime rate, this variable suffers from a simultaneity problem. The appropriate exogenous variable would reflect underlying crime-generating conditions.

[10] This U-shaped relationship between local expenditures and the rate of population change was first documented for Massachusetts communities in Ladd

(1980). It should be noted that the rate of population change could be considered a cost factor. To the extent that higher per capita costs in a city losing population reflect the costs of maintaining a public capital stock built to serve an earlier, larger population, these above-average costs are outside the control of current public officials. Treating population change as a cost variable has the disadvantage, however, that additional aid based on this variable might weaken cities' incentives to reduce discretionary expenditures as their populations decline. Since we are unable to separate which costs associated with population change are controllable by local officials and which are uncontrollable, we have taken the conservative approach of not treating the population change variables as cost factors.

[11]Brazer et al. (1971) and Knickman and Reschovsky (1981) have used the same procedure to predict fiscal costs.

[12]Dropping insignificant cost variables and estimating the equation without Boston in the sample result in only minor changes in both the magnitude of the cost index and the rank ordering of cities and towns by cost level.

A similar cost index was calculated to measure differences in non-school costs. This cost index is based on the same regression, but weighted pupils were excluded from the list of cost variables in calculating the index. This form of the cost index could be used in a formula designed to offset non-school cost disparities.

[13]This objective is similar to objectives proposed by Musgrave (1961) and by Thurow (1970).

[14]Using a calculus approximation, the two objectives are the same. Consider an indirect utility function, $V(C,Y)$, for the decisive voter, where environmental costs, C, play the role of prices and intergovernmental aid is treated as an increase in income. Now to find the aid required to hold real income (that is, utility) constant when C changes, totally differentiate the utility function, set dV equal to zero, and solve for dY. The answer: $dY = [(\partial V/\partial C)/(\partial V/\partial Y)]dC$. Furthermore, according to Roy's Law, $S = -(\partial V/\partial C)/(\partial V/\partial Y)$. Combining these two equations yields $dY = S(dC)$. In other words, the increase in income from intergovernmental aid must equal the starting service level multiplied by the change in costs—which is exactly the objective we defined earlier. Figure 1 shows why this derivation is only an approximation. The value of $S(dC)$ is $(Z^* - Z_2)$. If a jurisdiction is given this much aid, its production possibility schedule will shift to the right by this amount, and because the high-cost production possibility schedule is flatter than the baseline schedule, it will be able to achieve a slightly higher indifference curve than I_2. Thus, the calculus derivation slightly overstates the aid required to hold utility constant.

[15]Consider a constant-elasticity demand function of the form: $S = AY^\alpha C^\beta$. To find the aid necessary to hold S constant with a change in C, totally differentiate this function, set dS equal to zero, and solve for dY. The result: $dY = (-\beta/\alpha)(Y/C)(dC)$. Comparing this result with the result in footnote 14, we find that the equal-real-income objective requires less aid than the constant-service-level objective whenever $\beta < -k$, where $k = CS/Y$ is baseline spending on local services as a proportion of income. Because k is a fairly small fraction, this condition will be met for any reasonable values of β and α.

[16]See Musgrave and Polinsky (1970) for an example of how the concept of a need-revenue gap was used to evaluate federal revenue sharing.

[17]In Massachusetts, the standard property tax effort can be defined as 2 1/2 percent to reflect the rate limit mandated by the voter-passed Proposition 2 1/2.

[18]This formula is similar to revenue sharing formulas developed by Musgrave (1961), Le Grand and Reschovsky (1971), and Le Grand (1975). These formulas all account for differences in both costs (or needs) and fiscal resources among recipient jurisdictions.

[19]It is not appropriate to include special purpose state aid if that aid serves to finance state programs implemented at the local level, rather than to supplement the resources of local jurisdictions.

[20]The two figures are not exactly comparable for two reasons. First, as noted in the text, the programs calculate need-revenue gaps somewhat differently. Second, $150 million is distributed under the hypothetical programs, compared to $137 million of additional FY 1985 aid.

BIBLIOGRAPHY

Advisory Commission on Intergovernmental Relations, 1971. *Measuring the Fiscal Capacity and Effort of State and Local Areas*, M-58, Washington, D.C., USGPO.

Advisory Commission on Intergovernmental Relations, 1980. *The State of State-Local Revenue Sharing*, M-121, Washington, D.C., USGPO.

Advisory Commission on Intergovernmental Relations, 1981. *Studies in Comparative Federalism: Australia, Canada, the United States and West Germany*, M-130, Washington, D.C., USGPO.

Bradford, D. F., R. A. Malt, and W. E. Oates, 1969. "The Rising Cost of Local Public Services: Some Evidence and Reflections," *National Tax Journal*, 22:2 (June).

Brazer, Harvey, et al., 1971. *Fiscal Needs and Resources: A Report to the New York State Commission on Quality, Cost and Financing of Elementary and Secondary Education*, Albany.

Brazer, Harvey and Ann Anderson, 1975. "A Cost Adjusted Index for Michigan School Districts," *Selected Papers in School Finance, 1975*, Washington, D.C., Department of Health, Education and Welfare.

Chambers, Jay G., 1978. "Educational Cost Differentials and the Allocation of State Aid for Elementary/Secondary Education," *Journal of Human Resources*, 12:4 (Fall).

Chambers, Jay G., 1980. "The Development of a Cost of Education Index: Some Empirical Estimates and Policy Issues," *Journal of Education Finance*, 5 (Winter).

Cuciti, Peggy, 1978. "City Need and the Responsiveness of Federal Grant Programs," Subcommittee Print, Subcommittee on the City of the Committee on Banking, Finance, and Urban Affairs, House of Representatives, Washington, D.C., USGPO.

Gonzalez, Maria Elena, 1980. "Characteristics of Formulas and Data Used in the Allocation of Federal

Funds," *The American Statistician*, 34:4 (November).

Inman, Robert P., 1979. "The Fiscal Performance of Local Governments: An Interpretive Review," in Peter Mieszkowski and Mahlon Straszheim, eds., *Current Issues in Urban Economics*, Baltimore, Johns Hopkins University Press.

Knickman, James and Andrew Reschovsky, 1981. "Municipal Overburden: Its Measurement and Role in School Finance Reform," *Selected Papers in School Finance 1981*, Washington, D.C., U.S. Department of Education.

Ladd, Helen F., 1975. "Local Education Expenditures, Fiscal Capacity, and the Composition of the Property Tax Base," *National Tax Journal*, 28:2 (June).

Ladd, Helen F., 1980. "Municipal Expenditures and the Rate of Population Change" in *Cities Under Stress: The Fiscal Crisis of Urban America*, edited by R. W. Burchell and D. Listokin, New Brunswick, N.J., Center for Urban Policy Research.

Le Grand, Julian, 1975. "Fiscal Equity and Central Government Grants to Local Authorities," *Economic Journal* 85 (September).

Le Grand, Julian and Andrew Reschovsky, 1971. "Concerning the Appropriate Formulae for Achieving Horizontal Equity Through Federal Revenue Sharing," *National Tax Journal*, 24:4 (December).

Le Grand, Julian, 1982. "Fiscal Inequalities in the United Kingdom," Report to the Ministry of Urbanism, Government of France, London School of Economics, London.

Musgrave, Richard A., 1961. "Approaches to Fiscal Theories of Political Federalism," in *Public Finances: Needs, Sources and Utilization*, A Conference of the Universities—National Bureau Committee for Economic Research, Princeton University, Princeton, N.J.

Musgrave, Richard A., and A. Mitchell Polinsky, 1970. "Revenue Sharing—A Critical View," in *Financing State and Local Governments, Proceedings of the Monetary Conference*, June 14–16, 1970. Boston: Federal Reserve Bank of Boston.

Thurow, Lester C., 1970. "Aid to State and Local Governments," *National Tax Journal*, 23:1 (March).

Wendling, Wayne, 1981. "The Cost of Education Index: Measurement of Price Differences of Education Personnel among New York State School Districts," *Journal of Education Finance*, 6 (Spring).

Yinger, John, 1983. "On Cost Disparities Across Cities," unpublished manuscript, Ann Arbor, Michigan.

[3]
Measuring Disparities in the Fiscal Condition of Local Governments

HELEN F. LADD

Local fiscal condition refers to the ease or difficulty a local government faces in providing a standard package of public services at a reasonable tax rate or tax burden on its residents. Within most U.S. states, fiscal condition varies greatly from one local government to another. To offset the effects of this variation in fiscal condition on local tax burdens or service levels, many states currently provide general purpose, or equivalently, revenue-sharing aid to their local governments. Such aid programs are intended to direct more aid (per capita) to jurisdictions in poor fiscal condition than to those in good fiscal condition.

To implement equalizing aid programs of this type, state policymakers require accurate measures of the fiscal condition of their local governments. Such measures are needed first to permit state policymakers to determine whether the disparities are sufficiently large to justify state action and second to design appropriate aid formulae to offset those disparities. Historically, state policymakers often used variation in local per capita property tax bases as a proxy for variation in local fiscal condition. However, several states have recently commissioned studies that take a more comprehensive approach to measuring fiscal condition, one that specifically accounts for variation across communities in their expenditure need as well as in their revenue-raising capacity. This chapter describes, evaluates, and compares the new approaches to measuring local fiscal conditions.

The chapter starts from the reasonable, but not undisputed, presumption that reducing inequalities in the fiscal condition of local governments is a laudable goal (see Oakland, this volume, for an alternative view). Underlying this presumption is the view that even with substantial redistribution of income among individuals, lower-income people and those who face discrimination in the housing market are more likely than higher-income, more-mobile households to live in jurisdictions with poor fiscal condition, and that this outcome is socially undesirable. Thus, the case for reducing local fiscal disparities relies either on empirical evidence documenting the limited mobility of disadvantaged households or on the judgment that the social costs of encouraging people to respond to poor fiscal conditions by moving may be unacceptably high, or some combination of both (see Ladd and Yinger (1991), chapter 12 for elaboration).

Given the goal of reducing fiscal disparities, the central problem is how to measure local fiscal conditions. The first section introduces the basic concepts and compares and contrasts two approaches to measuring each of the two components of local fiscal condition—revenue-raising capacity and expenditure need. The second section illustrates the application of these approaches in six states or metropolitan areas—Massachusetts, Nebraska, Minnesota, Wisconsin, Maryland, and Chicago. A final section describes the use of such measures in state policy debates.

BASIC CONCEPTS

Fiscal condition indicates the structural or underlying fiscal position of a local jurisdiction relative to other jurisdictions of the same type. In some cases, fiscal condition is used to refer not simply to a single governmental unit, but rather to all the units within a geographic area, such as the area defined by a county's boundary. The appropriate unit of measurement varies across studies depending on the local governmental structure of the state and the purpose for which the measure is to be used. For simplicity of exposition, I refer to cities throughout the conceptual discussion, but the reader should remember that the same concepts can be applied to other local governmental units or areas.

Need-Capacity Gap

More specifically, the fiscal condition of a local government is defined as the gap between its expenditure need and its revenue-raising capacity, where both need and capacity are expressed in dollars per capita and reflect the impact of socioeconomic factors, such as income and the poverty rate, that are outside the control of local officials.[1] As defined here, a city's fiscal condition reveals nothing about the city's current budgetary surplus or deficit or, more generally, about its current financial condition. This conclusion follows because expenditure need is not determined by a city's actual expenditures. Nor does revenue-raising capacity measure the city's actual revenues. Instead, as elaborated below, they represent standardized measures of the fiscal effects of forces outside the control of local officials. Although the fiscal condition and the financial condition of a city may sometimes be related, they need not be. Mismanagement or an unanticipated shortfall in revenues could produce a budget deficit in any one year regardless of the city's underlying fiscal condition. Similarly, provided the political will is there, any city, even a city in poor fiscal condition, can balance its budget, albeit at the cost of inadequate service levels or excessive tax burdens.

Because this measure of a city's underlying fiscal condition excludes the effects of political and managerial differences across cities, as well as variation in voters' preferences for services, it can serve as an objective guide for state assistance to local governments. That is, more state assistance can be given to those local governments experiencing structural fiscal problems, rather than to those that are mismanaged or whose residents choose to provide high- or low-quality services. Implicit in this approach is the view that an equalizing local assistance program should compensate local governments only for the effects of adverse conditions that are outside their control.

Central to the need-capacity gap approach is that it includes the expenditure side as well as the revenue-raising side of the local fiscal picture. Differences across cities in expenditure need should not be ignored. Consider, for example, the city of Boston. According to estimates that I made with others in 1984 (Bradbury et al., 1984), the city's revenue-raising capacity was about at the state average. However, according to our estimates, its expenditure need exceeded those of the average Massachusetts city by 40 percent. Combining these two facts meant that Boston had poor fiscal health relative to other cities. Had state policymakers focused only on revenue-raising capacity, they would have concluded incorrectly that Boston's fiscal condition was about average.

The challenge arises in measuring the two components—revenue-raising capacity and expenditure need. In the following sections, I first describe and compare the two main approaches used in recent studies to measure revenue-raising capacity. I then do the same for the two main approaches to measuring expenditure need. The description of recent state studies in the final section illustrates the implementation of the various approaches.

Revenue-Raising Capacity

Two basic approaches have been used to measure the capacity of each city to raise revenue from its own sources relative to other cities. The first starts with local tax bases and the second with the income of city residents. In each case, comparability across cities requires that something be standardized across cities. In the tax base approach, the calculations are based on an assumption of a similar tax structure and, in particular, one with similar tax rates. In the income-with-exporting approach, the calculations are based on an assumption of similar tax burdens on residents, where burden is defined as a share of the resident's income.

The Tax-Base Approach, Often Called the Representative Tax System Approach. If cities are empowered to use only the property tax, one could measure a city's revenue-raising capacity as the city's property tax base times a standard tax rate, such as the statewide average tax rate or, in the case of state with a stringent limit on tax rates, the maximum rate allowed. The city's revenue-raising capacity would then indicate the amount of revenue the city would raise if it chose to tax its property at the standard tax rate. Implicit in this approach is the assumption that the size of the tax base is invariant to the tax rate; that is, the base would be no different if the standard tax rate were applied than it is with the actual tax rate.

Generalizing this approach to the case of more than one tax base, city i's per capita revenue-raising capacity could be calculated as a weighted sum of each of its j tax bases per capita ($BASE_{ij}$), with the weights most naturally being average tax rates (t_j) as follows:

$$RRC_i = \Sigma_j t_j Base_{ij} \qquad (1)$$

This approach is the well-known representative tax or revenue system approach that the Advisory Commission on Intergovernmental Relations (ACIR) developed many years ago for measuring the revenue-raising capacity of states (ACIR 1962 and more recent publications such as ACIR 1990). When revenues other than taxes are included in the calculation, researchers typically use per capita income as a proxy for the "base" of each of these additional revenue sources and total statewide collections as a fraction of income as the "rate." In principle, there is no limit to the number of different revenue sources that can be included in the calculation.

Income-with-Exporting Approach. The income-with-exporting approach measures revenue-raising capacity as the per capita amount of revenue that city residents could raise if they imposed a standard tax burden on themselves, augmented by the amount that they would generate by exporting tax burdens to nonresidents (see Ferguson and Ladd, 1986, for a full discussion). This approach starts with city residents and standardizes across cities not in terms of average tax rates but rather in terms of the burden, expressed as a percent of income, on those residents. More precisely, the measure for the ith city is where K^* is the uniform percentage burden on residents, Y_i is the per capita income of city residents in i, and e_i is an

$$RRC_I = K^* Y_i(1+e_i) \qquad (2)$$

export ratio, defined as the dollars paid by nonresidents per dollar of tax borne by resident taxpayers.[2]

The starting point for this approach is the ability of city residents to pay taxes. An individual consumer's ability to pay is typically measured by her income. When individuals are grouped together in cities, and if for the moment we assume that each consumer works and shops only in the city where she lives, the income of the group would be an appropriate index of the group's ability to pay local taxes. Regardless of which tax bases are actually used, all taxes are ultimately paid out of the income of city residents. Hence, a city with poorer residents (low Y) would have less capacity to raise revenue than one with richer (higher Y) residents. Relaxing the assumption that consumers live, shop, and work in the same community opens up the possibility of tax exporting. When city residents impose tax burdens on themselves, they may also be generating revenue from nonresidents. Hence, if two cities have the same income, the one with the greater ability to export tax burdens to nonresidents will have the greater revenue-raising capacity.

How can one measure the ability to export tax burdens? Exporting through the sales tax provides the simplest example. Based on the plausible assumption that sales tax burdens are ultimately borne by consumers in the form of higher prices, the analytical task is to determine what portion of locally taxed purchases are made by nonresident tourists and other visitors to the city. With this information, one can calculate an export ratio as the sales to nonresidents per dollar of sales to residents. In general, the revenue-raising capacity of city residents would be augmented more in a city that had a big retail mall or one that was a tourist center rather than in one that did not attract outside shoppers.

Compared to the sales tax, the property tax is more complicated because economists disagree about who ultimately bears the burden of the tax. The simplest approach would be to assume that taxes on each of the classes of property such as owner-occupied housing, rental housing, or commercial real estate are borne either by residents or by nonresidents, but not by both. For example, one might assume that residents bear the full burden of the tax on residential property and nonresidents the full burden of the tax on business property. Export ratios would vary across cities because of variations in the composition of the property tax base. A city with a lot of business property relative to residential property would, based on these assumptions, be able to export a larger share of its property taxes than a city with less business property.

A more sophisticated approach to the exporting of property tax burdens would begin by using economic theory and reasonable assumptions about mobility to determine how the burden of each portion of the property tax is shared among various economic groups. For example, one reasonable assumption might be that capital is mobile and, therefore, that owners of capital can escape the burden of local property tax completely by shifting their investments from one metropolitan area to another. Consequently, other groups, such as consumers of housing services in the city, consumers of goods and services produced in the city, workers in the city, and city landowners share the burden of the tax. The second step is to allocate the resulting burdens to residents and nonresidents using city-specific data on the share of commuters into the city or the size of the city relative to the metropolitan area. (For more detail, see Bradbury and Ladd, 1985.)

For local governments that use income or local payroll taxes, the ability to export tax burdens to nonresidents will vary across cities depending on the structure of the tax (for example, whether it includes the earnings in the city of nonresident commuters) and the share of the taxable income accruing to nonresident commuters.

Conceptual Differences Between the Two Approaches. The tax-base approach provides an answer to the following question: How much revenue would the city raise if it taxed all its tax bases at average tax rates? As noted by Oakland (this volume), the concern underlying this approach is the maintenance of a competitive tax structure. If a city can finance a basic package of public services by applying average tax rates, it will not be at a competitive disadvantage relative to other cities.

In contrast, the income-with-exporting approach provides an answer to a different question: Given the set of taxes it is empowered to use and the assumption that it cannot impose differentially higher rates on nonresidents, what is the maximum amount of revenue the city could raise if it imposed a standard burden (defined as a percent of resident income) on city residents? In contrast to the tax-base approach, this approach starts from a model of political behavior and the insight that a city might not be willing to impose average tax rates on each base if the result were heavy tax burdens on residents. As elaborated in Ferguson and Ladd, 1986, the income-with-exporting approach emerges from a model in which local residents are assumed to maximize utility as they choose between publicly and privately provided goods and services. Thus, the income-with-exporting approach is firmly grounded in the economic theory of consumer demand.

If state policymakers are ultimately concerned with the welfare of city residents, as I believe they should be, they should standardize across communities by assuming a uniform tax burden on city residents, not by assuming uniform tax rates. From the resident-based perspective, the problem with the tax-base approach is that uniform tax *rates* need not lead to uniform tax *burdens* on city residents. If incomes are low relative to residential property values in one city compared to another, for example, the average tax rate will produce a greater burden on residents in the first city relative to the other city. Ferguson and Ladd (1986) illustrate through a national sample of large cities that the approach matters. For example, their estimates suggest that the representative tax system approach leads to burdens on residents that vary across major cities from less than 2 percent of income to more than 6 percent of income (Ferguson and Ladd, 1986, pp. 156–157).

Downes and Pogue (1992) argue that the weighted tax-base approach is superior to the income-with-exporting approach given the state policy goal of reducing fiscal disparities. In particular, they assert that the best way for a state to reduce revenue-related fiscal disparities is to direct aid to localities with low capacity as measured by the tax-base approach. Their reasoning proceeds as follows. First they assert that fiscal disparities arise when "individuals [have] to pay different taxes in one locality than in another for a given package of public services" (p. 468). They then criticize the income-with-exporting approach by showing that distributing aid to equalize tax effort according to that measure need not equalize tax rates across localities (a true statement). Finally, they conclude, "And for that reason, it will not, in general, preclude individuals bearing different taxes for a given service level simply because their economic activities take place at different locations" (p. 472).

One flaw in the Downes and Pogue argument can be illustrated with respect to property tax payments. Consider two households with identical incomes and comparable homes. One household is in community A, a centrally located community. The other household is in community B, a more distant community. Provided households value central locations, the price of the house in A will exceed that in B. If property tax rates were equal in A and B, the two identical households would pay different taxes, not the same taxes as implied by Downes and Pogue. Only if tax burdens (defined as a share of income) were equalized would they pay the same taxes and hence would disparities, even by Downes' and Pogue's definition, be eliminated. Another, more straightforward way of stating the same conclusion, is the fact that some households, such as those in A, choose to spend more of their income on access (in the form of higher housing prices) compared to those in B, does not mean they have greater ability to pay taxes, as would be implied by the tax-base approach.

More generally, however, the choice between the two methods turns on whether state policymakers are more concerned with the welfare of city residents and their ability to tax themselves for public services or with the competitive position of one city relative to another.

Implementation Issues. The tax-base approach is relatively straightforward to implement. It simply requires data on tax bases and on average tax rates.³ If the concept of revenue-raising capacity is expanded to included non-tax revenue sources, such as licenses and fees, the approach becomes much less precise, but still straightforward to implement. For license and fee revenue, analysts typically use resident income as a proxy for the tax base in each city and calculate an average tax "rate" as the ratio of total collections from licenses and fees as a fraction of aggregate income.

In contrast, the income-with-exporting approach poses the challenge of estimating export ratios for each local jurisdiction. Both theoretical considerations (such as the difficulty of determining who ultimately bears the burden of each local tax) and empirical considerations (such as the need to allocate the resulting burden among residents and nonresidents) make it difficult to calculate accurate ratios. However, experience from Minnesota, discussed below, illustrates the feasibility of calculating such ratios.

Consistency with Past Practice. Supporters of the tax-base approach emphasize its consistency with past practice and the political acceptability that comes with such consistency. This consistency stems from the fact that most states with equalizing aid programs distribute aid inversely with a local jurisdiction's property tax base (the single most important and often the only tax used by local governments, especially school districts). Hence, many policymakers in such states naturally tend to think in terms of tax bases as the measure of capacity. Moreover, if tax limitation laws or constitutional provisions restrict the rate at which property or other local tax bases can be taxed, local officials are likely to reject a value of capacity that exceeds what they are legally empowered to raise in taxes. The weighted tax-base approach precludes this politically unacceptable outcome provided one starts with actual tax bases and uses as weights tax rates that do not exceed the legal maximum.

In contrast, the income-with-exporting alternative, which ignores tax bases altogether, has been criticized for its inconsistency with past practice.⁴ However, precedent for the concept of using resident income (albeit not augmented by exporting) as a measure of capacity to raise revenue can readily be found in federal aid programs to local governments, including the general revenue sharing program (which existed from 1972 to 1986).

Summary. As discussed below in connection with the study for Minnesota, the choice between the two methods is not inconsequential in practice. In particular, across the set of Minnesota cities with population over 2500, the variation in revenue-raising capacity turns out to be twice as large when capacity is measured by the tax-base approach than when it is measured by the income-with-exporting approach.

Because I believe that state policymakers should be more concerned with the welfare of city residents and their ability, through the local political process, to generate revenue than with the competitive position of one city relative to another, I believe that the income-with-exporting approach is preferred on conceptual grounds to the weighted tax-base approach. However, this conceptual advantage of the income-with-exporting approach may be offset in some states by other practical considerations that favor the weighted tax-base approach.

Expenditure Need

Analogous to the two approaches to measuring revenue-raising capacity are two basic approaches to measuring a city's expenditure need. The first, the *representative expenditure* approach, follows the logic of the representative tax system, or weighted tax-base, approach. The second, the *regression-based cost* approach, is more in the spirit of the income-with-exporting approach in that it focuses on city residents. Both approaches attempt to provide an objective measure of the variation in expenditure need across jurisdictions that reflect, not variation in actual expenditure decisions, but rather variation in factors outside the control of local officials. Neither approach tries to provide a normative measure of how much spending is appropriate. Instead, they both start with average per capita local spending and model variations around that average.

The Representative Expenditure Approach. Recently developed by Robert Rafuse and the ACIR initially for states, the representative expenditure approach measures the ith jurisdiction's per capita expenditure need (EN_i) as the sum of the city's workload (WL_{ij}) for each of j services, weighted by average spending per unit of workload on each service $EXPWL_j$, and divided by city population (POP_i). Specifically,

$$EN_i = \Sigma_j (EXPWL_j)(WL_{ij})/POP_i. \tag{3}$$

According to this approach, expenditure need answers the question: How much would the jurisdiction have to spend per capita given the service-specific workloads it faces, if it spent an average amount per unit of workload on each service category?

Typical workload measures used to implement this approach include the local population, number of visitors to the jurisdiction, and the proportion of households with income below the poverty level. In some cases a single indicator of workload is used. In other cases, indicators are combined to construct more complex measures.

The Regression-Based Cost Approach. According to the regression-based approach, a local government's expenditure need is measured as the amount it must spend to provide a standard quality of public services given the set of services for which it is responsible and the costs it faces. Costs vary from one local government to another because of variation in local community characteristics such as population density. Relevant characteristics are those that are outside the immediate control of local officials and that can be shown to have a statistical impact on the cost of providing public services. Typically, regression analysis is used to determine the variation in cost indexes needed to implement this approach.[5] Through no fault of their own, local governments with relatively extensive service responsibilities or with relatively high costs must spend more than other local governments to achieve any given quality of public services.

According to this approach, the ith city's total expenditure need (EN_i) can be written as follows:

$$EN_i = \Sigma_j Q_j S_{ij} C_{ij} \quad (4)$$

where Q_j is standard per capita spending on the jth expenditure function, S_{ij} is the ith city's index of service responsibility for the jth spending category relative to the average over all cities, and C_{ij} is the ith city's index of per capita costs for the jth spending category relative to the average over all cities. In most of the applications discussed below, Q_j is measured by statewide average per capita spending on the designated function.

Variation in service responsibilities played a large role in research done by Ladd and Yinger (1991) on the fiscal condition of cities across the country. Such variation is less important for groups of similar governmental units within a state. Nonetheless, for a few services, such as transportation, variation in responsibilities cannot be ignored and will be discussed below.

The main determinant of variation in expenditure need is the cost of providing public services of a given quality, as reflected in the cost index. Costs vary because some local governments must pay more than others to attract workers away from the private sector. In addition, costs may vary because social and demographic characteristics of a locality affect the difficulty of providing public services. For example, a city that has a lot of old, densely packed wooden structures may find it more difficult to provide a given level of protection against loss from fire than a less dense city with brick structures. Similarly, a city or county with a high poverty rate may need to provide more social services than a city or county with a lower poverty rate.

Sorting out the effects of these social and economic characteristics on the per capita costs of providing a given quality of public services requires the statistical technique of multivariate regression analysis. This statistical tool can be used to measure the average impact of each of a variety of cost factors such as population density, the poverty rate, or the age of the housing stock on local public expenditures controlling for differences across localities in wealth or the preferences for public services.

To implement this approach, a regression equation is estimated for each major expenditure category using actual spending data for all the cities in the study. The reduced-form equation takes the following general form:

$$EXPPC_i = f(DEMAND_i, AID_i, PREF_i, COSTFACT_i) \quad (5)$$

That is, per capita spending in the ith city ($EXPPC_i$) is explained as a function of demand variables ($DEMAND_i$) such as the income or wealth of city residents and the tax price of a decisive voter; intergovernmental aid variables (AID_i) that measure the resources available to the city from other levels of government; preference variables ($PREF_i$) that account for the preferences of local voters for public services; and cost factors ($COSTFACT_i$) that reflect characteristics of the city outside the control of local officials. Differences in the efficiency with which services are provided and unmeasurable preferences are assumed to be randomly distributed among cities and are captured in an error term.[6] The criteria for a city characteristic to be included as a cost factor is that an intuitively plausible story can be told about how it would affect public spending and that it produce a statistically measurable effect in the regression equation.

Cost indexes are generated as follows. First, the estimated coefficients of the regression equation are used to predict, or simulate, what the level of per capita spending would have been in each city if the city had average values of all the DEMAND, AID, and PREF variables, but its own values of cost factors such as the poverty rate or population density. Thus, simulated expenditures (EXPPCSIM) vary across cities only because of variation in the cost factors. The cost index for the ith city is then calculated as follows:

$$C_i = EXPPCSIM_i / EXPPC, \quad (6)$$

where EXPPC is average per capita spending.

Thus, the cost index for each locality indicates the impact of the locality's social and economic characteristics relative to those of an average city on the costs of providing public services. For example, a city with a harsh environment for providing public safety might have a cost index of 1.5, which means that its social and economic characteristics raise the per capita costs of providing a standard quality of public safety relative to the average city by 50 percent.[7]

Relationship between the two approaches. A small amount of algebra helps illuminate the relationship between the representative expenditure and the regression-based cost approach.[8] The subscript i continues to designate the city. For expositional simplicity, I assume that there is only one spending category. Hence no j subscript is needed.

Expanding the first element (average spending per workload) given above for the representative expenditure approach, expenditure need in the ith city can be written as

$$EN_i = (\Sigma_i EXP_i / \Sigma_i WL_i) WL_i / POP_i \qquad (7)$$

where EXP_i is spending by the ith city. Multiplying the right-hand side by

$$\Sigma_i POP_i / \Sigma_i POP_i,$$

and rearranging terms yields

$$EN_i = (\Sigma_i EXP_i / \Sigma_i POP_i)[(WL_i / POP_i)/(\Sigma_i WL_i / \Sigma_i POP_i)]. \qquad (8)$$

Simplifying the notation, we have

$$EN_i = (EXPPC)(WLPC_i) \qquad (9)$$

where EXPPC is average per capita spending in the state and $WLPC_i$ is the workload relative to population in the ith city expressed relative to the average for all cities.

This form of the representative expenditure approach facilitates the comparison to the regression-based cost approach which can be simplified as follows: ignoring variation in service responsibilities and assuming that Q is proxied by average per capita spending, the regression-based cost approach for a single spending category can be written

$$EN_i = (EXPPC)(C_i) \qquad (10)$$

where, as before, C_i is an index of per capita costs in the ith city relative to the average over all cities.

Comparing the last two expressions clarifies that the representative expenditure approach and the regression-based approach will yield similar results for a particular city only if the workload index is similar to the cost index. In general, these two indices are likely to differ, with the cost-index yielding the more general and more precise results.

Consider the following example. For the spending category, general government, the obvious workload measure is population (see below for evidence that this measure is typically used). The use of this workload measure implies that, according to the representative expenditure approach, per capita expenditure need is constant across cities. Implicit in this conclusion is the *assumption* that there are no economies or diseconomies of scale in the provision of general government with respect to population. However, regressions of general government spending on demand, aid, preference, and cost-factor variables typically indicate that per capita spending on general government decreases with population. This finding provides empirical evidence of economies of scale which are then incorporated directly into the cost indexes. Thus, the regression approach is more general than the workload approach in that it allows for the possibility of economies or diseconomies of scale with respect to population or with respect to any other workload measure.

The major challenge of the representative expenditure approach is choosing appropriate workload measures. A number of problems arise. The first is that typically no single best measure, such as population, emerges as the ideal workload measure. Consequently, often two or more measures, such as resident population and city employment, must be combined into a single workload measure, but the approach provides no coherent and conceptually defensible means of defining weights. Hence, any combined measure is based on an ad hoc set of weights. A related problem is that the approach provides no explicit way to incorporate the harshness of the environment for providing public services. Consequently, most of the workload measures reflect easy-to-quantify aspects of the burden on city governments, such as the number of pupils. Measures that reflect variation in the harshness of the environment, such as the proportion of school-age children from disadvantaged households, can sometimes be identified and included, but often such measures are hard to define within the representative expenditure framework, and are hard to incorporate into the workload measure in a theoretically defensible manner.

In summary, the regression-based cost approach rests on a more solid conceptual foundation than the representative expenditure approach and, consequently, is the preferred approach. One potential drawback is the difficulty of explaining regression analysis to those unfamiliar with the technique. However, despite the complexities of the technique, the basic ideas underlying the regression-based cost approach are straightforward and intuitively plausible. The Massachusetts experience (described below) illustrates that the method can be explained to and accepted by state policymakers.

Need-Capacity Gaps Revisited and Intergovernmental Aid

With various combinations of these measures, a city's fiscal condition is straightforward to calculate as the difference between the city's expenditure need and its revenue-raising capacity. It is useful to pause at this point to recall the main purpose for calculating such need-capacity gaps, namely to determine how large a claim one city (or any other type of local government) has on state equalizing aid relative to other cities (or local governments of the same type). Before turning to how such gaps might be used in designing local aid policy, two issues remain: one related to the measurement and the other to the reporting of gaps.

To what extent should a city's relative claim to state equalizing aid depend on how much money the local government receives through other forms of intergovernmental aid? In particular, in calculating need-capacity gaps should a local government's revenue-raising capacity be augmented by the amount of federal aid and the amount of categorical aid it receives from the state? The main consideration here is the extent to which local receipts from other aid programs are directed toward narrowly defined categorical services that the local government might not otherwise provide. Thus, for example, federal aid for a specific program such as school breakfasts should be excluded from a local government's revenue-raising capacity on the grounds that it may not free up any local funds for other spending, while federal block grants, such as those received through the Community Development Block Grant program, should be included. The same logic holds for other state aid programs, except to the extent that state policymakers choose to consolidate a variety of existing aid programs into a single new equalizing aid program, in which case aid received through those existing aid programs should not be treated as part of local revenue-raising capacity for the purposes of designing a new aid program. Thus, the measures of local revenue-raising capacity discussed earlier should be augmented to account for intergovernmental aid.

Before reporting need-capacity gaps, it is wise to express each gap relative to the average gap, that is, as the difference between each city's gap and the gap in the average city. In contrast to the absolute gaps, these relative need-capacity gaps focus attention where it belongs, namely on the disparities among cities. If absolute gaps are presented, some people may inappropriately try to use the average gap as an argument for or against additional state aid to cities. This use of the gaps is inappropriate. Need-capacity gaps are neither intended nor designed to inform policymakers about whether local governments as a group are spending too much or too little or require more or less state aid to meet their service responsibilities. Instead, their sole purpose is to measure each city's fiscal condition relative to that of others.

These relative gaps can be used by policymakers in three ways. First, policymakers can use them to determine whether disparities among local governments are so large as to require state action. While the relative gaps themselves do not resolve the issue, evidence on the magnitude of the disparities is crucial input to informed policy debate. Second, the distribution of relative gaps can provide a benchmark against which an existing aid program can be evaluated. Assuming that an existing program is intended to be equalizing, policymakers can evaluate the extent to which the program is in fact equalizing by correlating the per capita distribution of aid dollars among cities with the index of relative gaps. A large positive correlation would suggest that the program distributes aid in an equalizing manner; a small or negative correlation would indicate the reverse.

Third, they can be used as the basis for designing a new formula for distributing equalizing aid among local governments. However, even with an accurate set of relative need-capacity gaps and a fixed aid budget, policymakers still have an important role to play. To fashion an aid formula based on need-capacity gaps, state policymakers must first determine how targeted they want the aid to be. In particular, they need to decide whether the program will be directed to all cities or just to the cities in the poorest fiscal condition. For example, the cities in the state could be ranked by their relative need-capacity gaps and aid given only to the 50 or 75 percent of the cities with the greatest need. In this case, aid might be distributed in proportion to each city's gap relative to the gap in the baseline city, where the baseline city is the city whose fiscal condition just barely eliminates it from receiving aid. Alternatively, all cities could be given per capita aid with the neediest city getting the most aid and the least needy city getting the least aid. The advantage of this approach is that all cities receive some aid; the disadvantage is that because the aid is spread thin, the neediest cities would receive much less assistance than in the previous case (see Bradbury et al., 1984, for additional discussion).

EXPERIENCE WITH THESE APPROACHES

Six recent studies illustrate the application of these approaches to the measurement of local fiscal condition or its components. The six studies are summarized in table 2.1, grouped by their approach to measuring expenditure need. The earliest study using the regression-based cost approach was done by Bradbury and others for cities and towns in Massachusetts. Their 1984 paper not only describes how the need-capacity gaps were measured, but also describes how the gaps were used by the state to distribute incremental aid to cities and towns during the early to mid 1980s. Subsequent studies that built on the Massachusetts methodology (and also on the more detailed methodology in Ladd and Yinger [1989 and 1991]) include the studies by John Yinger for Nebraska counties, municipalities, and school districts; by Ladd, Reschovsky, and Yinger for Minnesota; and by Reschovsky and Green for Wisconsin. Although similar in approach on the expenditure side, the four studies differ in their approach to measuring revenue-raising capacity.

TABLE 2.1
Overview of Six Studies

	Expenditure Need	Revenue-Raising Capacity
Massachusetts-cities and towns Bradbury, Ladd, Reschovsky, Perrault, and Yinger (1984)	Regression-based cost	Tax base (property only)
Nebraska-counties, municipalities, and school districts Wasylenko and Yinger (1988)	Regression-based cost	Income with exporting
Minnesota-cities Ladd, Reschovsky, and Yinger (1991)	Regression-based cost	1) Income with exporting 2) Tax base (property only)
Wisconsin-cities Green and Reschovsky (1993)	Regression-based cost	Tax base (property only)
Maryland-county areas Rafuse, Marks, Cohen (1990)	Representative expenditure	Not applicable
Chicago Metro Region-40 city areas Rafuse and Marks (1991)	Representative expenditure	Representative tax system

Sources:

Massachusetts: Katherine L. Bradbury, Helen F. Ladd, Mark Perrault, Andrew Reschovsky, and John Yinger, "State Aid to Offset Fiscal Disparities Across Communities," *National Tax Journal*, June 1984, pp. 151-170.

Nebraska: Michael Wasylenko and John Yinger, Co-directors, *Nebraska Comprehensive Study, Final Report*, Metropolitan Studies Program, The Maxwell School, Syracuse University, Syracuse, New York, July 1988.

Minnesota: Helen F. Ladd, Andrew Reschovsky, and John Yinger, *Measuring the Fiscal Condition of Cities in Minnesota, Final Report*. Prepared for The Minnesota Legislative Commission on Planning and Fiscal Policy, March 1991.

Wisconsin: Richard K. Green and Andrew Reschovsky, *An Analysis of The State of Wisconsin's Shared Revenue Program*. Report prepared for the Department of Revenue, State of Wisconsin, 1993.

Maryland: Robert W. Rafuse, Jr., Lawrence R. Marks, and Carol E. Cohen, *Local Government Spending in Maryland: Needs and Performance*, Final Report for the Commission on State Taxes and Tax Structure, State of Maryland, October 1990.

Chicago: Robert W. Rafuse, Jr. and Lawrence R. Marks, *A Comparative Analysis of Fiscal Capacity, Tax Effort & Public Spending Among Localities in the Chicago Metropolitan Region*, U.S. Advisory Commission on Intergovernmental Relations, March 1991.

The last two studies, one of Maryland counties and one of the Chicago metropolitan region, both by Robert Rafuse and colleagues, use the representative expenditure approach for measuring expenditure need.[9] In the Chicago study, revenue-raising capacity was calculated using the representative tax system approach. The Maryland study was limited to the expenditure side of the equation. These two studies also differ from the other four in focusing on spending and taxes within the designated geographic areas, counties in Maryland and cities in Chicago, rather than on city or county governments alone.[10]

Expenditure Need

The most interesting and most innovative aspect of the new studies is their attempt to measure the variation in expenditure need. Tables 2.2 and 2.3 summarize how the two approaches have been implemented in practice.

Regression-based Cost Approach. According to the regression-based cost approach, a jurisdiction's expenditure need for any spending category is the product of its service responsibility for that function and its service-specific cost index. Service responsibilities are expressed in dollars per capita and are equal to statewide average per capita spending provided all jurisdictions in a given class have the same service responsibility. Table 2.2 summarizes the key elements of these two components for the relevant studies. The information in the column headed service responsibilities reflects decisions of the analysts based on the availability of data and resources available for the study. For example, it reflects analysts' decisions about how much to disaggregate the spending categories, how to incorporate some variation in responsibility, and how to treat capital outlays. In contrast, the cost factors in the final column emerge from the empirical analysis. They and other intuitively plausible potential cost factors were initially included in expenditure regressions. The factors listed for each study emerged as empirically relevant factors.

The Massachusetts study is the earliest of the studies. Compared to most other states, Massachusetts' governmental structure is very simple. Cities and towns cover the entire state and have responsibility for all local government services, including in most cases elementary and secondary education. Even the limited amount of county services are financed out of city and town budgets, as is spending by regional school districts. Hence, the units of observation for the Massachusetts study, the state's 351 cities and towns, cover virtually all local government activity in the state, including elementary and secondary education. Welfare spending, however, is a state, not a local, responsibility in Massachusetts. This simple governmental struc-

TABLE 2.2
Expenditure Need: Regression-Based Cost Approach

	Service Responsibilities (dollars per capita)	Cost Factors
Massachusetts Cities and Towns	Average current spending per capita	Density Poverty rate Weighted pupils per resident Crime rate Old housing Manufacturing employees per resident Trade and Services employees per resident Government employees per resident Road miles per vehicle
Nebraska Counties	Average per capita spending on basic services weighted by municipal-rural mix of population + (Average per mile cost of county roads) x (number of miles per resident) + Average net cost of county hospital per resident if county has a hospital	Total area per capita Number of farms per capita Share of population on farms Poverty rate Crime rate
Municipalities	Average cost of police and fire services per capita + (Average per mile cost of streets) x (number of miles) + Average net cost of sewers if city provides sewers	Density[a] Poverty rate[b] Rental share of housing[c] Old housing[d]
School Districts	Average spending per pupil	Number of students Number of handicapped students Transportation costs Ratio of secondary to elementary students Type of school district

TABLE 2.2 (continued)

	Service Responsibilities (dollars per capita)	Cost Factors
Minnesota Cities	*Public Safety* Average current spending per capita + 4-year average capital spending per capita	Proportion of 1980 housing built before 1940 Accidents on all city roads per resident Cost of living in the city's county Crime rate (total reported crimes per 1,000 people)
	Transportation Spending[5] (Average current spending per lane mile) x lane miles per resident	1988 Population Lane mile owned by the city (reduces costs) Heating degree days (reduces costs) Population density (and density squared) Change in population
	Economic and Social Services Average current spending per capita + 4-year average capital spending per capita	Population density Proportion of 1980 housing built before 1940 1988 population (in logarithmic form) 5-year rate of population change (and rate squared)
	Administration Average current spending per capita + 4-year average capital spending per capita	1988 population (in logarithmic form) 5-year rate of population change (and rate squared) Cost of living in the city's county Number of subsidized family housing units per capita
Wisconsin Municipalities	*Public Safety (Fire Protection)* 5-year average current and capital spending per capita	Density (and density squared) Old housing Area wage level Government employment per capita[f]
	Law Enforcement 5-year average current and capital spending per capital (0 for police in towns)	Density (and density squared) Population growth rate (and rate squared) Area wage level

TABLE 2.2 (continued)

Service Responsibilities (dollars per capita)	Cost Factors
Transportation (5-year average current and capital spending per city-owned street mile) x miles per capita	Population squared Density (and density squared) Employment in trade and services per capita
Economic Programs 5-year average current and capital spending per capita	Population under age 18 Employment in trade and services per capita
Social Programs 5-year average current and capital spending per capita	The poverty rate Employment by government per capita[6]
General Government 5-year average current and capital spending per capita	Population (and population squared) Area wage level

Footnotes:

1. Cost factor for per mile spending on streets and for per capita spending on fire protection.
2. Cost factor for per capita police spending.
3. Cost factor for per capita police spending and per capita spending on fire protection.
4. Cost factor for per capita spending on fire protection.
5. The cost factors for transportation spending represent factors that affect the cost of transportation per lane mile.
6. Excludes municipal employment.

Source: See Table 2.1.

ture led the analysts to treat all cities and towns as if they had the same service responsibilities. Hence the main task involved deciding on cost factors and measuring their impacts.

As shown in the table, nine factors were interpreted as cost factors, all of which exerted positive impacts on aggregate local spending.[11] Higher density and higher crime rates presumably increase the cost of providing a given amount of public safety. A greater proportion of old housing may increase the costs of fire protection and may also serve as a measure of disadvantaged households who typically are disproportionately dependent on the public sector. The number of pupils (weighted according to factors used by the Massachusetts Department of Education) relative to the population is an obvious cost factor given the large share of local spending attributable to elementary and secondary education. The three employee variables are intended to measure the pressure on local public spending that comes from having workers commuting into the community. Finally the road miles variable crudely captures the spending pressure in rural areas that have many miles of roads to maintain. (Subsequent studies treat miles as a responsibility variable, rather than as a cost factor.)

The more complicated governmental structure in Nebraska partially accounts for the more disaggregated approach used in that state to determine expenditure need. First, the analysts had to examine counties, municipalities, and school districts separately.[12] Second, they could not assume that service responsibilities were similar across counties. In particular, they had to account for the different proportions of county residents living in municipalities, and thereby receiving municipal rather than county services, and for variation in responsibility for county hospitals. In addition, both for counties and for municipalities, the analysts chose to treat miles of streets per resident as a measure of responsibility, rather than as a cost factor. Third, for municipalities, they chose to run three different expenditure regressions, one for per capita police spending, one for per capita spending on fire protection, and one for spending on streets per mile of municipally owned streets. This more refined treatment of spending on streets yields intuitively plausible results: rural areas have higher expenditure burdens because of the larger number of street miles relative to population, but urban areas experience higher costs per mile because of their greater population densities.

Most of the complexities associated with Minnesota's system of overlapping governments were not directly addressed in the Ladd, Reschovsky, and Yinger, study which focused exclusively on Minnesota's municipalities with population over 2500. However, the analysts were careful to adjust the raw spending data collected by the state auditor to assure comparability across cities. For example, spending on trash collection was not included as a spending item in any city since it typically does not appear in city budgets. Similarly, adjustments were made for spending functions that appear in enterprise funds in some cities but in general funds in other cities. After these adjustments, the analysts concluded that they could view all cities as having the same set of service responsibilities for three of the four spending categories listed in the table. In calculating average spending for each category, they included both current spending and the four-year average of capital spending per capita. Similarly to the Nebraska study, they treated lane miles per resident as a responsibility measure for transportation spending. Hence, the cost factors for that category refer to the costs of providing transportation per lane mile, while cost factors for the other three categories relate to per capita spending.

One cost variable of particular interest in the Minnesota study is the cost of living in the city's county. That such a variable should be included as a cost factor has been recognized by other researchers; a higher cost of living means that the local governments must pay more to attract workers away from the private sector. The usual problem is that local cost-of-living data are not available. The data used in this study were from a special report that had recently been completed in the state (program evaluation division, 1989).

The different signs across spending categories of the population variable illustrate the power of the regression-based approach. For example, population (in logarithmic form) has a positive impact on per capita spending for economic and social services but a negative impact on per capita spending for administration. The former result provides evidence of diseconomies of scale in the provision of economic and social services. The latter, that there are economies of scale in the provision of administration.

Most of the other cost factors listed in the table for Minnesota are self-explanatory. In several cases, cost factors were entered in quadratic form to allow for the possibility of nonlinear impacts. For example, the finding of a positive coefficient on density but a negative coefficient on the square of density in the transportation spending equation suggests that costs per lane mile increase at a decreasing rate. Similarly a negative coefficient on the square of the five-year rate of population growth in the economic and social services category suggests that per capita spending on that category increases at a decreasing rate with the rate of population growth.

The Wisconsin study of municipalities is modeled closely on the Minnesota study. One difference is that Reschovsky and Green split economic and social programs into two categories: economic programs which include spending on sanitation (except sewerage services), housing, and economic development and social programs which include spending on health and human services, culture, recreation, and some education (but not public schools). For economic programs, the percent of the population under eighteen and per capita employment in trade and services emerge as cost factors. For social programs, the poverty rate and government employment (excluding municipal employment) emerge. Cost factors for the other functional categories include density, old housing, area wage level, and the rate of population growth.

The Representative Expenditure Approach. To implement the representative expenditure approach, Rafuse and his colleagues used similar methods for the county areas of Maryland and city areas in the Chicago metropolitan area. Hence, table 2.3 provides illustrative examples of workload measures from the Maryland study alone. Neither state has any relevant local cost-of-living data comparable to the Minnesota data. Hence, the analysts were not able to adjust the workload measures for cost-of-living differences, although they would have liked to do so.

Implicit in the Rafuse approach is an assumption of constant returns to scale in production. The significance of this assumption emerges with respect to the first spending category listed in table 2.3, general government. By using population as the only workload measure, Rafuse is implicitly arguing that all counties could provide a given level of general government services at the same per capita expenditure. Yet, the Minnesota regression results provide evidence in favor of economies of scale for this spending category. Hence, the Rafuse approach is likely to overstate the expenditure need related to general government spending in large counties and to understate it in small counties.

For many of the service categories, a basic workload measure is constructed as the sum of the resident population, average daily visitors to the county, and total employment in the county. Together these three population figures are intended to measure the total number of people placing claims on public sector services. Although the visitor category excludes commuters, the argument made by the authors to counter the criticism that this measure involves double counting is not fully convincing. Nor is the argument that each component should be weighted equally in forming the workload measure. However, the combined population measure appropriately recognizes the limitations of the use of resident population alone as a workload population measure.

As shown in the table, the workload measure for most services is a weighted average of more than one indicator. In some cases the combined measure provides a way for the analysts to account for the workloads of two different aspects of the service. For example, consider the spending category of sanitation and waste disposal. The nonresident population serves as the workload measure for the sanitation component, and the number of people served by treatment plants serves as the workload measure for the waste disposal component. In other cases, the combined measure reflects an effort to incorporate some of the effects of hard-to-measure cost factors. In the highway category, for example, vehicle miles traveled is intended to capture the effects of usage on highway deterioration and hence on maintenance spending, while lane miles capture the effects of weather on deterioration. Based on national studies, the weights reflect the relative contributions of the two sources of deterioration. (Capital spending is not included in the analysis.) Another effort to include cost factors is in the workload measure for elementary and secondary education in which pupils from disadvantaged households are weighted more heavily than other pupils to reflect the higher cost of educating them.

TABLE 2.3
Expenditure Need: Representative Expenditure Approach
Illustrative Examples from the Maryland Study

Spending Category	Workload Measures[1]
General Government	Population
Police	1/3(Population + Visitors + Employment) + 1/3(Number of violent crimes) + 1/3(Expected arrests for violent crime, given age distribution)
Fire Protection[2]	Population + Visitors + Employment
Health and Hospitals	.06(Population + Visitors + Employment) + .94(Population in households with income <125 percent of poverty level)
Highways	0.825 Vehicle miles traveled on locally maintained roads + 0.175 Lane miles of locally maintained roads and bridges x 20
Sanitation and Waste Removal	0.333 Population + 0.667 Population served by municipal and county-run sewage treatment plants
Social Services	0.667 Population of households with income below poverty level + 0.333 Population of households with income below 125 percent of poverty level
Elementary and Secondary Education	0.60 Pupils (age 5-14) + 1.00 Pupils (age 15-17), with pupils from households in poverty weighted 1.25

Footnotes:

1. The population measures are defined as follows: population = resident population as of midpoint of fiscal year; visitors = average daily number of visitors (excluding commuters) in calendar year; employment = total employment in the county.
2. The expenditure figure is adjusted upward to account for the value of volunteer fire fighters.

Source:

Robert W. Rafuse, Jr., Lawrence R. Marks, Carol E. Cohen, *Local Government Spending in Maryland: Needs and Performance*, Appendix A. Study prepared by the ACIR for the Commission on State Taxes and Tax Structure, State of Maryland, October 1990.

Despite the amount of work and thought that has gone into the development of these workload measures, one cannot help being struck by the absence of a procedure for determining their validity or plausibility. How can the analyst determine whether the measures make sense and are the best that can be developed given available data? In contrast to the regression-based approach in which a cost factor must pass the test of exerting a significant average impact on spending, there is no comparable test for the workload measures in the context of the representative expenditure approach.

Revenue-Raising Capacity

In principle, it makes sense to combine the representative expenditure approach on the spending side with the representative tax system or weighted tax base approach on the revenue side, and that is exactly what was done in the Chicago study. Similarly, it makes sense to combine the regression-based cost approach with the income-with-exporting approach. However, for a variety of reasons, this latter pairing did not always occur. Table 2.4 summarizes the measurement of revenue-raising capacity in the five studies that measured capacity.

Massachusetts. Bradbury and her colleagues measured revenue-raising capacity as .025 times each city's or town's per capita property tax base. The authors chose this approach because of Massachusetts' stringent property tax limitation measure, Proposition 2 1/2, which limited tax rates to 2 1/2 percent of market value. With the property tax as the only broad-based tax that cities and towns could use, their revenue-raising capacity was clearly constrained by the 2 1/2 percent rate limit. However, even this straightforward approach was not without controversy. Some communities with rates well below 2 1/2 percent protested that the measure overstated their capacity to raise revenue since a local referendum was needed for them to raise their effective tax rates.

In addition to property taxes, Massachusetts municipalities also rely on user charges for revenue. However, Bradbury and her colleagues chose not to include revenue from user charges as part of local own-source capacity. This decision was based on the policy judgment (supported by public officials involved in the discussions) that the state should in no way discourage the use of user charges. They were concerned that, in the absence of an appropriate potential base for calculating the capacity to generate user-charge revenue, actual user-charge revenue would be used as a proxy. If so, cities that relied more heavily on user charges would appear to be in stronger fiscal condition relative to others, all else constant, and would receive less equalizing aid. Instead, the authors treated user charges

TABLE 2.4
Revenue-Raising Capacity from Own Sources

Massachusetts	*Tax base approach*
Cities and Towns	.025 x (Property tax base per capita)
Nebraska	*Income-with-exporting approach*
Counties	Property tax capacity - (Adjustment for capacity "used up" by municipalities and townships) + Other capacity
Municipalities	Property tax capacity + Sales tax capacity + Other capacity
School Districts	Property tax capacity (adjusted for payments into and out of the district)
Minnesota Cities with population over 2,500	1) *Income-with-exporting approach* Property tax capacity (adjusted for fiscal disparities and tax increment financing additions) + Electricity and liquor transfers 2) *Tax base approach* Property tax capacity + Tax increment financing addition + Electricity and liquor transfers
Wisconsin	*Tax base approach*
Municipalities	t x (Property tax base per capita) + Portion of revenue from tax increment financing
Chicago	*Representative-revenue approach*
40 City Areas	$\Sigma_i t_i BASE_i$ 6 tax categories plus interest earnings, current charges, other general revenues, utility and insurance trust revenue

Sources: See Table 2.1.

like prices. That is, they ignored them on the revenue side, but subtracted them from spending. Hence, the average spending numbers used in the Massachusetts study and two of the three subsequent studies that built on it (studies for Minnesota and Wisconsin) treat spending as spending net of user-charge revenue.

Nebraska. The Nebraska study is more ambitious than the others in terms of the number and classes of governmental units covered. For each category, Yinger (and others) used the income-with-exporting approach to measuring revenue-raising capacity.

Yinger calculated standard tax burdens (K^* in the formal expression) separately for each revenue source as the ratio of total statewide taxes collected (by type of tax) by all governments of a particular type to the income of local residents.[13] For the county calculations, he adjusted for the capacity "used up" by other governments in the county. At a given tax burden on county residents, less revenue is available for *county* governments in counties where many people live in municipalities (which also levy taxes) than where most people live in unincorporated parts of the county. This adjustment was necessary to account for the differing role of municipalities from county to county. In contrast, no adjustment was made for capacity "used up" by school districts because such districts blanket all counties.

Yinger crudely estimated export ratios for the property tax (for all three classes of governments) and the sales tax (for municipalities), but assumed export ratios of zero for miscellaneous taxes and user charges that make up the "other" category.

Minnesota. On conceptual grounds, Ladd, Reschovsky, and Yinger strongly preferred the income-with-exporting approach to measuring the revenue-raising capacity of Minnesota cities. However, many state officials, strongly preferred the tax-base approach. Consequently, the authors presented results based on both approaches.

Minnesota undoubtedly has one of the most complicated systems of local property taxation in the country. These complications arise from the use of a classified property tax in which higher valued residential property is taxed more heavily than lower valued property and both types are taxed less than business property, a system of tax credits for residential taxpayers, a program of tax-base sharing in the Twin Cities metropolitan area, heavy reliance on special assessments especially in fast-growing areas, and extensive use of tax increment financing (TIF). Each of these institutional features had to be addressed in measuring the relative capacities of Minnesota cities to raise revenue.

Because the state's system of property tax classification is a relatively permanent feature of the state fiscal environment, Ladd, Reschovsky, and Yinger treated it as given and outside the control of local officials. Consequently, they based the measures of revenue-raising capacity not on market values of property, but rather on assessed values, that is, on values after the application of the appropriate classification rates. Also not controversial was the need to adjust for contributions and distributions to the tax-base sharing program, and to adjust for homestead credits. After careful examination of the data and discussion with state and local officials, Ladd, Reschovsky, and Yinger augmented local fiscal capacity with revenue captured by a city through the TIF program and with transfers into the general fund from liquor stores and electric utilities. Most difficult conceptually and most controversial in practice was the treatment of special assessments. In light of both the conceptual and empirical complexities associated with the treatment of special assessments, the authors ultimately chose to treat revenues from special assessments as comparable to revenues from the property tax (see Appendix E of Ladd, Reschovsky, and Yinger, 1991, for full discussion of the special-assessment issue).

The main challenge in implementing the income-with-exporting approach involved the calculation of export ratios. The task was facilitated by the availability of excellent data on the composition of the property tax base. It was hindered by the conceptual and empirical difficulties of calculating city-specific export ratios by property type. The compromise was to combine average export ratios by property type from a previous study (Bradbury and Ladd, 1985), adjusted for the income tax deductibility of property taxes, with the city-specific data from Minnesota on property tax bases. In contrast, the tax-base approach was quite straightforward to implement and involved no additional complications beyond those discussed in the previous paragraph that applied to both approaches.

The results for the two approaches turned out to be highly correlated across cities. The simple correlation coefficient between the two measures of 0.92 suggests that the measures move closely together.[14] However, the deviations across cities of each measure from their respective means present a different picture. As mentioned earlier, the tax-base approach exhibits much greater variation around the mean than does the income-with-exporting approach. Of particular interest are the deviation results for Minneapolis and St. Paul, the two most populous cities in the state. The substantially larger positive deviations for both cities under the tax-base approach imply that both cities would appear better off when the tax-base approach rather than the income-with-exporting approach is used to calculate revenue-raising capacity. Consequently, use of the tax-base approach weakens the claim on state aid of these two Minnesota cities.

Wisconsin. For the Wisconsin study, Green and Reschovsky focused on the major local revenue source, the property tax, and measured revenue-raising capacity in each municipality simply as the amount of property tax revenue that would be generated from the local tax base assuming the municipality used an average tax rate (calculated as the average for the 585 municipalities in the sample). They added to this amount some of the revenue generated by local tax increment financing programs. Lack of data and quantitative unimportance justified their decision to ignore any revenue-raising capacity associated with the local hotel tax or municipally owned utilities.

Chicago. The Chicago study illustrates the application of the representative tax system to local jurisdictions. For forty city areas in the Chicago metropolitan area, Rafuse and Marks calculated representative revenues for each area for ten categories of own-source revenue based on 1987 census data. With the exception of intergovernmental revenue, for which the actual data were used, an average "rate" was applied to each area's "potential base," for each revenue category, where the average was calculated not just over the forty city areas, but rather over the entire Chicago metropolitan area. This approach allows the authors to measure the revenue-raising capacity of each of their forty city areas against the average for the whole area, not just for the forty cities.

For property tax and sales tax capacity, Rafuse and Marks use as the potential tax base in each municipality, the equalized assessed value of real property and total retail sales, respectively. However, for other local revenue sources, the potential tax base is less clear. Consequently, Rafuse and Marks simply use resident income as the default base and area-wide tax collections divided by income as the relevant average rate.[15] Revenue sources treated in this way include motor fuel taxes, motor vehicle license taxes, other taxes, current charges, interest earnings, all other own general revenues, utility revenue, and insurance trust revenue. Whether resident income is the best possible indicator of the potential yield of each of these sources is debatable. For example, it is hard to find a compelling conceptual argument for using resident income as the base for the somewhat anomalous categories of interest earnings and insurance trust revenue. Moreover, the implicit assumption that a city has the same sort of flexibility to change its interest earning or insurance trust revenues as it has for tax revenues is questionable.

Summary. The representative tax base approach appeals to some people because it is easy to implement and because many local revenue sources can be included. The evidence reviewed here confirms that it is relatively easy to implement provided, however, that the focus is primarily on the property tax. It becomes much more difficult to implement in a conceptually coherent way when additional revenue sources are included. As illustrated by the Chicago study, crude and perhaps inappropriate procedures, must be used to accommodate some of the miscellaneous revenue sources. Moreover, the connection between such approaches and the underlying model that requires equal tax rates is weak at best.

More fundamentally, the tax-base approach is flawed to the extent that willingness to raise revenue for public services rather than on the competitive position of one city relative to another.

USES OF STUDIES OF LOCAL FISCAL CONDITION

The types of studies discussed in this chapter can be used to evaluate current programs of assistance to local governments and to design new ones. By comparing the pattern of existing local aid to the pattern that would emerge if the state's sole goal were to equalize local fiscal condition, one can determine the extent to which the state's current aid programs target assistance to the neediest local governments. The experiences of Massachusetts, Nebraska, Minnesota, and Wisconsin suggest that existing aid programs are not very equalizing. This type of information is important to state policymakers and can stimulate productive discussion about the extent to which the state wishes to equalize the fiscal condition of local governments and how it might achieve that goal.

Of the studies discussed in this chapter only the Massachusetts study has had a direct impact on state legislation. That state used the need-capacity gap concept developed by Bradbury and others, including a modified version of the regression-based measure of expenditure need, to distribute incremental aid to cities and towns for several years during the mid 1980s. (See Reschovsky and Schwartz, 1992, for an evaluation of the equalizing impact of the program.) The Minnesota study generated substantial interest in that state and spawned substantial additional work by various local groups, but as yet no legislation has been enacted. None of the other studies appear to have had much legislative impact, although the Wisconsin study is so recent that it is too early to predict its impact.

Whether a state should use the measures of fiscal condition directly in an aid formula is a tricky question. Had Massachusetts chosen to distribute all aid in line with local fiscal condition as it was measured by Bradbury and her colleagues, aid to many wealthy communities would have had to be cut to zero so that sufficient aid could be targeted to the neediest communities. Politically, this outcome was unacceptable, as it is likely to be in other states. Instead, Massachusetts chose to use a modified version of this approach to distribute new to aid to local governments. This decision reflected a consensus first, that new aid should serve to equalize fiscal condition and second, that any measure of local fiscal condition should incorporate expenditure need as well as revenue-raising capacity. I should note here, however, that the use of regression analysis to generate local expenditure need made it difficult for interested people to fully understand the formula and provided leeway for policymakers to manipulate the cost index somewhat from year to year.

Even if states are not ready to use the results from such studies directly in aid formulas, I believe that many states would benefit from periodic studies of the fiscal condition of their local governments. First, such studies document the importance of considering disparities generated on the spending side as well on the revenue side. Second, they illustrate that objective measures of local expenditure need can be generated. Third, they inform the policy debate by providing state policymakers with new and better evidence on the magnitude of fiscal disparities across local governments and benchmarks against which existing aid programs can be evaluated. In sum, such studies take time and resources, but can provide state policymakers with useful information for evaluating and designing state policies toward local governments.

NOTES

1. In one of the studies discussed below, the authors focus initially not on the gap expressed in dollars per capita, but rather on the ratio of an index of revenue-raising capacity to an index of expenditure need. However, they also report the per capita gaps as defined here, but with the sign reversed so that a positive number indicates strong fiscal condition. As they point out, the gap approach is more directly useful to state policymakers interested in knowing how much it would cost the state to offset gaps between each locality's ability to raise revenue and its expenditure need. See Rafuse and Marks (1991).

2. This approach includes the exporting, but not the importing, of tax burdens. In principle, tax burdens imported into the jurisdiction should be included, but, in practice, they can usually be ignored because of the asymmetric way in which exported and imported burdens affect capacity. This asymmetry arises because exported burdens directly augment city revenues while imported taxes affect net disposable income. Consider an increase in the local earnings tax rates, say from 0 to 1 percent. If 50 percent of the tax is borne by commuters, then exporting augments the amount raised from residents by 100 percent. If 30 percent of the earnings of city residents are earned outside the city, a corresponding rise in earning taxes in nearby jurisdictions lowers the net-of-tax income of these "reverse commuters" by 1.0 percent, a reduction that amounts to only 0.3 percent of all earnings in the city. Thus, imported taxes in this example reduce the capacity of the city to raise revenue by 0.3 percent while the potential to export taxes increases it by 100 percent. Moreover, if one is willing to assume that imported tax burdens account for approximately the same share of income across local districts, ignoring tax importing has no effect on the

revenue-raising capacity of one city relative to another.

3. In principle, these tax bases should be potential tax bases not actual bases. That is they should reflect what state law allows the city to tax, not what the city has chosen to tax.

4. This assertion is based on my experience with policymakers in Minnesota.

5. This approach is developed most fully by Ladd and Yinger (1989 and 1991) for a national sample of cities. As discussed below, the approach has also been used by Ladd and Yinger and various other researchers to measure the fiscal condition of local governments within particular states.

6. To the extent that inefficiencies are not randomly distributed across communities, but instead vary with one of the cost factors, that cost factor will capture not only the effects on costs of that factor were all cities to produce public services efficiently, but also some inefficiency-related cost differences. For example, local population often emerges as a cost factor with a positive sign. To the extent that larger communities have larger governmental organizations than smaller communities and large organizations are less efficient than small ones, one explanation for the positive effect of population on estimated costs may be the greater inefficiency associated with large, rather than with small, governmental organizations. Note that this observation does not weaken the power of the cost-based regression approach. It simply highlights the fact that the approach need not imply that all jurisdictions are providing a given package of services at least cost, where least cost is the cost that jurisdictions might be forced to achieve if they were all small communities facing market-like pressure from the potential movement of local residents.

7. This approach might be described as an indirect method of estimating costs. A more direct approach requires data on outputs. Such data are often available for elementary and secondary education in the form of test scores, but are not available for most local public services. Fortunately, Downes and Pogue's results for education in Arizona indicate that the two statistical approaches yield similar results. See Downes and Pogue (1992a and 1992b).

8. Jerry Fastrup provided the initial insights for this comparison. See Fastrup (1990).

9. This approach was also applied to four county governments in Hawaii in 1989, but that study has not been released.

10. As an additional component of their work, the authors of the Chicago study also compared actual spending to their calculated measure of expenditure need. To do so, they had to devote tremendous effort to allocating appropriate shares of the spending by overlying districts to city areas.

11. However, it should be noted that not all of them were statistically significant. The two least significant variables were government employees per resident and the poverty rate. These variables were left in the equation for completeness and to avoid biasing any of the other coefficients.

12. Separate studies were completed by John Yinger for counties and municipalities, and by Kerri Ratcliffe, Bruce Riddle, and John Yinger for school districts. All are reported in Wasylenko and Yinger (1988).

13. In principle, the numerator should include taxes borne only by residents.

14. If the revenue capacity associated with tax increment financing and the transfers into the general fund from liquor stores and electric utilities are excluded from both measures, the correlation falls slightly to 0.87. See Ladd, Reschovsky, and Yinger (1991, p. 71).

15. Note that this procedure makes that part of their capacity measure similar to what would emerge from a crude income-with-exporting approach, with the assumption of zero exporting.

References

Bradbury, Katharine L., and Helen F. Ladd. "Changes in the Revenue-Raising Capacity of U.S. Cities, 1970–1982." *New England Economic Review* (March/April 1985), 20–37.

Bradbury, Katharine L., Helen F. Ladd, Mark Perrault, Andrew Reschovsky, and John Yinger. "State Aid to Offset Fiscal Disparities Across Communities." *National Tax Journal* 37 (June 1984), 151–170.

Downes, Thomas A., and Thomas F. Pogue. "Financing Local School Districts." In Therese J. McGuire and Dana Wolfe Naimark, eds., *State and Local Finance for the 1990s: A Case Study of Arizona.* Tempe, AZ: School of Public Affairs, Arizona State University, 1991.

Downes, Thomas A., and Thomas F. Pogue. "Intergovernmental Aid to Reduce Fiscal Disparities: Problems of Definition and Measurement." *Public Finance Quarterly*, 20 (October 1992), 468–82.

Fastrup, Jerry C. "Estimating the Cost of Local Public Services." Washington, D.C.: U.S. General Accounting Office, 1990.

Ferguson, Ronald F. and Helen F. Ladd. "Measuring the Fiscal Capacity of U.S. Cities." In H. Clyde Reeves, ed. *Measuring Fiscal Capacity.* Boston: Oelgeschlager, Gunn & Hain, Publishers, Inc., 1986, 141–68.

Green, Richard K., and Andrew Reschovsky. *An Analysis of The State of Wisconsin's Shared Revenue Program*. Report prepared for the Department of Revenue, State of Wisconsin, 1992.

Ladd, Helen F., Andrew Reschovsky, and John Yinger. *Measuring the Fiscal Condition of Cities in Minnesota, Final Report*. Prepared for the Minnesota Legislative Commission on Planning and Fiscal Policy, 1991.

Ladd, Helen F., and John Yinger. *America's Ailing Cities: Fiscal Health and the Design of Urban Policy*. Baltimore: Johns Hopkins University Press, 1989 and 1991 (1991 is updated paperback edition).

Program Evaluation Division, Office of the Legislative Auditor, State of Minnesota. *Statewide Cost of Living Differences*, 1989.

Rafuse, Robert W. Jr., and Lawrence R. Marks. *A Comparative Analysis of Fiscal Capacity, Tax Effort & Public Spending Among Localities in the Chicago Metropolitan Region*. Washington, D.C.: U.S. Advisory Commission on Intergovernmental Relations, 1991.

Rafuse, Robert W., Lawrence R. Marks, and Carol E. Cohen. *Local Government Spending in Maryland: Needs and Performance*. Final Report for the Commission on State Taxes and Tax Structure, State of Maryland, 1990.

Ratcliffe, Kerri, Bruce Riddle, and John Yinger. "The Fiscal Condition of School Districts in Nebraska: Is Small Beautiful?" In Michael Wasylenko and John Yinger, eds., *Final Report of the Nebraska Comprehensive Tax Study*. Syracuse, NY: Syracuse University, Maxwell School, Metropolitan Studies Program, 1988.

U.S. Advisory Commission on Intergovernmental Relations. *Measures of State and Local Fiscal Capacity and Tax Effort*. Washington, D.C., Report M-16, 1962.

U.S. Advisory Commission on Intergovernmental Relations. *1988 State Fiscal Capacity and Effort*. Report M-170. Washington, D.C., 1990.

U.S. Advisory Commission on Intergovernmental Relations. *The Structure of State Aid to Elementary and Secondary Education*. Report M-175. Washington, D.C., 1990.

Wasylenko, Michael, and John Yinger. *Nebraska Comprehensive Study, Final Report*. Metropolitan Studies Program. Syracuse, NY: The Maxwell School, Syracuse University, 1988.

[4]

THE CASE FOR EQUALIZING AID
HELEN F. LADD* & JOHN YINGER**

Equalizing aid can be used by the federal government to equalize fiscal outcomes or resources among subnational governments, or by states to equalize outcomes or resources among local governments. Although equalizing aid can sometimes be justified in part on efficiency grounds, we focus on its primary function, namely, to achieve equity objectives.[1] The equity objective of a donor government can take many forms. The central theme of this paper is that the appropriate design for an equalizing aid program depends on the form of this objective.

Intergovernmental aid is not, of course, the only tool higher-level governments can use to assist poor or troubled lower-level governments. State governments, for example, can achieve equity objectives by altering the fiscal arrangements within which local governments operate. A state could take over from local governments the financing of certain services, such as social services, that place large burdens on a few jurisdictions,[2] or, to counter fiscal disparities in education financing, a state could encourage the merger of school districts. Hence, intergovernmental aid should be viewed as

*Duke University, Durham, NC 27708.
**Syracuse University, Syracuse, NY 13244.

only one tool, and not always the best tool, to achieve fiscal equity.

We place equity objectives into two classes: categorical equity, which relates to public sector spending, either on specific functions or on all functions, and distributional equity, which is aimed at equalizing the real incomes of local residents. In the following discussion, we focus on state aid to local governments.[3] For simplicity of presentation, we assume that local governments have access to only one local revenue source, a local property tax, and recognize that the local tax base *per capita* varies across jurisdictions.

Many of the specifics of what follows are well known to public finance experts. Our contributions are as follows: to incorporate cost considerations into the various aid formulas, to highlight the similarities and differences among formulas in a common framework, to highlight the role of capitalization in the discussion of equalizing real incomes, and to argue that equalizing aid is a valuable policy tool under some circumstances.

As we use the term, a local government's public service costs indicate how much a jurisdiction must spend to provide a given package of public services at a given quality level. These costs reflect both the cost of inputs and the harshness of the environment for providing public services.[4] Local governments that must pay more to attract employees from the private sector obviously have higher public service costs than other governments, all else equal.[5] Moreover, as first pointed out by Bradford, Malt, and Oates (1969), a jurisdiction with a harsh environment must pay more, all else equal, to obtain the same service quality. Extensive old housing, for example, raises the cost of fire protection, and a concentration of poor or disadvantaged residents raises the cost of most local public services.

In practice, costs can be derived from the coefficients of input and environmental cost factors in a multivariate regression analysis of local public spending that controls for income, price, and taste variation across jurisdictions.[6] To facilitate their inclusion in an equalizing aid formula, these estimated costs are best expressed in index form, with the index equal to one in a jurisdiction with average costs. To avoid giving inappropriate incentives to recipient jurisdictions, the cost factors included in this index should be largely, if not totally, outside the control of local public officials.

CATEGORICAL EQUITY ARGUMENTS FOR EQUALIZING AID

The most fundamental equity argument for equalizing aid is categorical equity, which exists when all citizens have fair access to public services that are thought to be particularly important to their opportunities in life.[7] Although policy makers at any higher level of government may have categorical equity objectives, the attainment of categorical equity is particularly important to states, each of which bears the primary responsibility for its system of local governments and the resulting distribution of local public services. This section presents several possible categorical equity objectives for a donor government (that is, several possible definitions of fair access), and describes the grants needed to achieve them.[8]

Ensuring a Minimum Outcome

One widely applied categorical equity standard requires that all citizens (or students) have access to a minimum quality of public services. This standard can be applied to an individual public service, such as education or public safety, or to local public services in general.

The most direct way to achieve this standard is with a foundation grant, which ensures that each jurisdiction can reach some minimum level of spending per capita, labeled E^*, if it is willing to levy a property tax rate, labeled t^*, that is considered to be a fair minimum.[9] Both the minimum level of spending and the minimum fair tax rate are policy parameters that must be set by public officials.

With this approach, the state grant per capita to jurisdiction j, A_j, equals the minimum spending minus the local revenue that can be raised at the fair tax rate. If V_j is the property tax base per capita in jurisdiction j, then the foundation formula is

$$A_j = E^* - t^* V_j.$$

An alternative version of this formula highlights the fact that a foundation grant is a block grant, which means that it does not vary with a jurisdiction's chosen spending level, and that it is larger for jurisdictions with relatively small tax bases.[10] If V^* is defined as the tax base at which A_j equals zero, it follows immediately that $E^* = t^* V^*$ or $t^* = E^*/V^*$. Substituting this result into equation 1 yields

2

$$A_j = E^* \left(1 - \frac{V_j}{V^*}\right).$$

Note that negative grants are not allowed; jurisdictions with tax bases above V^* receive no aid.

This approach easily can be extended to include public service costs. In this case, the first policy parameter is the minimum acceptable service quality, S^*; C_j is a cost index for jurisdiction j; and state aid is the difference between the spending needed to achieve S^*, namely S^*C_j, and local revenue at the fair tax rate. In practice, S^* can be set equal to the minimum acceptable spending in a community with average costs, that is, with $C_j = 1$. In symbols,

3

$$A_j = S^* C_j - t^* V_j.$$

Now redefine V^* to be the tax base at which state aid would equal zero assuming a cost index equal to unity, so that $t^* = S^*/V^*$ and

4

$$A_j = S^* \left(C_j - \frac{V_j}{V^*}\right).$$

This formula describes a block grant that depends both on a jurisdiction's costs and tax base. Remember that the cost index, C_j, is defined as a jurisdictions's costs relative to the average jurisdiction; hence the terms in brackets are both expressed in relative terms.

A foundation grant makes it possible for a jurisdiction to provide the minimum acceptable service level at the fair minimum tax rate. It does not guarantee, however, that a community actually will provide this level unless it is accompanied by the requirement that the jurisdiction levy at least the minimum tax rate, t^*, to support the relevant service or services.[11]

Easing the Burden of Providing Standard-Quality Public Services

Sometimes a donor government is unwilling to require local governments to provide a specific service level on the grounds that local governments should be free to make their own decisions. Nevertheless, because some jurisdictions are fiscally disadvantaged relative to others and some service or services are viewed as particularly important, the donor government may want, without imposing a spending requirement, to help equalize the ease with which jurisdictions can achieve a specified service level. Fiscal disadvantages arise from two sources: below-average capacity to raise revenue, as measured by V_j, and above-average costs of providing the standard service quality, as measured by C_j. Hence, to successfully ease the burden of providing standard-quality public services, the donor government should give more aid to jurisdictions that have larger fiscal disadvantages, measured by what we call the *need-capacity gap*.[12] This approach makes it possible for all jurisdictions to move toward standard-quality services at a standard tax rate.

To be specific, we define a jurisdiction's need-capacity gap as the difference between its *expenditure need* and its *revenue-raising capacity*, all defined in *per capita* terms. Expenditure need is the amount of money required for the jurisdiction to provide the standard-quality services and is calculated as the standardized service quality, S', multiplied by the jurisdiction's cost index, C_j.[13] Revenue-raising capacity is the amount of money a jurisdiction could raise at a standard tax rate given its own tax base, which equals the standard tax rate, t', multiplied by V_j.[14] The need-capacity gap indicates the extent to which the revenue the jurisdiction can raise at a standard tax rate falls short of the amount it must spend to provide standard-quality public services. The meaning of "standard" must be set by policy makers; that is, S' and t' are policy parameters.

Once the need-capacity gap has been defined, the natural grant system is to close a certain portion of the gap in each jurisdiction. In symbols,

$$A_j = a + b\,G_j = a + b\,(S'\,C_j - t'\,V_j), \quad (5)$$

where a and b are policy parameters that define the aid program. Defining G' as the gap at which aid equals zero, we find that $a = -bG'$. Substituting this result into equation 5 yields:

$$A_j = b(G_j - G') = b(S'\,C_j - t'\,V_j - G'). \quad (6)$$

As before, negative aid is not allowed, so jurisdictions with a gap less than G' receive no aid.

Foundation grants are a special case of this formula, in which b is set equal to one (that is, the entire gap is closed); S' is set at the minimum acceptable level of services, S^*; t' is set at what is believed to be the minimum fair tax rate, t^*; and G' is set to zero (that is, jurisdictions that can afford the minimum service quality at the fair tax rate receive no aid).

The more general form in equation 6 allows a grant program to close only part of the gap between expenditure need and revenue-raising capacity and to give some aid to jurisdictions that have negative need-capacity gaps. With b less than one and without a requirement that each jurisdiction impose at least the standard tax rate, t', the grant program helps jurisdictions move toward the selected service level at a fair tax rate, but neither fully funds the move to this outcome nor requires it. Moreover, the amount appropriated for the grant program determines the extent of equalization. In general, there is an inverse relationship between b and the program's budget, holding G' constant; raising G', that is, excluding more jurisdictions from aid, increases the value of b that can be achieved for a given budget.[15]

Ensuring Equal Service for a Given Sacrifice

Another widely discussed categorical equity objective is to ensure that every jurisdiction willing to make a certain level of sacrifice will receive the same level of public services, regardless of its own tax base. In this context, "sacrifice" is defined as the effective property tax rate.[16] Grants to achieve this objective are called "power-equalizing" grants. In 1991–2, eight states used some form of power-equalizing grant, usually with severe restrictions, to help finance local education (Gold et al., 1992).

In equation form, this objective is to set

$$E_j = t_j \hat{V} \quad (7)$$

where $\hat{V}$ is a policy parameter. Since local revenue equals $t_j V_j$ and state aid equals the difference between spending and local revenue, this formula leads directly to

$$A_j = E_j - L_j = t_j(\hat{V} - V_j). \quad (8)$$

Now solving equation 7 for t_j and substituting the result into equation 8 yields

$$A_j = E_j\left(1 - \frac{V_j}{\hat{V}}\right). \quad (9)$$

This equation defines a matching grant in which the state's share of total spending, which is the term in brackets, is higher for jurisdictions with lower tax bases. Note that when the two policy parameters, V^* and $\hat{V}$, are equal, the term in brackets is the same as for a foundation formula, but this term is multiplied by actual spending in equation 9, not by the state-determined minimum spending as in equation 2. With a power-equalizing formula, in other words, a jurisdiction's aid depends both on the spending level it selects and on the divergence between its tax base and the tax base designated by policy makers.

Note also that the policy parameters in equations 9 and 2 need not be the same. The derivation of equation 9 does not assume that power-equalizing grants go only to a subset of jurisdictions. Thus, if $\hat{V}$ is set at any level below the tax base of the richest jurisdiction, the formula implies that some jurisdictions will have negative matching rates, an outcome that usually is politically unacceptable.[17] Negative matching rates can be eliminated by raising $\hat{V}$, but this action would increase the cost of the program. Instead, power-equalizing grants, as implemented, virtually always override the formula to assure a minimum amount of aid for each jurisdiction and thereby limit the extent of equalization relative to equation 9.

This type of grant also can be modified to account for a jurisdiction's costs.[18] In particular, the defining equation can be restated to say that service quality, or real spending, will depend only on sacrifice. In symbols,

(10)

$$\frac{E_j}{C_j} \equiv S_j = t_j \hat{V}.$$

Following the same steps as before, this equation leads to the grant formula

(11)

$$A_j = S_j \left(C_j - \frac{V_j}{\hat{V}} \right).$$

Now the matching rate, that is, the state's share of total spending, depends on a jurisdictions's cost index as well as its tax base. Equation 11 differs from the cost-adjusted foundation formula, equation 4, because it is based on a jurisdiction's actual real spending (or service quality), not on a fixed minimum real spending.

Wealth Neutrality

In some of the early school finance cases, courts ruled that the wealth of the local school district should be viewed as a "suspect category," which constitutionally cannot serve as the basis for differences in the quality of education services, often measured by per pupil spending, available to pupils across the state.[19] These rulings express another possible equity objective, called wealth neutrality, which requires that variation across districts in per pupil spending, or preferably in school service levels, be uncorrelated with variation in the per pupil property tax base, a measure of wealth. Wealth neutrality could be an objective for other public services as well.

One way to achieve this outcome is to redefine school districts so that they all have the same tax base per pupil. By eliminating variation in district tax bases, this nonaid approach would assure that any remaining variation in spending or service levels was uncorrelated with district wealth.[20] Given the obvious political difficulties of redrawing district boundaries, the challenge is to design an intergovernmental aid formula that achieves the same goal.

By assuring that every jurisdiction, regardless of the size of its tax base, can generate the same revenue *per capita* (or per pupil) as the district with base V^*, power-equalizing grants appear at first to generate wealth neutrality. As pointed out by Feldstein (1975), however, this statement is not generally true. Although higher matching rates for lower-wealth jurisdictions are likely to push a system toward wealth neutrality, they also may induce lower-wealth jurisdictions to select lower (or higher) tax rates than high-wealth jurisdictions, so that a correlation between service outcomes and wealth remains despite the rule imposed by equation 7.

Feldstein (1975) also shows that, assuming a particular algebraic form for the demand for education, a wealth-neutralizing matching grant is defined by

12

$$A_i = E_i(1 - kV_i^{\beta_w/\beta_p}),$$

where k is a scale parameter, which roughly corresponds to $1/\bar{V}$ in equation 9 and which determines the overall level of spending; β_w is the elasticity of spending with respect to wealth; and β_p is the (negative) elasticity of spending with respect to price.[21] As in equation 9, the term in brackets defines a matching rate. Comparing equations 9 and 12 reveals that a power-equalizing grant is wealth-neutral only when the two elasticities in equation 12 are equal in absolute value. If they are not equal, a jurisdiction's response to the matching grant, which is determined by the price elasticity, does not exactly offset the existing impact of its wealth on service demand.

Feldstein (1975) estimates that the required exponent for V_i in this formula equals about 0.33 for cities and towns in Massachusetts in 1970. According to this estimate, the implicit unitary exponent on wealth in the power-equalizing formula, equation 9, is too large, in the sense that it leads to a negative correlation between wealth and spending. Feldstein's estimated price elasticity is, however, much greater in absolute value than the price elasticity estimated by most other studies of local spending.[22] With a more widely accepted value for this parameter, one might conclude that the implicit exponent in a power-equalizing formula is about right or even too small to generate wealth neutrality.

The Feldstein (1975) formula is general enough to encompass public service costs. Cost factors that are uncorrelated with wealth do not influence the formula at all; if costs are uncorrelated with wealth across school districts, achieving wealth neutrality with respect to spending implies achieving wealth neutrality with respect to service quality. Moreover, so long as all cost variables that are correlated with wealth are included in the empirical analysis, and therefore influence the estimate of β_w, equation 12 leads to wealth neutrality with respect to service quality.[23]

Another way to achieve wealth neutrality would be to equalize voters' budget constraints in all jurisdictions. A constraint-equalizing grant program would consist of lump-sum grants to offset income differences across districts and matching grants to offset tax-price differences.[24] This approach has the advantage over the Feldstein (1975) approach that it does not require the incorporation of estimated elasticities into the grant formula. It costs the state more than the Feldstein approach, however, because it uses block grants instead of relying exclusively on matching grants. Given the low price elasticities found by most studies, however, the cost difference might not be too large.[25]

In conclusion, no state has attempted to implement a program that would literally be wealth-neutral. Foundation and power-equalization programs move toward this objective, at least if implemented in pure form, but they cannot achieve it. Programs that could achieve wealth neutrality are either too complicated, in the sense that they must be based on estimated elasticities, or too expensive, in the sense that they involve extensive redistribution, to be politically feasible—at least so far.

Ensuring Equal Outcomes

An even stronger equity objective than wealth neutrality is complete equality in service levels. This objective is based on the view that certain public services (education, police, or fire, for example) are so important to a person's life chances that all citizens should have equal access to them, regardless of their circumstances or the circumstances of their community.[26]

None of the plans described so far meets this objective. If they are implemented without limits and loopholes, they all move toward it, but none of them achieves full equality of outcomes. A foundation grant places no limit on the spending by rich districts; power-equalizing grants do not even achieve wealth neutrality, which is a necessary condition for equal outcomes; and wealth-neutral grants do not eliminate spending variation that is uncorrelated with wealth.

The only way we know of to meet this objective through grants is to use a foundation plan that requires each jurisdiction to set its tax rate exactly at t^*.[27] However, attempts to restrict the school tax rates of wealthy jurisdictions have proved to be unpopular and could, as emphasized by Reschovsky (1994), encourage wealthy taxpayers to send their children to private schools.[28] In principle, these political problems could be avoided if the "minimum acceptable level" were set above the spending that any jurisdiction would select, but this approach would run into another political problem: its prohibitive expense.

The Case for Equalizing Grants

In our judgement, a strong case can be made for equalizing grants to achieve categorical equity, although the appropriate form of the grants depends on the circumstances. According to their constitutions, many state governments are explicitly responsible for the character of the system that provides elementary and secondary education (see Reschovsky, 1994). We believe that a state's most fundamental responsibility in education is to ensure that every student receives a minimum acceptable level of educational services. Thus, we agree with Reschovsky (1994) that the best grant program for education is a "complete" foundation plan with a required minimum tax rate, with costs in the formula, and, we would add, with a relatively high minimum service quality.

Compared to ensuring a minimum acceptable education, the objectives of equal service per unit sacrifice, of wealth neutrality, or of equal outcomes are stronger in the sense that they require adjustments by all districts, including those that would provide high-quality education without additional assistance. However, controversy surrounding these stronger objectives inevitably leads to compromises that severely limit the extent of equalization. Some people support programs to promote equal service per unit sacrifice or wealth neutrality because those programs allow some variation in service quality even at low levels of wealth and thereby enhance choice for parents.[29] We believe that this extra choice comes at a high equity cost imposed on the students who consequently receive inadequate services. Thus, we prefer a complete foundation plan to the most widely discussed alternative, a power-equalizing grant, as well as to wealth-neutral or equal-outcome grants, and we strongly prefer a complete foundation plan to power-equalizing grants as they are typically implemented with no consideration of costs, with hold harmless clauses, and with a minimum amount of aid to each district.

Although state constitutions do not specifically mention local services other than education, this case for a complete foundation plan also can be extended to other key local public services, such as public safety. Outside of education, however, the minimum acceptable service quality may prove to be difficult for state officials to define, and a practical alternative to a foundation plan is a plan based on the need-capacity gap. This approach makes it possible to give more help to the jurisdictions that face the most severe constraints in providing these services, but it does not literally require a minimum service level. Moreover, unlike a foundation plan, this approach has the practical advantage that, holding constant the state's budget, the number of jurisdictions receiving aid (and hence the political support for the program) can be increased by lowering the extent to which state aid actually closes measured need-capacity gaps. Because the state may want to treat other local services, such as social services, the same way it treats public safety, a grant program based on the need-capacity gap also might be appropriate for all local spending.

EQUALIZING REAL INCOMES THROUGH EQUALIZING AID

Another possible objective for an equalizing grant program is to make more equal the distribution of households' real incomes. Although more direct methods for achieving this objective, such as transfer programs, social insurance, and progressive income taxation, are available, a possible role remains for equalizing grants. This role arises because low-income people cannot directly select the level of public services or taxes in their jurisdiction, and indeed may not have enough votes or political power to influence their jurisdiction's choices. If a jurisdiction in which a low-income household lives provides a service level that is far below what the household prefers, federal or state resources might have a larger impact on the household's utility if they were devoted to increasing the quality of public services than if they were devoted to transfers that directly increase the household's income. This possibility is magnified if local services are characterized by nonrivalry in consumption. Moreover, if the local tax system is regressive, so that tax reductions yield the greatest benefits to people at the bottom of the income distribution, intergovernmental grants that lead to reduced local taxes also might be worth more to low-income people than higher transfers. These are theoretical arguments; we know of no empirical work that determines whether these conditions are met.

Even if these conditions are satisfied, however, the potential of intergovernmental aid programs to boost the real incomes of low-income households may be limited by capitalization, which arises when local service quality and local tax rates affect property values.[30] In the presence of capitalization, which has been documented by many empirical studies,[31] increases in real income associated with higher service quality or lower taxes may be partially or totally offset by higher rents or housing prices.[32]

To be more specific, full capitalization implies that the benefits to tenants from grant-induced increases in service quality are canceled by rent increases and that the benefits to homeowners are confined to people who currently own property in the community. Homeowners who arrive in the future must pay a higher price to enter the community and therefore are no better off as a result of the improved services. With capitalization, therefore, an equalizing grant program appears likely to help many current low-income homeowners and current landlords (some of whom may have low incomes), but appears unlikely to help low-income renters or future low-income homeowners.

Moreover, the existence of capitalization undercuts to some degree an implicit premise in the basic objective of equalizing real incomes, namely that a person's real income depends in part on the service quality and tax rate in the jurisdiction where she lives.[33] If all households are mobile, every household with a given set of skills and preferences can achieve the same real income. Hence, because of compensation in the form of lower housing prices, low-income households who live in jurisdictions with poor public services or high taxes already are no worse off than low-income households who live in jurisdictions with excellent services or low taxes.

For two reasons, however, this capitalization argument neither completely invalidates the premise that real incomes depend on public service quality nor completely eliminates the possibility of using intergovernmental grants to equalize real incomes. The first reason is that age, disability, poverty, and discrimination reduce the mobility of many low-income people.[34] With barriers to mobility, differences in service quality or tax rates need not be fully reflected in housing prices.

The second reason is that even if low-income people are mobile, the impact of grants on housing prices depends on the solution to a complex general equilibrium problem, which does not always yield offsetting housing price changes. A general treatment of this problem is not available, but this point can be illustrated by examining several special cases.

Suppose, for example, that all low-income people live in central cities with poor public services, that these central cities contain only low-income people, and that all of these central cities receive equalizing grants. Because capitalization reflects competition among households of a given type for housing in communities with different public service levels, there is nothing to capitalize in this case. Hence, the real incomes of all low-income households are depressed by the fact that they receive low-quality public services, and raising the quality of public services in all these central cities boosts the real incomes of all low-income households without having any impact on prices. In other words, if a grant program raises service quality in every jurisdiction where low-income people live, a capitalization effect does not arise, and capitalization has no impact either on the validity of the objective or on the ability of grants to achieve it.

Wyckoff (1992) analyzes an alternative case in which there are two communities and three income classes. One community (call it the central city) contains all low-income households, the other (call it the suburb) contains all high-income households, and both contain some of the middle-income households. In this case, capitalization reflects the service demands of the middle-income households who are the households at the moving margin. Raising service quality in the central city therefore boosts the price of housing enough to keep middle-income households in equilibrium, that is, enough to offset middle-income households' valuation of the increment in service quality. This change in housing price could be higher than, lower than, or equal to the value of the public service increment to low-income households. It follows that the real income of low-income households could go down, go up, or be unchanged by equalizing grants. Wyckoff also shows that if the central city contains "a large fraction of the population of the metropolitan area, most of the relative price changes between housing prices in the two communities necessary to restore middle class indifference are accomplished by price changes in the" suburb (p. 22). In this case, intergovernmental aid has the desired effect; that is, it raises the real income of low-income households.

We conclude that capitalization weakens, but does not eliminate, the case for using intergovernmental grants to equalize real incomes. Further research is needed to determine the extent to which capitalization offsets the redistributional benefits of these grants.

Conclusions

Both state governments and the federal government have a long history of attempting to meet equity objectives through intergovernmental grants. The key step in designing an equalizing grant program is deciding on the form of this equity objective. Many different categorical equity objectives, including the guarantee of a minimum service quality and wealth neutrality, can be attained with an appropriately designed equalizing aid program, and under some circumstances equalizing grants can make a contribution to a fairer distribution of real incomes. Moreover, because all relevant equity objectives are concerned with service quality, not spending as such, grant formulas to achieve them must account for public service costs. Although few grant programs account for costs in a systematic way, methods for doing so are readily available.

Different equity objectives and grant programs are appropriate under different circumstances. In our judgement, a complete foundation plan, that is, a foundation plan that requires a minimum tax rate, accounts for costs, and sets a relatively high minimum service level, is appropriate for elementary and secondary education. For police, fire, and other local services, grants based on the need-capacity gap provide a flexible way to focus aid on the jurisdictions that, through no fault of their own, need help the most.

ENDNOTES

[1] For a discussion of some of the efficiency arguments in favor of equalizing aid, see Ladd and Yinger (1991) and Oates and Schwab (1988). For some efficiency arguments against equalizing aid, see Oakland (1994).

[2] Around 1970, for example, many states moved the responsibility for welfare services from the city to the county or state level. See Ladd and Yinger (1991).

[3] For an analysis of the extent of equalization in existing state aid to local governments, see Yinger and Ladd (1989).

[4] The fact that household characteristics may influence the environment for providing public services leads to an important efficiency argument for equalizing grants, namely, to offset the externality imposed on jurisdictions when low-cost individuals leave. See Oates and Schwab (1988).

[5] Note that actual public wages are a poor measure of costs because they are influenced by local officials. Cost measures—and hence aid formulas—should be based on factors outside the control of local officials. For more on this issue, see Ladd and Yinger (1991).

[6] For examples of this procedure, see Bradbury et al. (1984), Ratcliffe, Riddle, and Yinger (1990), Ladd and Yinger (1991), and Ladd, Reschovsky, and Yinger (1991). Oakland (1994) states that because "spending is not a valid measure of output . . . the coefficients

produced by spending studies measure handicap only if actual budget policy compensates exactly for the handicap." This argument is not correct. The regression-based method is rigorous and requires no such assumption. See Yinger and Ladd (1991, chapter 10).

[7] Oakland (1994) discounts categorical equity objectives (except, apparently, in the case of education) because he sees no reason to think that public services are worth more to people than are private goods and services. We find categorical equity worthwhile not only because certain public services, such as education and public safety, are important to a person's opportunities, but also because a person cannot directly select the level of public services he or she receives.

[8] If many citizens believe in any of these equity objectives (or the one in the next section), then there is an efficiency gain to equalizing grants that parallels each equity objective. This is an application of the well-known theory of efficiency-improving redistribution (Hochman and Rogers, 1969). See also Ladd and Doolittle (1982).

[9] The issue of property tax capitalization, which is discussed at length in a later section, is not relevant here. The minimum service objective (along with most of the other categorical equity objectives) includes a statement about the share of a jurisdiction's tax base that represents a fair contribution to the provision of the relevant public services. The fact that a jurisdiction's property tax base may reflect the tax rate that it actually selects has nothing to do with selection of this share. One might object, however, to the use of the property tax base as a measure of a jurisdiction's capacity to raise revenue, because it reflects the jurisdiction's actual tax decisions. This problem can be solved by using a more general measure of revenue-raising capacity, which is discussed in endnote 14.

[10] Grants inversely related to a jurisdiction's tax base also may have efficiency consequences. Oakland (1994) argues that they may either offset distortions that arise when location decisions are based on tax or service levels or lower efficiency by lowering interjurisdictional variation in service-tax packages. Others have argued that these grants undercut a jurisdiction's incentive to attract more property. Because broad economic and social forces have a much larger influence on a city's tax base than anything the city can do, we do not find this argument compelling. See Ladd and Yinger (1991).

[11] An equivalent requirement is that the jurisdiction spend at least S^*C_j on the service. Note that if t^* is defined as the minimum tax rate required for a jurisdiction to be eligible for the program, instead of the minimum tax rate permitted, then some low-spending jurisdictions might choose not to participate in the grant program at all.

[12] Grants of this type were implemented by the state of Massachusetts in 1980. See Bradbury et al. (1984). Grants of this type also are described in Ratcliffe, Riddle and Yinger (1990) and Ladd, Reschovsky, and Yinger (1991).

[13] In some cases, a measure of expenditure need also must account for differences across jurisdictions in service responsibilities. See Ladd and Yinger (1991).

[14] An alternative approach to revenue-raising capacity is given by Ladd and Yinger (1991). In this approach, a jurisdiction's capacity is the amount it could raise at a standard tax burden on its residents. Ladd and Yinger show how this measure of capacity depends on a jurisdiction's income and its ability to export tax burdens to nonresidents. This approach is more complicated to implement, however, largely because export ratios are difficult to estimate, and it appears to be highly correlated with the tax-base approach used in the text. In Minnesota, for example, the correlation between the two approaches across municipalities is 0.92. See Ladd, Reschovsky, and Yinger (1991).

[15] These claims can easily be proven by substituting the formula for aid per capita, equation 6, into the program's budget constraint and rearranging the terms. This budget constraint can be written as follows:

$$B = \sum_{j=1}^{J} N_j A_j$$

where B is the total budget for the program, J is the number of jurisdictions that receive aid, and N_j is the population of jurisdiction j.

[16] This notion of sacrifice is not without problems. Jurisdictions may have other sources of revenue, for example. Philosophical objections to this notion also can be raised. See Feldstein (1975).

[17] An experiment with negative matching rates was attempted by the state of Maine but was quickly overturned by a referendum.

[18] This point was made, although not implemented, by Feldstein (1975, p. 77): "expenditure per pupil could be modified to reflect local differences in input prices or student abilities."

[19] In the 1973 Texas case of Rodriguez v. San Antonio, the U.S. Supreme Court, in a 5–4

decision, held that education was not a fundamental right and that school district wealth was not a suspect category under the United States Constitution. See Odden and Picus (1992, p. 27). Rulings by state courts have not been so definitive. For more on these issues, see Reschovsky (1994).

[20] A extreme version of this approach is to provide schools at the state level, as is done in Hawaii.

[21] Feldstein's demand function expresses the log of spending as a function of the log of wealth, the log of price (as determined by the matching rate), and the log of other variables, which may be correlated with wealth. The elasticity of spending with respect to wealth includes the direct elasticity for the wealth variable and the indirect elasticity for all other variables that affect demand and are correlated with wealth. In principle, a weaker form of wealth neutrality could be achieved with the Feldstein approach if the components of the wealth elasticity are confined to variables that are thought to be systematically, not incidentally, related to wealth.

[22] Feldstein's estimate price elasticity is −1.0. Most estimates for education fall between −0.1 and −0.5. See Inman (1979) and Bergstrom, Rubinfeld, and Shapiro (1982).

[23] As it turns out, Feldstein's equations contain no cost variables, so substituting his estimated elasticities into his formula will not yield wealth neutrality with respect to service quality, given that many other studies have found that cost factors influence education. See Hanushek (1986) or Ratcliffe, Riddle, and Yinger (1990).

[24] The precise forms of the block grant and matching grant can be found from the median voter's budget constraint. In a standard model, the block grant equals the difference between the target income (a policy parameter) and the median voter's actual income divided by the median voter's tax share (which is her house value divided by house value *per capita* in the jurisdiction). Assuming constant costs in the production of service quality, the matching rate equals the jurisdiction's cost index divided by the median voter's tax share and by the target tax price (another policy parameter). For a derivation of this type of grant in a more complex model, see Yinger (1986). Strictly speaking, this approach raises two new issues. First, it removes all systematic correlation between wealth and service outcomes, but not literally all correlation, as does the Feldstein approach. Preference differences that are correlated with wealth, for example, still might influence outcomes. Second, it assumes that it is appropriate to base grants on a majority rule (or median-voter) framework even if actual decisions diverge from what the median voter would choose. Moreover, it assumes that the median voter can be identified as the person with median income and median preferences. The conditions under which this is true are stated by Bergstrom and Goodman (1973).

[25] In addition, this approach achieves only the weaker form of wealth neutrality described in the previous endnote, which may or may not satisfy courts in school equity cases.

[26] Reschovsky (1994) points out that several state courts appear to be requiring this objective for education.

[27] One way to achieve this objective without a grant is for a state to take over provision of the service, and then to provide the same service level in each community. In Hawaii, for example, education is provided at the state level and, in principle, the same level of education could be (but undoubtedly is not) provided in each school. Another way is for the state to "take over" the local property tax. See Giertz and McGuire (1992). In Kansas, for example, every district must levy the same state-determined property tax rate and return any revenue above a certain amount to the state. Districts also can supplement their revenue with an additional local levy, although this option is scheduled to phase out. See Myers (1992).

[28] A description of a debate over restrictions on the tax levy for high-wealth districts can be found in a case entitled "Funding Schools in Washington State" in Gomez-Ibanez and Kalt (1990).

[29] Oakland (1994) criticizes equalizing aid programs for diminishing efficiency-enhancing variation in public service outcomes. However, efficiency does not require variation in outcomes associated with income or wealth; instead, it requires that communities with different preferences at any given level of income or wealth be allowed to make different choices.

[30] For more detailed discussions of this issue, see Yinger (1986) or Wyckoff (1992).

[31] For a review of existing studies with a focus on tax capitalization, see Yinger et al. (1988).

[32] Although the impact of public service quality on rents is not literally an example of "capitalization," because it does not involve an asset price, it generally is included in the concept of capitalization. In addition, note that when many urban areas are considered, service quality or tax differences also could be

partially or fully offset by wage differences. Moreover, one cannot get around capitalization by giving higher transfers to individuals in low-service or high-tax jurisdictions. Any program in which benefits depend on residence runs into the problem of capitalization.

[33] A similar point is made by Oakland (1994). In discussing differences resulting from higher wage costs, he says: "To equalize for these premia would be to doubly compensate individuals for disamenities."

[34] Racial and ethnic discrimination continues to be a severe barrier to mobility. For a review of evidence from the 1989 Housing Discrimination Study, see Yinger (1993).

REFERENCES

Bergstrom, Theodore C. and Robert Goodman. "Private Demand for Public Goods." *American Economic Review* 53 (June, 1973): 280–96.

Bergstrom, Theodore C., Daniel L. Rubinfeld, and Perry Shapiro. "Micro-Based Estimates of Demand Functions for Local School Expenditures." *Econometrica* 50 (September, 1982): 1183–1205.

Bradbury, Katharine L., Helen F. Ladd, Mark Perrault, Andrew Reschovsky, and John Yinger. "State Aid to Offset Fiscal Disparities Across Communities." *National Tax Journal* (June, 1984): 151–70.

Bradford, David F., R. A. Malt, and Wallace E. Oates. "The Rising Cost of Local Public Services: Some Evidence and Reflections." *National Tax Journal* 22 (June, 1969): 185–202.

Feldstein, Martin S. "Wealth Neutrality and Local Choice in Public Education." *American Economic Review* 65 (March, 1975): 75–89.

Giertz, J. Fred and Therese J. McGuire. "Regional and State-Wide Property Tax Base Sharing For Education." In *Proceedings of the 85th Annual Conference of the National Tax Association—Tax Institute of America* (1992): 190–94.

Gold, Steven, David Smith, Stephen Lawton, and Andrea C. Hyary. *Public School Finance Programs of the United States and Canada.* Albany, NY: The Nelson A. Rockefeller Institute of Government, 1992.

Gomez-Ibanez, Jose A. and Joseph P. Kalt. *Cases in Microeconomics.* Englewood Cliffs, NJ: Prentice-Hall, 1990.

Hanushek, Eric. "The Economics of Schooling." *Journal of Economic Literature* 24 (September, 1986): 1141–75.

Hochman, H. M. and J. D. Rogers. "Pareto Optimal Redistribution." *American Economic Review* 59 (September, 1969): 542–57.

Inman, Robert P. "The Fiscal Performance of Local Governments: An Interpretative Review." In *Current Issues in Urban Economics*, edited by P. Mieszkowski and M. Straszheim, 270–321. Baltimore: Johns Hopkins University Press, 1979.

Ladd, Helen F. and Frederick C. Doolittle. "Which Level of Government Should Assist Poor People?" *National Tax Journal* 35 (September, 1982): 323–36.

Ladd, Helen F., Andrew Reschovsky, and John Yinger. "City Fiscal Condition and State Equalizing Aid: The Case of Minnesota." In *Proceedings of the 84th Annual Conference of the National Tax Association—Tax Institute of America, 1991.* 42–49.

Ladd, Helen F. and John Yinger. *America's Ailing Cities: Fiscal Health and the Design of Urban Policy.* Updated ed. Baltimore: Johns Hopkins Press, 1991.

Myers, Will S. "Local Government Implications of Recent Trends in State Education Finance." In *Proceedings of the 85th Annual Conference of the National Tax Association—Tax Institute of America* (1992): 184–89.

Oakland, William. "Fiscal Equalization: An Empty Box?" *National Tax Journal* 47, No. 1 (March, 1994).

Oates, Wallace E. and Robert Schwab. "Economic Competition Among Jurisdictions: Efficiency Enhancing or Distortion Inducing?" *Journal of Public Economics* 35 (1988): 333–54.

Odden, Allan R. and Lawrence O. Picus. *School Finance: A Policy Perspective.* New York. McGraw-Hill, 1992.

Ratcliffe, Kerri, Bruce Riddle, and John Yinger. "The Fiscal Condition of School Districts in Nebraska: Is Small Beautiful?" *Economics of Education Review* (January, 1990): 81–99.

Reschovsky, Andrew. "Fiscal Equalization and School Finance." *National Tax Journal* 47, No. 1 (March, 1994).

Wyckoff, Paul Gary. "Capitalization, Equalization, and Intergovernmental Aid." Unpublished Manuscript, 1992.

Yinger, John. "Access Denied, Access Constrained: Results and Implications of the 1989 Housing Discrimination Study." In *Clear and Convincing Evidence: Measurement of Discrimination in America*, edited by M. Fix and R. Struyk, 69–112. Washington, D.C.: The Urban Institute Press, 1993.

Yinger, John. "On Fiscal Disparities Across Cities." *Journal of Urban Economics* 19 (May, 1986): 316–37.

Yinger, John, Axel Boersch-Supan, Howard S. Bloom, and Helen F. Ladd. *Property Taxes and House Values: The Theory and Estimation of Intrajurisdictional Property Tax Capitalization.* New York: Academic Press, 1988.

Yinger, John and Helen F. Ladd. "The Determinants of State Assistance to Central Cities." *National Tax Journal* 62 (December, 1989): 413–28.

[5]

THE DETERMINANTS OF STATE ASSISTANCE TO CENTRAL CITIES***

JOHN YINGER* AND HELEN F. LADD**

ABSTRACT

This paper examines the determinants of state assistance to 70 major central cities in 1982. State assistance is broadly defined to include both intergovernmental grants and institutional assistance, such as granting a city access to a tax with export potential or state takeover of city service responsibilities. Two key hypotheses are derived: states direct assistance to cities that need help the most, and states regard grants and institutional assistance as substitutes. Both hypotheses are strongly supported by the data. A third hypothesis, that high federal aid to a city is offset by low state assistance, receives no support.

THE past ten years have witnessed a lively debate on the nature of the U.S. federal system. Many policymakers want to shift fiscal responsibilities away from the federal government toward the states; other policymakers want to maintain or even strengthen the role of the federal government.

Unfortunately, however, this debate has been hampered by a lack of information about the behavior of key participants in the federal system, particularly state governments. In this paper we address one aspect of this problem by examining the determinants of state assistance to central cities. Do states provide more assistance to cities with greater needs? What are the forms of state assistance to cities? What is the impact of federal assistance to cities on state assistance to cities?

This analysis is made possible by a data set we created for a study of the fiscal health of major U.S. central cities (Ladd and Yinger, 1989). This data set contains a comprehensive measure of each city government's fiscal condition, as well as measures of state assistance to cities through both intergovernmental grants

*Syracuse University, Syracuse, NY 13244.
**Duke University, Durham, NC 27706.

and fiscal institutions. The concept of assistance through fiscal institutions is crucial for understanding state assistance to cities. A state obviously can help its cities by giving them intergovernmental grants, but it also can assist cities by allowing them to use taxes, such as commuter taxes, that shift some of the city tax burden to nonresidents or by taking over public services previously provided by cities. Our data set provides a unique opportunity to examine the determinants of state assistance through both grants and institutions and to ask whether state policymakers regard these two types of assistance as substitutes.

We begin by explaining the measures of city fiscal condition and of state and federal assistance to cities that we develop in Ladd and Yinger. In the following two sections, we present our model of state assistance to cities and test it using data for 70 major central cities in 1982. In the final section, we discuss the policy implications of our results.

Measuring State Assistance and City Fiscal Condition

Our analysis is built on the distinction, clearly made by Bradbury (1982, 1983), between a city's budgetary condition and its underlying or structural fiscal condition. A city's budgetary condition reflects the current state of its financial affairs and is heavily influenced by the political and management decisions of city officials. In contrast, a city's structural fiscal condition is its ability to provide public services at reasonable tax rates, as determined by economic and social factors that are outside city officials' control. This paper is concerned with structural fiscal condition, or fiscal condition for short.

A city's fiscal condition reflects the balance between its revenue-raising capacity and its expenditure need. Revenue-raising capacity is defined to be the amount of money a city could raise (per capita) at a given tax burden on its residents. Expenditure need is the amount a city must spend (per capita) to provide public services of a given quality. For the purposes of this paper, we measure a city's overall fiscal condition by its need-capacity gap, which is the difference between expenditure need and revenue-raising capacity.[1]

Both revenue-raising capacity and expenditure need are influenced by a city's economic and social structure and by its fiscal institutions. Economic and social factors determine the potential taxable resources in the city and the cost of providing city services, whereas state-determined fiscal institutions determine which taxes a city is allowed to employ and the extent of a city's responsibilities for providing public services. Our approach is to separate these two types of factors. First, we define a standard set of fiscal institutions and calculate the need-capacity gap each city would have if these institutions were in place. This gap measures the impact of economic and social factors on a city's fiscal condition. Second, we calculate an alternative need-capacity gap that incorporates each city's actual fiscal institutions. The difference between the need-capacity gaps with standard and actual institutions is our measure of the assistance each city receives from the fiscal institutions created by its state.

A city's need-capacity gap with a standard set of fiscal institutions, which we call its *standardized need-capacity gap,* is the difference between the expenditure need the city would have with national average service responsibilities, which we call its standardized expenditure need, and the revenue-raising capacity it would have with three broad-based taxes (property, earnings, and sales), which we call its full revenue-raising capacity.

A city's standardized expenditure need is determined by its costs of providing public services. As first explained by Bradford, Malt, and Oates (1969), public service costs vary from one jurisdiction to another because of variation in both input prices and environmental factors. For example, a city with a relatively high poverty rate or with other environmental characteristics associated with criminal behavior, must spend more than other cities to obtain a given level of protection against crime. Building on the work of Bradbury et al. (1984), we develop (in Ladd and Yinger, 1989) indexes of public service costs and standardized expenditure need for each major central city.

Full revenue-raising capacity is the amount a city could raise from three broad-based taxes at a standard tax burden on its residents. In a closed city economy, this capacity is determined entirely by resident income; the higher is resident income, the greater is the revenue the city could raise at the standard tax burden. With economic flows in and out of the city, however, revenue-raising capacity also is influenced by the city's ability to export its tax burden to nonresidents.[2] This ability to export depends on tax incidence. In the case of the property tax, for example, exporting depends on the shares of the tax that fall on workers, consumers, and property owners—and on the residential locations of these three groups. We calculate each city's ability to export taxes on the basis of a detailed analysis of the incidence of city property, income, and sales taxes (see Bradbury and Ladd, 1985).

A state influences its cities' expenditure needs through its assignment of public service responsibilities. All else equal, for example, a city government must spend more to meet its service responsibilities at a given quality level if the city itself, instead of an independent school district, is responsible for local education, or if the city operates a hospital. In Ladd and Yinger we develop a service responsibility index for each major city. Combining this index with our index for public service costs yields each city's actual expenditure need, which is the amount it would have to spend to meet its actual service responsibilities at an average quality level.

Several state-determined fiscal institutions also directly influence a city's revenue-raising capacity. The state decides which taxes the city can levy and may place restrictions on city tax base definitions and tax rates. These rules are key determinants of tax exporting. In most cases, for example, an earnings tax that applies to commuters into the city allows the city to export a large share of its tax burden; by prohibiting such a tax, therefore, a state may be severely restricting a city's actual revenue-raising capacity. A state also gives taxing authority to other local jurisdictions, such as counties, whose boundaries overlap with a city's. These overlying jurisdictions also draw on the taxpaying ability of city residents; the greater is the taxing authority of overlying jurisdictions, the lower is the capacity left over for the city government to draw on. A city's restricted revenue-raising capacity (before grants) is its capacity after these fiscal institutions have been accounted for.

A city's actual need-capacity gap (before grants) is the difference between its actual expenditure need and its restricted revenue-raising capacity (before grants). Because this actual gap accounts for a city's fiscal institutions whereas the standardized gap assumes uniform fiscal institutions, we interpret the difference between these two gaps as a measure of the impact of fiscal institutions on a city's fiscal condition. If a state assigns heavy service responsibilities to a city but does not provide it with access to taxes with export potential, for example, then the state's fiscal rules may add more to the city's expenditure need than to its revenue-raising capacity. In this case, state institutional "assistance" actually makes things worse; that is, it adds to the city's need-capacity gap. Other cities' fiscal conditions are improved because their states allow them to use a tax with high export potential while assigning them limited service responsibilities. Note that state institutional assistance varies both within and across states. San Francisco, for example, is the only city in California with access to a tax on commuter earnings, and Albany, unlike the other major cities in New York, does not have responsibility for schools.

States (and the federal government) also assist their cities by giving them intergovernmental grants. These grants do not raise such complex conceptual issues and data on grants can be obtained from published sources.[3]

In summary, data taken from Ladd and Yinger (1989) can be used to calculate a city's standardized need-capacity gap, state assistance to a city through institutions and through grants, and federal grants to cities. All of these variables are expressed in dollars per capita. An algebraic description of our calculations and some illustrations are in the appendix.

A Model of State Assistance to Cities

Our model of state behavior focuses on the trade-off between assistance to cities and other state objectives, including political ones. It builds on the observation that many state aid programs include equalizing provisions that direct more aid to local governments in poorer fiscal condition, as indicated by their tax bases or public service costs (see Bradbury et al., 1984).

Key Assumptions

The model is based on three key assumptions. First, we assume that state policymakers care about the actual fiscal condition of each city in their state, as they perceive it. In particular, we assume that one of their objectives is to lessen differences across cities in actual fiscal condition by providing more assistance to cities whose fiscal condition before state assistance is relatively poor.

Second, we assume that the standardized need-capacity gap summarizes state policymakers' perceptions about city fiscal condition before state and federal assistance. State policymakers obviously do not carry out the same calculations that we do, but the basic elements of our calculations have been widely discussed and some of them have been incorporated into existing state grant formulas.

Third, we assume that state policymakers recognize that state and federal grants and state assistance through institutions all can contribute to a city's fiscal health, although they may not believe that $1 of state grants makes the same contribution as $1 of state institutional assistance or $1 of federal aid. State grants may be perceived to make a relatively high contribution to a city's fiscal condition, for example, because they can be directed toward types of city spending that state policymakers believe are particularly important for a city's fiscal health. In contrast, state institutional assistance, which is less focused and more difficult to measure, may be perceived to make only a modest contribution to a city's fiscal condition, and some federal grants may be tied to city programs that state policymakers do not value—or at least do not value as much as the programs supported by state aid.

These assumptions lead to the concept of a city's perceived need-capacity gap after state and federal assistance. This gap equals a city's standardized need-capacity gap minus the perceived contributions to city fiscal condition of state and federal grants and of state institutional assistance. Let us define

SGAP = A city's standardized need-capacity gap;
GAP = A city's need-capacity gap after state and federal assistance, as perceived by the state;
G = State assistance to a city in the form of grants;
I = State institutional assistance to a city;
F = Federal grants to a city;

where all of these variables are measured in dollars per city resident. Moreover, suppose that state policymakers believe that $1 of assistance of type a contributes Θ_a dollars to a city's fiscal condition. Then we can write

$$\text{GAP} = \text{SGAP} - \Theta_G G - \Theta_I I - \Theta_F F. \quad (1)$$

A Formal Model

According to our first assumption, lowering the post-assistance need-capacity gap is a key objective of state policymakers. A simple way to express this objective algebraically is to say that state policymakers want to increase the difference between the maximum observed pre-assistance gap, MAX, and each individual city's post-assistance gap, GAP. (MAX need not be an observed gap. It can be interpreted as a reference gap used by state policymakers—as long as it is greater than or equal to the highest actual post-assistance gap.)

State policymakers can achieve the objective of lowering a city's GAP by raising grants, G, or by raising institutional assistance, I. In deciding how to use these policy tools, however, they must trade off this objective against other state objectives. We summarize these other objectives by assuming that type a assistance to cities must compete with the amount spent (per city resident) on another set of state activities, Z_a. In addition, we assume that B_a is the state budget (per city resident) allocated for Z_a and city assistance of type a. The notion of a budget for assistance through institutions is somewhat abstract. No such budget literally exists, but all forms of institutional assistance involve some shifting of the burden of city services onto noncity residents. An abstract budget is a convenient way to express the trade-off between institutional assistance and alternative uses of limited resources that is implicit in this type of shifting.

To capture the trade-off between assistance to cities and other state objectives, we assume that state policymakers' preferences are defined by a Cobb-Douglas welfare function with Z_G, Z_I, and (MAX − GAP) as arguments. They maximize this welfare function subject to their perceptions about the contributions of various forms of assistance to a city's fiscal condition and to their budget constraints for grants and for institutional aid.

Thus, the state policymaker's problem is to select Z_G, Z_I, G, and I to:

Maximize $W = (Z_G^{\alpha_G})(Z_I^{\alpha_I})$

$(\text{MAX} - \text{GAP})^\beta \quad (2)$

Subject to $\text{GAP} = \text{SGAP} - \Theta_G G$

$- \Theta_I I - \Theta_F F$

$B_G = Z_G + G$

$B_I = Z_I + I.$

The first-order conditions of this problem yield the following two structural equations, which indicate how G and I are determined:

$$G = b_{0G} + b_{1G}B_G + b_{2G}SGAP + b_{3G}I + b_{4G}F \quad (3)$$

$$I = b_{0I} + b_{1I}B_I + b_{2I}SGAP + b_{3I}G + b_{4I}F, \quad (4)$$

where for a = G, I (and a' = I, G)

$$b_{0a} = -\alpha_a MAX/[\Theta_a(\beta + \alpha_a)]$$
$$b_{1a} = \beta/(\beta + \alpha_a)$$
$$b_{2a} = \alpha_a/[\Theta_a(\beta + \alpha_a)]$$
$$b_{3a} = -\Theta_a b_{2a}$$
$$b_{4a} = -\Theta_F b_{2a}$$

These two equations contain three principal hypotheses about the way states design grants and institutional assistance to cities. The equations indicate that a city with a higher SGAP receives more G and more I. The first hypothesis, therefore, is that states give more grants and more institutional assistance to cities with higher standardized need-capacity gaps. Moreover, a higher level of G leads to a lower level of I (and vice versa). Thus the second hypothesis is that states view grants and assistance through institutions as substitutes for each other. Finally, both G and I are negative functions of federal grants, as long as those grants are perceived to improve a city's fiscal condition. Consequently, the third hypothesis is that relatively high federal grants may lead to relatively low state assistance—of both types.

Equations (3) and (4) can be estimated with linear regression techniques for a sample of cities. Our measures of SGAP, G, I, and F can be introduced into Equation (3) or (4) in exactly the form derived from our model, and their coefficients can be interpreted as the indicated functions of the model parameters. Because the reference gap, MAX, is constant, it is estimated as part of the constant term. Although B_G and B_I cannot be observed directly, we identify and measure a variety of factors, both economic and political, that influence these "budgets."

The coefficients of SGAP test the hypothesis that state officials attempt to direct each form of assistance toward cities in poor fiscal condition, as measured by their standardized need-capacity gap. To be specific, these coefficients measure the dollar increase in assistance that accompanies a dollar increase in this gap. The coefficient of I in the regression to explain G and the coefficient of G in the regression to explain I test the hypothesis that the two forms of state assistance are substitutes for each other. The perceived contributions of each form of state aid toward city fiscal health, Θ_G and Θ_I, also can be calculated from these coefficients.[4]

In this model, G and I are jointly determined. Equations (3) and (4) therefore must be estimated with a simultaneous equations procedure. As reported below, we estimate the model with both two- and three-stage least squares. The factors that influence B_I but do not influence B_G are excluded instruments in the regression to explain G; factors that influence B_G but not B_I are the excluded instruments in the regression for I.

Implementation of the Model

To implement our model, we divide federal aid into two types: categorical aid and general revenue sharing. The coefficients of these aid variables can be interpreted like those of the state assistance variables; the absolute value of each coefficient, divided by the coefficient of SGAP, is the perceived contribution of that form of aid toward city fiscal health.[5]

Federal aid to central cities might be influenced by state aid to central cities. For example, the federal government might give more categorical grants to cities that are in poor fiscal health as a result of low assistance from their state.[6] In our judgment, however, state assistance is unlikely to have a significant impact on federal grants. Our strategy, therefore, is to assume that both types of federal grants are exogenous in our basic models and to examine this assumption with the appropriate specification tests.

State grants to cities are the product of

the state's budgetary process, so the exogenous factors that influence B_G reflect voter demand and politics. To account for the two key demand factors, namely income and price, we include state per capita income and the share of state population that is in central cities (all central cities—not just those in our sample). The higher is the per capita income in the state, the higher is the demand for state services, including services supported by grants to cities; and the higher is the central city share of state population, the higher is the cost per state resident of providing a certain level of per capita grants to central cities.[7]

We also include state population as a type of price variable, although we cannot determine its sign *a priori*. To the extent that state-provided public services are public goods, larger states can provide the same service quality at a lower cost per capita. A likely response to this lower cost is an increase in the quality of state services, including those supported by grants to cities. To the extent that state-provided public services face diseconomies to scale (from congestion or administrative costs), larger states will have higher per-capita costs and lower service quality.

Several political factors also might influence the outcome of a state's budgetary process. Because they are elected officials, city mayors may have more leverage in obtaining grants than do city managers. Cities with a large share of a state's population have more representation in a state legislature and may have more influence on state budgetary decisions. Moreover, the competition for state funds may be particularly severe in states with many local governments. To control for these three possibilities, our grant regression includes the city's share of state population, the number of local governments with taxing authority relative to state population, and a dummy variable for cities with mayors.

Finally, several city characteristics might influence state grants. City/counties are much more likely than separate cities to have responsibility for welfare and schools. State legislatures may have a particular interest in supporting these two services and may therefore give more grants to city/counties than to other cities with the same standardized need-capacity gap.[8] In addition, cities in which many state government employees work may be treated differently than other cities. This effect could work in either direction. Cities with many state government employees per capita might have extra influence in a state legislature and therefore receive more grants, or locating state employees in a city may be seen as a form of assistance to that city and may therefore be regarded as a substitute for state grants. (The latter possibility implies that the number of state employees per capita is an endogenous variable; we examine this possibility with a specification test.) State capitals also may receive more grants, in part because they have many state government employees and in part because they are the city in which the legislators work and perhaps live. Thus, the control variables in the state-grants regression include the number of state government employees per capita and dummy variables for city/counties and for state capitals.

The exogenous factors that affect B_I reflect state officials' long-run decisions about the nature of their state/local fiscal system. States with higher incomes are likely to be more generous in providing institutional assistance to cities. All forms of institutional assistance shift some of the burden of providing city services onto noncity residents; the higher are state incomes, the higher is the burden that noncity residents will accept.

In addition, we hypothesize that states will take advantage of existing opportunities to provide institutional assistance to cities. First, if a city is small relative to its metropolitan area, then the burden of institutional assistance to a city can be spread out over the relatively large number of noncity residents. In this case, giving a city access to taxes with high export ratios or shifting service responsibility to counties that encompass several cities will not place a large burden on individual suburbanites. Second, a state that does not rely heavily on an income tax itself may find that the additional burden of a city's earnings tax is acceptable and may therefore allow its cities to levy such a tax and hence to boost their tax exporting. To control for these factors, we include the city's share of metropolitan population and the share of state tax revenue from an income tax.

Finally, state decisions about assistance through institutions are likely to be influenced by several characteristics of the institutional setting. As in the case of state grants, state assistance through institutions may favor city/counties, which tend to have high service responsibilities, even controlling for city fiscal condition. A dummy variable for city/counties is included to account for this possibility. Moreover, states with complex fiscal arrangements may find it more difficult to design and obtain agreement on effective institutional assistance. We measure the complexity of a state's fiscal arrangements with a dummy variable for states in which some central cities are city/counties and others separate cities with overlying counties.

Our model is summarized in Table 1. This table lists the explanatory variables (including endogenous ones) in the regressions for state assistance through both grants and institutions, gives the sample mean for each variable, and states the hypothesized sign of each coefficient in each regression.

Empirical Results

We estimate our model using data for 70 major central cities in 1982. This sample consists of the subset of the 86 major central cities in the U.S. for which we could find complete data. A major central city is defined as a city with a population above 300,000 or the central city of one of the 50 largest metropolitan areas in 1970 or 1980. After presenting our regression results, we explore the implications of the simultaneity between the two types of state assistance, and test several of the hypotheses that are built into our econometric specification.

Regression Results

Our regression results are presented in Table 2. We estimate our model with 2-stage least squares. For comparison, 3-stage least squares results are also presented.[9]

Table 2 provides strong support for our two key hypotheses. First, states direct both grants and institutional assistance toward cities in poor fiscal health. If city A's standardized need-capacity gap is $1 higher than city B's, then, all else equal, city A can expect to receive $0.22 more in state grants and $0.42 more in state assistance through institutions. Both of these estimates are significant at the 1 percent level or above. These results indicate that, to some degree, states give more assistance through both grants and institutions to cities with larger standardized need-capacity gaps. Moreover, assistance through institutions is more equalizing than assistance through grants. Indeed, state assistance through institutions offsets, on average, almost twice as much of a city's need-capacity gap as do state grants. One clear illustration of this role for state institutional assistance is given by Ladd and Yinger (1989): 5 of the 6 cities with the poorest standardized fiscal health (and 11 of the 20 least healthy cities) are allowed to tax the earnings of nonresident commuters.

Second, states regard assistance through grants and assistance through institutions as substitutes for each other. In the grants regression, the coefficient of assistance through institutions is −0.40; if, because of exogenous factors, city A receives $1 more than city B in state assistance through institutions, it will also receive, on average, $0.40 less in state grants. In the institutions regression, the coefficient of grants is −0.88; differences across cities in grants caused by exogenous factors are almost fully offset by differences in assistance through institutions. Both of these coefficients are statistically significant at the 1 percent level.

Remember from our discussion of Equations (3) and (4) that we can solve for the weight, Θ, that state policymakers place on each form of assistance to cities. We find that state policymakers perceive that $1 of assistance through grants lowers a city's actual need-capacity gap, as

TABLE 1

VARIABLE DEFINITIONS AND HYPOTHESIZED SIGNS

Variable	Definition	Mean	Hypothesized Sign GRANTS	Hypothesized Sign INSTIT
	1. Endogenous Variables			
GRANTS	State grants per capita	$81.94	n.a.	−
INSTIT	State assistance through institutions per capita	$10.85	−	n.a.
	2. Exogenous Variables			
SGAP	Standardized need-capacity gap per capita	$32.94	+	+
FCAT	Federal categorical grants per capita	$44.75	?	?
FGRS	Federal general revenue sharing per capita	$ 9.60	−	−
SEMP	State government employment in the city per capita	0.025	?	excl.
SPCY	State per capita income (Thousands)	$11.147	+	+
COUNTY	Dummy for city/counties	0.286	+	+
SCCTOS	Share of state population in central cities	0.302	−	excl.
SPOP	State population (Millions)	10.167	?	excl.
MAYOR	Dummy for cities with mayors	0.471	+	excl.
RELPOP	City share of state population (Percent)	8.480	+	excl.
CAPIT	Dummy for state capitals	0.229	?	excl.
SLOCAL	Local governments per 1000 people in the state	0.241	−	excl.
METPOP	City share of metropolitan population (Percent)	30.700	excl.	−
SRELYY	State's reliance on an income tax	0.218	excl.	−
MIXED	Dummy for states with mixed fiscal system	0.457	excl.	−

Notes: The entry "excl." indicates that a variable is excluded from the final or second-stage regression for the indicated dependent variable. However, all exogenous variables, including those marked "excl.", are used as instruments in the simultaneous equations procedure.

perceived by state policymakers, by (.877/.421) = $2.08, whereas $1 of assistance through institutions, as we measure it, lowers this gap by (.403/.221) = $1.82. Apparently, state policymakers value those aspects of city finances that are supported by state assistance, through grants or institutions, more highly than city fiscal condition in general. Moreover, despite the complexity of fiscal institutions, state policymakers perceive that $1 of assistance through institutions contributes almost as much to a city's fiscal condition as $1 of state grants.

Federal general revenue sharing to cities does not have a statistically significant impact on either form of state assistance. According to our conceptual model, this result implies that state policymakers do not believe that general revenue sharing improves a city's fiscal condition. Federal categorical grants to cities also do not have a statistically significant impact on state assistance through institutions, but they do have a significant impact on state grants. In particular, we find that a $1 increase in federal categorical grants leads to a $0.43 increase in state grants. This positive effect contradicts our conceptual model, and we do not have a compelling interpretation of it. Perhaps programs supported by federal grants

TABLE 2

ESTIMATION RESULTS FOR 1982

	Dependent Variable			
	Two-Stage Least Squares		Three-Stage Least Squares	
Variable	GRANTS	INSTIT	GRANTS	INSTIT
GRANTS	--	-0.877 (2.80)	--	-0.858 (2.97)
INSTIT	-0.403 (4.98)	--	-0.389 (5.32)	--
SGAP	0.221 (3.81)	0.421 (3.41)	0.208 (4.08)	0.433 (3.84)
FCAT	0.430 (2.20)	-0.253 (0.57)	0.491 (2.87)	-0.246 (0.60)
FGRS	0.414 (0.20)	-0.575 (0.13)	-0.130 (0.07)	0.089 (0.02)
SEMP	213.529 (1.13)	--	192.407 (1.30)	--
SPCY	27.677 (5.45)	11.988 (1.18)	26.526 (5.99)	10.743 (1.15)
COUNTY	47.658 (3.46)	66.273 (1.83)	46.853 (3.88)	65.193 (1.97)
SCCTOS	-47.778 (0.68)	--	-88.843 (1.58)	--
SPOP	-5.553 (5.08)	--	-5.089 (5.56)	--
MAYOR	4.254 (0.38)	--	7.002 (0.78)	--
RELPOP	-1.788 (2.76)	--	-1.322 (2.52)	--
CAPIT	-17.710 (1.19)	--	-17.825 (1.53)	--
SLOCAL	-38.096 (2.04)	--	45.951 (3.03)	--
METPOP	--	-1.538 (2.59)	--	-1.730 (3.40)

TABLE 2 (CONT.)

	Dependent Variable			
	Two-Stage Least Squares		Three-Stage Least Squares	
Variable	GRANTS	INSTIT	GRANTS	INSTIT
SRELYY	--	-457.679 (3.35)	--	-500.847 (4.20)
MIXED	--	-86.984 (3.74)	--	-74.274 (3.66)
Constant	-174.326 (3.11)	119.926 (0.99)	-153.638 (3.17)	136.783 (1.24)
R-squared	0.845	0.625	0.845	0.618
Number of Observations	70	70	70	70

Notes: Absolute values of asymptotic t-statistics are in parentheses. The 2-tailed (1-tailed) 95 percent critical value is 2.00 (1.67). A 2-tailed test is appropriate unless the coefficient has the sign predicted in Table 1.

sometimes attract state funds.

Most of the control variables in the state grants regression perform well. State income, the dummy for city/counties, and the number of local governments per capita are significant at the 5 percent level or above with the expected signs. State population, the sign of which is indeterminate on conceptual grounds, is negative and significant. This result indicates diseconomies of population scale in the delivery of state grants. The share of state population in central cities and the dummy for cities with mayors have the predicted signs but are not significant. The only variable that is significant with the wrong sign is the city's share of state population.

In the assistance-through-institutions regression, all of the control variables have the expected signs, and all except for state per capita income are statistically significant. Of particular interest are the coefficients of the state's reliance on the income tax and the city's share of metropolitan population. The former coefficient suggests that states relying heavily on an income tax are indeed reluctant to allow a city to levy an earnings tax as a way to boost its revenue-raising capacity; the latter coefficient suggests that states are more likely to assist cities through institutions if the burden of that assistance can be spread out over a relatively large number of suburbanites.

The Simultaneity Between the Two Types of State Assistance

The results in Table 2 describe the way state officials design each form of assistance to cities. Because the two forms of assistance are simultaneously determined, however, these results do not fully describe the variation in assistance received by cities in different circumstances. To obtain a complete answer, we must solve Equations (3) and (4) for the two unknowns, G and I.[10]

Consider, for example, the exogenous factors that are unique to each equation. Suppose that because of a difference in one of the exogenous factors that is unique to our grants regression, City A receives $1 more in state grants than does City B. As shown in the first row of Table 3, this positive $1 difference in grants will lead to a negative $1.36 difference in institutional assistance, which will add, in turn, $0.55 to the original difference in grants. The ultimate impact of the original $1 difference in grants, therefore, is only a $0.19 net advantage for City A in total state assistance; in other words, the feedback effects eliminate most of City A's original advantage.

Similarly, a $1 advantage in state assistance through institutions for a city that is caused by one of the exogenous factors unique to our institutions regression will lead to a $0.62 disadvantage in state grants, which will add, in turn, $0.55 to the original advantage in assistance through institutions. In this case, the feedback effects roughly cancel out, and City A's original $1 advantage in institutional assistance becomes a net advantage of $0.92.

We can also determine the impact on total assistance to a city of differences across cities in exogenous factors that appear in both regressions, such as the standardized need-capacity gap (or gap for short). If City A has a gap that is $1 higher than City B's, then the results in Table 2 indicate that city A will receive $0.22 more in state grants and $0.42 more in institutional assistance than will City B. But these results overstate the link between a city's need-capacity gap and its state assistance because they do not consider the fact that the differences in state grants will lead to differences in institutional assistance—and vice versa. After accounting for these feedback effects, we find that City A will receive $0.08 more in state grants and $0.35 more assistance through institutions than will City B, which implies a net advantage in state assistance of $0.43 (see the third row of Table 3). In other words, state assistance eliminates over two-fifths of the differences in need-capacity gaps across cities.[11] Although most of the public debate has focused on the equalizing role of grants, we find that state assistance through institutions, not state grants, does most of the equalizing.

State income is another key exogenous factor in both equations. The results in Table 2, which ignore feedback effects, indicate that if per capita income is $10 higher in State A than in State B, cities in State A will receive $0.28 more in

TABLE 3

NET IMPACTS OF EXOGENOUS FACTORS
ON STATE ASSISTANCE

One-Dollar Exogenous Difference in:	Net Impact on:		Total Assistance
	GRANTS	INSTIT	
GRANTS	1.55	-1.36	0.19
INSTIT	-0.62	1.55	0.92
SGAP	0.08	0.35	0.43
SPCY/10	0.35	-0.19	0.16

grants and $0.12 more in assistance through institutions than the cities in State B. After accounting for feedback, we find that cities in State A will receive $0.35 more in grants and $0.19 less in institutional assistance, for a difference in total state assistance of only $0.16.

Specification Tests

To shed further light on our results, we also test two types of hypotheses about our specification: Are any variables that are assumed to be exogenous really endogenous? Are the excluded exogenous variables in each regression (which are the variables that identify the simultaneous equations system) appropriate instruments, that is, are they truly exogenous?

As noted earlier, three of the variables we assumed to be exogenous might be endogenous. Federal aid to a city might be influenced by state assistance to that city, and state government decisions about the location of state government employment and about state assistance to cities may be made simultaneously. We examined the endogeneity of these three variables using the chi-squared test developed by Hausman (1978). As explained by Bowden and Turkington (1984), this test can be applied to right-side variables or to excluded instruments.[12] Thus, we also apply the test to each of the instruments identified as "excluded" in Table 1.

On the basis of our test results, we cannot reject the hypotheses that both forms of federal aid and state government employment are indeed exogenous and that all of our instruments are appropriate.[13] In other words, our results in Table 2 do not appear to be based on inappropriate assumptions about endogeneity.

Conclusions and Policy Implications

In this paper we present two key hypotheses about the behavior of state policymakers. First, state policymakers want to improve the fiscal condition of their cities and therefore give more assistance, through both grants and institutions, to cities in poorer fiscal condition. Second, state policymakers regard state grants and state assistance through institutions as substitutes for each other; that is, both types of state assistance are believed to improve a city's fiscal condition. Both of these hypotheses are strongly supported by our results.

We also find that, on average, state assistance makes a major contribution toward eliminating differences in fiscal condition across cities. If the standardized need-capacity gap is $1 higher in City A than in City B, City A can expect to receive $0.08 more in state grants and $0.35 more in state institutional assistance than City B—after accounting for the feedback effects between the two types of state assistance. Overall, therefore, state assistance offsets over 40 percent of the differences in fiscal condition across cities. This important equalizing role of overall state assistance has not been observed in previous studies, which do not consider state institutional assistance.

In addition, our results indicate that in the view of state policymakers either $1 of state grants or $1 of institutional assistance contributes more to a city's fiscal condition than a $1 decline in the standardized need-capacity gap, as we measure it. The large perceived impact of institutional assistance is particularly surprising, given the complexity of state institutional assistance. However, $1 of state grants is perceived to contribute more to a city's fiscal condition than $1 of assistance through institutions.

We find no evidence that state policymakers consider federal aid to cities to be a substitute for state assistance to cities. Cities with higher federal categorical grants and cities with higher general revenue sharing do not receive less state assistance (through grants or institutions) than others.

These results have several implications for the design of our federal system and in particular for federal policy toward cities.

Although states give more assistance to cities with larger standardized need-capacity gaps, 60 percent of the differences in these gaps remains, on average, after state assistance. Moreover, some cities in relatively poor fiscal condition receive relatively little help from—and may even be harmed by—state actions. Ladd and Yinger (1989) find, for example, that very large cities and cities with relatively poor residents are in much poorer fiscal health than other cities even after state grants and state institutional assistance. Thus, federal grants or other federal policies may be required to bring the fiscal condition of some cities up to an acceptable level.

We also discover that state assistance to cities depends on state characteristics, and in particular on state income. Every $1000 increase in state per capita income is associated with a $16 increase in net state assistance to cities (per city resident), after accounting for the feedback between the two types of state assistance. Otherwise identical cities may receive different levels of assistance because of differences in their states' per capita incomes. To the extent that federal policymakers want to insure that all cities are able to provide some minimum level of public services, they may want to provide additional assistance to cities in low-income states, all else equal.

Our regressions examine state assistance to a cross-section of major central cities in 1982—not changes in state assistance over time. To the extent that the 1982 situation is an equilibrium, however, our results also provide some insight into the possible effects on cities of various changes in federal urban policies. For example, differences in federal categorical and in general revenue sharing do not appear to cause differences in state assistance to cities—either through grants or institutions. This finding implies that state actions are unlikely to offset the impact on cities of the recent cuts in federal categorical aid or the recent elimination of general revenue sharing.[14]

Overall, our results suggest federal grants still have an important role to play in our federal system.[15] Even after state grants and institutional assistance, many cities are in poor fiscal condition and federal policymakers may want to help the neediest cities. Although we find no evidence that state assistance to cities changes in response to changes in federal assistance to cities, the federal government may want to minimize the possibility of such offsetting behavior by employing grant provisions, such as state matching requirements, that discourage a state from reducing assistance to cities.[16] We also believe that the federal government should not reward states that are miserly toward their cities. To avoid such rewards, federal grants should be directed toward cities with high standardized need-capacity gaps—not high post-assistance gaps.

ENDNOTES

***The authors are grateful to Jan Ondrich and Gary Solon for econometric advice and to Roy Bahl, Stephen D. Mullin, and two anonymous referees for helpful comments.

[1] In Ladd and Yinger (1989), we use a related measure of city fiscal health, namely (capacity-need)/capacity, which is standardized to be zero in the average city in 1972.

[2] Revenue-raising capacity also is influenced by tax importing, that is, by taxes residents pay to other jurisdictions. We account for taxes residents pay to overlying jurisdictions, but not for the few taxes they pay to nonoverlying jurisdictions. See Ladd and Yinger (1989).

[3] One relatively minor adjustment is necessary, however. Our two measures of need-capacity gap, and hence our measure of state assistance through institutions, are comparable across cities because they are based on a standard state and local tax burden. To make state grants comparable in the same sense, we multiply each city's grants by the ratio of the standard tax burden to the state and local tax burden in that city's state. Our adjusted grants are higher for cities in states that spend a large share of their budget on grants or that tilt their grants more heavily toward large cities, but unlike actual grants they are not higher in cities that receive more grants simply because state taxes (and the programs they support, including grants) are high. See Ladd and Yinger (1989).

[4] In each regression, the absolute value of the coefficient of the other form of aid divided by the coefficient of SGAP can be interpreted as Θ_a.

[5] The division between state and federal assistance is not always clear. Some federal grants are given to the states and then passed through to cities. The Census treats these grants as state aid to cities. The two principal examples of this form of "pass-through" aid are education and welfare programs. In the case of education, the state's only role is administrative; the federal government determines the size of each city's grant and the state simply acts as an intermediary. As a result, we subtracted education pass-through aid from state grants to cities and added it to federal categorical grants to cities. In the case of Aid to Families with Dependent Children, the guidelines are determined by the federal government, but the amount of welfare assistance a city receives is determined largely

by state decisions. A state's decisions about eligibility criteria and benefit levels (along with the state's demographic characteristics) determine the amount of federal welfare aid flowing into the state, and the state's decisions about the assignment of welfare responsibilities determine whether that aid flows to cities or counties or remains with the state itself. During the last twenty-five years, for example, most states have taken over responsibility for welfare programs; by 1982, only 9 of the 70 central cities in our sample retained major welfare responsibilities. Moreover, federal matching provisions imply that the state's decisions about welfare affect its budget. Because a state plays a crucial role in determining the federal welfare aid received by its cities and because this aid affects the state budget, we followed the Census procedure of treating welfare pass-through aid as state aid.

[6] Programs supported by state grants also might attract federal aid. In addition, the general revenue sharing formula gives more aid to cities with relatively high tax effort; higher state assistance enables a city to lower its tax effort and might lead therefore to a lower revenue sharing grant for that city.

[7] In a standard model of local voting, a voter's tax price equals her property tax share multiplied by the marginal cost of public services (see Ladd and Yinger, 1989). We have not included tax shares in our analysis because they are poorly defined at the state level (shares of which tax?) and because they seem unlikely to affect state officials' decisions about aid to cities.

[8] Another possibility is that because a city's fiscal condition is difficult to measure, state legislatures give assistance on the basis of easily obtained indicators that are perceived to be correlated with fiscal condition. Thus, because city/counties tend to have higher responsibilities, they may be given relatively high state assistance, even when their fiscal condition, as measured by their need-capacity gap, is relatively good.

[9] If our specification is correct, 3-stage least squares will yield asymptotically more efficient parameter estimates than will 2-stage least squares, but 2-stage least squares appears to be less sensitive to specification error than is 3-stage least squares (see Hausman (1978, p. 1265) or Fomby, Hill, and Johnson (1984, p. 507)). Because this type of state behavior has not been widely studied, we are not confident that our specification is correct (and we will examine it with specification tests), so we believe that results obtained using 2-stage least squares should be given more weight. In fact, however, the two methods yield very similar results.

[10] The simplest way to solve Equations (3) and (4) is to collapse all the exogenous factors (including their coefficients) in Equation i into X_i, define the matrix transposes $A' = [G, I]$ and $X' = [X_3, X_4]$, and define the coefficient matrix

$$B = \begin{bmatrix} 1 & -b_{3G} \\ -b_{3I} & 1 \end{bmatrix}.$$

Then these equations can be written $BA = X$, and their solution is $A = B^{-1}X$. The impact of a change in any exogenous factor on A is B^{-1} multiplied by the derivative of X with respect to that factor. With the 2-stage least squares estimates in Table 2,

$$B^{-1} = \begin{bmatrix} 1.547 & -0.624 \\ -1.356 & 1.547 \end{bmatrix}.$$

Thus, as shown in Table 3, a one unit exogenous change in G—that is, in X_3—would ultimately raise G by $1.55 and would lower I by $1.36.

[11] Ladd and Yinger (1989) report, based on a preliminary version of this paper, that state assistance offsets almost two-thirds of the differences in need-capacity gaps across cities. Since that version of the paper was written, we have revised the calculations for state assistance through institutions and now find a somewhat smaller offset.

[12] The form of the test is as follows: We run two regressions, one with the variable in question treated as endogenous and one with it treated as exogenous. We then subtract the coefficient vector of the second regression from that of the first regression and the variance-covariance vector of the second regression from that of the first regression. The test statistic is a quadratic form calculated using the differenced coefficient vector and the inverse of the differenced variance-covariance matrix. This statistic has a chi-squared distribution with degrees of freedom equal to the number of coefficients. A high value of the statistic implies rejection of the null hypothesis of no endogeneity. See Hausman (1978) and Bowden and Turkington (1984).

[13] In fact, no test comes close to rejecting the null hypothesis of exogeneity. The 95 percent critical value for the chi-squared test with 12 degrees of freedom (about the number of coefficients in each regression) is 21, whereas all the text statistics are below 2.5, except that of the excluded instrument RELPOP, which is 8.7.

[14] We ran supplementary regressions to investigate another possibility, namely that federal aid directly to the state government leads to higher assistance from that state to its cities. These regressions included an additional exogenous right-side variable, namely federal aid to the state (which, as defined by the Census, includes pass-through aid) adjusted for the state's share of state-local spending. The coefficient of this variable is negative and insignificant in both the grants and institutional assistance regressions. Thus, the federal government should not count on state governments to act as its agents.

[15] For a more detailed discussion of the role of federal grants, see Ladd and Yinger (1989).

[16] A more speculative possibility is for the federal government to design grants that, unlike current grants, encourage states to provide institutional assistance. For example, federal grants could be designed to reward states for taking over welfare or other services from cities or for allowing their cities to use earnings taxes that apply to commuters. Because institutional assistance is regarded by state policymakers as less powerful than grants, increases in it are not likely to induce large decreases in state grants.

REFERENCES

Bradbury, Katharine L. 1982 "Fiscal Distress in Large U.S. Cities." *New England Economic Review* (November/December): 33–44.

Bradbury, Katharine L. 1983 "Structural Fiscal Distress in Cities: Causes and Consequences." *New England Economic Review* (January/February): 32–43.

Bradbury, Katharine L., and Helen F. Ladd. 1985. "Changes in the Revenue-Raising Capacity of U.S. Cities, 1970–82." *New England Economic Review* (March/April).

Bradbury, Katharine L., Helen F. Ladd, Mark Perrault, Andrew Reschovsky, and John Yinger. 1984. "State Aid to Offset Fiscal Disparities Across Cities." *National Tax Journal* 37 (June): 151–170.

Bradford, D. F., R. A. Malt, and W. E. Oates. 1969. "The Rising Cost of Local Public Services: Some Evidence and Reflections." *National Tax Journal* 22 (June): 185–202.

Bowden, Roger J., and Darrell A. Turkington. 1984. *Instrumental Variables.* Cambridge, England: Cambridge University Press.

Fomby, Thomas B., R. Carter Hill, and Stanley R. Johnson. 1984. *Advanced Econometric Methods.* New York: Springer-Verlag.

Hausman, J. A. 1978. "Specification Tests in Econometrics." *Econometrica* 46 (November): 1251–1271.

Ladd, Helen F., and John Yinger. 1989. *America's Ailing Cities: Fiscal Health and the Design of Urban Policy.* Baltimore: The Johns Hopkins University Press.

Appendix

This appendix describes our calculations of the standardized need-capacity gap and of state assistance through institutions. We begin with five variables from Ladd and Yinger (1989); all expressed in dollars per capita:

RRC = Full revenue-raising capacity (with three broad-based taxes and no overlying jurisdictions)

RRRC = Restricted revenue-raising capacity (with actual taxes, actual overlying jurisdictions, and adjusted state aid)

SAID = Adjusted state aid (with no education pass-through aid and an adjustment for overall state tax effort)

SEN = Standardized expenditure need (based on actual public service costs and average service responsibilities)

AEN = Actual expenditure need (based on actual public service costs and actual service responsibilities)

The standardized need-capacity gap, SGAP, equals [Q(SEN) − RRC], where Q is a service quality level that is held constant across cities. We use the value of Q derived in Ladd and Yinger, which insures that SGAP, expressed as a percentage of RRC, equals zero in the average city in 1972. Thus, a positive (negative) SGAP indicates fiscal health below (above) the 1972 average.

The actual need-capacity gap without grants, AGAPNG, equals [Q'(AEN) − (RRRC − SAID)]. This gap is affected by actual service responsibilities, actual access to taxes, and actual overlying jurisdictions, but it is not affected by state aid. The value of Q' is selected so that AGAPNG, expressed as a percentage of (RRRC − SAID), equals zero in the average city in 1972.

State assistance through institutions, SINST, is the improvement (or deterioration) in the need-capacity gap due to actual service responsibilities, access to taxes, and overlying jurisdictions. It equals (SGAP − AGAPNG).

The fiscal health measures in Ladd and Yinger equal these gap measures multiplied by minus one and divided by the appropriate capacity measure. In a few cities, AGAPNG is less than SGAP, which implies that state assistance through institutions is negative, whereas AGAPNG/(RRRC-SAID) is greater than SGAP/RRC, which implies that state assistance through institutions is positive. These results are perfectly consistent. Fiscal institutions can increase the need-capacity gap in absolute terms while increasing capacity so much that they decrease the need-capacity gap in percentage terms.

A city's actual need-capacity gap, AGAP, which is not explicitly considered in this paper, equals [Q*(AEN) − RRRC]. As before, Q* is set so that AGAP as a percentage of RRC equals zero in the average city in 1972. Because Q* is greater than Q', AGAP does not equal (AGAPNG + SAID).

The values of variables for selected cities are presented in Table A1.

TABLE A1

NEED-CAPACITY GAPS AND STATE ASSISTANCE IN SELECTED CITIES, 1982

City	SGAP	AGAPNG	AGAP	SINST	SAID
Buffalo	187.02	314.65	193.13	-127.63	420.88
Cleveland	243.64	30.18	125.51	213.46	83.21
Ft. Lauderdale	-289.75	-209.56	-196.39	-80.19	65.80
Oakland	7.94	33.16	103.44	-25.22	63.26
Providence	44.56	-182.69	-115.83	227.25	224.68
70 Major U.S. Cities					
Average	32.94	22.09	23.33	10.85	182.65
Maximum	385.53	754.24	871.54	245.41	895.03
Minimum	-289.75	-308.82	-282.34	-426.45	9.63

Note: All entries are expressed in 1982 dollars per capita.

[6]

WHICH LEVEL OF GOVERNMENT SHOULD ASSIST THE POOR?

HELEN F. LADD* AND FRED C. DOOLITTLE*

I. Introduction

MOST economists assert that income redistribution should be a function of the highest possible level of government and therefore urge a greater federal role in public assistance programs for the poor. Although the argument has focused primarily on the financing of public assistance, some analysts argue that the federal government should administer the programs as well.

During the postwar period, the federal role in public assistance increased dramatically. In the late 1960s and early 1970s, changes in eligibility standards and a sharp increase in participation rates induced a major expansion of Aid to Families with Dependent Children (AFDC). Federalization of aid to the aged, blind and disabled in 1974 under the Supplemental Security Income (SSI) program also contributed to the trend. Most recently, the federally financed food stamp program and the jointly financed Medicaid program have offered more generous benefits to more people and represent the fastest growing program areas.

The Reagan administration, however, contends that many redistributive functions should be returned to state and local governments. By increasing the use of block grants and cutting federal welfare eligibility, the 1982 federal budget has already brought changes, especially in the federal role in aiding the working poor. The President's New Federalism proposal calls for even more sweeping changes, including a federal pullout from AFDC and food stamps, two of the nation's basic aid programs. This renewed debate forces us to reconsider the proper roles of federal, state and local governments in aiding the poor.

This analysis begins with a brief review of the role each level of government

---

*Kennedy School of Government, Harvard University.

now plays in public assistance. The paper then presents the case for federal financing of income redistribution as well as the two major arguments against federal responsibility. The final section discusses the issue of which level of government should administer the programs, examining administrative capacity, bureaucratic control, fraud prevention, and the provision of in-kind aid.

II. Current Division of Responsibilities

A. Overview of Public Assistance

Federal, state, and local governments together spent almost $65 billion on income-tested public welfare programs in FY1980.[1] Of this total, expenditures by state governments were more than 50 percent, by the federal government about 30 percent, and by local governments somewhat less than 20 percent. The distribution of financing responsibilities, however, is skewed toward the federal government. As Table 1 indicates, nearly three out of four dollars came from federal taxes, 22 percent from state taxes, and only 4 percent from local taxes. The federal government thus plays the primary role in financing aid to the poor but plays a secondary role in direct spending.

The division of financing, spending, and administrative responsibilities for five income-tested transfer programs, shown in Table 2, demonstrates how diverse the institutional arrangements are for providing assistance. At one extreme are general assistance programs in which financing, spending, and service delivery functions are all performed at the state and local levels with no federal subsidy. At the other is the food stamp program, which is paid for primarily by federal taxes and which has nationally uniform eligibility standards and benefit levels; even this program, however, is adminis-

101

TABLE 1. Public Welfare Expenditures in 1980
Distribution by Level of Government

	Percent of Total ($64,764 million)		
	Federal	State	Local
Distribution of Direct Expenditures	29.7%	51.3%	19.0%
Distribution of Financing	73.7%	22.0%	4.3%

Source: U.S. Department of Commerce, Bureau of the Census, Governmental Finances, 1979-80, Table 9. Breakdown of state and local financing is based on 1979 data from the Advisory Commission on Intergovernmental Relations, Significant Features of Fisical Federalism, 1980-81 Edition. (Washington, D.C.: U.S.G.P.O., 1981), Table 15.

tered through state and local welfare offices.

As in the food stamp program, the federal government finances benefits and is responsible for setting eligibility standards for the basic Supplemental Security Income program. The states are free to supplement SSI benefits, however, and may set eligibility standards if they choose to administer their own supplements. The basic SSI program is the only major assistance program to be administered by the federal government.

All three levels of government share fiscal responsibility for AFDC and Medicaid. Open-ended federal grants, with matching rates that vary between 50 and 83 percent, give the federal government a significant financial stake in the two programs. Since the states may set their own eligibility standards and benefit levels, and choose whether to participate or not, the federal government nevertheless has little control over total spending, benefit levels, and the distribution of grant funds across states. AFDC benefit levels for a family of three with no income, for example, vary from $96 per month in Mississippi to $492 in Vermont, a range that far exceeds the difference in the cost of living between the two states.

The division of financing responsibility for the non-federal share of AFDC and Medicaid also varies across states. In 1979, 11 states required their local governments to contribute at a rate between 4 to 25 percent of the total costs of AFDC. Many of these same states also required a local contribution for the Medicaid program, although only four required a contribution greater than 5 percent of the costs.

Although Table 2 demonstrates a wide range of possibilities, it should be noted that some combinations of authority are not represented. Federal minimum standards paid for by state taxes, for example, is missing. Such a combination would presumably be opposed by the states, and as, discussed further below, would impose unfair burdens on taxpayers in different states. Also missing is the combination of full federal financing of state determined eligibility and benefit levels since this arrangement would provide no incentive for the states to restrain spending.

B. *A Closer Look at the Federal Role*

The categories of spending discussed so far exclude many programs designed, at least in part, to help the poor, such as social security, compensatory education and legal aid. Table 3 illustrates the federal role as of 1981 in this more comprehensive set of programs. The table includes three types of information: outlays on all federal programs oriented at least in part to the alleviation of poverty, federal grants to state and local governments in each of these program areas and rough estimates of the share of the expenditures in each category that benefit the poor. Because the estimates are based on a study of 1972 expenditures, they should be viewed as illustrative only.[2]

In 1981, federal expenditure on the relevant programs totalled $346 billion. Excluding social insurance and related programs, the total falls to $154 billion. Income-tested transfer programs such as AFDC and SSI account for only about 15 percent of this non-social-insurance total; expenditures for in-kind programs—including Medicaid and other health programs, food stamps, housing subsidies, employment and training programs, social services and education—represent about 85 percent. We estimate that at least 70 percent of the expenditures for the in-kind programs other than education benefit the pre-transfer poor. This range of programs for poor people should be borne in mind; it clearly indicates that any discussion of which level of government should take care of poor people must focus on more than cash-transfer programs alone.

The information presented in Table 3 also illustrates the distinction between financing and spending responsibilities. Only in social insurance programs and SSI does the federal government directly spend more than 70 percent of program outlays; in the rest, federal expenditures are primarily intergovernmental grants that are spent by state and local governments. In many program areas—including

Table 2: Division of Responsibilities for Major Income-Tested Transfer Programs

Programs	Financing	Spending Eligibility	Spending Benefit Levels	Administration and Service Delivery
General Assistance	State or local funds, or some combination of each	State or local standards	State or local governments set levels	State or local administration
Food Stamps	Federal financing of all benefits and 50 percent financing of administrative costs	Federal standards	Federal government sets levels	Administered through state and local welfare offices
Supplemental Security Income (SSI) (Assistance for the aged, blind, and disabled)	Federally financed minimum levels State financed supplements	Federal standards for basic program States can set eligibility for supplements, provided they administer their own supplementation program	Federal government sets minimum level States can supplement	Federal administration of basic program Choice of state or federal administration of the state supplements
Aid to Families With Dependent Children (AFDC)	Federal matching grants to states States are required to participate in financing Local participation varies across states	States set eligibility standards subject to federal guidelines	States set benefit levels	State and local administration, subject to federal quality controls on error rates
Medicaid (Medical assistance for the poor and the medically indigent)	Federal matching grants to states States (and in some cases, local) financing of the non-federal share	Federal eligibility requirements with state options	Determined by medical costs	State administration, often by Departments of Health

TABLE 3. Federal Poverty Budget, 1981
(millions of dollars)

Expenditure Category	Federal Outlays	Federal Grants	Percent to Poor[a]
A. CASH TRANSFER PROGRAMS			
Income-tested transfer programs			
AFDC and related assistance.	$8,504	$8,462	93%
Supplemental security income	7192	45	76
Other[b]	7781	2249	42-100
Total (47% through grants)	23,477	10,756	86
Non-income tested social insurance, and related programs			
Social Security	137,970	0	58
Other[c]	53,419	0	21-58
Total (0% through grants)	191,389	0	52
B. IN-KIND PROGRAMS			
Health Care: Income tested			
Medicaid	$16,948	16,833[d]	76
Other	4,254	1,982	65
Total (89% through grants)	21,202	18,815	74
Health Care: Non-Income tested			
Medicare	$42,482	0	48
Other	7,591	75	22-75
Total (0% through grants)	50,073	75	45
Food and nutrition assistance			
Food stamps	11,253	489	85
Child nutrition	4,949	4,391	46
Total (30% through grants)	16,202	4,880	73
Housing and community development.			
Subsidized housing	5,747	3105	74
Community development block grants	4,042	4,042	75
Other	1,396	954	75
Total (72% through grants)	11,185	8,101	75
Employment and training			
General training and employment	4,150	0	NA
Other[e]	4,998	7,979	NA
Total (89% through grants)	9148	7,979	86[h]

TABLE 3 (Continued)

Expenditure Category	Federal Outlays	Federal Grants	Percent to Poor[a]
Social services.			
Block grant	2646	2646	NA
Other[f]	3885	2946	NA
Total (86% through grants)	6531	5592	81[i]
Education-total.			
Elementary and secondary education for the disadvantaged	3,354	3,345	52
Other[g]	12,742	2,702	28-40
Total (38% through grants)	16,096	6,047	36
Justice			
Legal aid	324	0	96
TOTAL	$345,627		
TOTAL (excluding social insurance and related programs)	$154,238		

Sources: Executive Office of the President, Office of Management and Budget, *Budget of the United States Government, Fiscal Year 1983* and "Special Analysis of Federal Aid to State and Local Governments."

a. Entries in this column are based on estimates for 1972 reported by Robert D. Plotnick and Felicity Skidmore, *Progress Against Poverty* (New York: Academic Press, 1975). In some cases the estimates have been adjusted to incorporate recent program changes.

b. Includes income-tested veterans' pensions, refugee assistance, energy and emergency assistance, earned income tax credit and "other."

c. Includes railroad retirement, federal employees retirement, service-connected pensions for veterans, other retirement benefits and unemployment compensation.

d. Includes Indian health and hospital and medical care for veterans.

e. Includes special target groups, job corps, public service employment, federal-state employment service, and work incentive program.

f. Includes rehabilitation services, child welfare, services for children, youth, female and elderly.

g. Includes education for the handicapped, higher education and veterans education.

h. Estimate based on aggregate of 1972 training programs.

i. Estimate based on 1972 public assistance and social service category.

housing and community development, income-tested health services, social services, and employment and training—the federal share of direct expenditures is 25 percent or less. As observed above, the federal government thus plays a major role in the financing of many programs for the poor, but is much less involved in the actual delivery of services.

III. Who Should Assist Poor People?

The various financing, spending and administrative arrangements that already exist in public assistance programs suggest that spending and financing responsibilities are logically separable from administration. This does not rule out the possibility, however, that certain administrative arrangements may be superior to others for any given spending and financing scheme; in general, though, the optimal assignment of administrative responsibility need not influence that of spending and financing authority. Hence, we first resolve the issue of how spending and financing authority ought to be distributed and then, in light of that resolution, discuss the appropriate division of administrative responsibilities.

A. Financing and Spending

The Case for Federal Responsibility

The case for federal financing of a nationally-determined standard of welfare benefits proceeds from the presumption that the welfare level in any particular jurisdiction ought to reflect the redistributive preferences and attitudes of residents throughout the country, not just those within the local jurisdiction. Implicit in this presumption is either the assumption that the concern of local voters for the poor extends to poor people living elsewhere in the country, or alternatively, the value judgement that, regardless of their actual views, people *ought* to be concerned about the poor in other states because poverty is a national problem. Two recent national polls by the Advisory Commission on Intergovernmental Relations provide indirect support for the assumption about voter preferences. The polls show that only 15 to 17 percent of the respondents would like the federal government to withdraw in favor of state and local governments from programs to aid the needy. More than four out of five respondents thus apparently believe the federal government has a responsibility to help needy people, which in turn suggests that they believe poverty is a national concern.[3]

Support for the value judgement is grounded in the complex causes of poverty. Part of the country's poverty reflects limited employment opportunities due to national economic conditions and policies. Employment opportunities differ across states because some states are more sensitive than others to fluctuations in the national economy and past national economic development strategies have had differential impacts. The main cause of unemployment-related poverty, however, relates to national rather than local conditions; similarly, the causes of poverty for the remaining poor reflect problems and social trends affecting the entire nation such as employment discrimination and increases in the number of divorces and out-of-wedlock births.

From the presumption that poverty is a national concern, it directly follows that national standards for assistance payments are appropriate. Only national standards can assure potential beneficiaries of a minimum level of benefits regardless of where they live and regardless of the wealth and generosity of other state residents. A national standard of assistance, however, need not imply uniform benefit levels in dollar terms; indeed, cost-of-living differences both across and within states mean that uniform consumption levels can only be achieved by varying cash or voucher payments. Cost-of-living adjustments are clearly appropriate for alleviating poverty as defined in an absolute sense, that is, an inability to command access to a minimum acceptable bundle of goods and services. Provided the frame of reference is the national distribution of *real* income, such adjustments are also appropriate when the standard is defined in a relative sense—that is, as some fraction of, for example, median household income.

Given the desirability of national standards, why should responsibility for financing minimum benefit levels be lodged at the federal, rather than at the state or local, level? Could not the federal government simply mandate minimum standards for welfare payments or, alternatively, use appropriately designed matching aid to induce poor or miserly states to increase their benefit levels up to the national standard? The conclusion that full federal financing is preferable to the alternative financing arrangements follows directly from the presumption that poverty is a national concern. As is the case for all national programs, fair treatment of taxpayers requires that the distribution of tax burdens be in line with ability to pay regardless of the state of residence. Subnational financing would approximate this outcome only if poor people and taxable resources were evenly distributed across states.

In reality though, the incidence of poverty ranges widely: in 1975, over 15 percent of the population in many southern states were needy, or more than twice the level in states such as Connecticut and Minnesota. Although overstated somewhat because the poverty data are based on a national standard that is not adjusted for cost of living differences across states, the interstate variation is sufficiently large to suggest that assigning the states major financial responsibility for the poor would lead to uneven and, hence, horizontally inequitable tax burdens across states. The mismatch between states' needs, as measured by the number of poor people, and their fiscal resources, as measured by per capita income, reinforces this conclusion. State per capita income ranges from 70 percent of the national average in Mississippi to 128 percent in Alaska. Of the 26 states with more than 10 percent of their populations living in poverty, 22 have per capita incomes below the national average. The mismatch is even greater when the broader ACIR Representative Tax capacity measure is used.[4]

Taxpayer mobility only exacerbates the unevenness of fiscal burdens across states. In a decentralized system, taxpayers in states with large concentrations of poor people would have fiscal incentives to move to other states; by moving they could avoid responsibility for financing public assistance, but would leave the burden to fall unfairly on those who remain.

Macro-economic considerations also contribute to the case for federal financing. To the extent that poverty reflects an unhealthy economy, welfare burdens tend to rise at the same time that tax revenues decline. At the federal level this relationship may be advantageous in that payments to the poor exert an automatic stabilizing effect on the economy. Unlike the federal government, however, state and local governments are required to balance their budgets. Hence, with decentralized financing, increasing welfare burdens at a time of recession would require states to raise taxes in a cyclically counter-productive manner.

This completes the basic case for a substantial federal role in the setting of benefit levels and the financing of welfare programs. The thrust of the argument is that because poverty is, or ought to be, a national concern, national standards of welfare assistance are appropriate and fair treatment of taxpayers requires that the financial burden be distributed among households throughout the country in line with ability to pay. The following two sections discuss the extent to which variations across states in attitudes toward the poor and in local wage rates modify this conclusion.

Variations in Preferences

Opponents of national welfare programs argue that only by locating fiscal responsibilities at the state and local level will public assistance programs reflect the diverse preferences and attitudes of residents in different jurisdictions. According to this view, it is appropriate for welfare benefits to vary from place to place just as do service levels for many other public programs such as local parks and police. How much do attitudes toward the poor actually vary across states and to what extent do these variations weaken the argument for federal fiscal responsibility?

The diversity across states in attitudes toward the poor is illustrated by variations in AFDC benefit levels and eligibility standards. As noted above, variations in benefit levels across states are large; and they remain large when expressed in real terms or as a percent of state household income. Moreover, as Larry Orr concludes in his 1976 statistical study of benefit levels "systematic regional differences in taxpayers preferences" apparently play an important role in explaining the variation across states even after controlling for differences in income, federal matching rates and the characteristics of recipients.[5] Diverse views about how to define the deserving poor are illustrated by the variations in eligibility provisions across states shown in Table 4. States vary in their treatment of unborn infants and children between 18 and 21, their willingness to provide assistance to households with unemployed parents and their work requirements. Although some of this variation may reflect differences in the ability of states to finance welfare programs, much probably represent actual differences in attitudes. This follows because setting eligibility standards is not the only way to limit welfare spending; states can also control welfare spending by limiting benefit levels.

By analogy to the Tiebout model of local public goods, it is tempting to believe that because of these differences in attitudes toward the poor, fully decentralized decision-making and financing of welfare benefits would be preferable in terms of economic efficiency to a uniform national standard financed by federal taxes. With decentralization, the diverse attitudes and preferences would be reflected in different welfare programs across states. Taxpayers would then be able to choose the state whose welfare policy most closely matched their own preferences.

In an important 1973 article, Mark Pauly proves formally that, under certain conditions, local decision-making about redistributive programs can lead to efficient outcomes.[6] A close examination of the necessary conditions, however, indi-

TABLE 4: State AFDC Eligibility Requirements, 1980

Eligibility Provision	# of States
Age	
Aid is available until child is 21	40
Aid ends when child is 18	10
Unborn Child	
Medically verified pregnancy establishes eligibility	33
Eligibility only at birth of child	17
Unemployed Parent	
Unemployment of parent can establish eligibility	27
Unemployment is not a basis of eligibility	23
Work Requirements	
Job search and work requirement beyond federal requirements	18
None	32

Source: U.S. Dept. of Health and Human Services, Social Security Administration, Office of Family Assistance, <u>Characteristics of State Plans for Aid to Families with Dependent Children, 1980.</u>

cates that such an outcome is not likely. The two conditions of interest here are first, that non-poor residents are concerned only about poor people in their own jurisdiction and second, that potential welfare recipients do not move in search of higher welfare benefits. The first assumption rules out benefit spillovers from one jurisdiction to another and makes welfare payments analogous to other local services such as police and fire that provide benefits primarily to local residents. Because the alleviation of poverty in a particular jurisdiction is assumed to be valued only by the people living in that jurisdiction, taxpayers with the strongest preferences for income redistribution end up in communities with the most poor people, while those with weaker preferences select communities with few poor people. As Pauly correctly notes, once the assumption that people are concerned only about the poor in their own jurisdiction is relaxed to allow for concern, but at a lower level, for poor people in other jurisdictions, matching grants from a higher level of government are required to induce local jurisdictions to make efficient spending decisions. Relaxing the assumption further by positing that people are equally concerned about poor Americans wherever they live leads once again to the conclusion that poverty is a national concern.

Thus, the central difference between the Pauly analysis and the view that national preferences ought to take precedence over local preferences relates to how much taxpayers value the alleviation of poverty in jurisdictions other than their own. The extreme Pauly assumption is that residents place no value on welfare expenditures made by other jurisdictions; the assumption underlying the national view is that they value such expenditures as much as they value expenditures on the poor in their own jurisdiction. Pauly gives two rationales for his approach. The first relies on altruism, with the desire to do good being conditional on the perception of bad circumstances. Because people are more likely to have contact with the local poor than with the national poor, altruistic concern, he argues, is likely to demonstrate the posited spatial relationship. The second relies on self-interest and the desire to minimize the adverse manifestations of poverty. Thus, taxpayers may expect to receive benefits from income transfers in the form of reduced crime or upgraded neighborhoods. Once again, this would lead to a spatial dimension of the benefits from income redistribution.

How compelling are these arguments for a spatial dimension to concern about poor people? First, the altruism argument for a spatial dimension is less convincing in an era of television and advanced communications than it might have been at an earlier time. Furthermore, the argument is substantially weakened when applied to jurisdictions as large as states rather than to local neighborhoods. It is plausible, for example, that non-poor people living in a large city have as much or more concern for poor people living in other cities than they do for poor people living in rural parts of their own state. In addition, a certain romanticism about poverty may even lead people to be more concerned about the distant poor than about the poor living nearby whose faults are better known. Finally, the validity of the altruism argument may vary with the degree of poverty; taxpayers may value the alleviation of the most obvious cases of poverty in all states while reserving concern for the less severe cases for the poor in their own state. Together, these considerations weaken the argument for the Pauly position, especially insofar as it is based on altruism.

This in turn weakens the basic efficiency argument for decentralization of fiscal responsibility for welfare programs. Nonetheless, because the self-interest justification for providing welfare may well have a spatial dimension, the efficiency argument should not be completely ignored. This suggests that efficiency may well be enhanced by state supplementation of federally funded minimum welfare levels. Because of the differences in the capacities of states to finance such supplements, however, even here a federal financing role may be appropriate; federal matching of state supplements with the matching rates varying inversely with state fiscal capacities would promote both efficiency and equity in the provision of welfare benefits.

The second condition required for efficiency in the Pauly model of decentralized decision-making is that potential welfare recipients not be free to move from one jurisdiction to another in search of higher benefit levels. Within Pauly's model, migration induced by the level of welfare payments imposes social costs without providing offsetting social benefits. In a more complete model, migration of beneficiaries would have the additional effect of inducing jurisdictions to provide lower welfare benefits than they otherwise would.

Although poor people are apparently not very mobile in response to economic opportunities, statistical evidence suggests that they are quite responsive to different benefit levels across states. A recent study by Lawrence Southwick, Jr. documents the strong response of AFDC mothers.[7] One of his tests shows, for example, that a ten percent increase in benefit levels in one census division would increase in-migration of welfare recipients by 25 percent. Moreover, the strong effect remains with the estimation of a simultaneous model which allows the payment level itself to be influenced by migration. These statistical results are confirmed by anecdotal evidence from states currently reducing welfare payments. Oregon, for example, reports a loss of one quarter of its Indo-Chinese AFDC population to California as a direct result of its reduction in benefit levels. One response to this mobility by poor people would be to limit their rights of free movement or impose durational residency requirements as a condition of receiving public assistance. Although these approaches have been common in the past, clear and strongly-worded Supreme Court opinions now have found them unconstitutional.

Thus once again, we are left with the conclusion that the federal government should take primary fiscal responsibility for welfare and other programs for poor people. The efficiency argument for decentralization of fiscal responsibilities is not compelling, except as the basis for state supplementation of a federal minimum.

Labor Market Considerations

A second common argument against a nationally determined welfare standard centers on the diversity of labor market conditions across states. Because a given level of welfare benefits would be likely to affect work effort more in low-wage rural areas than in high-wage industrial areas, the adverse effects on labor supply of a national welfare program are likely to vary by geographic area.

This argument against a national program is ironic since concern about work effort partially motivated the push for full federalization of welfare during the 1970s. Proponents of a national negative income tax or family assistance program argued that, compared to existing welfare programs, the reform would increase recipients' incentives to work by reducing marginal tax rates on earned income. The defeat of these proposals for a national system can be attributed in part to the opposition of people from low wage areas who were concerned more about the size of the basic payment relative to local wages than they were about the work disincentive effects of high marginal tax rates.

Adjusting a national benefit standard to reflect cost-of-living differences, as recommended above, would partially offset this concern. In addition, one could design a national program that specifically incorporated differences in wage rates across labor market areas. Such a program is not likely to pass the test of political acceptability, however, since it would implicitly acknowledge the legitimacy of low wage industries and be seen as penalizing those with poor employment prospects. Given this, people who are especially concerned about work disincentives in low wage areas should logically prefer that subnational governments have control over eligibility requirements and benefit levels. The authors' value judgment, however, is that national recipient equity should take precedence.

B. Administration

The conclusion that the federal government should take primary financial responsibility for welfare programs need not imply that it also administer them. In making the choice between federal and state or local administration, four issues deserve attention: administrative capacity; managerial control; the balance between recipients' privacy and fraud control; and the special considerations that arise with in-kind, as opposed to cash, assistance. Since federal administration dominates state and local administration in some ways but not in others, the optimal division of administrative responsibilities depends in part on the weight attached to the various considerations.

Differences in Administrative Capacity

Experience has shown that the federal government does in fact have the capacity to administer large and complex assistance programs successfully. For many years it has operated the social security system, and now, after initial transition problems, it is also successfully administering the Supplemental Security Income program. The capacity of state and local governments to manage public assistance programs, however, varies across jurisdictions. A detailed study of AFDC error rates in the late 1970s indicates that differences in the social and economic environments in which state programs are operated, such as the degree of urbanization and the characteristics of the case load, account for only one third of the differences in error rates across states, with the balance attributable to differences in administrative practices and managerial capacity.[8] The capacity of local governments to administer AFDC programs also varies significantly across jurisdictions even within a single state. Although state monitoring and supervision may reduce somewhat these intrastate differences, error rates in programs directly administered by the states are lower than those in state-supervised local programs.[9]

Economies of scale in welfare management help explain these differences in administrative performance. The fixed costs of staff training programs are one cause of such economies. In small jurisdictions without the capacity to develop formal training modules, the informal instruction provided to new workers introduces significant variation into the interpretation of regulations. Economies of scale also exist in data management since, above a fairly small scale of operations, keeping track of information on eligibility is a substantial undertaking. Even without precise data on the magnitude of these economies, it seems safe to conclude that state or federal administration is preferable to local administration.

Maintaining Bureaucratic Control

Assuring that the output of a bureaucracy conforms to the intentions of policymakers is never an easy task. Managers often attempt to make the interests of service delivery bureaucrats coincide with policymakers' goals so that they will freely choose to work for organizational objectives. When this approach fails, managers must monitor performance and offer explicit incentives to affect output.

Programs that are administered by one level of government but designed and financed by another exacerbate the problem of managerial control by introducing another level of government. The interstate differences in attitudes toward the poor mentioned above mean that in many cases the federal agency's goals will differ from those of grantee jurisdictions. Moreover, the current federal practice of subsidizing different costs at different rates within grant programs for public assistance sometimes hinders the federal manager's attempt to induce recipient jurisdictions to operate in the national interest. For example, if the local share of assistance costs is 25 percent and of administrative costs is 50 percent, local bureaucrats have a financial incentive to resist federal efforts to implement an administrative procedure costing $1,000 that would save $1,900 in erroneous assistance payments; the local cost of the change would be $500 while the local savings would be only $495. An extreme example of this problem occurs in the food stamp program, where the federal government pays all assistance but only half the costs of state administration, an arrangement that invites administrative problems.

Given this conflict between the interests of federal policymakers and local administrators, the grantor must rely on formal systems to monitor and control program implementation. Although recent federal efforts to improve auditing practices and institute quality control systems have met with some success, implementing these changes in grant programs poses legal and political problems. If repeated noncompliance with federal requirements is found, the final sanction is to cut off funds to the grantee. This action is often counter-productive, however, because it imposes immediate costs on the intended beneficiaries of the program rather than on the program administrators. Federal administrators thus face a dilemma: once the threat of a fund cutoff has failed to prevent grantees from violating requirements, there is little point in actually cutting off the grant. Unless the cutoff is occasionally enforced, however, the control system will collapse. Even if the sanction is actually imposed, the grantee can nevertheless avoid any financial penalty by agreeing to change its practices, since typically there are no retroactive fund cutoffs or financial penalties for deliberate violations that are later corrected.

States have sometimes refused to provide benefits to people who were eligible under federal regulations or to provide all federally mandated benefits to eligible recipients, thus creating an especially difficult control program for federal administrators. For a time during the late 1960s and early 1970s, recipients successfully challenged these violations in the federal courts and won numerous awards of retroactive benefits. In recent years, however, litigation has become less important because the Supreme Court weakened the statutory requirements on states and ruled that the federal courts did not have the power under the constitution to order the states to make retroactive payments to recipients unlawfully denied benefits.[10]

On balance, concern about managerial control argues for concentrating administrative responsibility at the governmental level having primary responsibility for program design and financing. Given our previous argument that fiscal responsibility for the poor ought to be concentrated at the federal level, this consideration implies federal administration. The strength of this argument, however, is difficult to determine without more detailed analysis of these issues of managerial control. Moreover, the case for federal administration rests in part on current federal practices such as differential cost reimbursement that could be changed. Finally, the reader should remember that the argument for state supplementation of federal basic benefits clouds the issue further. While the federal government could easily administer programs that varied across states in benefit levels, it would have more difficulty administering programs with differing eligibility standards.

Recipients' Privacy vs. Control of Fraud

Many of the most controversial issues in welfare concern efforts to control abuses of the system by recipients. Until the late 1960s, both state and local governments commonly raided the homes of recipients suspected of fraud, while the federal government only timidly defended recipients' rights to privacy. In recent years, the federal government has urged the states to develop computer systems to check reported income against other state and federal records, and seek child-support payments from absent fathers.

To the extent that surveillance is necessary to prevent welfare fraud, the choice between local and federal administration requires balancing the fear of a national police power against the economies of scale that the federal government can achieve in fraud investigation. Traditionally, the investigation and control of individual behavior has been a function of local governments in the United States because of a concern about the potential abuses of a national police force; indeed, the Department of Justice has explicitly opposed proposals to shift responsibility for investigation of welfare fraud and abuse to the federal government on just these grounds. On the other hand, the federal government has data-processing resources for cross checking of records and tracking recipients and absent fathers across state lines.

Thus, while people will continue to hold differing views on the appropriate balance between recipient privacy and fraud control, the implications of this choice for the division of administrative responsibilities among levels of government is less clear now than in the past because of recent changes in federal policy. In some program areas, the federal government probably now can do a better job than local governments at minimizing rates of fraud; in other program areas, such as those that include work requirements, however, the subnational governments may be better suited to this task.

In-Kind Aid

Providing certain types of in-kind aid such as housing and health care involves different administrative problems than a system of cash payments or vouchers. Because the direct provision of services requires specific knowledge about local conditions and needs, local administration is probably preferable to federal administration. It should be noted, however, that administration by local non-profit agencies may be as effective and efficient in some cases as administration by local governments.

Summary

This analysis of administrative considerations implies that administrative structures should vary from program to program depending on how policymakers weight the factors discussed above. On balance, they appear to suggest that cash assistance programs and voucher programs should be administered by the federal government (or at the very least by state governments) and programs that provide direct services should be run by local government or non-profit agencies.

IV. Conclusion

In sum, we have reaffirmed the long-standing argument of economists that the federal government should take primary fiscal responsibility for assisting poor people. Regardless of differences in attitudes across states, if taxpayers value benefits to poor people living in other jurisdictions as much as they value benefits to the poor in their own jurisdictions, alleviation of poverty is a national concern. Consequently, national standards for public assistance are appropriate. Moreover, as is the case for all national programs, taxpayer equity requires that fiscal burdens be fairly distributed among taxpayers throughout the country. Movement of potential beneficiaries in search of higher public assistance levels strengthens the case for centralizing fiscal responsibilities at the national level. Concern that nationally determined benefit standards would have significant adverse effects on work effort in low-wage states weakens the case for centralization; adjusting benefit levels for state cost-of-living differences, however, would reduce the force of this concern.

We have also argued that state supplementation of national programs may be appropriate and that, especially for assistance programs that provide direct services, state or local administration may be preferable to federal administration. Which level of government should administer other public assistance programs is not fully resolved here, but considerations of administrative capacity and managerial control seem to point toward federal administration of cash assistance and voucher programs.

FOOTNOTES

[1] As defined by the United States Census Bureau, public welfare programs include cash assistance payments to needy persons; vendor payments for medical care and other services provided under welfare programs; and other expenditures for welfare purposes.

²The share of expenditures in each program area going to the pre-transfer poor is based on 1972 estimates reported by Robert D. Plotnick and Felicity Skidmore, 1975. In some cases, we have incorporated more recent information about particular programs.

³ACIR, 1981.

⁴The ACIR approach calculates tax capacity by estimating the amount of revenue each state would raise if it taxed all its state and local tax bases at average national rates. For a full discussion of this Representative Tax System approach, see ACIR, March 1982.

⁵See Orr, 1976, p. 369. Orr recognizes that the dummy variables used in his analysis may capture a variety of regional affects, but argues that it is plausible to believe that the large differentials that he finds by region reflect systematic regional differences in taxpayers' preferences for income redistribution.

⁶Pauly, 1973.

⁷Southwick's empirical tests are based primarily on data from a 1967 study of 66,577 AFDC families conducted by the U.S. Department of Health, Education and Welfare. See Southwick, 1981.

⁸See M. Bendick et al., Chapter 2. In January–June 1976, case error rates ranged from 5.7 percent in Nevada to 44.6 percent in the District of Columbia while payment errors ranged from 1.5 percent in Nevada to 23.3 percent in the District of Columbia.

⁹Martha Derthick (1970) documents the variation in error rates across communities in Massachusetts before the state took over welfare in 1968. See Bendick et al. 1978, pp. 113–117, for their analysis of state administration versus state supervision.

¹⁰See Doolittle, 1982.

REFERENCES

Advisory Commission on Intergovernmental Relations, "Changing Public Attitudes on Governments and Taxes, 1981," S-10. Washington, D.C., 1981.
———, "Tax Capacity of the Fifty States: Methodology and Estimates," M-134, Washington, D.C., 1982.
Bendick et al., *The Anatomy of AFDC Errors*. Washington, D.C.: The Urban Institute, 1978.
Derthick, Martha, *The Influence of Federal Grants*. Boston: Harvard University, 1970.
Doolittle, Fred C., "State-Imposed Nonfinancial Eligibility Condition in AFDC," *Harvard Journal on Legislation*, Vol. 19, No. 1 (Winter, 1972), pp. 1–48.
Orr, Larry L., "Income Transfers as a Public Good: An Application to AFDC," *American Economic Review*, June 1976, pp. 359–371.
Pauly, M. V., "Income Redistribution as a Local Public Good," *Journal of Public Economics*, Vol. 2, No. 1 (February, 1973), pp. 35–58.
Plotnick, Robert D. and Felicity Skidmore, *Progress Against Poverty*. New York: Academic Press.
Southwick, Lawrence, Jr., "Public Welfare programs and Recipient Migration," *Growth and Change*, Vol. 12, No. 4 (October 1981), pp. 22–32.

[7]

THE STATE AID DECISION: CHANGES IN STATE AID TO LOCAL GOVERNMENTS, 1982–87**

HELEN F. LADD*

ABSTRACT

This paper provides evidence on several policy issues about state aid to local governments. With state-specific changes in state aid between 1982 and 1987 as the dependent variable, the estimated equations show that state aid to local governments grew less than proportionately with exogenously determined changes in state own-source revenue and that changes in the amount of aid were influenced by the state's initial financial condition. In addition, state governments apparently did not view federal aid to state governments as general funds from which they could provide additional aid to local governments. Most surprising is the finding that, controlling for other determinants of aid, state governments apparently offset substantial amounts of the 1982–87 changes in direct federal aid to local governments.

RECENT changes in the U.S. federal system have focused attention on the role of state governments in our three-tiered federal system. As the federal government has eliminated, cut, or consolidated into block grants many of the intergovernmental aid programs that had been introduced in the early 1960s and expanded during the 1970s, attention has shifted to the states. How would the states respond to the cutbacks in federal aid and would they have the capacity and the willingness to fill the gaps left by the federal cutbacks? Optimists have noted significant changes in states' capacity to deal with their new fiscal responsibilities. State governments' more extensive reliance on broad-based sales and income taxes, it is argued, gives them the capacity to do more than in the past. At the same time, however, states are also facing growing expenditure pressures in the form of higher Medicaid costs, rapidly rising corrections needs, and pressure to improve the quality of elementary and secondary education. This paper focuses on one aspect of state governmental responsibilities, that of providing assistance to their local governments. In 1987, state governments devoted on average about one-third of their general spending to intergovernmental aid to local governments.[1] Not only is this aid important as a share of state spending, it is equally important as a revenue source for local governments; in 1987, for example, state aid accounted for about one-third of all local general revenues and more than 50 percent of the general revenues of independent school districts. Not surprisingly, these aggregate figures mask tremendous diversity in the role of state aid across states. For example, leaving aside Hawaii because of it extremely centralized governmental structure, state aid varied from about 15 percent of state general expenditures in New Hampshire and Vermont to 47 percent in California. On the revenue side, state aid accounted for 12 percent of local general revenue in New Hampshire and 26 percent in Vermont, but over 40 percent in California, Delaware, New Mexico, North Carolina, and Wisconsin. These magnitudes imply that changes in state aid to local governments can have big impacts on the finances of both state and local governments.

Interpreting state aid figures and developing empirical models of the aid decision in the state-local context are complicated by the fact that state-local fiscal structures differ greatly from one state to another and that the monetary aid flows between state and local governments are part of a larger set of decisions about the design of state-local intergovernmental relations. These decisions include how spending responsibilities are divided between state and local governments and how spending by local governments is to be financed. Because the differences across states in intergovernmental relationships

*Duke University, Durham, NC 27706.

reflect differences that are firmly rooted in each state's historical development and have evolved only slowly over time, they are not very amenable to economic modeling. Consequently, the empirical work in this paper focuses on changes in, rather than levels of, state aid.

The research reported here provides evidence on several policy-related questions about this significant component of state government spending and local revenues. The article begins with the policy questions. Subsequent sections describe the underlying model, discuss the data, and report the results. The paper ends with a summary and conclusion.

Policy Questions

Based on data on changes in state aid between 1982 and 1987, the empirical work described below is designed to shed light on the following five policy questions. The first three relate to state government resources and budgets. The third and fourth relate to the role of resources available to local governments.

1. How responsive is state aid to exogenous changes in the state's own-source revenues?

The more responsive state aid is to changes in the state's revenues, the more closely linked is the fiscal condition of local governments to that of the state government. Of course, when the state economy is booming and state expenditure pressures are minimal, local governments benefit from this close relationship. But when the economy declines and revenues from relatively income elastic state income and sales taxes decline or when pressures rise for more state-provided services, local governments are adversely affected by this close relationship and might be better off relying on their own revenue sources. This conclusion follows provided that local tax sources are less responsive than state taxes to the economic downturn or local government officials have the political will to raise tax rates when the economy weakens.

The analysis in this paper uses data only from a period of economic expansion. Consequently, it sheds light primarily on the effect on aid on increases in state revenues. The main issue is whether aid grows more slowly or more rapidly than state revenues. To appreciate the importance of this question, consider the following situation. Assume that in an initial year, the appropriate balance between own-source local revenues and state aid is deemed appropriate, with aid accounting for 50 percent of local general revenues, and that over time the desired level of local spending (and hence local revenues) rises at the same rate as the desired level of state spending. Then, if aid grows more slowly than state revenues, local government revenues will be restricted relative to state revenues unless local officials increase own-source revenues at a faster pace and shift the mix between own-source and external funds toward own sources. Or, alternatively, if the growth of locally-generated revenues is capped, the disproportionately slow growth in state aid will reduce the level of local public services.

2. How is state aid affected by state budgetary stress?

A related question is how states change the amount of aid they give to their local governments at a time of state budgetary stress. Compared to cutbacks in direct state spending, cutbacks in aid may be more palatable to state politicians because they require no layoffs of state employees and no reductions in the services for which state governments are directly responsible. While cutbacks in aid to local governments will eventually show up in the form of higher local taxes, reductions in local services, or layoffs of local employees, these effects are dispersed throughout many local governments and frequently are hard to attribute directly to the actions of state politicians. Thus, the empirical question is the extent to which short-run fiscal pressures at the state level translate into cutbacks in state aid. This study is not well designed to provide a complete answer to this question, but can shed some light by exploring how differences across states in their budgetary conditions in 1982 affected subsequent aid decisions.

3. Do changes in the amount of federal aid distributed to state governments affect how much aid states give to their local governments?

An increase in federal aid to states could lead to higher state aid to local governments for two reasons. The first, which is grounded in economic theory, is simply that an increase in federal assistance increases the resources available to the state and consequently would make it possible for the state to increase its spending on all state activities, including aid to local governments.[2] The size of the predicted impact depends on the nature of the federal aid. The more restricted is the federal aid to narrowly-defined programs that the state would not otherwise have funded, the less flexibility the state government has to use the money for its own priorities, including state aid to local governments.

The second reason is grounded in the accounting practices of the Governments Division of the Census. The census counts federal aid that is distributed initially to states but which is then passed through to local governments as federal aid to state, rather than to local, governments. Because the amount that is passed through is reported as state rather than federal aid, the census data should show a positive relationship between changes in the amount of aid labeled federal aid to states and that labeled state aid to local governments. For example, consider a state that delegates to county governments responsibility for health care. If the census reports that the state receives an increase in federal aid under the health block grant program, we would expect to see a corresponding increase in state aid (by the census definition) to counties. Similarly, with the shift in 1983 of administration of the Community Development Block Grants for small cities to the states, census figures should show a simultaneous increase in federal aid to states and state aid (in the form of pass-through aid) to local governments. However, even with the census treatment of pass-through aid, total state aid to localities need not be positively associated with federal aid to states; state governments could choose to offset the increased pass-through aid by decreasing aid from their own resources or to offset decreased pass-through aid by increasing aid from their own resources.[3]

As discussed below, the main source of state aid data in this study is the National Association of State Budget Officers (rather than the census), which excludes federal pass-through aid. This fact should lead to cleaner estimates of the effect of federal aid to states on state aid than would be obtained from census data alone.

4. To what extent did states offset cutbacks in federal aid to local governments by increasing state aid?

Recent years have witnessed major changes in direct federal aid to local governments. After a dramatic increase in federal aid during the 1960s and 1970s, such aid was dramatically reduced during the 1980s as President Reagan tried to reduce the size of government and the involvement of the federal government in state and local affairs. Intergovernmental aid bore a disproportionate share of the federal spending cutbacks in the early 1980s and, within the category of intergovernmental aid, grant programs directed toward local governments tended to be harder hit than those to states. This outcome occurred in part because the programs most vulnerable to cuts were the new programs of direct aid to localities introduced during the Johnson and Nixon years (Gold, 1990). Another factor was that many narrowly-defined categorical programs were consolidated into block grants designated for states. Of the 77 grants that were consolidated into block grants in 1981, 47 formerly delivered federal funds directly to localities (Ladd 1984, p. 190). Between 1980 and 1987, most of the federal grant programs of special importance to urban areas were significantly reduced or, as in the case of general revenue sharing, eliminated completely. One estimate suggests that, including revenue sharing, grants of special importance to urban areas fell 47 percent in current dollars between 1980 and 1987 at the same time that all other grants, including AFDC and Medicaid, increased by 47 percent (Cuciti, 1990, Table 3).

Early evidence based on field research suggested that states did little to replace cutbacks in federal grants, but subsequent evidence suggests relatively complete replacement in some states for some programs (see Peterson 1982, Peterson et al. 1986, Nathan and Doolittle 1983, and Nathan, Doolittle and Associates 1987). The difficulty with these studies is determining what the state would have done in the absence of the federal changes. Moreover, none focuses directly on the state aid decision.

Behavioral models of how states adjust their own intergovernmental aid in response to federal aid to local governments are found in Craig and Inman (1982 and 1986) and Yinger and Ladd (1990). Unfortunately, no clear answer emerges from these studies. Craig and Inman's ambitious papers based on pooled cross-sectional data across states over time focus not on all state aid, but only on the largest component, state aid to education, and place it in the context of other state decisions about spending and taxing. In their 1982 paper, the authors concluded that states reduced state aid to education by one dollar (or more) for each dollar of direct federal aid to local school districts (Craig and Inman 1982, p. 547). This large offset contrasts with their 1986 finding that state aid to education was unaffected by the one component of direct federal aid to local school districts, namely federal impact aid, included in their model.[4] Thus, two contradictory results emerge from the same authors.

Yinger and Ladd's recent study (1990) of state aid to major cities based on 1982 cross-sectional data finds no evidence that state policymakers treat federal aid to cities as a substitute for state assistance to cities. In other words, Yinger and Ladd find that, controlling for other factors, cities with higher federal categorical grants and those with higher general revenue sharing in 1982 received no less assistance than other cities. The authors suggest that their findings might apply to changes over time. If so, their results would imply that state actions probably did not offset the impact on cities of the recent cuts in federal aid to cities.

The empirical model discussed below is in the spirit of the Yinger-Ladd paper, but differs by focusing on state aid to all local governments rather than to major central cities alone, and examines changes in, rather than levels of, state aid.

5. Do states change their aid to local governments in response to exogenously determined changes in local own-source revenues?

Local taxes can go up for many reasons. Except when they are raised to offset cutbacks in intergovernmental aid, increases in local taxes are associated with increases in local spending, although not necessarily with increases in service levels. One hypothesis would be that state officials feel the political heat of rising local taxes and try to offset them by providing additional aid to their local governments. Alternatively, state officials may perceive no state interest in local decisions about local own-source revenues and may therefore ignore changes in local own-source revenues when making state aid decisions.

According to the simple model presented in the next section, how states respond to changes in local taxes is an empirical question that turns on how state policymakers value additional local services financed out of local own sources relative to the political costs they bear from higher local taxes.

A Model of the State Aid Decision

By focusing on changes in aid over time, this paper takes the institutional context as given and thereby obviates the need to explain the large variation across states in aid levels. As a consequence, the model described in this section makes no reference to the magnitude of disparities or spillovers that could be important determinants of variation across states. Moreover, the model is partial in that it focuses on the allocation of an exogenously determined amount of state resources. (However, the empirical work allows for the endogeneity of state revenues.)

State policymakers are assumed to allocate an exogenously determined level of budgetary resources (B) between state aid to local governments (STAID) and direct state services (G) in order to maximize a welfare function whose arguments are direct state services (G) and the level of local services net of taxes as perceived by state policymakers (NLS). More specifically, state policymakers maximize

W = W(G, NLS)

subject to

B = G + STAID

NLS = STAID + (a − c) LTAX + b FAID

LTAX = f(STAID, X) with

δLTAX/δSTAID ≤ 0.

where LTAX is local taxes, FAID is federal aid to local governments, X is a vector of exogenous determinants of local taxes, and a, b, and c are perception parameters.

The innovative part of this model is the introduction of the perceived level of local services net of taxes. Clearly, state policymakers value the public services (summarized by G), such as highways and higher education, that they provide directly using state government employees. In addition, they derive value from the actions of local government officials. The challenge is to specify how they view local fiscal outcomes. The starting assumption for this model is that state policymakers' perception of local services depends on how they are financed. Assuming that the price of local services is $1 and that spending on local services is financed by three revenue sources—locally-generated taxes (LTAX), aid received from the state (STAID), and aid received from the federal government (FAID)—this assumption implies that states perceive the value of local services (LS) to be:

LS = STAID + a LTAX + b FAID

where a and b represent the values that state officials place on dollars of local spending (and hence services) financed by each revenue source relative to the value they place on local services financed with state aid. Consider first the valuation parameter b. In general, we would expect b to be less than one. That is, for most programs, we would expect state policymakers to value services financed by federal aid less highly than those services financed by state aid. This relative valuation is most clearly predicted when intergovernmental aid is restricted to narrowly-defined categorical programs. Because the programs targeted by federal aid are determined by national, rather than state policymakers, in most cases their value to state policymakers is likely to fall short of that for programs that the state has explicitly chosen. However, the more unrestricted are the aid programs, the less difference we would expect in the two valuation parameters. For example, state policymakers might value equally those local services financed by federal general revenue sharing and those financed by a state revenue sharing program.

The magnitude of the valuation parameter a is harder to predict. At one extreme, state policymakers might care little about the service level provided by local governments out of their own revenues. In this case, a would be close to zero. At the other extreme, state policymakers could view locally-financed services as perfect substitutes for services directly financed by the state. In this case, a would have the value 1. But there is more to the story. A value of 1 on locally-financed services would imply that states would have incentives to shift extensive responsibilities onto local governments, since locally-provided services would not consume scarce state budgetary resources. Hence, state policymakers must also care about the local tax burden; a higher local tax burden decreases the welfare of local taxpayers, who in turn may complain to state policymakers. Thus, a higher local tax burden has potential political costs and decreases the welfare of state policymakers. This addition leads to the concept of local services net of the local tax burden perceived by state policymakers (NLS):

$$NLS = STAID + a\,LTAX + b\,FAID - c\,LTAX$$
$$= STAID + (a - c)\,LTAX + b\,FAID$$

where c (defined as a positive number) represents the perceived political cost to state policymakers of local taxes. The expression $(a - c)$ represents the net value to state officials of local services financed by local taxes. If $a = c$, state officials are indifferent to the level of services that local governments provide out of their own resources.

If the state's welfare function is expressed in Cobb-Douglas form and certain other simplifying assumptions are made, this model yields an equation in which changes in state aid are a linear function of exogenous changes in state budgetary resources, exogenous changes in local own source revenues, and changes in federal aid to local governments. (See appendix for the details.) The model predicts first that changes in state aid are likely to be positively related to changes in state budgetary resources. Only a large offsetting reduction in local taxes combined with a high valuation of local public services relative to local tax reduction would alter this prediction. Second, the predicted effect of exogenous changes in local taxes depends directly on the value of $(a - c)$. If state policymakers place equal value on locally-financed public services and local tax reduction, local taxes will have no impact on the state aid decision. Third, the model predicts that changes in state aid will be negatively related to changes in federal aid to local governments, but that the offset will vary positively with the valuation parameter b. If b were equal to zero, no offset would be expected.

This model provides the basic framework for the empirical work presented below, justifies the linear form of the estimating equations, and helps one interpret the estimated coefficients.

Data and Equations

Equations are estimated for per capita changes (deflated by the national deflator for state and local public sector purchases) between 1982 and 1987 for 44 states. Alaska and Hawaii were excluded because their governmental structures differ significantly from those of other states, Wyoming was excluded because of its small size, and Louisiana because of its extreme fiscal stress during the period. Two other states—Arizona and Nevada—were excluded because of incomplete data.

The basic equation takes the following form:

$$STAID_i = \beta_0 + \beta_1\,SOSREV_i$$
$$+ \beta_2\,FEDSTOTH_i + \beta_3\,FEDSTSS_i$$
$$+ \beta_4\,BAL82_i + \beta_5\,LOSREV_i$$
$$+ \beta_5\,FAIDOTH_i + \beta_6\,FAIDSS_i + u_i$$

where all variables other than BAL82 are defined as per capita changes over the 1982–87 period. (See Table 1 for variable definitions, means, and standard deviations.) With a few important exceptions, most of the fiscal data come from the census publication, *Government Finances*.

The dependent variable takes four different forms, two of which are based not on census data but rather on survey data collected by the National Association of State Budget Officers (NASBO) for 1982 and 1987. These data are better suited than those from the Governments Division of the Census for two reasons. The first and most important is that the NASBO survey specifically asked state officials to exclude from their state aid figures aid passed through from the federal government. Second, NASBO collected data on the state takeover or assumption of local services between 1982 and 1987.[5] Courts and jails were the local service most commonly taken over by the states. Other services taken over in a few states include parks and recreation, high-

TABLE 1
VARIABLE NAMES, DEFINITIONS, MEANS AND STANDARD DEVIATIONS[a]

Variable	Definition	Mean	Standard Deviation
State Aid Variables			
NSTAID	Change in total state aid to local governments including state takeover of local services, per capita. 1982-87 in 1987 dollars. NASBO-1	$60.49	$66.65
CSTAID	Change in total state aid to local governments including NASBO information on state takeover of local services, per capita. 1982-87 in 1987 dollars. CENSUS-1,2.	$40.37	$58.08
NSTAIDU	Change in unrestricted state aid to local governments, per capita. 1982-87 in 1987 dollars. NASBO-1	$8.34	$19.56
CSTAIDGEN	Change in general-purpose state aid to local governments, per capita. 1982-87 in 1987 dollars. CENSUS-4,5.	$2.58	$22.02
Explanatory Variables			
SOSREV[b]	Change in state government own-source revenues excluding interest earnings, per capita. 1982-87 in 1987 dollars. CENSUS-1,2.	$185.04	$177.55
LOSREV[b]	Change in local government own-source revenues excluding interest earnings, per capita. 1982-87 in 1987 dollars. CENSUS-1,2.	$149.37	$79.74
BAL82	State general fund balances as a share of general fund expenditures in 1982. NASBO-2	0.04	0.08
FAIDOTH	Change in federal non-education and non-welfare aid to local governments, per capita. 1982-87 in 1987 dollars. CENSUS-1,2.	-$27.05	$17.58
FAIDSS	Change in federal education and welfare aid to local governments, per capita. 1982-87 dollars. CENSUS-1,2.	$1.22	$5.88

TABLE 1 (continued)
VARIABLE NAMES, DEFINITIONS, MEANS AND STANDARD DEVIATIONS*

Variable	Definition	Mean	Standard Deviation
FEDSTOTH	Change in federal non-education and non-welfare aid to the state government, per capita. 1982-87 in 1987 dollars. CENSUS-1,2.	$20.00	$20.63
FEDSTSS	Change in federal education and welfare aid to the state government, per capita. 1982-87 dollars. CENSUS-1,2.	$18.44	$25.42
Other Exogenous Instrumental Variables			
GSPPC	Change in gross state product, per capita. 1982-87 in 1987 dollars. SPT.	$671.00	$1475.00
CHUR	Change in state unemployment rate, in percentage points. 1982-87. SPT.	-3.25	2.10
POP	Change in state population as a fraction of 1982 population. 1982-87. SPT.	0.04	0.04
INCPC	Change in income per capita. 1982-87 in 1987 dollars. SPT.	$1511.00	$1115.00
MEDRECIP	Change in number of Medicaid recipients, as a fraction of 1982 recipients. 1982-86. HHS-1 and STABST-1.	0.04	0.15
PRISONERS	Change in number of adults in prisons and jails as a fraction of 1981 prisoners. 1981-86. STABST-1,2.	0.42	0.18
TAXEXP	Dummy for expansion of local tax authority. Takes on value 1 if number of local governments using local sales or income taxes increased by more than 10 percent between 1982 and 1987, and 0 otherwise. ACIR-2.	0.36	0.49
LIMITS	Dummy for stringent property tax limit. Takes on value 1 if state has enacted broad limitations on property tax levies since 1978, and 0 otherwise. ACIR-1.	0.32	0.47

TABLE 1 (continued)
VARIABLE NAMES, DEFINITIONS, MEANS AND STANDARD DEVIATIONS[a]

Variable	Definition	Mean	Standard Deviation
CRIME	Change in property crimes per 100,000 persons. 1982-87. SPT	-0.02	0.10
PUPILS	Percent change in fall public school enrollment, expressed as a decimal. 1982-87. NEA	-0.04	0.06
PROPBUR82	Property tax burden per $1000 of personal income. 1982 SPT	$0.39	$1.21
Other Variables			
FAIDOTHA	FAIDOTHA minus change in per capita general revenue sharing aid to local governments. 1982-87 jin 1987 dollars. CENSUS-1,2.	-$2.70	$17.37
GRS86	Change in general revenue sharing aid to local governments, per capita. 1981-86 in 1987 dollars. CENSUS-1,2.	-6.61	2.05
NSTAID82	Total state aid to local governments, per capita 1982 in 1987 dollars. NASBO-1	$393.75	$167.75
FAIDOTH80-82	Change in federal non-education and non-welfare aid to local governments, per capita. 1980-82 in 1987 dollars. CENSUS-2,3.	-$12.34	$14.10

Notes: [a] Source references listed at end of each definition refer to the appendix table on data sources
[b] Endogenous variables

way and street maintenance, food stamp administration, and portions of the local responsibility for medical services. Although not included in the census definition of state aid, state takeover of local expenditure responsibilities has effects that are very similar to those of grants and should not be ignored.[6]

A possible disadvantage of the NASBO data is that consistency across states cannot be fully assured. Although NASBO worked hard to insure that state officials defined state aid in a uniform manner, undoubtedly some nonuniformities remain. Within each state, however, the figures should be comparable over time and thus appropriate for this study of changes in state aid between 1982 and 1987. The two state aid variables based on this NASBO data are denoted NSTAID for the change in total state aid, adjusted upward to include expenditure takeovers, and NSTAIDU for unrestricted state aid. Unrestricted aid includes revenues from state income, sales, or cigarette taxes that are shared with local governments, general purpose aid, and payments in lieu of taxes.

For comparison purposes, regressions based on state aid data from the Census are also reported. The two relevant variables are denoted CSTAID for total state aid, adjusted upward by the state takeover amounts from the NASBO survey, and CSTAIDGEN for general purpose state aid. As defined by the Census Bureau, general purpose aid is the amount distributed to local governments without restriction of function or purpose. Table 1 indicates relatively large discrepancies between the two data sources, with the mean per capita change in the NASBO total aid figures exceeding that of the census figures by about 50 percent. Presumably, this discrepancy largely reflects the reduction in federal pass-through aid during this period.

The regressions use three measures of state budgetary resources: state government revenues from own sources excluding interest earnings (SOSREV), federal aid to the state for social services defined as welfare and education programs (FEDSTSS), and federal aid to the state government for all other purposes (FEDSTOTH), all of which are measured as per capita real changes and are available from annual census publications. In contrast to the stylized model in which state budgetary resources were assumed to be exogenous, in the estimated model, state revenues from own sources are assumed to be simultaneously determined with the level of state aid; a decision to give more aid to local governments could lead the state to increase its tax revenues. Thus, changes in state own-source revenues are treated as an endogenous variable in the state aid equation, which is estimated using two-stage least squares. However, federal aid to the state is treated as exogenous to the state aid decision. This treatment is most reasonable for the NASBO definition of state aid, which excludes the federal pass-through money.

In addition to the annual flow of its budgetary resources, the state's initial budgetary condition could also affect the state aid decision. This initial budgetary condition is measured by BAL82, which is defined as the 1982 General Fund balances as a fraction of 1982 expenditures as reported by the National Association of State Budget Officers.[7] States with higher balances are deemed to be in stronger financial health and in a better position to assist their local governments. Hence, a positive sign on the BAL82 coefficient is expected.

Changes in locally-generated revenues excluding interest earnings (LOSREV) are also treated as an endogenous variable, since changes in state aid are likely to lead to changes in locally-generated revenues. Changes in direct federal aid to local governments are exogenous to the state aid decision and in all the reported regressions are separated into two categories; federal aid for social services such as public welfare and education (FAIDSS), and federal aid for all other purposes including general revenue sharing (FAIDOTH). As shown in Table 1, the average change in the direct social services aid variable is tiny compared to the change in the other aid. The $27 per capita change in other aid largely reflects the 1986 elimination of general revenue sharing grants. As discussed below, however, most of the variation across states in this variable reflects not the changes in revenue sharing but rather the changes in federal aid programs in areas such as housing, highways, and natural resources.

The other variables listed in Table 1 are used either as instruments to identify the state and local own-source revenue variables in the state aid equation or to refine the model as discussed below.

Results—State Aid Equations

Table 2 summarizes the basic regression results for the state aid regressions. These equations were estimated using two-stage least squares with the full set of instrumental variables listed at the bottom of the table. Appendix Table A1 reports a similar set of results based on a more limited set of instrumental variables.[8] Col-

STATE AID DECISION

TABLE 2
STATE AID TO LOCAL GOVERNMENTS: ESTIMATED EQUATIONS
(Per Capita Changes, 1982–87)

	NSTAID State Aid Total (NASBO) (1)	CSTAID State Aid Total (CENSUS) (2)	NSTAIDU State Aid Unrestricted (NASBO) (3)	CSTAIDGEN State Aid General Purpose (CENSUS) (4)
Endogenous Variables				
SOSREV	0.296** (4.23)	0.217** (2.87)	0.044** (1.60)	0.038 (1.27)
LOSREV	0.114 0.83	0.066 (0.44)	-0.032 (0.58)	-0.030 (0.51)
Exogenous Variables				
FAIDOTH	-0.979** (2.06)	-0.951** (1.86)	-0.240 (1.29)	-0.380** (1.89)
FAIDSS	-0.166 (0.10)	1.812 (1.01)	0.735 (1.13)	0.155 (0.22)
FEDSTOTH	0.152 (0.39)	0.214 (0.51)	-0.044 (0.29)	-0.119 (0.72)
FEDSTSS	0.424* (1.38)	1.812 (1.02)	-0.082 (0.68)	-0.098 (0.744)
BAL82	167.22* (1.34)	161.27 (1.20)	45.83 (0.93)	72.99* (1.38)
Constant	-54.48* (1.56)	-46.55 (1.24)	-1.67 (0.12)	-8.89 (0.60)
R^2	.54	.29	.17	.23
Mean Square Error	49.64	53.48	19.49	21.15
F-Statistic	5.93 (p=0.00)	2.10 (p=0.04)	1.04 (p=0.40)	1.51 (p=0.16)

Notes: Estimated by two-stage least squares; absolute value of t-statistics in parentheses; two asterisks (**) and one asterisk (*) denote coefficient is statistically significant at the 5% and 10% one-tailed levels, respectively. The instruments used to identify SOSREV and LOSREV are GSPPC, CHUR, POP, INCPC, MEDRECIP, PRISONERS, TAXEXP, LIMITS, CRIME, PUPILS, PROPBUR82.

umns 1 and 2 refer to total state aid, while 3 and 4 refer to unrestricted aid. Looking initially at column 1, the preferred regression, we see that the results are reasonable and consistent with the theoretical model. As predicted, the main measure of state budgetary resources (SOSREV) has a positive impact on state aid; the major direct federal aid variable (FAIDOTH) enters with a negative sign; and changes in the locally-generated revenue variable (LOSREV), the predicted coefficient of which depended on the relative values of locally-financed services and local taxes to state policymakers, has a coefficient that is statistically indistinguishable from zero.[9] In brief, these results imply that state budgetary resources affect the local aid decision, that states almost fully offset changes in non-social service aid to local governments, and that the value to state policymakers of additional locally-financed public services is balanced by the political costs of higher local taxes.

Column 2 shows results for CSTAID, which is based on the census definition of state aid. With some minor differences, the results are quite similar to those in column 1. In general, the equations for unrestricted or general aid in columns 3 and 4 have less explanatory power than those for total aid, but have signs and magnitudes that, given the smaller quantities of aid, are roughly comparable to those for total aid.

State Response to Changes in Federal Aid to Local Governments

The estimated response of total state aid to changes in direct federal aid to local governments is striking. The -0.98 coefficient for FAIDOTH implies that between 1982 and 1987, state governments on average offset each 1 dollar decline in federal aid (other than that for education and public welfare) to local governments by increasing state aid by 98 cents. This result represents a larger offset that has been found in previous studies. The results in column 2 confirm that this finding is not a quirk of the NASBO data. Even when the census measure of state aid is used, the average estimated offset is more than 95 cents per dollar decline in federal aid. As shown in columns 3 and 4, between 24 and 38 cents of the offset is in the form of unrestricted or general aid. The rest is in the form either of monetary grants restricted to particular functions or state assumption of certain local spending responsibilites.

The finding that states offset almost on a dollar-for-dollar basis changes in non-education and non-public welfare federal aid is surprising and deserves further discussion. First, the response should not be interpreted as the state response to the elimination of general revenue sharing. Instead it represents the response to changes in a variety of other federal programs that were cut throughout the 1982–87 period. As readers of an earlier version of this paper pointed out, the 1986 elimination of federal revenue sharing occurred after states had already put together their 1987 budgets. Although states could have adopted 1987 budgets that anticipated the elimination of revenue sharing, people familiar with state governments argue that few states behaved in this way.[10] Moreover, the similarity in the changes in revenue sharing across states makes it unlikely that there would be sufficient variation to yield precise estimates of the state behavioral response to its elimination.

In light of these observations, the basic regression was rerun with FAIDOTH replaced by FAIDOTHA, defined as per capita changes in federal aid other than education, public welfare, and general revenue sharing, and GRS86, changes in per capita general revenue sharing lagged one year. The results for the new aid variables are shown in the second section of Table 3. The coefficient of the new other federal aid variable falls to $-.871$ but is still significant at the 5 percent one-tailed level, while the coefficient of the 1981–86 changes in general revenue sharing is not significant.[11]

Second, the data do not support two competing explanations for the large estimated response. One alternative explanation relates to the fact that the variables are all expressed as absolute rather than percentage changes. Assume, for example, that all states increase their aid at approximately the same rate and do not vary their aid in response to changes in federal aid. Then if it were the case that the states providing the largest amounts of state aid also faced the largest cutbacks in federal aid to local governments, a negative sign on the federal aid variable would emerge despite the assumed lack of behavioral response. This alternative explanation was ruled out by adding to the equation the 1982 level of per capita state aid (NSTAID82). As shown in section 3 of Table 3, its coefficient is virtually zero and the coefficient of the federal aid variable hardly changes. An alternative explanation posits that between

TABLE 3
IMPACT ON ESTIMATED STATE RESPONSE
TO FEDERAL AID OF ALTERNATIVE SPECIFICATIONS[a]

	Variable	Regression Coefficient (absolute value of t-statistic)
1.	FAIDOTH	-0.979** (2.06)
2.	FAIDOTHA	-0.871** (1.79)
	GRS86	1.089 (0.23)
3.	FAIDOTHA	-0.887** (1.84)
	NSTAID82	0.030 (0.57)
4.	FAIDOTHA	-0.843** (1.73)
	FAIDOTH80-82	0.360 (0.592)

Note: [a] Each entry represents the estimated coefficient of the designated variable (and absolute value of its t-statistic) in an NSTAID equation of the form presented in column 1 Table 2. Two asterisks (**) denote that the coefficient is statistically at the 5% one-tailed level.

1982 and 1987, states could have been responding not only to the changes in federal aid during that period but also to the large reductions in federal aid prior to 1982. To test for this possibility, the change in other federal aid between 1980 and 1982 (FAIDOTH80-82) was added to the equation. Table 4 shows that this new variable has a small and insignificant coefficient and that the coefficient of FAIDOTHA is only slightly reduced. Hence, we maintain our previous conclusion that states offset a large portion of changes in non-education and non-public welfare direct aid to local governments between 1982 and 1987.

The findings differ for the other federal aid variable. The small negative coefficient on FAIDSS in the NSTAID regression is reasonable, but imprecisely estimated. Taken at its face value, it suggests that during the 1982-87 period, state governments essentially offset none of the decline in direct federal aid to local governments for education and social services. In terms of the theoretical model, this finding is consistent with state officials placing a low value on certain locally-provided services financed by the federal government. Thus, while state officials clearly value education and social services in general (as is evident from high state spending in those areas), they apparently place little value on the specific local programs financed by the federal government, such as impact act and aid for students in disadvantaged households. The large positive (but statistically insignificant) coefficient for this variable in the CSTAID equation probably reflects the inclusion of federal pass-through aid in the CSTAID variable; in states where local governments take on substantial responsibility for social services, local governments are likely to receive above-average amounts of direct federal aid for social services as well as above-average amounts of federal pass-through funds.

TABLE 4
RESPONSIVENESS OF STATE AID TO STATE OWN SOURCE REVENUES

	Estimated Elasticity	
	From Table 2	From Table A1
NSTAID	.77	.78
CSTAID	.51	.51
NSTAIDU	.99	1.05
CSTAIDGEN	.84	.99

Note: Based on the coefficients of SOSREV from Table 2 and Table A1 multiplied by the average level of per capita state own-source revenues (calculated as 1982 plus 1987 revenues divided by 2) and divided by the average level of per capita aid (calculated as 1982 plus 1987 aid divided by 2) for each aid category.

State Response to Changes in Budgetary Resources

Both total and unrestricted aid vary positively with the growth in state own-source revenues. For each 1 dollar increase in state revenues, total state aid increases by about 30 cents using the NASBO definition and about 22 cents using the census definition. The smaller coefficient for the census variable is explained by the fact that the federal pass-through funds that are included in the census variable are likely to be less responsive to the budgetary condition of the state than is state aid financed from own sources.

Table 4 translates the estimated coefficients into response elasticities using mean values of average state own-source revenues and state aid. Elasticities are reported both for the preferred set of equations in Table 2 and those in Table A1. The interesting result is that the elasticities for total aid are all below 1. In particular, a 10-percent increase in state own-source revenues, associated for example with growth in the state economy, leads to about a 7.7 percent increase in state aid. Once again, the lower .51 estimate for the census variable reflects its inclusion of pass-through funds. In contrast to the results for total aid, the elasticities for unrestricted or general aid are close to one. These higher elasticities emerge because much of this unrestricted aid takes the form of shared state tax revenues that are expected to grow at the same rate as other state tax revenues. The lesson for local officials is that they are more likely to share in the growth of the state economy when aid is in the form of shared taxes than when it is dependent on state appropriations.

Another component of state budgetary resources is federal aid to the state government. As shown near the bottom of Table 2, most of the coefficients on the two state federal aid variables (FEDSTOTH and FEDSTSS) are small and insignificant, signifying little impact of such aid on the state aid decision. In none of the equations does FEDSTOTH have any discernible effect on state aid. This finding suggests that the federal government should not expect state governments to act as its agents in assisting local governments to provide services other than social services. The positive coefficient of the social service aid variable (which includes aid for education and public welfare) in the NSTAID equation is somewhat surprising, given that pass-through aid is not included, and deserves further investigation.

Finally, as expected, the general fund balances variable (BAL82) enters all the equations with a positive sign. These results suggest that the stronger is a state's financial condition at the beginning of the period, the more additional assistance it is able to give to its local governments in following years. At the risk of drawing too strong a conclusion from imprecisely estimated coefficients, this finding suggests that when local governments rely heavily on state aid, they become vulnerable to the vagaries of state government financial management and fiscal pressures.

Discussion and Conclusion

The analysis in this paper is based on changes in state aid to local governments between 1982 and 1987. This period was determined by the availability of the NASBO data and represents a time of large changes in federal aid to state and local governments. Unfortunately, states were not in equilibrium in 1982. Not only had they just experienced major cuts in federal aid, but also the economy was in deep recession. But how that disequilibrium affects the behavioral estimates reported here is unclear. In general, one is hard pressed to predict in which direction, if any, widespread disequilibrium would bias the estimated elasticities of state aid with respect to changes in state revenues. Moreoever, the 1982 General Fund balance variable helps control for differences across states in their 1982 fiscal condition, thereby minimizing potential biases associated with variation in the degree of fiscal disequilibrium across states. The question of bias with respect to the responsiveness of state aid to changes in direct federal aid to localities has already been addressed; the inclusion in the equation of the 1980 to 1982 changes in federal aid has little or no effect on the results. In summary, while the 1982 starting year is potentially problematic, I am not persuaded that it has much impact on the behavioral estimates reported here.

The model of the state aid decision developed in this paper sheds light on five policy issues related to the understudied question of state aid to local governments. First, the elasticity of total state aid with respect to state own-source revenue appears to be less than one. Thus, during the period of the study, the growth in state economies and exogenously determined state tax revenues was not translated into proportionate increases in state aid to local governments. Only when aid is in the form of shared taxes rather than annual appropriations do local governments share fully in the growth of the state economy. Second, the equations suggest that changes in the amount of state aid appear to be influenced by the state's initial financial condition. Together, these two findings suggest that local governments have good reason to be wary of becoming too dependent on state governments for their revenue.

Third, state governments apparently do not view federal aid to the state government as general funds from which they can provide additional aid to local governments. Such aid appears to be used primarily for state direct expenditures rather than for state aid to local governments. Federal aid to states, therefore, is not an effective way for the federal government to assist local governments.

A fourth and surprising (to me at least) conclusion is that state governments apparently were quite responsive to changes in certain types of direct federal aid to local governments; in particular they appear to have offset each dollar change in federal aid by changing their own aid to local governments by more than 80 cents in the other direction. As noted earlier, the conclusions from previous research on this issue have been mixed. This new finding implies that the cutbacks in federal aid to local governments during the early 1980s put significant pressure on state government finances.

Fifth, the estimated equations are consistent with the view that between 1982 and 1987 state policymakers on average paid little attention to changes in local own source revenues in making state aid decisions. One possible explanation is that during this period the value they placed on locally-financed public services was offset on average by the costs they experienced from local taxes. An alternative explanation is that state policymakers placed little or no value either on the services financed locally or on the taxes used to pay for those local services.

The strength of this study is that it focuses on changes in, rather than levels of, state aid. As emphasized in the introduction, historically rooted differences across states in the distribution of responsibilities between state and local governments make it difficult to explain variation in levels of aid across states. The limitation of this study is that it is based on a single cross section of changes. A larger panel data set would produce a larger sample and more variation in the explanatory variables. Consequently, the larger panel data set would allow for a richer set of hypotheses to be explored. Of particular interest might be hypotheses about asymmetric responses. For example, with a larger panel data set one might be able to explore whether the elasticities reported in Table 4 are applicable to a declining economy as well as to the expanding economy examined in this paper or whether states respond differently to changes in federal aid when that aid is increasing than when it is decreasing as it was between 1982 and 1987.

ENDNOTES

**An earlier version of this paper was completed while I was a Senior Fellow at the Lincoln Institute of Land Policy. I appreciate the support of the Institute and also want to thank Linda McCarthy for assistance with data collection, Jerry Miller and Karen Farrell of the National Association of State Budget Officers for help with the NASBO data, and three referees of this journal.

[1] This and the following numbers in this paragraph were calculated from U.S. Department of Commerce, Bureau of the Census, *Government Finances in 1986-87*, Table 29.

[2] See Gramlich and Galper (1973) for a model of state and local budgetary decisions and a careful analysis of the different types of federal aid.

[3] A recent study for the U.S. Treasury determined that for a sample of 10 states, non-education pass-through aid accounted for about 20 percent of non-education state aid. This ratio varied from a low of 7 percent in Illinois to a high of 41 percent in Minnesota. Because education aid accounts for about 60 percent of all state aid, this 20 percent translates into about 8 percent of total aid. Added to this would be small amounts of education pass-through aid. Thus, on average pass-through aid probably accounts for about 10 percent of state aid to local governments but this percentage varies substantially across states because of differing divisions of responsibilities between state and local governments. See Fiscal Planning Services, 1986.

[4] Craig and Inman's failure to include other direct federal aid to local governments for education in their 1986 paper is perplexing. Also curious is their failure to include federal general revenue sharing aid to local governments in either of their models. Despite the fact that revenue sharing was distributed to general-purpose governments rather than school districts, the logic of their overall state decision models would seem to call for the inclusion of local revenue sharing as an explanatory variable.

[5] In fact, the NASBO survey reported figures as of 1988 in 1988 dollars, but these were adjusted back to 1987 dollars for this study. During the 1982–87 period, state takeovers as a fraction of total 1987 state aid (including these takeovers) varies from 0 in most states to 13 percent in New Hampshire, which assumed responsibility for children and youth placement services. In evaluating this New Hampshire figure, the small amount of regular state aid should be kept in mind. In most other states, state assumptions accounted for less than 5 percent of total aid in 1987.

[6] Yinger and Ladd (1990) show that state assistance to central cities through grants and through the design of fiscal institutions are substitutes. Assistance through institutions includes state takeover of spending responsibilities such as welfare or the courts and the expansion of local taxing authority. In their cross-sectional analysis of state assistance to 70 major central cities in 1982, Yinger and Ladd find that each dollar difference in institutional assistance leads to a 40 cent offsetting difference in state grants and that each dollar difference in state aid leads to an 88 cent offsetting difference in institutional assistance.

[7] These figures are superior to those reported by the National Conference of State Legislatures in that they reflect revisions made after the end of the fiscal year. These balances do not include money in budget stabilization funds, because such information is not readily available for 1982; NASBO did not begin reporting information about budget stablization funds until 1984.

[8] My strategy was first to include as identifying instruments all the additional exogenous variables that might influence the change in either state or local own source revenues. For state own-source revenues, these variables included changes in per capita gross state product (GSPPC) and in the state unemployment rate (CHUR) to represent the condition of the state economy and changes in state population (POP), in Medicaid recipients (MEDRECIP), and in adults in prisons and jails (PRISONERS) to represent pressures on state government spending. For local own-source revenues, the variables included changes in per capita income (INCPC), changes in population (POP), expanded use of sales and income taxes (TAXEXP), the

existence of limits on the growth of local property tax levies (LIMITS), changes in school enrollments (PUPILS), changes in the state's crime rate (CRIME), and the level of property taxes as a fraction of income in 1982 (PROPBUR82). The variables that turned out to be insignificant in structural equations for SOSREV and LOSREV were then excluded from the smaller set of instruments used in the appendix table.

All the identifying instruments met the two-fold basic test for exogeneity, namely (1) the variable does not belong in the state aid equation, and (2) conditional on (1), it is not correlated with the error term. See Lugar and Stahl (1986) and Hausman (1978).

[9] Note that the asterisks in the table refer to statistical significance based on one-tailed tests. The decision to use one-tailed tests reflects the fact that the model predicts specific signs for the key variables and that the relatively small sample size yields less precise estimates than would a larger sample.

[10] This statement is based on information from Steven Gold of the National Conference of State Legislatures and on information published by the National Association of State Budget Officers in their annual *Fiscal Survey of the States.*

[11] As indicated by the summary statistics in Table 2, FEDOTHA did not decline in all states. In fact, the interquartile range is from −$9.29 to +$8.99.

REFERENCES

Break, George F. 1980. *Financing Government in a Federal System.* Washington D.C.: Brookings Institution.

Craig, Steven G. and Robert P. Inman. 1982. "Federal Aid and Public Education: An Empirical Look at the New Fiscal Federalism," *Review of Economics and Statistics.* LXIV, 4 (November 1982): 541–552.

Craig, Steven G. and Robert P. Inman. 1986. "Federalism, Welfare, and the "New" Federalism: State Budgeting in a Federalist Public Economy." In Harvey S. Rosen, ed. *Studies in State and Local Public Finance.* Chicago: The University of Chicago Press.

Cuciti, Peggy. 1990. "A Non-Urban Policy: Recent Policy Shifts Affecting Cities." In Marshall Kaplan and Franklin James, eds., *The Future of National Urban Policy.* Durham, N.C.: Duke University Press. pp. 235–250.

Ellwood, John William. 1982. *Reductions in U.S. Domestic Spending.* New Brunswick, New Jersey: Transaction Books.

Fiscal Planning Services, Inc. 1986. "The Local Distribution of Federal Pass-Through Grants-in-Aid:

An Empirical Study of Ten States." In US. Department of the Treasury, Office of State and Local Finance, *Federal-State-Local Fiscal Relations: Technical Papers,* Vol. II.

Gold, Steven D. 1990. "State Finances in the New Era of Fiscal Federalism." In Thomas Swartz, ed., *The Changing Face of Fiscal Federalism.* M. E. Sharpe.

Gold, Steven D. and Brenda M. Erickson. "State Aid to Local Governments in the 1980s," *State and Local Government Review.* Winter 1989: 11–22.

Gramlich, Edward M. and Harvey Galper. 1973. "State and Local Fiscal Behavior and Federal Grant Policy," *Brookings Papers on Economic Activity.* 15–65.

Hausman, J. A. 1978. "Specification Tests in Econometrics," Econometrica, 46 (6), 1251–1271.

Inman, Robert P. 1979. "The Fiscal Performance of Local Governments: An Interpretive Review." In P. Mieszkowski and M. Straszheim, eds., *Current Issues in Urban Economics.* Baltimore: Johns Hopkins University Press, pp. 270–321.

Ladd, Helen F. 1984. "Federal Aid to State and Local Governments." In Gregory B. Mills and John L. Palmer, eds., *Federal Budget Policy in the 1980s.* Washington, D.C.: Urban Institute Press.

Ladd, Helen F. 1990. "State Assistance to Local Governments: Changes During the 1980s." *American Economic Review,* vol 80, no 2 (May), pp. 171–175.

Ladd, Helen F. 1990. "State Aid to Local Governments in the 1980s." Working paper. Lincoln Institute of Land Policy. Cambridge, Massachusetts.

Lugar, Michael I. and Dale O. Stahl, II. 1986. "Specification Errors in Models of Aggregate Labor Supply," *The Review of Economics and Statistics,* LXVIII (2), pp. 274–283.

Nathan, Richard P. and Fred C. Doolittle. 1983. *The Consequences of Cuts.*

Nathan, Richard P., Fred C. Doolittle, and Associates. 1987. *Reagan and the States.* Princeton, N. J.: Princeton University Press.

Peterson, George. 1982. "The State and Local Sector." In John Palmer and Isabel Sawhill, eds., *The Reagan Experiment.* Washington, D. C.: The Urban Institute Press, pp. 157–218.

Peterson, George et al. 1986. *The Reagan Block Grants.* Washington, D. C.: The Urban Institute Press.

Shapiro, Perry. 1981. "Popular Response to Public Spending Disequilibrium: An Analysis of the 1978 California Property Tax Limitation Initiative." In Helen F. Ladd and T. Nicolaus Tideman, eds., *Tax and Expenditure Limitations.* Washington, D. C.: The Urban Institute Press.

Yinger, John and Helen F. Ladd. 1990. "The Determinants of State Assistance to Central Cities." *National Tax Journal,* vol. XLII, no. 4, 1990, pp. 413–28.

DATA SOURCES

Fiscal Data

NASBO-1 — National Association of State Budget Officers. 1989 survey of state aid to local governments (includes data for 1982 and 1987).

NASBO-2 — National Association of State Budget Officers. Information on year-end General Fund Balances and Total Expenditures, annually.

CENSUS-1 — U.S. Department of Commerce, Bureau of the Census, *Government Finances in 1986–87,* Series GF-87-5. Washington, D.C.: USGPO (1988). Table 29.

CENSUS-2	U.S. Department of Commerce, Bureau of the Census, *Governmental Finances in 1981–82*, Series GF82, No. 5. Washington, D.C.: USGPO (1983). Tables 5 and 13.
CENSUS-3	U.S. Department of Commerce, Bureau of the Census, *Governmental Finances in 1979–80*, Series GF 82, No. 5. Washington D.C.: USGPO (1981), Table 5.
CENSUS-4	U.S. Department of Commerce, Bureau of the Census, *State Government Finances in 1982*, Series GF82, No. 3. Washington, D.C.: USGPO (1988). Table 11.
CENSUS-5	U.S. Department of Commerce, Bureau of the Census, *State Government Finances in 1987*, GF-87-3. Washington, D.C.: USGPO (1988). Table 14.

Other Data

SPT	State Policy Trends—Data on diskettes from Brizius & Foster, McConnellsburg, PA. Source for population, per capita income, gross state product, property tax burden in 1982, unemployment rate and crime rate.
NEA	National Education Association—fall enrollments in public schools.
ACIR-1	U.S. Advisory Commission on Intergovernmental Relations, *Significant Features of Fiscal Federalism*, 1984 edition, M-141. Washington, D.C.: USGPO (1985), Table 93. Source for data on property tax limits.
ACIR-2	U.S. Advisory Commission on Intergovernmental Relations, *Significant Features of Fiscal Federalism*, 1988 Edition, Vol. 1, M-155. Washington, D.C.: USGPO (1987). Tables 19 and 23.
HHS-1	U.S. Department of Health and Human Services, *Medicare and Medicaid Data Book*, 1984. Washington, D.C.: USGPO. Source for Medicaid recipients in 1982.
STABST-1	U.S. Department of Commerce, Bureau of the Census, *Statistical Abstract of the United States: 1988*. Washington, D. C.: USGPO (1987). Table 578. Source for Medicaid recipients and prisoners in 1986.
STABST-2	U.S. Department of Commerce, Bureau of the Census, *Statistical Abstract of the United States: 1984*. Washington, D.C.: USGPO (1983). Table 320. Source for prisoners in 1981.
STABST-3	U.S. Department of Commerce, Bureau of the Census, *Statistical Abstract of the United States: 1989*. Washington, D.C.: USGPO (1988). Table 321. Source for prisoners in 1986.

Appendix—The Model

Assuming for simplicity that state policymakers' preferences are defined by a Cobb-Douglas welfare function, the state policymakers' problem is to

Maximize $W = G^a NLS^\beta$

Subject to

$B = G + STAID$

$NLS = STAID + (a - c) LTAX + b FAID$

$LTAX = f(STAID, X)$ with

$\delta LTAX / \delta STAID \leq 0$

where G is direct state services, NLS is the perceived level of local services net of the state political costs of local taxes, B is state budgetary resources, STAID is state aid to local governments, LTAX is local taxes, FAID is federal aid to local governments, and X is a vector of exogenous determinants of local taxes.

Based on this formulation, the state government can "buy" more net local spending by providing additional aid to local governments. The price to the state of purchasing an additional dollar of net local spending is

$1/(1 + (a - c) \delta LTAX / \delta STAID)$.

Consider the following special cases. Assume first that $(a - c)$ is zero so that the value state policymakers place on locally-financed public services is fully offset by the political cost to the state of the local taxes used to finance those services. In this case, the price of obtaining more local services through additional state aid is one dollar. An additional dollar of state aid raises the level of net local services, as perceived by state policymakers, by one dollar in this case because state policymakers are indifferent to how the local governments use the grant money. If in contrast, $(a - c)$ exceeds zero, that is, the value to state policymakers of local services exceeds the political cost to them of higher local taxes, then the price to the state of an additional dollar of net local services is greater than one dollar. How much greater it is depends on how much the local governments reduce their own taxes in response to the aid. Because of the local offset, the state government must devote more than one dollar to local aid to increase net local services by one dollar. If $(a - c)$ is less than zero, the price to the state of increasing net local services could be less than 1 dollar. This result reflects the high value the state would be placing on local tax reduction.

Taking the total differential of the first order conditions and assuming that (δLTAX/δSTAID) is constant yields the following equation:

$$dSTAID = \delta \left(\frac{1 + (a - c)\frac{\delta LTAX}{\delta STAID}}{Z} \right) dB$$

$$- \frac{\alpha(a - c)\frac{\delta LTAX}{\delta X}}{Z} dX - \frac{\alpha b}{Z} dFAID$$

where d denotes the differential and $(Z) = \alpha +$
$\beta \left(1 + (a - c)\frac{\delta LTAX}{\delta STAID} \right)$.

Rewriting δLTAX/δX dX as dLTAX*, where dLTAX* designates the change in local taxes resulting from change in the exogenous variable X, yields

$$dSTAID = \beta \left(\frac{1 + (a - c)\frac{\delta LTAX}{\delta STAID}}{Z} \right) dB$$

$$- \frac{\alpha(a - c)}{Z} dLTAX^* - \frac{\alpha b}{Z} dFAID.$$

In general, the denominator is expected to be positive.[1] Hence the model predicts first that changes in state aid are likely to be positively related to changes in the state budget. Only a large offsetting reduction in local taxes combined with a high valuation of local public services relative to local tax reduction could alter this prediction. Second, the predicted effect of exogenous changes in local taxes depends directly on the value of $(a - c)$. If state policymakers place equal value on locally-financed public services and local tax reduction, local taxes will have no impact on the state aid decision. Third, the model predicts that changes in state aid will be negatively related to changes in federal aid.

[1] If $(a - c)$ is less than or equal to 0, the sign is unambiguously positive. If $(a - c)$ is greater than 0, the sign is positive provided that $(a - c) \delta$LTAX/δSTAID ≥ -1.

TABLE A1
STATE AID TO LOCAL GOVERNMENTS
(Per Capita Changes, 1982–87)

	NSTAID State Aid Total (NASBO) (1)	CSTAID State Aid Total (CENSUS) (2)	NSTAIDU State Aid Unrestricted (NASBO) (3)	CSTAIDGEN State Aid General Purpose (CENSUS) (4)
Endogenous Variables				
SOSREV	0.302** (4.17)	0.219** (2.80)	0.047* (1.67)	0.045* (1.47)
LOSREV	0.126 (0.85)	0.100 (0.61)	0.030 (0.52)	-0.033 (0.51)
Exogenous Variables				
FAIDOTH	-0.99** (2.05)	-0.98** (1.88)	-0.240 (1.28)	-0.38** (1.84)
FAIDSS	-0.097 (0.05)	1.83 (1.02)	0.77 (1.18)	0.253 (0.35)
FEDSTOTH	0.149 (0.38)	0.212 (0.50)	-0.045 (0.30)	-0.122 (0.74)
FEDSTSS	0.430* (1.39)	-0.037 (0.11)	-0.081 (0.66)	-0.098 (0.74)
BAL82	174.42* (1.39)	167.58 (1.23)	49.48 (1.00)	80.36* (1.50)
Constant	-57.90* (1.62)	-53.25 (1.37)	-2.68 (0.19)	-9.99 (0.65)
R^2	.53	.28	.17	.23
Mean Square Error	49.81	53.92	19.50	21.19
F-Statistic	5.85 (p=0.00)	1.98 (p=0.05)	1.03 (p=0.40)	1.50 (p=0.16)

Notes: Estimated by two-stage least squares with small set of instruments; absolute value of t-statistics in parentheses; two asterisks (**) and one asterisk (*) denote coefficient is statistically significant at the 5% and 10% one-tailed levels, respectively. The instruments used to identify SOSREV and LOSREV are GSPPCC, INCPC, POP, TAXEXP, LIMITS, and PUPILS.

PART II

TAX STRUCTURE AND TAX LIMITATIONS

STATE TAX STRUCTURE AND MULTIPLE POLICY OBJECTIVES

WILLIAM M. GENTRY* & HELEN F. LADD**

Abstract - We use a portfolio model of state tax structure to examine how a state's economy and the nature of its taxes affect the choices available to state policymakers. Data from North Carolina and Massachusetts indicate that the income tax is the dominant tax in both states, that the two states differ in the nature of the trade-offs between characteristics such as growth and instability and between progressivity and instability, and that differences in the economies of the two states and their characteristics lead to differing prescriptions about the optimal mix of taxes. We conclude that policy recommendations about state tax structures may not be transferable across states.

INTRODUCTION

The goals of tax policy are typically to provide a fair, efficient, and predictable means of financing government expenditure. To achieve these multiple objectives, policymakers choose a mix of taxes. Separately, each tax has its own

*Department of Economics, Duke University, Durham, NC 27708-0097.
**Sanford Institute of Public Policy, Duke University, Durham, NC 27708-0243.

characteristics of fairness, efficiency, and predictability. Together, the properties of each tax and the interactions between the taxes determine the characteristics of the tax system. These characteristics of the overall tax system are the starting point for our analysis of state decisions about the composition of state taxes. Specifically, we view state policymakers as having preferences over the characteristics of the tax system, which in turn generate a demand for specific taxes. The desired mix of taxes will vary from one state to another, both because of differences in policy preferences and because of variation across states in the characteristics of individual taxes and how they interact with the state economy.

We focus our attention on two states—Massachusetts and North Carolina—and four characteristics of state tax structures. Our goal is to compare and contrast the characteristics of different possible tax structures for each state and the choices made by the two states. The four characteristics are revenue growth, stability, equity, and competitiveness with other states.[1] Each of these characteristics is likely to be important to state policymakers who are faced with the challenge of raising money to finance public services with limited information about the future of the economy and how agents will respond to a given tax structure. Because short-term changes in the tax system generate political and economic costs, revenue shortfalls or excesses impose costs on policymakers. Hence, policymakers will strive to design a tax system that provides growth in revenue that corresponds to the predicted growth in expenditures and provides a stable source of revenue. Equity is clearly of concern, although the acceptable amount of progressivity will typically vary from one state to another. Competitiveness with other states loosely accords with notions of economic efficiency in that a tax burden that is out of line with those of other states can create economic distortions.

As a methodology for comparing the characteristics of different tax structures, we use a portfolio choice model of tax structure. Pioneered by White (1983) for Georgia, this approach modifies the portfolio model of finance theory to construct an efficiency frontier to depict the trade-off between revenue growth and stability in a state's tax structure.[2] Using data from New York, Harmon and Mallick (1994) extend White's methodology to include equity considerations. Our analysis advances this line of research further by incorporating into the analysis a broader set of characteristics, directly comparing two states, and addressing three specific policy questions: What is the mix of state taxes in an efficient portfolio? What changes in its tax mix are required for the state to move to its frontier? And are there trade-offs between policy goals?

Our research is motivated in part by the observation that economists have devoted considerable attention to the characteristics of individual taxes, but little attention to the broader question of the appropriate mix of taxes within a governmental jurisdiction. In addition, it is motivated by previous policy prescriptions of the Advisory Commission on Intergovernmental Relations (ACIR). Kleine and Shannon (1986) and Shannon (1987) recommend that states adopt relatively uniform state-local tax structures and that these structures be balanced in the sense that about one-third of tax revenues come from each of three major taxes—property, sales, and income. Ladd and Weist (1987) counter that neither recommendation necessarily improves tax policy. If the composition of economic activity or the value that policymakers place on different tax policy goals varies across states, then variation, rather than uniformity, in state tax structures is appropriate. Furthermore, data suggest that moving toward a more balanced state tax structure will not promote the standard goals of tax policy in all states. Missing from the Ladd and Weist analysis was a comprehensive and integrated model, such as a portfolio choice model, of the state tax decision. As developed further below, our analysis based on such a model supports the Ladd and Weist conclusion that tax structures need not be similar across states.

We begin by comparing the portfolio approach to other models of tax structure. The following section describes the characteristics of state tax structures in North Carolina and Massachusetts. Subsequent sections describe the derivation of the efficiency frontier, compare the frontiers for Massachusetts and North Carolina, and discuss the policy implications of the results. We end with a brief evaluation of the portfolio approach.

COMPARISON OF THE PORTFOLIO MODEL WITH OTHER MODELS OF TAX STRUCTURE

The centerpiece of the portfolio approach is the derivation of a frontier that depicts the trade-offs among characteristics of a state's tax system. Thus, the focus is on how the tax structure interacts with the state economy to constrain the choices available to state policymakers. As the approach has been implemented by others and as we implement it in this paper, the preferences of the policymakers among the characteristics are left unspecified. Hence, most of the conclusions about whether one portfolio of taxes is better than another are conditional on the specification of one of the characteristics, such as the growth rate of revenue, and on the reasonable assumption that certain characteristics, such as equity, are desirable and others, such as instability, are undesirable.

The main alternative to the portfolio approach is optimal taxation theory (see Auerbach (1985) and the references therein). According to this theory, an optimal tax structure maximizes an explicit social welfare function, defined as some aggregation of the welfare of individuals. Underlying the approach is the view that tax-induced inefficiencies are potentially large and must be considered in the design of policy. Standard optimal tax models prescribe a tax system by specifying (1) a model of economic behavior based on consumer preferences, technology, and market structure (almost always perfect competition), which generates the deadweight loss associated with taxes; and (2) a social welfare function, which captures equity concerns. While these models have offered numerous theoretical insights into the design of a tax system, their level of abstraction limits practical implementation.[3] Measuring the full efficiency losses associated with taxes requires a large amount of information on preferences and technology and empirical estimates of how people respond to taxes. Moreover, although the social welfare function succinctly models fairness, its usefulness depends on the analyst's ability to specify the concavity of society's welfare function.

Compared to the optimal tax models, the portfolio approach requires less information and puts less emphasis on economic efficiency. Instead of requiring a full specification of behavioral responses to taxes and the parameters of the social welfare function, the portfolio approach can be based on the historical interaction of different taxes with the state's economy and simple measures of progressivity to capture equity considerations. Although additional information on behavioral responses to taxes could beneficially be incorporated into the portfolio model, its absence does not prevent the implementation of the model. The reduced attention to efficiency is justified by the challenges of measuring deadweight losses, the fact that policymakers appear to put less emphasis on minimizing deadweight losses than do economists, and the observation that other considerations such as the stability of the tax system, which are not incorporated into static optimal taxation models, are important to policymakers.

We incorporate some elements of efficiency by including the competitiveness of a state's tax structure as one of a state's policy goals. To maintain a competitive tax structure, a state must avoid imposing taxes at rates that greatly exceed those in other states, thereby minimizing tax-driven economic distortions associated with location decisions. However, our approach ignores distortions not associated with differential tax rates across states. For example, by not explicitly measuring deadweight loss, we fail to capture the advice from economic theory that source-based taxes are undesirable on efficiency grounds (see Dixit (1985) and references therein).

In contrast to the explicit statement of a social welfare function in the optimal tax approach, the objective function of state policymakers is less well-specified in the portfolio approach. Nonetheless, an optimizing framework is implicit in that the policymaker is assumed to be trying to maximize an objective function defined across several policy goals. In particular, the policymaker is assumed to be striving to design a tax system that provides growth in revenue that corresponds to the predicted growth in expenditures, provides a stable source of revenue, and satisfies other goals such as equity and competitiveness. Specifying how the policymaker weighs one goal relative to another would be arbitrary. Hence, we leave the preference function unspecified and focus instead on the nature of the trade-offs among policy goals.[4]

Our analysis also departs from the purely positive, predictive models of state tax behavior developed by Hettich and Winer (1984, 1985, and 1988). These models are predicated on the assumption that state officials minimize the political costs of raising revenues. Their work is intriguing and has served as the basis for empirical work by themselves and others (see, for example, Chernick (1991); Alm and McCallin, 1992). However, the purely positive focus of their approach limits its usefulness as a tool for evaluating state tax structures and providing policy guidance.[5]

CHARACTERISTICS OF THE TAX STRUCTURES OF NORTH CAROLINA AND MASSACHUSETTS

We analyze North Carolina and Massachusetts partly because of our familiarity with both states, but also because they have certain similarities and differences that are relevant for this study. The two states have approximately the same population. Despite more rapid population growth in North Carolina, taxes have grown at similar rates in the two states during the past two decades.[6] Moreover, neither state is an outlier with respect to the mix of taxes. In particular, both states have income and general sales taxes and neither relies on severance taxes, heavy reliance on which would complicate the analysis because of the potential for exporting the burden to nonresidents. In 1990, *per capita* state and local tax revenues were $2,360 in Massachusetts, about 40 percent higher than the $1,675 level in North Carolina. However, because *per capita* income in Massachusetts exceeds that in North Carolina also by about 40 percent, taxes as a percent of income are almost identical—10.8 percent in Massachusetts and 10.9 percent in North Carolina.[7]

In this paper, we focus on state, rather than state and local, tax revenues. This focus is sensible because state policymakers have full control over state tax revenues but much less control over local taxes. However, because state and local tax decisions are closely intertwined, a case can also be made for focusing on the combined state and local sector. While we appreciate the arguments for examining state and local governments together, the logic underlying our estimates of growth, instability, and equity cannot be readily applied to local property taxes.[8]

We exclude from the analysis federal aid to states because, unlike taxes, it is not directly controlled by state government officials. In addition, we exclude charges and fees because reliance on them across states varies with a state's decisions about expenditures, such as whether to have a large public university system.

Table 1 reports the 1991 mix of state taxes in each state. Three differences emerge: compared to North Carolina, Massachusetts relies more heavily on in-

The Challenge of Fiscal Disparities for State and Local Governments 141

TABLE 1
ACTUAL TAX PORTFOLIO SHARES FOR 1991

Tax	Massachusetts	North Carolina
Income	0.564	0.489
Sales	0.213	0.233
Corporate	0.068	0.068
Insurance	0.029	0.027
Energy	0.059	0.139
Wealth	0.028	0.012
Other	0.039	0.033

Notes: Revenues from each tax as a fraction of total state revenues. See Appendix A for data sources and details about tax categories.

dividual income taxes and wealth taxes (defined as estate, gift, and inheritance taxes) but less on energy taxes (defined as motor fuel taxes and utility taxes). Reliance on general sales taxes, corporate income taxes, insurance taxes and other taxes does not vary much between the two states. However, as elaborated further below, the differences between the tax structures in the two states are substantially greater than this table suggests. This conclusion follows because of variation in the way each state defines its tax bases, as most graphically illustrated by the sales tax: Massachusetts' narrow base excludes food and most clothing, while the North Carolina tax base includes food and clothing. (See Appendix A for definitions of tax bases.)

An alternative, and in our view more useful, way to classify tax structures is in terms of their characteristics. Table 2 presents data on four main characteristics: revenue growth, instability, equity, and competitiveness. As elaborated below, the estimates of revenue growth and instability are based on historical data in each state and reflect the combination of the characteristics of each tax, changes in the state economy, and small discretionary changes in tax rates and tax bases. The measures of equity and competitiveness are calculated for 1991. The table shows that the two states' tax structures differ along these four dimensions.

The first characteristic, revenue growth, primarily reflects growth in demand for spending. The expected rates of real revenue growth reported in Table 2 are weighted averages of tax-specific growth rates estimated over a 21-year period, with the weights equal to the 1991 portfolio shares. (Details on the calculation of this and the other characteristics by tax are discussed below in the context of the derivation of the efficiency frontier). For 1991, the expected real growth rate was about 3.6 percent per year for North Carolina and 2.85 percent per year for Massachusetts.

Instability refers to the short run variability of the tax portfolio around its expected growth rate and accounts for both the variance of the trend-adjusted residuals of individual taxes and their covariances. To make the units comparable, we report instability as a standard deviation rather than as a variance. Because states are required to balance their budgets and because they find it hard to maintain sufficient reserves in the form of "rainy day funds" to offset unanticipated revenue shortfalls, we assume that unstable tax systems are less desirable than stable ones, all else held constant. The table shows that the Massachusetts tax structure has greater instability than the North Carolina tax structure.

Our measure of equity is intended to capture the progressivity of the tax

TABLE 2
CHARACTERISTICS OF STATE TAX STRUCTURES FOR 1991

Characteristic	Massachusetts	North Carolina
Real growth rate	2.85 percent	3.63 percent
Instability (percentage points)	4.99	3.81
Equity	1.65	1.08
Competitiveness		
Income	1.31	1.47
Sales	0.65	0.90[a]
Corporate	1.43	1.18
Insurance	1.03	1.18
Energy	0.59	1.02
Wealth	2.56	1.05

Notes: The calculations of growth, instability, and equity are discussed in the text. Competitiveness is based on the average effective tax rates relative to averages for all states (ACIR data for 1988).
[a] Includes local sales taxes. Without local two percent tax, the North Carolina value would be 0.60.

structure. In particular, we use one of several standard measures of tax progressivity, namely, the elasticity of tax payments with respect to annual income.[9] As applied to discrete income spans, this measure is calculated as the percentage change in tax revenues divided by the percentage change in income. An elasticity greater than one indicates a progressive tax system, while an elasticity less than one indicates a regressive system. We apply the measure to relatively high-income households (those with income in the $40,000 and $50,000 range) and to relatively low-income households (those with incomes between $10,000 and $20,000),[10] with the calculation based only on those taxes that are intended to be borne by residents. This measure, it should be noted, is based on burdens in relation to annual income rather than the alternative of permanent income. While annual income may be a reasonable measure of ability to pay for middle-income households, it is probably a poor measure for many people in the lowest and the highest income classes. By avoiding the very lowest and the highest income classes, our selection of income classes minimizes the limitations of using annual income.[11]

Along this equity dimension, Massachusetts and North Carolina have made significantly different choices. The index value of 1.65 indicates that Massachusetts' state tax structure is highly progressive, while the value of 1.08 indicates that North Carolina's is only slightly progressive. However, the reader should note that both states appear to have regressive structures when local taxes are added.[12]

Finally, we characterize the competitiveness of a state's tax structure in terms of effective tax rates relative to the national average for each of several taxes. At this point, we simply report measures for each tax for each state. Below, we introduce competitiveness into the model as a constraint on the effective tax rates that states can impose. The state's effective tax rate is calculated as the tax collections from the tax divided by the potential tax base, as measured in a consistent way across states by the U.S. Advisory Commission on Intergovernmental Relations (1992). Because states vary in how they define tax bases, the use of nominal tax rates would be misleading. A ratio greater than one implies that the state imposes an average effective rate greater than the national average. To the extent that individuals or firms evaluate the effective tax rate in their own state by comparing it with tax rates in other states, the higher is a state's tax rate relative to the national average, the less competitive by definition is that state in terms of that tax.[13] The bottom part of Table 2 shows that both states tax personal income, corporate income, insurance, and wealth at above-average effective rates. In contrast, both states tax sales at below-average effective rates. The relative effective sales tax rate of 0.90 for North Carolina is based on the sum of state and local sales taxes, rather than on state taxes alone. Because firms and individuals do not distinguish between state and local taxes as they compare rates across states, the relevant effective rate is based on revenue generated by the uniform two percent local rate as well as that by the four percent state rate.[14] Compared to Massachusetts, the effective tax rates in North Carolina are somewhat higher for income, sales, insurance, and energy.

THE EFFICIENCY FRONTIER

A major purpose of this paper is to understand and evaluate the decisions that the two states have made about these four dimensions, especially the latter three. Central to this analysis is the concept of an efficiency frontier, namely, the boundary of the set of characteristics that are feasible given the nature of the state economy and the values of state residents. One set of questions revolves around the position and shape of this frontier. A second set involves the relationship between the state's actual choices and the frontier.

Following portfolio theory from finance, we begin by describing the frontier for the tax portfolio in terms of revenue growth and instability. These two characteristics of a state's tax portfolio are the most similar to the relevant characteristics of asset portfolios in the finance literature, namely, the rate of return on assets and the riskiness of the portfolio. However, in contrast to asset models for which it is reasonable to assume that the investor cares about only the mean and the standard deviation of portfolio returns, models of the state tax decision must incorporate other policy objectives. Specifically, the models must, at a minimum, incorporate considerations of equity and competitiveness. Following Harmon and Mallick (1994), we incorporate these other considerations into the construction of the frontier in the form of constraints.

Revenue Growth and Instability

The expected growth rate of revenue generated by a tax system can be calculated as a weighted average of the expected real growth rates of each tax, where the weights are the shares of total tax revenue attributable to each tax. For both Massachusetts and North Carolina, we estimate tax-specific growth rates using annual data for the past 21 years.

One issue that arises in estimating growth rates is whether to adjust annual revenues for discretionary changes in tax rates and tax bases to assure that the dependent variable represents revenue from a tax that is defined uniformly over time. For major, infrequent discretionary changes, such an adjustment is clearly desirable. If the adjustment were not made, the resulting estimates of growth rates would confound the effects of legislated changes with growth in the tax base. Stated differently, the estimated growth rates would represent biased estimates of the expected growth in revenue that would be generated from growth in the tax base alone. However, the case for adjusting revenues for discretionary changes is much less compelling when such changes are frequent and relatively small. In this situation, one might appropriately view the expected growth in a revenue source as the combination of growth arising from a uniformly defined tax augmented (or diminished) by legislated changes. Thus, this approach explicitly accounts for growth due to systematic legislative activity as well as for growth due to economy-related changes in the tax base.

The preferred approach for each tax category depends on each state's legislative history.[15] Our criteria for determining which changes required adjustment were that the growth rate in a year was substantially greater or smaller than the average growth rate over the period and that the outlier could be matched with a clearly specified policy change. Based on these criteria, we did not adjust the North Carolina data. A close examination suggests that legislated changes in that state were, in general, relatively frequent and relatively small.[16] For some of the minor taxes, such as cigarette taxes, the changes were more significant. However, because we group several small taxes together, legislated changes that may appear large for an individual tax are often small in the context of the larger category.

Using the same methodology, we identified and adjusted for four significant policy changes in Massachusetts. These were an increase in the state sales tax rate from three to five percent, which affected revenues in 1976; changes that lowered corporate tax revenue in 1975 (an increase in the investment tax credit and a reduction in the rate on tangible property); a 50 percent increase in the gasoline tax rate that affected energy taxes in 1991; and a change in the structure and rates of the income tax in 1972. In each case, we adjusted the data by setting the growth rate for the relevant year at the average for the sample period.[17]

We estimate growth rates for each tax using the following equation:

$$d \log R_{it} = b_i + e_{it}$$

where $d \log R_{it}$ is the change in the natural logarithm of real revenue (deflated using the implicit price deflator for state and local services) from the ith tax between year $t - 1$ and t, b_i is the estimated growth rate, and e_{it} is a random error term, which we assume is stationary. According to this specification, the expected growth rate for each tax is simply the geometric average growth rate of actual revenue during the period.[18]

The instability of a tax refers to the variation in revenue growth around its average. Hence, tax-specific measures of instability can be calculated as the standard deviation of the error term, e_{it}, or, equivalently, as the standard deviation of the dependent variable. The greater the variation around the average growth rate, the greater the instability of a tax. For the portfolio as a whole (as shown for 1991 portfolios in Table 2), the measure of instability takes account of the covariances between the residuals as well as their variances.

Table 3 presents tax-specific measures of growth and instability for the seven tax categories for each state. In both states, the income tax clearly exhibits the fastest real growth (3.8 percent per year in Massachusetts and 6.0 percent in North Carolina). The fact that revenue from these taxes grows faster than real income in both states can be explained both by the progressivity of each tax and the accumulation of small legislated changes in rates and bases. The table also shows that sales tax revenue grows faster in Massachusetts than in North Carolina both absolutely and relative to

The Challenge of Fiscal Disparities for State and Local Governments

TABLE 3
REAL EXPECTED GROWTH AND INSTABILITY BY TAX FOR 1991

	Massachusetts		North Carolina	
Tax	Growth (Percent)	Instability (Percentage Points)	Growth (Percent)	Instability (Percentage Points)
Income	3.8	5.7	6.0	5.0
Sales	3.2	8.0	2.6	5.7
Corporate	0.4	10.6	0.9	10.7
Insurance	2.9	13.0	2.7	6.8
Energy	−1.2	8.3	−0.1	7.5
Wealth	1.9	14.8	0.9	15.5
Other	−2.2	6.1	−1.5	6.2
Addendum				
Real income	2.2	2.4	3.0	1.7

Note: See the text for details on these calculations.

income growth, a finding which is consistent with the differing definitions of the tax base. The narrow base in Massachusetts makes the tax into a tax on consumer durables, spending on which grows faster than personal income. In North Carolina, the broader base, which includes food and all clothing, grows more slowly than personal income. In both states, the lowest growth rates arise for the corporation income tax, energy taxes, and other taxes.

The differences between the two states reflect both differences in how each tax is defined and how it interacts with the state economy. The most striking finding is the greater instability of most of the Massachusetts taxes relative to the North Carolina taxes. The largest differences appear for the general sales tax (with a standard deviation of 8.0 percentage points in Massachusetts *versus* 5.7 percentage points in North Carolina), the taxes on insurance (13.0 *versus* 6.8) and the energy taxes, which include motor fuel and utility taxes (8.3 *versus* 7.5). Part of this greater instability reflects the greater instability in state real income in Massachusetts. As shown in the addendum to the table, the Massachusetts economy was approximately 50 percent more unstable than North Carolina's during the period, despite its lower average growth rate.

Equity

Regardless of the statutory placement of taxes, the burden ultimately falls on individuals. Hence, equity refers to the pattern, usually by income class, of tax burdens on individuals. The distributional effects of taxes by income class depend first on which functional groups—*e.g.*, people in their capacity as consumers, wage earners, or landowners—bear the ultimate burden of the tax and second on the patterns of spending or earnings by income class. The incidence of taxes on state residents is complicated further by the possibility that some of the tax burden may be shifted to taxpayers outside the state. To allocate taxes among income classes, we assume that policymakers believe that taxes on income are not shifted at all and that taxes on consumer goods are fully shifted forward to consumers.

For the purposes of this analysis, we assume that state policymakers care only about perceived burdens on state residents from taxes intended to be borne by state residents such as the personal income tax, general sales taxes, and selective sales taxes. For business taxes for which the ultimate incidence is unclear (to economists as well as to policymakers and residents), we assume that in making their equity calculations, state policymakers either perceive no burden on state residents or that they ignore such burdens. Thus, our equity analysis ignores business taxes.

Using data from the most recent regional Consumer Expenditure Survey (1988), we calculated the incidence by income class of the following taxes: income, general sales, tobacco, alcohol, gasoline, and utilities.[19] Appendix B details our methodology for estimating progressivity. Tobacco and alcohol taxes are part of the category of taxes labeled "other." Taxes on gasoline and utilities together make up the energy category. Given our assumptions about incidence, burdens for the income tax were distributed among income classes in line with actual tax payments (adjusted for deductibility against the federal income tax), and burdens for both general and selective sales taxes were distributed in line with consumption of taxed items. The resulting burdens by tax by state for two types of households are shown in Table 4. The third column of the table for each state indicates our summary measure of progressivity, the elasticity of the tax burden between the two income classes.[20]

Differences in state tax rates and bases, plus some variation in spending patterns in the Northeast and the Southeast, account for the different relative burdens on high- and low-income households. The income tax is highly progressive in both states. Although Massachusetts does not have progressive tax rates, the rate on unearned income, which disproportionately accrues to higher-income households, exceeds that on earned income. North Carolina has a relatively flat rate schedule but minimizes the burden on low-income households by using a tax base that mimics quite closely the federal tax code. The sales tax is regressive in both states, but more so in North Carolina, which includes food in the tax base. Similarly the gasoline tax is regressive in both states. Its greater absolute burden in North Carolina reflects the state's slightly higher tax rate and much heavier reliance on travel by automobile, especially among low-income households. As indicated at the bottom of the table, the Massachusetts state tax structure in 1989 was significantly more progressive than the North Carolina structure.[21] Of interest is that the greater progressivity in Massachusetts is

TABLE 4
EQUITY MEASURES BY TAX FOR 1989

	Massachusetts			North Carolina		
Tax	$10,000–$20,000 (Percent)	$40,000–$50,000 (Percent)	Elasticity	$10,000–$20,000 (Percent)	$40,000–$50,000 (Percent)	Elasticity
Income	1.53	3.79	3.22	1.01	3.10	4.10
Sales	1.95	1.62	0.75	3.04	1.93	0.45
Tobacco	0.37	0.19	0.27	0.02	0.01	−0.04
Alcohol	0.12	0.11	0.86	0.24	0.12	0.26
Gasoline	0.31	0.24	0.64	1.25	0.74	0.39
Utilities	0.11	0.05	0.21	0.51	0.25	0.23
Total	4.39	6.00	1.55	6.08	6.15	1.02
Addendum Average income	$14,867	$44,443		$14,752	$44,493	

Notes: This information is based on revenue data for 1988–89 and Consumer Expenditure Survey expenditure patterns for 1988. The elasticity is defined as the percentage change in tax payments divided by the percentage change in income. See Appendix B and the text for details about the derivation of equity measure. The average income refers to the average income within the income bracket from the regional Consumer Expenditure Survey.

achieved not through significantly higher tax burdens on high-income households but rather through substantially lower burdens on low-income households. The higher average income in Massachusetts and smaller percentage of low-income households apparently make it easier for Massachusetts than for North Carolina to afford to be generous to its low-income households.

As explained further below, we incorporate equity into the frontier of efficient tax portfolios in the form of a constraint. Specifically, we allow the degree of progressivity to vary around its 1991 level within a limited range. The basic range is plus or minus 0.15, a range that roughly approximates the historical variation in the progressivity of taxes over time in these two states.[22]

Competitiveness

Competitive pressures across states may limit policymakers' tax structure choices and their ability to reach desired levels of growth, stability, or fairness in the tax system. Competitive pressures can come either from the threat of relocation by businesses or individuals or through "yardstick" competition by which voters compare their state's performance with that of other states (see Besley and Case, forthcoming). This competitive pressure might also push states toward choosing tax structures that reduce economic inefficiency. We interpret these competitive pressures as putting limits on a state's maximum reliance on each of the following six types of taxes: personal income, general sales, corporate income, insurance, energy, and wealth.

As a measure of the limits imposed by competing with other states, we compare each state's reliance on each of these taxes with the hypothetical revenues it would receive if it relied heavily on the tax. For interstate comparisons, we turn to ACIR data on tax effort for each tax in each state for 1988 (the latest year for which data are available). A state's tax-specific effort index is calculated as the ratio of its actual revenue from the tax to its tax capacity, where capacity is defined as the national average tax rate multiplied by the state's tax base assuming it used the ACIR's uniform tax base. A tax effort index greater than one implies that the state imposes an above-average effective tax rate on that revenue source.

To construct the competitiveness constraint, we limit the effective tax rate on each tax to the tax effort of the state at the 95th percentile of tax effort.[23] We use the 95th percentile instead of the state with the highest tax effort, because each tax typically has some outliers in terms of tax effort.[24] For each tax, we define each state's maximum potential revenue as the competitive limit on tax effort multiplied by each state's own tax capacity. Since we formulate the tax structure choice problem in terms of portfolio shares, we divide the state's maximum potential revenue from each tax by the state's total 1988 tax revenue to measure the state's maximum potential reliance on each tax.

Table 5 lists the resulting maximum shares for the corporate, insurance, energy, personal income, and general sales taxes for Massachusetts and North Carolina. The limits differ across the two states because of differences in the size of the tax bases of the different states and differences in total revenues. A comparison of these maximum shares with the actual choices in Table 1 shows that both states could double their reliance on corporate and sales taxes and could substantially increase insurance taxes without the competitiveness constraint binding. In contrast, neither state could substantially increase reliance on the income tax without the constraint binding.[25]

148 The Challenge of Fiscal Disparities for State and Local Governments

TABLE 5
COMPETITIVENESS CONSTRAINT MAXIMUM SHARES

Tax	Massachusetts	North Carolina
Income	0.604	0.492
Sales	0.589	0.447[a]
Corporate	0.137	0.170
Insurance	0.054	0.043
Energy	0.074	0.161
Wealth	0.032	0.027

Notes: The competitiveness constraints are based on ACIR data for 1988. See the text for details on the derivation of the maximums.
[a]Two-thirds of maximum sales tax revenue allocated to the state.

The Frontier

We initially summarize the options facing each state in the form of a trade-off between growth and instability. For any specified growth rate, the frontier indicates the minimum amount of instability that can be achieved by changing the mix of taxes given the equity and competitiveness constraints. While the optimization problem can be set up either in terms of maximizing revenue growth or minimizing instability, we prefer the latter approach because it is more consistent with the reality that demand for spending growth determines expected growth rates of revenue. Thus, for any growth rate, the challenge for the state policymaker is to choose a portfolio of taxes that minimizes instability consistent with other tax goals.

Policymakers minimize instability by choosing the portfolio weights for different taxes. Their constrained minimization problem for the frontier can be expressed as follows:

(2)

$$\min \sum_i \sum_j w_i w_j \sigma_{ij}$$

subject to

(3)

$$\sum_i w_i g_i = \text{constant}$$

(4)

$$w_i \leq c_i$$

where i = corporate, insurance, income, sales, energy, and wealth.

(5)

$$E_{\min} \leq \dfrac{\dfrac{\sum_j w_j K_j^{40} - \sum_j w_j K_j^{10}}{\sum_j w_j K_j^{10}}}{\dfrac{I^{40} - I^{10}}{I^{10}}} \leq E_{\max}$$

where j = income, sales, energy, and other.

(6)

$$w_i \geq 0 \quad \forall i$$

(7)

$$\sum_i w_i = 1$$

where w_i is the portfolio weight for each tax, σ_{ij} is the covariance between the percentage changes in the tax revenues (when $i = j$, this term is the variance of tax i), g_i is the expected growth rate for each tax, c_i is the competitiveness constraint for corporate, insurance, income, sales, energy, and wealth taxes described above, K_i^m is the percentage of tax i borne by a household in income class m, and $E_{\min}$ and $E_{\max}$ are the minimum and maximum levels of acceptable progressivity. The objective in equation 2 is the instability of the portfolio of taxes. Equation 3 specifies the expected growth rate for the portfolio. Changing the growth rate generates points along the frontier. Equation 4 is the set of competitiveness constraints for the personal income, corporate income, insurance, sales, energy, and wealth taxes described above. In equation 5, the expression between the inequality signs reduces to the elasticity expression with the portfolio weights included. Hence, the equation places limits on the degree of progressivity for the set of taxes with an intended incidence on state residents. Equation 6 is a set of non-negativity constraints for the portfolio shares. Equation 7 specifies that the portfolio shares sum to one, which ensures that the state receives the appropriate level of revenue.

This approach summarizes the options facing each state in growth-instability space. By setting up alternative constrained optimization problems, we can also characterize the trade-off between other characteristics, such as progressivity and instability. We refer to these alternative characterizations below in the discussion of policy implications.

Figure 1 illustrates two growth-instability frontiers for each state. The top line for each state depicts the results of the minimization problem just described. The lower line for each state depicts the results of a modified minimization problem, namely, one which incorporates neither the equity nor the competitiveness constraint. The difference between the two frontiers illustrates how considerations of equity and competitiveness influence the trade-offs available to each state. Because instability is viewed as undesirable and growth is desirable, movements in a southeasterly direction represent improvements and movements in a northwesterly direction represent less desirable outcomes.

Emerging from the graph are four insights about tax policy options and choices in the two states. First, the Massachusetts frontiers indicate that Massachusetts faces much higher levels of instability than North Carolina for any expected growth rate. This finding is not surprising in light of the greater instability associated with most of the individual taxes shown in Table 3. Second, equity and competitiveness considerations are more constraining in North Carolina than in Massachusetts. Such considerations raise the amount of instability in the efficient portfolio by 12.0 percent (a 0.4 percentage point increase) in North Carolina at its 1991 expected growth rate of 3.6 percent, but hardly at all in Massachusetts at its 2.85 percent expected growth rate.

Third, after accounting for equity and competitiveness considerations, North Carolina faces a trade-off between growth and instability in the relevant range. That is, to get more revenue growth, the state must accept more instability. For example, an increase in the growth rate from 3.6 to 3.9 percent requires that North Carolina accept 6.3 percent (0.21 percentage points) more instability, and an increase in the growth rate from 3.9 to 4.2 percent requires 13.2 percent more instability. Massachusetts faces much less of a trade-off between growth and stability. An increase in the expected growth rate from 2.85 percent (the 1991 value) to 3.3 percent requires an increase in instability of only 2.5 percent (0.12 percentage points). The less favorable trade-off in North Carolina is associated in large part with equity and competitiveness considerations. In the absence of such considerations, greater growth would require very limited increases in instability in that state.

FIGURE 1. Massachusetts and North Carolina Growth-Instability Frontiers

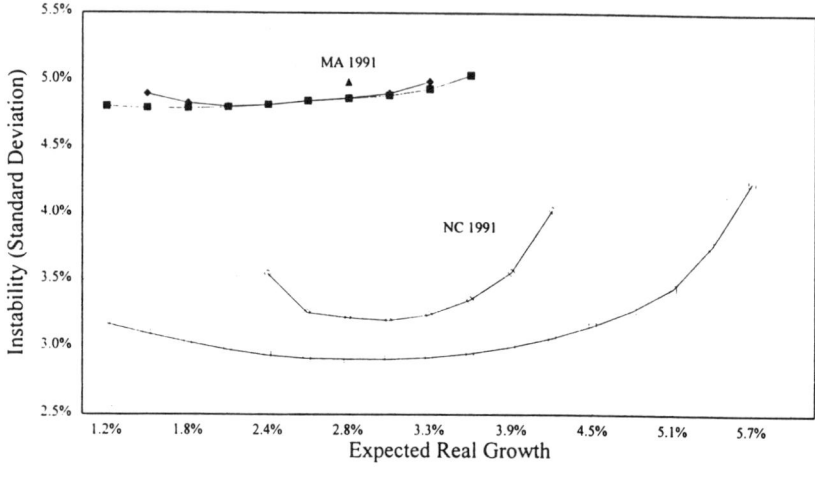

- MA Without Equity & Competitiveness Constraints
- MA With Equity & Competitiveness Constraints
- NC Without Equity & Competitiveness Constraints
- NC With Equity & Competitiveness Constraints

Fourth and finally, neither state was on its frontier in 1991. In other words, each state could have rearranged its mix of taxes to reduce instability without any loss in expected revenue or, alternatively, to achieve greater growth in revenue with no additional instability. Relative to North Carolina, this difference is small for Massachusetts.

Caveats

The frontiers indicate the efficient combinations of characteristics available to state policymakers in each state. In general, without some knowledge of the relative preferences of policymakers for the various characteristics, one cannot judge the desirability of one combination on the frontier relative to another. However, it is not unreasonable to assume in this tax context that policymakers have preferred levels of expected revenue growth that are determined by nontax considerations such as the desired rate of growth of spending. From this perspective, the model yields normative conclusions of the following form: for any specified growth rate, an optimal or efficient portfolio is one that puts the state on the relevant frontier.

Before elaborating the policy implications of the model, we note here some of the limitations of this portfolio approach to the analysis of state tax structures. First is the possibility that we have not included all the major considerations that drive the tax portfolio decision. In contrast to finance models for which it is reasonable to assume that investors care only about the mean and variance of returns, these tax models have no comparable theory to guide the analyst in the set of relevant portfolio characteristics. Thus, the best the analyst can do is to avoid excluding an obvious characteristic, such as equity or competitiveness.

Second, the characteristics of the taxes are not fully exogenous to the decision maker. For an investor picking stocks, the characteristics (expected return and risk) of any one company's stock are exogenous to the individual investor. In contrast, if a state chooses to double its reliance on the sales tax by changing the definition of the tax base, it changes the equity and stability characteristics of the tax. Thus, the tax model works best under the assumption that states are not in a position to make major changes in the design of individual taxes.[26]

A related point, but one that applies to finance models as well as to tax models, follows from estimating the growth rate and instability for each tax from historical data. Like changes in the design of taxes, changes in the underlying structure of the economy may render the historically based estimates of growth and instability invalid. Also, it is difficult to determine whether the state's actual portfolio differs sufficiently from the portfolios on the frontier to be statistically significant. Like the previous limitation, this one applies to finance models as well as to tax models.

Finally, as we have implemented it, the portfolio model ignores some potentially important fiscal interactions between states and the federal government. Consider first the deductibility of state income taxes from the federal income tax base. Although we incorporate such deductibility into our equity measures, we do not account for the fact that by reducing the burden on state taxpayers, the ability to deduct the income tax, but not the sales tax, increases the attractiveness to state policymakers of the income tax relative to the sales tax. Nor do we capture the fact that some state tax bases are used by the federal government. The use by the federal government of the income tax but not the sales tax raises the political and economic costs to state policymakers of using the income tax relative to the sales tax, costs that are not included in our model. Because these two excluded effects work in opposite directions, one encouraging greater reliance on the income tax and the other less reliance, the best we can hope is that they approximately cancel each other out.

Given these limitations of the approach, we proceed with caution in using the portfolio choice model to make policy recommendations about state tax structures. Nonetheless, we are convinced that, at a minimum, the model provides a convenient way of summarizing the various characteristics that are important in states' decisions about tax structures.

POLICY DISCUSSION

This portfolio approach provides policy-relevant information of three types: information about the optimal mix of taxes at given growth rates and the changes in portfolio shares that would be appropriate in each state, the effect of growth rates on the optimal mix of taxes, and the nature of the trade-offs among policy goals.

Optimal Mix of Taxes, at the Current Growth Rate

Underlying each point of each frontier in Figure 1 is a set of portfolio shares. We focus first on the optimal portfolio shares in each state associated with its 1991 expected real growth rate (3.6 percent in North Carolina and 2.85 percent in Massachusetts). These shares, which are shown in columns 1 and 4 of Table 6, correspond to the relevant points on the frontiers that are marked by diamonds in Figure 1, namely, the frontiers that incorporate the equity and competitiveness constraints.

For both states, the optimal portfolio calls for heavy reliance on personal in-

TABLE 6
OPTIMAL TAX PORTFOLIO SHARES

	Massachusetts			North Carolina		
Tax	Optimal Portfolio (1)	Optimal Minus Actual (2)	Percent Change in Revenue (3)	Optimal Portfolio (4)	Optimal Minus Actual (5)	Percent Change in Revenue (6)
Income	0.604[a]	0.040	7.1	0.492[a]	0.003	0.6
Sales	0.220	0.007	3.2	0.245	0.012	5.1
Corporate	0.072	0.004	6.5	0.000	−0.068	−100.0
Insurance	0.000	−0.029	−100.0	0.043[a]	0.016	59.3
Energy	0.035	−0.024	−41.5	0.161[a]	0.022	15.8
Wealth	0.000	−0.028	−100.0	0.000	−0.012	−100.0
Other	0.069	0.030	77.9	0.059	0.026	79.2
Addendum						
Instability	0.049	−0.001	−2.3	0.034	−0.004	−10.7
Equity	1.681	0.031	1.9	0.995	−0.085	−7.9

Notes: The "optimal portfolio" columns indicate the tax portfolio shares implicit in the growth-instability frontier for a 3.6 percent expected growth rate in North Carolina and a 2.85 percent expected growth rate in Massachusetts. The "optimal minus actual" columns are the differences between shares in the frontier portfolio and the actual portfolio. The third column for each state is the implied change in revenue from each tax. The addendum reports the levels and changes of instability and progressivity associated with these optimal portfolios.
[a] Denotes a portfolio share at the maximum of the competitiveness constraint.

come taxes. In fact, the share of income taxes in the optimal portfolio in each state is the maximum share allowed by the competitiveness constraint—0.604 in Massachusetts and 0.492 in North Carolina. Higher income in Massachusetts allows the state to rely more heavily on income taxes than North Carolina while still remaining competitive with other states. The heavy reliance on the income tax in these two portfolios stems from the characteristics of each state's income tax: for both states, the income tax is the most progressive tax (see Table 4), the fastest growing tax, and the most stable tax (see Table 3, though Table 3 does not adjust for covariances among taxes).

In contrast, the optimal portfolios for both states call for no use of wealth taxes, which are the most unstable taxes in both states.[27] Compared to that for Massachusetts, the optimal portfolio for North Carolina calls for much heavier reliance on energy and insurance taxes and somewhat higher reliance on the general sales tax. North Carolina apparently needs to rely more heavily on these taxes to offset the smaller share of revenues than can be raised from the income tax. Moreover, such taxes are apparently more acceptable in North Carolina than in Massachusetts because of North Carolina's historical willingness to accept less progressivity, as embodied in its equity constraint.

Columns 2 and 5 in Table 6 show the changes in the mix of taxes required for each state to attain the optimal mix (at the 1991 expected growth rate), and columns 3 and 6 indicate the required changes in revenues. The table shows, first, that both states should increase their reliance on income, sales, and taxes in the "other" category. However, neither state has much leeway to increase income taxes very much, since the shares in the actual portfolio are close to the maximum allowed by the competitiveness constraint. Second, both states should eliminate wealth taxes, which are characterized by the undesirable combination of relatively low growth and high instability.[28]

Third, with respect to energy, corporate, and insurance taxation, the model yields different advice for the two states. Massachusetts should reduce reliance on energy taxes, which have an expected growth rate of −1.2 percent and are quite regressive; North Carolina, on the other hand, should increase reliance on energy taxes to the limit allowed by the competitiveness constraint, presumably to offset in part the lower share of revenue it can garner from the income tax. Massachusetts should retain (and slightly increase) its corporate tax but decrease its reliance on insurance taxes to zero. Conversely, North Carolina should slightly increase its insurance taxes up to the competitive maximum but reduce its corporate income taxes to zero. This prescription probably reflects the differing patterns of instability of the two types of taxes in the two states. For Massachusetts, insurance taxes are second only to wealth taxes in terms of instability and hence should be avoided. For North Carolina, insurance taxes have the second highest growth rate and only moderate instability, while corporate taxes are quite unstable relative to most other taxes.

The divergent prescriptions for these taxes in the two states highlight the importance of measuring state-specific characteristics: a tax can have a relatively attractive set of characteristics in one state but a poor set of characteristics in another state. In addition, these prescriptions indicate the importance of accounting for the whole tax picture: for example, North Carolina's inability to raise as great a share of revenue from the income tax affects its reliance on other taxes.

Optimal Mix of Taxes, Differing Growth Rates

In addition to varying across states, the optimal portfolio shares for each state also vary with the expected growth rate, that is, with movements along the frontier. To illustrate, Figure 2 plots the optimal portfolio shares along the growth-instability frontier for the income, sales, energy, insurance, and "other" taxes for North Carolina. Since the figure for Massachusetts is quite similar, we omit it to save space.[29] The figure does not include wealth taxes, since it has a zero share along this portion of the frontier (growth rates from 2.4 to 4.2 percent). Throughout the range of expected growth rates, income and insurance taxes are at or near the limits imposed by the competitiveness constraint. In contrast, the shares for the sales and "other" taxes change substantially with movements along the frontier, and the share for energy falls at high growth rates. For example, increasing the expected growth rate from 3.6 percent to 3.9 percent raises the optimal sales tax share from 0.25 to 0.33, lowers the energy tax share from 0.16 to 0.14, and eliminates the use of "other" taxes. To attain higher growth rates, North Carolina would need to replace the relatively low-growth categories of energy and "other" taxes with revenue from the faster growing sales tax.

To summarize, the different income levels and other characteristics of Massachusetts and North Carolina generate differences in the optimal portfolio mix in the two states. This result implies that uniformity need not achieve goals of growth, stability, competitiveness, and equity. As for balance, neither state's frontier suggests a balanced portfolio of taxes: both states' frontiers require a heavy reliance on income taxes. Furthermore, the balance between taxes for each state varies with the desired expected growth rate of revenues. Hence, we find little support for the ACIR's proposals for either uniformity or balance among revenue sources.[30]

FIGURE 2. Tax Shares along Growth-Instability Frontier—North Carolina

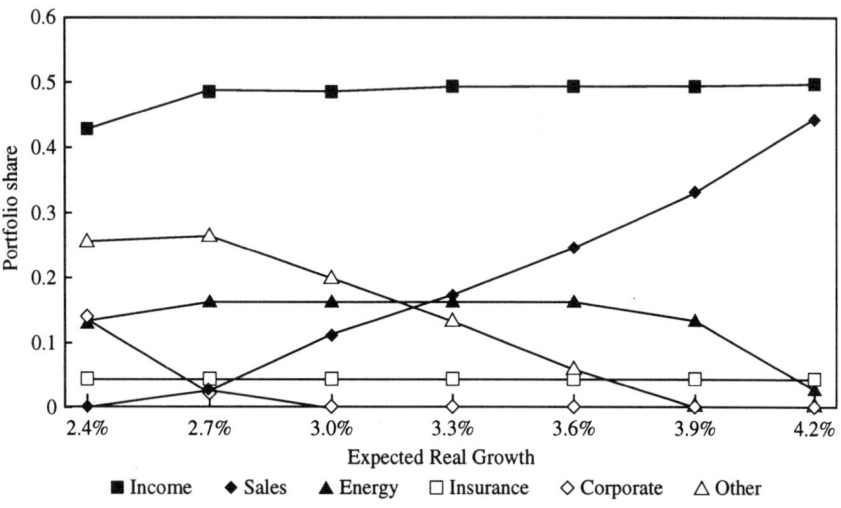

■ Income   ♦ Sales   ▲ Energy   □ Insurance   ◇ Corporate   △ Other

The tax share for the wealth tax is zero throughout this range.

Trade-offs Between Policy Characteristics

As noted above, Figure 1 shows that, around its 1991 expected growth rate, North Carolina faces a clear trade-off between growth and instability along the frontier: higher growth requires greater instability. In contrast, the trade-off in Massachusetts is much smaller. By setting up alternative optimization problems, we can examine the trade-offs between other policy characteristics. To capture the trade-off between instability and progressivity, the optimization problem involves minimizing instability for each level of progressivity given constraints on competitiveness and expected growth. With respect to competitiveness, we use the same constraint as for Figure 1. With respect to growth, we calculate a different frontier for each specific expected growth rate.[31]

Figure 3 displays the instability-progressivity frontiers for each state, with expected revenue growth set at the 1991 value for each state.[32] Each state's frontier is drawn in the neighborhood of current progressivity choices so that actual choices can be compared with the frontiers. The relatively flat instability-progressivity frontier for Massachusetts in the range of the actual index suggests that changes in tax structures that alter progressivity need not affect the instability of revenue. In contrast, for North Carolina, increases in progressivity along the frontier clearly increase instability. These increases in progressivity in North Carolina are achieved by increasing unstable corporate taxes (which are neutral

FIGURE 3. Massachusetts and North Carolina Progressivity-Instability Frontier

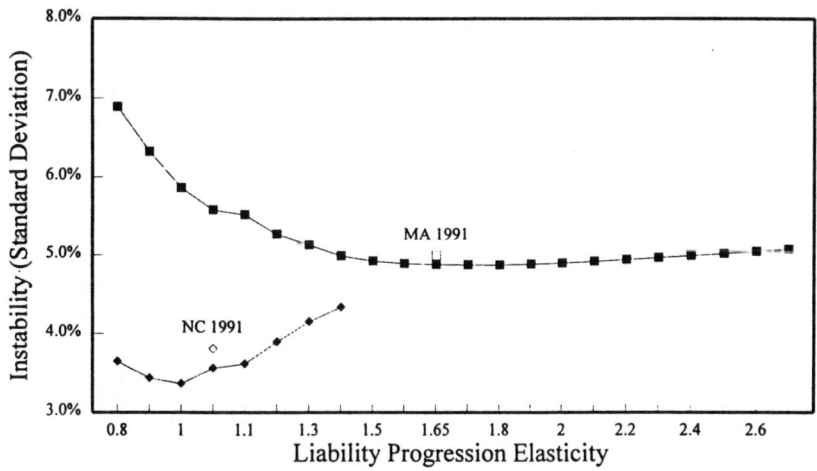

■ MA Progressivity-Instability Frontier ◆ NC Progressivity-Instability Frontier

'Expected growth rate is 3.6% in NC and 2.8% in MA

Conclusions

This portfolio choice approach to modeling the choice of state tax structures appears to be promising. By focusing attention on the characteristics of a tax system, such as growth, stability, equity, and competitiveness, this approach helps state policymakers think clearly about trade-offs (which may be small or large) among policy goals. Aside from information about covariances, most of the information needed to think about such trade-offs is available from the characteristics of the individual taxes. However, without some systematic way to combine that information, the various trade-offs are hard to discern. Thus, the main contribution of this approach is that it provides a means of combining a lot of information in a systematic manner.

Our comparison of two states yields some interesting findings and suggestions for further research. One finding is the large difference in the progressivity of the two state tax structures. Keeping in mind that the differences in progressivity between the two states are much smaller when state and local taxes are combined, the differences are still worth exploring. Additional research is needed to explore the extent to which this difference reflects differences in the income levels of the two states, and hence the ability of a state to afford to be relatively generous to low-income residents, or differences in values, independent of income. A second interesting finding is the dominance of income taxes in both states' optimal portfolios over a wide range of growth rates. Of interest is that this dominant role for the income tax also emerges for other studies, such as those for New York (Harmon and Mallick, 1994) and Georgia (White, 1983). A third set of findings relates to the trade-offs between characteristics along the frontier. For North Carolina, more growth or more progressivity typically requires more instability. In contrast, Massachusetts faces much smaller trade-offs between these characteristics.

Finally, within the context of the portfolio choice model, differences in the economies of the two states and in the characteristics of their taxes lead to differences in their tax structures. This finding argues against the policy prescription that states should use similar tax structures and that this uniform tax structure should be balanced in terms of the tax shares of the major taxes. Moreover, differences between the frontiers of the two states suggest that specific policy recommendations for these two states should not be extrapolated to other states. Instead, differences in state economies and characteristics of each tax emphasize the need for state-specific analysis.

ENDNOTES

We are extremely grateful to Ed Harris for his exceptional research assistance. We thank David Crotts of the Fiscal Research Division, North Carolina General Assembly, and Susan Persons, Chief Economist, Department of Revenue, Commonwealth of Massachusetts, for providing data; Joel Slemrod, seminar participants at Duke University, and three anonymous referees provided very helpful comments. In addition, we thank the Arts and Sciences Research Council of Duke University for financial support.

This list of characteristics is not exhaustive. For specific taxes, policymakers may care about other characteristics. Examples include (1) corrective taxation in the case of energy taxes, (2) exportability in the case of severance taxes, and (3) the distribution of wealth for inheritance taxes.

[2] The political and economic costs of instability may be linked to state constitutional requirements for balanced budgets, which limit a state's ability to engage in stabilization policy. Hence, the assumption that policymakers view instability in revenues as undesirable applies most clearly at the state level. This situation contrasts with the federal level, where tax policy may have a stabilization role. In theory, the portfolio model could handle stabilization; however, this extension would require replacing the goal of minimizing the instability of revenues with the goal of reducing business cycle fluctuations. While conceptually feasible, this extension would require a macroeconomic model of stabilization. For this reason and others, we view the portfolio approach as most applicable to state tax systems.

[3] See Haveman (1994) for a general critique of the policy usefulness of optimal tax theory. Deaton (1987) highlights the econometric difficulties of implementing optimal tax models.

[4] To complete the model, one would need to specify an objective (or loss) function over the characteristics of the tax system. This approach differs from the social welfare function approach in the sense that the policymaker is assumed to have preferences over observable characteristics of the tax system rather than individuals' utilities.

[5] Recent theoretical work by Van Velthoven and Van Winden (1991) begins to unify these political economy concerns with the efficiency costs of taxation.

[6] Contrary to this assertion, our analysis below indicates a slower rate of growth in Massachusetts than in North Carolina. This discrepancy is explained by the fact that, for the basic analysis, we adjusted the Massachusetts tax data to eliminate major discretionary changes in tax bases and tax rates during the period.

[7] Figures are from ACIR, *Significant Features of Fiscal Federalism*, vol. 2, 1992.

[8] Because local property tax revenues, especially in North Carolina, are driven almost exclusively by the growth in local spending, our approach to measuring growth and stability is not readily extended to local taxes. In the context of local property taxes, the approach would yield something closer to the growth and instability of local spending rather than the growth and instability of the tax. This link between spending growth and tax growth presents less of a problem for state taxes given the large number of such taxes. For Massachusetts, we could develop reasonable measures of the growth and instability of the property tax because of the state's property tax limitation measure, Proposition 2-1/2, which severely limited the rate of growth of local property tax revenues during the 1980s.

However, to incorporate local property taxes would require that we limit the time frame for that state to the 1980s. Our inability to develop reasonable measures of growth and stability for North Carolina local property taxes and this restriction in the time frame for Massachusetts largely account for our decision to focus exclusively on state taxes.

[9] This measure is referred to as *liability progression*. Two alternative measures are *average rate progression*, which is calculated as the ratio of the change in effective tax rate to the change in income, and *residual income progression*, which is calculated as the percentage change in after-tax income to the percentage change in before-tax income. See Musgrave and Tin (1948) and the discussion in Musgrave and Musgrave (1989, pp. 358–61).

[10] Specifying the relatively low-income group as households with incomes between $5,000 and $15,000 yields very similar results in terms of the overall frontier.

[11] An alternative approach would be to use current consumption as a measure of permanent income. Full implementation of this approach would require microdata for households so that they could be grouped by permanent income classes. In the absence of microdata, we could partially implement this approach by substituting current consumption for annual income in the denominator of the burden expressions. However, this substitution would not affect our results, because it would have the same effect on each specific tax.

[12] Determining the effects by income class for the local property tax poses a challenge. The statement in the text is based on the assumption that only the residential portion of the tax is relevant and that it is borne fully by the owners and users of housing services. As a result, the property tax, which accounts for 35 percent of total state and local tax revenue in Massachusetts and 23 percent in North Carolina, adds a very regressive component to the tax system. The regressivity of the North Carolina state-local tax structure is augmented further by the local sales tax. Based on 1991 portfolio shares, the combined state-local equity index for Massachusetts is 0.83 and that for North Carolina is 0.82.

[13] Our focus on average effective rates rather than marginal rates is largely determined by data availability. However, we also believe that the relevant rate both for discrete location decisions and for the yardstick comparisons alluded to below is an average, rather than a marginal, rate.

[14] Among all the taxes examined in this paper, only the sales tax is used by both state and local governments, and only in North Carolina.

[15] For each state, we compiled lists of changes in tax rates and tax bases for each tax from the *State Tax Reporter*, distributed by the Commerce Clearing House; state published sources including the *North Carolina Statistics of Taxation*, Biennial Report of the Tax Research Division, North Carolina Department of Revenue; and information from state officials.

[16] One specific change deserves attention, namely, the 1989 change in the structure of the North Carolina income tax described in Appendix A. This structural change had little impact on revenue but could conceivably alter the growth and stability of the tax in the future. Unfortunately, we have no way to adjust the data for these possible changes. In contrast, our equity measure fully reflects the 1989 change.

[17] While our adjustment method is simplistic, the resulting data series represents a clear improvement over the unadjusted data.

[18] We chose this form of the relationship primarily because the constant geometric growth rate is more intuitively plausible than the alternatives. Statistical tests based on the lagged term in a model in which the logarithm of revenue is regressed on a constant, time, and the log of lagged revenue confirmed that this difference stationary specification was reasonable.

[19] We were not able to construct progressivity measures for wealth taxes because of data limitations, especially for North Carolina, which uses an inheritance tax rather than an estate tax. Taxes on estates are paid to North Carolina by the heirs who inherit the estate, regardless of whether they live inside or outside the state. Alternatively, we could have followed Phares (1980) and allocated all wealth taxes to the top income group. However, this treatment would not affect our measure of liability progression, which does not incorporate any information on households in the top income group.

[20] The elasticity for 1989 in Table 4 differs from that for 1991 in Table 2 because the portfolio shares are different in the two years.

[21] Note that we used the 1988 Consumer Expenditure Survey, but the revenue data was for the fiscal year 1988–89.

[22] The historical variation in each state was crudely estimated based on the variation in the progressivity of each state's tax structure over time accounted for by variations over time in the state's mix of taxes. Allowing a

wider band (plus or minus 0.25 around the 1991 level) yields only small differences in the results.

[23] We compare each state with all of the other 50 states. Using all 50 states avoids the sticky issue of choosing a relevant smaller comparison group of states. See Case, Hines, and Rosen (1993) for an attempt to determine the relevant comparison group empirically.

[24] Neither Massachusetts nor North Carolina is an outlier for any of the taxes.

[25] We focus on specific taxes rather than the overall tax structure. This approach is consistent with the following story. Each tax is particularly unattractive to specific groups of taxpayers. For example, retailers are particularly concerned about sales taxes, high-income people about high income taxes, and corporations about corporate income taxes. Each group is likely to compare the tax rate with which it is most concerned with tax rates in other states and to complain to state policymakers when the state's tax rate exceeds those in other states. Implicitly, this approach assumes that a change in one tax rate need not affect public expenditures in that it will be offset by a change in another tax rate which affects other people. Alternatively, one might focus on the net package of taxes paid and services received by households or by firms. This alternative approach introduces a whole set of new issues that are beyond the scope of this analysis. For individual taxes (income and sales), we were able to specify the competitiveness constraint as individuals worrying about the combined burden of income and sales taxes. We replaced the limit on each tax with a limit on the sum of the two shares based on the combined sales and income tax burdens of other states. This change in the constraint caused a slight substitution of income for sales taxes in each state but did not radically change our results.

[26] Another key difference from finance models is that stock prices may adjust so that there is a trade-off between risk and return; however, state tax structures do not have an equivalent market mechanism.

[27] As noted earlier, we were not able to include progressivity measures for wealth taxes.

[28] Wealth taxes may, however, serve a purpose not included in our model, such as explicitly wanting to affect the wealth distribution.

[29] The major differences are that energy taxes have a much smaller portfolio share throughout the range in Massachusetts, and at expected growth rates below 3.6 percent, corporate income taxes are included in the optimal portfolio.

[30] To be fair to the ACIR position, we note that Shannon and others do not call for strict uniformity or balance. Instead, they call for some flexibility around the recommended shares.

[31] We could also constrain the policymaker to tax structures that generate growth rates within a range. However, since instability tends to increase with the expected growth rate, the solution to the optimization problem with a range of growth rates typically has the minimum allowed expected growth rate along the entire frontier. Thus, allowing a range of growth rates yields the same solution as fixing the growth rate at the minimum growth rate in the range.

[32] For each state, frontiers for different expected growth rates are similar. Higher growth rates shift the frontiers upward (more instability for any level of progressivity); lower expected growth rates shift the frontier downward. These shifts are consistent with the growth-instability trade-off in Figure 1.

REFERENCES

Alm, James and Nancy J. McCallin. 1992. The Determinants of State Government Tax Structures. University of Colorado. Photocopy.

Auerbach, Alan J. "The Theory of Excess Burden and Optimal Taxation." In *Handbook of Public Economics*, vol. 1, edited by Alan Auerbach and Martin Feldstein, 69–127. Amsterdam: North-Holland, 1985.

Besley, Timothy and Anne C. Case. "Incumbent Behavior: Vote Seeking, Tax Setting and Yardstick Competition." *American Economic Review*: forthcoming.

Case, Anne C., James R. Hines, and Harvey S. Rosen. "Budget Spillovers and Fiscal Policy Interdependence: Evidence from the States." *Journal of Public Economics* 52 (October, 1993): 285–307.

Chernick, Howard. 1991. The Effect of Distributional Constraints and Interstate Tax Competition on State Decisions to Tax: An Econometric Model. Hunter College. Photocopy.

Deaton, Angus. "Econometric Issues for Tax Design in Developing Countries." In *The Theory of Taxation for Developing Countries*, edited by David Newbery and Nicholas Stern, 92–113. New York: Oxford University Press, 1987.

Dixit, Avinash K. "Tax Policy in Open Economies." In *Handbook of Public Economics*, vol. 1, edited by Alan Auerbach and Martin Feldstein, 313–74. Amsterdam: North-Holland, 1985.

Gieseman, Raymond. "The Consumer Expenditure Survey: Quality Control by Comparative Analysis." *Monthly Labor Review* (March, 1987): 8–14.

Harmon, Oskar R. and Rajiv Mallick. "The Optimal State Tax Portfolio Model: An Extension." *National Tax Journal 47* (June, 1994): 395–401.

Haveman, Robert. "Optimal Taxation and Public Policy." In *Modern Public Finance*, edited by Eugene Smolensky and John Quigley, 247–56. Cambridge, MA: Harvard University Press, 1994.

Hettich, Walter and Stanley L. Winer. "A Positive Model of Tax Structure." *Journal of Public Economics 23* (June, 1984): 67–87.

Hettich, Walter and Stanley L. Winer. "Blueprints and Pathways: The Shifting Foundations of Tax Reform." *National Tax Journal 38* (December, 1985): 423–45.

Hettich, Walter and Stanley L. Winer. "Economic and Political Foundations of Tax Structure." *American Economic Review 78* (September, 1988): 701–12.

Kleine, Robert J. and John Shannon. "Characteristics of a Balanced and Moderate State-Local Revenue System." In *Reforming State Tax Systems*, edited by Steven D. Gold, 31–54. Washington, D.C.: National Conference of State Legislatures, 1986.

Ladd, Helen F. and Dana Weist. "Balance Among Taxes vs. Policy Goals." In *The Quest for Balance in State-Local Revenue Structures*, edited by Frederick D. Stocker, 39–64. Cambridge, MA: Lincoln Institute of Land Policy, 1987.

Musgrave, Richard A. and Peggy M. Musgrave. *Public Finance in Theory and Practice.* 5th edition. New York: McGraw-Hill, 1989.

Musgrave, Richard A. and Tun Thin. "Income Tax Progression, 1928–48." *Journal of Political Economy 56* (December, 1948): 498–514.

Phares, Donald. *Who Pays State and Local Taxes?* Cambridge, MA: Oelgeschlager, Gunn, and Hann, 1980.

Ring, Raymond J., Jr. "The Proportion of Consumers' and Producers' Goods in the General Sales Tax." *National Tax Journal 42* (June, 1989): 167–79.

Shannon, John. "State Revenue Diversification—The Search for Balance." In *The Quest for Balance in State-Local Revenue Structures*, edited by Frederick D. Stocker, 9–38. Cambridge, MA: Lincoln Institute of Land Policy, 1987.

U.S. Advisory Commission on Intergovernmental Relations. *State Fiscal Capacity and Effort, 1988.* Washington, D.C., 1990.

U.S. Advisory Commission on Intergovernmental Relations. *Significant Features of Fiscal Federalism*, vol. 2. Washington, D.C., 1992.

Van Velthoven, Ben and Frans Van Winden. "A Positive Model of Tax Reform." *Public Choice 72* (1991): 61–86.

White, Fred C. "Trade-Off in Growth and Stability in State Taxes." *National Tax Journal 36* (March, 1983): 103–14.

APPENDIX A: STATE TAX DEFINITIONS

Massachusetts tax data are from *Massachusetts Economic Indicators, Annual Data Supplement* (September, 1992); North Carolina tax data are from the Office of Fiscal Analysis, North Carolina General Assembly. For each state, we aggregated tax revenues into seven categories. The taxes in each of the seven categories for each state are defined as follows. Definitions are for 1992 unless otherwise noted.

Massachusetts

1. *Personal income:* Taxable income is divided into two parts, unearned income which is taxed at 12 percent and earned income which is taxed at 5.95 percent. Unearned income is total interest, dividends, and capital gains other than income earned from Massachusetts savings accounts. Earned income is all other Massachusetts income. For married taxpayers filing jointly, personal exemptions are $4,400 plus $1,000 per dependent.

2. *General sales:* Includes the five percent general sales tax on retail sales and the five percent tax on motor vehicles and meals away from home. Exempt from the tax are food purchased for home consumption, purchases of clothing under $175, prescription drugs, and electricity and gas for residential use. Custom computer programs and repair charges are not taxed.

3. *Corporate income:* A tax rate of 9.5 percent applies to net corporate income and a rate of $2.60 per $1,000 applies to the value of taxable tangible property or of net worth. The allocation is based on local-to-total payrolls, property, and sales (with sales weighted 50 percent).

4. *Insurance:* Domestic and foreign insurance companies pay taxes on gross premiums. In addition, domestic casualty insurance companies pay a tax on gross investment income, and domestic life insurance companies pay an investment privilege tax.

5. *Energy:* Includes taxes on the net income of public utilities and taxes on motor fuels. The tax rate on public utilities is 6.5 percent of net income. This grouping essentially treats the tax on the net income of utilities as if it were a gross receipts tax, based on the rationale that regulators allow the tax to be shifted forward to consumers in the form of higher prices. The tax rate on motor fuels is 19.1 percent of the average wholesale price, with a 21 cent per gallon minimum.

6. *Wealth:* Taxable estates (after expenses, debts, losses, exemptions, charitable, and marital deductions) taxed at rates between 5 and 16 percent.

7. *Other:* Includes taxes on cigarettes, alcoholic beverages, racing, beano, deeds, and miscellaneous other taxes. The tax rate on cigarettes is $0.26 per 20-count package. The tax rate per gallon of alcoholic beverages more than 50 percent proof is $4.05. In 1992, revenue from cigarettes and alcoholic beverages accounted for more than 70 percent of the "other" category, the bulk of which was from the tax on cigarettes.

North Carolina

1. *Personal income:* Starting in 1989, the tax is based on the federal government's definition of taxable income. The rates are close to flat, with a six percent marginal tax rate for low incomes and a seven percent marginal tax rate for high incomes. The top tax bracket starts at $21,251 of taxable income for married taxpayers filing jointly. Prior to 1989, no joint returns were allowed, and the tax rates ranged from three to seven percent, with the top rate starting at $10,000.

2. *General sales:* A state tax rate of four percent applies to retail sales including food, clothing, and utility fuels sold for residential use. Prescription drugs, custom computer programs, and repair charges are exempt. In general, admission charges are not taxable. After 1989, motor vehicles are exempt from the sales tax but are subject to the highway use tax equal to three percent of the purchase price, with a minimum tax of $40 and maximum tax of $1,000.

3. *Corporate income:* A rate of 7.75 percent applies to the net income of corporations and savings and loan associations. Allocation rules are based on local-to-total property, payroll, and sales, with sales weighted at 50 percent. Treatment of S-corporations conforms with federal treatment starting in 1989. Before 1989, S-corporations were taxed as corporations.

4. *Insurance:* The tax is based on gross premiums. The tax rate is 1.875 percent (1.9 percent starting in 1992). Some forms of insurance pay different tax rates. In addition, companies pay a regulatory charge calculated as a percentage of the company's premium's tax liability (currently 6.5 percent).

5. *Energy:* This category includes the special franchise tax on utilities and the tax on motor fuels. The franchise tax is a privilege excise tax imposed on the gross receipts (minus some deductions) of electric power, natural gas, water, and sewerage companies. In addition, it includes a gross receipts tax on local telecommunications service. Part of the franchise tax is a tax on all corporations' net worth. This portion of the tax accounts for about one-third of the revenue. Following the Census of Governments, we classify all franchise tax revenue as a tax on utilities. The tax rate on motor fuels is 22.6 cents per gallon. After 1989, revenue reported from the motor fuels tax includes that from the highway use tax (an excise tax on the purchase of automobiles, see the definition of the sales tax).

6. *Wealth:* These include inheritance and gift taxes and are due from heirs independent of where they live. Rates vary from 1 to 17 percent.

7. *Other:* This category includes cigarettes taxes, beverage taxes, the privilege license tax, the soft drink tax, and other miscellaneous taxes. In 1991, revenue from the beverage tax and the cigarette tax accounted for about 70 percent of the revenue from this category. However, in contrast to Massachusetts, the bulk comes from alcoholic beverages, with only six percent from cigarettes. As of 1991, the tax rate on cigarettes is $0.05 per pack.

APPENDIX B: MEASURING EQUITY

As discussed in the text, our equity analysis applies to the following taxes: general sales, taxes on utilities, motor fuels, alcohol, and tobacco and the personal income tax. The analysis involves three steps. First, we calculated the incidence by income class for each tax intended to be borne by consumers. Second, we collapsed the incidence for each tax into a summary measure. Third, we specified the equity constraint in terms of portfolio shares consistent with the optimization model.

Incidence by Income Class

The basic methodology is straightforward. For each of the taxes on spending, we assumed that the tax was borne in line with taxable spending. We used the Consumer Expenditure Survey (CES) to allocate burdens by income class. For North Carolina, we used the Southeast Region CES, and for Massachusetts, we used the Northeast Region CES. The major task for the general sales tax involved matching taxable spending categories with CES spending categories. For the income tax, the major task involved converting CES money income to state adjusted gross income.

When tax rates were known, such as with the general sales tax, we applied that rate to average taxable spending in the class. When tax rates were not known or were not *ad valorem* taxes, such as taxes on cigarettes or alcoholic beverages, we allocated the total tax revenue generated from the tax among income classes in line with taxable spending. When the tax is levied on a per unit basis, this approach may understate the regressivity of the tax since lower income consumer units may buy more of the cheaper products: generic cigarettes, lower grade gasoline, and cheap liquor.

The following sections describe various issues that arose and how we dealt with them.

Insufficient detail in the regional survey: In several cases, where the breakdown in the regional survey was insufficient for defining taxable spending, we used the breakdowns by income class from the national survey to allocate spending totals on regional categories by income class into subcategories. For example, we used the national survey to divide total spending on food between consumption at home and away from home. In addition, we used it to supplement regional data for spending on each of the goods subject to selective sales taxes, namely, tobacco, alcohol, and gasoline.

Households versus consumer units: The CES focuses on the consumer unit as the unit of observation. The CES provides information on the number of consumer units by income class but only for the sample within each region. Hence, for state-specific distributions of consumer units, we had to use Census information on households. The major difference between a Census household and a CES consumer unit is the treatment of unrelated individuals who live together. The Census treats people living in the same housing unit as one household. The CES treats people who live together but who are financially independent as separate consumer units. Hence, there are fewer households than consumer units. We estimated the number of consumer units in each income class as the number of family households plus the number of one-person nonfamily households plus 1.5 times the number of multiple person nonfamily households. This adjustment generates a number of consumer units by income class that is two to three percent larger than the number of households.

Shortfall in calculated general sales tax revenue: The average sales tax burdens on residents (calculated as the sum across all income classes of the state tax rate times average spending on taxable goods in each income class) appeared to be too low. Specifically, the estimated revenue generated by multiplying the average burdens by the number of consumer units in each income class amounted to only about 50 percent of the total revenue collected by the state. Some shortfall was to be expected since business firms and nonresident visitors also buy goods subject to the general sales tax. Nonetheless the underestimate seemed too large. (Using a similar methodology, Ring (1989) finds large underestimates for Massachusetts and North Carolina using data for 1979. We disagree with his conclusion that the difference between allocations using CES data and actual revenue collections are solely due to sales to businesses and nonresidents.) Because the major reason for the large underestimate appears to be under-reporting on the CES (see Giesemari, 1987), we inflated the sales tax burdens in both states by 33 percent, so that we could account for approximately 75 percent of the sales tax revenue. Note that this adjustment has no effect on the indices of equity reported in Table 4 for the general sales tax because those indices are based on ratios of burdens not absolute burdens. The adjustment's only impact is on the overall equity index and constraint.

Income tax: The starting point for calculating income tax burdens is average money income for each income class, as reported in the CES. To convert CES money income to state adjusted gross income (AGI), we subtracted contributions to Individual Retirement Accounts or Keogh plans, Social Security Income, Workman's Compensation, Veterans benefits, public assistance, food stamps, 75 percent of postdivorce support received, and other income (such as in-kind payments of food and room), based on data from the regional CES supplemented with data from the national survey. We included 25 percent of postdivorce payments as income, since alimony is taxable but child support is not. To add capital gains income to money income, we estimated state-specific capital gains by income class from federal tax return data reported in various issues of the Internal Revenue Service's *Statistics of Income Bulletin*. For each income class, we calculated the ratio of capital gains to precapital gains income based on the IRS data and then multiplied that ratio by precapital gains income calculated from CES money income. This procedure yields an estimate of capital gains income for each income class that can be added to precapital gains income to generate an average AGI for each CES income class.

Tax burdens are taken from state distributional tables for the income tax. The Massachusetts figures are based on 1989 data. North Carolina figures are based on 1989 data, the latest year with state-level distribution tables. The dollar value of the income tax burden is the average effective tax rate within the AGI class times the average AGI for each CES money income class. Dividing this burden by average CES money income yields an effective tax burden relative to CES money income that is comparable to the burdens of other taxes. This method closely approximates tax revenue for Massachusetts but overstates tax revenues for North Carolina, possibly because of the 1989 changes in the state tax code. To correct this overstatement, we deflated the estimates of dollar tax burdens by a constant 30 percent; this correction does not affect the relative tax burdens of income classes for the income tax.

We account for the federal deductibility of state income taxes by reducing the state income tax burden by the value of the reduction in federal taxes. For each income class in each state, we multiply the average state income tax burden times the fraction of tax returns that itemize in the income class (from the *Statistics of Income Bulletin*) and the marginal federal tax rate for the income class. We subtract this amount from the state tax burden to reflect the average burden on state residents.

The Equity Index

As a summary measure of equity, we chose the liability progression elasticity. We measure this elasticity between two income groups, the $10,000 to $20,000 group and the $40,000 to $50,000 group. The elasticity is the percentage change in average tax burdens divided by the percentage change in average income between the two groups. We constructed this elasticity for each tax and for the overall tax system.

To convert this measure of progressivity into an expression which includes portfolio shares, we use the following relationship between the total amount of tax a paid by the average household in income class b (T_a^b):

$$T_a^b = w_a T K_a^b$$

where T is total tax revenue; w_a is portfolio share (fraction of total revenue generated by tax a); and K_a^b is an allocation factor, the percentage of tax a borne by a household in income class b.

Some algebra leads to an overall elasticity:

$$\frac{\sum_{j=1}^{n} w_j K_j^{40} - \sum_{j=1}^{n} w_j K_j^{10}}{\sum_{j=1}^{n} w_j K_j^{10}}$$
$$\frac{}{\frac{I^{40} - I^{10}}{I^{10}}}$$

where I^{10} is the average income for households in the $10,000 to $20,000 income class and I^{40} is the average income for households in the $40,000 to $50,000 income class.

The Equity Constraint

As described in the text, each state faces a permissible range of possible values of progressivity. In our base case, the total elasticity of the tax system is allowed to vary by plus or minus 0.15 of the 1991 value for each state. Alternatively, we allowed the total elasticity to vary by plus or minus 0.25 of the 1991 value for each state. This difference did not substantively change the results.

This article contributes to the small literature on the determination of local taxes by testing hypotheses about whether local officials consider the tax burdens of neighboring counties when making their own decisions about taxes on residents. Based on data for large U.S. counties, evidence of tax mimicking appears first in comparisons of the degree of clustering of tax burdens among neighboring counties within metropolitan areas to that among nonneighboring counties within states. In addition, regression equations based on both 1978 and 1985 data confirm the presence of tax mimicking for total local tax burdens and for property tax burdens, but not for sales tax burdens.

MIMICKING OF LOCAL TAX BURDENS AMONG NEIGHBORING COUNTIES

HELEN F. LADD
Duke University

The economics literature is replete with models of the demand for local public services and the determination of local public spending. However, much less has been written about the level and composition of state or local taxes. Exceptions include the recent work by Hettich and Winer (1988), Inman (1989), and Chernick (1991), who posit political choice models in which policymakers are assumed to try to minimize the costs — broadly defined to include the political costs — of raising revenue.

This article contributes to the small but growing literature on the determination of local taxes by testing hypotheses about tax mimicking. Specifically, the question is whether local governments take into account the tax burdens in other jurisdictions when making their own tax decisions. To the extent that they do, we would expect to observe less variation in the tax burdens of

---

AUTHOR'S NOTE: *This article was initially prepared for the 1991 Conference of Taxation, Resources, and Economic Development (TRED), "Financing Local Government in the 1990s," sponsored by the Lincoln Institute of Land Policy, Cambridge, Massachusetts, Oct. 4-5, 1991. The data for this article were assembled as part of a larger project during 1989-1990 while I was a Senior Research Fellow at the Lincoln Institute of Land Policy. I am grateful to the Lincoln Institute for support during that year and also for the expert research assistance of Russ LaMotte. Peter Mieszkowski provided useful comments and suggestions on the earlier version of this article.*

neighboring jurisdictions than in comparable nonneighboring jurisdictions. Although not discussed much in the academic literature, tax mimicking is often mentioned by policymakers as a justification for particular tax decisions. For example, local officials might defend a decision to raise the local sales tax rate on the grounds that the new rate will not be out of line with those in neighboring jurisdictions, or they may oppose an increase in the property tax rate because the resulting tax burden will be excessive relative to those in nearby jurisdictions.

When making tax decisions, local officials might be influenced by the rates in neighboring jurisdictions because of concern about the loss of business activity. This concern motivates much of the theoretical literature on tax competition that explores how competition among jurisdictions for a mobile tax base, such as industrial property, affects the nature of the equilibrium and the efficiency of public sector choices (see Oates and Schwab 1988; Wildasin 1988; Wilson 1986; Zodrow and Mieszkowski 1986). In contrast to that theoretical work, this article shifts the focus away from business taxes onto individual tax burdens.

With respect to burdens on people, one might try to explain local officials' concern with tax burdens in neighboring jurisdictions in terms of the Tiebout model and its emphasis on voting with one's feet. However, the Tiebout mechanism need not lead one jurisdiction to copy the tax burdens in neighboring jurisdictions. According to that mechanism, fiscally related movement among jurisdictions is motivated not by tax burdens alone, but rather by the entire fiscal package, that is, by the level of public services relative to tax burdens. Potential residents may be willing to pay higher taxes in one jurisdiction than another if the higher taxes are offset by higher services. Stated differently, some jurisdictions may purposely keep tax and spending burdens low relative to their neighbors specifically to differentiate their community fiscally from the others. Tiebout movement would lead to clustering of tax burdens only if there were clustering of expenditure packages.

Alternatively, the political "voice" mechanism (see Hirschman 1970) may lead jurisdictions to keep their taxes in line with those of their neighbors. According to this mechanism, resident voters may use tax burdens in other jurisdictions as a yardstick with which to evaluate the fiscal performance of their own government. By threatening to punish at the polls those officials who impose tax burdens out of line with those in other jurisdictions, voters set the stage for local tax burdens to be influenced by the burdens in neighboring jurisdictions. A similar mechanism could also operate with respect to public services: Voters could demand that their local government keep up with the service expansions in nearby communities.

The most interesting and innovative recent empirical work on fiscal copycatting focuses on the behavior of states. In an unpublished paper, Case, Hines, and Rosen (1989) use panel data from states to examine the extent to which states copy their "neighbors" when making their spending decisions, where "neighbors" are defined as states to which the state compares itself. And in a more recent paper, Case (forthcoming) continues this line of research by using panel data on individual tax burdens to examine the extent to which states copy their "neighbors" in the setting of income tax rates. One difficulty with this state- based research arises in determining a state's neighbors, that is, the set of states to which the state compares itself. In the first paper, Case et al. let the data determine the appropriate dimension, such as income or racial composition of the population, along which neighbors should be defined. In the second paper, Case simply assumes that a state's neighbors are those that share state boundaries. Neither approach is fully satisfactory; the first because what emerges from the data, namely the racial composition of the state, is hard to justify intuitively, and the second because geographic proximity is clearly not the key dimension in many situations. For example, residents in Massachusetts are presumably more likely to compare their tax burdens to those in other industrialized states rather than to those in the geographically contiguous, but rural, state of Vermont.

This article contributes to the empirical literature on fiscal copycatting behavior by focusing on tax mimicking at the local, rather than the state, level. A major advantage of the local focus is that the concept of neighboring jurisdictions is relatively straightforward. In contrast to the state level, where geographic proximity is at best a crude measure of a state's "neighbors" for the purposes of tax competition, geographic proximity within the same metropolitan area provides a natural way of defining potentially competitive jurisdictions at the local level. However, for a national study such as this one, local government comparisons can be treacherous because of the variation across states in the fiscal role of local governments and the division of responsibilities among different types of local governments, such as counties, municipalities, and school districts. Fortunately, the availability of Census of Governments data aggregated to county areas makes it possible to avoid this potential problem. As elaborated below, the unit of observation for this study is the county (or county equivalent), and tax burdens are based on the taxes levied by all types of local governments within the geographic boundaries of each county.

The first section describes the county data on which the analysis is based. The second section looks for evidence of tax mimicking by comparing the degree of clustering of tax burdens among neighboring counties within metropolitan areas to that among nonneighboring counties within states. The third section continues the investigation of mimicking using regression models in the spirit of those developed by Case. The fourth section discusses the plausibility of the results and considers alternative formulations. The article ends with a brief conclusion.

THE COUNTY DATA

The data used in this study are drawn from a larger national data set for 248 large counties or county equivalents that I put together to look at various questions about the interrelationship between growth and taxes. The 248 counties represent all the counties for which complete data on taxes and spending and on population measures were available for both 1978 and 1985. The years 1978 and 1985 were chosen to minimize the effects of the national economy on the data; both years are in the expansion phase of the national economic cycle and follow a recession by three years. In 1985, these 248 large counties contained 59% of the nation's population.

The sample was determined primarily by the availability of fiscal data, the major source for which is the annual Census of Governments publication on local government finances in major county areas.[1] The information in this publication differs from that of other census publications on local finances in that taxes and spending are aggregated for all local governments within the geographic area defined by county boundaries. Because states differ in how they divide responsibilities for local spending on functions such as education or social services among types of local governments such as municipalities, counties, or school districts, this aggregation assures comparability across the country in the treatment of local spending. Most of the population and economic data by county were provided on diskette by the National Planning Association.

Much of the empirical work presented in this article is based on subsets of this data. The regressions in the third section are based on data for the 94 counties that are located in metropolitan areas represented by at least three large counties in the 248-county data set. This set of 94 counties is the largest set of counties for which information on geographic neighbors can be constructed. The 94 counties are located in the 26 metropolitan areas listed in the appendix.[2] A somewhat smaller set of 72 counties is used in the next section. This smaller set excludes the counties in metropolitan areas that cross state lines, namely, Cincinnati, Philadelphia, St. Louis, and Washington, DC.

CLUSTERING OF LOCAL TAX BURDENS

As defined above, tax mimicking implies that local officials take into consideration the tax burdens of neighboring counties when making their own tax decisions. Regardless of the motivation for this behavior, the manifestations are clear: namely, local tax burdens will be more clustered than they would be in the absence of tax mimicking.

To test for copycatting behavior, my strategy in this section is to compare variation in tax burdens among counties within metropolitan areas — that is, among neighbors — with that among counties, at least some of which are not neighbors, within states.

Tables 1 and 2 provide information on tax clustering for 1978 and 1985. Each table presents results for seven tax or revenue burdens where burdens are calculated as revenues divided by the personal income of county residents. I would prefer to use effective tax rates rather than tax burdens as defined here, but statutory tax rates are not available by county and differences in the definitions of tax bases across the country would render the statutory tax rates meaningless.[3] I have chosen to express taxes relative to resident income rather than on a per capita basis because the resulting burden measures are more like tax rates (albeit average, rather than marginal, rates). However, they are at times imperfect measures of the burden on residents. Consider, for example, the measure of total property tax burdens. The more nonresidential property in the area that is owned by nonresidents, the less well this measure approximates the burden on county residents. This conclusion follows because some of the property taxes would ultimately be paid by nonresidents rather than by residents. Hence the measure overstates the burden of local property taxes on residents.[4] Fortunately, this particular limitation can be dealt with by constructing a more refined measure of the property tax burden, the amount of the property tax burden attributable to property taxes on residential property alone. Such adjustments are not feasible for other burden measures.[5]

The burden measures all begin with the prefix TB and end with a 2-digit year suffix. The first two measures are aggregates: total taxes (TBTTAX) and personal taxes and charges (TBPERS). This second aggregate is constructed as the sum of residential property tax burdens (TBRES); sales taxes (TBSALE); other taxes (TBOTH), which includes selective sales taxes, income taxes, and miscellaneous taxes; and current charges (TBCHAR).

Consider initially the first column in Table 1. The entries are based on the 72 counties in the 22 metropolitan areas in single states described above. To construct each entry in column 1, the counties were first grouped into their 22 metropolitan areas, a metropolitan-specific coefficient of variation was

TABLE 1: Clustering of Tax Burdens, 1978: Metropolitan Areas Versus States (average coefficients of variation)

	All Counties		Suburban Counties		
	MSA (1)	State (2)	MSA (3)	State (4)	t statistics (5)
TBTTAX78	0.1830	0.1878	0.0781	0.1436	3.06
TBPERS78	0.1972	0.2018	0.1131	0.1417	1.22
TBPROP78	0.1593	0.1723	0.0933	0.1533	2.52
TBRES78	0.1730	0.1882	0.1241	0.1770	2.31
TBSALE78	0.5951	0.5551	0.3613	0.3842	0.14
TBOTH78	0.5829	0.5370	0.2275	0.2879	1.17
TBCHAR78	0.3543	0.4205	0.2433	0.3256	1.35
Number of observations	22	26	20	21	

TABLE 2: Clustering of Tax Burdens, 1985: Metropolitan Areas Versus States (average coefficients of variation)

	Suburban Counties		
	MSA (1)	State (2)	t statistics (3)
TBTTAX85	0.0887	0.1294	1.73
TBPERS85	0.1341	0.1732	1.19
TBPROP85	0.0768	0.1319	2.71
TBRES85	0.0967	0.1463	1.78
TBSALE85	0.2772	0.4006	0.81
TBOTH85	0.2653	0.3111	1.01
TBCHAR85	0.2350	0.3784	1.80
TBSS85	0.5428	1.0044	3.91
TBINC85	0.5428	1.7546	6.69
Number of observations	20	21	

calculated for each area for the relevant type of tax burden, and the coefficients of variation were averaged over the 22 metropolitan areas. Thus the first entry indicates that the typical standard deviation for total local taxes is about 18% of the mean within a metropolitan area.[6]

The goal is to compare this variation in local taxes within metropolitan areas (that is, among neighbors) to the variation across large counties within states. States are the logical unit for this comparison because all local governments within a state operate within the same state-local fiscal environment. Thus column 2 differs from column 1 in that counties are first grouped by state rather than by metropolitan area. The reader should note that the set of counties included in this calculation differs from that in the previous column. Starting with the sample of 248 large counties, the criterion for a state, and consequently for all its large counties, to be included is that the state be represented by 3 or more large counties located in more than one metropolitan area. This criterion is met in 26 states.

A comparison of column 1 with column 2 provides little support for the hypothesis of tax mimicking. Contrary to expectations, the variation among neighboring counties is not consistently smaller than the variation among counties within a state. Additional reflection, however, provides a plausible explanation for these results and suggests the need for more refined comparisons. The problem is that some of the large counties are either primarily or exclusively large central cities. Such counties may be sufficiently different from suburban counties that the relevant neighbors—that is, the set of counties to which a large suburban county compares itself—should exclude any county that contains a central city.

Columns 3-5 implement this refinement by reporting the within-metro area and within-state variations only for large suburban counties. Metropolitan areas and states were retained in the sample provided that there were at least two large suburban counties in the metropolitan area and, in the case of states, that the counties were located in more than one metropolitan area.

Contrary to the earlier findings, a comparison of the measures of variation in columns 3 and 4 suggests that tax mimicking is alive and well. Consistent with such behavior, in all seven categories of tax burden, the variation of local tax burdens among suburban neighbors within a metropolitan area is smaller than that of nonneighboring counties in other parts of the state. The largest proportional difference is for total taxes (0.08 vs. 0.14), but differences are also quite large for residential property taxes (0.12 vs. 0.18) and for current charges (0.24 vs. 0.33). In three of the comparisons, TBTTAX78, TBPROP78, and TBRES78, the differences are sufficiently large relative to the standard errors to be statistically significant (see the t statistic for difference of means in the final column).

Table 2 replicates the right-hand side of Table 1 for 1985 data and adds two more burden categories, namely two subcategories of the "other" category: selective sales taxes (TBSS85) and income taxes (TBINC85). For the basic seven categories, the 1985 pattern is similar to that for 1978. Once again, the variation among neighboring suburban counties (column 1) in all cases is smaller than the average variation among counties within states (column 2). Although the 1985 differences are slightly smaller relative to their standard errors than the 1978 difference, three continue to be statistically significant.

The two additional subcategories provide the most dramatic evidence of clustering among neighbors, and, hence, provide the strongest support for the presence of tax competition. The average coefficient of variation within metropolitan areas for selective sales tax burdens (0.54) is just over half that for states (1.00), and the average coefficient of variation within metropolitan areas for income taxes (0.46) is less than one third that for states (1.75). Both differences are highly significant.

A competing explanation for this clustering is that counties in the same metropolitan area have similar tax rates not because of mimicking but rather because they share similar characteristics, such as population density, that affect tax burdens. Table 3 helps rule out this alternative hypothesis by focusing on changes in, rather than levels of, tax burdens. Because changes during the 1978 to 1985 period were both positive and negative, mean changes are not very meaningful. Hence the measure of variation used in this table is the standard deviation, rather than the coefficient of variation.

The hypothesis here is that tax mimicking would lead counties to change tax burdens in line with changes in neighboring counties. If this were the case, we would expect to find more clustering (as evidenced by smaller average deviations) of tax rate changes within metropolitan areas than within states. As is evident from a comparison of columns 5 and 6, the results are generally consistent with the hypothesis. For example, the average standard deviation of the total tax burden is only 0.0021 in MSAs, which is significantly smaller than the 0.0037 deviation in states. However, the differences for residential property taxes, sales taxes, and other taxes are small or nonexistent.

In sum, Tables 1-3 are generally consistent with the existence of tax mimicking. The consistency of the patterns for the two years of data plus for the change data are strongly suggestive of the hypothesized behavior. Because this analysis does not control for the other characteristics that influence tax burdens (or changes in tax burdens), however, it cannot stand alone. The following section reinforces these results with results from a regression model.

TAX BURDEN REGRESSIONS

Regression analysis provides an alternative means of determining the magnitude of tax mimicking. The basic model takes the following form:

TABLE 3: Clustering of Changes in Tax Burdens, 1978-1985: Metropolitan Areas Versus States (average standard deviations)

	Suburban Counties		
	MSA (1)	State (2)	t statistics (3)
TBTTAXCH	0.0021	0.0037	2.83
TBPERSCH	0.0039	0.0058	1.72
TBPROPCH	0.0018	0.0033	2.76
TBRESCH	0.0022	0.0025	0.62
TBSALECH	0.0008	0.0009	0.18
TBOTHCH	0.0007	0.0007	0.13
TBCHARCH	0.0021	0.0030	1.74
Number of observations	20	21	

$$TB_i = a + \sum_h b_h X_{hi} + \sum_k c_k SD_{ki} + d \sum_j w_j TB_{ji} + u_i,$$

where TB_i is the tax burden in the ith county, each X_h is county characteristics that affect tax burdens, SD_k is an indicator variable for each state in which one or more of the sample counties is located, and $\sum_j w_j TB_{ji}$ is a weighted average of tax burdens in neighboring counties, where wj is the weight, and u_i is a random error term. The coefficient d measures the degree of tax mimicking.

Case (forthcoming) provides a theoretical foundation for this type of regression equation based on a political voice model. According to Case's formulation, when making tax rate decisions, local officials try to increase tax revenues beyond the amount needed to meet the service demands of county residents. They are constrained, however, by the ability of voters to compare the fiscal performance in their county to that in other counties. It is this fiscal comparison that explains the presence in the tax burden equation of tax burdens in neighboring jurisdictions.

The regressions are estimated separately for 1978 and 1985 data. Five different tax burden variables are used as the dependent variable, with yy indicating the final two digits of the year: total taxes (TBTTAXyy), property taxes (PBPROPyy), residential property taxes (TBRESyy), general sales taxes (TBSALEyy), and other taxes (TBOTHyy). The X variables in the regressions include per capita income (INCPCyy), public school enrollments as a fraction of the population (PUPPCyy), population density (POPDENyy), and two indicator variables: one that takes on the value 1 if the county embraces a central city (CC) and another that takes on the value 1 if the county is in a metropolitan area that crosses state boundaries (DS). The first three variables are potential determinants of local spending and hence of tax burdens. The state dummy variables are needed to control for the tremendous variation across states in the division of taxing responsibilities between state and local governments and in the general level of taxation. For example, local tax burdens are likely to be higher in New York, with its strong preferences for public services and large role for local governments, than in many other states. Because New York State is treated as the base state in the regressions, the coefficients of many of the state dummy variables are expected to be negative.

Of central interest is the variable representing the tax burdens in neighboring counties. Based on the findings in the previous section, neighbors are defined exclusive of central cities. For simplicity, the weights are assumed to be equal so that the neighbor variable in each equation is simply the average tax burden for the relevant type of tax in all other large noncentral city counties in the metropolitan area. The idea is that individual counties, whether they be counties with central cities or suburban counties, compete with the suburban counties. This variable is indicated by NEIGH and differs from one equation to another depending on which type of tax is being investigated.

Estimating the tax burden equation by ordinary least squares would be problematic. The possibility that counties in a single metropolitan area may be subject to similar shocks potentially leads to spatial correlation of the errors. To counter this statistical problem, the equations were estimated using instrumental variables. The instruments used to identify the coefficient of the neighborhood variable are weighted averages of the per capita income, pupils per capita, and population of the county's neighbors. The results for 1978 are reported in Table 4 and for 1985 in Table 5. The sample includes the 94 counties for which neighbor variables can be constructed as described earlier.

Consider first the 1978 regressions. Of primary interest are the result for the NEIGH variable in the first row. For the total tax burden, the property tax burden, and the residential property tax burden (columns 1, 2, and 3), the equations provide clear and striking support for the hypothesis that counties mimic their neighbors. For example, the first entry implies that if the burden of total taxes on a county's neighbors increases by $1 per $100 of income, the burden in the county will increase by $0.59 per $100. The comparable degree of tax mimicking for total property taxes is $0.45 and for residential property tax burdens is $0.55 per dollar change in the county's neighbors. The plausibility and robustness of these results are discussed below.

The results for the general sales tax burden and other tax burden (columns 4 and 5 in Table 4) are much less supportive of the view that counties try to emulate their neighbors. Taken literally, the negative coefficients on the neighborhood variable imply that counties try to differ from them. But neither coefficient is statistically significant. In the case of the sales tax regression, this statistical insignificance may reflect the limited role of income, pupils, and population density in explaining the county sales tax burden. However, the addition of other explanatory variables, such as employment density, neither changes nor improves the results. Not all counties in the sample use sales taxes. Nor do all make use of the taxes in the "other" category. This lumpiness in use makes it difficult to sort out the role of tax mimicking at the margin. One possible interpretation is that counties do not compete on the basis of individual taxes, but rather on the basis either of the overall tax burden or of widely used taxes such as property taxes.

The 1985 equations in Table 5 are similar to those for 1978, but the explanatory power of the regressions is a bit lower and the neighborhood variable for residential property taxes is now tiny and not significant. The coefficients of the NEIGH variable for total taxes and total property taxes remain positive and statistically significant. For total taxes, the mimicking effect rises to .82, and for property taxes, to 0.58. The coefficients on TBSALES and TBOTH remain negative.

Some of these differences may be explained by the nationwide "tax revolt" of the late 1970s and early 1980s. Starting with a California initiative (Proposition 13) in 1978 that significantly reduced local property tax rates and made them more uniform, other states moved to limit local taxes either through referenda or by a political unwillingness to raise taxes. The resulting public focus on tax burdens at the local level could plausibly account for the greater sensitivity of counties to the tax burdens of neighboring counties in 1985 compared to 1978. The anomalous findings for residential property taxes most likely reflect data limitations associated in part with the tax revolt. Recall that the residential tax burden is constructed by multiplying the total property tax burden by the estimated residential share of assessed value in each county. Changes over time in assessing practices can lead to errors in the estimates. Because some states responded to the tax revolt of the early 1980s by changing their assessing practices, the residential property findings are potentially subject to error.[7]

TABLE 4: Tax Burden Regressions, 1978

	TBTTAX78	TBPROP78	TBRES78	TBSALE78	TBOTH78
NEIGH	0.585**	0.451**	0.546**	−0.734	−1.21
	(2.72)	(2.72)	(3.30)	(0.43)	(0.92)
INCPC78	0.037×10^{-5}	0.024×10^{-5}	0.061×10^{-5}*	0.015×10^{-5}	0.025×10^{-5}
	(0.76)	(0.59)	(1.89)	(1.16)	(0.62)
PUPPC78	0.037	−0.001	0.008	0.007	0.043**
	(1.29)	(0.06)	(0.44)	(0.59)	(2.40)
POPDEN78	0.080×10^{-5}**	−0.029	-0.077×10^{-5}**	0.006×10^{-5}	0.106×10^{-5}**
	(2.70)	(1.20)	(3.90)	(0.74)	(6.04)
CC	0.013**	0.007**	0.004**	0.003**	0.004**
	(6.40)	(4.18)	(3.18)	(3.48)	(2.87)
DS	0.004*	0.001	0.001	0.000	0.000
	(1.74)	(0.75)	(0.58)	(0.48)	(0.22)
State dummy variables	[21]	[21]	[21]	[21]	[21]
Constant (NY)	0.009	0.020**	0.003	0.006	−0.002
	(0.73)	(2.24)	(0.58)	(1.26)	(0.27)
Adj. R^2	0.84	0.83	0.79	0.82	0.81
Mean of dependent variables	0.045	0.035	0.023	0.003	0.006
Number of observations	94	94	94	94	94

NOTE: Regressions estimated by instrumental variables; absolute value of t statistics in parentheses. TBTTAX78 = Total taxes as a fraction of personal income, 1978. TBPROP78 = Property taxes as a fraction of personal income, 1978. TBRES78 = Residential property taxes (= total property taxes times percentage of gross annual value that is residential) as a fraction of personal income, 1978. TBSALE78 = General sales taxes as a fraction of personal income, 1978. NEIGH = Neighborhood variable as described in the text; different variable for each type of tax. INCPC78 = Per capita income in 1978 in 1982 dollars. PUPPC78 = Public school enrollment in 1978 (estimated) as a fraction of 1978 population. POPDEN78 = Population density per square mile, 1978. CC = Indicator variable that takes on the value 1 if the county contains a central city and 0 otherwise. DS = Indicator variable that takes on the value 1 if the metropolitan area is located in more than one state. State dummy variables = Indicator variables that take on the value 1 if the county is in the specified state and 0 otherwise. Number in brackets indicates number of state dummies included in the equation.
*statistical significance at the 10% level, **statistical significance at the 5% level.

TABLE 5: Tax Burden Regressions, 1985

	TBTTAX85 (1)	TBPROP85 (2)	TBRES85 (3)	TBSALE85 (4)	TBOTH85 (5)
NEIGH	0.815** (2.71)	0.577** (3.78)	0.007 (0.03)	−0.143* (1.78)	−0.231 (0.19)
INCPC85	-0.013×10^{-5} (0.31)	0.003×10^{-5} (0.13)	0.009×10^{-5} (0.47)	0.002×10^{-5} (0.13)	-0.015×10^{-5} (0.47)
PUPPC85	0.001 (0.02)	0.021 (0.88)	0.014 (0.79)	0.004 (0.26)	0.016 (0.58)
POPDEN85	0.052×10^{-5} (1.61)	−0.061** (3.14)	-0.017×10^{-5} (1.23)	−0.015 (1.38)	$0.122 \times 10^{-5**}$ (6.44)
CC	0.014** (5.54)	0.008** (5.31)	0.005** (4.91)	0.004** (4.34)	0.003** (1.98)
DS	0.002 (0.74)	−0.000 (0.16)	−0.001 (0.87)	0.001 (0.72)	0.000 (0.17)
State dummy variables	[21]	[21]	[21]	[21]	[21]
Constant (NY)	0.010 (0.61)	0.011 (1.36)	0.020** (2.78)	0.021** (3.57)	0.002 (0.23)
Adj. R^2	0.76	0.75	0.69	0.86	0.78
Mean of dependent variables	0.042	0.031	0.020	0.004	0.006
Number of observations	94	94	94	94	94

NOTE: Regressions estimated by instrumental variables; absolute value of t statistics in parentheses. For definition of variables, see Table 4.
*Statistical significance at the 10% level; **statistical significance at the 5% level.

DISCUSSION

One might legitimately wonder if the key results of this study, namely, those for the neighbor variables, are spurious. Perhaps the NEIGH variables are picking up not the behavior of geographically defined neighbors but rather the effects of tax burdens in any random set of counties in the state. To explore this possibility, a new set of "neighbors" was defined as follows. Within each state, the 248 counties were ranked alphabetically. Then, for each large county in the 94-county sample, the county's neighbors were defined to be the three other counties in the state that follow the county in the alphabetical ordering.[8] The question then becomes whether the tax burdens of neighbors based on this essentially random set of neighbors exert the same impact on the county's tax burden as the geographically defined NEIGH variables in Tables 4 and 5. The answer is clear. In every case, the alphabetically defined neighbor variable has a coefficient indistinguishable from zero. For example, in the total tax burden equation for 1978, the coefficient is –0.12 with a t statistic of 0.75. This finding helps confirm that the original NEIGH variables are measuring something meaningful.

A second issue is whether the estimates of tax mimicking might be refined. The reported results are for the 94 counties for which data on neighbors were available, including those counties in metropolitan areas that cross state lines. The equations account for these MSAs in more than one state with the DS indicator variable. This approach is advantageous because it permits use of the full 94-county sample. An alternative is to rerun the equations with the smaller set of counties in single-state MSAs. This modification for 1978 yields results for the NEIGH coefficients that are similar to those reported in Table 4. The pattern of coefficients is identical, with somewhat larger estimated impacts for total taxes and property taxes and somewhat lower statistical significance.[9]

Another refinement is to eliminate from the sample the counties that include central cities. The assumption implicit in the model as initially estimated is that both central city-counties and suburban counties mimic suburban counties. The fact that tax burdens are typically higher in central cities than in suburban counties is accounted for by the central city indicator variable. This approach seems to be reasonable; eliminating the central city-counties reduces the sample size to 67 counties, but has virtually no impact on the NEIGH variable. Also implicit in the basic methodology is the assumption that suburban counties mimic other suburban counties but not central city-counties. To examine this assumption, the regressions based on the suburban subsample were rerun with an additional tax burden, namely, the tax burden in the central city of the MSA, in the equation. The results confirm the assumption. Specifically, the coefficient on the NEIGH variables in the 1978 total tax, property tax, and residential property equations remains about 0.50, whereas the coefficient on the city tax burden variable is much smaller and statistically insignificant.[10]

Finally, one might ask if the estimated magnitudes of mimicking are reasonable. They appear to me to be intuitively plausible. Moreover, they are consistent with estimates presented in the other empirical study of this type, the study by Ann Case of state income taxes. She finds that a $1 increase in the income taxes on a state's neighbors leads to about a $0.50 increase in the state, with the results varying somewhat by income class and whether it is before or after the federal Tax Reform Act of 1986.[11]

CONCLUSION

This study provides support for the view that local tax decisions in one jurisdiction are influenced by the tax burdens in neighboring jurisdictions. Given these initial, but relatively strong, findings of tax mimicking, the next step is to explore in more detail the underlying reasons for this behavior. As discussed in the introduction, two potential motivations need to be examined, the voice and the exit mechanism. In her work on states, Case is currently examining the voice mechanism by exploring the extent to which governors who preside over tax increases that exceed those in neighboring states are rebuffed at the polls. The county data used in this article are not amendable to a similar analysis because tax decisions involve too many local public officials. However, with the county data, indirect evidence on the views of residents toward taxes can be gleaned by examining their location decisions. In particular, one could look at the extent to which population changes by county are influenced not only by the tax burden in the specific county but also by the tax burdens in neighboring counties, controlling for public service levels in both places. My preliminary work on that topic is consistent with the story that emerges from this article, namely, that residents appear to care about tax burdens in neighboring counties. However, more work remains to be done.

APPENDIX
Metropolitan Areas That Include
Three or More Large Counties

Albany, Schenectady, and Troy, New York
Atlanta, Georgia
Baltimore, Maryland
Boston, Lawrence, and Salem, Massachusetts, NECMA
Chicago, Illinois
Cincinnati, Ohio, Kentucky, and Indiana
Cleveland, Ohio
Dallas, Texas
Denver, Colorado
Detroit, Michigan
Greensboro, and Winston-Salem, North Carolina
Houston, Texas
Kansas City, Missouri and Kansas
Minneapolis-St. Paul, Minnesota
New Orleans, Louisiana
New York, New York
Newark, New Jersey
Philadelphia, Pennsylvania and New Jersey
Pittsburgh, Pennsylvania
Portland, Oregon
Sacramento, California
Salt Lake City, Utah
San Francisco, California
St. Louis, Missouri and Illinois
Tampa-St. Petersburg, Florida
Washington, DC

NOTES

1. For fiscal year 1984-85, fiscal data are available in the U.S. Department of Commerce, Bureau of the Census, *Local Government Finances in Major County Areas: 1984-85* (GF85, April 1987) for all 410 counties with population greater than 100,000 regardless of the metropolitan area in which they are located. Because of a change in the criteria for selecting counties, only about 260 of these counties were included in the comparable 1978 publication, *Local Government Fiances in Selected Metropolitan Areas and Large Counties: 1977-78* (GF78, no. 6, April 1980).

2. Initially, there were 95 counties, but Rockland, New York was eliminated because it proved to be a significant outlier in the regression analysis.

3. In the context of individual states, one can look more closely at tax rates or tax bases. For Arizona, for example, where individual cities have the power both to define their tax bases and to set tax rates, Dana Weist and I have provided evidence that city decisions about the taxation of food appear to be influenced by the actions of nearby cities. See Ladd and Weist (1991).

4. Implicit in this assertion is the assumption that property taxes on business property are borne by the owners of the business. With other incidence assumptions, the situation becomes more complicated, but the basic logic remains.

5. The residential share of total property taxes is approximated by multiplying the total by the residential share of the gross assessed value in each county. With respect to sales taxes, even if one knew what share of local sales taxes accrued from sales of intermediate goods to firms rather than final sales to consumers, determining the share of the tax borne by residents would be complicated by the possibility that firms might be able to shift large portions of the burden to local residents in the form of higher prices.

6. The counties in metropolitan statistical areas (MSAs) in more than one state were excluded because differences across states in the state share of state and local taxes could lead to significantly larger variation across counties in these MSAs than in the typical MSA. However, such counties are included in the regressions reported in this section. In the regression, an indicator variable is included to control for this institutional difference.

7. Massachusetts is the clearest example. In response to the state's 1980 tax limitation measure, Proposition 2½, many communities for the first time found it advantageous to assess all property close to 100% of market value. The resulting movement to 100% assessment typically resulted in a major redistribution of the property tax burden away from business property onto residential property in many big cities.

8. If a county is near the bottom of the alphabet, the contiguous counties are assumed to be those at the beginning of the alphabet.

9. The coefficients of the NEIGH variable in the 1978 regressions are as follows with absolute values of t statistics in parentheses: TBTTAX78 = 0.854(1.95); TBPROP78 = 0.504(1.61); TBRES78 = 0.577(1.96); TBSALE78 = –0.886(1.18); NTBOTH78 = –0.250(–0.25).

10. One other variation is to redefine all the dependent variables and the NEIGH variables in Tables 4 and 5 in per capita terms. The pattern of results on the NEIGH variables are identical to those reported in the tables. The major difference is in the somewhat smaller, but still statistically significant, estimates of tax mimicking. However, the smaller estimated magnitudes simply reflect the somewhat different question that is being asked. In one case, the question refers to movements in taxes relative to income, and in the other, taxes relative to population.

11. Based on a related methodology, Chernick (1991) finds a different pattern, one that is more suggestive of a tax haven model of interstate tax competition than of tax mimicking. However, his analysis may be subject to potential problems of spatial correlation.

REFERENCES

Case, Ann C. Forthcoming. Interstate tax competition after TRA86. *Journal of Policy Analysis and Management*.

Case, Ann C., James R. Hines, Jr., and Harvey S. Rosen. 1989. Copycatting: Fiscal policies of states and their neighbors. Working Paper, No. 3032, National Bureau of Economic Research, Cambridge, MA.

Chernick, Howard. 1991. The effect of distributional constraints and interstate tax competition on state decisions to tax: An econometric model. Mimeo.
Hettich, Walter, and Stanley Winer. 1988. Economic and political foundations of tax structure. *American Economic Review* 78:701-12.
Hirschman, A. D. 1970. *Exit, voice, and loyalty*. Cambridge, MA: Harvard University Press.
Inman, Robert P. 1989. The local decision to tax: Evidence from large U.S. cities. *Regional Science and Urban Economics* 19:455-91.
Ladd, Helen F., and Dana Weist. 1991. General sales taxes. In *State and local finance for the 19901: A case study of Arizona*, ed. Therese J. McGuire and Dana Wolfe Naimark. Tempe: Arizona State University, School of Public Affairs.
Oates, Wallace E., and Robert M. Schwab. 1988. Economic competition among jurisdictions: Efficiency enhancing or distortion inducing? *Journal of Public Economics* 35:333-54.
Wildasin, David E. 1988. Nash equilibria in models of fiscal competition. *Journal of Public Economics* 19:229-40.
Wilson, John D. 1986. A theory of interregional tax competition. *Journal of Public Economics* 19:296-315.
Zodrow, George, and Peter Mieszkowski. 1986. Pigou, Tiebout, property taxation, and the underprovision of local public goods. *Journal of Urban Economics* 19:356-70.

Helen F. Ladd is a professor of public policy studies and economics at Duke University. Prior to moving to Duke in 1986, she taught at Harvard University's John F. Kennedy School of Government. She specializes in state and local public finance and intergovernmental fiscal relations. Her most recent book (with John Yinger) is America's Ailing Cities: Fiscal Health and the Design of Urban Policy, *updated edition (Johns Hopkins University Press, 1991).*

Property Tax Revaluation and Tax Levy Growth Revisited

HELEN F. LADD

Institute of Policy Sciences and Public Affairs, Duke University, 4875 Duke Station, Durham, North Carolina 27706

Received January 30, 1989; revised August 25, 1989

I. INTRODUCTION

In an earlier paper, Bloom and Ladd used pooled time-series data for Massachusetts cities and towns to test the hypothesis that local public officials take advantage of the confusion created by jurisdiction-wide revaluation of property to raise taxes by more than they otherwise would have [3]. The authors found that revaluation led to higher-than-predicted tax levies during the revaluation year in the state's cities, but not in its towns. These results imply that the median voter model, with its assumption of no discretionary power for local officials, was a better predictor of short-run government behavior in Massachusetts cities with their town-meeting form of government than in Massachusetts cities with their mayor–council form of government.[1]

The Bloom–Ladd analysis also sheds light on whether state governments should require some form of "full disclosure" or "truth in taxation" to accompany jurisdiction-wide revaluation of property.[2] If the process of revaluation allows local officials to increase levies excessively during the revaluation year and to maintain that increase over a longer period of time, one might support state legislation to strengthen the link between the demands of taxpayer voters and local budgetary decisions. The Bloom–Ladd finding that revaluation had no impact on a typical town's tax levies during the revaluation year and possibly no long-run effect in cities provides at best only limited support for such legislation.

---

[1]Because it was based on the tax levy data for years prior to 1980, the Bloom–Ladd study was not affected by the state's stringent tax limitation measure that passed in November 1980.

[2]Full disclosure or truth in taxation laws refer to procedures designed to promote public discussion and political accountability by requiring local government bodies to hold public hearings before raising tax rates above what would be necessary to collect a fixed percentage of the previous year's levy. Information on states with laws of this type can be found in U.S. Advisory Commission on Intergovernmental Relations," Significant Features of Fiscal Federalism" [1, Table 78] and comparable tables for other years. Also see reference in [3].

This paper replicates and extends the Massachusetts study using pooled time-series data for North Carolina counties from 1960 to 1984. Three arguments justify replicating the study for North Carolina. First, given the way North Carolina administers the local property tax, jurisdiction-wide revaluations are even more nearly exogenous to the local decision-making process in North Carolina than in Massachusetts and thereby provide a cleaner test of the basic hypothesis. Second, North Carolina's reliance on county governments makes its governmental structure more similar to that of other states than of Massachusetts with its limited reliance on counties and its heavy reliance on the town-meeting form of government. Hence, results from North Carolina should be more generalizable to other states than those from Massachusetts. Third, the North Carolina data allow for tests of a richer set of hypotheses than was true for Massachusetts.

Section II summarizes the basic conceptual and methodological framework of the earlier study. Section III then discusses similarities and differences between North Carolina and Massachusetts and Section IV presents the new results and their implications.

II. CONCEPTUAL FRAMEWORK OF PREVIOUS STUDY

Many models of local government expenditures start from the assumption that local public officials seek simply to satisfy the demands for services of local taxpayer voters. In the most restrictive form of these models, local officials are assumed to provide the services demanded by the median voter, the voter whose desired level would gain majority support. (See, for example, Bergstom and Goodman [2] and Borcherding and Deacon [4].) In more general models, officials respond to a somewhat more vaguely defined decisive voter or to a weighted average of all voters. Following from these demand-oriented models is the conclusion that local tax levies are determined solely by factors that affect the demand for public services, and not by institutional factors, such as revaluation, that might operate through local officials' decisions about what quantity or quality of public services to supply.

An alternative view of the local political process posits that public officials exercise discretion over tax and spending levels and consequently may choose levels that differ temporarily or permanently from those desired by taxpayer voters. Examples of this view include the bureaucratic model of Niskanen [8], the surplus maximizing model of Brennan and Buchanan [5], and the agenda setter models of Romer and Rosenthal [9] and Mackay and Weaver [7a]. Typically these models assume that public officials use their discretion to increase the budget beyond what would be chosen by the median voter.[3] According to this view, jurisdiction-wide

---

[3]For a full discussion of these and other models, see Inman [7].

revaluations are likely to lead to higher local tax levies by giving public officials more discretionary power than they normally have.

This discretionary power comes from voter confusion. Because revaluation redistributes tax burdens within a jurisdiction, taxpayer voters find it difficult to distinguish between changes in their tax liability due to revaluation and changes due to an increase in the tax levy. Moreover, the increase in assessed valuation resulting from revaluation makes it possible for local officials to increase tax levies without increasing the nominal tax rate; tax levies increase provided only that officials do not lower the nominal tax rate enough to offset the rise in assessed values. The resulting confusion enables local officials to increase public expenditures during revaluation years without incurring the full political costs of the corresponding tax increase.

To determine the impact of revaluation in Massachusetts, Bloom and Ladd used the following covariance model for pooled time series.

$$\ln(L_{kt}/L_{k,t-1}) = \alpha_0 + \sum_{j=-2}^{+2} \beta_j D_{kt}^j + \sum_{i=1}^{T-1} \gamma_i Y_{kt}^i + \sum_{m=1}^{N-1} \delta_m C_{kt}^m + \mu_{kt}, \quad (1)$$

where

L_{kt} = community k property tax levies in year t;

D_{kt}^0 = a dummy variable that takes on the value 1 if community k revalued in year t, and 0 otherwise;

D_{kt}^j = a dummy variable that takes on the value 1 if year t is the jth year before or after revaluation in community k, and 0 otherwise. $j < 0$ indicates years before revaluation and $j > 0$ indicates years after revaluation.

Y_{kt}^i = a year dummy that takes on the value 1 when t equals i, and 0 otherwise;

C_{kt}^m = a community dummy that takes on the value 1 when k equals m, and 0 otherwise;

$\alpha_0, \beta_j, \gamma_i, \delta_m$ = parameters to be estimated;

T = the length of each time series; and

N = the number of time series.

The coefficient of primary interest is β_0, the coefficient of the dummy value for revaluation. A positive value of β_0 implies that during revaluation years levies grow faster than they otherwise would. The dummy variables for years preceding and following revaluation allow for the possibility that pressures from taxpayer voters might offset the short-run effect of revaluation. The long-run effect of revaluation can be measured by the sum of the five coefficients $\sum_{j=-2}^{+2} \beta_j$.

The variables Y_{kt}^i for each year i in the sample (except the baseline year) control for variation over time in statewide factors influencing property taxes (such as general economic conditions and intergovernmental aid). The variables C_{kt}^m for each community m (except for an arbitrarily selected baseline community) control for variations in local factors that affect the growth of property taxes such as population growth, industrial and commercial development, and changing preferences for public services. Combined with the constant term, the coefficients of these variables allow one to predict how much property tax levies would have grown in community k during year t in the absence of revaluation based on statewide year-specific trends and community-specific patterns over time.

Despite its simplicity, the model yields unbiased estimates of the parameters of primary interest; the year and community variables eliminate potential bias due to the correlation of the revaluation variable with either year-specific or community-specific factors that influence property tax growth and eliminate autocorrelation across years and communities. Consequently, it is reasonable to assume that the error term, μ_{kt}, meets all the distributional requirements for ordinary least-squares estimation. Essential to this conclusion is the assumption that the timing of the revaluation is outside the control of local public officials. Bloom and Ladd argued that this exogeneity assumption was reasonable in Massachusetts because revaluations took several years to implement and were carried out by independent assessing firms. Nonetheless, the possibility cannot be ruled out that local public officials in some cases might have had some control over the date at which the revaluation was made effective.

III. REVALUATION IN NORTH CAROLINA

The relevant observations for the Massachusetts study were the state's 351 cities and towns because these units have almost complete responsibility both for assessing property and for levying taxes on that property. The situation is more complicated in North Carolina with its county–municipality governmental system. The state's 100 counties serve as agents of the state government and typically are responsible for services available to all state residents such as local schools, public welfare, social services, and health services. The state's 435 municipalities provide additional services such as public safety, sanitation, and parks for residents. County governments in North Carolina have responsibility for assessing all property subject to taxation within their boundaries. The county-assessed property is then subject to property taxes levied by county governments, municipalities, and in some cases, separate school districts and special districts. Hence, in North Carolina, the state's 100 counties are the basic units for examining revaluation. Within each county, however, county government officials could conceivably respond differently than municipal government officials to a rise in property values due to county-wide revaluation.

A 1959 North Carolina law requires that each county revalue all its real property every 8 years, with approximately 12 counties required to revalue each year. Unlike Massachusetts, where legal mandates for revaluation were honored mainly in the breach, North Carolina counties have met the requirements of the law every year since 1960. Moreover, in stark contrast to Massachusetts, North Carolina counties have no authority to postpone the date at which revaluation becomes effective. Although counties are permitted to accelerate the revaluation schedule, during the 24-year period of this study only 12 revaluations were implemented earlier than required under the law. (See Table A2 for distribution of revaluations.)

Between 1961 and 1984, 287 revaluations were spread relatively evenly over time and among counties. The large number of revaluations permits a rich natural experiment for examining the impact of an exogenous institutional change on the growth of local tax levies. Moreover, the even distribution across counties and through time permits examination of subperiods and subsets of counties, as discussed further below.

The regular revaluations make it easy for the state Department of Revenue to monitor their effects. In its biennial report, the Department provides information on changes in tax bases, tax rates, and tax levies in each of the counties revaluing in a particular year. For example, counties that revalued as of January 1, 1981, experienced an average 69% increase in assessed values and an 11% increase in fiscal year 1981-1982 tax levies. Comparable figures for the following year were 62 and 13%.[4] In addition, the regularity of revaluations makes them understandable to the media and the public, especially during the later years of this study.

Because most Massachusetts communities underassessed residential property relative to business property prior to revaluation, one could be quite sure that revaluation in that state would redistribute tax burdens from business taxpayers to residential taxpayers. Indeed, concern about this predicted tax shift was what made many Massachusetts politicians so reluctant to proceed with the revaluation process. For communities that did revalue, one could predict that the redistribution caused by revaluation would increase the tax price of services to local residents and thereby depress their demand for public services and reduce the growth rate of

---

[4]"1984 North Carolina Statistics of Taxation" [10, pp. 163–64]. Because real estate is revalued on an 8-year cycle while personalty is reassessed annually, the assessed value of real estate increases more than that for all property, which includes personalty, during the revaluation year. Comparable growth rates for real property were 121% in 1982 and 97% in 1983.

taxes. Thus, on the demand side, the effect of revaluation would be to dampen the growth of total tax levies. Hence, the demand effect is clearly distinguishable from the supply side hypothesis, namely, that discretionary behavior by suppliers led them to increase the growth rate of tax levies.

The redistributive effects of revaluation are less clear in North Carolina, but appear to work in the same direction as those in Massachusetts. This conclusion follows in part from the fact that personalty, most of which is business property, is assessed annually rather than on the 8-year cycle used for real estate. When revaluation occurs in a county, it increases the valuation of real estate relative to personalty and thereby reduces the business share. How revaluation affects the residential share of real estate in each county is harder to determine. Aggregate statewide figures, however, are suggestive; they show that residential real estate was assessed well below commercial and industrial real estate in 1961, but by 1981 was assessed 25% higher, thereby implying a shift away from business taxes to residential taxes.[5]

IV. RESULTS—100 COUNTIES

Table 1 summarizes results for the key parameters for the full sample of 100 countries over 25 years. Estimating Eq. (1) for this large sample would be unwieldy because it would require 99 county-specific independent variables. To eliminate these variables, standard procedures were used to express each variable as the deviation from its county-specific mean. Hence, whenever the sample covers the full set of 100 counties, the results are based on the transformed equation,

$$\ln(L_{kt}/L_{k,t-1}) - \theta_k$$
$$= \sum_{j=-2}^{2} \beta_2(D_{kt}^j - D_k^j) + \sum_{i=1}^{T-1} \gamma_i(Y_{kt}^i - Y_k^i) + \mu_{kt}, \quad (2)$$

where θ_k, D_k^j, Y_k^i = county-specific means for the dependent and independent variables, respectively.

To allow for differences in behavior between county and noncounty governments, separate equations were estimated for property tax levies by type of government. The dependent variables for the results reported in the first two rows of Table 1 are the property tax levies of county governments and those of all noncounty governments within each county. The third row refers to the total property taxes levied by all governments

---

[5]U.S. Department of Commerce, "Census of Governments," Vol. 2; "Taxable Property Values," 1962 and 1982.

TABLE 1
Estimated Revaluation Coefficients
(100 Counties)

[Sample size]	Pre-revaluation		Revaluation	Post-revaluation		Cumulative Effects	
	β_{-2}	β_{-1}	β_0	β_{+1}	β_{+2}	$\sum_{j=-1}^{+1}\beta_j$	$\sum_{j=-2}^{+2}\beta_j$
County governments [2400]	0.007 (1.13)	−0.006 (−0.95)	0.020* (3.03)	0.001 (0.19)	0.002 (0.25)	0.015 (1.15)	0.024 (1.38)
Non-county governments [2375]	−0.013 (−0.19)	−0.026* (−2.31)	0.069* (6.24)	−0.018 (−1.16)	−0.001 (−0.91)	0.025 1.16	0.011 (0.11)
All governments [2396]	−0.001 (−0.12)	−0.007 (−1.25)	0.031* (5.702)	−0.002 (−0.24)	−0.001 (−0.11)	0.022* (3.85)	0.020 (1.59)

Note. Results are based on Eq. (2). Numbers in parentheses in the first five columns are *t*-statistics; numbers in parentheses in the final two columns are *F*-statistics. An asterisk (*) denotes the coefficient is statistically significant at the 0.05 level.

in each county.[6] Statewide, county taxes account for about 66% of total property taxes. This fraction is lower in urban counties and higher in rural counties.

The results in Table 1 for the revaluation year provide support for the hypothesis of discretionary behavior. In particular, they indicate that local officials increase property taxes on average more during revaluation years than during other years. To clarify, if revaluation becomes effective on January 1, 1981, the revaluation year is the fiscal year that begins on July 1, 1981 and ends on June 30, 1982. This is the year for which local officials can increase the effective tax rate simply by not reducing the nominal tax rate enough to offset the rise in assessed valuation. In all three equations, the estimated β_0 for the revaluation year is positive and statistically significant. Moreover, the estimated effect, especially for noncounty governments, is large. The 0.069 coefficient implies that property taxes were 7.1% higher than they would have been had it not been a revaluation year. The effects are smaller for the other categories of governments, but they are positive and statistically significant.

To test whether the positive revaluation effect reflects the spurious effect of other factors influencing revenue growth, a fourth equation for county government tax revenues other than property taxes was also estimated (not reported in table). Revaluation of the property tax base should

---

[6] See Appendix Table A.1 for the coefficients of the year dummies.

have no effect on such revenues. The finding of a small negative and statistically insignificant coefficient for the revaluation year dummy in this equation supports the view that it is revaluation, not some other factor, that caused the positive coefficients in the property tax equations.[7]

The other coefficients reported in Table 1 shed light on the longer-term effects of revaluation. One hypothesis is that local officials, knowing that they have leeway to raise taxes during the revaluation year, raise taxes less than they otherwise would during the years just before revaluation. By altering the timing of tax increases in this way, local officials minimize the political heat of raising taxes. A second hypothesis is that once the confusion of the revaluation year is past, taxpayer voters are able to reassert pressure on local officials to force them to bring tax burdens back in line with the preferences of taxpayer voters.

The signs of the coefficients of the anticipation variables (β_{-2} and β_{-1}) and of the post revaluation variables (β_{+1} and β_{+2}) in the equations for noncounty governments and for all governments are consistent with these hypotheses. However, with the exception of the coefficient of the 1-year anticipation variable in the equation for noncounty governments, the coefficients are not statistically significant. According to that equation, municipal officials apparently anticipate the revenue-raising potential of the revaluation process by raising tax levies less than they otherwise would during the year prior to revaluation.

The final two columns of the table show the cumulative effects of local officials' behavior during both the 3-year and 5-year periods surrounding revaluation. The cumulative effects over these longer periods are all positive and fall in the range of 0.011 to 0.025. Although we cannot rule out the possibility that for the county governments and the noncounty governments taken separately, the cumulative effects reflect chance factors rather than revaluation, an F-test indicates that the 3-year cumulative effect for all governments is significant at the 0.05 level. The cumulative effect for all governments over the 3-year period implies that revaluation leads to total tax burdens on county residents that are 2.2% higher than they would have been had there been no revaluations.

Before 1974, North Carolina counties were allowed to assess property at a ratio less than 100%, provided all types of property were assessed at the same fraction. Since 1974 they have been required to assess property at full market value. How this fact affects the main hypothesis is not clear. Less than full value assessment might exacerbate the hypothesized confusion effect during the revaluation year but the a priori case for this outcome is not strong. In any case, 1974 is a reasonable year to divide the

---

[7]The coefficient of β_0 is -0.004 and the t-statistic is 0.22.

TABLE 2
Estimated Revaluation Coefficients by Time Period
(100 Counties)

[Sample size]	Pre-revaluation		Revaluation	Post-revaluation		Cumulative effects	
	β_{-2}	β_{-1}	β_0	β_{+1}	β_{+2}	$\sum_{j=-1}^{+1} \beta_j$	$\sum_{j=-2}^{+2} \beta_j$
County governments							
1962–1974	0.020*	0.004	0.030*	−0.001	0.000	0.033*	0.053*
[1300]	(2.72)	(0.53)	(3.75)	(−0.10)	(0.04)	(3.92)	(4.81)
1975–1985	−0.006	−0.015	0.009	0.003	0.003	−0.003	−0.006
[1100]	(-0.60)	(−1.45)	(0.85)	(0.25)	(0.27)	(0.04)	(0.06)
Non-county governments							
1962–1974	−0.020	−0.008	0.084*	−0.022	0.005	0.054	0.039
[1277]	(−0.144)	(−0.57)	(5.76)	(−1.46)	(0.32)	(3.02)	(0.74)
1975–1985	−0.003	−0.048*	0.048*	−0.017	−0.009	−0.017	−0.029
[1098]	(−0.14)	(−2.18)	(2.93)	(−1.02)	(−0.56)	(0.23)	(0.31)
All governments							
1962–1974	0.008	0.003	0.043*	−0.005	−0.001	0.041*	0.048*
[1298]	(1.57)	(0.56)	(7.66)	(−0.79)	(−0.13)	(12.30)	(7.97)
1975–1985	−0.010	−0.017	0.010	−0.000	−0.001	−0.007	−0.017
[1098]	(−1.04)	(−1.77)	(1.67)	(−0.01)	(−0.07)	(0.01)	(0.19)

Note. Results are based on Eq. (2). Numbers in parentheses in the first five columns are t-statistics; numbers in parentheses in the final columns are F-statistics. An asterisk (*) denotes the coefficient is statistically significant at the 0.05 level.

sample to examine whether the response to revaluation has changed over time.

Table 2 shows that for all three dependent variables, both the revaluation-year effect and the cumulative effect are much larger during the early period than during the later period. In contrast to large and statistically significant coefficients for the revaluation dummy in the early period, the coefficients for the later period are much smaller, and except for non-county governments are not statistically significant. For the earlier period, the estimated 3-year and 5-year cumulative effects for all governments are 0.041 and 0.048 and are statistically significant; for the later period they are about zero. These results imply that whatever leeway the revaluation process provided for local officials to raise property taxes has diminished over time and is virtually zero in the post 1974 period. Further insight into the behavior of local officials over the sample period appears in Fig. 1 and Appendix Table A2. The figure shows that prior to 1975 the average growth of property tax levies in revaluing counties exceeded that in

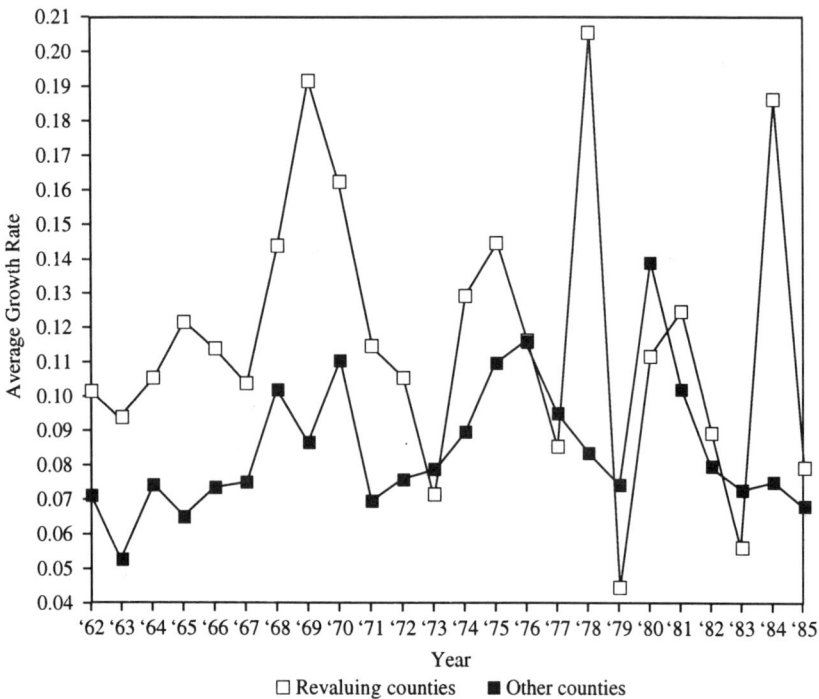

Fig. 1

nonrevaluing counties in 12 of the 13 years. Thus, the positive revaluation effect reflects relatively consistent behavior by revaluing counties throughout the period. After 1975, in contrast, revaluing counties raised levies faster than nonrevaluing counties in only 6 of the 11 years.

Part of the explanation for the different behavior over time may be attributed to a learning effect, namely that taxpayer voters learn from experience what to expect from revaluation. As a result of this learning process they are less willing to let local officials take advantage of them in the later period than in the earlier work. An examination of the behavior over time of each of the eight cohorts of revaluing counties (that is, the group that revalues together on an 8-year cycle) provides support for this view in that in three of them the difference in the average growth rate between revaluing and nonrevaluing counties declines monotonically over the revaluations in the sample period.[8] On the other hand, the existence of some very large positive revaluation effects for some years in the later

---

[8]This comparison is adequate but is not quite right since the cohorts change slightly over time as a result of accelerated revaluation schedules in some cases.

period (for example, 1977–1978 and 1983–1984) suggests that such learning does not operate the same way in all counties.[9]

V. RESULTS FOR COUNTIES GROUPED BY INCOME AND POPULATION GROWTH

Pressures on the property tax vary greatly from one county to another. Some counties, especially those in the middle of the state, experienced rapid population and economic growth during the study period while others remained relatively rural. Rapid population growth brings with it the demand for more local public services and urban infrastructure that must be financed primarily from the local property tax. At the same time, such growth also raises property values. As a result, the average annual growth of property tax levies across counties during the study period ranged from 6 to 17%.

Conceivably, local officials in counties experiencing different degrees of fiscal pressure might respond differently to revaluation. Officials in counties facing the greatest demands on property taxes relative to the property base, for example, might be more willing to behave in a discretionary manner than those in less pressured fiscal situations. If these differences exist, equations based on the full sample of 100 counties might conceal even greater discretionary effects in subsets of this sample.

In light of this possibility, equations were estimated for subsets of counties grouped by population growth rates and levels of resident income. In general, counties with higher rates of population growth or lower resident income are likely to be more pressured than those with slower population growth or higher income. In each case the counties were ranked in descending order of the relevant characteristic and divided into quintiles. The presence of only 20 counties in each sample makes it feasible to estimate Eq. (1), with 19 county dummies included in each regression. Based on equations that use property taxes of all county governments as the dependent variable, the results for the revaluation variables are reported in Tables 3 and 4.

The overall patterns are almost identical to those for the full 100-county sample. In particular, positive and statistically significant effects emerge for the revaluation year for the early period in all subsets, but there is almost no evidence of a revaluation effect in the latter period; the only statistically significant positive effect in the post 1974 period is for the richest quintile. Moreover, no clear differences of coefficients emerge across the quintiles. The revaluation-year effects in the early period range

---

[9]The reader is reminded that the large observed differences in 1977–1978 and 1983–1984 between revaluating and other countries may not reflect the effects of revaluation alone. Unlike the regression model, the figure does not control for characteristics of the revaluing counties that could account for rapidly growing tax levies.

TABLE 3
Estimated Revaluation Coefficients by Quintiles of Counties
Grouped by Population Growth and by Time Period

[Sample size]	Pre-revaluation β_{-2}	Pre-revaluation β_{-1}	Revaluation β_0	Post-revaluation β_{+1}	Post-revaluation β_{+2}	Cumulative effects $\sum_{j=-1}^{+1}\beta_j$	Cumulative effects $\sum_{j=-2}^{+2}\beta_j$
			I. Rapid growth				
1962–1974	0.015	−0.016	0.042*	−0.009	−0.017	−0.127	−0.129
[259]	(1.04)	(−1.09)	(2.76)	(−0.55)	(−1.07)	(0.28)	(0.09)
1975–1985	−0.019	−0.028	0.031	0.007	−0.038	0.010	−0.047
[217]	(−0.72)	(−1.12)	(1.27)	(0.30)	(−1.53)	(0.84)	(0.35)
			II. Moderate growth				
1962–1974	0.014	0.015	0.032*	0.001	0.018	0.048	0.080*
[259]	(1.22)	(1.25)	(2.58)	(0.06)	(1.32)	(3.14)	(3.98)
1975–1985	−0.014	−0.016	−0.003	−0.022	0.016	−0.041	−0.039
[219]	(−0.79)	(−0.97)	(−0.18)	(−1.44)	(1.01)	(1.55)	(0.60)
			III. Medium growth				
1962–1974	−0.005	−0.005	0.056*	0.006	0.001	0.057*	0.053
[259]	(−0.46)	(0.43)	(4.98)	(0.051)	(0.10)	(7.54)	(2.97)
1975–1985	0.000	−0.002	−0.000	−0.011	−0.005	−0.013	−0.018
[219]	(0.24)	(−0.09)	(−0.14)	(0.068)	(0.35)	(0.14)	(0.12)
			IV. Slow growth				
1962–1974	0.010	0.002	0.058*	−0.004	0.012	0.056*	0.078
[259]	(0.79)	(0.159)	(4.23)	(−0.28)	(0.83)	(3.88)	(3.50)
1975–1985	0.006	−0.010	−0.033*	0.017	0.012	−0.026	−0.008
[219]	(0.32)	(−0.60)	(−2.07)	(1.07)	(0.72)	(0.057)	(0.03)
			V. Slower growth				
1962–1974	0.014	0.014	0.032*	−0.022	−0.014	0.024	0.024
[259]	(0.93)	(0.93)	(2.24)	(−1.48)	(−(0.092))	(0.60)	(0.26)
1975–1985	−0.060	−0.063	0.061	−0.015	0.003	−0.017	−0.074
[219]	(−1.48)	(−1.62)	(1.64)	(−0.42)	(0.08)	(0.05)	(0.39)

Note. Results are based on Eq. (1). Dependent variable is the natural logarithm of property taxes levied by all governments in each county in year t divided by those levied in year $t-1$. Numbers in parentheses in the first five columns are t-statistics; numbers in parentheses in the final columns are F-statistics. An asterisk (*) denotes the coefficient is statistically significant at the 0.05 level.

TABLE 4
Estimated Revaluation Coefficients by Quintiles of Counties
Grouped by Per Capita Income and by Time Period

[Sample size]	Pre-revaluation		Revaluation	Post-revaluation		Cumulative effects	
	β_{-2}	β_{-1}	β_0	β_{+1}	β_{+2}	$\Sigma_{j=-1}^{+1}\beta_j$	$\Sigma_{j=-2}^{+2}\beta_j$
I. Highest income							
1962–1974	0.019	−0.006	0.044*	−0.001	0.011	0.037	0.067
[259]	(1.51)	(−0.41)	(3.30)	(−0.06)	(−0.82)	(1.72)	(2.68)
1975–1985	0.006	−0.003	0.020*	−0.000	−0.011	0.017	0.012
[217]	(0.63)	(−0.026)	(2.02)	(−0.00)	(−1.12)	(0.62)	(0.14)
II. High income							
1962–1974	0.009	−0.001	0.055*	−0.009	0.022	0.045	0.076
[259]	(0.62)	(−0.05)	(3.99)	(−0.61)	(1.49)	(2.22)	(2.80)
1975–1985	−0.024	−0.004	−0.012	−0.004	0.006	−0.020	−0.050
[219]	(−1.54)	(−0.26)	(−0.79)	(−0.026)	(0.38)	(0.39)	(0.67)
III. Middle income							
1962–1974	0.002	0.009	0.037*	0.003	0.007	0.049	0.058
[259]	(0.15)	(0.74)	(2.99)	(0.25)	(0.49)	(3.38)	(2.07)
1975–1985	−0.044	−0.087*	0.017	−0.041	−0.018	−0.111	−0.173
[219]	(−1.18)	(−2.21)	(0.46)	(−1.08)	(−0.50)	(1.93)	(2.18)
IV. Low income							
1962–1974	−0.003	0.013	0.048*	0.001	−0.011	0.062*	0.048
[259]	(−0.22)	(1.03)	(3.71)	(0.06)	(−0.82)	(5.04)	(1.36)
1975–1985	−0.030	−0.014	0.019	0.003	−0.017	0.008	−0.039
[219]	(−1.12)	(0.53)	(0.79)	(0.14)	−(0.67)	(0.03)	(0.26)
V. Lowest income							
1962–1974	0.026	0.004	0.047*	−0.011	−0.021	0.040	0.045
[259]	(1.77)	(0.30)	(3.02)	(−0.70)	(−1.22)	(1.45)	(0.81)
1975–1985	−0.014	0.006	0.014	0.007	0.013	0.027	0.026
[219]	(−0.64)	(0.31)	(0.74)	(0.39)	(0.69)	(0.45)	(0.19)

Note. Results are based on eq. (1). Dependent variable is the natural logarithm of property taxes levied by all governments in each county in year t divided by those levied in year $t-1$. Numbers in parentheses in the first five columns are t-statistics; numbers in parentheses in the final columns are F-statistics. An asterisk (*) denotes the coefficient is statistically significant at the 0.05 level.

from 0.032 to 0.056 across the population growth quintiles and from 0.037 to 0.055 across the income categories. The largest effects emerge in counties experiencing medium and slow population growth and in counties with relatively high income. For the subsets for which the cumulative effects of revaluation are statistically significant, these effects range from 0.057 to 0.080.

VI. CONCLUSIONS

North Carolina local officials and taxpayer voters in each county have experienced many country-wide revaluations. As a phenomenon that occurs regularly on an 8-year cycle for each county, revaluation is a common occurrence that is closely monitored by the Department of Revenue and the public. This study shows that prior to 1975, the degree of monitoring was not sufficient to keep local officials from taking advantage of the confusion created by revaluation to raise tax levies by more than they otherwise would have. This finding replicates the finding of the earlier study for Massachusetts cities. Since 1975, in contrast, local officials apparently have had somewhat less leeway than they had in the earlier period to capitalize on the confusion created by the revaluation process.

Prior to 1975, county-wide revaluations of property in North Carolina allowed both county and municipal officials to raise tax levies on average by 3 to 8% more than they otherwise would have during the revaluation year. In addition, even after potentially offsetting behavior in the years before and after revaluation is allowed for, revaluation tended to have a long term effect on tax levies; property taxes of all local governments in each county on average were 2.2% higher as a result of each revaluation than they otherwise would have been. Examination of local officials' behavior by year and across subsets of counties indicates that the observed discretionary behavior was widespread and was not limited to certain types of counties in certain years. Thus, institutional characteristics of local revenue systems apparently can have permanent effects on local tax revenues.

In contrast to the pre-1975 period, the evidence for discretionary behavior on the part of local officials since 1975 is much weaker. Some support for the hypothesis appears for noncounty governments and for the total property taxes collected in the richest countries. In general, however, the relevant coefficients estimated with data for the recent period are small and statistically insignificant. Apparently, as voters became more accustomed to the process of revaluation, they were better able to restrain the behavior of local officials and to keep them from using their discretion to raise tax levies. One interpretation of these findings is that the demand-based model of local tax decisions may be reasonable as a long-run equilibrium model, but only if voters have had sufficient time to become accustomed to changes in institutional procedures.

With respect to policy, this study provides somewhat more support than the Massachusetts study for formal truth-in-taxation laws or full disclosure laws to tighten the link between taxpayer voter demand and local budgetary decisions. Because the monitoring done by the State of North Carolina was not sufficient to keep local public officials from taking advantage of the confusion created by revaluation to raise tax levies excessively prior to 1975, the state's taxpayers would have benefitted from legislation making it more difficult for local officials to increase effective tax rates during the revaluation year. Admittedly, the current case for such legislation for North Carolina is less strong than it would have been in the 1960s. Nonetheless, this study suggests that such legislation might make sense in other states that have had less experience with regular revaluations.

APPENDIX

Table A.1
Estimated Coefficients of Year Dummies
(100 Counties)

	County governments	Non-county governments	All governments
DUM62	0.011(0.79)	−0.007(−0.28)	0.008(0.70)
DUM63	0.005(0.37)	−0.055(−2.3)	−0.11(−0.90)
DUM64	0.003(0.22)	0.019(0.79)	0.010(0.81)
DUM65	0.004(0.28)	−0.002(−0.08)	0.004(0.30)
DUM66	0.017(1.2)	0.019(0.80)	0.010(0.86)
DUM67	0.010(0.69)*	−0.012(−0.47)	0.011(0.90)
DUM68	0.046(3.2)*	0.042(1.7)	0.040(3.3)*
DUM69	0.040(2.8)*	0.016(0.65)	0.034(2.8)*
DUM70	0.055(3.9)*	0.016(0.64)	0.048(4.0)*
DUM71	0.005(0.34)	0.006(0.26)	0.006(0.52)
DUM72	0.007(0.52)	0.015(0.62)	0.010(0.88)
DUM73	0.002(0.12)	0.028(1.1)	0.009(0.75)
DUM74	0.028(2.0)*	0.012(0.49)	0.027(2.2)*
DUM75	0.049(3.5)*	0.033(1.4)	0.047(3.9)*
DUM76	0.059(4.2)*	0.002(0.07)	0.048(4.0)*
DUM77	0.036(2.5)*	−0.026(−1.1)	0.024(2.0)*
DUM78	0.037(2.6)*	0.030(1.2)	0.032(2.7)*
DUM79	0.002(0.15)	−0.010(−0.43)	0.005(0.39)
DUM80	0.074(5.2)*	0.027(1.12)	0.065(5.4)*
DUM81	0.038(2.7)*	0.020(0.81)	0.037(3.2)*
DUM82	0.017(1.2)	−0.000(−0.01)	0.011(0.91)
DUM83	−0.003(−0.23)	0.041(1.7)	0.004(0.34)
DUM84	0.025(1.7)	0.006(0.25)	0.021(1.8)
DUM85	BASE	BASE	BASE

Note. Results are based on Eq. (2). Numbers in parentheses are t statistics. An asterisk (*) denotes the coefficient is statistically significant at the 0.05 level.

Table A.2
Comparison of Average Growth Rates
in Tax Levies by Year

Fiscal year	Number of revaluations	Average growth rate in revaluing counties	Average growth rate in nonrevaluing counties
1961–62	11	0.102	0.073
1962–63	6	0.094	0.053
1963–64	15	0.105	0.074
1964–65	12	0.122	0.064
1965–66	18	0.114	0.073
1966–67	9	0.104	0.075
1967–68	13	0.143	0.102
1968–69	16	0.190	0.086
1969–70	13	0.162	0.110
1970–71	8	0.115	0.069
1971–72	15	0.105	0.075
1972–73	13	0.071	0.078
1973–74	16	0.129	0.089
1974–75	11	0.144	0.110
1975–76	14	0.116	0.116
1976–77	13	0.084	0.093
1977–78	14	0.204	0.082
1978–79	10	0.044	0.074
1979–80	15	0.111	0.138
1980–81	12	0.124	0.102
1981–82	19	0.089	0.079
1982–83	9	0.056	0.072
1983–84	12	0.185	0.075
1984–85	15	0.079	0.068

Note. The number of revaluations in a particular year refers to revaluations that became effective as of January 1, six months prior to the start of the specified fiscal year. For example, the 11 revaluations listed for 1961–62 became effective on January 1, 1961. The growth rate is defined as the logarithm of the tax levies of all governments within each county in the specified fiscal year divided by tax levies in the previous fiscal year. The entries in column 2 and 3 are simple unweighted averages for the specified group of countries.

ACKNOWLEDGMENTS

I thank the Duke University Research Council for financial support; Howard Bloom, Philip Cook, and Don Liner for comments on an earlier version of this paper; and Jack Strauss for research assistance.

REFERENCES

1. Advisory Commission on Intergovernmental Relations, "Significant Features of Fiscal Federalism, 1987 Edition," Report M-151, U.S. Government Printing Office, Washington, DC (1987).
2. T. C. Bergstrom and R.P. Goodman, "Private Demands for Public Goods," *Am. Econom. Rev.*, **43** (3), 280–297 (1973).

3. H. S. Bloom and H. F. Ladd, Property tax revaluation and tax levy growth, *J. Urban Econom.*, **11**, 73–84 (1982).
4. T. E. Borcherding and R. T. Deacon, The demand for the services of non-federal governments, *Am. Econom. Rev.* **42** (5), 891–901 (1972).
5. G. Brennan and J. Buchanan, "The Power to Tax: Analytical Foundations of a Fiscal Constitution," Cambridge Univ. Press, New York (1980).
6. R. T. Deacon, A demand model for the local public sector, *Rev. Econom. Statist.*, **60** (2). 184–92 (1978).
7. R. P. Inman, Markets, governments, and the 'new' political economy, *in* "Handbook of Public Economics" (A. Auerbach and M. Feldstein, Eds.), Vol. II, Elsevier, Amsterdam/New York (1987).
7a. R. Mackay and C. Weaver, Agenda control by budget maximizers in a multi-bureau setting, *Public Choice*, **37**, 447–472 (1981).
8. W. Niskanen, "Bureaucracy and Representative Government," Aldine–Atherton. Chicago (1971).
9. T. Romer and H. Rosenthal, Political resource allocation, controlled agenda, and the status quo, *Public Choice*, **33** (4), 27–44 (1978).
10. "Statistics of Taxation," State of North Carolina, various years.

[11]

State Responses to the TRA86 Revenue Windfalls: A New Test of the Flypaper Effect

Helen F. Ladd

In our U.S. federal system, the income tax structures used by the three levels of government are interrelated in complicated ways. Many states link various components of their income tax codes to the federal income tax code; state and local income taxes are deductible at the federal level; and several states permit federal income taxes to be deducted at the state level. Consequently, changes in the federal tax system, such as those embodied in the Tax Reform Act of 1986 (TRA86), are likely to have significant ramifications for lower levels of government. In some cases, policymakers may propose federal tax reforms specifically to change state and local behavior. For example, the proposal to eliminate the federal deductibility of state and local taxes was justified in part as a way to put downward pressure on state and local spending. However, many of the consequences of federal tax reform for subnational governments are probably more appropriately viewed as unintended, although sometimes predictable, by-products of the federal action.

This paper focuses on one set of the potential unintended effects of TRA86 on state governments, namely, those associated with the so-called windfall gains (or, in some cases, losses) that occurred because many state tax structures are linked by definition to various components of the federal tax code. TRA86 both broadened the base of the federal personal income tax and lowered marginal tax rates. Base broadening by itself would have raised federal income taxes; the combined effect of base broadening and rate reduction was to reduce federal personal income taxes by about 10 percent.[1] This broadening of the base of the federal personal income tax "automatically" increased state tax revenues in any state that tied its tax base to the federal base. As discussed further below, the magnitude of these windfall gains (or losses) varied across states according to the mechanisms through which the state code is linked to the federal code; in many states, such windfalls accounted for a significant portion of state income tax revenues.

---

[1] Revenue neutrality was achieved by raising taxes on coporations. Whether or not the states experienced significant windfall gains from the increase in corporate taxes is not clear. See Gold [1990a] for the debate about the size of the corporate windfalls. In any case, the corporate windfalls were probably quite small and are not analyzed in this paper. However, they are included as a control variable in Table 4.

Journal of Policy Analysis and Management, Vol. 12, No. 1, 82–103 (1993)
© 1993 by the Association for Public Policy Analysis and Management
Published by John Wiley & Sons, Inc. CCC 0276-8739/93/010082-22

A simple economic model of state government behavior would predict that this type of interaction would be fully undone by state discretionary actions. According to this model, state officials would offset the windfalls by reducing tax rates or restructuring the state revenue system to maintain spending and state tax burdens in line with voter preferences. Supporting the predictions of this model are empirical studies suggesting that states with elastic revenue structures (i.e., those that would receive large "automatic" revenue increases during periods of economic growth) have no greater tendency to tax and spend than those with less elastic revenue structures. In other words, the windfall gains from automatic revenue growth apparently do not translate into higher taxes. Feenberg and Rosen [1987] provide the strongest statement of this view. (See also Oates [1975], who finds moderate effects.) To the extent that the predictions of this simple model are valid for windfalls generated by federal tax reform, the fact that a state tax code is linked definitionally to the federal code has few consequences for state revenues; any change in the federal code that could affect state revenues would simply be undone by state action.

However, another body of economic literature suggests a different conclusion. Empirical studies on the response to intergovernmental grants find that recipient governments spend (and consequently tax) more than would be predicted by the simple economic model. In other words, local officials treat resources coming into a locality in the form of grants to the local government differently than additional local resources in the form of private incomes. This phenomenon has been labeled the "flypaper effect" to indicate that money sticks where it hits.[2] To the extent that the flypaper effect is operative with respect to the TRA86 windfalls, one would predict that the windfalls would not be fully offset; some of the windfall would remain in state government coffers rather than all being returned to state taxpayers. In that case, federal tax reform could have significant ramifications for state tax levels and should not be ignored in discussions of federal tax reform. Similarly, in state tax debates, state policymakers would have to weigh the advantages and disadvantages of this revenue link against the simplicity and equity advantages of maintaining a close tie between federal and state tax bases.

The extent to which the flypaper effect operates with respect to windfalls generated by federal tax reform can best be answered empirically. Hence, the main purpose of this paper is to test for the existence of a flypaper effect on state income tax decisions, using the TRA86 windfalls as a natural experiment. Like the other papers in this symposium, this one relies heavily on the tax simulation (TAXSIM) model for state income taxes developed by the National Bureau of Economic Research (NBER). This simulation model is well suited to the task at hand. First, TAXSIM can be used to generate estimates of the windfall gains by state. These estimates are reported and discussed in the first section of this paper. Second, TAXSIM can be used to generate estimates of the magnitude of the discretionary tax changes made by states during the years immediately following the Tax Reform Act. These magnitudes, discussed in the following section, provide a first cut on the state response to the TRA86 windfalls. However, one should not interpret all the

---

[2] This term was originally coined by Arthur Okun. See Gramlich [1977] and Fisher [1982] for reviews of the empirical work on intergovernmental grants and the flypaper effect.

discretionary tax changes made by states during 1987 and 1988 as responses to the TRA86 windfalls. States presumably were responding as well to other pressures and to other incentives resulting from TRA86. To isolate the effect of the windfalls, the paper's third section embeds the windfalls in a more complete pooled time-series model of state discretionary tax changes.

Throughout the paper, the windfall estimates generated by TAXSIM are compared to windfall estimates reported in two previous studies. One study was completed by Peat Marwick and Main & Co. for the Advisory Commission on Intergovernmental Relations (ACIR) and published by the ACIR in January 1988. As elaborated in the first section, below, the ACIR estimates are based on simulations similar to those done with TAXSIM. The other study is an amalgam of two reports, one published by the National Association of State Budget Officers (NASBO) in March 1987 and updated in September 1987, and the other by the National Conference of State Legislatures (NCSL) in July 1987. Because the NCSL report draws heavily on the NASBO report, the two sets of estimates have been merged for the purposes of this analysis. In contrast to the TAXSIM and ACIR windfall estimates, the NASBO/NCSL estimates are based on reports from state officials.

NATURE AND MAGNITUDE OF THE WINDFALLS

According to the dictionary, a windfall is something (as fruit from a tree) blown down by the wind. That is, it is an unexpected or sudden gift, gain, or advantage. For the purposes of this study, a state's windfall is defined as the additional annual individual income tax revenues that the state government would receive given the TRA86, assuming no discretionary change in state tax behavior.[3] This windfall is expected to be positive in most states. However, those states that couple state tax liabilities directly to the federal liability would experience revenue losses, or negative windfall gains. States without income taxes or with tax systems that are not coupled in any way to the federal code would experience no windfall.

Consider the case of windfall gains. Clearly, state taxpayers as a group experience no windfall. Indeed, the windfall occurs precisely because state taxes are higher (before any offsetting discretionary state action) than they would be without the TRA. We simply have a transfer between taxpayers and the state government. Thus, such a windfall is a gain only from the narrow perspective of the state government treasury. In a sense, it might be viewed as a political dividend to state legislators.

The TRA86 produces a one-time gain in the sense that it reflects the federal actions of a single year. However, in another sense, the windfall is a gain for all future periods; without discretionary offsetting state action, the new broader tax base would yield higher revenues not only in FY 1987 but also in future years as well. Because little would be gained from defining the windfall in terms of the present value of the gain, it seems appropriate to use the

---

[3] Some states automatically adopt federal tax changes into the state code. Other states tie their code to the federal code as of a certain date. For most states in this latter category, updating the state code to the federal code is a routine matter that is done annually or biannually, depending on the state's legislative calendar. In calculating the windfalls in the next section, I treated these routine updates as automatic, nondiscretionary changes.

annual definition. Nonetheless, the phasing in of the TRA86 provisions lead to alternative ways of measuring the size of the annual windfall.

One approach would be to measure the effect of the fully implemented TRA86 on a state's 1986 revenues. This approach ($W1$ for windfall measure 1) can be expressed as

$$W1 = R(Y_{86}, S_{86}, F_{89}) - R(Y_{86}, S_{86}, F_{86})$$

where R refers to simulated revenue based on the year of the income data (Y), the state tax rules for the indicated year (S), and federal rules for the indicated year (F). Thus the first revenue term is the amount of state income tax revenue that would have been generated in 1986 had the 1986 state laws been in effect along with the federal laws as of 1989.[4] The 1989 federal rules correspond to full implementation of TRA86. The second term corresponds to simulated revenues in 1986 under federal and state tax laws for that year. Notice that only the federal laws differ in this formulation; the state laws are held constant in their 1986 form because the windfall is defined as the revenue change associated with the change in the federal rules in the absence of discretionary state action.

An alternative formulation measures the effect of TRA86 on a state's 1987 revenues assuming federal law as of 1987. This measure ($W2$ for windfall measure 2) can be expressed as

$$W2 = R(Y_{87}, S_{86}, F_{87}) - R(Y_{87}, S_{86}, F_{86}).$$

The main point to notice is that the new federal law in this formulation includes only those provisions enacted for 1987. Comparable one-year measures can be simulated for other years, such as 1988. A 1988 windfall would represent the additional revenues in 1988 that accrue to the state as a result of changes in the federal tax code between 1987 and 1988.

The first two columns of Table 1 report the TRA86 windfalls generated from the TAXSIM model according to these two definitions. The windfall estimates are based on income data from the 1985 Statistics of Income file (SOI) aged to the relevant year. The file was aged by increasing the weights for each return by the growth in the state's population and monetary amounts by the growth in the state's nominal income per capita. This aged 1985 data seems most appropriate given the contamination of the income data in more recent SOI files, especially income from capital gains as taxpayers changed their realization behavior in anticipation of or in response to the Tax Reform Act.[5]

The last two columns of Table 1 represent the ACIR and NASBO/NCSL estimates. Like the TAXSIM estimates, the ACIR estimates are based on a

---

[4] 1989 is the latest year for which the federal tax rules are programmed into TAXSIM. Most, but not all, of the provisions of TRA86 were scheduled to take effect by 1989.

[5] State tax codes are missing from the SOI data for taxpayers with income greater than $200,000. These high-income filers were allocated by state (and by income bracket) based on the 1985 distribution of high-income taxpayers. A less tractable problem, but one that fortunately has less impact on the liability estimates used in this paper, arises because low-income taxpayers who need not file federal tax forms are excluded from the sample despite the fact that they may be subject to state taxes.

Despite concerns about small sample sizes in some states, TAXSIM does a reasonable job of simulating tax liabilities in states with broad-based income taxes. Bearing in mind that liabilities differ somewhat from collections, the finding that the average absolute difference between the liabilities generated by TAXSIM and actual collections was 10 percent for 1986, 14 percent for 1987, and 11 percent for 1988 means that TAXSIM performs quite well.

Table 1. Windfalls (in millions of dollars, ranked by column 1).

	TAXSIM windfall W1 (1)	TAXSIM windfall W2 (2)	ACIR windfall 1986 (3)	NASBO/NCSL windfall FY1988 (4)
New York	3271.9	3135.2	1014.8	1100.0
California	1981.7	1847.5	951.5	1407.0
Ohio	819.3	436.8	221.1	262.0
Minnesota	513.6	458.3	325.5	304.0
Colorado	371.0	308.0	223.7	264.8
Virginia	339.6	291.5	208.7	147.0
Oregon	338.8	311.7	162.2	184.0
Oklahoma	297.3	253.9	160.6	122.4
Georgia	285.8	273.2	237.4	200.0
Maryland	275.1	239.9	155.2	152.8
Missouri	266.4	263.3	168.7	157.0
Arizona	264.4	215.3	102.4	117.0
Michigan	258.5	238.0	241.1	170.0
Connecticut	253.0	271.0	34.7	150.0
Kansas	245.3	199.8	151.1	143.0
Iowa	243.4	212.0	112.3	155.0
Illinois	199.7	179.3	102.4	100.0
Louisiana	180.2	138.9	142.4	40.0
Kentucky	174.0	140.3	115.4	141.0
Utah	143.9	118.2	90.6	50.0
North Carolina	139.9	104.5	−32.4	15.0
Wisconsin	139.4	115.8	70.7	185.8
Hawaii	136.4	122.8	71.9	50.0
Indiana	110.8	104.0	38.6	50.0
West Virginia	102.6	92.0	47.6	47.0
Alabama	101.8	75.2	30.0	10.0
Arkansas	75.2	61.0	−6.8	26.0
Maine	73.3	74.7	38.5	13.0
New Mexico	73.0	64.7	61.9	54.0
Delaware	67.1	60.4	34.2	22.6
Montana	59.5	49.2	28.4	22.6
South Carolina	48.5	49.1	−8.7	−9.0
Mississippi	42.5	30.3	7.2	10.0
Idaho	13.0	19.7	0.8	13.3
Vermont	3.7	−1.1	−16.4	−14.9
Tennessee	0.0	0.0	−0.7	0.0
Pennsylvania	0.0	0.0	−32.9	0.0
New Jersey	0.0	0.0	−51.5	0.0
New Hampshire	0.0	0.0	−0.1	0.0
Massachusetts	0.0	0.0	10.3	80.0
North Dakota	−0.0	0.0	−8.3	−2.8
Rhode Island	−10.5	−0.8	−34.4	−24.3
Nebraska	−19.1	−6.9	−29.8	−22.5
Alaska		No state income tax		
Florida		No state income tax		
Nevada		No state income tax		
South Dakota		No state income tax		
Texas		No state income tax		
Washington		No state income tax		
Wyoming		No state income tax		
Total	11880.0	10546.7	5169.7	5915.3

simulation model. More specifically, the ACIR windfalls represent the effects of TRA86 (assuming full implementation) on 1986 tax revenues. The ACIR results are thus most comparable to the TAXSIM estimates in the first column, the main difference being that the income data used in the ACIR estimates are from the 1981 SOI file aged to 1986. This simulation approach contrasts significantly with the approach used by NASBO/NCSL. Their windfall estimates represent the amounts reported by state officials for fiscal year 1988.[6]

The entries are ranked by the absolute size of the windfalls in the first column. According to the TAXSIM estimates in that column, the windfalls ranged from $3.27 billion in New York to negative $19.1 million in Nebraska. Seven states have no income tax and hence have no windfalls. Another three states (Connecticut, New Hampshire, and Tennessee) have narrowly defined income taxes. Of these three, only Connecticut has a significant windfall because its tax is on capital gains, which became fully taxable under TRA86. New Jersey and Pennsylvania define their tax bases more broadly than the federal government, so they were unaffected by TRA86. According to the NASBO/NCSL estimates, five states (North Dakota, South Carolina, Vermont, Nebraska, and Rhode Island) experienced negative windfalls, largely because they "piggyback" their taxes on federal tax payments, which under TRA86 declined for individuals. By all four windfall measures in Table 1, California and New York, both large states with high marginal tax rates, experienced the largest windfalls.

The total TAXSIM windfall estimates are substantially higher than the total ACIR and NASBO/NCSL estimates, ranging from $10.5 to $11.9 billion in contrast to the $5.2 billion for the ACIR and $5.9 billion for NASBO/NCSL. The reasons for this discrepancy are not completely clear. However, before concluding that the TAXSIM model grossly overstates the windfalls, one should note that the NASBO/NCSL estimates are probably too low. State officials have much stronger incentives to understate the magnitude of the windfalls than to overstate them.[7] Understatement minimizes taxpayer expectations about the potential for discretionary state tax reductions and provides flexibility for state budgeteers. As for the discrepancy between the ACIR and the TAXSIM estimates, about two-thirds apparently reflects the use of different SOI files. As reported in Table A-1 (appendix), TAXSIM generates a total windfall of $7.6 billion when aged 1981 SOI data are used rather than aged 1985 SOI data.

As a share of income tax revenues, windfalls are not inconsequential. The first column of Table 2 shows that TAXSIM windfalls exceed 10 percent of income tax revenues in 27 states. Even according to the smaller ACIR or NASBO/NCSL estimates, windfalls represent more than 10 percent of income

---

[6] The NASBO/NCSL estimates are drawn from the September 1987 NASBO report with the following exceptions: Because the September report included no negative windfalls, the value for South Carolina was drawn from the July 1987 NCSL report and the remaining negative values were drawn from the March 1987 NASBO report. Values for Oregon, Arkansas, and Kentucky were drawn from the July 1987 NCSL report because these values correspond more closely to the results described subsequently by Gold [1988, 1990b].

[7] Steven Gold, the former director of fiscal studies for the National Conference of State Legislatures, acknowledges the underestimation of the windfalls. "The $6.3 billion figure for the total potential personal income tax windfall was derived by aggregating estimates prepared by individual states. Because numerous states made these estimates conservatively, it is probably an underestimate to some degree [Gold, 1990b, footnote 2].

Table 2. Windfalls as a fraction of income tax revenue (ranked by column 1).

	TAXSIM windfall W1 (1)	TAXSIM windfall W2 (2)	ACIR windfall 1986 (3)	NASBO/NCSL windfall FY1988 (4)
Connecticut	0.622	0.347	0.099	0.426
New Mexico	0.475	0.184	0.466	0.178
Louisiana	0.426	0.199	0.312	0.069
Kansas	0.391	0.298	0.256	0.173
Oklahoma	0.359	0.197	0.237	0.147
Colorado	0.338	0.229	0.231	0.228
Arizona	0.303	0.174	0.139	0.136
Minnesota	0.303	0.184	0.164	0.116
Ohio	0.286	0.134	0.078	0.078
New York	0.285	0.241	0.085	0.081
Maine	0.278	0.151	0.108	0.023
Utah	0.273	0.164	0.173	0.078
Oregon	0.270	0.212	0.132	0.143
West Virginia	0.265	0.177	0.108	0.119
Montana	0.261	0.140	0.164	0.093
Missouri	0.259	0.175	0.146	0.104
Iowa	0.256	0.180	0.131	0.146
Hawaii	0.238	0.163	0.147	0.080
Delaware	0.207	0.148	0.087	0.060
California	0.191	0.145	0.079	0.109
Kentucky	0.182	0.105	0.138	0.140
Mississippi	0.158	0.078	0.027	0.028
Virginia	0.158	0.100	0.093	0.053
Maryland	0.141	0.098	0.078	0.063
Georgia	0.140	0.108	0.117	0.084
Alabama	0.137	0.077	0.035	0.011
Arkansas	0.127	0.082	−0.013	0.044
Indiana	0.084	0.057	0.029	0.028
Michigan	0.082	0.065	0.071	0.047
Illinois	0.076	0.056	0.037	0.032
Wisconsin	0.070	0.049	0.031	0.080
South Carolina	0.070	0.045	−0.009	−0.008
North Carolina	0.062	0.037	−0.014	0.005
Idaho	0.053	0.065	0.003	0.047
Vermont	0.019	−0.006	−0.096	−0.074
Tennessee	0.000	0.000	−0.010	0.000
Massachusetts	0.000	0.000	0.003	0.020
New Jersey	0.000	0.000	−0.023	0.000
Pennsylvania	0.000	0.000	−0.012	0.000
New Hampshire	0.000	0.000	−0.004	0.000
North Dakota	−0.000	0.000	−0.119	−0.025
Rhode Island	−0.040	−0.002	−0.116	−0.063
Nebraska	−0.057	−0.017	−0.083	−0.052
Washington		No state income tax		
Alaska		No state income tax		
South Dakota		No state income tax		
Texas		No state income tax		
Florida		No state income tax		
Nevada		No state income tax		
Wyoming		No state income tax		

Table 3. Determinants of the windfalls (dependent variable: windfall as a fraction of income tax revenue; absolute value of t-statistics in parentheses).

	TAXSIM windfall	ACIR windfall 1986	NASBO/NCSL windfall FY1988
Federal liability	−0.088	−0.109	−0.077
	(2.13)	(3.95)	(3.43)
AGI with deductions	0.048	0.038	0.024
	(1.82)	(2.12)	(1.60)
Capital gains	0.098	0.060	0.037
	(3.16)	(2.93)	(2.22)
Exemptions	−0.096	−0.075	−0.029
	(1.92)	(2.25)	(1.05)
Deductibility of federal taxes	0.092	0.078	0.046
	(3.30)	(4.21)	(3.00)
Constant	0.068	0.008	0.022
	(3.04)	(0.57)	(1.77)
R^2	0.73	0.81	0.70
No. of observations	39	39	39
Mean of dependent variable	0.171	0.076	0.063

Note: TAXSIM windfall is based on 1985 SOI data aged to 1986, and reflects the effects of the federal provisions through 1989. The TAXSIM windfall is expressed as a fraction of 1986 simulated income tax revenue, based on 1985 SOI data aged to 1986. The ACIR windfall is expressed as a fraction of calendar year 1986 income tax revenues. The NASBO/NCSC windfall is expressed as a fraction of FY 1988 income tax revenue. All the explanatory variables are 0–1 variables that take on the value 1 when the tax code is linked to the federal tax code in the specified manner. The sample is the 40 states that have a broad-based income tax, excluding New Mexico.

tax revenues by one of the two measures in 18 states and exceed 50 percent in New Mexico and 49 percent in Connecticut.[8] However, the ACIR and NASBO/NCSL windfalls (and by extension, the TAXSIM estimates) loom much less large when expressed as a share of total revenues, reaching a maximum of only 5.82 percent (based on NASBO/NCSL estimate) in Colorado (not shown in a table). In New Mexico and Connecticut, where windfalls represent very large shares of income tax revenues, they represent only 1.60 percent and 2.36 percent, respectively, of total revenue (based on NASBO/NCSL estimates), because income taxes in those states are narrowly defined and account for small portions of state revenue.

By regressing the fractions reported in Table 2 on the mechanisms through which the state code is coupled to the federal code, the effects on the windfall of each type of coupling can be determined. Descriptive regressions of this type are reported in Table 3. The dependent variable is the windfall as a share of income tax revenues for three estimates of the windfall: the TAXSIM W1 measure, the ACIR measure, and the NASBO/NCSL measure. The first two equations are expected to fit better than the NASBO/NCSL equation since

---

[8] The TAXSIM windfalls are expressed as a fraction of the simulated income tax liability in the relevant year. The ACIR windfalls are expressed as a fraction of 1986 calendar year collections and the NASBO/NCSL windfalls are expressed as a fraction of 1988 fiscal year collections.

the TAXSIM and ACIR windfall measures were both generated from models that explicitly take into account these provisions. The extent to which the NASBO/NCSL estimates are based on sophisticated simulation models at the state level is unclear.

All the explanatory variables are indicator variables that take on the value 1 if the state code is coupled to the federal code in the specified way. Thus, the first variable, Federal liability, indicates whether tax liabilities under the state tax code are tied directly to the taxpayer's federal liability. The coefficient of this variable implies that piggybacking on the federal code in this way reduces state liabilities on average by 8.8 percent, 10.9 percent, or 7.7 percent, depending on the windfall measure used.

According to the TAXSIM measure, those states that use the federal definition of AGI plus most of the federal deductions experienced, on average, a 4.8 percent rise in their revenues, while reliance on the federal definition of capital gains increased revenues by about 9.8 percent. Using the federal definition of exemptions, in contrast, reduced state liabilities by about 9.6 percent because of the substantial expansion of the federal exemption under TRA86.[9] The final variable, which measures whether federal taxes are deductible at the state level, is predicted to have a positive sign; because the TRA reduced federal income taxes for individuals, the value of this deduction to state taxpayers fell, thereby raising state liabilities.[10]

STATE DISCRETIONARY ACTIONS

Only one previous study has attempted to quantify state actions at the time of the windfalls. Based on questionnaires to the states asking them what actions they took in 1987 and 1988, NASBO generated estimates of the proportion of the windfalls returned to state taxpayers. NASBO treats any state that reported a tax reduction of more than 100 percent as if it returned exactly 100 percent. Of the 34 states with positive windfalls, NASBO reports that 13 returned 100 percent, 15 returned none, and 6 returned less than 100 percent but more than zero. Those states that took discretionary offsetting action typically either reduced tax rates or increased exemptions. According to the NASBO estimates, states returned, in the aggregate, about 81 percent of the windfall to state taxpayers. However, because states (like New York and California) with the largest windfalls tended to offset their windfalls by reducing taxes by 100 percent (or more) of the windfall while smaller states appeared to retain their windfalls, the NASBO estimates imply that the "average" state experiencing a positive windfall returned about 60 percent of the windfall to state taxpayers.

With the help of TAXSIM, more refined estimates of discretionary tax changes can be simulated. One-year discretionary changes (labeled $D87$ and

---

[9] The regression includes the major categories of changes under TRA86. Other more specific provisions that were changed by TRA86, such as the reduction of the IRA deduction and the deduction for two-earner households, were included in supplemental regressions but were not statistically significant.

[10] The one potentially disturbing aspect of the TAXSIM regression is the large positive constant term. This positive coefficient is consistent with the view that the TAXSIM estimates of the windfalls may be somewhat too large.

$D88$) can be simulated as

$$D87 = R(Y_{87}, S_{87}, F_{87}) - R(Y_{87}, S_{86}, F_{87})$$
$$D88 = R(Y_{88}, S_{88}, F_{88}) - R(Y_{88}, S_{87}, F_{88})$$

where the first term in each expression indicates simulated actual revenue in 1987 (or 1988) and the second term indicates how much revenue the state would have collected in 1987 with its 1986 tax code (or in 1988 with its 1987 tax code), allowing for the changes in the federal code that affect state provisions.

The TAXSIM results suggest that total net discretionary reductions in state income taxes in 1987 and 1988 *exceeded* the total windfall for the same two years by 9 percent.[11] In other words, states took discretionary actions that, in the aggregate, more than offset the windfall. If the TAXSIM results are adjusted to conform with NASBO's somewhat arbitrary decision to cap TRA86-related tax reductions at the size of the windfall and to ignore discretionary increases in taxes, the TAXSIM results imply that, in the aggregate, 67 percent of the windfall was returned to taxpayers and that the "average" state returned about 43 percent of the windfall.

These results are at best descriptive and tell us little about whether the windfalls caused the discretionary tax changes. To the extent that other state-specific effects of TRA86 were correlated with the windfalls or that states that experienced the largest relative windfalls also experienced other pressures to reduce taxes, the state discretionary changes observed between 1986 and 1988 should not be attributed fully to the TRA86 windfalls.

MODEL OF STATE DISCRETIONARY TAX CHANGES

A more complete model of state discretionary tax changes is needed to isolate the effects of the windfall. This model, to be estimated with pooled data for all states with broadly based income taxes for the period 1982–1988, can be written in general form as

$$D_{it} = F(W_{it}, X_{it}) \qquad (1)$$

where D_{it} is the per capita discretionary tax change in the ith state in year t, W_{it} is the per capita windfall in the ith state in year t, and X_{it} is a vector of control variables. The challenge is to determine the set of variables to be included as control variables and to specify a straightforward test of the flypaper effect.

Income tax collections (T) in any year in any state can be viewed as the product of an income tax rate (r), or more generally a structure of rates; a coverage ratio (C), which can be interpreted as the ratio of the income tax base to personal income; and state personal income (Y). Consequently, changes in income tax collections can be decomposed as follows, where d denotes change:

$$dT = dr(CY) + dC(rY) + dY(Cr) \qquad (2)$$

The first term to the right of the equals sign denotes the change in income tax collections associated with discretionary changes in state tax rates. The

---
[11] I am focusing here on two years of windfalls and discretionary changes in order to make the results comparable to the NASBO analysis.

second term indicates changes in collections associated with changes in the definition of the tax base, and the third term indicates changes in revenue associated with changes in state income. This expression can be written more simply as

$$dT = D + W + A \qquad (3)$$

where D stands for discretionary changes in state tax policy and includes $dr(CY)$ plus the portion of $dC(rY)$ that reflects state discretionary changes in the state tax base; W denotes windfall, namely the remaining portion of $dC(rY)$; and A denotes automatic revenue growth and is equal to $dY(Cr)$.

Rewriting this expression to focus on state discretionary decisions yields:

$$D = dT - W - A \qquad (4)$$

We can make this into a behavioral model of state discretionary tax changes by replacing dT with the desired change in income taxes (dT^*), where the desired change reflects individual preferences as aggregated through the political process, and adding a random error term to reflect errors in translating desired into actual changes (u). These adjustments produce the following model where the i and t subscripts denote state and year, respectively:

$$D_{it} = dT^*_{it} - W_{it} - A_{it} + u_{it} \qquad (5)$$

The desired change in income taxes is unobservable. Hence, it must be replaced by its determinants. According to the standard median voter model, state policymakers choose the level of income taxes preferred by taxpayer voters, given their demands for public services and the tax price of income taxes relative to other revenue sources. In the standard stylized change form of this model,

$$dT^*_{it} = f(d\text{INCOME}_{it}, d\text{TAXPRICE}_{it}, d\text{GRANTS}_{it}, d\text{RELPRICE}_{it}) \qquad (6)$$

where dINCOME is the change in income of the decisive voter, dTAXPRICE is the change in the decisive voter's tax price,[12] dGRANTS is the change in federal grants to the state (normally specified per capita), and dRELPRICE is the change in the price of income taxes relative to other broad-based taxes such as sales taxes. The first three independent variables influence the desired change in spending. The income variable is expected to enter with a positive sign and the tax price with a negative sign. In addition to increasing the desired spending level, a larger amount of federal aid also reduces the need for funding from the state's own sources, including the state income tax. Hence, the expected sign of dGRANTS in this equation is negative. Finally, the decision about whether to finance public services from income taxes or other revenue sources depends in part on the relative price of raising revenue from various sources, as accounted for here by the relative tax price term.

Substituting equation (6) into equation (5) yields the following model of discretionary changes:

$$D_{it} = f(d\text{INCOME}_{it}, d\text{TAXPRICE}_{it}, d\text{GRANTS}_{it}, d\text{RELPRICE}_{it}) \\ - W_{it} - A_{it} + u_{it} \qquad (7)$$

Notice that according to this stylized model, the desired change in income taxes is independent of the components of the change; that is, state policymak-

---

[12] A tax price is the cost to the state taxpayer of an additional dollar of state tax collections. See "Tax-Price Variables," below, for more discussion.

ers are assumed to be indifferent to how the overall change in state income taxes is achieved. The implications for the coefficients of both the automatic growth and the windfall are clear; both should be equal to minus 1.

Of course, the political economy of state tax changes may make the composition of the tax change pertinent. Assuming that policymakers are interested in maximizing spending, fiscal illusion on the part of taxpayer voters may provide some flexibility for policymakers to seize the opportunity presented by automatic revenue growth to increase state spending more than would otherwise be desired. For example, policymakers may find it politically easier to raise taxes when the tax increase occurs automatically than when it comes in the form of discretionary changes in tax rates that face the bright light of public scrutiny. The argument is that people are generally aware of explicitly enacted tax changes, but are less aware of tax increases that occur with, say, a progressive income tax during a period of economic growth. (See Wagner [1976] for the hypothesis, and Feenberg and Rosen [1987] for evidence against this view.) Thus, fiscal illusion would lead to a flypaper effect in that some of the automatic increases would remain in the public treasury.

The fiscal illusion hypothesis is most fully developed in the literature on intergovernmental grants. In this literature, the illusion takes the form either of voter confusion between the fall in the averge price of public services and the marginal price (see Courant et al., [1979]; Oates [1979]) or incorrect perceptions about how much aid is received (see Filimon et al. as described in Fisher [1982]). According to the Filimon et al. model, the budget-maximizing bureaucrat hides the grant from voters and then spends it on top of the amount desired by the median voter. This last model seems the most potentially applicable to the windfall case. One could imagine state policymakers making state tax decisions on the basis of revenues in the absence of the windfall, and then spending the windfall on top of the amount desired by the median voter. Compared to some grants, however, the revenue from tax windfalls is less closely associated with specific spending programs. Thus the politics surrounding the use of the windfall may differ somewhat from that surrounding grants.

Stated more formally, the vector of potential political determinants of dT^* may include A and W. The larger the windfall or the greater the automatic change in revenue, the greater may be the politically desired change in state taxes. Letting a be the coefficient of W and b the coefficient of A in the desired tax change equation, and X' the vector of other determinants of desired changes, we can write this more general model as

$$D_{it} = f(X'_{it}) + (a - 1)W_{it} + (b - 1)A_{it} + u_{it}. \qquad (8)$$

Bureaucratic behavior aimed at keeping some of the revenue from the windfalls or automatic growth in the public treasury would generate positive values for a and b. This formulation provides a direct test of the flypaper effect, both for windfalls and for automatic revenue increases. In addition, it allows one to compare the magnitude of the flypaper effects for W and A. The test for the existence of a flypaper effect with respect to windfalls is simply whether a is greater than zero. This test is equivalent to testing the null hypothesis that the estimated coefficient of W is equal to -1 against the alternative that it is closer to zero. To test the null hypothesis that state officials retained the entire windfall, we would test the null hypothesis that the coefficient of W equals zero against the alternative hypothesis that it is less than zero. Similar tests can be made for automatic growth.

REGRESSION RESULTS: WINDFALL AND TAX GROWTH EFFECTS

Table 4 reports the results for the pooled-time series model. Each regression is based on data for the 40 states with broad-based income taxes pooled for the years 1982–1988. The dependent variable in all four equations is the annual discretionary tax change (similar to windfall measure W2) as generated by TAXSIM for each year of the sample. The regressions were estimated by ordinary least squares, with standard errors corrected for heteroscedastic-

Table 4. Discretionary tax change equations[a] (pooled data: 40 states, 1982–88; standard errors in parentheses).

	(1)	(2)	(3)	(4)
WINDFALL[b]	−0.724**	−0.989**		
	(0.171)	(0.107)		
WFTRA86[c]		−0.598**		−0.620**
		(0.259)		(0.264)
POSWIND			−0.740**	−1.118**
			(0.198)	(0.139)
NEGWIND			−0.574**	−0.479**
			(0.214)	(0.198)
TAXGRWTH	−0.962**	−0.994**	−0.956**	−0.977**
	(0.291)	(0.295)	(0.298)	(0.298)
INCOMECH	0.025**	0.026**	0.025**	0.026**
	(0.011)	(0.012)	(0.012)	(0.012)
GRANTCHL	−0.016	−0.023	−0.017	−0.029
	(0.083)	(0.082)	(0.083)	(0.082)
BALANCEL	−0.045	−0.047	−0.046	−0.050
	(0.037)	(0.036)	(0.037)	(0.036)
CORPWIND	0.113	0.109	0.133	0.111
	(1.105)	(1.097)	(1.100)	(1.097)
TXPR75CH	−62.79	−46.59	−68.12	−63.36
	(73.17)	(70.42)	(74.68)	(73.50)
RLPR75CH	43.60	52.27	44.69	56.80
	(106.80)	(108.16)	(106.01)	(107.07)
YEAR82	2.76	5.80	2.95	7.83
	(5.25)	(5.60)	(5.30)	(5.92)
YEAR83	10.98**	11.31**	11.04**	12.15**
	(5.13)	(5.14)	(5.13)	(5.18)
YEAR84	−2.60	−1.43	−2.75	−1.20
	(4.63)	(4.74)	(4.65)	(4.82)
YEAR85	−14.78**	−14.01**	−15.07**	−14.37**
	(5.94)	(5.85)	(5.90)	(5.86)
YEAR86	−11.66**	−11.16**	−11.89**	−11.32**
	(2.14)	(5.41)	(5.43)	(5.44)
YEAR87	18.02	14.36	18.53	15.60
	(11.92)	(12.08)	(11.87)	(11.99)
CONSTANT	18.18**	18.17**	18.38**	18.40**
	(5.72)	(5.65)	(5.66)	(5.61)
Adj. R^2	0.44	0.44	0.44	0.44

[a] Dependent variable is the discretionary change in income taxes in year t per capita (DISC). Each equation is based on 280 observations. Two asterisks (**) denote that the coefficient is significantly different from 0 at the 5-percent level; one asterisk (*) denotes statistical significance at the 10-percent level.

ity using White's method.[13] The equations differ in terms of the specification of the windfall variable. All the regressions include year indicator variables to control for changes in nationwide factors such as national economic conditions that might affect state discretionary income tax changes. The excluded baseline year is 1988.

The results of primary interest are those for the windfall and the TAXGRWTH variables. The basic windfall variable (WINDFALL) in the first regression is the annual windfall associated with federal tax changes throughout the sample period. The −0.724 point estimate of its coefficient in column 1 implies that states reduced taxes by 72 cents and retained 28 cents in the public treasury per dollar of windfall. We can rule out with confidence the null hypothesis that the coefficient equals zero, namely that states retained all the windfalls. With somewhat less confidence (slightly less than 90 percent) we can also rule out the hypothesis that the coefficient is −1, namely that states returned all the windfall. This last finding provides support for the existence of a flypaper effect.

To determine if states responded to the large TRA86 windfalls any differently than to the smaller windfalls in previous years, the second equation includes a measure of the windfalls associated with TRA86. This variable (WFTRA86) takes the value 0 for years before 1987 and the value of the windfall in 1987 and 1988. To simplify the interpretation of the results, the

---

[13] This method is described in William H. Greene [1990, ch. 14].

---

^b This variable is redefined for equation (2) to exclude the windfalls in 1987 and 1988.
^c This variable represents only positive windfalls in regression 4.

Definition of variables (All dollar figures are in 1982 dollars per capita, based on the implicit price deflator for state and local government purchases):

Dependent variables

DISC	Discretionary change in income taxes in year t, based on TAXSIM, per capita (mean = -5.93).

Independent variables

WINDFALL	Windfall in year t, based on TAXSIM, per capita (mean = $7.31; mean for variable excluding 1987 and 1988 = $1.61).
WFTRA86	Windfall in year t = 1987 or 1988, per capita, otherwise 0 (mean for 1987 = $31.28; mean for 1988 = $2.03).
POSWIND	Windfall in year t if windfall is positive (mean = $8.31; mean for variable excluding 1987 and 1988 windfalls = $2.39).
NEGWIND	Windfall in year t if windfall is negative (mean = -1.00).
TAXGRWTH	Growth in income taxes in year t from income growth alone, based on TAXSIM, per capita (mean = $22.78).
INCOMECH	Change in per capita income (mean = $189.64).
GRANTCHL	Change in per capita federal grants to the state, lagged one year (mean = -2.61).
BALANCEL	General fund balance in year $t - 1$, per capita (mean = $31.41).
CORPWIND	Corporate windfall in year t, if t = 1987 or 1988, from NASBO, per capita. Adjusted for amount returned in 1988. Otherwise 0 (mean for 1987 = $2.35; mean for 1988 = $1.16).
TXPR75CH	Change in tax price of filer at 75th percentile, from TAXSIM (mean = 0.006).
RLPR75CH	Change in tax price of income taxes relative to tax price of sales tax of filer at 75th percentile in year t, from TAXSIM (mean = -0.0017).
YEARXX	Indicator variable that takes on value 1 if year is XX and 0 otherwise, for XX = '82 ... '87 (mean for each variable = 0.142).

basic windfall variable in this equation has been redefined to exclude the TRA86 windfalls. This adjustment means that the coefficient of WFTRA86 can be interpreted analogously to that of the WINDFALL variable, namely as the proportion of the windfall returned to taxpayers. The results are quite striking. The -0.989 coefficient of the basic windfall variable is sufficiently close to -1 that it provides no support at all for the presence of a flypaper effect in state responses to typical windfalls. The -0.598 coefficient on the TRA86 windfall variable, however, is consistent with a flypaper effect of 40 cents on the dollar.

Regressions 3 and 4 allow for the possibility that states might respond differently to windfall gains than to windfall losses. Equation (3) suggests a differential response, but the difference is not statistically significant. The estimated coefficients imply that states reduce taxes by 74 cents per dollar of windfall gain but increase taxes by only 57 cents per dollar of windfall loss. Equation (4) refines the analysis by distinguishing the positive windfalls associated with TRA86 from other positive windfalls throughout the period. (POSWIND has been redefined to exclude the TRA86 windfalls.) A comparison of regressions 2 and 4 indicates quite similar coefficients for the TRA86 windfall variable. Both equations suggest a flypaper effect of about 40 cents with respect to the TRA86 windfalls.[14]

To summarize, evidence for a flypaper effect emerges for the TRA86 windfalls but not for the smaller windfalls in previous years. In one sense this differential pattern is a bit curious. The extensive publicity associated with the large TRA86 windfalls suggests that the potential for fiscal illusion would be less for the TRA86 windfalls than for previous windfalls. That is, the TRA86 windfalls presumably should have been harder to hide and consequently harder to retain than the smaller windfalls of previous years. Consequently, the less-than-100-percent offset of the TRA86 windfalls cannot be explained solely on the basis of the potential for hiding revenue from taxpayers. One alternative explanation relates to uncertainty. To the extent that state officials were uncertain about the magnitude of the TRA86 windfall, we would expect them to return less than 100 percent of the actual windfall.[15] But uncertainty is far from the whole story. As mentioned earlier, some states apparently returned 100 percent and some 0 percent. This observation suggests that many states made explicit decisions about whether to take any action at all. In the concluding section below, I speculate about the nature of legislative decisionmaking that might explain this result.

The coefficients of TAXGRWTH in all equations provide no evidence whatsoever of a flypaper effect with respect to automatic growth of tax revenues. The coefficients, which range from -0.96 to -0.99, are all consistent with the hypothesis that the true coefficient is -1. This finding supports the conclusions of Feenberg and Rosen [1987] who find no evidence that the elasticity of the state's tax base affects revenue growth.

---

[14] Of interest is the observation that these estimated coefficients are almost identical to the average return percentage of 60 percent implicit in the NASBO study. Thus, despite large differences in the magnitudes of the estimated windfalls and in methodology, the TAXSIM model and the NASBO study yield similar conclusions.

[15] I thank Edward Gramlich for suggesting this point.

RESULTS FOR OTHER VARIABLES

Non-Tax-Price Variables

Most of the other variables enter with the expected signs, but the presence of the year indicator variables in the equation makes some of them insignificant. As predicted, the change in per capita income (INCOMECH) enters positively and significantly in all equations. These results support the view that rising income increases the demand for public services and for the taxes to finance the additional services. Note that this behavioral demand effect emerges even after controlling for the automatic change in income tax revenues associated with changes in state income.

To minimize simultaneity problems, the change in grants variable (GRANTCHL) has been lagged one year. Its negative sign is consistent with the hypothesis that grants increase the desired level of services by less than they increase the non-tax funding for those services, but the coefficients are unexpectedly small and imprecise. If the year variables are excluded from the equations, the estimates become more reasonable. For example, in a specification comparable to equation (1), the coefficient of the grants variable is -0.224 with a t-value of -3.21. Apparently the variation across states in the change in grants is insufficient to separate the year effects from the grant effects.[16]

Two additional variables not discussed earlier have also been included. The first is the state's general fund balances as a percentage of spending at the end of the previous year (BALANCEL). This variable is intended to measure the short-run fiscal condition of the state. Low year-end balances could put pressure on state officials to raise income (and other taxes) more than would be consistent with changes in the fundamental factors affecting the demand for spending. Similarly, high fund balances in one year reduce the need to increase taxes the next year. The negative coefficients in all equations are consistent with this short-run fiscal pressure effect. Once again, however, the inclusion of the year variables weakens the results; presumably, the year-end balances are highly correlated with specific events, such as the national recession. When the year variables are excluded from the equation, the estimated effect is about 50 percent greater and significant at the 10-percent level.

The other additional variable, CORPWIND, controls for the possibility that corporate windfalls associated with TRA86 might influence state decisions about the personal income tax. As is true for personal income taxes, many states link the base for the state corporate income tax to the federal code. Hence, the 1986 changes in the federal code produced windfalls in many

---

[16] In other empirical work, inferences are made about the magnitude of the flypaper effect with respect to grants by comparing coefficients of the grants variable and the income variable. One should resist the temptation to make any inferences of that type based on these equations for three reasons. First, the grants variable is not sufficiently well specified to provide a good test of the flypaper effect. As specified for these equations, it includes grants of all types, not just the lump sum grants that are needed to test the theory. One would expect the state response to matching grants or narrowly defined categorical grants to differ from that of broadly defined block grants. Second, the inability to separate the grant effects from the year effects makes it difficult to determine the true behavioral response to the grants. Third, the standard theory refers to effects of grants on spending, not on one specific revenue source as is the case here.

states.[17] Based on estimates from NASBO, these corporate tax windfalls are much smaller than those for the personal income tax, and as shown by the regression results have virtually no impact on discretionary changes in personal income taxes.

Tax-Price Variables[18]

I have singled out the tax-price variables for separate discussion because they are the vehicle through which many of the behavioral effects of TRA86 on state governments were predicted to occur. By increasing the net cost of additional state taxes to state taxpayers, TRA86's reduction in federal marginal rates and decreased incentives for filers to itemize were predicted to lead to downward pressure on state taxes. In addition, the elimination of the deductibility of state and local sales taxes under TRA86 was expected to encourage states to shift away from the now more-expensive sales tax toward the still-deductible income tax. The results presented here are at best suggestive; for a more complete and definitive analysis of the tax-price effects of TRA86 on income and sales taxes, see Gilbert Metcalf [1993].

The tax price is defined as the cost to state taxpayers of an additional dollar of state tax collections. For a nonitemizing taxpayer, this price is simply equal to $1. For a taxpayer who itemizes, the price of the state taxes is reduced by the associated reduction in federal tax payments, with appropriate adjustments for whether federal taxes are deductible at the state level. TAXSIM was used to generate expected tax prices for a random 1-in-5 sample of all filers included in the 1985 SOI data.[19] Following Metcalf [1993], we generated an average tax price for all filers as well as for groups of filers at various percentiles of the income distribution, such as the 50th, 75th, 95th percentiles.[20]

The regressions include two tax-price variables, both calculated for taxpayers at the 75th percentile. This percentile was chosen based on Metcalf's finding that high income groups appear to be decisive for the personal income tax. The first variable (TXPR75CH) is the change in the tax price of state income taxes for filers of this type. The second variable, denoted RLPR75CH, is the change in the price of raising revenue through the income tax relative to raising it through a general sales tax. Negative coefficients are expected on both variables. TRA86 should make the value of the first tax-price variable positive; the reduction in marginal tax rates and lower probabilities of itemiz-

---

[17] See Steven D. Gold [1990a] for an analysis of the aggregate size of the corporate income tax windfall.

[18] Jonathan Jacobson took primary responsibility for estimating the tax price terms, based on data from TAXSIM generated by Daniel Feenberg.

[19] To implement this approach, an estimate of the probability of itemizing in each state that does not depend on state-specific information is required. We estimated these probabilities by regressing a 0–1 itemization variable on AGI and AGI squared and using that equation to predict the probability of itemization, limiting the predictions to the 0–1 range. This approach differs somewhat from that used by Gilbert Metcalf [1993].

[20] Metcalf [1993] calculates tax prices for certain percentiles by averaging estimated tax prices for filers with AGIs within $1000 or $2000 of the nth percentile filer's AGI. In contrast, we calculate tax prices by averaging all of the tax prices for filers within 2.5 percentiles of the nth percentile filer. For example, the 75th percentile tax price is an average of tax prices of filers with AGI between the 72.5th and the 77.5th percentiles in each state.

ing under TRA86 raise the tax price of state taxes. TRA86 makes the second tax-price variable negative; the elimination of the deductibility of sales taxes relative to income taxes lowers the tax price of income taxes relative to sales taxes.

Contrary to the predictions of economic theory, the tax-price results in equations (1) and (2) indicate little behavioral effect of the changes in tax prices. Although the negative sign of TXPR75CH is consistent with Metcalf's finding that a higher income tax price reduces the use of income taxes, the coefficient is not significant. The very insignificant coefficient on the relative tax-price change variable is also consistent with Metcalf's conclusion that the tax price of sales taxes has no impact on the decision to use the income tax. Experimentation with changes in other tax-price variables, including changes in the average tax price and in that of the 50th, 90th, and 95 percentiles, yields no stronger results.

Only if the change variables are replaced by levels do the tax-price results change in any important way. In equations not shown, the change variable (TXPR75CH) was replaced with the average tax price in year t and the change in relative prices (RELPR75CH) was replaced with the level of average tax prices in year t. In this formulation, the average tax price becomes negative and statistically significant.[21] In other words, discretionary income tax changes in states with high average tax prices are likely to be smaller on average than those in states with low average tax prices. Based on this result, we would conclude, along with Metcalf, that by raising tax prices, TRA86 led to smaller discretionary income tax increases than would otherwise have occurred. Why the levels of average tax prices should affect *changes* in taxes, however, is not fully clear. Moreover, the relative tax-price term enters with a large and significant positive coefficient that is difficult to justify. Its large impact on the year coefficients suggests that it may be measuring a year effect rather than a tax-price effect. Hence, given the theoretical criticisms of using levels rather than changes and the difficulty of interpreting the relative tax-price variable, the regressions as reported are preferred. In any case, the choice of tax-price variable has virtually no effect on the windfall coefficients.

CONCLUSION

When states link their state income tax codes to the federal income tax code, they minimize compliance costs for state taxpayers and buy into the nationally determined equity notions implicit in the federal code. To be weighed against these advantages is the possibility that such definitional linkage will affect the amount of state income taxes collected. Because the Federal Tax Reform Act of 1986 made major changes in the federal tax base and, consequently, in many state tax bases as well, it provides a natural experiment for determining how these definitional linkages affect state revenues in practice. Thus, an important policy question for both federal and state policymakers is the extent to which the windfalls generated by TRA86 affected state decisions about income taxes.

[21] The coefficient on the average tax price is −267 with a standard error of 104. The coefficient of the average relative tax-price term is 480 with a standard error of 250. The coefficients on the windfall variables are essentially unchanged.

As a by-product of examining the state response to the TRA86 windfalls, the analysis in this paper also provides new evidence on the so-called flypaper effect. As observed frequently in the vast literature on intergovernmental grants, money tends to stick where it hits. That is, recipient jurisdictions tend to retain for public spending a greater-than-predicted share of lump-sum grant funds. The question for this paper is the extent to which a flypaper effect operates with respect to windfalls generated by federal tax changes.

An additional dollar of TRA86 windfalls appears to have led states to retain, on average, about 40 cents—that is, to increase their income tax revenues by 40 cents more than they would have in the absence of the windfalls.[22] This finding of a flypaper effect contrasts sharply with the findings for the smaller windfall gains experienced by states in previous years and for the changes in revenues that occur automatically with changes in state personal income. No evidence emerges to support the view that a flypaper effect operates with respect to these other revenue changes.

How can we reconcile these two findings? That is, why does a flypaper effect emerge for the large and well-publicized windfalls associated with the Tax Reform Act, but not for other tax-related windfalls? Two differences between tax-related windfalls and intergovernmental grants may help explain the absence of a flypaper effect for the non-TRA86 windfalls. In contrast, the anticipation of large windfalls associated with the Tax Reform Act of 1986 appears to have created a political situation more similar to that of grants and one that favors the emergence of a flypaper effect.

The first difference between grants and windfalls relates to the source of funds. Additional tax revenues associated with tax windfalls or automatic revenue growth are not really net gains to state taxpayers. In fact, they simply represent higher taxes, the only distinguishing characteristic of which is that they do not require explicit changes in tax rates. This situation contrasts to that for intergovernmental grants which, because the money comes primarily from taxpayers in other states, may appear relatively cost-free to state policymakers. This difference between the two sources of funds could easily generate a lesser flypaper effect for tax-related windfalls than for intergovernmental grants.

A second difference between grants and tax-related windfalls relates to the applicability of the assumptions underlying the flypaper effect. The most plausible explanations for the flypaper effect, such as that of Filimon et al. (as described in Fisher [1982]), require the assumption of budget-maximizing bureaucrats with control over the agenda. In general, such an assumption seems more applicable to grants than to tax windfalls. For example, consider lump-sum grants designated for social services. One can easily imagine a process in which the proponents of social-service spending gain control of the agenda and are able to use the grants to raise spending beyond levels that would otherwise be desired. The fact that tax windfalls are not linked to any specific spending item makes this process less likely for tax windfalls, especially when the windfalls are relatively small and not well publicized.

However, when windfalls are large and well publicized, as they were in 1986 and 1987, the process just described for grants may also operate for

---

[22] Because this study focuses on income taxes alone, we do not know for certain that the 40-cent increase in income taxes translates into a 40-cent increase in total state revenues.

windfalls. With large windfalls, lobbyists have something to fight about. In particular, advocates of higher spending have an incentive to form coalitions to push for higher spending. The outcome of the resulting bargaining process between proponents of higher spending and advocates of tax reduction is likely to vary from state to state, but on average could lead to results quite similar to that for grants.

The finding of a flypaper effect for the large TRA86 windfalls means that state actions do not fully offset the unintended windfall gains for state governments associated with large-scale federal tax reform. Consequently, definitional linkages between state and federal tax codes matter in the sense that they affect the total amount of income tax revenue raised at the state level. The linkages between federal and state tax codes affect the political economy of state tax policy in another way as well. The windfalls provide fiscal dividends to state policymakers that can be distributed back to state taxpayers. In the process of returning the windfalls, state policymakers have to grapple with the distributional consequences of their decisions. As a result, federal tax reform may well affect the structure as well as the level of state income taxes. For future research, TAXSIM would appear to be a useful tool for exploring the political economy of the distributional choices that states made in returning the windfalls.

APPENDIX

Table A-1. Comparison of windfalls: 1981 and 1986 SOI data.

	Windfall ($ million) $W1$		Windfall/ estimated revenue	
	SOI 85	SOI 81	SOI 85	SOI 81
Alabama	101.8	91.4	0.137	0.130
Alaska	0.0	0.0		
Arizona	264.4	189.3	0.303	0.247
Arkansas	75.2	33.8	0.127	0.053
California	1981.7	1606.7	0.191	0.167
Colorado	371.0	285.7	0.338	0.260
Connecticut	253.0	122.5	0.622	0.401
Delaware	67.1	34.6	0.207	0.101
Florida	0.0	0.0		
Georgia	285.8	188.3	0.140	0.102
Hawaii	136.4	84.5	0.238	0.149
Idaho	13.0	−22.8	0.053	−0.080
Illinois	199.7	121.1	0.076	0.042
Indiana	110.8	57.2	0.084	0.041
Iowa	243.4	202.5	0.256	0.172
Kansas	245.3	193.7	0.391	0.269
Kentucky	174.0	158.5	0.182	0.156
Louisiana	180.2	137.1	0.426	0.286
Maine	73.3	36.8	0.278	0.103
Maryland	275.1	170.3	0.141	0.083
Massachusetts	0.0	0.0	0.000	0.000
Michigan	258.5	152.8	0.082	0.048

Table A-1. (Continued)

	Windfall ($ million) W1		Windfall/ estimated revenue	
	SOI 85	SOI 81	SOI 85	SOI 81
Minnesota	513.6	349.6	0.303	0.190
Mississippi	42.5	27.1	0.158	0.086
Missouri	266.4	187.2	0.259	0.156
Montana	59.5	57.1	0.261	0.226
Nebraska	−19.1	−47.4	−0.057	−0.118
Nevada	0.0	0.0		
New Hampshire	0.0	0.0	0.000	0.000
New Jersey	0.0	0.0	0.000	0.000
New Mexico	73.0	56.5	0.475	0.367
New York	3271.9	2071.3	0.285	0.167
North Carolina	139.9	48.8	0.062	0.021
North Dakota	−0.0	0.0	−0.000	0.000
Ohio	819.3	246.4	0.286	0.068
Oklahoma	297.3	151.0	0.359	0.193
Oregon	338.8	256.7	0.270	0.196
Pennsylvania	0.0	0.0	0.000	0.000
Rhode Island	−10.5	−35.6	−0.040	−0.112
South Carolina	48.5	−60.5	0.070	−0.080
South Dakota	0.0	0.0		
Tennessee	0.0	0.0	0.000	0.000
Texas	0.0	0.0		
Utah	143.9	99.3	0.273	0.200
Vermont	3.7	−29.0	0.019	−0.149
Virginia	339.6	207.7	0.158	0.091
Washington	0.0	0.0		
West Virginia	102.6	66.2	0.265	0.143
Wisconsin	139.4	74.3	0.070	0.030
Wyoming	0.0	0.0		
Total average	11880.0	7570.6	0.180	0.102

I thank the NBER for financial support, Elisabeth Coutts for her TAXSIM programming, and Daniel Feenberg for his help with the tax-price variables. In addition, I am extremely grateful to Jonathan Jacobson for his excellent research assistance.

HELEN F. LADD is Professor of Public Policy Studies and Economics at the Terry Sanford Institute of Public Policy, Duke University.

REFERENCES

Advisory Commission on Intergovernmental Relations (1988), "The Tax Reform Act of 1986: Its Effects on Both Federal and State Personal Income Tax Liabilities." Staff Information Report (SR-8) (January).

Baumgardner, James R. (1991), "Tests of Median Voter and Political Support Maximization Models: The Case of Federal/State Welfare Programs." Unpublished manuscript, Duke University.

Courant, Paul N., and Gramlich, Edward M. (1990), "The Impact of the Tax Reform Act of 1986 on State and Local Fiscal Behavior," in Joel Slemrod (ed.), *Do Taxes Matter? The Impact of the Tax Reform Act of 1986* (Cambridge, MA: MIT Press), pp. 243–277.

Courant, Paul N., Gramlich, Edward M., and Rubinfeld, Daniel (1979), "The Stimulative Effects of Intergovernmental Grants: Or Why Money Sticks Where It Hits," in P. Mieszkowski and W. Oakland (eds.), *Fiscal Federalism and Grants in Aid* (Washington, DC: The Urban Institute Press).

Feenberg, Daniel R., and Rosen, Harvey S. (1987), "Tax Structure and Public Sector Growth," *Journal of Public Economics* 32, pp. 185–201.

Fisher, Ronald C. (1982), "Income and Grant Effects on Local Expenditure: The Flypaper Effect and Other Difficulties," *Journal of Urban Economics* 12, pp. 324–345.

Gold, Steven D. (1987), "The State Government Response to Federal Income Tax Reform: Indications From the States That Completed Their Work Early," *National Tax Journal* 40(3), pp. 431–444.

Gold, Steven D. (1988), "The Blizzard of 1987: A Year of Tax Reform Activity in the States," *Publius* 18(3), pp. 17–35.

Gold, Steven D. (1990a), "Comments on 'The Impact of the TRA on State and Local Fiscal Behavior,'" in J. Slemrod (ed.), *Do Taxes Matter? The Impact of the Tax Reform Act of 1986* (Cambridge, MA: MIT Press).

Gold, Steven D. (1990b), "Did the Windfall Stay or Blow Away?" *The Fiscal Letter*, 12(1) (Jan/Feb), pp. 3–4.

Gramlich, Edward M. (1977), "Intergovernmental Grants; A Review of the Empirical Literature," in Wallace Oates (ed.), *Political Economy of Fiscal Federalism* (Lexington, MA: D.C. Heath), pp. 219–240.

Greene, William H. (1990), *Econometric Analysis* (New York: Macmillan).

Metcalf, Gilbert E. (1993), "Tax Exporting, Federal Deductibility, and State Tax Sructure," *Journal of Policy Analysis and Management* (this issue).

National Association of State Budget Officers (1987a), *Fiscal Survey of the States* (March).

National Association of State Budget Officers (1987b), *Fiscal Survey of the States* (September).

National Conference of State Legislatures (1987a), *State Budget Actions in 1987* (July).

National Conference of State Legislatures (1987b), "The Budding Revolution in State Income Taxes." Legislative Finance Paper No. 61 (December).

National Conference of State Legislatures (1988), *State Budget Actions in 1988* (July).

Oates, Wallace E. (1975), "Automatic" Increases in Tax Revenues: The Effect on the Size of the Public Budget," in Wallace E. Oates (ed.), *Financing the New Federalism* (Baltimore, MD: Johns Hopkins University Press), pp. 135–160.

Oates, Wallace E. (1979), "Lump-Sum Intergovernmental Grants Have Price Effects," in P. Mieszkowski and W. Oakland (eds.), *Fiscal Federalism and Grants in Aid* (Washington, DC: The Urban Institute Press).

Tannenwald, Robert (1975), "The Effects of Federal Tax Reform on New England's State Income Tax Revenues," *National Tax Journal* 40(3), pp. 445–459.

Wagner, Richard E. (1976), "Revenue Sructure, Fiscal Illusion, and Budgetary Choice," *Public Choice*, pp. 45–61.

AN ECONOMIC EVALUATION OF STATE LIMITATIONS ON LOCAL TAXING AND SPENDING POWERS

HELEN F. LADD*

ABSTRACT

This paper analyzes and evaluates from an economic perspective expenditure limitation and property tax relief as motivations for the recent resurgence of interest in state imposed controls on local taxing and spending powers. A systematic analysis of the possible causes of excess local spending leads to the conclusion that the benefits from expenditure restriction are likely to be limited while the costs are potentially significant. A partial adjustment model of the local public sector expenditure process shows that in some cases temporary controls may be justified as a supplement to new state aid intended for property tax relief.

THE 1970's have witnessed a resurgence of interest in state imposed controls on local taxing and spending power. In contrast to earlier controls that generally took the form of property tax rate limitations, the new controls place limits on the rate of growth of property tax levies, total tax levies, or in one case, on total appropriations, thereby reducing the leeway for uncontrolled tax and expenditure growth. While included in many states as part of the new controls, voter-override provisions are not the central element of the new statutes. Since the new controls are described in a recent study by the Advisory Commission on Intergovernmental Relations (ACIR), no further description is provided here.[1]

The purpose of this paper is to analyze and evaluate the rationales for the recently enacted tax and expenditure controls. In Section I, cross section regression equations demonstrate that rapid local expenditure growth and heavy property tax burdens increase the probability that a state will impose such controls on its local governments, results consistent with the view that expenditure limitation and property tax relief are major motivations for controls. In the following two sections, we analyze and evaluate these motivations from the perspective of an economic model of the local public decision making process. Section II focuses on the potential economic benefits and costs of controls intended to limit local expenditures, while Section III focuses on the role of controls in achieving property tax relief.

I. Motivations for Controls

Historically, tax and expenditure controls were motivated by the desire to limit the rate of growth of local government expenditures as in the late 19th century or to provide property tax relief as during the Depression.[2] As recently noted by the ACIR, both motivations appear to be important in the widespread movement toward more stringent controls in the 1970's.[3] The authors of the ACIR report reach this conclusion by examining statements in support of controls and by making logical deductions from time series data on state-local relations. As the study notes, the rapid increase in local as well as state-local public expenditures during the 1960's and early 1970's provide substance to the argument that local expenditures are out of control and require limitation from above. In addition, the recent period has witnessed growing concern at the state level about the burden of the property tax, evidenced by the widespread introduction of circuit breaker legislation, state takeover of certain local government expenditure categories, provision of additional state aid to local governments, and statutes enabling local governments to use sales or income taxes. More stringent property tax limits appear to be a logical component of these policies that are intended to secure property tax relief by

*Department of City and Regional Planning, Harvard University. The author would like to thank Howard Bloom, Karl Case, John Yinger, and the Wellesley College economics department faculty seminar for comments and suggestions on earlier versions of this paper.

shifting away from the property tax to some other revenue source.

Further support for the view that expenditure limitation and property tax relief motivate the new controls can be deduced from a cross-sectional analysis of the probability of states imposing new controls during the 1970's. If expenditure limitation and property tax relief are the goals, states imposing controls are likely to be characterized by high rates of local expenditure growth in the recent past and heavy property tax burdens or both. To test these hypotheses, a linear probability model was estimated across states with the results reported in Table 1.[4] In both the reported equations, the dependent variable (DUM) takes on the value 1 if the state enacted new controls during the 1970's and 0 if it did not. The states imposing new controls are listed in the table.[5] The explanatory variables are property tax revenues per dollar of personal income in 1971 (PROPY), the rate of growth of local expenditures per capita 1967-71 (DPCEL) and (in equation 2) a dummy variable taking on the value 1 if the state imposed some form of controls in 1962 (DUM62). This last variable is intended to control for differences across states in the political willingness of state legislatures to impose controls on local governments. The positive coefficient of DUM62 is consistent with the hypothesis that states historically willing to impose property tax controls are more willing to impose new, more stringent controls in the 1970's than are other states.

The equations show that states relying heavily on the property tax in 1971 are more likely to attempt to reduce the burden by imposing controls during the subsequent period than are other states. The coefficient of PROPY in equation 2, the preferred specification, implies that a state having a property tax burden one standard deviation (i.e., $15 per 1000 of personal income) above the nationwide average (i.e., $43 per 1000) has a probability of imposing new controls 12.3 percentage points higher than the state with an average tax burden, *ceteris paribus*.

Similarly, rapid rates of local expenditure growth during the period 1967-71 increase the probability that a state will impose controls as is demonstrated by the positive coefficient of DPCEL. The .95 value of the coefficient in equation 2 implies that a state with a rate of local expenditure growth one standard deviation (.125) above the average (.47) has a probability of imposing controls 12 percentage points higher than the state with average local expenditure growth, other factors held constant.

Thus, in conjunction with the time series evidence of rapid nationwide local expenditure growth and evidence of widespread efforts to reduce the burden of the property tax in the 1970's, this cross-sectional evidence strongly suggests that expenditure limitation and property tax relief are two major goals of the statutory restrictions imposed on local governments during the 1970's. This leaves unanswered two basic questions. First, why do state legislatures want to limit local public sector expenditures? Presumably expenditures provide services from which local taxpayer voters derive benefits. What then is gained by limiting such expenditure? Second, are controls needed for property tax relief, assuming the goal is to shift the balance among tax sources rather than to limit expenditures? Is additional state aid, for example, insufficient by itself to achieve property tax relief? These two issues are the focus of the following sections.

II. Controls to Limit Expenditures

This section focuses on the contributions of economic analysis to the explanation of why state legislatures might want to limit the growth of local expenditures. Although political factors undoubtedly play a role as well, the economic perspective taken here provides the framework for an evaluation of the economic benefits and costs of controls. The central element of the economic approach is that local taxpayer voters receive benefits from and have demands for public services analogous to their demands for private goods and services.[6] The issue then becomes one of how well the local budgetary process translates these individual demands into

TABLE I
PROBABILITY OF IMPOSING CONTROLS

---

1) DUM = −.4778 + 6.879 PROPY + .8608 DPCEL
        (.3020) (3.734)   (.4655)

2) DUM = −.7682 + 8.296 PROPY + .9494 DPCEL + .2240 DUM62
        (.3640) (3.854)   (.4652)   (.1604)

(Standard errors in parentheses)

DUM = 1 for states imposing new controls during the 1970's (Alaska, California, Georgia, Indiana, Iowa, Kansas, Ohio, Minnesota, New Jersey, Washington, Wisconsin) and 0 otherwise. Source: Advisory Commission on Intergovernmental Relations, *State Limitations of Local Taxes & Expenditures*, A-64 (Washington, D.C.: U.S.G.P.O., February 1977).

PROPY = Property tax revenue per dollar of personal income (1971). Source: Bureau of the Census, *Governmental Finances*, 1970-71.

DPCEL = Rate of growth of local expenditures per capita 1967-71. Source: Bureau of the Census, *Governmental Finances*, 1966-67, 1970-71.

DUM62 = 1 for states with some form of local tax limit in 1962 and 0 otherwise. Source: Advisory Commission on Intergovernmental Relations, *State Constitutional and Statutory Restrictions on Local Taxing Powers*, A-14 (Washington, D.C.: U.S.G.P.O., October 1962).

---

local public services. Since expenditures are the product of price times quantity, the initial discussion is divided into two parts: the desire to limit service levels that are excessive (part 1) and the desire to limit costs or the rate of growth of costs that are excessive (part 2). In each case, the potential benefits from controls are evaluated. In part 3, we demonstrate the potential efficiency costs of controls using an analytical model of the demand for local public services. The section concludes with a discussion of equity considerations.

1. Excessive Service Levels

Unlike privately provided goods and services where consumers are free to choose directly their most desired quantities of goods and services, provision of public services through the budget mechanism rather than the market mechanism may result in service levels considered by some to be excessive. One implication of the budget mechanism is that the community decides on a single level of service of each type which presumably is distributed equally among all recipients within the jurisdiction.[7] Even if every household within a jurisdiction pays the same amount in taxes, most members of the community are likely to be in disequilibrium because of differing preferences and differing capacities to enjoy public services varying, for example, with the number of public school children in the household. Complicating the matter further is the variation in tax payments across households within a jurisdiction. Only if tax liabilities, or more precisely, tax prices, vary across households in line with the marginal valuation of benefits of public services, is it possible for all residents to be content with the level of public services provided.[8] The more common result is the presence within each jurisdiction of groups with above average demands for public services and of groups with below average demands. To the extent that groups with below average demands for public services have more political power in state legislatures than in the local budgetary process, the equal service provision aspect of public goods (with a given tax structure) may be one explanation of the willingness of state legislatures to impose controls. That is, controls are designed to benefit particular interest groups rather than the state population as a whole.

The local taxation of business property complicates the situation further. The direct local voting power of business owners is limited because resident business owners are outnumbered locally by other resident voters and non-resident owners have no direct voting power. Except insofar as owners of firms can influence the ratio to market value at which their property is assessed or can influence the level of local expenditures by threat of exit or of tax shifting, firms have little control over the level of taxes they pay locally in relation to services received.[9] Hence, owners of firms, like resident voters with below average demands for public services given their share of the tax bill, may have incentives to exert pressure on state legislators for limitation of local taxing and spending powers.

An alternative explanation is that pressure for controls comes from the local majority rather than groups with below average demands for locally provided public services. In the public sector context, the level of services provided may differ from the level desired by the local majority for several reasons: excess local political power of certain interest groups such as municipal unions; lags in the adjustment of actual expenditures to desired expenditures caused in part by infrequent elections; "automatic" revenue increases that are politically easier to translate into expenditure increases than are revenue increases requiring a change in the tax rate; bureaucratic behavior; and the imperfections associated with voting for city officials representing a complex bundle of issues.[10]

Thus, because of imperfections in the political process through which household demands for public services are translated into community demands, the actual service level provided by locally elected public officials may not correspond to the level desired by the local majority. To the extent that circumstances result in service levels in excess of majority preferences, the local majority conceivably may try to impose controls on elected officials from above through state action.

Implicit in the previous two concepts of excessive service levels is the view that households have individual demands for public services analogous to their demands for private goods and services and that a desirable social outcome can occur provided that the individual demands are correctly aggregated. A third view asserts that the individual demand functions themselves are incorrect on the grounds that voters either seriously under or over estimate benefits or costs because of the tenuous link between taxes paid and benefits received.[11] According to this perspective, if costs are underestimated or benefits are overestimated or both, majority rule will lead to an expenditure level in excess of the efficient level even if there are no lags or imperfections in the political process.[12] Note, however, that in this case local taxpayer voters, unaware of their incorrect perceptions, have no incentive to pressure state legislatures for controls. Hence, this concept of excessive expenditures is best interpreted as a rationale for expenditure control given by people who advocate controls for other reasons.

Thus, three possible senses in which local public service levels may be deemed excessive have been identified: service levels that exceed the desired level of groups with below average demands for local public services, service levels in excess of the demands of the majority caused by imperfections in the political process, and majority determined service levels that exceed efficient levels because of misperceived benefits or costs. In light of these possibilities, are controls desirable?[13] The answer is generally no.

In the first case, restrictions on the level of growth of local public services may indeed make certain groups better off, but at the cost of reducing the welfare of the local majority. Even if some legitimate state equity goal could be achieved by helping these groups, control of local expenditures is likely to be a less efficient means of achieving the goal than direct alleviation of the tax burden of these groups as has been accomplished in many states for groups such as the elderly and the farmers.[14]

In the case of imperfections in the political process that cause a divergence between actual and desired service levels, state imposed controls that interfere with local choice are counterproductive. Here, the goal of state action should be to strengthen the political mechanism rather than weaken it. This can be achieved through procedural controls as in full disclosure legislation recently enacted in several states or perhaps in referenda requirements. Full disclosure laws require the local government to advertise publicly and to hold a public hearing before increasing the tax rate above the rate required to raise some percentage (95-100%) of the previous year's levy, thereby ruling out "automatic" revenue increases caused by assessment increases.[15] As such, full disclosure legislation is a reasonable means of dealing with one of the several imperfections mentioned above.

Procedural controls in the form of requiring local officials to submit expenditure requests above a certain amount to a local majority rule referendum have the potential to improve the decision-making process but their success depends on 1) providing the appropriate information to enable voters to make the link between taxes and expenditures, 2) nonbiased voter turnout, and 3) either allowing for multiple referenda or designing a substitute procedure to promote the competitive rather than the monopoly outcome.[16] The gains from such procedural controls will vary by community depending on the extent to which imperfections of representative democracy currently result in excessive service levels and on the design of the referendum system. The costs include 1) the direct cost of referenda, 2) the additional opportunity costs to individuals of informing themselves and voting, and 3) costs associated with the delays inherent in a democratic decision-making process.

State interference with the local decision-making process can be justified from a social welfare point of view only when the cause of excess service levels is overestimation of benefits or underestimation of costs by household voters. As noted above, however, no local public support for controls will be forthcoming when excessive spending is of this type. The practical argument for controls even in this case remains weak. First, state legislatures are unlikely to be good judges of the proper or efficient level of services, and second, even if they were, they are unlikely to design a system of controls sophisticated and flexible enough to improve the situation. The solution in this case is to provide more information to voter taxpayers to enable them to make better decisions rather than to interfere with those decisions.

2. Excessive Cost Increases

Rapidly rising public sector costs provide a second set of rationales for local public expenditure controls. Since price increases in excess of income increases lower household real income, households have an incentive to try to contain rising prices both in the private sector and the public sector. Cost increases in the local public sector have been especially acute in the post-war period.[17] At least three explanations of this cost growth are possible. First, cost increases may result from the absence of the discipline imposed in a competitive market economy. This lack of market pressure, it has been argued, weakens the incentives for the public sector to innovate and to encourage cost-saving technological change. This argument should be distinguished from a similar one: lack of market pressure encourages mismanagement, bureaucratic inefficiencies, and corruption. In the former case, the rate of growth of costs is affected, in the latter only the level of costs is affected unless inefficiency and corruption are growing over time. In addition, provision through the budget mechanism rather than the market mechanism has potential implications for the power of municipal unions. Because a governmental body, unlike a perfectly competitive firm, can levy additional taxes to pay for increased wage settlements and because elected officials are vulnerable at the polls to the voting power of union members, elected officials may be unable to resist the wage and fringe benefit demands of municipal unions.

As has been pointed out by W. Baumol, and others, however, the technological character of the services provided through the public sector rather than public sector provision *per se* provides an alternative and more powerful explanation of low productivity and high cost growth in the local public sector.[18] Specifically, unstandardized outputs and a close connection between the quantity of labor input and the quality of the service provided make technological progress difficult and limit the potential for improvements in productivity in the public sector (and more generally in the personal service sector as a whole). To the extent that the public sector must compete for labor with the rest of the economy where technological change results in productivity growth reflected in rising wages, per unit costs of production in the public sector are bound to rise. Thus, the major insight of this argument is that a competitive labor market will cause the growth of wages in the public sector to follow the rate of growth in the rest of the economy in spite of differential rates of productivity growth, making the inevitability of lagging productivity growth the major cause of rising costs in the public sector. Moreover, to the extent that municipal unions merely facilitate the transfer of wage increases in the private sector to the public sector, unions should not be considered the cause of local public sector cost increases.

A third explanation for rising costs in the public sector employs the conceptual distinction made by Bradford, Malt, and Oates between C-outputs and D-outputs.[19] C-outputs refer to the level of services actually consumed by local residents such as security from crime while D-outputs refer to the services directly produced such as police patrol hours, which in turn are produced with the factor inputs labor (policemen) and capital (patrol cars). The final consumption level (C) is a function of direct outputs (D) plus environmental factors such as the level of congestion. This distinction explains why over time it may be necessary to increase direct outputs (requiring more capital and labor) just to maintain a given level of final output. For example, growing urbanization and congestion requires countervailing increases in police services to maintain a constant level of security from crime, thereby increasing the cost of protection from crime.

In light of these three explanations for rising costs: provision through the budget mechanism, the inevitable lagging productivity in the service sector, and the growth in direct service requirements per unit of output associated with deteriorating environmental factors, what is the role of tax and expenditure controls? From the point of view of the local taxpayer voters such controls are "successful" to the extent that they reduce the level or the rate of growth of costs rather than the level or rate of growth of services.

Tax and expenditure controls are unlikely to be effective in limiting costs, especially when the cause of rising costs is either the lagging productivity associated with the service sector of the economy or the deteriorating environmental situation. From these perspectives, the per unit costs of public services are determined by the underlying production function for public services combined with a reasonably competitive labor market. In response to state imposed limitations, the local communities have no choice except to reduce services.

Whether controls can induce local governments to reduce waste, inefficiency, and corruption, thereby lowering per unit costs, or to be more innovative, thereby lowering the rate of growth of costs, are debatable questions. More extensive knowledge of the bureaucratic process is required to determine the relationship between productive efficiency, both static and dynamic, and the tightness of the budgetary constraint. But even if controls were to have some impact on production efficiency, surely more effective means of achieving the goal are available. Direct measures such as management and accounting reforms and changes in the incentive structure now enshrined in the civil service system are undoubtedly superior to the crudeness of tax and expenditure controls as a means of increasing production efficiency.

The power of controls to reduce cost excesses associated by some with the strength of municipal unions is also debatable. Three overlapping groups are involved: local taxpayers, local service recipients, and members of municipal unions. Tax controls that limit tax revenues, clearly strengthen the position of local taxpayers *vis à vis* the unions, but the outcome still depends on the bargaining strength of unions versus that of service recipients. The more powerful the unions, the higher will be the per unit cost of services and the lower will be the level of services that can be provided within the limited budget constraint. Since there is no compelling reason to believe that the power of service recipients, many of whom are poor, will be greater than that of the municipal unions, the desired outcome of reducing public sector costs cannot be assumed.

3. Efficiency Costs of Expenditure Limitations

The discussion so far has focused on the limited potential gains from tax and expenditure controls intended to control expenditure growth. We now turn to the major potential cost of controls, the efficiency loss resulting from interference with the local public sector decision making process. Because of the nature of the costs, their magnitude depends on how well the local political process currently aggregates individual preferences for public services. For example, if actual service levels are currently five percent above the level desired by the local majority and controls succeed in reducing service levels to the desired level, the result is an efficiency gain rather than an efficiency cost. Therefore, to discuss potential costs, we take the extreme position that in the absence of controls, services would be provided at the desired level and that controls have no impact on the rate of growth of public sector costs. That is, we assume away all potential benefits from controls to determine the potential costs. Actual costs would be less than the potential costs to the extent that controls succeed in bringing actual service levels closer to the desired level or in reducing the level or rate of growth of public sector prices.

To determine the potential efficiency costs of tax and expenditure controls, estimates are needed of the impact of controls on local public service levels. In its recent study, the ACIR concluded that, for the average state, local expenditures would have been 6–8 percent higher in the absence of controls.[20] This conclusion is based on a cross section regression model of locally financed own expenditures estimated across states for the year 1974, using dummy variables to represent the presence of tax and expenditure controls. For several reasons, the ACIR results are not helpful for the present purposes. First, since the newly imposed restrictions are potentially more restrictive than the traditional rate limitations, the ACIR results, based on all existing limitations, do not apply to the new levy and appropriation limitations.[21] Second, the absence of a carefully specified model makes the results suspect. In particular, the ACIR equation specification and estimated coefficients imply that high income states imposing controls have *higher* local expenditures than high income states not imposing controls. This raises the broader question of whether cross sectional analysis as undertaken by the ACIR correctly sorts out the direction of causation. It may well be that the level of local expenditures affects whether or not a state has controls, thereby creating a problem of simultaneous equations bias. This suggests that time series analysis of local expenditures within a particular state would be preferable to cross-state analysis, were the necessary data available. Moreover, as noted above, actual expenditure reduction may reflect some efficiency gains and price reduction in addition to the service level distortions that reduce welfare.

In light of the difficulties involved in estimating the impact on service levels of tax and expenditure controls and in interpreting the results, we turn to an analytical model of the local expenditure decision. Let the demand for public services within a jurisdiction take the form:

$$Q = Y^\alpha \left(\frac{P_g}{P_c}\right)^\beta$$

where Q = quantity demanded per household by the median voter,

Y = real household income of the median voter,

P_g = price of publicly provided goods,
P_c = price of all other goods and services,
α, the income elasticity of demand, is positive
and β, the price elasticity of demand, is negative.

Assuming that the political process perfectly responds to majority preferences, Q represents the level of services actually provided.[22] Expenditures on public services per household are consequently equal to

$$P_g Q = Y^\alpha P_g^{\beta+1} P_c^{-\beta}$$

In the absence of expenditure controls, the level of expenditures desired in subsequent years will depend on the desired expenditures in the first year; the growth rates of real income, of local public sector prices, and of all other prices; and the price and income elasticities of demand. More specifically, desired expenditures in the tth year can be expressed as:

$$P_{gt} Q_t = Y^\alpha P_g^{\beta+1} P_c^{-\beta} [(1+\gamma)^{\alpha \cdot t} (1+\delta)^{(\beta+1) \cdot t} (1+\rho)^{-\beta \cdot t}]$$

where γ = annual rate of growth of real income
δ = annual rate of growth of public sector prices
ρ = annual rate of growth of all other prices

Provided again that the political budgetary process fully responds to the demand for public services in the absence of controls, $(P_{gt} Q_t)$ represents the actual level of expenditures in year t.

Now consider the effect of expenditure controls that allow expenditures to rise at the rate of 5% annually. At the end of t years, expenditures are permitted to be $[(1.05)^t - 1] \cdot 100\%$ higher than they were the first year.

By specifying values for the demand equation parameters and for the growth rates of income and prices, we can compare the desired level to the restricted level of expenditures. Note that this expenditure difference translates directly into a service level difference provided we assume that controls have no effect on public sector prices. The first row of Table II presents the service level effects in the 5th year of controls for specific values of α, γ, δ, and ρ, and three different values of β, the price elasticity of demand. The values chosen for γ, δ, and ρ, the three growth rates, are based on historical trends while the value of α, the income elasticity of demand, and the range of values for β, the price elasticity of demand, are based on empirical studies of the demand for local public services. Since the specified values (as listed in Table II) of δ and ρ imply that the relative price of publicly provided services is growing over time, the higher the (absolute value of the) price elasticity of demand, the smaller the percentage reduction in expenditures caused by the controls. As reported in the table, the percentage reduction in service levels is substantial and varies in the 5th year of controls from 13 percent to 20 percent depending on the value of the price elasticity.

This service reduction implies a loss in consumer surplus as shown by the triangle abc in Figure 1 where D is the demand or marginal benefit curve for public services and MC is the marginal cost of provision, assumed to be constant. Expressed as a fraction of total public expenditures, the efficiency loss can easily be shown to be positively related to the square of the percentage reduction in service levels and inversely related to the price elasticity of demand for public services.[23] Row 2 of Table II shows that the calculated efficiency loss varies from 10 percent of expenditures for the lowest elasticity to .8 percent of expenditures for the highest elasticity. Since quantities are being distorted rather than prices, the less price-elastic the demand, the greater the welfare loss. This follows because low elasticity implies that the marginal valuation to consumers rises steeply as services are cut back.

An alternative, and perhaps more meaningful, way of looking at the adverse effect of the controls is to look at the value of the marginal dollar to local resident voters at the restricted level of services.

Table II
Effects of Controls in the 5th Year For Three Price Elasticities of Demand

	$\beta = -.2$	$\beta = -.5$	$\beta = -1$
% Reduction in Service Levels	20%	17%	13%
Welfare Loss as a Fraction of Expenditures	10%	2.9%	0.8%
Value of Marginal Dollar	$3.05	$1.45	$1.15

Assumptions

$\alpha = 1$ (Y elasticity of demand)
$\gamma = .02$ (growth of real income)
$\delta = .08$ (growth of P_g)
$\rho = .06$ (growth of P_c)

Controls allow 5% growth per year.

Figure 1

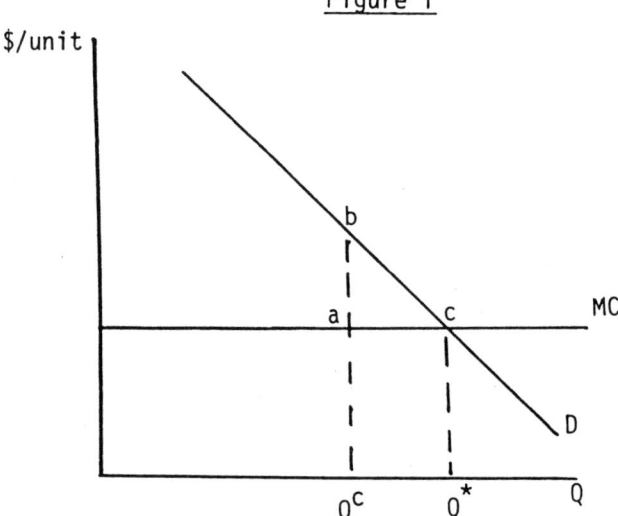

Q^* = quantity of services provided without controls
Q^c = quantity of services provided with controls

This is shown in Figure 1 by the height of the demand curve at point b. Row 3 of the table shows, for example, that for a price elasticity of −.5, residents value $1 of services at $1.45. That is, they would be willing to pay an additional $1.45 to have the level of public services increased by $1. For the low price elasticity case, the value of the marginal dollar rises to $3.05. These calculations demonstrate the incentives municipalities have to avoid the controls by whatever means available. These include shifting to non-controlled revenue sources, juggling expenditure accounts, pressuring state legislatures for additional state aid, and testifying against controls in legislative hearings.

In summary, the potential gains from expenditure control are slight while the potential costs are significant. Only to the extent that service levels exceed efficient levels or that high or rising costs are the result of imperfections in the budgetary process rather than production or market considerations, is there leeway for controls to improve the situation. Even in these cases, controls may not achieve the desired result or may not be the best means of achieving the goal. As has been shown, the costs in terms of service level distortions are potentially significant.

4. Income Distributional Considerations

We now turn briefly to the income distributional consequences of controls on local taxing and spending powers. Providing the controls succeed in reducing the rate of growth of own financed local expenditures below what it would be in the absence of controls, households in their capacity of local property taxpayers are made better off. At the same time, however, households in their capacity of public service recipients are made worse off by the reduced expenditures except when expenditure reduction is achieved through reduced inefficiency or lower public sector wages rather than reduced service levels.

The determination of the effects by income class of the lower tax and lower service levels is a complex matter. On the tax side, the benefits of controls by income class depend on the incidence of the property tax, an issue not fully resolved. Let us take the position most favorable to controls, the view that the burden of the property tax is regressive.[24] In this case, a reduction in property taxes would benefit low income households more than high income households, a movement in the direction of greater equity. But, as noted above, this is not the entire picture. Associated with the reduction in taxes is likely to be a reduction in service levels. While further research would be useful in identifying the services most likely to be cut back in the event of controls and the distributional consequences of such cutbacks, the presumption must be that the impact of service level reductions will fall more heavily on poor households than on rich within any one jurisdiction. Hence, at best, the net incidence of controls is unclear and requires detailed research in the context of particular jurisdictions subject to expenditure limitations.

An additional consequence is the potential differential effects of controls on jurisdictions within a particular state. If state-imposed controls are more restrictive in central cities where there are large concentrations of low income households than in wealthy suburban areas, the effects of the controls will be distributionally adverse. Without detailed knowledge of the form of the controls in a particular state, no equity judgment can be made. It should be noted, however, that controls specifically designed to be more restrictive in high tax than in low tax jurisdictions will impact most heavily in large cities which, in part because of the low income population, have high tax rates.[25] Moreover, controls that restrict the rate of growth of levies per capita will also have their most severe impact in large cities, especially those experiencing declining population growth.

III. Property Tax Relief

The role of controls in securing property tax relief in the 1970's differs significantly from the Depression period. In contrast to the earlier period, controls in the more recent period are generally part of a larger package of policy changes, the purpose of which is to achieve property tax relief by shifting away from the property tax to some other revenue source. By increasing state aid or by allowing local governments to tap new revenue sources, state legislatures hope to reduce the burden of the property tax.

The question then arises of whether controls are needed as part of the package. Why, for example, isn't additional state aid by itself sufficient to induce communities to reduce reliance on the property tax? Consider the case of non-matching lump sum grants. According to the individualistic collective choice model of the local public expenditure process used throughout this paper, lump sum aid is theoretically equivalent to an increase in the disposable income of local taxpayer voters.[26] As in response to any increase in disposable income, voters, including the median voter, will respond to increased aid by increasing their demands for public services, the extent of the increased demand depending on the income elasticity of demand for public services. Thus, economic theory predicts that the new state aid will induce higher local expenditures because of the increased resources of the individuals in the community. In light of the empirically estimated magnitudes of the income elasticity of demand for public services, however, the predicted increase in expenditures is likely to be small, in the range of 5-10¢ per dollar of aid, thereby implying a 90-95¢ reduction in property tax revenues for each dollar of aid.[27] Hence, substantial property tax relief theoretically can be achieved simply by increasing lump sum aid. Controls on local taxing and spending power are not necessary, according to this view, unless state legislators wish to restrict expenditures to levels below those desired by the majority of local taxpayers in order to achieve dollar for dollar property tax reduction. But if expenditure control is the goal, the analysis of the previous section is again relevant.

This standard economic argument, however, assumes away all lags or imperfections in the response by public officials to the changing service demands of local taxpayer voters. In this section, we present a model that explicitly introduces partial adjustment to changing service demands. The case for using controls to supplement additional state aid intended for property tax relief is then re-evaluated in the context of this model. It should be noted that the results of the model depend heavily on the underlying assumption about the behavior of local public officials. While the key behavioral assumptions employed in the model are plausible, further research into the dynamic response of local public officials to increases in aid would be useful.

1. Basic Model—No Change in State Aid.

First we present a partial adjustment model of the local decision making process for the case of no change in state aid. The model can be written as follows:

$$E_t^* = a + bY_t + cAID_t \qquad (1)$$

$$E_t - E_{t-1} = \lambda [E_t^* - E_{t-1}]$$

where $0 < \lambda < 1$ \qquad (2)

or $\quad E_t = \lambda E_t^* + (1 - \lambda)E_{t-1}$ \qquad (2a)

where E_t^* = expenditure level per household desired by the median taxpayer voter in year t
Y_t = all factors other than lump sum aid in year t affecting demand for local public services
AID_t = state lump sum aid per household in year t
E_t = actual expenditures per household in year t
λ = a partial adjustment parameter

In this simplified model, E_t^* represents the expenditure level desired by the median voter and consequently the level preferred by the majority of local taxpayer voters. This desired level is assumed to be a linear function of intergovernmental lump sum aid and all other factors, including tastes, the tax price of public services relative to other prices, and household income. For simplicity of exposition, these other factors are compressed into a single variable Y, which might conveniently be thought of as real disposable income.[28] While a more complicated formulation would be more correct, little would be gained since the current discussion focuses on the adjustment effects of a change in aid. Actual expenditures can diverge from the desired level because we assume that local public officials only partially adjust actual expenditures to changes in desired expenditures each year. This partial adjustment, expressed in equation (2), states that the change in actual expenditures from one year to the next is some constant fraction of the difference between the desired level and the current actual level. Equivalently, actual expenditures in year t can be expressed as a weighted average of desired expenditures and actual expenditures of the previous year with the weights equal to λ and $(1 - \lambda)$ as in equation (2a).

The adjustment parameter λ reflects the reluctance on the part of local officials to change actual expenditures because of the potential political costs involved, costs that arise from imperfect information and uncertainty on the part of voters and officials. More specifically, local officials are assumed to be hesitant to satisfy fully the demand for additional services for fear of suffering the adverse political consequences of raising local taxes without gaining the political benefits of increasing service levels. This appears irrational in that the majority of local taxpayer voters, by definition of the desired level, are willing to pay the taxes necessary to finance that level. But local public officials may fear that when city elections next occur, voters will remember the increase in taxes and not the increase in services.[29] Similarly, local officials may be reluctant to reduce expenditures for fear of losing the support of people whose services are reduced without gaining the support of taxpayers who benefit from the lower taxes.[30]

The implications of this model are developed more fully in the appendix and are shown graphically in Figure 2. We start at an initial level of expenditure E_0 assumed to be equal to the desired level E_0^* consistent with aid equal to AID_0 and other factors equal to Y_0. Now assume that the only change is an increase in other factors to Y_1 in year 1 and remaining constant thereafter. The solid line in Figure 2 portrays the adjustment from time to the new desired level of expenditure E_1^*. Because of the partial adjustment assumption, only the proportion λ of the gap between desired and actual is removed each year. For purposes of the figure, λ is set equal to $1/2$.

2. Partial Adjustment Model with Increased State Aid.

Now consider a change in the desired level of expenditures brought about by some combination of changes in other factors and increased aid in year 1. Specifically, we have:

Year	Aid	Other factors
0	AID_0	Y_0
1	AID_1	Y_1
2	AID_1	Y_1
3	AID_1	Y_1
.	.	.

where the desired level of expenditures in every year after the initial year equals $E_1^* = a + bY_1 + AID_1$. For expositional simplicity, we will consider any combination of AID_1 and Y_1 that results in the same desired expenditure level E_1^* portrayed in Figure 2.

With the introduction of a change in aid, the partial adjustment parameter must be respecified to vary by periods as follows:

$$\lambda_t = \lambda + (1 - \lambda) \frac{AID_t - AID_{t-1}}{E_t^* - E_{t-1}}$$

where λ is defined as in the previous model. Because of the assumption that AID changes only in the first period, however, λ_t reduces to just two distinct adjustment parameters. For all years after year 1, λ_t is equal to λ since $AID_t - AID_{t-1} = 0$ for $t \neq 1$. Only in period 1, the period during which aid is increased, does the

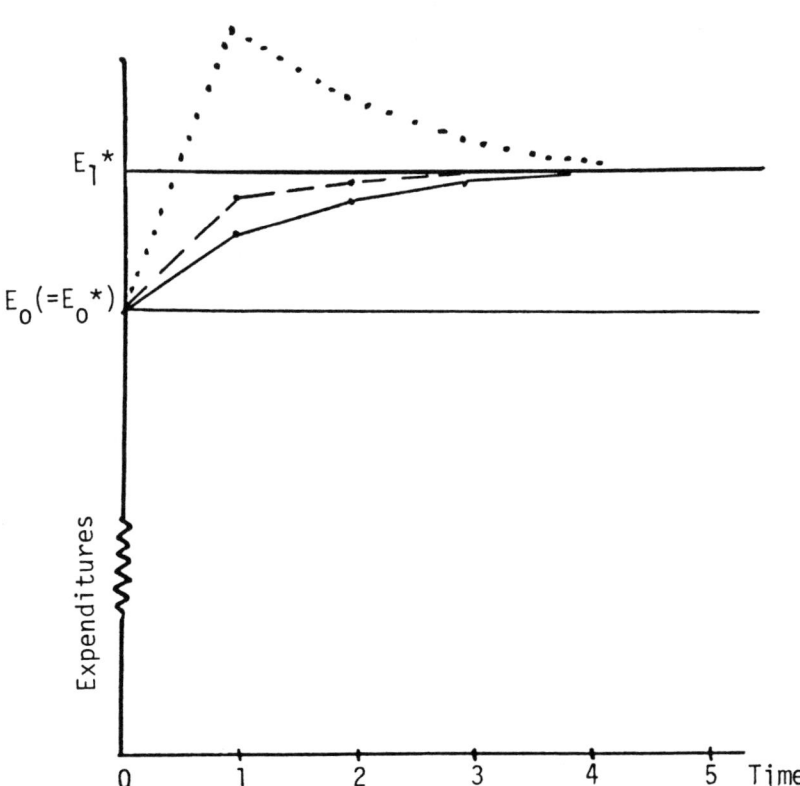

Figure 2

adjustment parameter differ from λ. In that year, the response by local public officials to a change in the desired expenditure level is assumed to depend on the proportion of the desired increase that is financed by new state aid, which, unlike new local tax revenue, is assumed to be costless from the point of view of elected local officials. The particular specification of the adjustment parameter implies that if the new aid in year 1, ($AID_1 - AID_0$), is just equal to the desired change in expenditure ($E_1^* - E_0$), then $\lambda_1 = 1$. That is, in year 1, public officials will fully adjust actual expenditure to desired expenditures if the additional expenditures are completely financed by additional aid, there being no reason to delay adjustment given the "free" aid. More generally, whenever the change in aid is less than ($E_1^* - E_0$), the first period adjustment parameter is greater than λ but less than 1. Note that if the change in aid exceeds the desired change in expenditures, the proportion of the gap filled the first year can exceed 1. An example of this is given below.

The implications of this model, developed more fully in the appendix, are suggested by the dotted and dashed lines in Figure 2. Consider first an increase in aid during a period of growth in desired expenditures sufficient to ensure that $AID_1 - AID_0/E_1^* - E_0 < 1$. Hence, λ_1 is greater than λ and less than 1. The path to equilibrium can be portrayed by a line such as the dashed line in the figure. In the first period, public officials satisfy a greater proportion of the gap between desired and actual expenditures compared to the previous case because of the new intergovernmental aid that eases the financing problem. In subsequent periods, however, the pattern of adjustment is similar to the previous case. In year 2, for example, the proportion λ (= 1/2 for the purposes of the diagram) of the remaining gap is satisfied and so on for subsequent periods.

As noted above, λ_1, the first period adjustment parameter, can exceed 1. Consider, for example, an increase in aid with no change in other factors affecting the demand for expenditures. According to equation (1), desired expenditures increase by $b\Delta AID$. Hence, $\Delta AID/(E^* - E_{t-1}) = 1/b$. Assuming desired expenditures increase by 5¢ to 10¢ per dollar of aid, $1/b$ will be 10 to 20, making $\lambda_1 > 1$. In other words, the increased aid induces local public officials to overadjust actual expenditures to desired expenditures in the first period. More generally, first period actual expenditures will exceed desired expenditures whenever the additional aid exceeds the desired change in expenditures. For all subsequent periods, however, the adjustment parameter again becomes $\lambda (<1)$ because of the constant aid and the perceived political costs of reducing expenditures. This results in a gradual approach to the equilibrium level of expenditures as shown by the dotted line adjustment path in Figure 2.

We now re-evaluate in the context of this model the argument for using tax and expenditure controls as a supplement to state aid intended for property tax relief. As has been shown, during a period of non-aid-induced growth in desired expenditures, increases in aid speed up the adjustment process, thereby resulting in expenditure levels higher in the early years than they would be in the absence of new aid. Significantly, however, actual expenditures never exceed desired expenditures. These higher expenditure levels imply that less property tax relief is attained in the early periods than would occur if the adjustment process were not speeded up. From a social welfare point of view, however, this acceleration of the adjustment of actual expenditures to desired expenditures is desirable and, consequently, provides no economic justification for controls.

The conclusion differs when aid is increased during a period of zero or limited growth in desired expenditures so that the new aid induces local officials to spend more than the desired level in the early years as shown by the dotted line in Figure 2. In this situation, temporary controls on local taxing power are justified as a means of preventing the new aid from allowing local officials to increase actual expenditures above the desired level. It should be emphasized, however, that the justification for controls in this connection is based on a modified lagged adjustment model that is only as good as its underlying behavioral assumptions. Moreover, the model provides a justification for temporary controls only. In the long run, even without controls, total expenditures will approach the desired level as shown in the figure and the full property tax relief predicted by the standard economic model will be achieved.

IV. Conclusion

On the basis of this economic analysis and evaluation of state imposed controls on local taxing and spending powers, we conclude, first, that the economic benefits from controls motivated by the desire to limit local public expenditures are likely to be slight, while the costs, in terms of service level distortions, are potentially significant. Second, with respect to the goal of securing property tax relief, our partial adjustment model of the local decision making process provides a justification for *temporary* controls in some cases although the results depend crucially on the key behavioral assumption. The partial adjustment model, while not definitive, is suggestive and demonstrates the need for further investigation of the dynamic response of local public officials to changes in desired expenditures in the presence of increasing intergovernmental aid.

Appendix

In this appendix, we develop more fully the lagged adjustment model presented in the text.

Case 1. $\Delta AID = 0$ and $E_1^* > E_0^*$
The model is:

$$E_t^* = \alpha Y_t + \beta AID_t \qquad (1)$$

$$E_t - E_{t-1} = \lambda(E_t^* - E_{t-1}) \text{ where } 0 < \lambda < 1. \qquad (2)$$

where E_t^* = expenditure level per household desired by local taxpayer voters in year t.
Y_t = all factors other than lump sum aid in year t affecting the demand for local public services.
AID_t = state lump sum aid per household in year t.
E_t = actual expenditures per household in year t.
λ = a partial adjustment parameter.

Substituting equation (1) into equation (2) and solving for E_t yields:

$$E_t = \lambda[\alpha Y_t + \beta AID_t] + (1 - \lambda)E_{t-1}. \qquad (3)$$

For a first period increase in Y and no change in aid, we have for all $t > 0$:

$$E_t = \lambda[\alpha Y_1 + \beta AID_0] + (1 - \lambda)E_{t-1}. \qquad (4)$$

By setting $E_t = E_{t-1}$, we obtain the new long-run equilibrium level of expenditures E_e:

$$E_e = \alpha Y_1 + \beta AID_0 = E_1^*. \qquad (5)$$

To determine the time path of adjustment to equilibrium, we solve the difference equation (4), obtaining:

$$E_t = [E_0 - E_1^*][1 - \lambda]^t + E_1^* \qquad (6)$$

where E_0, the initial level of expenditures, is assumed to be the desired level in the initial period. Since $(1 - \lambda)$ is positive and less than 1 and E_0 is less than E_1^*, actual expenditures converge to the desired level from below.^-1 For the purposes of Figure 2 in the text, we set $\lambda = 1/2$, yielding:

$$E_1 = E_1^* - 1/2[E_1^* - E_0]$$
$$E_2 = E_1^* - 1/4[E_1^* - E_0]$$
$$E_3 = E_1^* - 1/8[E_1^* - E_0]$$

Case 2. $\Delta AID > 0$ and $E_1^* > E_0^*$
In this case, the adjustment parameter in each year t is expressed as:

$$\lambda_t = \lambda + (1 - \lambda)\frac{AID_t - AID_{t-1}}{E_t^* - E_{t-1}} \qquad (7)$$

Assuming that aid only increases in the first period, $\lambda_t = \lambda$ for all $t > 1$. For $t = 1$,

$$\lambda_1 = \lambda + (1 - \lambda)\frac{AID_1 - AID_0}{E_1^* - E_0} \qquad (8)$$

Incorporating the first period increase in both aid and income, the long-run equilibrium is again

$$E_e = \alpha Y_1 + \beta AID_1 = E_1^*. \qquad (9)$$

For the purpose of Figure 2 in the text, this E_1^* is assumed to be the same as the E_1^* of Case 1 necessitating a smaller increase in Y. This assumption is not important to the analysis.

The time path of adjustment must be analyzed in two steps. First, we determine actual expenditures in year 1 from

$$E_1 = \lambda_1 E_1^* + (1 - \lambda_1)E_0 \qquad (10)$$

Substituting for λ_1 from equation (8), we obtain

$$E_1 = \lambda E_1^* + (1 - \lambda)E_0$$
$$+ (1 - \lambda)[AID_1 - AID_0]. \qquad (11)$$

The last term expresses the amount by which actual expenditures in year 1 exceed what they would have been in the absence of new state aid for any given levels of E_0 and E_1^*. For an increase in aid, this difference is necessarily positive.

Once actual expenditures in the first period are determined, we can find the remaining time path of adjustment by solving the relevant difference equation for subsequent time periods. The solution is:

$$E_{t-2} = [E_1 - E_1^*][1 - \lambda]^{t-2} + E_1^*. \qquad (12)$$

Since $[1 - \lambda]$ is positive and less than one, actual expenditures again converge to the desired level. At this point, we must consider the two cases $E_1 < E_1^*$ and $E_1 > E_1^*$ corresponding to the two situations depicted in Figure 2 of the text. E_1 less than E_1^* requires λ_1 to be less than 1. Referring to the definition of λ_1 in equation (8), we see this will be true provided the increase in aid is less than the increase in desired expenditures. In this instance, $[E_1 - E_1^*]$ is negative and, according to the solution given in equation (12), actual expenditures converge to desired expenditures from below.

Similarly, for E_1 to exceed E_1^*, the parameter λ_1 must be greater than 1. This will be true if the increase in aid exceeds the increase in desired expenditures. Referring again to equation (12), we see that when $[E_1 - E_1^*]$ is positive, actual expenditures approach desired expenditures from above.

Case 3. $\Delta AID > 0$ and $E_1^* < E_0^*$

In both the previous cases, it was assumed that the desired expenditure level in year 1 was higher than in year 0. We now consider the case in which a first period increase in aid is more than offset by a first period change in other factors affecting demand so that the new desired expenditure level is lower than the initial one. Since we are still dealing with a positive increase in aid, the analysis of case 2 remains relevant. In particular, equations (11) and (12) are still valid. Equation (11) shows that actual expenditures in the first period are higher than what they would be in the absence of any new aid, for any given E_1^* and E_0, by an amount $(1 - \lambda) [AID_1 - AID_0]$. This implies unambiguously that $[E_1 - E_1^*]$ is positive so that after the first period, expenditures converge gradually from above to the desired level according to equation (12). Note, additionally, that the gap between E_1 and E_1^* may exceed the gap between E_0 and E_1^*. It can easily be shown that this will be the case if the change in aid exceeds $\lambda/(1 - \lambda)$ times the change in desired expenditures implying that local officials increase first period expenditures in spite of the decline in desired expenditures.

FOOTNOTES

[1] See Advisory Commission on Intergovernmental Relations (ACIR) (1977) and a condensed version of the report in Shannon et al. (1976).

[2] For a discussion of the history of tax and expenditure controls, see ACIR (1962).

[3] ACIR (1977), p. 26. An additional motivation discussed by the ACIR but not dealt with in this paper relates to school finance reform. With the introduction of new state matching aid for education, controls may be used to limit the cost of the aid to the state and to limit the school expenditures of wealthy districts in an attempt to equalize expenditures across jurisdictions. Since equalization of school expenditures raises a host of additional issues, this motivation is not discussed here. For a descriptive summary of the use of controls in this context, see Cattanach, Lang, Hooper (1976).

[4] Although the use of ordinary least squares to estimate probability models leads to heteroscedastic errors, the estimated coefficients are still unbiased and consistent. For a discussion of the advantages and disadvantages of linear probability models in relation to some of the more sophisticated alternatives, see Pindyck and Rubinfeld (1976), pp. 237-64.

[5] Excluded from this list are states introducing full disclosure legislation as defined by the ACIR and states enacting limits solely on school districts in connection with school finance reform.

[6] A growing economic literature supports this proposition. For example, see Peterson (1975), Bergstrom and Goodman (1973), Borcherding and Deacon (1972), Barr and Davis (1966).

[7] This is not always the case. There is increasing evidence that within large cities the quality of public service varies markedly across neighborhoods, but the assumption that the same level of services is provided to all resident households is generally acceptable, especially for small, homogeneous communities.

[8] This is known as a Lindahl equilibrium.

[9] Some of ways firms exert their influence over local taxes and expenditures are discussed in Ladd (1975) and Ladd (1976a).

[10] Theoretical and empirical studies examining some of these points include Courant, Gramlich, and Rubinfeld (1977); Oates (1975); Niskanen (1975); Buchanan (1967); and Jackson (1972).

[11] For an example of this view see Uhler (1973), p. 383, where he refers to a survey by W. C. Stubblebine that found people substantially underestimate costs of public services.

[12] It should be noted that even when individuals correctly perceive the tax price they face for public services, majority rule may lead to an inefficient outcome. This argument has been made by, among others, Buchanan and Tullock (1962) and Lovell (1975).

[13] Throughout the remainder of this section, we assume that controls can be designed to be effective in the sense of altering public sector outcomes.

[14] The issues relevant to the appropriate local tax treatment of business property have been discussed elsewhere. See Brazer (1961) and Ladd (1976).

[15] For a more complete description of full disclosure laws, see ACIR (1977).

[16] An example of such a procedure is reported in Holcombe (1977). When the local officials have monopoly power to determine the new expenditure level to be submitted to the electorate, a majority rule referendum does not necessarily lead to the expenditure level desired by the local majority of taxpayer voters. This point is shown in a theoretical paper by Romer and Rosenthal (1976).

[17] For a detailed discussion of the evidence, see Bradford, Malt, and Oates (1969).

[18] See Baumol (1967), Baumol and Oates (1976), and Bradford, Malt and Oates (1969).

[19] Bradford, Malt, and Oates (1969).

[20] ACIR (1977).

[21] In the study, an attempt is made to distinguish between levy and rate restrictions. The recent introduction of most of the levy restrictions, however, precludes the finding of meaningful results from this separation.

[22] As long as preferences are single peaked, the budget preferred by the median voter is the only budget that will get at least a majority of the votes when paired against any other budget. See Duncan Black (1948).

[23] The welfare loss (L) can be expressed as follows: $L = -1/2 \Delta P \Delta Q$ where ΔP is the change in the marginal benefit to consumers and ΔQ is the service level reduction. Hence, $L = -1/2 \; \Delta P/P \; \Delta Q/Q \; PQ$ and by substitution of $\Delta P/P = (\Delta Q/Q)/\beta$ where β is the price elasticity of demand, $L/PQ = -(\Delta Q/Q)^2/2\beta$.

[24] From the perspective of an individual municipality in contrast to the nation as a whole, this view of the incidence of the property tax is consistent both with the "new view" and the "old view" of property tax incidence. See McLure (1977).

[25] The system of controls recently proposed by the Massachusetts Taxpayers Foundation for Massachusetts' communities would have precisely this effect. Under the proposal, high tax rate cities would have a more stringent restriction than do low tax rate municipalities. (Massachusetts Taxpayers Foundation, Mimeo, December 7, 1976).

[26] Oates, (1972), pp. 105-18.

[27] This estimate is based on a survey paper by Gramlich (1976).

[28] The relevant disposable income measure is income net of all nonlocal taxes.

[29] When the increase in desired expenditures reflects an increased cost of services rather than a higher level of services, residents are even less likely to remember the benefit side when next voting for public officials. They are unlikely to reward local officials for providing a constant (or declining) level of services at a higher cost.

[30] Implicit in this formulation of the partial adjustment model is the assumption that the costs of adjustment, in this case the political costs of raising taxes or lowering service levels, increase at an increasing rate. In a more complete discussion, other adjustment cost functions should be considered. See Rothschild (1971) for an analysis of adjustment cost functions in the context of firms' investment decisions.

[A.1] If E_t^* is less than E^0, actual expenditures would converge to the desired level from above.

REFERENCES

Advisory Commission on Intergovernmental Relations, *State Constitutional and Statutory Restrictions on Local Taxing Powers*, Report A-14. Washington: U.S. Government Printing Office, 1962.

Advisory Commission on Intergovernmental Relations, *State Limitations on Local Taxes and Expenditures*, Report A-64. Washington: U.S. Government Printing Office, 1977.

Barr, James L. and Otto A. Davis, "An Elementary Political and Economic Theory of the Expenditures of Local Governments," *Southern Economic Journal*, 33, No. 2 (October, 1966), pp. 149-65.

Baumol, William J., "Macroeconomics of Unbalanced Growth: The Anatomy of Urban Crises," *American Economic Review*, 57 (June 1967), pp. 415-26.

Baumol, William J. and Wallace E. Oates, "The Cost Disease of the Personal Services and the Quality of Life" in *The Urban Economy*, edited by Harold M. Hochman. New York: W. W. Norton & Co., Inc., 1976.

Bergstrom, T. C. and R. P. Goodman, "Private Demands for Public Goods," *American Economic Review*, LXIII, No. 3 (June, 1973), pp. 280-97.

Black, Duncan, "On the Rationale of Group Decision Making," *Journal of Political Economy*, LVI, No. 1 (February, 1948), pp. 23-34.

Borcherding, Thomas E. and Robert T. Deacon, "The Demand for the Services of Non-Federal Governments," *American Economic Review*, LXII, No. 5 (December, 1972), pp. 891-901.

Bowen, Howard S., "The Interpretation of Voting in the Allocation of Economic Resources," *Quarterly Journal of Economics*, 58 (November 1943).

Bradford, D. F. and R. A. Malt, and W. E. Oates, "The Rising Cost of Local Public Services: Some Evidence and Reflections," *National Tax Journal*, XXII, 2 (June 1969), pp. 158-202.

Brazer, Harvey E., "The Value of Industrial Property as a Subject of Taxation," *Canadian Public Administration*, IV, No. 2 (June, 1961), pp. 137-47.

Buchanan, James M., *Public Finance in Democratic Process*. Chapel Hill: University of North Carolina Press, 1967.

Buchanan, J. M. and G. Tullock, *The Calculus of Consent*. Ann Arbor: The University of Michigan Press, 1962.

Cattanach, Dale, Robert Lang and Lloyd Hooper, "Tax and Expenditure Controls: The Price of School Finance Reform" in *School Finance Reform: A Legislators Handbook*. The National Conference of State Legislatures, 1976.

Courant, Paul N., Edward L. Gramlich, and Daniel L. Rubinfeld, "Public Employee Market Power and the Level of Government Spending." University of Michigan, Institute of Public Policy Studies discussion paper, July 1977.

Gramlich, Edward M., "Intergovernmental Grants: A Review of the Empirical Literature" in Wallace E. Oates, *The Political Economy of Fiscal Federalism*. Lexington, Mass.: D. C. Heath & Co., 1977, pp. 219-39.

Holcombe, Randall G., "The Florida System: A Bowen Equilibrium Referendum Process," *National Tax Journal*, XXX, No. 1 (March, 1977), pp. 77-84.

Jackson, John E. "Politics and the Budgetary Process," *Social Science Research*, I, No. 1 (April, 1972), pp. 35-60.

Ladd, Helen F., "Local Education Expenditures, Fiscal Capacity, and the Composition of the Property Tax Basis," *National Tax Journal*, XXVIII, 2 (June, 1975), pp. 145-58.

Ladd, Helen F. "Municipal Expenditures and the Composition of the Property Tax Base," in *Property Taxation, Land Use, and Public Policy*, edited by Arthur D. Lynn. Madison: University of Wisconsin Press, 1976a.

Ladd, Helen F., "State-Wide Taxation of Commercial and Industrial Property for Education," *National Tax Journal*, XXIX, No. 2 (June, 1976b), pp. 143-54.

Lovell, Michael C., "The Collective Allocation of Commodities in a Democratic Society," *Public Choice*, XXIV (Winter, 1975), pp. 71-92.

McLure, Charles E., "The New View of the Property Tax: A Caveat," *National Tax Journal*, XXX, No. 1 (March, 1977), pp. 69-76.

Mueller, Dennis C., "Public Choice: A Survey," *Journal of Economic Literature*, XIV, No. 2 (June, 1976), pp. 395-433.

Niskanen, W. A., "Bureaucrats and Politicians," *Journal of Law and Economics*, XVIII, No. 3, (December, 1975).

Oates, Wallace, "Automatic Increases in Tax Revenues—The Effect on the Size of the Public Budget" in *Financing the New Federalism*, edited by Wallace E. Oates. Baltimore: Johns Hopkins Press for Resources for the Future, Inc., 1975.

Oates, Wallace, *Fiscal Federalism*. New York: Harcourt, Brace, Jovanovich, Inc., 1972.

Peterson, George, "Voter Demand for Public School Expenditures," in *Public Needs and Private Behavior in Metropolitan Areas*, edited by John E. Jackson. Cambridge, Mass.: Ballinger, 1975.

Pindyck, Robert S. and Daniel L. Rubinfeld, *Econometric Models and Economic Forecasts*. New York: McGraw Hill, 1976.

Romer, Thomas and Howard Rosenthal, "Bureaucrats vs. Voters: On the Political Economy of Resource Allocation by Direct Democracy." Carnegie Mellon University discussion paper, 1976.

Rothschild, Michael, "On the Cost of Adjustment," *Quarterly Journal of Economics*, 85, No. 4 (November 1971).

Shannon, John, et al., "Recent Experience With Local Tax and Expenditure Controls," *National Tax Journal*, XXIX, No. 3 (September, 1976), pp. 276-85.

Uhler, Lewis K., "A Constitutional Limitation on Taxes," National Tax Association—Tax Institute of America, Proceedings of Sixty-sixth Annual Conference, 1973, pp. 379-88.

[13]

WHY VOTERS SUPPORT TAX LIMITATIONS: EVIDENCE FROM MASSACHUSETTS' PROPOSITION 2-1/2**

HELEN F. LADD* AND JULIE BOATRIGHT WILSON*

ABSTRACT

Like two recent papers in this journal about tax limitation votes in California and Michigan, this paper uses survey data to examine why voters support tax limitations. The study uses data from a large 1980 survey of Massachusetts household heads to measure the importance of several policy-relevant reasons for supporting or opposing Proposition 2-1/2, a measure to limit local property taxes. The effects of views toward services (disaggregated by service category), spending and taxes, tax reform, government efficiency and the relative fiscal status of the household are distinguished from one another. The results indicate that the favorable vote was more an attempt to obtain lower taxes and more efficiency in government than to reduce the level of services or to substitute other revenues for the property tax. The consistency of these findings with those from other states implies a certain commonality to the tax revolt and suggests that findings can be generalized from one state to another.

O N November 4, 1980 Massachusetts voters followed California's lead by passing a stringent tax limitation measure. Commonly known as Proposition 2-1/2, the measure severely restricts the ability of Massachusetts cities and towns to raise tax revenue for local public services. Cities and towns with high tax rates are required to reduce property tax levies by at least 15 percent per year until they reach the maximum allowable rate of 2-1/2 percent; communities with rates below that level are allowed to raise property taxes, but by no more than 2-1/2 percent per year.

While high property taxes in Massachusetts set the stage for the passage of Proposition 2-1/2, a variety of goals

*John F. Kennedy School of Government, Harvard University

—including but not limited to property tax reduction—may have motivated individual voting behavior.[1] Support for property tax reduction, for example, may have been motivated by a desire to reduce service levels, to increase government efficiency, or to achieve tax reform in the sense of shifting away from local property taxes in favor of state sales or income taxes. Similarly, opposition to the tax limitation measure may have indicated satisfaction with existing service levels, the way government operates, or with the division of financing responsibilities among levels of government. In addition, some voters may have supported Proposition 2-1/2 to improve their fiscal status relative to other groups and others may have opposed it to preserve their public sector jobs.

This paper uses data from a large statewide survey of Massachusetts residents to measure the relative importance of these motivations in influencing the overall statewide vote on Proposition 2-1/2. The survey consisted of half-hour telephone interviews conducted by a professional survey firm during the two weeks following the vote and was based on a survey instrument that was written by the authors specifically for this purpose. The full sample includes 1,561 male and female household heads randomly selected from 58 Massachusetts cities and towns.[2] The sampling design assures that the 58 communities are representative of cities and towns throughout the state in terms of per capita property wealth, per capita expenditures, population, and percent of owner-occupied housing.[3]

Although based on a single state, the results reported here should be useful to policy makers in other states and researchers in other areas trying to understand the message of the nationwide "tax revolt." The Massachusetts experience is particularly enlightening for a number of reasons. First, a vigorous campaign together with thorough media coverage assured that residents were well informed both of the proposition's provisions and of the issues. This means that the case of Massachusetts is an appropriate setting for examining the link between voting behavior and complex public sector issues. Second, the absence of a state surplus meant that passage of Proposition 2-1/2 would force state and local governments to make budget reductions immediately. This contrasts with the well studied California situation where a large state surplus enabled people to believe that the tax limitation measure would not result in fewer public services. Third, the choice before the voters was clear-cut. Although the Massachusetts Teachers' Association had placed an alternative tax limitation measure on the ballot, it chose to campaign against Proposition 2-1/2 rather than for its own proposal; with no organized support for the Association's proposal, its existence apparently played little role in the vote on Proposition 2-1/2.[4] This situation is quite unlike the 1978 Michigan experience where the presence of alternatives and confusion about what would happen if two or more of the measures received majority support may have influenced voting behavior in a non-generalizable way.[5]

It should be noted that Massachusetts' Proposition 2-1/2 is an initiative law rather than a constitutional amendment; once passed by the voters, it became a regular law subject to change by the legislature. Although this characteristic of Proposition 2-1/2 should be borne in mind when interpreting the results of this study, the distinction between an initiative law and a constitutional amendment need not be overemphasized; state legislators are generally reluctant to undo what the majority of the voters support, particularly when the majority is large.[6]

The following section provides an overview of the voting model, Section II reports and interprets the results, and Section III summarizes the conclusions.

I. Model Overview

Proposition 2-1/2's main thrust is to roll back or limit the growth of property taxes in Massachusetts' 351 cities and towns.[7] Combined with the proposition's reduction in the motor vehicle excise tax, these provisions reduced local tax revenues by almost $500 million between fiscal years 1981 and 1982, or about 14 percent of 1981 tax revenues.[8] Proposition 2-1/2 also removes fiscal autonomy of school committees, ends binding arbitration for police and fire personnel, prohibits the state from mandating programs without providing funds, and allows renters to deduct one-half of their rent payments from their state taxable income.[9]

Because it neither made explicit provision for new state aid to replace lost property taxes nor restricted the state government from raising state taxes, Proposition 2-1/2's impact on spending and taxes by level of government was uncertain at the time of the election. The impact on local spending of a fall in property taxes depended on the extent to which the state responded with new state aid. The impact on spending for state purposes depended on whether the new aid would be financed by higher state taxes or by lower state spending. In addition to uncertainty about spending levels, there was tremendous uncertainty about how spending changes would be allocated across functional categories and about the implications of spending changes for service levels.

The voting model for Proposition 2-1/2 fully incorporates this wide range of potential effects and the uncertainty associated with them. As Table I indicates, the model addresses six issues that might motivate support for or opposition to the tax limitation measure: service levels, inefficiency and waste, spending and taxes, tax reform, relative fiscal status, and public sector job status. For each of the first four, the model includes variables capturing voters' preferences, perceptions, or attitudes (column 2) and their expectations about what Proposition 2-1/2 would accomplish (column 3). The former represent voters' desired changes in service or spending levels, government operations, and financing arrangements, regardless of Proposition 2-1/2. The latter reflect voters' expectations about Proposition 2-1/2's impacts on the behav-

Table I. OVERVIEW OF VOTING MODEL

Issues Motivating Voting Behavior (1)	Variables	
	Preferences, Perceptions and Attitudes (2)	Expectations about Effects of Proposition 2-1/2 (3)
1. Service levels	Preferences for clusters of services	Expected effects on clusters of services; expected effects on services used by respondent's household.
2. Inefficiency and waste (cost of public services)	Perceptions of inefficiency or waste - state government - local government - local public schools	Expectations of more responsible government, more efficiency in local government, more voter control over schools.
3. Spending and taxes	Desired spending and taxing by - state government - local government - local public schools	Expected effects on state and local taxes; expected effects on taxes paid by respondent's household.
4. Tax reform (tax shift)	Desired tax shifts. Attitudes toward taxes.	Expectations about state aid and about tax reform.
5. Relative fiscal status	Perceptions of how other groups fare relative to household.	- -
6. Public sector job status	- -	Public sector employee as proxy for fear of job loss or decline in quality of work environment.

ior of state and local governments and on the services consumed and the taxes paid by their households.

Relative fiscal status and public employee job status represent two additional aspects of self-interest that might motivate support or opposition to Proposition 2-1/2. In addition to caring about specific service or tax levels, voters may care about the relative size of the net benefits they receive from the public sector. The model controls for and tests this motivation with a set of variables representing respondents' perceptions of how they fare relative to other groups of taxpayers. Unfortunately, there is no comparable measure of expectations about how Proposition 2-1/2 would alter the respondent's relative fiscal status. Inclusion of public sector job status identifies the self-interest of voters who oppose the proposition to preserve their jobs, income, or quality of work environment.[10]

The full model explaining the probability that a voter voted "yes" on Proposition 2-1/2 includes 45 variables and is based on the responses of the 1,114 sample voters for whom complete information is available.[11,12] Two forms of the model—a linear probability model estimated by ordinary least squares and a logit model estimated using maximum likelihood techniques—yield similar results. The discussion that follows focuses on the results of the linear form because its coefficients are simpler to interpret and it allows a simpler approximation of the relative contribution of each of the six issues listed in Table I to the statewide vote on Proposition 2-1/2.[13] Comparable results for the logit model are reported in the appendix.

Overall, the linear probability model does an excellent job of explaining the vote on Proposition 2-1/2. The R^2 of 0.54 is high for linear probability models given the binary nature of the dependent variable. More importantly, using a cut-off probability of 0.5 to separate "yes" voters from "no" voters, the model correctly predicts 85 percent of the sample voters. This represents a substantial gain over the 51 percent that would be correctly predicted by chance or the 58 percent that would be correctly predicted by projecting a "yes" vote for everyone in the sample.[14]

II. Empirical Results

The six issues identified in Table I as likely to influence voting behavior on Proposition 2-1/2 provide the framework for presentation and interpretation of the model results. For each issue, we first report the coefficients of the relevant variables. These coefficients show how preferences and expectations about the particular issue influenced the probability that an individual would vote for or against Proposition 2-1/2, controlling for all other variables. We then present estimates of the impact of each specific view on the statewide vote for the proposition. Derived by weighting the marginal impacts from the estimated equation by the sample distribution of each variable, these "weighted impacts" show the difference between the actual percentage of respondents who voted in favor of Proposition 2-1/2 and what the statewide vote of household heads would have been had voters neither wanted nor expected any change in each specific variable.[15]

Service Levels

Like other surveys of voters' preferences for public services at the time of tax limitation votes, this study finds that a majority of Massachusetts voters wanted to maintain or increase the levels of most state and locally provided public services.[16] This does not rule out the possibility, however, that a substantial minority voted for tax limitation with the explicit goal of either reducing overall services or of reducing the levels of particular services.

To examine this possibility, preference and expectations variables were defined for each of the following five clusters of public services:[17]

o Education and recreation: includes public elementary and secondary education, after school programs such as music and athletics, adult education, and local parks and recreation.
o Public safety: includes police and firefighting services.
o Sanitation and street maintenance: includes garbage collection and street and sidewalk repairs.
o Human services: includes special education for children with learning problems, mental health programs, and services for the elderly.
o Welfare: welfare and other public assistance.[18]

Beyond reducing the number of separate services in the model to a manageable level, clustering also averages out the random errors associated with responses to a single item. The clusters nonetheless provide sufficient detail to isolate how views toward different types of services influenced the vote on Proposition 2-1/2.

For each cluster of services, preference variables were constructed by taking the mean response across items to a question about whether respondents would like a particular service cut back a lot, cut back a little, kept the same, increased a little or increased a lot.[19] The service level expectations variables are similarly constructed with the scale representing respondents' views on whether Proposition 2-1/2 will lead to a lot less or a little less, the same amount, a little more or a lot more of each public service. The five-point scales for preferences and expectations are treated as if they were interval scales. With respect to expectations, however, it is reasonable to suppose that voters might have viewed the difference between services that would be cut "a lot" and those that would be cut "a little" (i.e., the difference between a 1 and a 2 on the scale) as larger than the difference between services that would be cut "a little" and those that would be kept the same (i.e., the difference between a 2 and a 3).

Statistical tests provided support for a logarithmic specification for all the service expectations variables except welfare, for which the linear form was preferred.[20]

As Table II indicates, four of the five preference variables have negative coefficients. This finding supports the view that, for most types of services, respondents who prefer service cutbacks are more likely to support Proposition 2-1/2 than those who prefer the same or higher service levels. The clusters of locally provided services, i.e., education and recreation and public safety, exhibit the greatest effects. The desire to reduce education and recreation services a little (a lot), for example, increases the probability that a voter will support Proposition 2-1/2 by four (eight) percentage points compared to the desire to maintain services at their current level.

Although state and federal taxes fully finance welfare in Massachusetts, many people expected Proposition 2-1/2 to lead to welfare reductions. For some voters, this expectation may have reflected the incorrect belief that welfare is financed in part by local property taxes; for others it may have reflected the belief that the money for new state aid would come from existing public assistance programs. These views help to explain why the desire for less welfare assistance increases the probability of support for Proposition 2-1/2 even though its provisions apply only to local taxes.

Surprisingly, preferences for human services have a positive, though statistically insignificant, coefficient, suggesting that voters who wanted to increase human services may have been more likely to support Proposition 2-1/2 that those who did not. This finding is hard to explain. Both state and local governments finance and deliver human services in Massachusetts. It is possible, however, that voters wanting to increase human services supported Proposition 2-1/2 in the hope that a tax structure less dependent on local property taxes would be better suited to providing these services.

Comparison of the upper and lower sections of Table II reveals that expectations about the impacts of Proposition 2-1/2 on service levels influence voting behavior even more strongly than preferences. The positive signs of the first four service clusters—education and recreation, public safety, sanitation and street repairs, and human services—indicate that people expecting the measure to lead to cutbacks in these services were more likely to vote against the proposition than those who expected no change. The logarithmic specification for these four clusters captures the non-linear relationship between the expectations scale and the probability of voting yes. As the lower right section of Table II shows, the logarithmic form implies that expectations of large service cutbacks have more than twice the impact on the probability of voting "yes" on Proposition 2-1/2 than expectations of small cutbacks.

In contrast to the first four service clusters, expectations about welfare services enter the model linearly and have a negative sign. The coefficient of -0.043 implies that voters who expected welfare to be cut back a little (a lot) are 4.3 (8.6) percentage points more likely to support Proposition 2-1/2 than those who expected no change. We interpret this result to mean that voters, on average, viewed expected reductions in welfare as a desirable outcome of the tax limitation measure.[21]

To capture all possible service-related effects, the model also includes respondents' expectations about how Proposition 2-1/2 would affect overall service levels in their particular community as well as specific services directly used by their households. The positive and statistically significant coefficient for expectations about overall community services signifies that this variable exerts an independent influence on voting behavior; the larger the cutbacks expected, the lower the probability of a favorable vote. The small and statistically insignificant coefficient of the other variable, however, implies that voters' concerns about the impact of Proposition 2-1/2 on the services directly used by their households are already captured by the service cluster variables.

Table II. SERVICE LEVELS

Estimated Coefficients and Impacts on Probability of a "Yes" Vote[a]

Variable	Form[b]	Coefficient (Absolute value of t-statistic)	Effect on Probability of a "Yes" Vote of Expectation that Services Will be Cut Back:[c]	
			a little	a lot
Preferences				
Education and Recreation	Linear (1-5)	-0.040 (2.01)		
Public Safety	Linear (1-5)	-0.027 (1.57)		
Sanitation and	Linear (1-5)	-0.004 (0.22)		
Human Services	Linear (1-5)	0.024 (1.39)		
Welfare	Linear (1 5)	-0.023 (2.10)		
Expectations				
Education and Recreation	Ln(1-5)	0.151 (3.02)	-0.061	-0.166
Public Safety	Ln(1-5)	0.124 (2.98)	-0.051	-0.136
Sanitation and Street Repair	Ln(1-5)	0.041 (1.01)	-0.017	-0.045
Human Services	Ln(1-5)	0.119 (2.64)	-0.048	-0.131
Welfare	Linear (1-5)	-0.043 (3.12)	0.043	0.086
Total Community Services	Ln(1-5)	0.124 (3.81)	-0.050	-0.136
Services Used by Household	Ln(1-5)	0.031 (0.82)	-0.013	-0.034

[a] Based on the full model of voting behavior, which includes 45 independent variables and was estimated by ordinary least squares. The dependent variable is "1" if the respondent voted "yes" on Proposition 2½ and "0" if he or she voted "no."

[b] The preference and expectations scales are decrease a lot (1); decrease a little (2); no change (3); increase a little (4); and increase a lot (5). "Ln" signifies that the variable is expressed as a natural logarithm.

[c] Compared to the expectation that services will not change.

The results reported so far relate to individual behavior; the estimated impacts of these service-related views on the statewide vote for Proposition 2-1/2 are reported in Table III. Each "weighted impact" is the sum of the estimated effects on the probability of a "yes" vote weighted by the proportion of sample respondents in each response category. In each case, the implicit comparison is to a base case

Table III. PUBLIC SERVICES

PREFERENCES AND EXPECTATIONS

Weighted Impacts on Total Vote[a]

Variable	Weighted Impacts on Total Vote		
	For	Against	Net
Education and Recreation			
Preferences for less	0.008		
-- for more		-0.015	
Expectations of less		-0.061	
-- of more	0.001		
			-0.067
Public Safety			
Preferences for less	0.003[b]		
-- for more		-0.009[b]	
Expectations of less		-0.029	
-- of more	0.001		
			-0.034
Sanitation and Street Repair			
Preferences for less	0.001[b]		
-- for more		-0.001[b]	
Expectations of less		-0.011[b]	
-- of more	0.000[b]		
			-0.011
Human Services			
Preferences for less		-0.002[b]	
-- for more	0.017[b]		
Expectations of less		-0.034	
-- of more	0.002		
			-0.017
Welfare			
Preferences for less	0.020		
-- for more		-0.004	
Expectations of less	0.037		
-- of more		-0.002	
			0.051
Total Community Services			
Expectations of less		-0.056	
-- of more	0.002		
			-0.054
Services Used by Household			
Expectations of less		-0.008[b]	
-- of more	0.000[b]		
			-0.008

[a] Each entry is the difference between the actual statewide vote of household heads for Proposition 2½ and the predicted vote had no household head wanted or expected the specified change in service levels.

[b] Based on a coefficient that is not statistically significant at the 5 percent one-tailed level.

of "no change" in either a preference or an expectations variable (a value of 3 on the 5-point scale).[22]

The results are striking. On net, preferences and expectations about all the service clusters other than welfare decreased the favorable vote on Proposition 2-1/2 compared to what the voting outcome would have been had voters neither wanted nor expected changes in service levels. In addition, expectations of changes in services influenced the vote more strongly than preferences. Typically, the net effects result from small positive contributions to the favorable vote from people who desire fewer services or who expect more (shown in the "for" column) and larger negative contributions from people desiring more services or who expect fewer (shown in the "against" column). Views toward local education and recreation have the biggest impact of any cluster of services. These views reduce the overall favorable state vote by close to 7 percentage points. Taken together, the net effect of all service variables other that welfare is to reduce the favorable vote on Proposition 2-1/2 by 18.3 percentage points.[23]

These results for all services other than welfare reflect the fact that voters on average desired higher service levels but expected Proposition 2-1/2 to reduce them. As Table IV demonstrates, the percent of voters wanting cutbacks in particular service areas is substantially less than the percent expecting cutbacks.

Welfare stands out as the only service that more than half the voters wanted to see reduced. As noted above, it is also the only service for which the expectations variable has a negative sign in the voting model. These factors together imply that attitudes toward welfare contribute 5.4 percentage points to the favorable vote on Proposition 2-1/2.

Inefficiency and Waste

Massachusetts voters believe that both their state and local governments deliver public services inefficiently. Over 80 percent of the voting model sample believe, for example, that spending by each level of government could be reduced by five percent or more without reducing the quality or quantity of services provided. As reported elsewhere, 73 percent of the total sample of voters and non-voters believe state spending could be cut 15 percent or more, and 60 percent believe that local spending could be similarly cut, without service reductions. In addition, 88 percent of these respondents think corruption is common in state government while 63 percent believe that corruption is common in their particular local government. In response to two other questions related to the cost of providing local public services, 47 percent agree with the statement that "city or town employees are overpaid" and 67 percent agree that "local public employees do not work as hard as employees of private companies."[24]

The results of the voting model suggest that, controlling for other preferences, expectations, and attitudes, such perceptions of inefficiency and waste in public service delivery influence the vote on Proposition 2-1/2 somewhat, but that expectations about the measure's ability to alter the way government operates are a more powerful set of explanatory variables. Those believing that the tax limitation measure would make government more efficient and responsible are thus much more likely to support Proposition 2-1/2 than those less optimistic in this regard.

Starting with perceptions and attitudes, the model includes five variables to capture voters' views about the extent of government waste and inefficiency. Four of these are dummy variables that take on the value 1 if the respondent thinks state, local, school, or welfare spending can be reduced by five percent or more without service cutbacks.[25] Because school spending is such a large proportion of local budgets and welfare spending of the state budget, each is included as a separate spending category. Controlling for perceptions about school and welfare inefficiency in this way implies that the local inefficiency variable can be interpreted as local non-school inefficiency and the state government

Table IV. PUBLIC SERVICES

DISTRIBUTION OF PREFERENCES AND EXPECTATIONS[a]

Variable	Mean Response	Percent Wanting Decrease	Percent Expecting Decrease
Education and Recreation			
Preferences	3.17	31%	--
Expectations	2.12	--	87%
Police and Fire			
Preferences	3.19	13	--
Expectations	2.50	--	48
Street Repairs and Garbage Collection			
Preferences	3.17	17	--
Expectations	2.37	--	64
Human Services			
Preferences	3.61	12	--
Expectations	2.41	--	70
Welfare			
Preferences	2.32	57	--
Expectations	2.18	--	65
Overall Community Services			
Expectations	2.10	--	72
Services used by the respondent's household			
Expectations	2.33	--	49

[a] Based on 1114 respondents who voted on Proposition 2½. The preference and expectations scales are decrease a lot (1); decrease a little (2); no change (3); increase a little (4); and increase a lot (5).

inefficiency variable as nonwelfare state government inefficiency. The fifth variable measuring perceptions of inefficiency and waste is the respondent's extent of agreement with statements that local government employees are overpaid and that they work less hard than private sector employees. The higher the average response in the range 1 to 4, the more strongly the respondent agrees that the wage costs of locally provided public services are excessively high. The data presented in Table V show that only two of these five variables are statistically significant. In particular, respondents who believe that school services are inefficiently provided or who believe that wage costs are too high are more likely than others to support Proposition 2-1/2.[26]

In contrast, all three expectations variables are statistically significant and have large positive coefficients. Voters who expect Proposition 2-1/2 to make local government more efficient are 12.9 percent-

Table V. INEFFICIENCY AND WASTE
Estimated Coefficients and Weighted Impacts on Total Vote[a]

Variable	Form	Coefficient (Absolute value of t-statistic)	Weighted Impact on Total Vote		
			For	Against	Net
Perceptions of Inefficiency in:					
local government	0-1	-0.002 (0.05)		-0.002[b]	
state government	0-1	0.039 (1.03)	0.034[b]		
local schools	0-1	0.050 (2.01)	0.031		
welfare spending	0-1	0.018 (0.58)	0.015[b]		
Attitude					
Local government employees are overpaid and do not work hard	Linear (1-4)[c]	0.057 (4.23)	0.026	-0.015	
Expectations					
More efficiency in local government	0-1	0.129 (4.89)	0.084		
More efficient, responsible, or less corrupt government (single most important impact)	0-1	0.096 (3.638)	0.021		
More local voter control over school spending		0.129 (5.122)	0.090		
					0.284

[a] Based on the full model of voting behavior which includes 45 independent variables and was estimated by ordinary least squares. The dependent variable is "1" if the respondent voted "yes" on Proposition 2½ and "0" if he or she voted "no." The weighted impacts are the difference between the actual statewide vote of household heads for Proposition 2½ and the predicted vote had no household head perceived inefficiency or expected Proposition 2½ to make government more efficient.

[b] Based on a coefficient that is not statistically significant at the 5 percent one-tailed level.

[c] The base for the calculation of weighted impacts is a value of 2.5.

age points more likely to vote for the measure than those who are less optimistic about efficiency gains. Similarly, the belief that the most important effect of Proposition 2-1/2 will be to make government more responsible and efficient or less corrupt increases the probability of a "yes" vote by 9.6 percentage points. Moreover, the belief that Proposition 2-1/2 will increase voter control over school spending raises the probability of a "yes" vote by 12.9 percentage points. The additive form of the model implies that, controlling for other variables, these three expectations alone raise the probability of supporting Proposition 2-1/2 by 35 percentage points.

The weighted effects of the inefficiency variables, also presented in Table V, indicate the contribution of each variable to the overall state vote. Each weighted impact starts from a base case in which the respondent perceives little or no inefficiency in government (a value of zero for each perception variable), neither agrees nor disagrees that local government employees are overpaid or do not work hard (a value of 2.5 for the attitude variable), and expects no change in the way government operates (a value of zero for each expectation variable).

Unmistakably, these perceptions, attitudes, and expectations about government inefficiency and waste make a substantial contribution to the statewide vote in favor of Proposition 2-1/2. Most of the weighted effects are large and positive, the largest being the eight and nine percentage point impacts of the expectation that the measure would produce more efficiency in local government and allow more voter control over school spending. The net additive contribution to the statewide vote of all these beliefs and expectations is about 28 percentage points, a large contribution compared to the sample favorable vote of 58 percent.

Spending and Taxes

Sample voters are much more likely to prefer lower spending and taxes than to prefer fewer services. The fraction of voters desiring spending reductions in state government, for example, is 65 percent vs. 42 percent preferring service reductions. The comparable percentages for local government spending and service reductions are 59 and 22 percent; and for school spending and services, 47 and 18 percent. Beliefs that government spending can be cut without reducing the quality and quantity of services help reconcile these differences, but they do not explain them fully. The question here is the extent to which voters' preferences for lower spending and taxes influence the vote on Proposition 2-1/2, controlling for preferences for service levels and perceptions of government inefficiency and waste.

The three spending reduction variables, shown in the first three rows of Table VI, all have positive coefficients and make small contributions to the overall statewide favorable vote on Proposition 2-1/2; only the school spending coefficient, however, is statistically significant.[27] Although the desire to decrease school spending increases the favorable vote by 2.3 percentage points, fear of lower school spending—measured by a dummy variable representing the expectation that Proposition 2-1/2 would lead to a decrease in school funds—reduces the favorable statewide vote by 4 percentage points. On net, concern about decreased school spending thus outweighs the desire for that spending outcome in terms of its influence on the Proposition 2-1/2 vote.

Instead of asking respondents directly about what they expected to happen to state and local government spending, the questionnaire elicited respondents' expectations about how Proposition 2-1/2 would affect the major local tax, (the property tax) and the two major state taxes (sales and income taxes.) The results shown in Table VI indicate that the expectation of lower property taxes increases the probability of a "yes" vote by 13 percentage points, with a large weighted effect on the overall vote of 10.6 percentage points. The possibility that the state government might raise state taxes to offset the local revenue losses from the measure, however, was viewed as an undesirable outcome as shown by the fact that the expectation of higher state income or sales taxes enters the probability model with a negative sign and exerts a weighted impact of 6.3 percentage points against the proposition.

The final tax variable, respondents' expectations about the impact of Proposition 2-1/2 on household taxes, enters the voting model strongly with the predicted negative sign. The preferred logarithmic specification implies that expectations that household taxes would decrease "a lot"

Table VI. SPENDING AND TAXES

Estimated Coefficients and Weighted Impact on Total Vote[a]

Variable	Form	Coefficient (t-statistic)[c]	Weighted Impact on Total Vote		
			For	Against	Net
Want lower spending and taxes					
-- state government	0-1	0.028 (1.13)	0.018[b]		
-- local government	0-1	0.021 (0.83)	0.012[b]		
-- local schools	0-1	0.049 (1.96)	0.023		
Expect decrease in school funds	0-1	-0.060 (2.55)		-0.041	
Expect lower property taxes	0-1	0.131 (4.50)	0.106		
Expect higher state taxes	0-1	-0.079 (2.93)		-0.063	
Expect lower household taxes	Ln(1-5)[d]	-0.112 (4.14)	0.031	-0.007	
			0.190	-0.111	0.079

[a] Based on the full model of voting behavior which includes 45 independent variables and was estimated by ordinary least squares. The dependent variable is "1" if the respondent voted "yes" on Proposition 2½ and "0" if he or she voted "no." The weighted impacts are the difference between the actual statewide vote of household heads for Proposition 2½ and the predicted vote had no household head wanted or expected lower spending or taxes.

[b] Based on a coefficient that is not statistically significant at the 5 percent one-tailed level.

[c] t-statistics are in absolute-value form.

[d] "Ln" signifies that the variable is specified as a natural logarithm.

(a value of 1 on the five-point scale) has more than twice the effect on the probability of a "yes" vote than expectations that household taxes would decrease "a little" (a value of 2), relative to the expectation of no change (a value of 3). The weighted impacts indicate that expectations of lower household taxes contribute 3.1 percentage points to the favorable vote, while the less common expectation of higher taxes contributes a slight 0.7 percentage points against the vote.

In sum, compared to a base case of no desired or expected changes in spending and taxes, the desire for or expectation of lower spending or taxes contributes 19 percentage points to the favorable statewide vote on Proposition 2-1/2, while fears of higher state taxes or lower school spending reduce the favorable vote by 11 percentage points.

Tax Reform

The above discussion treats tax reform only in the sense of property tax or overall tax reduction. In this section, tax reform is defined as a shift away from reliance on the property tax to alternative taxes or fees, controlling for the level of government spending.

The four desired tax shift variables in the voting model are based on a series of questions of the form: "For each service I read, would you like to keep the financing the way it is now or see a greater share of the money come from local property taxes, from state income taxes, from sales taxes, or a greater share from fees paid by the users of the service?" The shift variables include:

SHIFT1 = 1 if respondent wants more state (sales or income tax) financing of elementary and secondary education, and 0 otherwise.

SHIFT2 = 1 if respondent wants more state (sales or income tax) financing of special education, and 0 otherwise.

SHIFT3 = Sum of responses indicating a desired shift to state income or sales taxes for police, parks, or after school programs, divided by the number of these services for which an answer was given. (Range is 0 to 1.)

SHIFT4 = Sum of responses indicating a desired shift to user charges for local transportation, adult education, and after school programs, divided by the number of these services for which an answer was given. (Range is 0 to 1.)

Table VII shows that SHIFT1, which captures the desire for more state financing of education, enters the voting model with a positive and statistically significant coefficient of 0.047. Compared to the base case of no desire to place heavier reliance on state taxes, however, these preferences contribute only about 1.6 percentage points to the statewide favorable vote on Proposition 2-1/2. The desire to rely more heavily on user charge financing plays a similar role in the overall vote, contributing about 1.5 percentage points. The coefficients for the other two SHIFT variables are small and insignificant. Although this minimal impact is not surprising for SHIFT3, the results for SHIFT2 refute the hypothesis that dissatisfaction with the financing of special education played an important role in the Proposition 2-1/2 vote.

Two additional attitude variables help represent respondents' views on tax reform. The first, a dummy variable that takes on the value 1 if the respondent believes the state should provide more aid to cities and towns to keep property taxes down, enters the voting model with a small negative and statistically insignificant coefficient. The second is a cluster of responses to two questions measuring respondents' attitudes toward redistributive taxes and state aid. The higher the average response (on a four-point scale), the more the respondent supports graduated income taxes or equalizing aid programs. The cluster's negative coefficient implies that those who favor using the state-local public sector to achieve redistributive goals are more likely to vote against the proposition. Presumably, these voters believe Proposition 2-1/2 will obstruct, rather than facilitate, the redistributive tax reform they desire. Compared to a base of no opinion on this issue (a value of 2.5 on the four-point scale), the weighted impact of the desire for more redistributive taxes and aid decreases the statewide favorable vote by 0.9 percentage points; this is exactly offset, however, by the impact of Proposition 2-1/2's supporters who oppose redistributive fiscal reform.

Expectations of a tax shift are difficult to isolate from expectations of tax reduction. In both cases, for example, people would expect Proposition 2-1/2 to lead to

Table VII. TAX REFORM
Estimated Coefficients and Weighted Impact on Total Vote[a]

Variable	Form	Coefficient (Absolute value of t-statistic)	Weighted Impact on Total Vote		
			For	Against	Net
Desired Shifts					
SHIFT1: Shift of education to state taxes	0-1	0.047 (1.93)	0.016		
SHIFT2: Shift of special education to state taxes	0-1	0.000 (0.39)	0.005[b]		
SHIFT3: Shift of other local services to state taxes	0-1[c]	-0.019 (0.46)		-0.004[b]	
SHIFT4: Shift of certain services to user charges	0-1[c]	0.053 (1.53)	0.015[b]		
Attitudes					
State should give more aid to reduce property taxes	0-1	-0.013 (0.51)		-0.010[b]	
Support for redistributive taxes and aid	Linear (1-4)	-0.025 (1.83)	0.009	-0.009	
Expectations					
Tax reform	0-1	0.057 (1.96)	0.046		
More state aid	0-1	0.024 (1.10)	0.010[b]		
			0.101	-0.023	0.078

[a] Based on the full model of voting behavior which includes 45 independent variables and was estimated by ordinary least squares. The dependent variable is "1" if the respondent voted "yes" on Proposition 2½ and "0" if he or she voted "no." The weighted impacts are the difference between the actual statewide vote of household heads for Proposition 2½ and the predicted vote had no household head wanted or expected tax reform or a shift in the financing of public services.

[b] Based on a coefficient that is not statistically significant at the 5 percent one-tailed level.

[c] Continuous variable with range 0 to 1.

lower property taxes. If respondents preferred shifting burdens away from property taxes onto state taxes, however, the expectation of higher state taxes would increase the probability of a "yes" vote on Proposition 2-1/2. Thus, the finding reported above that this expectations variable has a negative coefficient suggests that voters are more concerned with tax reduction than with actual tax reform.

In an attempt to incorporate more directly respondents' expectations about tax shifts, the model includes a dummy variable that takes on the value 1 if the voter expected Proposition 2-1/2 to "encourage the state legislature to reform Massachusetts taxes," and 0 otherwise. Expecting tax reform increases the probability of a "yes" vote by 5.7 percentage points compared to not expecting reform. Moreover, because so many respondents expected tax reform, the weighted impact of this variable is relatively large. Unfortunately, however, the possibility that this variable represents expectations of overall tax reduction rather than of a tax shift cannot be ruled out since "tax reform" means different things to different people.

Another approach to the tax shift issue is through respondents' expectations of new state aid. Aside from state takeover of local expenditure responsibilities or legislation enabling local communities to use non-property taxes, a tax shift can only occur if new state aid financed by state taxes replaces lost property tax revenues. This logic justifies interpreting a variable that takes on the value 1 if the respondent expects Proposition 2-1/2 to lead to more state aid and 0 otherwise as an indicator that the respondent expects tax reform. The variable makes a small positive, but statistically insignificant, contribution to the statewide favorable vote on Proposition 2-1/2.

To summarize, attitudes and expectations about tax reform in the sense of tax shift contribute an estimated 5.5 to 10.1 percentage points to the statewide favorable vote on Proposition 2-1/2, depending on how one interprets the variable for expectations of "tax reform." The desire for redistributive tax reform, however, works in the opposite direction; those who desire such reform are more likely to vote against the tax limitation measure.

Relative Fiscal Status

To what extent were voters motivated by the desire to improve or preserve the fiscal position of their households relative to that of other groups? To isolate this motivation, the model includes a set of variables representing respondents' views about their households' fiscal position relative to business firms, poor households, and minority households at the time of the vote, and perceptions of changes in relative status during the previous two years. Each current-status variable takes on the value of 1 if the respondent believes that the other group receives more public services in relation to taxes paid than his or her household, and 0 otherwise. Each change-in-status variable takes on the value of 1 if the respondent believes the fiscal status of the other group has improved relative to that of his or her household over the past two years. The weighted impacts of these six variables, reported in Table VIII, start from a baseline belief that the respondent's household is fiscally as well off as each of the other groups and that the relative positions have not been changing over time.[28]

Of particular interest are the change variables, all of which are statistically significant at the five percent level for all three categories. The belief that business firms have been improving their fiscal status relative to the respondent's household increases the probability of a "yes" vote by 4 percentage points and contributes 1.8 percentage points to the overall favorable vote in Proposition 2-1/2. Thus, while concern about the shift of taxes away from business firms onto individuals motivated some support for the tax limitation measure, the overall impact of this attitude on voting behavior appears to be small.

The coefficients for beliefs about the changing relative position of poor families and minorities are intriguing because they differ in sign. The view that poor households have been gaining relative to the respondent's household increases the probability of a "yes" vote on Proposition 2-1/2 by 7.1 percentage points while the comparable view about minorities decreases the probability by 5.5 percentage points. These results suggest that respondents disapprove of perceived fiscal gains among poor households at a time when their own income outlook is uncertain. At the same time, however, gains among minority households are apparently viewed as an appropriate outcome of public sector activity that tax limitation measures

Table VIII. RELATIVE FISCAL STATUS

Estimated Coefficients and Weighted Impacts on Total Vote[a]

Variable	Form	Coefficient (t-statistics)[c]	Weighted Impact on Total Vote		
			For	Against	Net
Perception of fiscal position relative to that of respondent's household					
Business firms are better off					
--today	0-1	-0.030 (1.34)		-0.018[b]	
--compared to 2 years ago	0-1	0.041 (1.77)	0.018		
Poor households are better off					
--today	0-1	0.015 (0.56)	0.007[b]		
--compared to 2 years ago	0-1	0.071 (2.18)	0.015		
Minority households are better off					
--today	0-1	0.035 (1.27)	0.018[b]		
--compared to 2 years ago	0-1	-0.055 (1.88)		-0.019	
			0.058	-0.037	0.021

[a] Based on the full model of voting behavior which includes 45 independent variables and was estimated by ordinary least squares. The dependent variable is "1" if the respondent voted "yes" on Proposition 2½ and "0" if he or she voted "no." The weighted impacts are the difference between the actual statewide vote of household heads for Proposition 2½ and the predicted vote had no household head perceived other groups were fiscally better off or had become better off relative to the respondent's household during the past two years.

[b] Based on a coefficient that is not statistically significant at the 5 percent one-tailed level.

[c] t-statistics are in absolute value form.

should not restrict. Because a smaller proportion of the sample respondents perceive fiscal gains for the poor than perceive gains for minorities, the positive weighted impact on the statewide vote of attitudes toward the poor is somewhat smaller than the negative impact of attitudes towards minorities.

The signs of the variables representing respondents' views of their current relative status complicate the net impact of voter attitudes toward other groups. The belief that poor or minority households are fiscally better off than the respondent's household leads to support for a change and, hence, for tax limitation. Neither coefficient, however, is statistically significant at the five percent level. One possible interpretation of the negative (but insignificant) sign of the variable representing perceptions about the current fiscal position of business is that voters who consider business taxes to be high in relation to services received (a low value of the variable) are more likely than others to support Proposition 2-1/2 and its promise of overall tax reduction. This interpretation is consistent with one of the campaign arguments used by the proposition's advocates. It also conforms to the finding that 74 percent of the total sample (voters and non-voters) agreed with the statement that Proposition 2-1/2 would attract more business and industry to Massachusetts.[29] It should be noted, however, that the variable actually expresses perceptions of the fiscal position of Massachusetts firms relative to the respondent's household rather than firms in other states.

Beliefs that business firms and poor households have improved their relative fiscal positions during the previous two years and that poor families and minorities receive greater net benefits from the public sector spending than the respondent's household thus contribute about 5.8 percentage points to the statewide favorable vote on Proposition 2-1/2. On the other hand, the view that firms are relatively well off today and that minority households are better off than two years ago contributed 3.7 percentage points to the overall vote against the proposition.

Public Sector Job Status

As shown in Table IX, the estimated equation implies that employment in the local public sector reduces the probability of a "yes" vote on Proposition 2-1/2 by 12 percentage points, while employment in either state government or local public schools reduces the probability by about 7 percentage points. Since the equation controls for preferred levels of and expectations about public services, taxes, and spending, these effects are relatively large and suggest that concern among local public employees about income reduction or morale loss strongly influenced their votes. The weighted effects on the overall vote are small, however, because only a small proportion of all Massachusetts households have a public sector employee.

III. Summary and Conclusions

Table X combines the preceding findings to present a complete picture of the relative importance of the six issues motivating the Proposition 2-1/2 vote, based on the concept of weighted impacts. The first line estimate indicates what the voting outcome would have been had voters neither wanted nor expected changes in the level and distribution of public services and taxes, neither perceived governmental inefficiency nor expected Proposition 2-1/2 to lead to more efficient or responsible government, and had no direct stake in the state-local public sector through a household member's employment in that sector. Under these assumptions, only about one quarter (26.7 percent) of Massachusetts household heads would have supported the tax limitation measure. In other words, most people would not have voted for change simply for the sake of change.

Among the factors leading to increases in the favorable vote, views toward inefficiency and waste in government are the most important. Included in these views are the effects not only of perceptions of existing inefficiency but also of expectations that Proposition 2-1/2 would improve the situation, with the latter play-

Table IX. PUBLIC SECTOR JOB STATUS

Estimated Coefficients and Weighted Impacts on Total Vote[a]

Variable	Form	Coefficient (t-statistic)[c]	Weighted Impact on Total Vote		
			For	Against	Net
State government employee	0-1	-0.076 (1.30)	-0.003[b]		
Local government employee	0-1	-0.121 (3.06)	-0.010		
Local school employee	0-1	-0.072 (1.69)	-0.005		
			-0.018		-0.018

[a] Based on the full model of voting behavior which includes 45 independent variables and was estimated by ordinary least squares. The dependent variable is "1" if the respondent voted "yes" on Proposition 2½ and "0" if he or she voted "no." The weighted impacts are the difference between the actual statewide vote of household heads for Proposition 2½ and the predicted vote had no household head lived in a household with an employee working in the state or local public sector.

[b] Based on the coefficient that is not statistically significant at the 5 percent one-tailed level.

[c] t-statistics are in absolute-value form.

ing the larger role. The 28.4 percentage point contribution of these views alone is large enough to turn the estimated 26.7 percent base favorable vote into majority support for Proposition 2-1/2. The proposition's orientation toward local, rather than state, government is reflected in the distribution of these effects by level of government; despite the finding that voters believe state government is less efficient than local government, views about inefficiency in state government contribute less to the favorable vote than do similar views about the operation of local government and public schools.

Preferences for and expectations of lower taxes and spending contribute another 19.0 percentage points to the favorable vote. Since more than half of this contribution reflects the expectation of lower property taxes, this might be interpreted as a tax reform effect. Tax reform in the sense of tax shift rather than reduction, however, adds another estimated 7.8 percentage points to the favorable vote. Overall, the model implies that concerns about the level and composition of taxes increase the "yes" vote on Proposition 2-1/2 by 26.8 percentage points.

In contrast to these large effects related to inefficiency and tax issues, the preference for lower levels of all services except welfare contributes only 1.0 percentage point to the favorable vote. This result clearly does not support the view that the success of Proposition 2-1/2 represents a general demand for fewer public services. Preferences for and expectations of lower welfare services, however, are estimated to increase the favorable vote by 5.7 percentage points. Finally, the desire to improve one's fiscal status relative to that of other groups also contributes 2.1 percentage points. Combining all of these

PROPOSITION 2-1/2

Table X. SUMMARY OF WEIGHTED IMPACTS ON TOTAL VOTE

A. Assume all voters neither want nor expect any public sector changes and no household member works in the state and local public sector

Base favorable vote		0.267

B. Issues increasing the favorable vote

Inefficiency and waste in			
--local government	0.093		
--state government	0.070		
--local schools	0.121		
		0.284	
Lower taxes and spending			
--lower property taxes	0.106		
--other	0.084		
		0.190	
Tax reform (net)		0.078	
Desire for lower public services (not welfare)[a]		0.010	
Lower welfare		0.057	
Relative fiscal status (net)		0.021	
Total additions to favorable vote			0.640

C. Issues decreasing the favorable vote

Fear of service loss[b]			
--education	-0.075		
--other[c]	-0.132		
		-0.207	
Fear of lower school funding		-0.040	
Fear of higher taxes			
--state taxes	-0.060		
--taxes paid by household	-0.007		
		-0.067	
Fear of loss of job security among public sector employees		-0.018	
Total subtractions from favorable vote			-0.332
Overall total			0.575

[a] This nets out the anomalous, but statistically insignificant, 0.002 negative impact on the favorable vote contributed by those who want to decrease human services.

[b] Net of the small effects of expected service increases.

[c] This nets out the anomalous, but statistically insignificant, 0.017 impact on the favorable vote contributed by those who want to increase human services.

factors leading to a favorable vote with the predicted base favorable vote of 26.7 percent yields a 90.7 percent statewide vote for Proposition 2-1/2.

Other preferences and expectations, however, motivated voters to oppose the tax limitation measure. As Table X indicates, fear of service loss is the most important cause of a "no" vote. Of this 20.9 percentage point impact, 7.5 points represent concern about reductions in education (and recreation) services. Combining this with evidence of concern about reduced education funding, fear of Proposition 2-1/2's adverse impact on local public schools reduces the favorable vote by 11.5 percentage points. The belief that Proposition 2-1/2 would lead to higher state taxes or higher taxes for the respondent's household contributes another 6.1 percentage points to the negative vote, while concern about the impact on public sector jobs adds 1.8 percentage points. Subtracting the sum of these negative effects from the predicted 90.7 favorable vote yields the sample of 57.5 percent in favor of Proposition 2-1/2.

Thus, the survey results clearly indicate that the vote for Proposition 2-1/2 was much more an attempt to obtain lower taxes and more efficient government than to reduce the level of public services. This conclusion is remarkably consistent with those from other states. From a survey-based analysis of the vote on Michigan's successful 1978 Headlee Amendment limiting state taxes, for example, Courant, Gramlich and Rubinfeld conclude that:

> ... 3 out of 4 voters responsible for the plurality of the Headlee Amendment were motivated by a desire for either efficiency gains or a free lunch. Only one out of 4 appears to favor a smaller-sized public sector where both spending and taxes are reduced.[30]

Using survey data gathered just before the 1978 vote on California's property tax limitation measure, Proposition 13, Jack Citrin also draws qualitatively similar conclusions; like voters in Massachusetts and Michigan, a majority of California residents were apparently satisfied with the existing levels of most public sevices at the time of the tax limitation vote. Moreover,

fully 38 percent of the California electorate believed that state and local governments could provide the same level of services as previously with a 40 percent reduction in their budget.[31]

The similarity of findings from Massachusetts, Michigan and California is striking in light of the different forms of their tax limitation measures and their differing fiscal and economic situations.

These findings need not imply that state and local governments were in fact any more inefficient in the late 1970's than in other periods. They do suggest, however, that, for whatever reason—high and rising property taxes, changing economic conditions or a shift in political ideology—voters in some states were particularly sensitive to issues of inefficiency and waste during this period.

FOOTNOTES

**This paper is part of a larger study funded by the National Institute of Education, grant no. NIE-G-81-0006, with supplemental funds from the Lincoln Institute of Land Policy, Cambridge, Massachusetts. The authors are grateful to Claire Christopherson for her expert computer programming.

[1] In 1979, property tax burdens in Massachusetts were the highest of any state in the continental United States, expressed both per capita and per $1000 of personal income. The 1979 per capita burden of $545 was almost double the United States average of $280.

[2] Because of the interviewing error, only 25 of the 55 interviews for the city of Salem were conducted. Hence, throughout the analysis, each Salem respondent is given a weight of two.

[3] A preliminary analysis and description of the survey results can be found in Ladd and Wilson, "Proposition 2-1/2: Explaining the Vote." Appendices A, B and C of that report describe the sampling plan, the questionnaire and interviewing procedure and present a demographic profile of the sample.

[4] The Massachusetts Teachers' Association proposal was defeated by a 36 to 64 percent vote.

[5] See Courant, Gramlich, and Rubinfeld (1980 and 1981) for an analysis of the Michigan vote and the comments by Oakland in Ladd and Tideman (1981), p. 76.

[6] To check whether people would have voted differently had Proposition 2-1/2 been a constitutional amendment, respondents were asked whether or not they thought Proposition 2-1/2 was an amendment to the constitution. Those respondents who answered correctly were then asked how they would have voted had it been a constitutional amendment. A comparison of these responses with their reported votes shows a small net shift of 40 votes against the proposition (out of our total voter sample of 1,253 respondents) had it been a constitutional amendment.

[7] In Massachusetts' relatively simple government structure, the 351 cities and towns of the Commonwealth levy all the property taxes. Both the county governments, which have few responsibilities, and the limited number of special districts finance themselves by assessing the cities and towns.

[8] The property tax is the only broad-based tax available to cities and towns. Aside from small amounts of revenue from the motor vehicle excise tax (about 6.5 percent of local tax revenues before Proposition 2-1/2), charges, fees, and intergovernmental aid provide municipalities' only other revenue.

[9] Most school district boundaries are coterminous with those of cities and towns. Before Proposition 2-1/2, school committees enjoyed fiscal autonomy in the sense that each city or town body was required to accept the proposed school budget and to raise the necessary property taxes as part of the municipal tax levy.

[10] If voters were perfectly rational, it would be desirable to interact each preference variable with an expectations variable. This would allow fiscal changes that are simultaneously preferred and expected to exert a larger impact on the probability of a "yes" vote on Proposition 2-1/2 than those that are either preferred but not expected or expected but not preferred. In addition to being unmanageable, a complete interactive specification would require many arbitrary assumptions. Hence, the basic model reported here eschews interactions in favor of a more inclusive range of possible fiscal motivations. But see footnotes 20 and 23 below.

[11] Of the (weighted) total of 1586 respondents, 1253 said they voted on Proposition 2-1/2. Of these, 139 were eliminated because of incomplete information.

[12] Throughout this paper we refer to the impact of a variable on the probability of a "yes" vote or on the statewide favorable vote for Proposition 2-1/2. These statements should be interpreted to refer to the population of Massachusetts household heads, rather than to the entire population of voters.

[13] This simplicity comes, however, from the imposition of a functional form that is theoretically inferior to the logit form. As noted in the appendix, the two forms have similar implications for the relative importance of the various motivating factors.

[14] The sample probability of a "yes" vote is .58 and of a "no" vote .42. Hence the percent that would be correctly predicted by chance using these aggregate probabilities is $(.58)^2 + (.42)^2 = .51$.

[15] For the simple case of a 0–1 variable, the weighted impact is calculated by multiplying the estimated coefficient by the proportion of the sample having the specified characteristic. See footnote 22 below.

[16] See Ladd and Wilson, "Proposition 2-1/2: Explaining the Vote"; Citrin "Do People Want Something for Nothing: Public Opinion Polls on Taxes and Government Spending"; and Courant, Gramlich and Rubinfeld, "Why Voters Support Tax Limitation Amendments: The Michigan Case."

[17] A combination of factor analysis and judgment were used to define the five service clusters. The responses to questions about preferred service levels for each of the 15 separate services included in the survey were first factor analyzed using a principal axis approach with quartimax rotation. Based on the factor loadings, the 15 services were initially grouped into six factors as follows (with factor loadings in parentheses):
1. Public elementary and high school education (0.51), after school programs (0.77), adult education (0.56), local parks and recreation (0.51) and state colleges and universities (0.74).
2. Police (0.78) and fire (0.80) services.
3. Garbage pick-up (0.73) and street and sidewalk repairs (0.68).
4. Special education (0.64), mental health programs (0.78) and services for the elderly (0.69).
5. Welfare and other public assistance (0.70), and support for local public transit (0.65).
6. Courts and judges (0.86).

Three services were then excluded: Courts and judges were eliminated to reduce the number of clusters; support for local public transit, because of the low correlation between voters' expectations about Proposition 2-1/2's impact on public transit and on welfare; and state and community colleges, because they are financed differently than the other services in the education and recreation cluster.

[18] The welfare cluster consists of a single item.

[19] Responses were averaged across those items in the cluster for which responses were given. This procedure makes it possible to keep in the sample those observations missing individual parts of the question, provided a response was given for at least one item in the cluster.

[20] The model was also estimated with preferences and expectations interacted by service category. Because dummy variables were used to construct the interaction variables (e.g., prefer but do not expect a reduction in public safety), this alternative specification has the advantage of not requiring any arbitrary assumptions about the intervals between response categories. Because response categories had to be collapsed to keep the total number of variables to a manageable number, however, the interactive model is also somewhat arbitrary. See footnote 23 below.

[21] This conclusion is confirmed by the interactive version of the model. Among voters who said they did not want welfare cuts, those who expected large cuts were more likely to support Proposition 2-1/2 than those who expected no cuts and were almost as likely to support it as those who both wanted and expected reduced welfare services.

[22] For variables taking on n discrete values, the expression for the weighted impact (M) for the ith variable takes the form:

$$M_i = \sum_{i=1}^{n} f_{ik} \hat{B}_i (V_{ik} - V_{io}).$$

where f_{ik} is the proportion of the sample in the kth value category of variable i, $\hat{B}_i$ is the estimated effect of the ith variable in the voting model, V_{ik} is the kth value of the ith variable and V_{io} is the value of the ith variable for the case of no change. (V_{io} equals 3 on a 5-point linear scale and ln3 on a 5-point logarithmic scale.) For multi-valued variables (e.g., variables that represent clusters of responses), M_i is approximated by letting k refer to intervals (each of length one standard deviation) and V_{ik} to the mean value in the kth interval. For most of the calculations, six intervals were used, three on either side of V_{io}.

[23] The comparable weighted impact from the interactive specification is 18.2 percentage points. The implications of the reported specifications are thus virtually identical to those of the richer interactive specification.

[24] Ladd and Wilson, pp. 30–33.

[25] Earlier versions of the model included two dummy variables for each spending category to represent perceptions of some inefficiency (5 to less than 15 percent possible spending reduction) and much inefficiency (greater than 15 percent possible spending

reduction). The similarity between the coefficients in each pair justifies the single set of dummy variables reported in the final equation.

[26] In the logit model, the variable representing perceptions of inefficiency in state government is also statistically significant at the five percent level.

[27] The school spending coefficient is not statistically significant in the logit model.

[28] These data are from responses to two questions: "Sometimes it seems that certain groups of people pay a lot in taxes but don't get very many services while others don't pay much in taxes but get a lot of services. Using the phrases in *list one*, please tell me whether _____ get a lot less than they pay for, a little less, the same amount as they pay for, a little more, or a lot more than they pay for"; and "Now we'd like you to think about two years ago. Taking into account services they get for the taxes they pay, are _____ better off, worse off, or about the same now as they were two years ago?" In the case of the first question, the responses were scored on a five-point scale, ranging from a lot less (1) to a lot more (5). In the case of the second question, the responses were scored on a three-point scale, ranging from better off (1) to worse off (3).

The variables used in the regression model were computed by subtracting respondents' scores for their households from their scores for other groups. The value 1 was given to those respondents who thought a specific group paid less for services or was better off now than the respondent's household.

[29] Ladd and Wilson, p. 19.

[30] Courant, Gramlich and Rubinfeld, "Why Voters Support Tax Limitations: The Michigan Case," (1980 and 1981), p. 18.

[31] Citrin, p. 115.

REFERENCES

Citrin, Jack "Do People Want Something for Nothing: Public Opinion on Taxes and Government Spending," *National Tax Journal* XXXII, 2 Supplement (June 1979), pp. 113–130.

Courant, Paul N.; Gramlich, Edward M.; and Rubinfeld, Daniel L. "Why Voters Support Tax Limitation Amendments: The Michigan Case," *National Tax Journal*, March 1980. Also in Helen F. Ladd and T. Nicolaus Tideman, eds., *Tax and Expenditure Limitations*. Washington, D.C.: The Urban Institute Press, 1981.

Oakland, William H. "Discussion of Paper by Courant, Gramlich and Rubinfeld," in Helen F. Ladd and T. Nicolaus Tideman, eds. *Tax and Expenditure Limitations*. Washington, D.C.: The Urban Institute Press, 1981.

Ladd, Helen F. and Wilson, Julie Boatright, "Proposition 2-1/2: Explaining the Vote," prepared for the National Institute of Education, January 1982. Also available as Research Report R81-1, John F. Kennedy School of Government, Program in City and Regional Planning, Harvard University, April 1981.

Ladd, Helen F. and Wilson, Julie Boatright, "Who Supports Tax Limitations: Evidence from Massachusetts' Proposition 2-1/2," *Journal of Policy Analysis and Management*, forthcoming.

Appendix A

Weighted Impacts by Model Type

The logit model is conceptually superior to the linear model but is more difficult to interpret. This appendix illustrates that the results from the linear model are similar to those from the logit model.

The weighted impacts from the logit model have been calculated from two starting points: the 9.6 percent favorable vote predicted to occur if voters had neither wanted nor expected any public sector changes and the favorable vote of 58.5 percent predicted to occur if everyone were characterized by mean values for all the variables included in the model. Thus, the logit entries in the following tables represent upper and lower bound estimates of the impact of the specified beliefs on the statewide vote of household heads for Proposition 2-1/2.

Table A-1: PREFERRED AND EXPECTED CHANGES IN SERVICE LEVELS
IMPACTS ON STATEWIDE VOTE FOR PROPOSITION 2½

By Model Type

Variable	Logit Model		Linear Model
	Base = 0.096[a] ($\hat{P}$ - 0.096)	Base = 0.585[b] (0.585 - $\hat{P}$)	Base = 0.0260[c] ($\hat{P}$ - 0.260)
Education and Recreation			
Preferences	-0.006	-0.017	-0.007
Expectations	-0.035	-0.111	-0.060
Combined	-0.039	-0.126	-0.067
Public Safety			
Preferences	-0.005	-0.014	-0.006
Expectations	-0.023	-0.069	-0.028
Combined	-0.027	-0.082	-0.034
Sanitation and Street Repair			
Preferences	-0.001[d]	-0.002[d]	0.000[d]
Expectations	-0.013[d]	-0.037[d]	-0.011[d]
Combined	-0.014	-0.039	-0.011
Human Services			
Preferences	0.012[d]	0.034[d]	0.015[d]
Expectations	-0.022	-0.065	-0.032
Combined	-0.003	-0.034	-0.017
Welfare			
Preferences	0.013	0.032	0.016
Expectations	0.034	0.080	0.035
Combined	0.050	0.109	0.051
Total Community Services			
Expectations	-0.040	-0.092	-0.054
Services Used by Household	-0.007[d]	-0.021[d]	-0.008[d]

[a] The entries in this column show the impacts on the predicted statewide vote for Proposition 2½ of the actual distributions of preferences and expectations separately by service category compared to the base case which assumes that voters neither want nor expect any public sector changes. For example, the first entry says that the actual distribution of preferences for education and recreational services lowered the vote by 0.6 percentage points compared to the 9.6 percent favorable vote predicted to occur if no one had wanted nor expected changes of any type including changes in the level of educational and recreational services. Note that the combined effect of preferences and expectations for each service category is not merely the sum of the two separate impacts because of the nonlinearity of the model.

[b] The entries in this column show the predicted impacts on the statewide vote for Proposition 2½ of the assumption that no one prefers (for the preference variables) or expects (for the expectations variables) a change in the particular service compared to the 58.5 percent favorable vote predicted to occur if everyone is characterized by mean values for all variables included in the model. To make the signs consistent with those in the other columns, the impact is defined as the predicted value for the base case (0.585) minus the predicted value for the specific simulation under consideration. Thus, the first entry shows that the favorable vote would have been 1.7 percentage points higher than the 0.585 vote predicted for mean values had no voter wanted changes in educational and recreational services.

(continued)

TABLE A-1 (continued)

[c] The entries in this column show the weighted impacts of each variable on the statewide favorable vote for Proposition 2½ derived from the linear model. See Table III.

[d] Based on a coefficient that is statistically insignificant at the five percent one-tailed level.

Table A-2. INEFFICIENCY AND WASTE

IMPACTS ON STATEWIDE VOTE FOR PROPOSITION 2½

By Model Type

Variable	Logit Model		Linear Model
	Base = 0.096[a] ($\hat{P}$ − 0.096)	Base = 0.585[b] (0.585 − $\hat{P}$)	Base = 0.0260[c] ($\hat{P}$ − 0.267)
Perceptions of Inefficiency in:			
local government	−0.004[d]	−0.012[d]	−0.002[d]
state government	0.065	0.147	0.034[d]
local schools	0.026	0.068	0.031
welfare spending	0.019[d]	0.051[d]	0.015[d]
Attitude			
Local government employees are overpaid and do not work hard.	0.009	0.026	0.011
Expectations			
More efficiency in local government	0.057	0.133	0.084
More efficient, responsible, or less corrupt government	0.016	0.043	0.021
More local control over school spending	0.083	0.178	0.090
Combined	0.480	0.486	0.280

[a] The entries in this column show the predicted impacts on the statewide vote for Proposition 2½ of the actual distribution of the indicated variable compared to the base case which assumes that voters neither want nor expect any public sector changes.

[b] The entries in this column show the predicted impacts on the statewide vote for Proposition 2½ of the assumption that no one expects a change or perceives a need for a change compared to the 58.7 percent favorable vote predicted to occur if everyone is characterized by mean values for all variables included in the model. To make the signs consistent with those in other columns, the impact is defined as the predicted value for the base case (0.585) minus the predicted value for the simulation under consideration.

[c] The entries in this column show the weighted impacts of each variable on the statewide favorable vote for Proposition 2½ derived from the linear model. See Table V.

[d] Based on a coefficient that is statistically insignificant at the five percent one-tailed level.

Table A-3. SPENDING AND TAXES

IMPACTS ON STATEWIDE VOTE FOR PROPOSITION 2½

By Model Type

Variable	Logit Model		Linear Model
	Base = 0.096[a] $(\hat{P} - 0.096)$	Base = 0.585[b] $(0.585 - \hat{P})$	Base = 0.0260[c] $(\hat{P} - 0.267)$
Want lower spending and taxes			
-- state government	0.015[d]	0.039[d]	0.018[d]
-- local government	0.009[d]	0.026[d]	0.012[d]
-- local schools	0.010[d]	0.027[d]	0.023
Expect decrease in school funds	-0.024	0.073	-0.041
Expect lower property taxes	0.117	0.229	0.106
Expect higher state taxes	-0.026	-0.143	-0.063
Expect lower household taxes	0.021	0.055	0.024

[a] The entries in this column show the predicted impacts on the statewide vote for Proposition 2½ of the actual distribution of the indicated variable compared to the base case which assumes that voters neither want nor expect any public sector changes.

[b] The entries in this column show the predicted impacts on the statewide vote for Proposition 2½ of the assumption that no one wants a change or expects a change compared to the 58.7 percent favorable vote predicted to occur if everyone is characterized by mean values for all variables included in the model. To make the signs consistent with those in other columns, the impact is defined as the predicted value for the base case (0.585) minus the predicted value for the simulation under consideration.

[c] The entries in this column show the weighted impacts of each variable on the statewide favorable vote for Proposition 2½ derived from the linear model. See Table VI.

[d] Based on a coefficient that is statistically insignificant at the five percent one-tailed level.

Table A-4. TAX REFORM
IMPACTS ON STATEWIDE VOTE FOR PROPOSITION 2½
By Model Type

Variable	Logit Model		Linear Model
	Base = 0.096 [a] ($\hat{P}$ − 0.096)	Base = 0.585 [b] (0.585 − $\hat{P}$)	Base = 0.0260 [c] ($\hat{P}$ − 0.260)
Desired Shifts			
SHIFT1: Shift of education to state taxes	0.018	0.047	0.016
SHIFT2: Shift of special education to state taxes	0.000[d]	0.001[d]	0.005[d]
SHIFT3: Shift of other local services to state taxes	−0.004[d]	−0.012[d]	−0.004[d]
SHIFT4: Shift of certain services to user charges	0.012[d]	−0.033[d]	−0.015[d]
Attitudes			
State government should give more aid to reduce property taxes	−0.007[d]	−0.019[d]	−0.010[d]
Support for redistributive taxes and aid[e]	−0.001	−0.003	−0.000
Expectations			
Tax reform	0.039	0.096	0.046
More state aid	0.011[d]	0.030[d]	0.010[d]

[a] The entries in this column show the predicted impacts on the statewide vote for Proposition 2½ of the actual distribution of the indicated variable compared to the base case which assumes that voters neither want nor expect any public sector changes.

[b] The entries in this column show the predicted impacts on the statewide vote for Proposition 2½ of the assumption that no one wants a change or expects a change compared to the 58.7 percent favorable vote predicted to occur if everyone is characterized by mean values for all variables included in the model. To make the signs consistent with those in other columns, the impact is defined as the predicted value for the base case (0.585) minus the predicted value for the simulation under consideration.

[c] The entries in this column show the weighted impacts of each variable on the statewide favorable vote for Proposition 2½ derived from the linear model. See Table VII.

[d] Based on a coefficient that is statistically insignificant at the five percent one-tailed level.

[e] Net effect of those who want and those who do not want a more redistributive fiscal structure.

Table A-5. RELATIVE FISCAL STATUS

IMPACTS ON STATEWIDE VOTE FOR PROPOSITION 2½

By Model Type

Variable	Logit Model		Linear Model
	Base = 0.096[a] ($\hat{P}$ − 0.096)	Base = 0.585[b] (0.585 − $\hat{P}$)	Based = 0.0260[c] ($\hat{P}$ − 0.260)
Perception of fiscal position relative to that of respondent's household			
Business firms are better off—			
Today	−0.012[d]	−0.036[d]	−0.018[d]
Compared to 2 years ago	0.009[d]	0.026[d]	0.018
Poor households are better off—			
Today	0.011[d]	0.029[d]	0.007[d]
Compared to 2 years ago	0.018	0.049	0.015
Minority households are better off—			
Today	0.009[d]	0.026[d]	0.018[d]
Compared to 2 years ago	−0.019	−0.055	−0.019

[a] The entries in this column show the predicted impacts on the statewide vote for Proposition 2½ of the actual distribution of the indicated variable compared to the base case which assumes that voters neither want nor expect any public sector changes.

[b] The entries in this column show the predicted impacts on the statewide vote for Proposition 2½ of the assumption that no one wants a change or expects a change compared to the 58.7 percent favorable vote predicted to occur if everyone is characterized by mean values for all variables included in the model. To make the signs consistent with those in other columns, the impact is defined as the predicted value for the base case (0.585) minus the predicted value for the simulation under consideration.

[c] The entries in this column show the weighted impacts of each variable on the statewide favorable vote for Proposition 2½ derived from the linear model. See Table VIII.

[d] Based on a coefficient that is statistically insignificant at the five percent one-tailed level.

Table A-6. PUBLIC SECTOR JOB STATUS IMPACTS ON STATEWIDE VOTE FOR PROPOSITION 2½

By Model Type

Variable	Logit Model		Linear Model
	Base = 0.096[a] ($\hat{P}$ − 0.096)	Base = 0.585[b] (0.585 − $\hat{P}$)	Base = 0.0260[c] ($\hat{P}$ − 0.260)
State government employee	−0.002[d]	−0.004[d]	−0.003[d]
Local government employee	−0.009	−0.025	−0.010
Local school employee	−0.004[d]	−0.010[d]	−0.005
Combined	−0.014	−0.040	−0.018

[a] The entries in this column show the predicted impacts on the statewide vote for Proposition 2½ of the actual distribution of the indicated variable compared to the base case which assumes that voters neither want nor expect any public sector changes.

[b] The entries in this column show the predicted impacts on the statewide vote for Proposition 2½ of the assumption that no one wants a change or expects a change compared to the 58.7 percent favorable vote predicted to occur if everyone is characterized by mean values for all variables included in the model. To make the signs consistent with those in other columns, the impact is defined as the predicted value for the base case (0.585) minus the predicted value for the simulation under consideration.

[c] The entries in this column show the weighted impacts of each variable on the statewide favorable vote for Proposition 2½ derived from the linear model. See Table IX.

[d] Based on a coefficient that is statistically insignificant at the five percent one-tailed level.

[14]

Who Supports Tax Limitations:
EVIDENCE FROM MASSACHUSETTS' PROPOSITION 2½

Helen F. Ladd
Julie Boatright Wilson

Abstract *The vote on Massachusetts' Proposition 2½—and by extension the votes to restrain or roll back taxes in other states as well—should not be interpreted simply as expressions of the narrowly defined self-interest of the voters. This study shows that other characteristics such as sex, race, religion, occupation, educational background, and political orientation also have an important influence on voting behavior. These characteristics combine with self-interest measures such as public sector employment and voters' likely gains from tax reduction to push individual voters in different directions on the issue of tax limitation. Consequently, we find little polarization in the electorate along demographic lines.*

The 1978 passage of California's Proposition 13, a constitutional admendment to reduce local property taxes, focused national attention on the question of who supports property tax limitations.[1] As voters across the country continue to use the referendum process to limit the tax and spending powers of their state and local governments, an additional question is raised: Is each tax limitation referendum unique or can patterns of support among population groups be observed across states despite differing fiscal and economic conditions and differences in the provisions included in each? This study addresses both questions by examining the bases of support for tax limitation in Massachusetts and comparing the results with those from similar studies for Michigan and California. In addition, this study examines whether Massachusetts voters—and by extension voters in other states as well—were polarized along demographic lines and the extent to which political orientations and attitudes exerted an independent influence on voting behavior. Finally, the study explores the consequences of a statewide referendum on a fiscal matter that primarily affects local governments.

In an earlier analysis, the authors used data from interviews

Journal of Policy Analysis and Management, Vol. 2, No. 2, 256–279 (1983)
© 1983 by the Association for Public Policy Analysis and Management
Published by John Wiley & Sons, Inc.   CCC 0276-8739/83/010256-23$03.30

with Massachusetts residents to determine the messages voters were trying to send elected officials when they overwhelmingly passed Proposition 2½, a measure reducing local property taxes to 2½% of market value. Our examination indicates that the electorate was essentially calling for lower taxes and more efficiency in government, but was not generally asking public officials to cut back the supply of public services.² Although useful in interpreting the vote and guiding the immediate policy response of public officials, this previous study provided no direct information on the demographic characteristics of voters or on the fiscal characteristics of the communities in which they live. The current study thus complements our previous work and also draws on its findings to ensure that all the relevant demographic and community characteristics are included.

PROPOSITION 2½ AND THE DATA

Proposition 2½ takes its name from its major provisions. Communities with high tax rates are required to reduce tax revenues by 15% each year until they reach the 2½% tax rate limit; communities with low tax rates may increase tax revenues but by no more than 2½% per year. An additional provision reduced the auto excise tax rate from 6.6 to 2½%; the rate is uniform across the state, but revenues from this tax accrue to local governments. At the time of the election, Massachusetts municipalities anticipated losing close to $500 million, about 14% of their total tax revenues, during the first year under the proposition. Many communities faced additional reductions in subsequent years as well. As with tax limitation referenda in other states, the measure made no explicit provision for new state aid or for state assumption of local expenditure responsibilities, and it offered no indication of which services might be reduced.

Data to explore the sources of support for Proposition 2½ were gathered in a comprehensive half-hour telephone survey administered to 1561 Massachusetts household heads during the two weeks following the November 1980 election. Survey respondents, half of whom were men and half of whom were women, were randomly selected from 58 cities and towns chosen to be representative of all cities and towns in the state in terms of per capita property wealth, per capita expenditures, population, and percent of owner-occupied housing. Of the 1243 respondents who reported that they voted on Proposition 2½, 58% voted for and 42% voted against it. These percentages are similar to the actual vote: 59% of Massachusetts voters supported the measure and 41% opposed it.

Despite the length and complexity of the interview, response rates were high for all questions except household income. For respondents failing to provide income information, the missing data were estimated using a multivariate model.³ The survey data were supplemented with census and other published data on the fiscal and population characteristics of the 58 communities from which the sample was selected.

Certain types of research questions can be answered simply by looking at how support for tax limitation varies among subgroups of voters. In a recent article in this journal, for example, the authors used this approach to compare the voting patterns of public sector employees, transfer recipients, and renters with those of the rest of the population.[4] But each voter is many things simultaneously—not only a state employee, but also, for example, a renter, a female, a resident of a town with low taxes, a conservative, and so on. Accordingly, a multivariate approach is required if the objective is to understand which of many overlapping characteristics actually motivated particular types of voters. Consequently, we use two analytic techniques in this study: (1) a cross-tabular analysis, which shows the proportion of voters in each subgroup who supported Proposition 2½ irrespective of differences among subgroup members, and (2) a linear probability analysis, which measures how the probability of support varied with membership in a subgroup after controlling for all other demographic, ideological, and community characteristics considered. The cross-tabular results are based on the number of respondents who answered each question. The full linear probability model is based on the 1182 sample voters for whom complete information was available and was estimated using ordinary least squares. Although the full model contains 50 variables, results are discussed in groups of a few variables at a time. The full model is reported in the Appendix.

Findings are discussed in four sections that focus on the following sets of characteristics:

- those associated with differences in the potential benefits of tax reduction (as implied by the fiscal characteristics of the respondent's community and homeowner–renter status);

- those that differentiate voters in terms of how they might be affected by the reduction in government revenues (as indicated by their role in providing public services and their use of public services);

- those that reflect differences in voters' views about the size and scope of government (respondents' political orientations and attitudes toward government);

- those that differentiate voters in terms of their access to resources and their preferences for specific services (as indicated by their social, economic, and demographic characteristics).

TAX REDUCTIONS

The major goal of Proposition 2½ was local tax reduction. Because it was designed to reduce taxes more in some communities than in others, however, the promised tax savings were larger for some voters than for others. In addition, within a given jurisdiction, the benefits for homeowners were more direct than those for renters.

Fiscal Characteristics of Communities

The prospective impact of Proposition 2½ on a community's taxes can be measured in various ways. We used two measures: the percentage decline in tax revenues that would occur in the first year following the passage of Proposition 2½, and the community's full-value tax rate as officially estimated by the Massachusetts Department of Revenue.[5]

The top half of Table 1 shows the relationship between support for Proposition 2½ and anticipated first-year revenue reductions in the respondents' communities. As the cross-tabular results indicate, a majority of voters in each of the various groups of communities supported the measure. In addition, as both the cross-tabular and linear probability results show, support for the measure increased with the size of the anticipated revenue reduction. The linear probability model indicates that, after controlling for the individual characteristics of the voter and for other characteristics of the community, the likelihood that a respondent would

Table 1. Support for Proposition 2½ in voter sample, classified by tax characteristics of communities in which they lived.

	Cross-tabular analysis[a]			Linear probability analysis[b]
	Number of voters in sample	Proportion voting "yes" on Proposition 2½	Difference in proportion between each category and base category	Probability of voting "yes" compared with base category
Total in sample	1243	0.580	NA[c]	
In communities with first year expected revenue losses				+0.0065[d]
Less than 10%	335	0.543	Base	
10–14.9%	385	0.590	+0.047	
15% or more	504	0.619	+0.076	
In communities with 1981 tax rate				
Less than 2.5%	160	0.538	Base	Base
2.5–3.9%	519	0.592	+0.054	−0.07
4.0–4.9%	270	0.633	+0.095	−0.06
5.0% or more	294	0.534	−0.004	−0.16

[a] The sampling errors for the differences in proportions decrease as the sample sizes increase and the differences being compared move away from 0.500 in either direction. As a rough guide, differences in proportions of 0.06–0.08 are a conservative estimate of the sampling error between any two subsamples, except where subsamples are small.

[b] The linear probability analysis is based on the 1182 respondents for whom complete information is available. The full linear probability model, presented in Appendix A, includes community characteristics, such as first-year revenue loss and 1981 tax rate; personal characteristics, such as sex, race, and religion; household characteristics, such as occupation of household head; use of public services; and the respondent's political ideology. The dependent variable takes on the value 1 for a "yes" vote. Variables enter the equation as continuous linear variables and binary 0–1 variables.

[c] NA = not applicable.

[d] To compare this result with those from the cross-tabular analysis, the differences in proportions reported in the column to the left of this figure should be divided by 5 to convert them from the effects of intervals that are approximately 5 percentage points long to the 1-percentage-point interval implicit in the continuous form of the variable in the multivariate model.

support the measure increased by 0.65 percentage points with each percentage point increase in the size of the local revenue loss. This finding suggests that the value voters placed on anticipated tax reductions outweighed whatever costs they expected to bear in the form of service reductions. Although not startling, this finding could not have been predicted *a priori* since the expected benefits of tax reduction might have been offset by expectations of service losses.

The lower portion of Table 1 shows the relationship between support for Proposition 2½ and the long-run impact of the tax limitation measure on the respondent's community. Each community's 1981 tax rate acts as a proxy for the total impact of Proposition 2½ on a community's property taxes; the more the 1981 tax rate exceeds 2½%, the more years taxes will have to be reduced to conform to the provisions of Proposition 2½.[6] Once again, a majority of voters in each of the different groups of communities supported Proposition 2½. Here, however, the data suggest that voters' reactions were not simply a function of anticipated tax savings. In communities with tax rates above 5.0%—that is, in communities that would be affected most severely in the long run—the disposition to support Proposition 2½ was weak. That fact is evident in the cross-tabular analysis, but even more striking in the linear probability analysis; after controlling for the individual characteristics of the voters and for other characteristics of the community, we find that taxpayers in communities with tax rates above 5.0% were 16 percentage points less likely than voters in communities with the lowest tax rates to vote for Proposition 2½. The highly taxed communities, of course, were those in which tax reductions—and presumably service reductions—were likely to be greatest. This result implies that voters in the most severely affected communities apparently believed that the possible disruptions in service were too great a price to pay for the anticipated tax savings.

The linear probability results have a second, more striking implication. If Proposition 2½ had required revenue reductions in all communities of the magnitude required in the most severely affected communities, support for the limitation measure would have been substantially less than it actually was. Assuming no other change, the model's results suggest that in such circumstances the vote in support of Proposition 2½ among our sample's respondents would have fallen from 58 to 50%.[7]

Renters versus Homeowners Expected benefits from lower taxes may also have varied from one group of households to the next within each community. In contrast to homeowners, renters could not expect to benefit from property tax reductions except to the extent that landlords passed the tax savings on in the form of lower rents. On the other hand, Proposition 2½ offered one direct benefit to tenants; the proposition provided that they would be allowed to deduct half their rent from their state income tax returns. Accordingly, it was not clear where their self-interest lay. Table 2 shows that 46% of the

Table 2. Support for Proposition 2½ in voter sample, classified by homeownership and renter status.

	Cross-tabular analysis[a]			Linear probability analysis[b]
	Number of voters in sample	Proportion voting "yes" on Proposition 2½	Difference in proportion between each category and base category	Prpbability of voting "yes" compared with base category
Total in sample	1243	0.580	NA[c]	
Renters—total	366	0.456	[d]	
Who never owned, no plans to	158	0.386	−0.248	−0.14
Who once owned	122	0.500	−0.134	−0.01
Who plan to own in next five years	86	0.523	−0.111	−0.07
Homeowners—total	848	0.634		
Whose property taxes relative to those paid in the local community are:				
Very low[e]	183	0.585	Base	Base
Low	221	0.670	+0.085	+0.07
High	157	0.605	+0.020	−0.01
Very high	202	0.698	+0.113	+0.07
Whose taxes were not reported	85	0.553	−0.032	−0.02
Voters who neither rent nor own	29	0.552	−0.082	−0.07

[a]See footnote a in Table 1.
[b]See footnote b in Table 1.
[c]NA = not applicable.
[d]The proportion of renters supporting Proposition 2½ is 0.178 less than that of all homeowners. The other entries in this column compare the various groups of renters with homeowners having very low tax shares; this makes the difference comparable to the results from the linear probability analysis.
[e]Local tax share is defined as the property taxes paid by the respondent's household as a percentage of average property taxes per household in the respondent's community. The four categories correspond to (1) less than 75% of the community average, (2) 75–100% of the community average, (3) 100–125% of the community average, and (4) greater than 125% of the community average.

renters—compared with 63% of the homeowners—voted in favor of the tax limitation measure. Thus, despite the income tax provision, renters viewed the proposition substantially less favorably than did homeowners.

Renters, however, are not a homogeneous group. Those renters who have never owned a house and have no plans for ownership differ much more from homeowners than do renters who have owned in the past or who plan to own in the future. Reflecting this difference, only 39% of the "permanent" renters supported the tax limitation measure, in contrast to about half of the other groups of renters. Moreover, this difference among renters remains in the multivariate analysis; even after controlling for all other characteristics, such as household income and service usage, the "permanent" renters prove much less supportive of tax reductions than those who identify more closely with the homeowner group.

The data in Table 2 also show the degree of support for Proposition 2½ among homeowners distinguished by the size of their local tax burden. The higher the homeowner's tax burden in relation to the average for the jurisdiction, the larger would be the homeowner's absolute savings from a given percentage reduction in local property taxes. We expected to find that as tax burdens increased, homeowners would be more likely to support the measure; instead we found that despite their larger savings expressed in dollars, homeowners with above-average tax burdens were no more likely than those with below-average tax burdens to support the tax limitation measure.

SPENDING AND SERVICE REDUCTIONS At the time of the election, voters were uncertain what the effects of the revenue reductions mandated by Proposition 2½ would be. Spending by local governments would certainly be reduced unless lost revenue was fully offset by new state aid or user charges. Voters, however, could not predict which, if any, local services would be cut back as a result of spending reductions. In addition, it was unclear whether spending reductions would be limited to local governments or would involve the state government as well; if the state increased local aid without increasing taxes, it too would have less money to spend on state programs.

Two groups—those who provided public services and those who used the services—may have been particularly concerned about the effects of revenue reductions and consequently more likely than others to oppose the measure. Public employees, particularly public school and local government employees, would be hurt if revenue reductions resulted in layoffs, lower wages, less favorable working conditions, or less bargaining power for workers. Service users would be adversely affected by revenue reductions that led to fewer or lower-quality services.

Service Providers Public employees, especially municipal and school employees, who would bear the brunt of any reductions in local spending, campaigned vigorously against the measure and opposed it at the polls. As Table 3 shows, seven out of ten respondents in households with municipal or school employees voted against Proposition 2½, making these the most strongly opposed of any demographic subgroup considered. The multivariate analysis indicates that, even after controlling for other characteristics, living in a household with a local government employee increased a voter's likelihood of opposing the measure by 32 percentage points and that living in a household with public school employees increased the likelihood by 27 percentage points.

Table 3. Support for Proposition 2½ in voter sample, classified by status as service providers.

	Cross-tabular analysis[a]			Linear probability analysis[b]
	Number of voters in sample	Proportion voting "yes" on Proposition 2½	Difference in proportion between each category and base category	Probability of voting "yes" compared with base category
Total in sample	1243	0.580	NA[c]	
Local public school employee in household	85	0.318	−0.320	−0.27
Other local government employee in household	106	0.292	−0.346	−0.32
State or county government employee in household	45	0.444	−0.194	−0.12
No local or state government employee in household	1007	0.638	Base	Base

[a]See footnote a in Table 1.
[b]See footnote b in Table 1.
[c]NA = not applicable.

Slightly more than five in ten voters in households with state government employees also opposed the measure. Presumably this group was concerned that any increase in state aid to cities and towns to make up for local revenue losses might be financed by reducing spending on state programs. Moreover, living in a household with state government employees increased the likelihood of opposing Proposition 2½ by 12 percentage points, even after other variables were controlled for. This is a sizable impact relative to other demographic variables, but less than half that associated with employment in local government or public schools.

Service Users Although the status of the respondent as a service provider had a substantial impact on voting behavior, the situation of the respondent as a recipient of services did not seem to affect voting behavior very much. We developed two measures of service use: the first, by asking respondents whether anyone in their household regularly used any of a variety of state and local services; and the second, by dividing the sample into groups defined by life-cycle stages. The second measure picks up an important distinction that the first does not. Some nonusers of services, primarily members of prefamily households and households with only preschool children, may nevertheless anticipate using the community's schools and other services in the future; at the same time other nonusers, primarily older childless households, may be past the stage of heavy use of local services, despite their heavy reliance on state or federally financed services such as Medicare or social security.

Although limitations of space have prevented us from presenting the data here, users of local services tended to be no more likely than nonusers to oppose Proposition 2½. Support was as strong among respondents in households with children attending public schools as among those without school-attending children, 58.2 versus 57.9%. In addition, there was hardly any difference in response between those with children attending private or parochial schools and those with children attending pulic schools, 59.0 versus 57.9%. Only those who used parks or after-school programs showed especially weak support for Proposition 2½. The strength of the opposition among this group, even after other household characteristics have been controlled for, may reflect the importance of publicity during the campaign about possible cuts in these park and after-school services. Even in the case of this group of users, however, 53.0% supported the measure.

Despite the local nature of Proposition 2½, the only strong opposition to the measure among service users came from users of welfare and other income-support services, all of which are provided in Massachusetts by state government. Although local governments finance no part of the welfare budget, more than half the respondents using welfare or other public assistance opposed the measure—55.4% of users versus 41.3% of nonusers. Their opposition was strong, even after controlling for income, occupation, and other demographic and municipal characteristics.

Further support for the assertion that service use had only a limited impact on voting behavior emerges from an examination of the relationship between life-cycle stage and support for Proposition 2½. The cross-tabular analysis shows that support increases with maturation of the households. As Table 4 illustrates, less than half the respondents in households at the prefamily stage supported the tax limitation measure compared with 70% in elderly households. The linear probability model suggests, however, that it is not family stage but other characteristics correlated with family stage, such as income and tenure status, that explain voting behavior. Once these other variables are included in the model, no differences in voting behavior emerge among household heads under 60.

Support for tax limitation among elderly households continues to stand out, however. Differences in income levels, general attitudes toward government, tax burdens, and service usage cannot account for this differential response on the part of the aged; the equation explicitly controls for differences along these dimensions. Instead, the differential may reflect the vulnerability of those living on fixed incomes to the pressures of inflation and rising

Table 4. Support for Proposition 2½ in voter sample, classified by life-cycle stage.

	Cross-tabular analysis[a]			Linear probability analysis[b]
	Number of voters in sample	Proportion voting "yes" on Proposition 2½	Difference in proportion between each category and base category	Probability of voting "yes" compared with base category
Total in sample	1243	0.580	NA[c]	
Stage in life-cycle				
Young adults, no children present in household	225	0.476	−0.116	−0.001
Children present in household, oldest under 6	120	0.550	−0.042	−0.01
Children present in household, oldest 6–17	432	0.579	−0.013	−0.01
Older adults, no children present in household	267	0.592	Base	Base
Elderly adults (60 or over), no children present in household	199	0.704	+0.112	+0.08

[a]See footnote a in Table 1.
[b]See footnote b in Table 1.
[c]NA = not applicable.

taxes. Because of the growing size of the elderly population, further investigation of this and other explanations would be desirable.

SPENDING REDUCTIONS AND LESS GOVERNMENT No matter how public officials chose to respond to reduced revenues, the result was bound to be less government—fewer services, fewer personnel, or less bureaucracy. Consequently, we hypothesized that respondents' political orientations would be important in explaining the vote, independent of other factors such as the respondent's age or service use. Respondents provided information on their political ideologies through their response to a series of questions. Table 5 identifies the questions and provides the data demonstrating the link between the voter's response and the voter's position on Proposition 2½. Most striking about these findings is the strong relationship between respondent's political orientations and support for Proposition 2½. Support ranges from 72% of those who are very conservative to 36% of those who are very liberal and from 66% of those who agree that welfare

Table 5. Support for Proposition 2½ in voter sample, classified by ideology and attitudes toward government.

	Cross-tabular analysis[a]			Linear probability analysis[b]
	Number of voters in sample	Proportion voting "yes" on Proposition 2½	Difference in proportion between each category and base category	Probability of voting "yes" compared with base category
Total in sample	1243	0.580	NA[c]	
Self-identified political ideology				
Very conservative	98	0.724	+0.104	+0.01
Fairly conservative	327	0.654	+0.034	
Middle-of-the-road	482	0.620	Base	Base
Fairly liberal	231	0.424	−0.196	−0.11
Very liberal	77	0.364	−0.256	
"Welfare recipients could find jobs if they really tried"				
Agree a lot	564	0.660	+0.216	+0.12
Agree a little	380	0.592	+0.148	
Disagree a little	180	0.444	Base	Base
Disagree a lot	95	0.284	−0.160	
"People expect too many services from government"				
Agree a lot	466	0.712	+0.297	
Agree a little	405	0.557	+0.142	
Disagree a little	253	0.415	Base	d
Disagree a lot	111	0.495	+0.080	
"The government should make sure that each family has enough to live on"				
Disagree a lot	196	0.684	+0.095	
Disagree a little	265	0.589	Base	
Agree a little	349	0.562	−0.027	d
Agree a lot	410	0.512	−0.077	

[a] See footnote a in Table 1.
[b] See footnote b in Table 1.
[c] NA = not applicable.
[d] In the linear probability model a single variable was formed from two attitude statements: "People expect too many services from the government," and "The government should make sure each family has enough to live on." Scores in the latter statement were reversed to make it consistent with the first statement. Respondents believing the government should have a more restrictive role, those with mean scores greater than 2.5, had a 0.10 greater probability of supporting the measure than those who think government should be more involved in helping individuals.

recipients could find jobs to 28% of those who strongly disagree. This variation across subgroups far exceeds that found for most of the demographic or community characteristic categories.

Results from the multivariate linear probability model are not directly comparable to the cross-tabular results since they are based on somewhat more aggregated variables; in the linear probability model, for example, "very conservative" and "fairly conservative" are combined to form one category labeled "conservative," and responses to the two questions about the appropriate role of government are combined into a single variable. Nonetheless, results from this analysis reinforce the cross-tabular results. The somewhat smaller magnitudes of the coefficients reflect the positive correlation between the attitude variables and certain demographic and community characteristics that push the voter in the same direction. Importantly, however, the model shows that political views and attitudes exert independent effects on voting behavior and that these effects are strong even after controlling for demographic and community characteristics.

PERSONAL CHARACTERISTICS Some commentators have referred to the tax limitation movement as a revolt of the "haves" against the "have-nots."[8] If this is a correct characterization, respondents with greater access to resources and to economic opportunities—those with higher incomes, more education, and higher-status occupations—would be more likely to support the tax limitation measure than those with more limited opportunities. The results reported in Table 6 provide some support for this view but suggest a more complex picture as well.

Economic Well-Being and Social Status Both the cross-tabular and multivariate analyses show that despite some inconsistencies in the middle ranges, respondents in high-income households were more likely to support Proposition 2½ than respondents in lower-income households, particularly households with incomes under $10,000. Moreover, for whatever reason—low expected tax savings or heavy dependence on public sector activities—a majority of low-income households opposed the measure. Thus, these results tend to support the interpretation of the revolt as one of "haves" versus "have-nots."

Higher educational attainment among voters, in contrast, decreased the probability that a voter would support Proposition 2½. Barely half the respondents with college degrees and fewer than half of those with graduate education supported the tax limitation measure. This may reflect these respondents' greater understanding of the link between services and taxes and their lesser willingness to believe in simple, quick solutions to fiscal problems; or it may simply reflect a stronger preference for maintaining elementary and secondary education. Whatever the reason, the positive correlation between educational background and income implies that both high- and low-income voters faced conflicting pressures as they considered the tax limitation measure.

Table 6. Support for Proposition 2½ in voter sample, classified by social and economic class.

	Cross-tabular analysis[a]			Linear probability analysis[b]
	Number of voters in sample	Proportion voting "yes" on Proposition 2½	Difference in proportion between each category and base category	Probability of voting "yes" compared with base category
Total in sample	1243	0.580	NA[c]	
Household income				
Under $10,000	107	0.467	−0.136	−0.08
$10,000 to under $20,000	368	0.603	Base	Base
$20,000 to under $30,000	375	0.560	−0.043	−0.04
$30,000 to under $50,000	313	0.617	+0.014	+0.04
$50,000 or more	60	0.683	+0.080	+0.07
Education				
Less than high school	107	0.626	Base	Base
High school degree	386	0.655	+0.029	+0.01
Some college	287	0.602	−0.024	−0.05
College degree	275	0.518	−0.108	−0.09
Graduate school	160	0.431	−0.195	−0.13
Occupation of household head[d]				
Managerial	268	0.664	+0.091	+0.09
Professional	322	0.512	−0.061	+0.03
Clerical, sales	154	0.623	+0.050	+0.05
Service	70	0.614	+0.041	+0.09
Blue-collar	302	0.573	Base	Base
Not reported, no occupation	127	0.520	−0.053	+0.01

[a] See footnote a in Table 1.
[b] See footnote b in Table 1.
[c] NA = not applicable.
[d] Household head is defined as the male in joint households and the respondent in single-adult households. Research suggests that in joint households status and economic situation are more likely to be defined by the male's occupation than the female's.

As an additional measure of social status, respondents were classified by the occupation of the head of their household. Respondents from households headed by someone in a management position were the most likely of all occupational groups to support Proposition 2½. This is consistent with the view that managers are more likely than others, particularly blue-collar workers, to be concerned about inefficiency in the public sector and to be willing to tolerate a reduction in public services in order to keep taxes down. Professionals contrast sharply with managers, however. As a group, those in households headed by professionals were the least likely of all occupational groups to support Proposition 2½; barely half of these respondents voted "yes." Some of the opposition to the measure among professionals can be explained by educational background and other characteristics, as indicated by the results from the linear probability model. After other characteristics are controlled for, respondents in professional households are slightly more likely than those in blue-collar households, but still 6 percentage points less likely than those in management households, to support the tax limitation measure. This difference between managers and professionals thus further clouds the interpretation of the vote as one of the "haves" versus the "have-nots."

Demographic Characteristics Sex, race, and often religion are inherited characteristics associated with patterns of socialization and life opportunities that may influence views on public sector issues. Nonwhites, for example, face more discrimination in all aspects of life than whites do; as a result, compared with whites they are both more likely to look to government for opportunities and protection from discrimination and less free to move to communities that could provide the package of services and taxes they prefer. To a much lesser extent this is also true of Jews, who have a long history of concern with education and social welfare. Women, too, can be expected to have special reactions, since despite other roles they may fill, they are traditionally more involved than men with the day-to-day lives of children and other family members.

The data in Table 7 are consistent with the hypothesis that women, Jews, and nonwhites were more concerned than others about possible service cuts as a result of Proposition 2½. As the table shows, more than half the nonwhite and Jewish respondents opposed the tax limitation measure; and women were far more likely than men to oppose the measure. These patterns hold even after controlling for other variables considered in the analysis, although, in the case of race, the difference between nonwhites and whites falls from 21 to 11 percentage points.

The overall influence of nonwhites and Jews on the outcome of the referendum was limited because these groups are such a small part of the Massachusetts population. The influence of women, in contrast, was considerable because they comprise half the electorate. Although a majority of women supported Proposition 2½, the large differential between men and women raises a number of questions for future research. Can the differential be fully explained by women's stronger preferences for particular public services such as elementary and secondary education and their differential concern about possible reductions in these services? Or does it reflect a complex set of factors that have a pervasive influence on how women view society and the role of government?

Table 7. Support for Proposition 2½ in voter sample, classified by inherited demographic characteristics.

	Cross-tabular analysis[a]			Linear probability analysis[b]
	Number of voters in sample	Proportion voting "yes" on Proposition 2½	Difference in proportion between each category and base category	Probability of voting "yes" compared with base category
Total in sample	1243	0.580	NA[c]	
Sex				
Male	616	0.635	Base	Base
Female	627	0.526	−0.109	−0.08
Race				
White	1193	0.588	Base	Base
Nonwhite	50	0.380	−0.208	−0.11
Religion				
Protestant	360	0.600	Base	Base
Catholic	605	0.612	+0.012	−0.02
Jewish	82	0.427	−0.173	−0.16
Other	196	0.510	−0.090	d

[a] See footnote a in Table 1.
[b] See footnote b in Table 1.
[c] NA = not applicable.
[d] An earlier analysis showed that "Other, no religion" had a coefficient close to zero. For this analysis we combined "Other, no religion" and "Protestant" to form the base case.

SUMMARY AND CONCLUSIONS

The findings for Massachusetts are similar to those from comparable studies of support for tax limitation in California and Michigan. Given the major differences in the provisions of each tax limitation measure and in the fiscal and economic climates of the three states, this similarity is striking. It implies a certain commonality to the tax revolt and suggests that findings from one state can be generalized to others.

California's Proposition 13, like Massachusetts' Proposition 2½, reduced local property taxes and capped their rate of growth; in contrast, Michigan's Headlee Amendment, which was approved in the fall of 1978, primarily limited the growth of state government revenues. At the time of its tax limitation vote in June 1978, California enjoyed a substantial state surplus; Michigan and Massachusetts did not. Compared with other states, Massachusetts relied more heavily on property taxes to finance local services. Moreover, California was in the midst of a boom in the housing market while Michigan was suffering from high unemployment caused by the depressed automobile market.

Table 8 compares the findings from the California and Michigan studies with those from the Massachusetts study.[9] For Massachusetts and Michigan, the equations are linear probability models; for California, the equation is a nonlinear model, technically called a probit model. Only the Massachusetts equation includes municipal characteristics. When the studies include comparable variables, the relationships between the variables and support for the specific limitations are similar. For example, sex, race, education, age, and political orientations affect voting behavior in the same way in the various states. Similarly, public sector employment consistently led voters to oppose tax limitations; not surprisingly, however, state employees were more opposed than local employees in Michigan where the tax limitation measure focused on state taxes. Aside from this difference, the form of the tax limitation measure appears to have had little influence on the voting patterns from one state to the next. In all three states, renters were less likely than homeowners to support tax limitation and, in Massachusetts and Michigan, receipt of welfare or other transfer income decreased support for tax limitation. All three studies show that high-income voters were more likely than middle-income voters to support tax limitation. The findings for low-income respondents, however, vary somewhat across states. This may reflect actual differences in behavior or, possibly, differences in model specification.

The results for Massachusetts indicate that after controlling for all other variables some of these characteristics pull voters more strongly toward support or opposition to tax limitation than others. Being in a household with a public school or local government employee, for example, increases the probability of opposing tax limitation relative to the base case (no state or local employee in household) almost twice as much as being a "permanent" renter, being Jewish, or having a graduate education (relative in each case to the appropriate base). Each of these characteristics, in turn, exerts a stronger impact on the probability of opposition than being female or nonwhite, having a college degree, or being politically conservative. For the most part, life-cycle stage and service usage exerted little influence on voting behavior. Old age and a management occupation pulled voters toward support for Proposition 2½ with effects comparable in magnitude to the effects in the other direction associated with being on welfare or being female.

To what extent do the effects of different characteristics reinforce one another and to what extent do they pull a particular voter in opposite directions? If the various characteristics were mutually reinforcing—if race, income, community, service use, and so on, all pushed a voter in one direction—the voting population would be split into two polarized groups defined along lines of personal and community attributes. To learn if this was the case, we used the complete set of demographic, attitudinal, and municipal characteristics in the linear probability model to predict the likelihood that each voter in the sample would support tax limitation. The distribution of these predicted probabilities resembles a slightly skewed bell-shaped curve; most voters were clustered

Who Supports Tax Limitations

Table 8. Comparisons of findings in studies of support for tax limitations in three states.[a]

	Massachusetts: Proposition 2½	California: Proposition 13[b]	Michigan: Headlee Amendment[c]
Demographic Characteristics			
Sex	Women less likely to support	Not included	Women less likely to support
Race	Nonwhites less likely to support	Blacks less likely to support	Blacks less likely to support
Religion	Jews less likely to support	Not included	Not included
Life-cycle stage/age	No effect at younger ages, but older are more likely to support	No effect, but entered as continuous variable	No effect, but older are somewhat more likely to support
Service usage	After-school program users and welfare recipients less likely to support	Not included	Public school users and transfer recipients less likely to support
Education	More educated less likely to support	More educated less likely to support	Not included
Household income	High-income more likely than middle-income and low-income to support	Higher-income and lowest-income more likely than middle-income to support	High-income and low-income more likely than middle-income to support
Occupation	Managers and service workers most likely to support	Not included	Not included
Unemployed	Not included	Not included	Less likely to support
Public employee in household	Less likely to support	Not included	Less likely to support
Renters	Less likely to support	Less likely to support	Less likely to support
Tax share of owners	Mixed relationship	Not included	Not included

Who Supports Tax Limitations

Attitudes			
Political ideology	Conservatives more likely to support	Conservatives more likely to support	Not included
Scope of government	Believers that government should limit its scope, more likely to support	Not included	Not included
Attitudes to welfare recipients	Believers that welfare recipients could work more likely to support	Not included	Not included
Party registration	Not included	Democrats less likely to support	Democrats less likely to support
Municipal Characteristics			
Anticipated revenue loss	Higher revenue loss, more likely to support	Not included	Not included
Prelimitation tax rate	Higher rate, less likely to support	Not included	Not included
Spending levels	Higher per capita noneducation spending more likely to support	Not included	Not included
Population diversity	Higher percentage nonwhite, less likely to support	Not included	Not included
Tax base diversity	Higher percentage commercial and industrial, less likely to support	Not included	Not included

[a] All findings are based on multivariate techniques and thus estimate the relationship between any one variable and support for the limitation measure controlling for all other variables included in the equation.
[b] Based on Citrin, Jack. "Do People Want Something for Nothing: Public Opinion on Taxes and Government Spending." *National Tax Journal* XXXII (2 Supplement) (June 1979): 113–129.
[c] Based on Courant, Paul M., et al., "Why Voters Support Tax Limitation Amendments: The Michigan Case." *National Tax Journal*, XXXIII (March 1980). Also printed in Ladd, Helen F., and Tideman, T. Nicolaus, Eds., *Tax and Expenditure Limitations* (Washington, DC: The Urban Institute Press, 1981). pp. 37–72.

around the average probability of supporting Proposition 2½. This implies that the Massachusetts electorate was not divided along demographic and attitudinal lines into two groups, one strongly opposed to and one strongly in favor of the tax limitation measure. It suggests instead that most voters are characterized by a combination of attributes that pulled them in opposite directions on the issue of tax limitation. This does not mean that the population was not split along other dimensions, however. In our earlier research, a clear division between supporters and opponents of tax limitation emerged in terms of voters' views toward tax reform, spending, and government efficiency.[10] The point is that these views about public sector issues and how Proposition 2½ would affect them are not highly correlated with the voters' personal and municipal characteristics examined here.

The conclusion of cross-cutting pressures on voters is consistent with the fact that support for tax limitation was distributed broadly across almost all demographic subgroups of the population. The exceptions, however, should not be ignored; being a renter, being black or female, receiving welfare, and living in a city with a high tax rate all contribute to the probability of a "no" vote. Thus, voters characterized by all these attributes had strong incentives to oppose the measure, with little offsetting pressure in the other direction. While the total number of such people may be small, the intensity of their opposition should not be overlooked.

The Massachusetts results also show that basic attitudes and political orientations play an important role in explaining voting behavior, even after controlling for demographic and municipal characteristics. This finding is consistent with other studies, especially those of political scientists, that emphasize the importance of "symbolic politics"—that is, political predispositions or attitudes that reflect an earlier socialization process—over narrow economic self-interest as a determinant of policy positions and voting behavior.[11] The line between narrow self-interest and "symbolic politics" is hard to draw in the case of tax limitation measures, however. Political orientations and views about the role of government fall into the latter category, while homeownership status and government employment fall into the self-interest category. Demographic characteristics such as sex, age, race, religion, and occupation may be proxies for economic self-interest, for prior socialization, or for both. Hence, precise quantification of the relative roles of self-interest and "symbolic politics" in the Massachusetts tax limitation vote is not possible. Nonetheless, the results imply that the vote in Massachusetts—and by extension in other states as well—should not be understood simply in terms of narrow self-interest.

Finally, Proposition 2½ passed in a statewide election, but its major intent was the reduction of tax revenues available to local governments. The variation in impacts across communities raises the possibility that the proposition imposed severe fiscal constraints on some communities against the wishes of local residents. There is little evidence to support that view. As Table 1 shows, in each of the categories of communities examined—categories defined by first-year revenue losses and pre-Proposition 2½ tax rates—a majority of voters supported the tax limitation measure. At the same time, however, the linear probability analysis indicates that if all voters had lived in communities subject to the severe cutbacks faced by the cities with the highest tax rates, the statewide vote might have turned out differently. In this sense then, the actual vote for Proposition 2½ can be interpreted in part as a way for voters in the fiscally strong communities to benefit at the expense of those in the fiscally weak communities.

APPENDIX Support for proposition 2½: Linear probability model.[a]

	Coefficient	t Value[b]
Community Characteristics		
First year revenue loss[c]	+0.0065	+1.87
Communities with 1981 tax rate[d]		
Less than 2.5%	Base	—
2.5–3.9%	−0.07	−1.10
4.0–4.9%	−0.06	−0.86
5.0% or more	−0.16	−2.02
Per pupil spending on public education[e]	−0.00003	−0.60
Per household spending on noneducation services[f]	+0.0001	+1.98
Percentage of households below poverty level[g]	+0.66	+0.79
Percentage of households headed by nonwhites[h]	−0.94	−1.77
Percentage of real estate revenue from commercial and industrial properties[i]	+0.27	+2.13
Personal Demographic and Household Characteristics		
Tenure status		
Renters—total		
Who never owned, no plans to	−0.14	−2.52
Who ever owned	−0.01	−0.17
Who plan to own in next five years	−0.07	−1.08
Homeowners (by local tax share)[j]		
Whose property taxes relative to those paid in the local community are:		
Very low	Base	—
Low	+0.07	+1.52
High	−0.01	−0.12
Very high	+0.07	+1.40

Appendix *(continued from previous page)*

	Coefficient	t Value[b]
Taxes not reported	−0.02	−0.30
Neither rent nor own	−0.07	−0.66
Government employee in household		
Local public school employee in household	−0.27	−4.95
Other local government employee in household	−0.32	−6.46
State or county government employee in household	−0.12	−1.61
No local or state government employee in household	Base	—
Services used		
Public elementary and secondary education	+0.01	+0.17
Private schools	−0.03	−0.52
Parks or after school programs	−0.07	−2.23
Elderly, mental health, or special education services	−0.05	−1.18
Welfare	−0.08	−1.25
Stage in life cycle		
Young adult, no young children present in household	−0.001	−0.02
Children present in household, oldest under 6	−0.01	−0.14
Children present in household, oldest 6–17	−0.01	−0.13
Older adults, no children present in household	Base	—
Elderly adults (60 or over), no children in household	+0.08	+1.67
Household income[k]		
Under $10,000	−0.08	−1.44
$10,000 to under $20,000	Base	—
$20,000 to under $30,000	−0.04	−1.21
$30,000 to under $50,000	+0.04	+1.07
$50,000 or more	+0.07	+0.96
Education of respondent		
Less than high school	Base	—
High school degree	+0.01	+0.25
Some college	−0.05	−0.90
College degree	−0.09	−1.46
Graduate school	−0.13	−1.86
Occupation of household head[l]		
Managerial	+0.09	+2.11
Professional	+0.03	+0.75

Appendix *(continued from previous page)*

	Coefficient	t Value[b]
Clerical, sales	+0.05	+1.14
Service	+0.09	+1.48
Blue collar	Base	—
Not reported, no occupation	+0.01	+0.28
Sex		
Male	Base	—
Female	−0.08	−2.88
Race		
Nonwhite	−0.11	−1.44
White	Base	—
Religion		
Catholic	−0.02	−0.67
Jewish	−0.16	−2.75
Protestant	Base	—
Attitudes and Ideology		
Self-identified political ideology[m]		
Conservative	+0.01	+0.18
Middle of the road	Base	—
Liberal	−0.11	−2.95
Attitude toward welfare recipients		
Believe welfare recipients could find jobs if they really tried	+0.12	+3.52
Believe welfare recipients could not find jobs if they really tried	Base	—
Government's role *vis-à-vis* individuals[n]		
Individuals should rely less on government	+0.10	+3.42
Government should help individuals	Base	—
Constant	+0.51	

[a] Based on 1182 respondents for whom complete information was available. Estimated using ordinary least squares. The dependent variable takes on the value of 1 for a "yes" vote and 0 for a "no" vote. Variables enter the equation in two forms—continuous linear variables and binary 0–1 variables.

[b] The standard tests for the statistical significance of the estimated parameters in a linear probability model are only approximate. Nonetheless, the entries in this column indicate the relative precision with which the coefficients have been estimated.

[c] Anticipated 1982 revenue loss, including both property taxes and auto excise taxes, expressed as a percentage of 1981 tax revenues in respondent's city or town.

[d] 1981 full-value tax rate in respondent's community as estimated by the Massachusetts Department of Revenue.

(continued on following page)

Support for proposition 2½: Linear probability model.[a]

[e] 1981 operating expenditures on elementary and secondary education per public school pupil in respondent's city or town.
[f] 1981 nonschool expenditures per household in respondent's city or town.
[g] Percentage of households in respondent's city or town with income below the poverty level.
[h] Percentage of residents in respondent's city or town who are not white.
[i] Assessed value of commercial and industrial property as a proportion of total assessed valuation in the respondent's city or town.
[j] Local tax share is defined as the property taxes paid by the respondent's household as a percentage of average per household property taxes in the respondent's community. The four categories correspond to (1) less than 75% of the community average, (2) 75–100% of the community average, (3) 100–125% of the community average, and (4) greater than 125% of the community average.
[k] Missing income data were estimated using a multivariate procedure described in Appendix C of Helen F. Ladd and Julie Boatright Wilson, *Tax Limitations in Massachusetts*, Report to National Institute of Education, 1982.
[l] Household head is defined as the male in joint households and the respondent in single-adult households. Research suggests that in joint households, status and economic situation are more likely to be defined by the male's occupation than the female's.
[m] Respondent's political self-description recorded on a five-point scale in which very conservative = 1, fairly conservative = 2, middle of the road = 3, fairly liberal = 4, and very liberal = 5.
[n] Dummy variable formed from two attitude statements: "People expect too many services from the government" and "The government should make sure that each family has enough to live on." Scores on the latter statement were reversed to make it consistent with the first statement. All attitude items were scored on a four-point scale: disagree a lot = 1, disagree a little = 2, agree a little = 3, agree a lot = 4. Respondents believing the government should have a more restrictive role, those with mean scores greater than 2.5 were assigned a value of 1.

This article is part of a larger study funded by the National Institute of Education, grant no. NIE-G-81-0006, with supplemental funds from the Lincoln Institute of Land Policy, Cambridge, Massachusetts. The authors are grateful to Claire Christopherson for her expert computer programming.

HELEN F. LADD is an associate professor of City and Regional Planning, Kennedy School of Government, Harvard University.
JULIE B. WILSON is an assistant professor of City and Regional Planning. Kennedy School of Government, Harvard University.

NOTES
1. This topic has also been studied by academicians. For a recent example, see Gramlich, Edward M., and Rubinfeld, Daniel L., "Voting On Public Spending: Differences Between Public Employees, Transfer Recipients and Private Workers." *Journal of Policy Analysis and Management*, 1(4) (Summer 1982): 516–534. See also Citrin, Jack, "Do People Want Something for Nothing: Public Opinion on Taxes and Government Spending." *National Tax Journal*, XXXII (2 Supplement) (June 1979): 113–130; Courant, Paul N., Gramlich, Edward M., and Rubinfeld, Daniel L., "Why Voters Support Tax Limitation Amendments: The Michigan Case." *National Tax Journal*, XXXIII(1) (March 1980): 1–20, and Lowery, David, and Sigelman, Lee, "Understanding The Tax Revolt: Eight Explanations." *The American Political Science Review*, 75(4) (December 1981): 963–974.
2. These results are reported in Ladd, Helen F., and Wilson, Julie Boatright, "Proposition 2½: Explaining the Vote." Research Report

R81-1, Urban Planning, Policy Analysis and Administration, John F. Kennedy School of Government, Harvard University, April 1981, and "Why Voters Support Tax Limitations: Evidence from Massachusetts' Proposition 2½." *National Tax Journal*, XXXV(2) (June 1982): 121–148.
3. The model expresses household income as a function of the age, education level, and race of the respondent and the sex, work status, and occupation of each adult head in the household. Sex, occupation, and work status are interacted to allow for the possibility that the contribution to household income made by a worker in a particular occupation varies by full- or part-time work status and with the sex of the worker. Details are available from the authors.
4. Gramlich and Rubinfeld, *op. cit.*, pp. 516–534.
5. For a complete description of Proposition 2½ and its first-year impacts, see Bradbury, Katharine L., Ladd, Helen F., and Christophersen, Claire, "Proposition 2½: Initial Impacts, Parts I and II." *New England Economic Review*, (January/February 1982): 13–24, and (March/April 1982): 46–62.
6. This measure overstates the effect in those communities that had not recently revalued their taxable property since the official estimates of true tax bases tend to be low and, hence, the estimates of tax rates tend to be high. Despite this overstatement, however, a community's 1981 tax rate captures what was known to voters at the time of the election about the proposition's full effects on property tax levies.
7. This estimate is simply a weighted average of the differences between the predicted probabilities of a "yes" vote in each tax rate category and the predicted probability in the high tax-rate category, where the weights are the proportions of the sample in each category.
8. See, for example, Kuttner, Robert, *The Revolt of the Haves* (New York: Simon and Schuster, 1980).
9. See Citrin, *op. cit.*, for the California results and Courant, Gramlich, and Rubinfield, *op. cit.*, for the Michigan results. See also Gramlich and Rubinfeld, *op cit.*, for further discussion of support for tax limitation in Michigan.
10. Ladd and Wilson, *op cit.*
11. See Sears, David O., et al., "Self-Interest vs. Symbolic Politics in Policy Attitudes and Presidential Voting." *The American Political Science Review*, 74(3) (1980): 670–684.

[15]

THE TAX EXPENDITURE CONCEPT AFTER 25 YEARS
Helen F. Ladd, President, National Tax Association

More than 25 years ago, Stanley Surrey, a well known tax administrator and professor of Law at Harvard Law School and also former president of the National Tax Association, introduced the concept which is the subject of my talk today, the concept of tax expenditures.

I take on this topic with some trepidation as many people in the audience and in the Association have had much more direct experience with the concept than I have. One advantage I have is a fresh perspective. Not being a player in the historical debate about and implementation of the concept, I have not staked out a position in the past. In addition, my perspective differs from that of some other participants in that my interests extend beyond the federal level, where most of the conceptual thinking has been focused, to the state and local level as well. I am aware that tax expenditure analysis is not the hottest topic among scholars at this point. Nonetheless, the question of tax expenditures is alive and well among the practitioner community. For example, a June 1994 General Accounting Office study calls for more scrutiny of tax expenditures at the federal level and a forthcoming study by the Center on Budget and Policy Priorities is about to call for much heavier use of the concept at the state level.

In one sense, tax expenditures can be viewed simply as a governmental accounting and reporting convention. Before 1967, we had no explicit way of accounting for a whole range of provisions in the tax code that functioned like expenditures. Surrey persuasively argued that many of these special provisions of the tax code were essentially equivalent to taxing people or activities at the full tax rate and then using the revenue to subsidize the taxpayer or activity, and hence that they functioned like expenditures. However, as pointed out by Surrey, the absence of an accounting mechanism for these components of the tax code meant that, compared to other budgetary elements, they received little attention and scrutiny. To deal with this limitation, Surrey, in his capacity as Assistant Secretary of the Treasury, produced the first tax expenditure "budget" or listing of these provisions in 1968. The requirement that federal tax expenditures be listed and published annually was subsequently enshrined in the Budget Control and Impoundment Act of 1974. Since then, many states have followed suit and published tax expenditure reports and many countries have done so as well.

However, as elaborated by Surrey (1973) and later by Surrey and McDaniel (1985), the concept of tax expenditures embodies much more than simply the provision of information in the form of a list of tax expenditures. It also represents an analytical approach to certain provisions of the tax code that contrasts sharply with the standard tax policy approach. By converting what might appear to be problems of tax reform to problems of spending reform, the tax expenditure mind set involves asking a new set of questions, namely those associated with spending programs such as: what is the goal of the program, how cost effective is the approach, what are the distributional implications of the program, and should the program be replaced with a direct expenditure program?

When I was first exposed to the concept of tax expenditures in the early 1970s, I found it a compelling and powerful idea, and in some ways I still do. In particular, I was excited by the prospect that such an apparently simple and obvious concept might open up a whole new way of thinking about the tax system that could potentially lead to some dramatic changes. People had long understood that tax preferences were hard to dislodge. I accepted — perhaps somewhat naively — the idea that if people could simply be induced to accept Surrey's proposition that tax preferences were virtually equivalent to expenditures, they might be easier to change. The logic was that not only would they be subject to more scrutiny, but the right questions about their effectiveness would be asked and opposition to their elimination would be muted by the substitution, when appropriate, of direct spending programs (Surrey and McDaniel, 1985, p. 25)

I am clearly not alone in finding the concept powerful. For example Richard Pomp (1988, p. 66) called it a "powerful analytical tool that has revamped traditional ways of viewing a tax system"; David Bradford, though critical of some aspects of tax expenditure reporting, nonetheless concludes that "there can be no doubt about the fundamental soundness of the enterprise" (1988, p. 428.); and in 1979 a Canadian former cabinet minister labeled the concept "the major innovation in tax and public finance during the last twenty or thirty years" (cited in Surrey and McDaniel, 1985, p. 29). However, although the listing of tax expenditures is now common procedure at the federal level and in many states, the concept has clearly not fulfilled the vision of Surrey and others of generating a major transformation of budgetary, tax policy and administration. My main goal today is to evaluate the tax expenditure concept in light of 25 years of experience.

My plan is to begin with a brief overview of the status of tax expenditure reporting at both the federal and state levels. The bulk of my talk then focuses on the evaluation of tax expenditure analysis — 1) as a reporting and accounting tool, 2) as a pathway to tax reform, and 3) as a way to achieve budgetary control. In order not to keep you in suspense about my conclusions, I will reveal some of them at this point. First, despite a number of shortcomings related to implementation, tax expenditure reporting is decidedly appropriate and useful as an accounting concept. Second, contrary to Stanley Surrey's hopes and expectations, tax expenditure analysis has been close to a complete failure as a pathway to tax reform. And third, it has been only marginally more successful as a tool of budget control. Despite some of its limitations, I remain a supporter of tax expenditure reporting and analysis, but without Stanley Surrey's passion, commitment to, and optimism about tax expenditures as an engine of tax reform.

Current Status of Tax Expenditure Reporting

As defined in the Budget Act of 1974,[2] tax expenditures are " . . . those revenue losses attributable to provisions of the Federal tax laws which allow a special exclusion, exemption or deduction from gross income or which provide a special credit, a preferential rate of tax or a deferral of tax liability" (P.L. 93-3, sec. 3(a)(3)). Of course, the concept of special exemptions or credits is meaningful only with respect to a baseline tax structure.

Consistent with the law, both the U.S. Treasury and the Joint Committee on Taxation have produced annual estimates of tax expenditures related to the individual and the corporate income tax since 1975. In addition, the Treasury lists tax expenditures related to estate and gift taxes.[3] However, because they use different baseline tax structures, their lists of tax expenditures differ slightly. The Joint Committee on Taxation defines tax expenditures with respect to a normal income tax structure patterned on a comprehensive income tax. The Treasury, in contrast, uses a reference tax as the baseline and limits tax expenditures to special exceptions in the tax code that serve programmatic functions. Starting with the 1982 budget, the Treasury complicated the situation further by adding a 8set of outlay equivalents which more accurately measure what comparable expenditure programs would cost. Although a conceptual step forward, these outlay equivalents may make the tax expenditure concept even more confusing to policymakers (Neubig, 1988).

Tax expenditure reporting is complicated further by the hazards of aggregating estimates of individual tax expenditures into totals, either by functional category or overall. The problem here is that the individual items interact with one another so that the removal of one tax expenditure may increase or decrease the revenue loss from another. Only by ignoring this aggregation problem can I say anything at all about the trends in federal tax expenditures relative to the other two main components of the budget, discretionary spending, and mandatory spending. As shown in figure 1, between 1975 and 1987, the reported sum of federal tax expenditures grew faster that either discretionary spending or entitlement spending so that in 1987 tax expenditures actually exceeded direct discretionary spending. The Tax Reform Act of 1986 then dramatically reduced tax expenditures. Since 1989, tax expenditures have been growing in real terms faster than discretionary spending, but noticeably less fast than entitlements.[4]

At the state level, California was the first state to adopt legislation calling for a tax expenditure report and published its first one in FY 1976. As of today, 17 states have relatively comprehensive tax expenditure reports. An additional 13 states have reports that are partial or are produced intermittently (Center for the Study of Budget and Policy Priorities, forthcoming report). Unlike the federal report which historically has focused on the individual income and the corporate income tax, the state reports typically cover a broader set of taxes, including general and selective sales taxes, and in some states, the local property tax. Putting together a tax expenditure budget at the state level can be a big task. Typically the task is performed by the Department of Revenue or the Budget Office or a combination of the two. First, the state needs to define what it means by a tax expenditure in the context of each tax. Unlike income taxes for which there is a relatively clear normative standard (which a state may or may not choose to use), the starting point for most of the other taxes is much less clear. For example, with respect to the general sales tax, how should one treat food, which is often exempted for distributional reasons, or services, which historically have not been included, but whose inclusion is increasingly under discussion? Or in Minnesota, how should one deal with the fact that the property tax is classified into more than 60 categories? As of 1985, most of the states with tax expenditure reports listed between 150 and 300 tax expenditures in contrast to about 135 at the federal level. For many of these categories, the state had never before collected the data and in many cases the data had to be developed from scratch. Some of the state reports include supplemental information beyond the revenue losses such as the purpose of the tax expenditure, a list of the primary beneficiaries, and conflicts with other state or tax programs. Others, however, are much more limited (Benker 1992).

To summarize, in one sense, we have come a long way with respect to tax expenditure reporting. The concept has been enshrined in federal law and many state governments have adopted tax expenditure reports. But a closer look suggests that the picture may not be quite so rosy as this description suggests and the full potential of tax expenditures as an analytical tool has not been achieved.

Tax Expenditures as a Budgeting and Accounting Tool

The most striking fact about tax expenditures is that they are taxes that are neither assessed nor collected. Putting aside for a moment the difficulties involved in measuring something that is not collected, the first question is do we need to account for them at all? The answer depends on the function of the public accounting system. Historically, its primary function was one of control. When individuals were giving up resources to the public sector, they presumably had a right to know how their funds were being spent. By this logic, tax revenues and the spending they financed had to be accounted for. In contrast, when tax provisions lead to taxes not being collected, nothing is being taken from individuals, and therefore there is nothing to account for.

However, if one takes a broader view of the functions of a public accounting system, as I do, a different conclusion emerges. In particular, if the function is to document the impacts of the public sector on the economy, and one accepts Surrey's crucial insight that many provisions of the tax code are functionally equivalent to expenditures, then it is clearly desirable to account not only for taxes that are collected but also for many of those that are not collected.[5] Moreover, such taxes not collected should be accounted for in the same way we account for public expenditures, namely grouped by functional spending category. In principle, the classification by functional spending area facilitates discussions about the role of tax policy in various policy areas, such as, for example, health reform (for example, see Henry Aaron, 1994).

More generally, the concept of tax expenditures represents only a partial response to the larger problem of an outdated division of accounts into spending and taxes. Historically, when the main function of government was the provision of goods and services, the distinction between spending and taxes was relatively clear cut (Allen Schick, 1986). With so much of government spending now in the form of transfers rather than purchases, the distinction between taxes and spending is blurred.[6]

I find myself agreeing with the conclusion of Neil Bruce in his summary of a 1988 conference in Canada on tax expenditures that "The enormous symmetry between the distributive function of tax policy and the distributive function of the transfer system begs for them to be reported in similar ways" (p.9). Perhaps, the ultimate solution is to follow his suggestion of a four-part grouping which would replace our current three part grouping of spending, taxes, and tax expenditures. The four groups would be defined by the following four objectives: 1) revenue raising 2) purchases of goods and services for government use 3) transfers of purchasing power, or goods in kind, for distributional purposes, and 4) providing economic incentives by altering relative prices. The latter two categories would include both tax and spending provisions. Thus, what we now call tax expenditures would be reclassified into two subgroups and paired with appropriate direct spending programs in those areas. I have no illusions that this approach would be easy to implement. For example, at the local level, one would have to decide if preferential treatment of agricultural land under the property tax is to be treated as a transfer of purchasing power to farmers or as an incentive to maintain land in farming. And we would need to rethink Surrey's original decision, which has been maintained, to define the graduated rates for the income tax as part of the basic tax structure rather than as a provision to redistribute income.

Even this four-part reclassification would not provide a complete accounting of the impact of the public sector on the economy. Like taxes not collected, government regulation and unfunded mandates also affect the economy. For example, if the federal government requires a private firm to install and pay for equipment to reduce pollution, the transaction is comparable to having the federal government collect taxes from the firm and then spend the money on the equipment. Consequently, the case for counting unfunded mandates as implicit spending may be as strong as the case for identifying in our accounting system implicit expenditures accomplished through the tax code.[7]

However, the observation that the tax expenditure concept does not solve all the problems of public sector accounting should not detract from the validity and potential power of tax expenditures as an accounting concept. Of greater concern in practice is the difficulty of measuring tax expenditures. The definitional problems are legion and were alluded to earlier. The key problem is the specification of the benchmark tax system, departure from which defines a tax expenditure. Even if one accepts the Haig-Simons normative standard as Surrey did, one has to make lots of compromises and pragmatic decisions such as how to treat unrealized capital gains or imputed income from owner occupied housing. If one rejects the Haig-Simons standard or focuses on taxes other than the income tax, defining the benchmark becomes somewhat arbitrary, but, I would argue not unmanageable. Unfortunately the disagreement between the Treasury and the Joint Committee on Taxation on how to define tax expenditures, plus Treasury's practice since 1982 of reporting outlay equivalents as well as revenue foregone, may have confused policymakers and may have limited the use of the tax expenditure concept as a policy tool (Neubig, 1988).

In sum, it makes a lot of sense to account for taxes not collected and I find Surrey's term for such tax provisions, tax expenditures, extremely useful. In my view, the term tax expenditure is far better than the more pejorative term, tax loophole, and more descriptive than the term, tax preference. Some conservatives object to the term tax expenditure *budget* because of its implication of governmental control over revenues that it has no claim over. I find myself in some sympathy with this objection, but it can be easily dealt with by forgoing the term budget in favor of a more neutral term such as tax expenditure report.

Tax Expenditure Analysis as a Pathway to Tax Reform

As spelled out eloquently and forcefully in his book, *Pathways to Tax Reform*, Stanley Surrey hoped that his new approach would lead to the ultimate elimination or replacement of most tax expenditures. The themes of the book were clear: 1) that, although many tax provisions function like spending programs, they are not subject to the same scrutiny as direct spending programs 2) that most tax expenditures are inherently unfair because they typically generate more benefits to higher income than to lower income households 3) that direct spending programs are almost always preferable to tax expenditures, and 4) finally, that most tax expenditures should be eliminated or replaced with more effective spending programs.

From today's perspective and the observation that most tax expenditures are alive and well, I was somewhat surprised as I reread Surrey's 1973 book at the strength of his opposition to specific tax expenditures. His argument was clearly not simply the one that I typically teach to my students, namely, that it makes sense to evaluate tax expenditures as expenditure programs so that tradeoffs can made between direct spending programs and tax expenditures. Instead, he went the next step of doing the analysis and concluding forcefully that most tax expenditures were undesirable and should either be eliminated outright or replaced with a direct spending program. By drawing attention to tax expenditures, he clearly hoped to reform the tax system, where reform meant simplifying the federal income tax to focus on its main goal of revenue raising and bringing the tax base in line with the Haig-Simons concept of comprehensive income.

A review of the evidence suggests that Surrey's aspirations for tax expenditure analysis as a tool of tax reform have not been met. One circumstantial piece of evidence is the growth in U.S. tax expenditures over time and, in particular, the new tax expenditures that were included in the 1981 Tax Act. But what, you might ask, about the Tax Reform Act of 1986 which eliminated or modified at least 10 major tax expenditures and indirectly affected the revenue losses from others by reducing marginal tax rates (see CBO, March 1988 and Neubig and Joulfaian,1988). Here the interpretations differ. On the one hand, previous analysis of specific tax expenditure provisions showing that particular subsidies were poorly targeted, excessive, or unnecessary undoubtedly influenced which provisions were cut or modified. On the other, the constraint that the Act be revenue neutral forced policymakers into the traditional tax policy approach of devoting all revenues from base broadening to the reduction in tax rates. In contrast, a tax expenditure mind set would have asked expenditure-type questions about each provision and would have explored the possibility of replacing certain tax expenditures with modified, more efficient direct expenditures (see McDaniel).[8]

A second type of evidence comes from Canada. There, the tax expenditure approach apparently had an impact, but in the wrong direction. The logic of the upside-down distributional effect of many tax expenditures led Canada to convert some deductions, including those for dependents, into tax credits. The Canadians erred, however, in that the provisions they changed were components of the basic tax structure rather than true tax expenditures and, therefore, should have remained as deductions (Richard Bird, 1988).

A third type of evidence comes from the state of California. In its 1983-84 report, the California Department of Finance recommended eliminating the 10-year old requirement to report tax expenditures. The first reason they cited was that the legislature had ignored over 90 percent of the recommendations for repeal of specific tax expenditures made by the Department over the previous 10 years and that special interest groups had continued to be effective in securing the enactment of new tax expenditures. In fact, some people believed that the publication of the reports had stimulated the demand for new tax expenditures. The report cited nearly one hundred new tax expenditures and extensions of existing tax expenditures enacted since 1972. Although the legislature responded by setting up legislative structures and procedures for regular review of tax expenditures, it still remains difficult in California to reduce or eliminate them.

While I make no claims for the completeness of this evidence, I personally am persuaded that, contrary to Surrey's view, the tax expenditure concept has not been the route to significant tax reform in the past and is not likely to be in the future. Is this outcome surprising? I think not, for four interrelated reasons.

The first reason is that tax expenditure items constitute an appropriate list of items for the purposes of tax reform discussions for the income tax only to the extent that people buy into the underlying normative standard that serves as the benchmark. At the time Surrey was writing, support was relatively widespread in the intellectual community for the Haig-Simons measure as a normative standard. However, even then, not all people bought into the concept as evidenced by the lively debate between Surrey and Bittker (1968). Since then the situation has become more murky as theoretical work in the field of optimal tax theory questioned the efficiency properties of a broad based tax of the Haig-Simons type and economists and tax lawyers became increasingly enamored of the consumption tax as a replacement for the income tax. If acceptance of the tax expenditure concept for purposes of tax reform means acceptance of the underlying normative standard, then more and more people have a reason to feel uneasy with the concept.

An alternative explanation starts from a more political perspective. According to this perspective (see Winer and Heltich, 1988), the tax system is the equilibrium outcome of a political process. Even if tax provisions are relabeled as spending items, there is often little incentive for anyone to try to change them. The political problem is exacerbated by the fact that the bulk of tax expenditures provide benefits to large groups of middle class taxpayers. The biggest tax expenditure items include, for example, deductibility of mortgage interest on owner-occupied housing, net exclusions of pension contributions, exclusions of employer contributions for health insurance premiums, exclusion of the bulk of social security benefits, and deduction of state and local income and property taxes. Eliminating any of these provisions in the name of tax reform is unlikely to be politically popular, to say the least. A third explanation deals with institutions and battles over political turf. Particularly problematic in the U.S. federal context, for example, is the fact that converting a tax expenditure into a direct spending program would require the tax writing committees to surrender jurisdiction to other committees. During the early 1980s, Canada tried to address the institutional challenge by setting up 9 envelopes of spending categories that included both direct expenditures and tax expenditures. The Canadian system was designed to force ministers to make tradeoffs between the two forms of spending. For a variety of reasons including some related to accounting problems and the lack of commitment from senior finance officials, the system did not last long (Poddar, 1988). Clearly some form of institutional mechanism is needed, but turf battles and political considerations being what they are, major changes in the near future are unlikely.

A fourth and final possibility is that Surrey may have been wrong in claiming the unconditional superiority of direct spending over tax expenditures. Critics of Surrey's position have purported to show various advantages of the tax expenditure mechanism in certain circumstances. These include, for example, that for means-tested programs, tax expenditures minimize stigma, that the absence of red tape often gives tax expenditures administrative advantages over direct subsidies, and the tax system provides a prompt and efficient mechanism for informing potential applicants of relevant government programs, such as broad-based business incentive programs. While these claims are not without criticism (see, for example, comments by Neil Brooks on Kesselman, 1988), I believe they have some merit.[9] Even more compelling is the political economy argument made by Ronald King (1984) that tax expenditures are often popular because they resolve the conflict between the liberals' desire to have the government do something and conservatives' inherent belief in the market mechanism. Recent support for the expansion of the earned income tax credit to help low-income workers but not for welfare spending illustrates the power of this argument. In sum, many tax expenditures are likely to be hard to dislodge because they serve an important political economy role.

The Concept of Tax Expenditures as a Budget Control Tool

The identification of tax expenditures serves as a tool for controlling budgets and deficits by broadening the set of options considered for deficit reduction. Thus, in addition to considering spending cuts or tax rate increases as a means of reducing deficits, policymakers can also consider reducing tax expenditures, which reduce the deficit by generating more tax revenue. The routine inclusion of many tax expenditure items on the Congressional Budget Office lists of options for deficit reduction confirms their role in national budgetary debates. Similarly at the state level, reductions in tax expenditures are often discussed as a revenue source (Harris and Hicks, 1992). In neither case is the potential of the concept fully developed.

Current federal budgetary procedures appropriately subject new or expanded tax expenditure programs to the pay-as-you go requirements of other direct spending programs in that revenue losses must be offset by revenue gains. However, existing tax expenditures receive differentially favorable treatment. Like entitlement programs, growth in tax expenditures caused by increases in the favored activity is not subject to pay-as-you-go provisions. Within the budget process, the major pressure for scrutiny of individual tax expenditures comes from the fact that the budget committees stipulate a minimum level of revenue the tax committees must raise. Various proposals for mechanisms to limit or roll back the aggregate amount of tax expenditures have been discussed but, for a variety of reasons, typically receive little support (see GAO, 1994). One basic problem is the difficulty of aggregating individual tax expenditure items into a total to be capped.

Even greater barriers exist in some states, as is illustrated by California. In that state, tax increases require a 2/3 favorable vote. Hence, because a reduction in tax expenditures is treated as an increase in taxes rather than a cut in spending, it is harder to cut tax expenditures than it is to cut direct spending. This 2/3 requirement plus other characteristics of tax expenditures have meant that during recessions and periods of budget deficits, the system is biased toward cuts in direct spending and away from cuts in tax expenditures. For example, during the state's budget shortfall in the early 1980s, tax expenditures were not reduced at all. During the 1991-92 recession, cuts in tax expenditures accounted for only 1/10 of the deficit reduction measures and in the following two years of budget shortfalls, tax expenditure cuts accounted for only 3 percent of the deficit reduction actions (Center on Budget Priorities and Policy, pp. 65-66.)

In summary, the identification of tax expenditures helps make them, along with direct expenditures, fair game for cuts in times of budgetary shortfalls. However, because they are still typically treated more like provisions of the tax code than like direct expenditures, they continue to be harder to cut than direct spending. I support the recent GAO report and a forthcoming report on state tax expenditures pushing for greater scrutiny of tax expenditures especially in times of budgetary shortfalls.

Conclusions

My first conclusion is that the tax expenditure concept is extremely useful as a conceptual tool for addressing a major component of government activity. Because these special tax provisions are functionally similar to direct spending, we need to keep track of and to scrutinize them despite the fact that no taxes are collected. Hence, I would encourage those states without tax expenditure lists to invest some resources in identifying and measuring tax expenditures. To conserve resources, states may want to identify all tax expenditures but attach dollar values only to the largest ones. Such lists should not be oversold as the panacea to budgetary or tax structure problems. Nonetheless such an investment should serve to improve the capacity of state officials to understand and analyze their tax and spending system.

My second conclusion is that, contrary to Surrey's hopes and aspirations, most tax expenditures themselves are here to stay. Some are hard to dislodge because they provide benefits to broad groups of people and others because they reflect the will of a powerful coalition of liberals who want to do something and conservatives who want to work through private market. As a consequence, we might as well accept the fact that we will never achieve Surrey's goal of a tax system that serves only the revenue raising goal. Somewhat ironically, the fact that we have not and will not meet his goal of eliminating them is what continues to make the tax expenditure concept so important. Given the strong historical, institutional, and political pressures to continue using the tax system not just as a revenue-raising device, but also as a policy tool, it is essential that we have a way to account for and to scrutinize the special provisions that provide incentives or subsidies to particular activities or groups of individuals.

Final Thoughts—Tax Expenditures and the Mission of the NTA

I chose to focus on tax expenditures today in part because, like the National Tax Association, the concept is potentially meaningful at all levels of government — federal, state, and local — as well as for governments around the world. In addition, the concept is of interest to all the constituent groups of the association: academics, government officials, and the business community. The concept highlights a number of fundamental questions that are central to our association.

1. Can or should tax policy ever be separated from expenditure policy?
2. What is the purpose of tax policy — revenue-raising alone, or revenue raising and as a policy tool to achieve other social goals?
3. How should we think about the size and impact of government?
4. Should a basic tax base be defined and, if so, how?
5. What is the role of governmental institutions in tax policy analysis and discussion?
6. How do accounting and estimating techniques affect the use and acceptability of tax policy concepts and practices?

The exciting thing about the National Tax Association is that it provides a forum where people with differing perspectives can ask and explore these types of fundamental questions. I am pleased to have been part of the Association for the past 20 years and proud to have served as its president this past year.

Thank you very much. [Applause]

[This concludes the Presidential Address.]

There being no further business, the President declared the meeting adjourned.

ENDNOTES

1. I thank the following people for their thoughtful comments on an earlier draft of this paper: Henry Aaron, William Gale, Rosemary Marcuss, Andrew Reschovsky, Pearl Richardson, Fritz Stocker, Emil Sunley, and Joseph White.

2. Officially the Congressional Budget and Impoundment Control Act of 1974.

3. In a recent article in the *National Tax Journal*, Bruce Davie (1994) of the U.S. Treasury has extended federal tax expenditure analysis by identifying 244 tax expenditure provisions in the federal excise tax code. These tax expenditures represent deviations from the "normal structure" of excise taxes serving nine different purposes.

4. It should be noted that the changes in the tax expenditure totals reflect not only explicit congressional decisions about tax expenditures but also many other factors such as changes in marginal tax rates, changes in the economy, and, in the recent period, rapid growth in health care costs.

5. There is no compelling reason to account for revenue foregone related to those provisions of the tax code that represent part of the basic structure of the tax code, such as personal exemptions and standard deductions.

6. The refundable earned income tax credit highlights the confusion. Because it is implemented through the tax side, it was initially viewed by the Joint Committee on Taxation (JCT) and the Congressional Budget Office (CBO) fully as a tax expenditure, albeit in two parts, the nonrefundable and the refundable portion given to those who had insufficient tax liability against which to credit the payment. Subsequently, however, the accounting was changed to treat the nonrefundable part as a tax expenditure and the refundable portion as a direct spending program under the category of income security to reflect its treatment under the First Concurrent Budget Resolution for the 1979 budget. (Surrey and McDaniel, 1985, p. 40)

7. In addition, Eugene Steuerle has highlighted another set of hidden transactions, namely the existence of tax measures within expenditure programs. These "expenditure taxes" which take back or recapture the benefits of expenditure programs as the beneficiary's income rises "may be far more insidious [than tax expenditures] in their effects on incentives and on individual behavior" (Steuerle, 1992, p. 3).

8. An example of a tax expenditure approach to tax reform in another context is discussion about the exclusion of interest on state and local bonds, where alternatives such as a subsidized taxable bond option were explicitly put on the table.

9. I have purposely not mentioned here the well known argument by Martin Feldstein in a 1980 analysis of charitable giving. Essentially, he argued that when public and private actions are close substitutes, tax subsidies will typically generate more charitable activity than direct government provision because they induce a substitution, as well as an income, effect. However, Feldstein's efficiency claims for the charitable deduction have been criticized for their narrow perspective (see Clotfelter, p. 284). Moreover, because Feldstein compares tax deductibility to direct provision of services rather than to the most comparable form of direct spending, namely a subsidy, his analysis contributes little to the debate about the superiority of direct versus tax expenditures as a means of providing subsidies.

REFERENCES

Aaron, Henry. 1994. "Tax Issues in Health Care Reform," *National Tax Journal* vol. XLVII, no. 2 (June), pp. 407-416.
Bird, Richard. 1988. "Comments," in Neil Bruce, editor, *Tax Expenditures and Government Policy* (Kingston, Ontario: Queen's University), pp.123-126.
Bittker, B. I., et al. 1968. *A Comprehensive Tax Base? A Debate*. Federal Tax Press.
Bradford, David. 1988. "Tax Expenditures and the Problem of Accounting for Government," in Neil Bruce, editor, *Tax Expenditures and Government Policy* (Kingston, Ontario: Queen's University), pp. 427-434.
Brooks, Neil. 1988. Comment on Kesselman, in Neil Bruce, editor, *Tax Expenditures and Government Policy* (Kingston, Ontario: Queen's University), pp. 324-329.
Bruce, Neil. 1988. "Introduction" In Neil Bruce, editor, *Tax Expenditures and Government Policy* (Kingston, Ontario: Queen's University), pp. 4-12.
Center on Budget and Policy Priorities. 1994. *A Tale of Two Futures: Restructuring California's Finances to Boost Economic Growth*. Washington, D.C.
Center on Budget and Policy Priorities, forthcoming report. Washington, D.C.
Clotfelter, Charles. 1985. *Federal Tax Policy and Charitable Giving* (Chicago: The University of Chicago Press).
Congressional Budget Office. 1988. *The Effects of Tax Reform on Tax Expenditures*. (March).
Davie, Bruce F. 1994. "Tax Expenditures in the Federal Excise Tax System," *National Tax Journal*, vol. XLVII, no. 1 (March), pp. 39-62.
General Accounting Office. 1994. *Tax Policy: Tax Expenditures Deserve More Scrutiny*. GAO/GGD/AIMD-94-122.
Harris, J.E. and S. A. Hicks. 1992. "Tax Expenditure Reporting," *Public Budgeting & Finance*, (fall), vol. 12, no. 3, pp. 32-49.
Kesselman, Jonathan R. 1988. "Direct Expenditures versus Tax Expenditures for Economic and Social Policy," in Neil Bruce, editor, *Tax Expenditures and Government Policy* (Kingston, Ontario: Queen's University), pp. 284-323.
King, Ronald F. 1984. "Tax Expenditures and Systematic Public Policy: An Essay on the Political Economy of the Federal Revenue Code," *Public Finance and Budgeting*, volume 4, no. 1 (spring), pp. 14-31.
McDaniel, Paul R.1988. "The Impact of The Tax Expenditure Concept on Tax Reform," in Neil W. Brooks, ed., *The Quest for Tax Reform: The Royal Commission on Taxation Twenty Years Later* (Toronto: Carswell), pp. 387-396.
Neubig, Thomas and David Joulfaian. 1988. "The Tax Expenditure Budget Before and After the Tax Reform Act of 1986," U.S. Treasury, Office of Tax Analysis, paper 60.
Poddar, Satya. 1988. "Integration of Tax Expenditures Into The Expenditure Management System: The Canadian Experience," in Neil Bruce, editor, *Tax Expenditures and Government Policy* (Kingston, Ontario: Queen's University), pp. 259-268.
Pomp, Richard D. 1988. "State Tax Expenditure Budgets — and Beyond," in Steven D. Gold, ed., *The Unfinished Agenda for State Tax Reform*. (Denver Colorado: National Conference of State Legislatures).
Schick, Allen. 1986. "Controlling Nonconventional Expenditure: Tax Expenditures and Loans," *Public Budgeting & Finance*, Vol 6, no. 1 (spring), pp. 3-19.
Steuerle, C. Eugene. 1992. "Toward an Expenditure Tax Budget," *NTA Forum*, summer 1992.
Surrey, Stanley S. 1973. *Pathways to Tax Reform* (Cambridge, MA: Harvard University Press).
Surrey, Stanley S. and Paul R. McDaniel. 1985. *Tax Expenditures* (Cambridge, MA: Harvard University Press).
Winer, Stanley L. and Walter Hettich. 1988. "Tax Expenditures and the Democratic Process," in Neil Bruce, editor, *Tax Expenditures and Government Policy* (Kingston, Ontario: Queen's University), pp. 379-406.

PART III

TAX POLICY AND LAND USE

Fiscal impacts of local population growth: A conceptual and empirical analysis

Helen F. Ladd

Terry Sanford Institute of Public Policy, Duke University, Durham, NC 27708-0243, USA

Received December 1992, final version received January 1994

Abstract

This paper examines the legitimacy of concerns of local residents about the adverse fiscal impacts of population growth. The conceptual discussion shows that economic theory provides no clear prediction of the impact of population growth on per capita spending. Based on a national data set of large counties, simple descriptive analysis indicates that greater population growth is associated with higher per capita current spending and interest outlays. More detailed analysis both of 1978–85 changes and of 1985 levels of current spending indicates that higher growth-related per capita spending primarily reflects the combined effects of greater density and increased local spending shares. In sum, established residents in fast-growing areas may experience declines in service quality as well as rising local tax burdens.

Key words: Local taxes; Spending; Population growth

JEL classification: H72; R11

1. Introduction

Many local governments, substate regions, and states are showing increasing interest in limiting or managing local population growth. For example, growth management is a burgeoning industry in communities throughout California, in many southern states, and even in parts of more stable states, such as Cape Cod in Massachusetts. In addition, several states, including Florida, Maine, Georgia, and Washington, have enacted statewide growth-management programs. This interest in managing local population growth reflects discontent with symptoms of rapid growth such as environmental degradation and changes in the character of the community. Also high among the expressed concerns of established residents are adverse fiscal effects, namely that population growth may raise tax burdens or reduce the quality of public services.

How legitimate are expressed concerns about the adverse fiscal impacts of population growth? Are they real or are they simply an excuse to keep people out of the community for other reasons? This paper uses a national data set on large counties to shed light on the nature and the magnitude of these fiscal impacts, impacts that have received scant attention in both the theoretical and empirical literature.

This paper contributes to our understanding of fiscal impacts by examining the effects of growth not directly on service quality and tax burdens, but rather on the related measure, per capita local public spending. My decision to focus on spending rather than service levels partially reflects the absence of adequate data on service quality. However, because spending can be conceptualized as an index of service quality times the cost per unit of quality, per capita spending is linked, albeit imperfectly and in ways discussed below, to service quality. Per capita spending is more closely linked to taxes. In the absence of rising intergovernmental assistance, a rise in per capita spending on current services necessarily requires an increase in revenue from local taxes or other local revenue sources. The focus on per capita spending rather than on tax burdens is analytically advantageous in that it permits one to draw on the extensive literature on the demand for, and costs of, providing local public services.

While most observers would probably agree with the prediction that local population growth puts upward pressure on total public spending, they are likely to disagree about its impact on per capita spending, that is, on whether spending will increase faster or slower than population. Moreover, the mechanisms through which growth may affect spending are not fully understood. Hence, the purpose of the first section is to describe systematically the various ways that population growth may affect local per capita spending. In the following sections, data from 248 large counties are used first to describe the simple empirical relationship between growth and spending and second to disentangle the various mechanisms. The final section links the analysis of spending to the issues that taxpayer voters ultimately care about, that is, tax burdens and service levels.

2. The conceptual framework

The strategy in this section is first to use economic theory to illuminate the determinants of per capita spending and second to build on that discussion to clarify the mechanisms through which population growth might affect spending.

2.1. Per capita spending

Local public spending is used to provide services for local residents. Hence, we can view per capita local public expenditures (EXP) as the product of a service level per resident (S), the unit cost per resident of providing services (C_s), and a measure of the division of service responsibilities between state and local governments (SR):

$$EXP = S * C_s * SR.$$

2.1.1. Service levels and their production technology

The service level (S) is defined as the goods and services that citizen voters value. For example, public safety should be viewed as protection from crime, and education as educational achievement. These service levels represent outcomes that should be distinguished from the direct, or intermediate, outputs produced by the public sector such as the number of blocks patrolled by police officers or the numbers of teachers per student. Letting X represent the total amount of the direct outputs, we can write the following production function for S:

$$S = f(X, N, E),$$

where N is population, and E is a vector of environmental factors that represent the conditions under which public services are provided. As initially discussed by Bradford et al. (1969), areas with harsher environments for providing public services require more direct outputs than other areas to produce a specified level of final services. For example, compared with a sparsely populated area, a densely populated area will require more stoplights and traffic control officers to provide a specified level of traffic safety. Similarly, in an area with a high poverty rate, more teachers may be needed per student to provide a specified level of educational achievement than in an area with fewer children living in disadvantaged households.

Controlling for other variables, the effect of population (N) on service levels depends on the publicness of the goods and services provided by the public sector.[1] More specifically, ignoring environmental factors, we can write

$$S = X/N^g,$$

---

[1] The concept of the environment in which public services are produced could easily be extended to include population size (see Ladd and Yinger, 1991). However, the centrality of population to the present study suggests that it should be dealt with separately.

where g is a measure of publicness. If g equals 0, the services are purely public. In this case, the service level enjoyed by each resident depends only on the total amount of direct outputs and consumption is non-rival; the presence of more residents does not diminish the benefits to existing residents. If g equals 1, the services are like private goods; to provide a constant level of services in counties of different size, direct outputs would have to vary in proportion to the population.

2.1.2. Costs of providing services

Turning now to the costs of providing the services that residents value, we can write

$$C_s = f(C_x, N, E),$$

where C_x is the cost per unit of direct output and N and E are defined as above.

(a) *Cost per unit of direct output.* The cost per unit of direct output depends on the prices of inputs such as land, labor, and capital and also on the production relation between inputs and output. The key production-related cost difference is one of economies or diseconomies of scale. For services with large fixed costs such as sewage plants and transportation systems, costs decline with output as large fixed costs are spread over a larger quantity. For services such as fire and police protection or elementary and secondary education, costs are more likely to be constant or possibly to rise with output.[2]

(b) *Publicness of publicly provided goods and services.* The significance of population for the costs per unit of final output depends on the publicness of the goods and services provided through the public sector. The costs per unit of S decline with population size in the case of public goods as the costs of the fixed direct outputs are spread among a larger population but are constant in the case of private goods as direct outputs are increased in line with population.

Empirical studies of local government expenditures typically estimate the publicness parameter (g) to be close to 1. Provided certain assumptions are made about the production technology, these findings suggest that publicly provided goods are characterized by congestion and, in effect, are similar to private goods.[3]

(c) *Environmental factors.* The cost implications of environmental factors follow directly from the previous discussion of how environmental factors

---

[2] For a classic discussion of cost functions for local public services, see Werner Z. Hirsch, 1968.

[3] See, for example, Begstrom and Goodman (1973). As elaborated by Inman (1979), the finding that g is close to 1 implies privateness only when accompanied by the assumption that the production of direct outputs or facilities is characterized by constant returns to scale. Interpreting population size as an environmental cost factor, Ladd and Yinger (1991) find that

influence service levels. A harsher local environment increases the amount of direct outputs needed per unit of final output and consequently raises the cost of that output. Several recent studies document the cost implications for cities of environmental factors such as population density, poverty, proportion of old housing, pupils per resident, and commercial employees per resident (see Bradbury et al., 1984; Ladd and Yinger, 1991; and Wasylenko and Yinger, 1988).

2.1.3. Service responsibilities

The final determinant of local public expenditures is the division of responsibilities between state and local governments. States differ in how they distribute responsibilities among levels of government. In Massachusetts, for example, the state government has had full responsibility for welfare since 1968 and, because of the limited power of counties, also has primary responsibility for health and social services. In contrast, other states often use county governments as agents of the state with the result that many social service and welfare programs are delivered by county rather than by state governments.

2.2. Population growth and changes in per capita spending

This framework implies that long-run equilibrium changes over time in the per capita spending of local governments will be influenced by three sets of factors: those that affect the demand for public services, those that influence the cost of providing services, and state decisions about the division of responsibilities. The demand for services can be expressed as

$$S^d = f(\text{income, preferences, tax price}),$$

where all the variables refer to characteristics of a representative or decisive voter.

The following discussion focuses initially on the long-run equilibrium changes that are related either directly or indirectly related to growth. Lags in the process by which communities respond to rapid population growth are introduced at the end.

---

for large cities g is greater than 1 for general and police services, which implies that these services exhibit diseconomies to population scale.

Oates (1988) provides an alternative explanation for the apparent congestion. Labeling it the 'zoo effect', Oates points out the tendency for cities to provide a wider range of services as they become larger.

2.2.1. Effects of population growth – identical residents

To simplify the discussion, consider first the situation in which an increase in population is achieved by replicating the existing population in all important ways. Thus the income and preferences of the new residents are the same as those of the established residents, the number of jobs in the county per resident does not change, and the new residents have most of the same socio-economic characteristics as the established residents. With these assumptions, population growth leads to no change in the demand for public services except, possibly, through a price effect related to a change in the cost of public services. Hence, any effects on spending of population growth occur as a result of changes in the cost of providing public services.

(a) *Role of publicness.* As I noted above, most publicly provided goods appear to be more similar to private goods than to public goods. To the extent that this finding is valid, public facilities must be increased in proportion to population, ceteris paribus, to maintain service levels. Consequently, the per capita costs of public services would be unaffected by population growth.

(b) *Effects on the cost of producing direct outputs.* Because the supply of land within each county is limited, population growth is likely to lead to higher land prices. These increases in land prices raise the cost of providing services to the extent that land must be purchased to provide additional services. Also, to the extent that population growth results in higher wages throughout the area, it might also increase the wages of public sector employees.

What about economies of scale in production? If economies exist, an increase in population that required more direct outputs could reduce average costs of production. In the presence of diseconomies of scale, population increases would lead to rising average costs. In counties that are not fully developed and incorporated, some of the population growth may be accommodated by setting up new jurisdictions rather than by expanding existing ones. The possibility of replication suggests that the relevant production function could well be characterized by constant costs in many areas.

Another production consideration is potential economies of density. Because county land areas are fixed, population growth leads to higher average density. The issue then is how this higher density affects the average costs of providing direct outputs. The most widely cited study on this topic, the Real Estate Research Corporation's (1974) study, *The Costs of Sprawl*, reports significant savings for the local public sector from high-density planned development. Using detailed data from *The Costs of Sprawl*, Downing and Gustely (1977) find that, compared with low-density development, high-density development significantly reduces both capital and operating costs for police, fire, solid waste collection and disposal, water supply, sanitary sewers, and storm sewers, but not for schools. However, these findings are based on the assumption of a given number of people and a fixed amount of land that produce a constant average density (see Windsor, 1979); indeed, the 'high-density' development might more accurately be labeled compact development plus open space. Nonetheless, higher density may indeed reduce the costs of providing some direct outputs. But even in this event, higher density resulting from population growth could well increase the average costs of providing public services (as distinguished from direct outputs) as discussed next under the rubric of environmental cost factors.

(c) *Environmental factors – population density*. Several recent empirical studies of the costs of providing public services in cities provide evidence to support the view that, potential savings through the production of direct outputs notwithstanding, higher average density *increases* the costs of providing public services (see Bradbury et al., 1984; and Ladd and Yinger, 1991).[4] The mechanism through which this outcome occurs can be understood in terms of the harshness of the environment. For example, increased density may require more traffic lights and traffic control officers to achieve a given level of traffic safety or traffic flow. Similarly, higher density may raise the social costs of inappropriately disposed waste and therefore may require more garbage pickup and disposal. Or increased density may provide an environment more conducive to crime that requires more police services to achieve a given level of protection from crime.[5] Thus, given that population growth increases average density, these studies predict that population growth will raise the per capita level of public spending for those services for which density is a relevant environmental cost factor.

(d) *Implications*. Because these considerations work in different directions, they lead to no clearcut prediction about how replicating the existing population will affect per capita spending on public services. Nonetheless the theory is suggestive. Population density appears to be a key determinant. To the extent that it puts upward pressure on land prices and that it adversely affects the environment for providing public services, a rise in population density will increase costs, and, provided demand is inelastic with respect to price, also per capita spending. To the extent that production of direct output is characterized by economies of density, and with the same proviso about the elasticity of demand, it will reduce pressures on spending.

---

[4] These cross-sectional studies typically use expenditure data but control for variations across communities in the factors that influence the demand for public services.

[5] Some authors label this phenomenon an increase in demand for services. The difference is only semantic. I am using demand to refer only to the demand for final outputs such as protection from crime. Any factor that affects the cost per unit of final output is labeled a cost factor. However, it is not unreasonable to talk about the intermediate outputs such as more police patrols that is derived from the more fundamental demand for police protection.

Thus, the effect of density on costs is an important empirical issue, and one that receives special attention in the empirical work discussed below.

2.2.2. Effects of population change – different characteristics

Relaxing the assumption that population change is achieved with no change in the composition of county residents or in other county characteristics adds additional considerations. The changing mix can influence both the desired level of public services and the environment within which services are produced.

(a) *Demand for services.* Population change often brings with it changing income and preferences for public services. To the extent that the income of new residents is higher than that of established residents, we would expect the demand for some public services to increase. Even with no change in income, however, new residents may have different preferences for public services. In some areas, for example, the new growth may include a larger proportion of two-worker households with greater demands for transit services or a greater proportion of elderly with greater demands for public safety or weaker preferences for education.

(b) *Environmental cost factors.* Two ways in which population change can alter the environment for providing public services are worth highlighting. First, population growth may bring with it a disproportionate increase in jobs or a changing mix of jobs. Either of these outcomes could mean that local governments will have to spend more money per resident to provide the direct outputs necessitated by the additional jobs and congestion they create.

Second, population decline that reflects the outmigration of middle and upper income households can bring with it a multitude of problems for the provision of public services. As people migrate out of the area, especially large cities, the vacant and abandoned buildings they leave behind increase the probability of fire and vandalism. To provide a constant level of protection to remaining residents, localities may need to increase expenditures on police and fire-fighting services. If the population decline also results in a shift toward a more dependent population, increased per capita expenditures may again be necessary just to maintain service levels. In many cities, for example, increasing proportions of pupils from disadvantaged or non-English-speaking households increase the costs of educating students. In all of these cases, higher per capita expenditures reflect the changed relationship between the direct outputs – police, fire-fighting, and education services – and public sector outputs – the services of particular interest to citizen consumers (see Peterson, 1976; Ladd, 1981). Analogously, to the extent that growing areas are characterized by falling proportions of disadvantaged households, such areas might experience declining costs of providing social services.

2.2.3. Disequilibrium or surge effects

Thus far, the discussion has been predicated on the assumption that somehow local governments are able to achieve the service levels desired by taxpayer voters. If they are not able to do so, observed spending reflects constrained, rather than desired, levels of services. Many local governments are subject to limitations on their revenues either because of state-imposed limits on their taxing authority or, as in California and Massachusetts, because of stringent voter-imposed limits on tax levies or rates. However, even if such limitations are binding for individual revenue sources, or for individual governments within a state, they may be less binding for the sum of all revenue sources (including intergovernmental aid) and for the combination of all local governments within each county; local government officials tend to be quite creative in circumventing limitations by finding alternative revenue sources and by setting up authorities or special districts outside the reach of the limitation measures.

Probably of more importance in rapidly growing areas are political or administrative constraints that may make it difficult for government officials to respond rapidly to the rising costs of providing services. In the presence of these constraints, the growth of actual spending will fall short of the growth of desired spending, with the shortfall emerging in the form of declining per capita spending and service quality. These disequilibrium or surge effects receive specific attention in the empirical work below.

2.2.4. Effects on the state–local division of responsibilities

Economic theory has little to say about the impacts of local population growth on the state–local division of spending responsibilities. Because the initial fiscal pressures of growth are felt at the local level, state governments may be slower than local governments to respond to growth-related pressures for more spending. If true, local governments in growing areas will face greater spending pressures than they would with a constant division of spending responsibilities between state and local governments.

2.2.5. Effects of population change – pressures related to infrastructure

In principle the foregoing discussion applies to local public spending defined as both spending on current operations and capital costs, where capital costs refer to the annual cost of using public capital in the county. Much of the empirical work reported below focuses on current account spending alone because the annual costs of using capital are difficult to approximate. Local governments, and also the Census of Governments which reports local spending data, account for capital in terms of outlays or investments, rather than in terms of annual economic costs as measured by depreciation and opportunity costs.

Rapid population growth and decline present special problems for local infrastructure – that is, the locality's roads and bridges, water and sewer systems, and public buildings – facilities that are financed primarily by municipal bonds and intergovernmental grants. Localities experiencing rapid economic growth at a time of rising interest rates or declining state or federal aid face higher debt service burdens for the new infrastructure than established residents faced for the existing infrastructure. Thus, even if the required infrastructure rises proportionately with population, population growth will lead to higher per capita interest costs.

A second reason for rising interest burdens in the case of rapid population growth reflects the institutional fact that bond lives are typically restricted to be shorter than the economic life of the infrastructure project. As spelled out by Snyder and Stegman (1987, p. 42), this restriction produces a higher interest burden on established residents whenever the rate of growth in the locality exceeds the real rate of interest. The restriction on bond lives means that the annual interest cost of new infrastructure exceeds the true annual economic cost of the infrastructure. When growth is slow, this burden is partially offset by the fact the new future residents share the costs of the infrastructure built to serve the established residents. However, established residents must also help pay the debt service for the capital expansions required to accommodate the new people. When population is growing rapidly, the burden on established residents of financing infrastructure for future residents exceeds the benefits they receive from sharing the burden of financing their own infrastructure.[6]

The fiscal problems associated with infrastructure differ for localities experiencing rapid population decline. Scaling down certain types of infrastructure in line with population loss is often difficult or impossible. Infrastructure, such as water and sewer or road systems, that is in the form of networks, is particularly difficult to cut back. Unlike individual buildings that can be sold or torn down, reducing the size of network facilities is technically impossible in some cases. The fiscal pressures associated with this excess infrastructure in declining areas is exacerbated by the fact that this infrastructure is typically old and requires high maintenance expenditures.

2.3. Summary

This conceptual framework highlights first that economic theory provides no clear prediction of the impact of population growth on per capita local public spending. Some factors push in one direction, and some push in the

---

[6] As pointed out by one of the reviewers, this burden on established residents may be offset to some extent by capitalization: the price of local land may rise to reflect the fact that payments have already been made for the future services of local capital facilities.

other direction. For example, to the extent that population growth creates a harsher environment for providing public services, it will increase per capita spending. To the extent that communities adjust their spending with a lag, population growth will reduce per capita spending. Hence, empirical work is needed to determine the direction and magnitude of the overall impact and the mechanisms through which the impacts arise.

In addition, the framework suggests that much of the upward pressure on spending reflects pressures on cost rather than increases in service quality. This observation implies that one should be careful not to interpret growth-related increases in per capita spending as increases in service quality.

3. Empirical estimates of the effects of growth on per capita spending

The theory is suggestive but does not yield a clear and unambiguous prediction about the relationship between population growth and per capita spending. Hence the first empirical task is to determine the overall relationship between population change and local public spending. Subsequent tasks involve first, separating the overall relationship into direct and indirect effects and second, distinguishing long-run from short-run disequilibrium impacts.

The data for this analysis are for the 248 large U.S. counties or county-equivalents for which complete data on taxes and spending and population measures were available for both 1978 and 1985. These years were chosen to minimize the effects of the national economy on the data; both 1978 and 1985 are three years into the expansion phase of the national economic cycle. The sample was determined primarily by the availability of fiscal data, the major source for which is the annual Census of Government publication on local government finances in major county areas.[7] The information in this publication differs from that of other census publications on local finances in that taxes and spending are aggregated for all local governments within the geographic area defined by county boundaries. This aggregation facilitates

---

[7] For the fiscal year 1984–85 (henceforth 1985), fiscal data are available in U.S. Department of Commerce, Bureau of the Census, *Local Government Finances in Major County Areas: 1984–85* (GF85, April 1987) for all 410 counties with population greater than 100,000, regardless of the metropolitan area in which they are located. Of these 410 counties, only about 260 were included in the comparable 1978 publication, *Local Government Finances in Selected Metropolitan Areas and Large Counties: 1977–78* (GF78, no. 6, April 1980). This discrepancy reflects a change in the criteria for selecting counties. In contrast to 1985 when inclusion was determined by county population alone, inclusion in 1978 was based on a two-part criterion: location in one of 74 major metropolitan areas regardless of county population or population greater than 200,000 regardless of location.

comparisons across states with differing divisions of responsibilities among local jurisdictions such as school districts, municipalities, townships, and counties.

Although the 248 county sample represents only 8% of the 3096 counties in the country, the large size of the included counties means that the sample includes more than 59% of the nation's population. Within the sample, the mean increase in population during the 7-year period was 9.5% and the median increase was 5.8%. Population change ranged from a 9% decline in St. Louis City to increases of more than 74% in Gwinnett, Georgia and Fort Bend, Texas. A quarter of the sample experienced population increases of more than 15%, but only 8 of the 248 large counties experienced increases greater than 40%.

3.1. Overall impact

The overall impact can be determined from the following regression model:

$$EXPPCH_i = a + bPOPPCH_i + cPOPPCH_i^2 + u_i, \qquad (1)$$

where $EXPPCH_i$ is the percent change in per capita spending in county i, $POPCH_i$ is the 1978–85% change in population in that county, and u_i is a random error term. The quadratic specification allows for potential non-linearity in the effects of population change on spending. Because this equation includes no control variables, the estimated coefficients reflect all the relationships between population growth and spending discussed above – not just those attributable to the replication of the existing population, but also those attributable to changes in other variables such as per capita income that were correlated with growth across counties during the sample period. Richer models are needed to sort out the various mechanisms through which population growth may affect spending and are discussed below.

Results for Eq. 1 are reported in the first three columns of Table 1 for three categories of real per capita spending: spending on current operations (*CURRPCH*), capital spending (*CAPPCH*), and interest on general debt. The first two categories include both general and utility spending; the third refers only to general debt.[8] As I indicated earlier, I would prefer to use a

---

[8] To make the categories for current spending reported by the Census comparable for the two years, current spending was calculated as direct current operation plus assistance and subsidies for the 1984–85 data and as current general expenditures minus interest on general debt plus current operation for utilities for the 1977–78 data. Thus the current spending measure does not include interest payments. All dollar figures were deflated by the implicit GNP deflator for personal consumption expenditure. See Ladd (1993) for comparable results for expenditure categories disaggregated by function.

Table 1
Effects of population growth and control variables: Regression results (percent change, in decimals; 248 counties; 1978-85)

Variable[a]	CURRPCH (1)	CAPPCH (2)	INTPCH (3)	CURRPCH (4)
Constant	0.111** (10.970)	−0.030 (0.710)	0.561** (7.450)	0.222** (6.320)
POPPCH	−0.070 (0.590)	1.339** (2.760)	3.992** (4.510)	−0.490** (3.700)
POPPCH2	0.493** (2.030)	−1.640* (1.660)	−4.195** (2.330)	0.838** (3.690)
INCPCPCH	–	–	–	−0.245** (2.030)
JOBPCPCH	–	–	–	0.236** (2.090)
AGE19	–	–	–	0.794 (0.820)
AGE65	–	–	–	−2.142** (1.990)
RPSCH	–	–	–	0.552** (2.380)
RSSCH	–	–	–	0.440** (5.000)
RHSGDECH	–	–	–	0.611** (3.960)
RTRANSCH	–	–	–	−0.099 (0.860)
R^2	0.031	0.031	0.089	0.260

Notes: Absolute values of t-statistics are in parenthesis. Two asterisks (**) denote statistical significance at the 5% level; one asterisk (*) denotes statistical significance at the 10% level. Each regression is based on 248 county observations minus outliers for that expenditure category. Omitted outliers, defined as having a residual more than five times the standard error, by category (with percent changes in parenthesis) are CURRPCH: Wake, NC (93%); Wauhesha, WI (96%); CAPPCH: Wake, NC (570%), Salt Lake City, UT (585%); INTPCH: Cleveland, OK (797%), Beaver, PA (699%).

[a] Dependent variables (percent change in real per capita spending, in decimals, 1978-85): CURRPCH – spending on current operations plus assistance and subsidies (general and utilities); CAPPCH – capital outlays (general and utilities); INTPCH – interest payments (general purpose). Independent variables (in decimals): POPPCH – percent change in county population; POPPCH2 – percent change in county population squared; INCPCPCH – percent change in real per capita income; JOBPCPCH – percent change in jobs per capita; AGE19 – change in share of population aged 19 and younger; AGE65 – change in share of population aged 65 and older; RPSCH – change in ratio of local spending to state and local spending, by state, in public safety; RSSCH – change in ratio of local spending to state and local spending, by state, on social services (welfare, wealth, and hospitals); RHSGDECH – change in ratio of local spending to state and local spending, by state, in housing and community development; RTRANSCH – ratio of local spending to state and local spending, by state, on transportation.

single measure of spending, namely one that includes both current spending and annual capital costs, but such a measure is not available because of the way governments account for capital.

As indicated by the low adjusted R^2s, none of the equations has much explanatory power. This finding is not surprising because many factors other than population growth account for changes in per capita spending. Nonetheless, assuming the functional form is reasonable, the equations accurately summarize the overall relationship between local spending and population growth during the 1978–85 period.

For current account spending, the estimated U-shaped relationship implies that the growth rate of per capita spending declines (but only very slightly) at very low growth rates to a minimum at a population growth rate of 7% (less than 1% per year) and then rises at an increasing rate (see the no-controls line in Fig. 1). The marginal impact of a percentage point increase in population evaluated at a 30% growth rate (3.8% annual rate) is 0.23; that is, a 10 percentage point positive difference in population growth (around this starting point) is associated with a positive difference in the growth of per capita spending of roughly 2.3 percentage points. Stated differently, for 7-year growth rates greater than 7%, total current spending

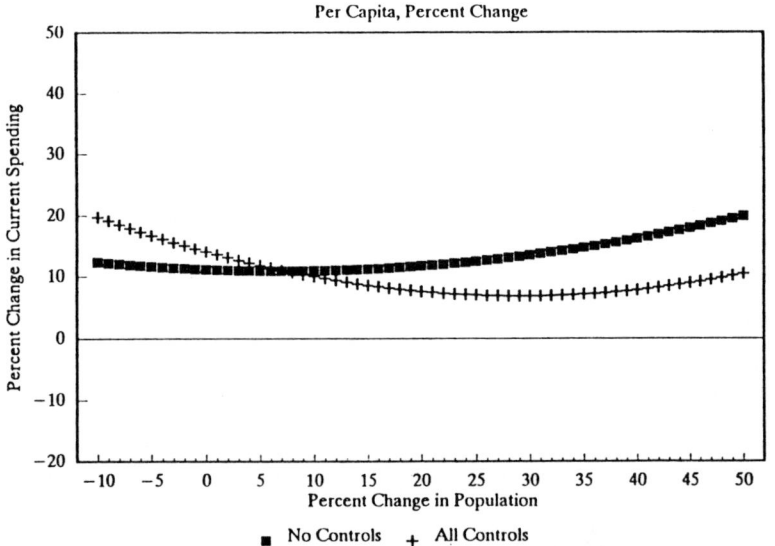

Fig. 1. Current spending. Per capita, percent change.

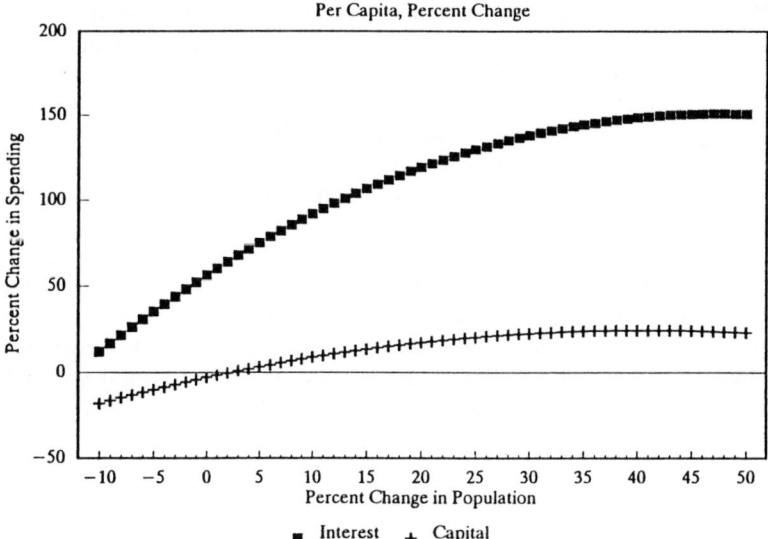

Fig. 2. Capital outlays and interest. Per capita, percent change.

increases faster on average than population, leading to rising real per capita expenditure.

Not surprisingly, the impacts of growth on capital spending are larger than those on current spending. Moreover, according to the estimated equation, per capita capital spending increases with population throughout most of the relevant range but at a decreasing rate (see the capital spending line in Fig. 2.) The marginal impact of a percentage point increase in population evaluated again at a 30% growth rate is 0.35, about 50% larger than for current account spending. Based on cumulative, rather than marginal, effects, the comparison becomes more dramatic. A county with a growth rate of 30% is predicted to experience an increase in its per capita capital spending that is 42 percentage points above that in a county with no population growth. This contrasts with a 2.3 percentage point cumulative difference over the same range for current spending. Clearly, population growth puts significant pressure on capital budgets as communities struggle to increase their investment in roads, water and sewer systems, and public buildings.[9]

---

[9] The largest impact by expenditure category is for transportation, much of which is capital spending. See Ladd (1993).

Because capital spending is financed in part by issuing bonds, we would expect to find that interest burdens rise faster in fast-growing areas than in slow-growing areas. The dramatic effects of growth captured by the interest equation (and shown in Fig. 2) reflect some notable factors affecting capital financing during the period, namely the extremely high double digit interest rates of the early 1980s and cutbacks in federal aid for capital projects.

In sum, rising per capita spending on current operations combined with rising interest burdens in rapidly growing areas lend legitimacy to claims by established residents that rapid population growth increases per capita spending, which in turn requires higher tax burdens. However, further analysis is needed to sort out the mechanisms through which the higher spending occurs. Because the conceptual model discussed above is more applicable to current account spending than to either capital spending or interest outlays, the remainder of the paper focuses on current account spending alone.

3.2. Distinguishing direct from indirect impacts

During the study period, population growth across counties was positively correlated with the growth in per capita income ($r = 0.15$) and with the growth of jobs per resident ($r = 0.26$). Moreover, visions of the elderly migrating to high-growth states such as Florida and Arizona notwithstanding, the elderly increased as a share of the population more in the slow-growth than in the high-growth counties, producing a correlation of -0.55 across counties between the percent change in population and the change in the share of population aged 65 years and older. These non-zero correlations imply that part of the spending pressures associated with population growth that emerged in column 1 of Table 1 may reflect changes in local economic growth and in the age composition of county residents.

The effects on spending of replicating the existing population (direct effects) can be distinguished from those caused by these growth-related changes (indirect effects) by adding variables to Eq. 1 to control for local economic growth and changes in the age distribution of county populations.[10] The four new variables are the percent change in income per capita (*INCPCPCH*); the percent change in jobs in the county per county resident (*JOBPCPCH*); the change in the share of the population aged 19 and younger (*AGE19*); and the change in the share of population aged 65 and older (*AGE65*).

---

[10] Data limitations preclude the inclusion of other demographic changes.

The spending measure throughout this analysis includes only that by local governments within each county. As noted earlier, a potentially important determinant of the growth of this local spending is changes in the division of spending responsibilities between the state and local governments within each state. For example, state assumption of responsibility during the period for services such as the court system or health care, formerly provided by local governments, would reduce the rate of growth of local spending. Analogously, a reduced state role in transportation could push more responsibilities onto local governments and thereby put upward pressure on local spending for transportation.

To capture these changes in the state–local division of responsibilities, changes in the local share of total state and local spending were calculated using statewide data and added to the current spending version of Eq. 1 for four service categories: public safety (*RPSCH*), social services (*RSSCH*), housing and community development (*RHSGDECH*), and transportation (*RTRANSCH*). Because local spending in any one county is typically small relative to that of all counties in the state, this measure of the changing division of responsibilities has the desirable characteristic of being relatively independent of the spending decisions made in a particular county. A positive sign is expected on each of these variables. Including these variables allows one to determine how population change would affect local spending in the absence of changes in the division of spending responsibilities in the county's state.

The augmented equation is reported in column 4 of Table 1. With respect to the measures of change in the local economy, different signs emerge for income and job growth. The negative sign on per capita income growth is inconsistent with its interpretation as a demand variable. However, income can also serve as a cost factor, especially with respect to social service expenditures; the greater is the increase in the income of county residents, the lower is the need for redistributive services. Indeed a disaggregated analysis by expenditure category corroborates this interpretation in that, contrary to most of the spending categories, the coefficient of income is negative and large in the social service equation (see Ladd, 1993). Growth in local jobs relative to the population has the expected positive impact on current spending; greater growth in jobs within county boundaries increases the costs of providing a given level of public services to residents. Consistent with other studies, an increasing proportion of elderly leads to a slower rate of growth of spending. As expected, three of the four local-share variables are positive and statistically significant.

The relevant question here is how the addition of the control variables affects the estimated impact of population change. As can be seen in Fig. 1, population change continues to exert a statistically significant U-shaped impact on current spending but the minimum point of the curve has moved to a higher growth rate, namely 29%. Thus, for counties experiencing growth rates less than 29%, a larger population achieved through replication of the existing population decreases per capita current spending (controlling for changes in the division of fiscal responsibilities). Only in counties experiencing extremely rapid increases in populations do high growth rates increase per capita spending. Various mechanisms could account for the observed decline in per capita spending at low and moderate growth rates. One is the possibility that the larger population produces economies of density. Another is that local spending adjusts with a lag to the larger number of people in the county. To the extent that this latter explanation, rather than economies of scale or density, explains the decline, the lower per capita spending would translate into lower service levels. (See cross-sectional analysis below for further discussion of this lagged response.)

Table 2 summarizes the direct and indirect effects of population growth that emerge from column 4 of Table 1, evaluated at 10% and 20% 7-year growth rates. The direct effect is calculated from the coefficients of $POPPCH$ and $POPPCH^2$ and represents the effect of population change alone after controlling for changes in the other variables. Each indirect effect can be interpreted as the effect of population growth on per capita spending that occurs because of its correlation during the sample period with

Table 2
Direct and indirect effects of population change

	Evaluated at $POPPCH =$	
	0.10	0.20
Direct effect	−0.323	−0.155
Indirect effects[a]		
INCPCPCH	−0.004	−0.002
JOBPCPH	0.046	0.052
AGE19	0.005	0.007
AGE65	0.069	0.059
RPSCH	0.044	0.033
RSSCH	0.140	0.115
RHSGDECH	0.089	0.065
RTRANSCH	−0.017	−0.013
Total indirect	0.372	0.316
Direct + indirect	0.049	0.161

[a] The indirect effect for the ith independent variable is $d_i \, \partial X_i / \partial POPPCH$, where d_i is the coefficient of X_i in the $CURR$ equation and $\partial X_i / \partial POPPCH$ is calculated from an auxiliary regression with X_i as the dependent variable and $POPPCH$, $POPPCH^2$, and the other X's as independent variables.

the indicated variable. For example, the 0.046 entry in the first column for *JOBPCH* indicates that an increase in the rate of population growth from 10% to 11% (a 10% increase) indirectly raises the growth rate of per capita spending by 0.46%. This positive impact reflects the positive correlations between population growth and job growth and between job growth per resident and spending per resident. The positive indirect impact associated with the *AGE65* variable reflects the multiplication of two negative coefficients; faster population growth reduces the share of the elderly who have lower demands for public services than working-age residents. Stated differently, the *AGE65* entry implies that local population growth puts upward pressure on spending by increasing the number of working-age residents relative to the elderly.

The clearest finding to emerge from Table 2 is the importance of the local share variables. In particular, the table indicates that the major reason why population growth increases per capita local current spending is the failure of state governments to maintain their share of state–local spending in the face of local population growth.

3.3. Distinguishing long-run from short-run disequilibrium effects

The study design implicit in the regressions in Table 1 is useful for determining the magnitude of the spending pressure faced by local governments in growing areas and sheds light on the sources of the pressure. However, it is not well designed to separate the long-run effects of population change from its short-run disequilibrium effects. Given the fixed boundaries of U.S. counties, when the population of a county increases, the gross population density of the county necessarily increases. As elaborated above, whether this increased density leads to higher or lower spending on public services cannot be determined a priori. Thus, a central empirical question for understanding the long-run fiscal effects of growth is how population density affects per capita spending.

This long-run effect of greater density on spending is independent of the rapidity of population growth; a larger population will have certain implications for local public spending independent of the rate at which the growth occurred. In contrast, the disequilibrium or surge effects of population change refer to the short-run effects on spending that occur either because rapid population growth forces communities to operate less cost-effectively than if they had a longer time to adjust to the change in population or because communities adjust their spending to the larger population only with a lag.

These two separate effects of population growth can be measured by embedding density and population change variables in a fully specified cross-section model of per capita local public spending consistent with the theoretical model discussed above. If measures of local public-sector outcomes were available, per capita expenditure could be specified as a function of public-sector outcomes, environmental cost factors, including density, and input prices. In the absence of outcome measures, the equation must be estimated in reduced form with the determinants of the demand for services replacing the outcome measures. A recent empirical study of K-12 education, for which outcome measures in the form of standardized test scores were available, shows that the direct and reduced-form approaches yield similar estimates of cost functions (see Downes and Pogue, 1992). In the context of the reduced-form approach, the impact on spending of a factor such as density includes both its impact on costs and its indirect impact on spending through a price effect. However, because most economists agree that the demand for local public services is inelastic with respect to price, a factor that increases costs will also increase spending.

The reduced-form model was estimated with 1985 data for all of the 248 large counties except Washington, DC (see appendix for results). The dependent variable in the regression model is the natural logarithm of per capita spending on current operations. Explanatory control variables include demand and taste variables such as per capita income, a proxy for tax price, and the percentage of the population with more than 12 years of education; a variety of cost and workload variables such as the manufacturing wage rate, public school enrolments per capita, the fraction of the population below the poverty level, and manufacturing and non-manufacturing jobs per resident; county population; and several intergovernmental fiscal variables that capture both the division of spending responsibilities between state and local governments and the distribution of state and federal aid to local governments. Most of the explanatory variables have the expected signs and many are statistically significant. The R^2 (adjusted for degrees of freedom) is about 0.64.

Both the density variables and the population change variables were specified in piecewise linear form to allow the data to determine the functional form of the relationship (see Ladd, 1992, for more detail). The implications of the estimated regression coefficients for spending are reported in Table 3. With respect to density, defined as population per square mile, the following results emerge. The lowest spending (and hence costs) occur at a density of about 250 people per square mile. For densities between 0 and 250 people per square mile, lower density raises costs; costs in a sparsely populated county with a density of only 125 people per square mile are predicted to exceed those in the minimum-cost county by about 14%. At densities above the minimum-cost density, costs rise monotonically up to a density of 1,250 people per square mile. At that density, costs are

Table 3
Current operations – predicted effects of density and population change[a]

	Predicted spending relative to base	Predicted spending (1982 dollars)
Density		
D 125	1.14	1,111
D 250	base	972
D 500	1.05	1,019
D 750	1.10	1,065
D 1250	1.19	1,153
D 1750	1.07	1,040
D 24,000	1.43	1,393
Population change		
P neg.	1.07	1,175
P 0	base	1,103
P 0.01	0.98	1,085
P 0.02	0.91	1,001
P 0.032	0.97	1,065
P 0.05	0.88	975
P 0.085	0.87	959

[a] Derived from appendix table.

approximately 19% above the minimum level. Somewhat counterintuitively costs then fall somewhat as density increases up to 1,750 people per square mile but then turn up again, reaching a level 43% greater than the minimum in the most dense counties. The basic message is that beyond the relatively low average density of 250 people per square mile, the costs of providing public services increase with population density.[11] Consequently, in all but the most sparsely populated large counties, population growth is predicted to raise the costs of providing public services through its impact on density. Because the higher spending reflects higher costs rather than higher demands, it does not translate into higher quality services for residents.

The surge effects of population change are less precisely estimated than those of population density, but nonetheless a general pattern emerges; controlling for other factors, the faster is the rate of population growth the lower is per capita spending.[12] This relationship emerges most clearly for the most rapidly growing counties. The point estimates suggest that per capita

---

[11] To provide some feel for the magnitudes, in 1985 Maricopa County (Phoenix, AZ) had a density of 199 people per square mile and Wake County (Raleigh, NC) had a density of 414 people per square mile.

[12] The one anomaly is at an annual rate of population change of 0.2%. For counties with growth rates in this vicinity, per capita spending is lower than that in counties with growth rates in the 3.5% range.

spending in counties growing at the rapid rates of between 5% and 8.5% per year are 12–13% below that in counties experiencing no population growth (but even these estimates have relatively large standard errors). Because the equation controls for the manifestations of population growth, such as a larger population, or a different mix of people, this negative relationship between rapid growth and per capita spending suggests that counties respond only sluggishly to a surge in population and in the process presumably allow their services to deteriorate.

4. Discussion and conclusion

This paper focuses on the effects of population growth on per capita local public spending. The decision to focus on spending reflects both data availability and the existence of a body of economic theory to guide the empirical analysis. Spending is of interest to analysts, taxpayer voters, and policymakers not for its own sake but because of its relationship to the level of services enjoyed by residents and to their tax burdens. The clearest and most unambiguous linkage is on the tax side; a rise in per capita current spending typically means higher per capita tax burdens. Only in the unlikely event that intergovernmental aid were to increase at a *faster* rate than local spending, would higher average burdens not emerge. With respect to services, the linkage is less clear; higher spending may simply reflect higher costs of providing services rather than a higher service level.

The simple descriptive analysis shows that in counties experiencing population growth of more than 7% during the 1978–85 period, faster growth is associated with higher per capita current spending. The combination of this finding with the dramatic growth-related increases in per capita interest payments provides empirical justification for the fiscal concerns of taxpayer voters in fast-growing areas; the sum of local spending on current operations plus interest increases at a faster rate than population. Consequently, average tax burdens also rise as counties grow.[13]

How population growth affects service quality is less clear. Nonetheless, the results suggest that most of the higher per capita spending associated

---

[13] One potential qualification arises with respect to business property. If growth is accompanied by an increase in business property relative to the population, some of the higher taxes might be shifted to the owners of business property or their customers, many of whom may be nonresidents. In practice, this qualification does not appear to be very important. As shown in Ladd (1993), per capita spending rises in most of the relevant range even when job growth (but nothing else) is controlled for. Also see that paper for a detailed analysis of population growth on taxes, by category of tax.

with population growth does not translate into higher-quality services for residents. As was shown in Table 2, the major contributors to the growth in per capita spending during the study period were, first, the inability or unwillingness of state governments to maintain their share of state and local spending burdens in states with rapidly growing counties; second, the positive association between population growth and the proportion of the population of working age; and third, the positive association between population growth and the ratio of jobs to the resident population. The cross-sectional regressions supplement these findings both by confirming that higher ratios of jobs to the resident population are associated with higher long-run equilibrium levels of per capita spending and by indicating that, in the long run, counties typically respond to the greater population density that necessarily accompanies population growth by spending more per capita. Only in sparsely populated counties does the greater density associated with population growth tend to reduce per capita spending.

Neither the increased local spending associated with a shift in responsibilities to local governments nor the growth-related increase in jobs translates into higher services for residents. In contrast, the higher spending associated with the growth-related changes in the age composition of the population could plausibly be interpreted as an increase in service quality. How to interpret the higher spending associated with density can be debated. As elaborated earlier, density is appropriately viewed as an environmental factor that raises the cost of providing public services. To the extent that these higher costs apply to the provision of standard services, such as public safety, they do not reflect improvements in service quality. However, to the extend that these higher costs reflect the provision of a wider range of public services to local residents – the 'zoo effect' identified by Oates (1988) – they could be interpreted as indicating a higher level of public services for county residents.

Finally, consider the surge effects of population growth. The cross-sectional analysis indicates that faster growing counties spend less per capita than slower growing counties, ceteris paribus. Apparently local governments are unable to raise public spending fast enough in rapidly growing counties to achieve the equilibrium level of public services. Consistent with this finding are the results from the change regression with controls. After the demographic, economic, and intergovernmental changes associated with population growth are controlled for, the growth of per capita spending declines throughout much of the relevant range of population growth. In other words, the short-run surge effect leads to a reduction in the growth rate of per capita spending. This short-run response implies that, in addition to facing higher tax burdens, residents in fast-growing areas may well experience reductions in service quality.

Acknowledgements

This paper is part of a larger research project investigating the interrelationship between population and economic growth on the one hand and local public spending and tax burdens on the other. The author is grateful to the Lincoln Institute of Land Policy for financial and institutional support and to K. Russell LaMotte for expert research assistance. An earlier version of this paper entitled 'Population Growth and Local Public Spending' is available as a Lincoln Institute Working Paper, 1990.

Appendix: Spending on current operations – LCURR85** (247 counties, 1985)

Variable	Coefficient	t-statistic
Demand, cost and taste variables		
PYPC85	0.343**	3.14
LRES86	−0.123	−1.39
LWAGE85	0.093	0.84
LPUPS85	0.209**	2.44
LPOV79	0.119**	2.09
LJMAN85	0.039*	1.75
LJNMAN86	0.121*	1.66
LCR17E85	0.004	0.12
LPOP85	0.004	0.19
L12ED80	0.362**	2.48
Intergovernmental		
LRDGE85	0.570**	4.88
LIFED85	0.085**	3.32
LIST85	0.167**	4.52
Density (pop./sq. mile)		
D 0	0.268**	2.91
D 250	base	
D 500	0.047	0.88
D 750	0.091*	1.86
D 1,250	0.171**	2.94
D 1,750	0.068	1.19
D 24,000	0.359**	2.51
Population change		
(annual rate, 1978–85)		
P neg.	0.063	0.84
P 0	base	
P 0.010	−0.016	0.30
P 0.020	−0.097**	2.20

P 0.035	−0.035	0.56
P 0.050	−0.123	1.58
P 0.085	−0.140	1.07
Constant	1.14	0.93
Adjusted R^2	0.639	
Standard error	0.160	

Notes: All dollar figures are in 1982 dollars, based on GNP implicit deflator for personal consumption expenditure; L signifies natural logarithm. Two asterisks (**) signify statistical significance at the 5% level; one asterisk (*) denotes statistical significance at the 10% level.

[a] *LCURR85* – spending on current operations per capita; *LYPC85* – income per capita; *LRES86* – residential share of arrived value of property tax base, 1986; *LWAGE85* – manufacturing wage rate (by state); *LPUPS85* – public school enrolments per capita; *LPOV79* – fraction of population below poverty level, 1979; *LJMAN85* – manufacturing jobs per resident; *LJNMAN85* – non-manufacturing jobs per resident; *LCRIME85* – crime rate; *LPOP85* – population; *L12ED80* – percent of population with more than 12 years of education, 1980; *LRD6E85* – ratio of local direct general expenditure to state and local direct general expenditure in the county's state; *LIFED85* – federal aid per capita; *LIST85* – state aid per capita; $D\ 0$ to $D\ 24{,}000$ – population density at the indicated level; $P\ neg$ – average annual population growth rate, 1978–85, of −0.013; $P\ 0$ to $P\ 0.085$ – average annual population growth rate, 1978–85, at the indicated level.

References

Bergstrom, T.C. and R.P. Goodman, 1973, Private demand for public goods, American Economic Review LXIII, no. 3, 280–297.

Bradbury, K.L., H.F. Ladd, M. Perrault, A. Reschovsky and J. Yinger, 1984, State aid to offset fiscal disparities across communities, National Tax Journal 37, 151–170.

Bradford, D.R., R.A. Malt and W.E. Oates, 1969, The rising cost of local public services: Some evidence and reflections, National Tax Journal 22, 185–202.

Downes, T.A. and T.F. Pogue, 1992, Intergovernmental aid to reduce fiscal disparities: Problems of definition and measurement, Public Finance Quarterly 20, no. 4, 468–482.

Downing P.B. and R.D. Gustely, 1977, The public service costs of alternative development patterns: A review of the evidence, in: P.B. Downing, ed., Local service pricing policies and their effect on urban spatial structure (University of British Columbia Press, Vancouver, BC).

Hirsch, W.Z., 1968, The supply of urban public services, in: Harvey S. Perloff and Lowdon Wingo, Jr. eds., Issues in urban economics (Johns Hopkins University Press, Baltimore) 477–526.

Inman, R.P., 1979, The fiscal performance of local governments: An interpretive review, in: P. Mieszkowski and M. Straszheim, eds., Current issues in urban economics (Johns Hopkins University Press, Baltimore) 270–321.

Ladd, H.F., 1981, Municipal expenditures and the rate of population change, in: Robert W. Burchell and David Listokin, eds., Cities under stress (Rutgers, The State University of New Jersey, Piscataway, NJ) 351–368.

Ladd, H.F., 1992, Population growth, density, and the costs of providing public services, Urban Studies 29, no. 2, 273–295.

Ladd, H.F., 1993, Effects of population growth on local spending and taxes, in: Robert Ebel, ed., People vs. places, Vol. 9: Research in Urban Economics Series (JAI Press).

Ladd, H.F. and J. Yinger, 1991, America's ailing cities: Fiscal health and the design of urban policy, updated edn. (Johns Hopkins University Press, Baltimore).

Oates, W.E., 1988, On the measurement of congestion in the provision of local public goods, Journal of Urban Economics 24, 85–94.

Peterson, G.E., 1976, Finance, in: W. Gorham and N. Glazer, eds., The urban predicament (Urban Institute Press, Washington, DC) 35–118.

Real estate research Corporation, 1974, The costs of sprawl: Environment and economic costs of alternative residential development patterns at the urban fringe (U.S.G.P.O., Washington, DC).

Snyder, T. and M. Stegman, 1987, Paying for growth (Urban Land Institute, Washington, DC).

Wasylenko, M. and J. Yinger, 1988, Nebraska comprehensive study, final report (Metropolitan Studies Program, The Maxwell School, Syracuse University) chs. 9–10.

Windsor, D., 1979, A critique of the costs of sprawl, Journal of the American Planning Association 45, no. 3, 279–292.

[17]

Urban Studies, Vol. 29, No. 2, 1992 273–295

Population Growth, Density and the Costs of Providing Public Services

Helen F. Ladd

[Paper received in final form, August 1991]

Summary. Recent policy interest in managing local population growth has drawn attention to the fiscal pressures that population growth imposes on local governments. This paper uses 1985 data for 247 large county areas to determine the separate impacts on local government spending of two dimensions of residential development patterns, the rapidity of population growth and the intensity of land use as measured by gross residential densities. Based on a regression model that controls for other determinants of per capita spending, this study provides careful estimates of the nonlinear impacts of population growth and population density on three types of local government spending: current account spending, capital outlays and spending on public safety. The study balances the engineering and planning view that greater population density lowers the costs of providing public services by documenting a U-shaped relationship between spending and density; except in sparsely populated areas, higher density typically increases public sector spending. In addition, the results suggest that rapid population growth imposes fiscal burdens on established residents in the form of lower service levels.

Many local governments, substate regions and states are showing increasing interest in managing local population growth. This interest in growth management reflects discontent with symptoms of rapid growth such as increased traffic congestion and environmental degradation (see Chinitz, 1990, for a thoughtful discussion of growth management). Among the concerns of established residents is that rapid population growth will have adverse fiscal effects either because it raises the costs of providing public services, and thereby raises taxes, or because it reduces the quality of public services. One manifestation of this fiscal concern in rapidly growing areas is the increased reliance of local governments on impact fees or exactions, financing tools that are specifically designed to shift the fiscal burden of growth onto developers or new residents. Another manifestation of fiscal concern is the remedy proposed by some advocates of growth management, to channel new development into more densely populated developments with the putative intent of reducing the costs of providing public services.

The starting point for this paper is the observation that we know very little about the average effects of population growth on local public sector spending.[1] As part of a larger research project investigating this question, this paper focuses on two separate effects of population growth. The first comprises the disequilibrium pressures associated with the rapidity of the popula-

---

Helen F. Ladd is at the Institute of Policy Sciences and Public Affairs, Duke University, Durham, NC 27706, USA. The paper is part of a larger research project investigating the interrelationships between population and economic growth on the one hand and local public spending and tax burdens on the other. The author is grateful to the Lincoln Institute of Land Policy for financial and institutional support, to K. Russell LaMotte for expert research assistance, and to Ben Chinitz for his support and warm friendship.

tion change. On the one hand, a surge in population is likely to increase the need for capital outlays as the community strives to provide the infrastructure necessary to support the current and projected future population. In addition, per capita spending would rise if rapid population growth increased the short-run marginal costs of providing services; when population is growing rapidly, communities may be forced to operate less efficiently than they could if they had a longer time to adjust to the change in population. On the other hand, rapid population growth could reduce per capita spending, with a concomitant decline in service levels, if communities were slow to adjust their spending to the larger population.

The second effect of interest for this paper works through population density. Because the boundaries of US counties are fixed, an increase in county population necessarily increases the population density of the county. Of interest here is how that increased density affects per capita public spending. Two opposite forces are at work. On the one hand, higher density is likely to increase per capita spending as more services, such as refuse collection, must be provided through the public rather than the private sector, and as more publicly provided goods, such as traffic lights, are needed to provide a given level of the outputs that consumers value, such as public safety. Working in the other direction, per capita costs could possibly fall if, as argued by many planners, there are economies of density in the production of certain public services. More analysis of how density affects spending would contribute both to our understanding of how population growth affects spending and to the policy question of whether to encourage higher-density development in order to reduce public sector costs.

The purpose of this paper is to isolate these two main effects of population change on per capita spending. The strategy is to estimate a fully specified cross-sectional model using data on spending by all local governments in 247 large US large counties, paying particular attention to the specification of the density and population-change variables. Results from this analysis shed light on two policy-relevant land-use issues: whether development pays its fiscal way, and whether denser development is fiscally more cost-effective than less dense development.

Data Sources and Results of Previous Work

The data for this study are for 247 large counties in 1985. Together with Washington, DC, which has been deleted from this study because of its unique position as the nation's capital, these counties account for more than 59 per cent of the nation's population. The data set was assembled as part of a larger project to explore the complex interrelationships between local population and economic growth on the one hand and local taxes and spending on the other, and represents all the counties for which complete data were available for both 1978 and 1985. The main sources for the fiscal data are US Department of Commerce, Bureau of the Census (1980, 1987) (see Ladd, 1990, for more discussion of the data.)

Two aspects of the data deserve emphasis. The first relates to the use of county areas as the unit of observation. In contrast to metropolitan areas or municipalities, county areas are uniquely suited for this analysis because their boundaries, and consequently their land areas, are fixed over time. Thus, a given percentage increase in population implies a corresponding percentage increase in population density. Secondly, the spending data for this study include spending by all local governments within the geographic area defined by county boundaries. More commonly, fiscal data are analysed by type of local government, such as cities, counties or school districts. The disadvantage of using data by type of local government for national fiscal comparisons is that the spending responsibilities of each type of local government differ from one state to another and sometimes within states, thereby making it difficult to define comparable spending measures. For example, in areas where municipalities have responsibility for local schools, spending by school districts would understate the true spending by local governments on elementary and secondary education. Using data aggregated across all local governments within the county ensures that all local spending on schools or any other function is included.

In a recent study, we used these data to examine the effects of changes in population on changes in per capita public spending by function and on local tax burdens for the 1978–85 period. Two sets of models were estimated (Ladd, 1990). In the first, the 1978–85 percentage change in per capita spending (by function) was simply regressed on the 1978–85 percentage change in population. In the second, statistical controls were added for the changes in the local economy (as measured by the change in per capita income and in jobs per resident); in inter-governmental fiscal relationships (as measured by the change in the share of state–local spending by function carried out at the local level); and in the age distribution of the population.

That research documents the substantial spending pressures that local population growth imposes on local governments. As an exercise in positive, predictive analysis, the results were clear: rapid population growth is associated with large increases in per capita public spending, especially in the areas of capital outlay, transportation spending and interest on general debt. But while that research was well designed to measure the fiscal pressures on local governments associated with population growth, it was not designed to separate the surge effects of rapid population growth from the effects on spending of having a larger and denser population. Hence, the present study complements the earlier work by using a study design that facilitates this separation.

Outputs and Costs: Concepts and Distinctions

Per capita public sector spending on current operations can be viewed as the product of the quantity or quality of public sector outputs and the costs of providing those outputs. Throughout this paper, the following definitions and distinctions are relevant. With respect to public sector outputs, the final outputs valued by citizen voters, such as protection from crime, should be distinguished from the intermediate or direct outputs produced by the public sector, such as police patrols (see Bradford et al., 1969). This distinction is relevant because the quantity of intermediate or direct outputs required to provide a given level of final outputs is likely to vary across counties according to the characteristics of the county; the harsher the environment for producing public services, the more direct outputs are needed to produce a given level of final outputs. In this research, we focus on the final output as valued by consumers.

The concept of costs can be confusing because it can refer either to the costs of producing a given level of direct outputs or, as in this research, a given level of final goods. As hinted at above and elaborated below, this distinction helps reconcile the planner's view that higher density is associated with lower production costs (of direct outputs) and the economist's view that higher density may increase the cost of providing final outputs.

The term costs is also sometimes used synonymously with per capita public sector spending. This usage is misleading for comparisons of costs across counties to the extent that differences in per capita spending reflect different levels of public services as well as differences in costs. However, provided that the factors that determine the demand for final outputs are adequately controlled for, differences in per capita spending on current operations can be roughly interpreted as differences in costs.[2] A similar statement cannot be made

Previous Work on Density

Many engineering studies investigate the link between population density and public sector costs, but one must be careful in interpreting them. Typically, these studies develop cost estimates for hypothetical developments of differing densities and other characteristics. One of the earliest, the study by Wheaton and Schussheim (1955), initially was widely interpreted as providing evidence that higher-density development reduces public sector costs. However, as noted by Kain (1967) in an unpublished survey, the authors' conclusions relate more to the placement of the development than to density.

The most widely cited study on this topic, the Real Estate Research Corporation's (1974) study, *The Costs of Sprawl*, reports significant savings for the local public sector from high-density planned development. Using detailed data from *The Costs of Sprawl*, Downing and Gustely (1977) find that, compared to low-density development, high-density development significantly reduces both the capital and operating costs of the police, fire and solid waste collection and disposal services, water supply, sanitary dewers and storm sewers, but not schools. These findings, however, are based on the assumption of a given number of people and a fixed amount of land which produce a constant average density (see Windsor, 1979); indeed, the 'high-density' development might more accurately be labelled 'compact development plus open space'. In addition, the findings focus quite narrowly on the costs of servicing the residential site alone with little attention to the costs of providing public services such as roads for all the activities, such as jobs, shopping and relaxation, that accompany residential development.[3] Finally, the findings refer to the costs of providing intermediate rather than final outputs.

An alternative approach involves the use of regression analysis. With this approach, the analyst typically uses cross-sectional data to examine the relationship between per capita local public spending and density, controlling for other determinants of public spending. This approach is advantageous in that it can pick up all the effects of density, not just those on the costs of providing direct outputs. Moreover, it provides a more comprehensive view in that the analysis extends beyond the typically site-specific perspective of the engineering studies. However, when implementing this approach, one must be careful to embed the density variables in a fully specified expenditure equation.

Several recent regression analyses of the costs of providing public services in cities provide evidence to support the view that, savings through the production of direct outputs notwithstanding, higher average density *increases* the costs of providing public services (see Bradbury et al., 1984; Ladd and Yinger, 1989). The mechanism through which this outcome occurs can be understood in terms of the harshness of the environment. For example, increased density may require more traffic lights and traffic control officers to achieve a given level of traffic safety or traffic flow. Similarly, higher density may raise the social costs of inappropriately disposed waste and therefore may require more waste collection and disposal. Increased density may also provide an environment more conducive to crime which requires more police services to achieve a given level of protection from crime.[4]

In summary, the findings on the effects of density on public service costs are still ambiguous. Moreover, the combination of potential economies of density in the production of direct outputs with the effect of density on the derived demand for intermediate outputs suggests that the relationship is probably not linear. Theoretical considerations alone are not sufficient to predict the precise functional form of the relationship between density and the costs of providing a given level of final outputs.

The Basic Model

The effects of population change and density on spending can best be determined by embedding those variables in a fully specified model of local public spending. The basic model used in this paper is derived from the extensive literature on local public spending in which the desired level of per capita spending is specified as a function of the demand for public services and their costs. Letting EXP_i represent desired per capita spending in the ith county, the model has the following general form:

EXP_i = f(demand, cost and taste variables; intergovernmental relations variables; population-density vector; population-change vector)

Following the literature, we specify all the variables in logarithmic form, except for the population-density and -change vectors, which are discussed below. Hence, the equation to be estimated takes the form:

$$LEXP_i = a + bLX_i + cLIGR_i + dDEN_i + ePOP_i + u_i$$

where:

LEXP is the natural logarithm of per capita expenditures;
LX is a vector of demand, cost and taste variables, all in natural logarithms;
LIGR is a vector of intergovernmental relations variables, all in natural logarithms;
DEN is a vector of density variables;
POP is a vector of population-change variables;
a is a parameter, and b, c, d and e are vectors of parameters to be estimated;
and u is a randomly distributed error term.

Specification of the Density and Population-change Variables

As the central focus of this study, the density and population-change variables deserve special attention. Throughout this study, density is defined as gross population density and is measured by the total population in the county divided by the county's land area in square miles. Population change is measured as an average annual rate of change over the 7-year period, 1978–85.

Other than indicating that a linear form, or even a log-linear form, would in general not be appropriate, conceptual considerations shed little light on the correct functional form for either variable. Hence, we have chosen to let the data determine the functional form using the technique of piecewise linear regression. With this approach, the statistical relationship between density or population change and per capita spending, controlling for other variables, is estimated in the form of a series of linear, connected segments as shown in Figure 1. The estimated regression coefficients, labelled b_0 to b_4 in the figure, indicate the height of the curve at each of the segment end-points.[5] With sufficient data, this approach allows a close approximation of the true functional relationship and avoids the awkward steps of the more common dummy-variable approach.

Regression Equations

Based on data for 247 counties in 1985, per capita spending equations were esti-

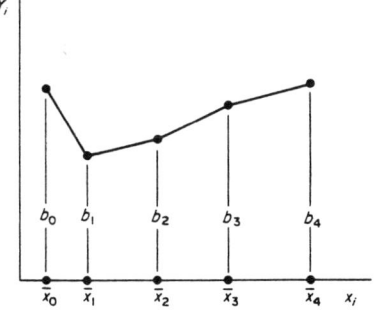

Figure 1. Piecewise linear regression form.

mated for three categories of spending: total current operations, capital outlays and public safety. As discussed more fully below, one must interpret with care the results for capital spending because local government accounting systems make no attempt to determine the annual user cost of capital (except in enterprise accounts). Instead, capital expenditures are recorded simply as outlays in the year in which they occur.

The following control variables are included in most of the regressions.

Demand, cost and taste variables. The primary demand variables are the income of county residents (LYPC85) and the tax price (LRES86) that they face for public services. Because property taxes are the major revenue source used by local governments and in many cases are likely to be the marginal revenue source, the tax price is specified as the residential share of local assessed valuation of property. The greater the residential share of assessed valuation, the higher the cost to local resident voters of an additional dollar of public services. The income elasticity of demand is hypothesised to be positive, while the price elasticity is expected to be negative.

Input costs are measured by the private sector manufacturing wage rate (LWAGE85); the higher the private sector wage, the higher the wage that public sector employers will have to pay to induce workers to work in the public sector.[6] Since the coefficient of this wage variable reflects both the effects of higher wages on spending and the negative price effect on the demand for services, the coefficient is expected to be positive but less than 1.

Other cost variables can be viewed as environmental cost factors. That is, they represent characteristics of the county outside the control of local public officials which affect the costs of providing a given level of public services. For example, to the extent that high poverty rates are associated with higher crime rates (either because poor people may turn to crime to support themselves or because poor people are more frequently the victims of crime), a county with a high poverty rate would have to spend more than a comparable county with a lower poverty rate to provide a given level of protection from crime. Similarly, a city with a large daytime population relative to its night-time or resident population may also need to spend more on police and fire protection to provide a given level of public safety. Included as environmental cost factors in the regressions reported below are the poverty rate (LPOV79), manufacturing and non-manufacturing jobs per resident to capture the daytime population (LJMAN85 and LJNMAN85), the number of pupils relative to the residents (LPUPS85) and in some equations the crime rate (LCRIME85).

Both population density and population itself can also be viewed as environmental cost factors. The specification of the density variable has already been discussed. Even controlling for population density, population (LPOP85) itself could affect per capita spending either because of the publicness of publicly provided services or because of economies or diseconomies of scale in production. In the extreme case of pure public goods (and constant returns to scale in production), the per capita costs of providing a given level of public goods vary inversely with the size of the population; the more people among whom the fixed costs of a given level of the pure public good can be spread, the lower are the per capita costs of the good. Working in the other direction is the possibility that providing services for a larger population could entail diseconomies of scale. Because our empirical analysis covers many governments within a county area, however, we are less likely to find evidence of diseconomies of scale than if the analysis focused on one governmental unit alone.[7]

Counties may also differ in the preferences of county residents for public services. To control for preference differences, the proportion of county residents with 12 or more years of education

Table 1. Variables: definitions and means (247 counties)[a]

Variable	Definition	Mean	Standard deviation
Expenditure variables			
LCURR85	Spending on current operations, per capita	6.97	0.26
LPS85	Spending on public safety, per capita	4.73	0.41
LCAP85	Capital outlays, per capita	5.02	0.59
LCAP78	Capital outlays, per capita, 1978	5.06	0.52
Demand, cost and taste variables			
LYPC85	Income, per capita	9.48	0.17
LRES86	Residential share of assessed value of property tax base, 1986	−0.43	0.15
LWAGE85	Manufacturing wage rate (by state)	2.27	0.13
LPUPS85	Public school enrolments, per capita	−1.82	0.17
LPOV79	Fraction of population below poverty level, 1979	2.22	0.41
LJMAN85	Manufacturing employment per resident	−2.61	0.59
LJNMAN85	Non-manufacturing jobs per resident	−0.85	0.27
LCRIME85	Crime rate	−3.02	0.46
LPOP85	Population	5.98	0.74
PL12ED80	Percentage of population with more than 12 years of education, 1980	4.25	0.11
Intergovernmental relations variables			
LRDGE85	Ratio of local direct general expenditure to state and local direct general expenditure in the county's state	−0.53	0.12
LRPS85	Ratio of local spending on public safety to state and local spending on public safety in the county's state	−0.33	0.10
LIFED85	Federal aid, per capita	4.05	0.64
LIST85	State aid, per capita	5.92	0.43
Regional dummy variables			
EAST	Dummy variable, takes on value 1 if county is in the East	0.27	0.44
MIDWEST	Dummy variable, takes on value 1 if county is in the Midwest	0.26	0.43
SOUTH	Dummy variable, takes on value 1 if county is in the South	0.30	0.45
WEST	Dummy variable, takes on value 1 if county is in the West	—	—
Density variables[b]			
D0	Population density equals 0 people per square mile	0.06	0.16
D250	Population density equals 250 people per square mile	0.26	0.33
D500	Population density equals 500 people per square mile	0.14	0.26
D750	Population density equals 750 people per square mile	0.14	0.27
D1250	Population density equals 1250 people per square mile	0.16	0.32
D1750	Population density equals 1750 people per square mile	0.02	0.10
D24000	Population density equals 24 000 people per square mile	0.10	0.21
D750[c]	Population density equals 750 people per square mile	0.13	0.26
D1000[c]	Population density equals 1000 people per square mile	0.13	0.26
D1500[c]	Population density equals 1500 people per square mile	0.21	0.36
D24000[c]	Population density equals 24 000 people per square mile	0.02	0.10
Population-change variables[b]			
Pneg.	Average annual population growth rate, 1978–85, −0.013	0.07	0.17
P0	Average annual population growth rate, 1978–85, 0	0.33	0.36

Table 1. *(Cont.)*

Variable	Definition	Mean	Standard deviation
P0.01	Average annual population growth rate, 1978–85, 0.01	0.26	0.32
P0.02	Average annual population growth rate, 1978–85, 0.02	0.19	0.31
P0.035	Average annual population growth rate, 1978–85, 0.035	0.10	0.22
P0.05	Average annual population growth rate, 1978–85, 0.05	0.05	0.18
P0.085	Average annual population growth rate, 1978–85, 0.085	0.01	0.09

[a] All dollar figures are in 1982 real dollars (based on gross national product implicit deflator for personal consumption expenditure); L signifies natural logarithm.
[b] See Note 5 for explanation of these variables.
[c] Part of alternative set of density variables.

(L12ED80) is included in the regressions. Educational background is an appropriate taste variable since the more highly educated local residents are, the more likely they are to spend on elementary and secondary education, an expenditure category that accounts for almost half of local public spending.

Intergovernmental relations variables. States vary as to how they divide spending responsibilities between state and local governments. In many states, for example, state governments take full responsibility for welfare and other social service programmes; in other states local governments take some responsibility for these programmes. To control for these differences across counties within the sample, local share variables (LRDGE85 and LRPS85) are included in each equation, where for each specific category of spending the local share of spending is measured as the ratio of spending by all local governments in the state on that category to total spending by state and local governments combined. Because the measure is based on state-wide rather than county data, it is exogenous to the county spending decision.

A second important aspect of intergovernmental relations is intergovernmental aid from both the state and the federal government. By increasing the financial resources available to local governments, such aid is likely to increase local spending. In the absence of detailed information on the type of such aid (e.g. matching versus non-matching) or on its specific provisions (e.g. maintenance of effort or 'no strings'), the equations simply include two aid variables: state aid (LIST85) and federal aid (LIFED85) per capita.

Regional dummy variables. To account for the possibility of systematic differences in local public spending not captured by the other control variables, some of the equations include three regional dummy variables (EAST, MIDWEST and SOUTH) that measure differences in spending in that region relative to the WEST.

The means and standard deviations of all the variables are reported in Table 1.

Empirical Results: Current Operations

To determine how population change and density affect the costs of providing services to current residents, we begin by focusing on current account spending alone. Capital spending should be excluded from the basic spending measure since it represents not the annual costs of using capital but rather the amount of gross investment in public sector infrastructure designed to serve both current and future residents.

The results for the current operations equations are reported in Table 2 for the control variables and Table 3 for the variables of primary interest, i.e. those relating to population change and density. Three regressions are reported: a basic equation, an equation with an alternative specification of the density variables and the basic equation supplemented by regional dummies. All three regressions perform well and explain about 64 per cent of the variation in per capita spending. The results for the control variables are similar across the equations, with the coefficients of the regional dummies being small and insignificant.

Control Variables

The signs of all the control variables are consistent with expectations, although a few of the coefficients are small and statistically insignificant. The estimated income and price elasticities are reasonable (0.34 for income and −0.12 for price), although the latter is not statistically significant. The coefficient of the wage variable is appropriately positive, but is smaller than expected. Among the cost variables, pupils and poverty come in most strongly, with more pupils and higher rates of poverty leading to higher per capita spending. Manufacturing and non-manufacturing employment are also positive as predicted, but are significant only in the first equation. The small and insignificant coefficient on population is consistent with other studies that imply that publicly provided services are more like private than like public goods (see, for example, Bergstrom and Goodman, 1973; Borcherding and Deacon, 1972).

All three intergovernmental variables are positive and highly significant. The greater the local share of a state's state and local spending, the greater the per capita spending by local governments within each county; a 10 per cent difference in the local share is associated with a 5.6 per cent difference in local spending. As expected, federal and state aid are also associated with higher spending. The elasticities reported in the table translate into marginal impacts of US\$1.58 for federal aid and US\$0.47 for state aid. In other words, each dollar of federal aid stimulates more than a dollar of spending while about half of each dollar of state aid shows up in higher spending and the other half in tax reduction.

These reasonable results for the control variables give one confidence in the equations and suggest that they should yield reliable results for the density and population-change variables.

The Effects of Density on Current Spending

The results for the density variables are reported in Table 3. The coefficient estimates are translated into more meaningful percentage effects and into dollar magnitudes in Table 4.[8] Because the equations control for the demand for public services, the coefficients of the density variables can be interpreted roughly as the effect of density on the costs of providing public services.[9] The end-points of the various line segments were chosen to provide a reasonable number of counties in each interval. The distribution of counties by interval, along with some representative counties, are reported in Table 5.

The following pattern emerges from the basic equation (equation (1) in Table 3). The lowest spending (and hence costs) occur at a density of about 250 people per square mile. For densities between 0 and 250 people per square mile, costs fall quite steeply with increasing density. Assuming a linear segment, the 0.268 coefficient at zero density implies that the cost would be about 14 per cent higher for a county with a density of 125 people per square mile than for one with 250 people per square mile. At densities above the minimum-cost

Table 2. Spending on current operations: effects of control variables (247 counties, 1985)[a]

Variable	Basic equation (1)	Alternative density (2)	Basic equation plus regions (3)
Density and population-change variables	See Table 3	See Table 3	See Table 3
Demand, cost and taste variables			
LYPC85	0.343**	0.343**	0.363**
	(3.14)	(3.13)	(3.16)
LRES86	−0.123	−0.114	−0.126
	(1.39)	(1.28)	(1.41)
LWAGE85	0.093	0.088	0.042
	(0.84)	(0.80)	(0.32)
LPUPS85	0.209**	0.209**	0.210**
	(2.44)	(2.43)	(2.37)
LPOV79	0.119**	0.116**	0.127**
	(2.09)	(2.04)	(2.18)
LJMAN85	0.039*	0.036	0.037
	(1.75)	(1.62)	(1.55)
LJNMAN85	0.121*	0.112	0.121
	(1.66)	(1.54)	(1.62)
LCRIME85	0.004	0.004	0.003
	(0.12)	(0.02)	(0.14)
LPOP85	0.004	0.009	0.001
	(0.19)	(0.24)	(0.02)
L12ED80	0.362**	0.366**	0.332
	(2.48)	(2.49)	(2.17)
Intergovernmental relations variables			
LRDGE85	0.570**	0.562	0.574
	(4.88)	(4.79)	(4.66)
LIFED85	0.085**	0.089**	0.082
	(3.32)	(3.47)	(3.16)
LIST85	0.167**	0.164**	0.164**
	(4.52)	(4.43)	(4.07)
Regional dummy variables			
EAST	—	—	−0.026
			(0.51)
MIDWEST	—	—	0.004
			(0.08)
SOUTH	—	—	0.031
			(0.69)
WEST	—	—	Base
Constant	1.14	1.17	1.21
	(0.93)	(0.95)	(0.92)
Adjusted R^2	0.639	0.636	0.635
Standard error	0.160	0.160	0.160
Number of observations	247	247	247

* Statistically significant at the 10 per cent level; ** statistically significant at the 5 per cent level.
[a] Results from regression with specified variables plus density and population variables listed in Table 3. Absolute values of t-statistics are in parentheses.

Table 3. Spending on current operations: effects of density and population change (247 counties, 1985)[a]

Variable	Basic equation (1)	Alternative density (2)	Basic equation plus regions (3)
Density variables			
D0	0.268**	0.274	0.254
	(2.91)	(2.96)	(2.68)
D250	Base	Base	Base
D500	0.047	0.052	0.047
	(0.88)	(0.95)	(0.87)
D750	0.091**	0.080	0.099**
	(1.86)	(1.40)	(1.95)
D1250	0.171**	—	0.173**
	(2.94)		(2.93)
D1750	0.068	—	0.070
	(1.19)		(1.19)
D2400	0.359**	—	0.357**
	(2.51)		(2.45)
D1000	—	0.164**	—
		(2.88)	
D1500	—	0.097*	—
		(1.78)	
D24000	—	0.343**	—
		(2.40)	
Population-change variables			
Pneg.	0.063	0.047	0.062
	(0.84)	(0.63)	(0.81)
P0	Base	Base	Base
P0.01	−0.016	−0.106**	−0.104**
	(0.38)	(2.40)	(−2.16)
P0.02	−0.097**	−0.016**	−0.019
	(2.20)	(0.37)	(0.56)
P0.035	−0.035	−0.032	−0.038
	(0.56)	(0.49)	(2.16)
P0.05	−0.123	−0.127	−0.123
	(1.58)	(1.63)	(5.53)
P0.085	−0.140	−0.139	−0.137
	(1.07)	(1.06)	(1.01)

* Statistically significant at the 10 per cent level; ** statistically significant at the 5 per cent level.
[a] Results from full regressions are reported in Table 2. Absolute values of *t*-statistics are in parentheses.

density, costs rise monotonically up to a density of 1250 people per square mile. At that density, costs are approximately 19 per cent above the minimum level. Somewhat counter-intuitively, costs fall slightly as density increases to 1750 people per square mile, but then rise again, reaching a level 43 per cent greater than the minimum in the densest counties.

Thus, the basic message is that beyond the relatively low average density of 250 people per square mile, the costs of providing public services increase with population density.

To examine the sensitivity of the results to the specific intervals chosen and in particular to determine whether the decline at the 1750 density level is a quirk of

Table 4. Current operations: predicted effects of density and population change[a]

	Equation (1)			Equation (2)	
	Predicted spending relative to base	Predicted spending (1982 dollars)		Predicted spending relative to base	Predicted spending (1982 dollars)
Density variables					
D125	1.14	1111	D125	1.15	1115
D250	Base	972	D250	Base	972
D500	1.05	1019	D500	1.05	1024
D750	1.10	1065	D750	1.08	1053
D1250	1.19	1153	D1000	1.18	1145
D1750	1.07	1040	D1500	1.10	1071
D24000	1.43	1392	D24000	1.41	1370
Population-change variables					
Pneg.	1.07	1175			
P0	Base	1103			
P0.01	0.98	1085			
P0.02	0.91	1001			
P0.035	0.97	1065			
P0.05	0.88	975			
P0.085	0.87	959			

[a] Based on Table 3. The base magnitude in each case is the average per capita spending for counties with population densities equal to 250 ± 125 for the density variables and with population growth equal to 0 ± 0.005 for the population-change variables; D125 indicates population density of 125 people per square mile.

the choice of interval end-points, equation (2) reports density coefficients for a different sequence of intervals above 750 people per square mile. The pattern is similar to that for the original sequence. In this case costs rise to 18 per cent above the minimum at a density of 1000 people per square mile, fall to 10 per cent at a density of 1500 people per square mile, and then rise to 41 per cent at the highest density. This pattern is comparable to the pattern for the basic equation. Experimentation with other interval sequences yields similar patterns.

Equation (3) differs from equation (1) only in the addition of the three regional dummies. As already noted, the coefficients of these three variables are small and statistically insignificant. Not surprisingly, therefore, their inclusion in the equation has virtually no effect on the density coefficients.

The Effects of Population Change on Current Spending

The effects of population change are estimated less precisely than those of population density, but nonetheless a general pattern emerges; controlling for other factors, the faster is the rate of population growth, the lower is per capita spending.[10] (See the first column of Table 3 and its translation in Table 4.) This relationship emerges most clearly for the most rapidly growing counties. The point estimates suggest that per capita spending in counties growing at rapid rates of between 5 and 8.5 per cent per year is 12 to 13 per cent below that in counties experiencing no population growth. Because the equation controls for the manifestations of population growth, such as a larger population or a different mix of people, this negative relationship between rapid population growth

Table 5. Distribution of counties by their population density (247 counties, 1985)

Density (people per square mile)	Number of counties	Representative counties	Density (people per square mile)
0–249	37	Riverside (CA)	113
		Maricopa (Phoenix, AZ)	199
250–499	73	Palm Beach (FL)	363
		Wake (Raleigh, NC)	414
500–749	37	Albany (NY)	541
		Orange (Orlando, FL)	609
750–1249	42	Morris (Newark, NJ)	889
		Cobb (Atlanta, GA)	1 087
1250–1750	22	Honolulu (HI)	1 361
		Suffolk (Long Island, NY)	1 433
> 1750	36	Los Angeles (CA)	1 998
		Saint Louis City (MO)	7 026
		Philadelphia (PA)	12 114
Total	247		7 026

and per capita spending suggests that counties respond only sluggishly to a surge in population and in the process presumably allow their services to deteriorate.

A comparison across regressions shows that these results are not sensitive to the use of the alternative set of density variables, nor to the inclusion of the regional dummies.

This finding that very rapid population growth is associated with *lower* per capita spending can easily be reconciled with the opposite conclusion from our earlier study (Ladd, 1990). First, this finding applies to current account spending alone, while the largest effects in the previous study were related to capital spending. As reported below, population growth exerts a strong positive impact on capital outlays. Secondly, the negative effect reported here captures only the surge effects of population change; the depressing effects on spending of the population surge might be more than offset by the other manifestations of population change (including, for example, higher density) which increase per capita spending.

Other Empirical Results: Capital Outlays and Public Safety

Comparable equations for capital outlays and public safety shed further light on the effects of population change and density on spending. The effects of population change emerge most clearly in the capital outlay equations and those of density most clearly in the public safety equations.

Capital Outlays

As already noted, capital outlays measure gross investment, not the annual costs of using capital. Hence, the capital outlay equations should not be interpreted as indicating the effects of population change and density on the annual cost of using capital. Instead they simply provide information on how population change and density affect investment spending.

The capital outlay equations take the same form as those for current spending and are reported in Tables 6 and 7. Two equations are reported, a basic equation and the basic equation with a dependent variable lagged 7 years to allow for the possibility of partial adjustment of actual to desired levels of capital spending.[11] The estimated coefficient on the lagged variable of 0.47 implies that 53 per cent of the difference between desired and actual capital spending is achieved during the 7-year time-period.[12] Because it is a model of the

Table 6. Capital outlays: effects of control variables (247 counties, 1985)[a]

Variable	Basic equation (1)	Partial adjustment (2)
Density and population-change variables	See Table 7	See Table 7
Demand, cost and taste variables		
LYPC85	−0.463*	−0.213
	(1.73)	(0.75)
LRES86	−0.317	−0.214
	(1.46)	(0.98)
LWAGE85	0.064	0.195
	(0.24)	(−0.72)
LPUPS85	0.438**	0.183
	(2.09)	(0.78)
LPOV79	−0.234*	−0.227*
	(1.69)	(1.67)
LJMAN85	0.088	0.108**
	(1.58)	(1.97)
LJNMAN85	0.939**	0.624**
	(5.25)	(2.79)
LCRIME85	0.087	0.070
	(0.98)	(0.80)
LPOP85	0.026	0.037
	(0.49)	(0.72)
L12ED80	0.600*	0.368
	(1.67)	(1.00)
Intergovernmental relations variables		
LRDGE85	0.686**	0.317
	(2.39)	(0.97)
LIFED85	0.370**	0.276**
	(5.86)	(3.70)
LIST85	0.090	0.113
	(0.99)	(1.27)
Lagged dependent variable		
LCAP78	—	0.47**
		(2.25)
Regional dummy variables		
EAST	—	—
MIDWEST	—	—
SOUTH	—	—
WEST	—	—
Constant	7.24**	3.15
	(2.41)	(0.91)
Adjusted R^2	0.556	0.573
Standard error	0.392	0.384
Number of observations	247	247

* Statistically significant at the 10 per cent level; ** statistically significant at the 5 per cent level.
[a] Results from regression with specified variables plus density and population variables listed in Table 7. Absolute values of *t*-statistics are in parentheses.

Table 7. Capital outlays: effects of density and population change (247 counties, 1985)[a]

Variable	Basic equation (1)	Partial adjustment (2)
Density variables		
D0	−0.002	0.025
	(0.01)	(0.13)
D500	Base	Base
D750	0.260*	0.233*
	(1.89)	(1.73)
D1250	−0.201*	−0.060
	(1.68)	(0.45)
D1750	0.131	0.088
	(1.06)	(0.71)
D24000	0.534	0.369
	(1.53)	(1.06)
Population-change variables		
Pneg.	0.097	−0.075
	(0.52)	(0.38)
P0	Base	Base
P0.01	0.158	0.116
	(1.51)	(1.10)
P0.02	0.335**	0.282**
	(3.09)	(2.58)
P0.035	0.672**	0.552**
	(4.39)	(3.47)
P0.05	0.878	0.674**
	(4.60)	(3.24)
P0.085	1.62**	1.115**
	(5.10)	(2.25)

* Statistically significant at the 10 per cent level; ** statistically significant at the 5 per cent level.
[a] Results from full equations as reported in Table 6. Absolute values of t-statistics are in parentheses.

demand for public services by current residents, the theoretical model on which the equations are based is less appropriate for capital outlays than for current spending. Hence, not surprisingly, the capital outlay equations perform somewhat less well than the current account equations, with values of R^2 hovering around 0.56, and fewer of the control variables are important.

The most important control variables are the amount of non-manufacturing employment per resident (LJMAN85), the number of pupils per resident (LPUPS85), the local share of state–local spending (LRDGE85) and federal aid (LIFED85), all of which increase capital outlays. Somewhat surprisingly, higher per capita income (LYPC85) is associated with lower capital investment. The negative sign on the poverty variable (LPOV79) suggests that counties with a high incidence of poverty favour current services at the expense of investment in infrastructure.

The results for the density variables are suggestive, but hard to interpret. Putting aside the counties with the lowest density, the relationship between density and capital outlays appears to be somewhat U-shaped, with a trough at a density of 500 people per square mile. In general counties with densities greater than 500 tend to

Table 8. Capital outlays: predicted effects of density and population change[a]

	Equation (1)			Equation (2)	
	Predicted spending relative to base	Predicted spending (1982 dollars)		Predicted spending relative to base	Predicted spending (1982 dollars)
Density variables					
D125	1.00	176	D125	1.01	178
D250	1.34	235	D250	1.27	224
D500	Base	176	D500	Base	176
D750	1.30	228	D750	1.26	222
D1250	1.22	215	D1250	1.06	187
D1750	1.14	201	D1750	1.09	192
D24000	1.71	300	D24000	1.45	254
Population-change variables					
Pneg.	1.10	133	Pneg.	0.93	112
P0	Base	121	P0	Base	121
P0.01	1.17	141	P0.01	1.12	136
P0.02	1.40	169	P0.02	1.33	160
P0.035	1.96	237	P0.035	1.74	210
P0.05	2.41	290	P0.05	1.96	237
P0.085	5.05	610	P0.085	3.05	368

[a] Based on Table 7. The base magnitude in each case is the average per capita spending for counties with population densities equal to 500 ± 125 for the density variables and with population growth equal to 0 ± 0.005 for the population-change variables.

have higher spending than those with a lower population density. However, because they tell us nothing about how density affects the annual costs of using capital, these results are not particularly interesting.

Of more interest are the effects on capital outlays of population change. Here the effects are clear and dramatic (see Tables 7 and 8). As the annual rate of population growth increases from 1 per cent to 8.5 per cent, capital spending rises monotonically from 17 per cent to 405 per cent above the typical amount of capital spending in a no-growth county according to the basic equation (which reflects the long-run adjustment) and from 12 to 205 per cent in the other equation (which reflects the partial adjustment over the 7-year period). Moreover, most of the coefficients are highly significant. Thus, the major stress on local public spending associated with a surge in population occurs in the capital, not the current, account budget.

Public Safety

The spending category of public safety illustrates quite clearly, once again, the U-shaped effects of population density on spending. Tables 9 and 10 report coefficients for four equations that differ one from another depending on the inclusion or exclusion of the crime rate variable and the three regional dummies.

The crime rate can be viewed as an environmental cost factor, and exerts a large positive impact on spending for public safety. Not surprisingly, the equations that include the crime rate perform slightly better than those that exclude it. However, two arguments can be made for estimating equations without the crime variable. First, it is not fully exogenous; the crime rate is presumably influenced in part by the level of spending on the police component of public safety. Secondly, to the extent that the crime rate is positively correlated with population density across

Table 9. Spending on public safety: effects of control variables (247 counties, 1985)[a]

Variable	Basic equation (1)	No LCRIME85 (2)	No LCRIME85 plus regions (3)
Density and population-change variables	See Table 3	See Table 3	See Table 3
Demand, cost and taste variables			
LYPC85	0.601**	−0.661**	0.779
	(4.28)	(4.33)	(5.24)
LRES86	−0.078	−0.139	−0.171
	(0.67)	(1.11)	(1.45)
LWAGE85	−0.065	0.180	0.075
	(0.44)	(1.17)	(0.44)
LPUPS85	0.069	−0.026	0.046
	(0.61)	(0.21)	(0.40)
LPOV79	0.004	0.192**	0.161**
	(0.06)	(2.62)	(2.25)
LJMAN85	−0.059**	−0.041	−0.033**
	(2.03)	(1.28)	(1.06)
LJNMAN85	0.233**	0.415**	0.320
	(2.43)	(4.16)	(3.31)
LCRIME85	0.304**	—	—
	(6.45)		
LPOP85	0.017	0.042	0.028
	(0.58)	(1.39)	(0.97)
L12ED80	0.049	0.057	−0.160
	(0.26)	(0.27)	(0.79)
Intergovernmental relations variables			
LRPS85	0.677**	0.539**	0.630**
	(3.93)	(2.90)	(3.26)
LIFED85	0.067**	0.063*	0.043
	(2.03)	(1.74)	(1.26)
LIST85	0.251**	0.234**	0.231**
	(6.37)	(5.48)	(5.55)
Regional dummy variables			
EAST	—	—	−0.356**
			(5.71)
MIDWEST	—	—	−0.213**
			(3.54)
SOUTH	—	—	−0.207**
			(3.41)
WEST	—	—	Base
Constant	−2.012	−4.405	−3.64
	(1.25)	(2.57)	(2.19)
Adjusted R^2	0.740	0.692	0.730
Standard error	0.207	0.225	0.211
Number of observations	247	247	247

* Statistically significant at the 10 per cent level; ** statistically significant at the 5 per cent level.
[a] Results from regression with specified variables plus density and population variables listed in Table 10. Absolute values of *t*-statistics are in parentheses.

Table 10. Spending on public safety: effects of density and population change (247 counties, 1985)[a]

Variable	Basic equation (1)	No LCRIME85 (2)	No LCRIME85 plus regions (3)
Density variables			
D0	0.254**	0.306**	0.167
	(2.15)	(2.38)	(1.35)
D250	Base	Base	Base
D500	0.015	0.071	0.079
	(0.22)	(0.96)	(1.13)
D750	0.147**	0.208**	0.255**
	(2.30)	(3.02)	(3.89)
D1250	0.235**	0.324**	0.328**
	(3.13)	(4.05)	(4.34)
D1750	0.196**	0.230**	0.246**
	(2.65)	(2.86)	(3.21)
D24000	0.369**	0.416**	0.474**
	(2.02)	(2.10)	(2.52)
Population-change variables			
Pneg.	0.093	0.074	0.147
	(1.02)	(0.74)	(1.55)
P0	0.093*	0.076	0.151**
	(1.68)	(1.27)	(2.59)
P0.01	Base	Base	Base
P0.02	0.060	0.147**	0.070
	(0.96)	(2.18)	(1.08)
P0.035	0.108	0.197**	0.116
	(1.43)	(2.43)	(1.48)
P0.05	−0.027	0.150	0.087
	(0.28)	(1.47)	(0.87)
P0.085	0.123	0.113	0.009
	(0.07)	(0.63)	(0.04)

* Statistically significant at the 10 per cent level; ** statistically significant at the 5 per cent level.
[a] Results from full regressions are reported in Table 9. Absolute values of *t*-statistics are in parentheses.

counties, excluding it provides a more complete measure of the total effects of density on spending.

In contrast to the other spending categories, the regional dummies enter the public safety equations with statistically significant coefficients. In particular, controlling for the other determinants, spending on public safety is lower in the East, Midwest and South than in the West. The disadvantage of including the regional dummies is that one does not know what they are measuring. In general, there is no compelling reason to prefer one of the public safety equations over another.

As shown in Table 10, density exerts an essentially U-shaped effect on spending (with the minor aberration at a density of 1750 people per square mile) in all three equations. Leaving out the crime variable has little impact on the estimated effects of density. Including the regional dummies affects the extremes; the coefficient of the lowest-density counties declines and that for the highest-density increases.

These effects are summarised in Table 11 for equations (1) and (2). The effects of

Table 11. Public safety: predicted effects of density and population change[a]

	Equation (1)			Equation (2)	
	Predicted spending relative to base	Predicted spending (1982 dollars)		Predicted spending relative to base	Predicted spending (1982 dollars)
Density variables					
D125	1.14	141	D125	1.17	144
D250	Base	124	D250	Base	124
D500	1.02	126	D500	1.07	133
D750	1.16	143	D750	1.23	152
D1250	1.26	157	D1250	1.38	171
D1750	1.22	151	D1750	1.26	156
D24000	1.45	179	D24000	1.52	188
Population-change variables					
Pneg.	1.10	120	Pneg.	1.08	118
P0	1.10	120	P0	1.00	109
P0.01	Base	109	P0.01	Base	109
P0.02	1.06	116	P0.02	1.16	126
P0.035	1.11	121	P0.035	1.22	133
P0.05	0.97	106	P0.05	1.16	126
P0.085	1.13	123	P0.085	1.12	122

[a] Based on Tables 9 and 10. The base magnitude in each case is the average per capita spending for counties with population densities equal to 250 ± 125 for the density variables and with population growth equal to 0.01 ± 0.005 for the population-change variables.

density are large. The most densely populated counties are estimated to have public safety costs that exceed those of the base counties by 45 to 52 per cent. The doubling of a county's density from 500 to about 1000 people per square mile increases per capita public safety costs by about 30 per cent.

Implications for Land-use Policy Issues

These results shed light on two current policy questions: whether denser developments are more cost-effective than less dense development, and whether development pays its way.

Density and Public Sector Costs

Controlling for other factors that influence spending, this study shows that population density exerts a U-shaped impact on current account spending. Comparing two counties with very low densities (fewer than 250 people per square mile), the county with the higher density is likely to have *lower* costs than the county with the lower density, ceteris paribus. But for counties with densities between 250 and 1250 people per square mile, higher density *increases* the current costs of providing public services. A county with 1250 people per square mile is predicted to have costs that exceed those in the minimum-cost county by 19 per cent, or by about US$180 per capita (1982 dollars), US$23 of which represents higher public safety costs (see Tables 4 and 11). Although we cannot rule out the possibility that increasing density beyond 1250 people per square mile could reduce spending somewhat either on total current operations or on public safety, extremely high density is associated with substantially higher spending.

The increasing per capita spending as the density of counties rises above 250 people per square mile provides important additional evidence to counter the view, which emerges from engineering and planning studies, that higher density reduces public sector costs. The difference between this finding and that of the engineering studies rests partially on the distinction between capital and current costs and more importantly on the distinction between direct and final outputs. Much of the planning literature reviewed earlier focuses on the capital costs of economic development patterns. Yet current costs are quantitatively much larger than capital costs.[13] This fact implies that the failure to consider the current costs of providing local public services, and the failure to distinguish between the concepts of final outputs and direct outputs, could lead to misleading conclusions about the fiscal effects of density.

The conclusions also differ because of the different questions being asked. In the planning literature, analysts focus on the narrow question of the costs of servicing residential developments of different densities. As already noted, such studies typically hold both population and land area constant. In other words, these studies focus on the fiscal effects of differing distributions of a given number of people in a given area; higher density in that context really means more compact development with compensating open space. In contrast, this study focuses on the fiscal effects of differing average densities, where the averages are calculated over a relatively large geographic area, the county.

Although they are quite large and diverse, counties nonetheless are a reasonable unit of observation for investigating how density affects public sector costs. Each county is big enough to include a variety of land uses. This variety is desirable because public sector activities serve people in their capacity not only as residents but also as employees, commuters and recreationists. Hence, a complete measure of the costs of different patterns of development should extend beyond the residential patterns alone to include the public sector costs of the other activities that residents engage in. Although an argument might be made for focusing on somewhat smaller, more uniform governmental units such as municipalities, the smaller the geographic area the harder it is to get a complete picture of the total amount of spending by local governments on behalf of area residents. Typically, small geographic areas are serviced by a variety of different governmental units. This variety greatly complicates the task of determining the total amount of public spending on behalf of the area.

In summary, this regression-based approach to determining the effects of density on public sector costs counters the engineering-based view that higher-density development is associated with lower costs of providing public services. While the engineering view may be valid at very low densities, for moderately populated counties an increase in population density apparently creates a harsher environment for, and thereby raises the costs of, providing public services.

Does Development Pay its Way?

Often, when analysts ask whether development pays its way, the reference is to a specific development project (see, for example, Altshuler et al., 1990, ch. 3). Here, we define development more generally as local population growth and ask whether development in the form of population growth imposes a fiscal burden on established residents. To the extent that growth imposes such a burden, it does not pay its way.

Population growth exerts two main effects on local government spending for current purposes—a surge effect and a population-density effect. This study shows that for counties that initially are moderately populated, the effects on spending work in different directions. Regardless of the *rate* of population growth, the higher density associated with a larger population is likely to increase the costs of public services and therefore spending.

Higher density represents a harsher environment for providing public services which requires more public sector inputs to provide a given level of service. The surge effects of rapid population growth work in the other direction; they tend to decrease per capita spending on current operations. However, this result suggests that local governments respond to rapid growth in part by allowing current service levels to decline. Thus, focusing on public sector burdens alone, established residents in moderately populated counties bear two forms of fiscal burdens from population growth: higher costs and reduced service levels. Only if the new development contributed significantly more than the average cost of providing services could it be said that development pays its fiscal way.

The situation differs for sparsely settled counties. Here, the net fiscal impact of population growth on established residents is ambiguous. On the one hand, the increased density associated with population growth reduces costs in these sparsely populated counties. On the other, very rapid growth could lead to a deterioration in service levels as local governments adjust slowly to the change in population. For these counties, moderate rates of population growth could provide fiscal benefits to established residents.

This study also documents the large impact of population growth on capital outlays. How this surge in capital outlays affects established residents depends largely on how it is financed. If the financing burden could be spread out over time fully in line with the receipt of services from the capital, high capital outlays in response to current and expected future growth need not burden current residents; each generation of service recipients and taxpayers would pay taxes equal to the full costs of the capital services it uses. However, this coincidence of the timing of burdens and benefits is not likely to occur. One reason is that bond maturities are typically restricted by law to periods shorter than the useful life of capital investments. As a result, current residents subsidise future residents by paying more in taxes than they use in capital services (for more details, see Snyder and Stegman, 1987).

Thus, the effects of rapid population growth on current spending and service levels as well as on capital outlays suggest that rapid population growth places a fiscal burden on established residents or, stated differently, that new development does not pay its way. Of course, the normative question of whether it *should* be asked to pay its way in order to hold harmless established residents is a different question, and one that is beyond the scope of this paper. One should note, however, that to the extent that the fiscal burden on established residents arises because of the higher overall density in the county, it is hard to make an economic argument for higher financing burdens on new residents alone; after all, the established residents are as much a cause of the higher density as are the new residents.

Notes

1. The major exception to this generalisation is the vast amount of applied analysis undertaken by local officials, commonly known as fiscal impact or cost–revenue analysis, of the budgetary impacts of specific development projects. See, for example, Burchell and Listokin (1978) and Altshuler et al. (1990, ch. 3).
2. For theoretical precision, the statement in the text needs to be qualified to account for the fact that costs influence the desired level of public services through the tax price term. In principle, it is easy to adjust the cost estimates for the price elasticity of demand (see, for example, Ladd and Yinger, 1989), but these adjustments have not been made in this paper and, in any case, are likely to be small given the low price elasticities of demand reported later in the text.
3. A recent survey of this literature by Frank (1989) concludes that "none of the studies are free of technical problems. None, furthermore, reach unassailable conclusions. The studies represent stimulating but faulty and ultimately unsatisfying attempts to define efficient patterns of development" (p. 1).

4. We are using demand to refer only to the demand for final outputs such as protection from crime. Any factor that affects the cost per unit of final output is labelled a cost factor. However, it is not unreasonable to talk, as does Altshuler (1990), about the demand for intermediate outputs such as more police patrols, which derived from the more fundamental demand for police protection.
5. The piecewise linear model takes the following form:

$$Y_i = \sum_j b_j g_j(x_i) + u_i$$

$$g_j(x_i) = (x_i - \bar{x}_{j-1})/(\bar{x}_j - \bar{x}_{j-1})$$
$$\text{if } \bar{x}_{j-1} \leq x_i < \bar{x}_j$$
$$= (\bar{x}_{j+1} - x_i)/(\bar{x}_{j+1} - \bar{x}_j)$$
$$\text{if } \bar{x}_j \leq x_i < \bar{x}_{j+1}$$
$$= 0 \text{ otherwise,}$$

where y and x are variables, $\bar{x}$ signifies an end-point of an interval, g is a function, and u is a random error. At the end-point of any interval, only one b will apply. At any x_i within an interval, we have a weighted sum of two b_j.
6. Unfortunately, the manufacturing wage is for the state rather than for the labour market area from which the county draws its workers. We also experimented with the ACCRA (American Chamber of Commerce Researchers Association) cost-of-living index for metropolitan areas put together by the Chamber of Commerce, but the results were not very interesting.
7. See Ladd and Yinger (1989) for evidence of diseconomies with respect to population size for major central cities.
8. Because of the functional form of the equations, each coefficient only roughly approximates the percentage impact on per capita spending. The more exact impacts reported in Table 4 were calculated by taking antilogs of the estimated coefficients. The estimated cost ratios were translated into dollar amounts (1985 levels in 1982 dollars) as follows. Spending for the base case is simply average spending for counties in the sample in that density category (with the category defined as the base case plus or minus 125). Predicted spending for the other categories is calculated by multiplying the predicted ratios by the base level average spending. Thus, predicted spending indicates what the spending for a county with the specified population density would be if the county were similar to the base county in all ways other than population density.
9. The reader is reminded that no adjustments have been made for the price effects of differing costs.
10. The one anomaly is at an annual rate of population change of 0.2 per cent. For counties with growth rates in this vicinity, per capita spending is lower than that for counties with growth rates in the 3.5 per cent range.
11. Because early tests with this data set indicated that the lagged dependent variable was correlated with the error term, the equation was estimated by two-stage least-squares regression using 1978 values of the independent variables as instruments.
12. The capital outlay equations were also run with the average outlay for the fiscal years 1983–84 and 1984–85 as the dependent variable. The goal here was to smooth out any lumpiness associated with capital outlays in a single year. The results were very similar to those reported in Tables 6 and 7. This result is not surprising. Although the Census treatment of capital spending can lead to some lumpiness over time in many local governments in each county and across all functional categories should lead to a relatively smooth series of capital spending over time in this data set.
13. This assertion is based on a comparison of the magnitudes for current spending and capital outlays in Tables 4 and 8. If data were available, we would prefer to make the comparison in terms of annual capital costs rather than capital outlays.

References

ALTSHULER, A. GOMEZ-IBANEZ, J. and HOWITT, A. (1990) *Developer provision of infrastructure: the political economy of exactions*. Draft manuscript, Lincoln Institute of Land Policy (Cambridge, MA) and the Taubman Center for State and Local Government, John F. Kennedy School of Government, Harvard University.

BERGSTROM, T.C. and GOODMAN, R.P. (1973) Private demand for public goods, *American Economic Review*, 63, pp. 280–297

BORCHERDING, T.E. and DEACON, R.T. (1972) The demand for the services of non-Federal governments, *American Economic Review*, 62, pp. 891–906.

BRADBURY, K.L., LADD, H.F., PERRAULT, M., RESCHOVSKY, A. and YINGER, J. (1984) State aid to offset fiscal disparities across communities, *National Tax Journal*, 37, June.

BRADFORD, D.F., MALT, R.A. and OATES, W.E. (1969) The rising cost of local public services:

some evidence and reflections, *National Tax Journal*, 22, pp. 185-202.
BURCHELL, R. and LISTOKIN, D. (1978) *The Fiscal Impact Handbook*. New Brunswick, NJ: Center for Urban Policy Research.
CHINITZ, B. (1990) Growth management: good for the town, bad for the nation?, *American Planning Association Journal*, 55, pp. 3-8.
DOWNING, P.B. and GUSTELY, R.D. (1977) The public service costs of alternative development patterns: a review of the evidence, in: P. B. DOWNING (Ed.) *Local Service Pricing Policies and Their Effect on Urban Spatial Structure*. Vancouver: University of British Columbia Press.
FRANK, J.E. (1989) *The Costs of Alternative Development Patterns: A Review of the Literature*. Washington, DC: Urban Land Institute.
KAIN, J. (1967) *Urban form and the costs of urban services*. Mimeograph. Cambridge, MA: MIT-Harvard Joint Center for Urban Studies.
LADD, H.F. (1990) *Effects of population growth on local spending and taxes*. Paper presented at the session on 'Growth Management: Fiscal and Policy Issues', of the 1990 Conference of the Association for Public Policy Analysis and Management, San Francisco, California, 19 October.

LADD, H.F. and YINGER, J. (1989) *America's Ailing Cities: Fiscal Health and the Design of Urban Policy*. Baltimore, MD: Johns Hopkins University Press.
REAL ESTATE RESEARCH CORPORATION (1974) *The Costs of Sprawl: Environmental and Economic Costs of Alternative Residential Development Patterns at the Urban Fringe*. Washington, DC: USGPO.
SYNDER, T. and STEGMAN, M. (1987) *Paying for Growth*. Washington, DC: Urban Land Institute.
US DEPARTMENT OF COMMERCE, BUREAU OF THE CENSUS (1980) *Local Government Finances in Selected Metropolitan Areas and Large Counties: 1977-78*. GF78. Washington, DC: USGPO.
US DEPARTMENT OF COMMERCE, BUREAU OF THE CENSUS (1987) *Local Government Finances in Major County Areas: 1984-85*. GF85. Washington, DC: USGPO.
WHEATON, W.L. and SCHUSSHEIM, M.J. (1955) *The Costs of Municipal Services in Residential Areas*. Washington, DC: US Department of Commerce.
WINDSOR, D. (1979) A critique of the costs of sprawl, *Journal of American Planning Association*, 45, pp. 279-292.

[18]
CITY TAXES AND PROPERTY TAX BASES***
HELEN F. LADD* AND KATHARINE L. BRADBURY**

ABSTRACT

This paper investigates the simultaneous relationship between tax rates and city property tax bases using data for 86 large U.S. cities in 1972, 1977, and 1982. We find that a 10 percent increase in a city's property tax rate decreases the property tax base by about 1.5 percent. Local income taxes and taxes levied by overlying jurisdictions also have negative impacts on the city's property tax base. We conclude that taxes affect local property values more than is typically implied by previous studies that have investigated the impacts of state and local taxes on firms' location decisions.

THE property tax has traditionally been and continues to be the major revenue source of U.S. cities. Although cities have increasingly turned to other local revenue sources such as sales and income taxes, they still rely heavily on the local property tax to finance their local public expenditures. Despite this heavy reliance, surprisingly little is known about the impact of a city's property tax rate on its tax base.

Many local public officials apparently believe that property taxes have significant adverse effects on city economic activity. Witness, for example, their frequent willingness to grant tax abatements to encourage economic investment in the city. Applied economists, in contrast, are nearly unanimous in their skepticism both about the wisdom of such tax breaks and, more fundamentally, about the magnitude of the adverse behavioral effects of state and local taxes. Many empirical studies appear to support the contention that differentials in state and local tax burdens are simply too small to offset differences in the more basic determinants of firm location such as labor costs and accessibility to markets. (See surveys by

*Duke University, Durham, NC 27706.
**Federal Reserve Bank of Boston, Boston, MA 02106.

Case, Papke, and Koenigsberg (1983); Kieschnik (1981); and Wasylenko (1981).

Recent econometric investigations of the link between state and local taxes and the location of economic activity fall into two categories. First are those that focus on particular types of location decisions, typically the branch plant decision which, one might argue, is the most likely to be affected by taxes. (See, for example, Carlton (1979), Bartik (1985, 1986), and Schmenner (1982).) This approach has the advantage of allowing the researcher to ground the empirical analysis in the microeconomic theory of firm behavior. The second approach takes a much broader definition of economic activity such as the level or change in employment or capital investment either for all industries or certain industrial sectors. (See for example, Papke (1986) who focuses on investment and Bradbury, Downs, and Small (1982) who focus on changes in employment.) These more aggregate variables are harder to model precisely because they reflect a variety of economic decisions including, for example, the decision to expand, to shut down, to set up a new branch plant, or to start a new firm.

Even if economists better understand the links between local taxes and the location and expansion decisions of firms, they would still be unable to answer the central question of this study, namely, what impact do local property taxes have on the size of a city's property tax base? The difficulty arises because the city tax base includes residential as well as business property and because the market value of such property reflects not only the intensity of economic development (the quantity of capital) but also location rents, that is, the prices that firms and households are willing to pay to invest in the central city rather than elsewhere. High property taxes may reduce the size of the tax base either by reducing the level of business or residential economic activity in the city or by being capitalized into lower property values, or by some combination of both. Whatever the mechanism, city officials and economists ought to care about the responsiveness of the city's property tax base to the property tax rate. To the extent that the current tax rate reduces the size of the base, the additional tax rate needed to finance a given increase in public expenditures will be higher.

Other state and local taxes such as income or sales taxes may also affect local property values despite their initial incidence on non-property factors of production or on other economic transactions. Hence, a secondary goal of this paper is to provide quantitative estimates of the effects of other state and local taxes on the size of a city's property tax base. This aspect of the study can be viewed as the first step in a larger and more ambitious study that would examine the effects of all major city taxes on each of a city's tax bases.

I. The Data and the Role of the Property Tax

Our empirical work focuses on the relationship between city property taxes and the market value of potentially taxable property in U.S. central cities. City governments, however, are often not alone in having the power to levy property taxes on the property located within city boundaries. In many metropolitan areas, independent school districts, county governments, and special districts are also authorized to tax city property if it falls within their jurisdictional boundaries. Moreover, the economic activity generated by the city's property may be subject to state or local sales and income taxes. Regardless of whether they apply specifically to property or are levied by overlying governments, all of these taxes (and the corresponding public services they finance) could affect the size of a city's tax base. Hence, all must be taken into account.

Our primary perspective, however, is the city government itself. As an independent decision-making entity, its decisions about local taxes can be modeled more easily than could those of an aggregated set of governmental units. Hence, our goal is to measure the impact of city property taxes on city property tax bases, controlling for all other taxes that may affect the amount of taxable property in the city.

The basic data are for 86 U.S. central cities for three years—1972, 1977, and 1982. The 86 comprise all those American cities with population over 300,000 in 1970 or 1980 plus all the central cities of the 50 largest SMSAs in either 1970 or 1980. Thus, the analysis includes all major central cities in the United States. The combined 1980 population of the 86 cities constitutes 21 percent of the 1980 U.S. population and 94 percent of the U.S. population in central cities containing 50,000 or more people.

Property taxes are less important for city governments than for other types of local governments such as counties and school districts, but they still accounted for over half of the 1982 tax revenues of the average city in our sample. Dependence on the property tax varies greatly across cities and regions; cities with population under 100,000 receive more than twice as large a share of revenues from the property tax as cities with population over 1 million and cities in the Northeast depend on property tax revenues twice as heavily as those in the West.

Effective property tax rates, like dependence on the property tax, also vary substantially across cities. We define an effective tax rate as

$t = T/B,$

where T is the city's total revenues from the property tax, and B is the market value of all potentially taxable property in the city. The tax base in this measure is intended to be independent of how each city defines its tax base in practice and to include all property other than that universally exempt from the property tax such as churches and government buildings. Data on property tax revenues are readily available from the Census of Governments, but the market value of each city's potential tax base had to be estimated from data on assessed values and assessment/sales ratios, supplemented, where possible, with data gathered directly from cities.[1] Because of missing data, information on tax bases is available for only 68 of the 86 cities for all three years, but a total of 202 city-year observations are available for the pooled regression analysis reported below.

Table 1 shows the level and variation in effective tax rates for the 68 cities with complete information. The average rate decreased from 0.9 percent in 1972 to 0.6 percent in 1982. (These rates may appear low, but they are averages of city tax rates alone. The inclusion of property taxes levied by overlying governments would raise the rates substantially in some cases.) The table shows that tax rates are generally highest for the smallest and the largest cities in the sample. This pattern reflects heavy dependence on the property tax relative to other revenue sources in the small cities and heavy overall taxation in the large cities. The table also shows that among regions, rates in northeastern cities are strikingly higher than those elsewhere.

This wide variation in effective tax rates provides a natural experiment for exam-

Table 1
Average Effective Property Tax Rates
(percent)

Cities by Group	Number Of Cities	1972	1977	1982
All	68	.86%	.80%	.64%
Population Size:				
Less than 100,000	6	1.42	1.17	1.12
100,000 - 250,000	18	.74	.69	.62
250,000 - 500,000	23	.68	.58	.45
500,000 - 1,000,000	16	1.00	1.01	.68
Greater than 1,000,000	5	1.00	1.05	.85
Region:				
Northeast	11	1.93	2.03	1.72
North Central	15	.63	.57	.47
South	22	.88	.72	.62
West	20	.42	.37	.20

Notes: Averages shown for cities with data available in all three years.

These effective property tax rates refer to property taxes of city governments alone; see text for definition of effective property tax rate and sources. Economic activity in these cities may also be subject to property taxes imposed by independent school districts or county governments.

ining the hypothesis that city tax rates affect the attractiveness of a city to households and firms and thereby directly influence the size of the city's potential property tax base. Correspondingly wide variation in city use of alternative revenue sources and in tax burdens imposed on city residents by overlying jurisdictions also provide the information needed to determine the effects of other taxes on city property tax bases.

II. Conceptual Framework

Our model has four structural components: 1) a tax base equation, 2) a balanced budget equation, 3) a demand equation for public spending, and 4) a tax mix equation. The tax base equation captures the effects of private sector decisions about locating and investing in the central city. The demand and tax mix equations describe the behavior of local public decisionmakers and, with the balanced budget requirement, determine the level of property tax revenues in each city. Our primary focus is on the tax base equation. For reasons discussed in the next section, however, careful attention to the other three components is needed to assure appropriate estimation of the effect of local property tax rates on city tax bases.

The Tax Base Equation

The size of a city's property tax base reflects investment decisions made over time by households and firms in response to the perceived costs and benefits of a city location. In modelling the outcome of these decisions, we focus on the local property tax rate, controlling for three sets of exogenous variables in addition to year dummies, and the lagged dependent variable. The first set of exogenous variables are those that emerge from a simple monocentric model of an urban economy. Second are those that control for taxes other than municipal property taxes levied on economic activity generated in the city. Third are measures of public services. The variables and reasons for including them are explained in the subsections that follow. Table 2 reports their mnemonic variable names, definitions, means, and standard deviations.

Property Tax Rate. A higher tax rate is expected to reduce the value of the city's property tax base in part because the land component of the tax will be capitalized into lower property values. In addition, the improvements component of the tax is expected to induce producers to shift away from capital toward labor and to reduce the attractiveness of the city as a place for investing capital. The reduced attractiveness of the city may manifest itself either in a change in land prices or in reduced economic activity or, most likely, in some combination of both.

Estimating the relationship between the market value of city property tax bases and city property tax rates would be relatively straightforward if tax rates could be viewed as exogenous. Such rates would be exogenous, for example, if state laws mandated binding limits on each city's property tax rate and all cities were at their specified legal limits so that city tax rates would not be affected by the size of the city tax bases. Perusal of the laws affecting city property taxes, however, suggests that in most cases a city's property tax rate, expressed as a fraction of full market value, is not independent of the city's tax base. While many cities are subject to tax limitations of some form, only rarely do these limitations determine the effective tax rate. The clearest exceptions are California cities in 1982 and Boston in 1982, each of which is subject to a binding limit expressed in terms of an effective tax rate.[2]

More commonly, the local property tax rate is determined in part by the size of the tax base. Consider, for example, the following model of city behavior. City government officials choose a level of expenditures in response to the demand of citizen voters for public services. They then levy sufficient property taxes to pay for whatever portion of total expenditures that they choose not to finance from other revenue sources. According to this model, a higher tax base would lead to a lower tax rate for any given property tax levy.

Assuming a log-linear specification of

Table 2
Variable Definitions and Means
(L denotes the natural logarithm)

Variable	Definition	Mean N=202	Standard Deviation
Endogenous Variables			
LPBASE	Market value of potential property tax base per capita in thousands of 1972 dollars.	2.55	.38
LPTAX	Property tax revenues per capita in 1972 dollars.	4.18	.79
Other Variables in the Base Equation			
LPCY	Per capita income of city residents in 1972 dollars.	8.29	.13
YR82	Dummy variable that takes on the value 1 for 1982 and 0 otherwise.	.36	.48
YR77	Dummy variable that takes the value 1 for 1977 and 0 otherwise.	.36	.48
LPBASE-1	LPBASE lagged one period (five years).	2.46	.35
LSMPOP	Population in the city's Standard Metropolitan Statistical Area - in thousands (1970, 1972, 1977, 1980)	7.18	.69
LLAND	City land area in square miles.	4.37	.99
KEYCC	Dummy variable that takes the value 1 for dominant central cities and 0 otherwise.	.74	.44
TRINC	Statutory tax rate for city income, earnings or payroll tax.	.0043	.0093
TRSAL	Statutory tax rate for city general sales tax.	.0064	.0082
LOVTAX	Overlying tax burden per capita in 1972 dollars.	5.90	.77
LCRIME	Total crimes (both property and violent as reported in Uniform Crime Reports) divided by private sector employees in the city.	-1.72	.36
LFIRESER	Total per capita state and local spending on fire protection in the city's state in 1972 dollars deflated by FCOST.	2.53	.50
LMISCSER	Total per capita state and local spending in the city's state on schools, health and hospitals, and sewers and sanitation in 1972 dollars deflated by MCOST.	5.67	.24

Table 2 - continued

Variable	Definition	Mean	Standard Deviation
Potential Instruments from the Tax Revenue Equation			
LTSRI	Total service responsibilities per capita in 1972 dollars.	4.81	.60
AVINC	Dummy variable that takes the value 1 if the city uses a local income, earnings, or payroll tax and zero otherwise.	.23	.42
AVGSAL	Dummy variable that takes the value 1 if the city uses a general sales tax and zero otherwise.	.48	.58
AVSSAL	Dummy variable that takes the value 1 if the city uses a selective sales tax and zero otherwise.	.88	.32
ERPROP	Export ratio for the property tax.	.35	.11
ERINC	Export ratio for the local income tax (0 if the tax is not used).	.082	.19
ERSAL	Export ratio for the general sales tax (0 if the tax is not used).	.077	.12
LMCOST	Cost index for miscellaneous services (Relative to 1972 average)	4.7	.21
LPCOST	Cost index for police services (Relative to 1972 average)	4.7	.55
LFCOST	Cost index for fire services (Relative to 1972 average)	4.6	.34
LFAID	Federal aid per capita in 1972 dollars.	3.64	.99
LSTAID	State aid per capita in 1972 dollars.	3.58	1.30

the tax base equation, we can eliminate part of the simultaneity by substituting the definitional relationship t = PTAX/PBASE (where t is the city's property tax rate, PTAX is per capita property tax revenues, and PBASE is the market value of property per capita) for the tax rate in the equation explaining the size of the base. Before the substitution we have

$$\ln \text{PBASE} = a + b \ln t + c \ln X + e, \quad (1)$$

where ln denotes natural logarithm, X is a vector of exogenous variables that influence the size the tax base, and e is a random error term. After substituting for t and solving for PBASE, the equation becomes

$$\ln \text{PBASE} = a/(1+b) + b/(1+b) \cdot \ln \text{PTAX} + c/(1+b) \ln X \quad (2)$$
$$+ e/(1+b).$$

Thus, treating property tax revenue, rather than the tax rate, as the explanatory variable removes one source of the simultaneity problem, yet still makes it possible to solve for b, the elasticity of the base with respect to the tax rate.

Even per capita tax revenue, however, may not be exogenous. A larger base means that the same amount of revenue can be raised with a lower tax rate, reducing the pain of raising taxes and thereby increasing the willingness of voters to vote for higher taxes. (See later sections of the paper for further discussion.) Thus we treat property tax revenue as an endogenous variable in the property tax base equation.

Variables Derived From an Urban Model. To capture the influence of the private economy on a city's property tax base, we begin with a monocentric model of an urban economy. This strategy of building on the descriptive implications of an urban model dramatically simplifies what is in fact an enormously complicated and not-very-well-understood problem, the behavioral modeling of economic activity in an urban area.[3] The following log-linear specification incorporates the essential implications of the standard urban model for the total value of property (B) per unit of land (LAND) in the portion of the metropolitan area designated as the central city:

$$\ln B/LAND = c_0' + c_1' \ln SMPOP + c_2' \ln LAND + e' \quad (3)$$

where e' is a random error. Controlling for the amount of land in the city, more activity in the metropolitan area as measured by metropolitan population (SMPOP) leads to a higher value of property in the city per unit of city land. According to the monocentric model, this occurs both because larger metropolitan areas have higher land prices at the center and also because the higher price of land induces more intensive economic development in the city in the form of business and residential structures.

More city land, controlling for metropolitan population, is predicted to reduce the value of property per unit of land; more land means that the city extends further down the rent and density gradients of the metropolitan area.

Expressing the dependent variable in per capita terms rather than per unit of land is more natural for the current empirical investigation. Hence, the dependent variable in equation 3 must be multiplied by the inverse of the population density (that is, by LAND/POP, where POP is the population of the city). One approach at this point would be to add the logarithm of density (with a predicted coefficient of -1) to the right-hand side of equation 3. The difficulty here is that population density is endogenous in that it, too, is determined by the exogenous determinants of land prices in the city, namely SMPOP and LAND. Hence, including population density as an exogenous variable in the estimating equation would not make sense. Instead, we specify the reduced form of the model in log-linear form as

$$\ln PBASE = a + c_1 \ln SMPOP + c_2 \ln LAND + e \quad (4)$$

where PBASE is the property tax base per capita and the coefficients c_1 and c_2 represent the combined effects of the exogenous variables on the base per unit of land and on population density. Provided the exogenous variables affect the population density gradient less strongly than the rent and business density gradients, we still predict a positive sign for SMPOP and a negative sign for LAND.[4]

The sample cities, and the metropolitan areas in which they are located, vary in how well they fit the simple monocentric model. Of most concern is that some of the central cities in the sample are not the primary centers of economic activity in their respective SMSAs. Thus, for example, Everett WA, with its 1982 population of 57,000, has far less claim to being the center of the Seattle-Everett metropolitan area than does Seattle with 490,000 residents. To help control for such variations, an additional variable (KEYCC) takes on the value one for those cities that dominate their SMSAs and zero otherwise. Dominant cities are defined as the central city in SMSAs with one central city and, somewhat arbitrarily, as those that have 60 percent or more of either population or employment in SMSAs with two central cities or 50 percent or more in SMSAs with three central cities. Dominant central cities are predicted to have larger tax bases per capita than do non-dominant central cities because of their positions as centers of urban economic activity.

Per capita income of city residents (PCY) completes the specification of this part of the equation. This variable is expected to have a positive sign because higher income increases the demand for housing.[5]

Nonproperty Tax Variables. Three additional tax variables control for the other taxes imposed on economic activity in central cities. Alternative taxes levied by the city itself are represented in the tax base equation by statutory city tax rates for income taxes (TRINC) and for general sales taxes (TRSAL), with a rate of zero if the city does not use the tax. Close to half the sample cities make no use of local general sales taxes and only 18 of the 86 sample cities had some form of a city income or payroll tax in 1982.[6] Negative signs are expected on both tax rate variables. A higher income tax rate lowers the net-of-tax income of city residents, and may induce firms to pay higher wages than they otherwise would, thereby reducing net profits and discouraging investment in the city. These effects will reduce the demand for property in the city except in the unlikely event that the incentive for firms to substitute away from labor in favor of land and capital is large enough to offset the output effect. A higher sales tax rate may reduce the demand for taxed goods, and, similarly, lead to less investment in the city.

The tremendous complexity and variation in the division of taxing responsibilities among city and non-city governments across states makes it impossible to control separately for each of the non-city taxes imposed on city economic activity. Instead, we constructed a single variable (OVTAX), based on statewide data, as a proxy for the burden of overlying taxes. The variable is calculated as the average state and local per capita tax burden in the city's state multiplied by the "non-city" share of taxes in the state, and is based on the following logic. If the city itself imposed no taxes, all residents (including residents of the city) could be viewed as being subject to the average state and local tax burden in the state. But since each city's major taxes (property, income, and sales) are modeled separately, city taxes must be removed from the total state and local burden. This adjustment is accomplished by using statewide data to subtract the average per capita taxes collected by all those jurisdictions in the state that perform the same functions as the city in question. Thus, for example, in constructing the overlying tax variable for a city such as San Francisco which has responsibility for county functions as well as municipal functions and hence has no overlying county, care is taken to make sure that the calculated overlying burden does not include county taxes.[7] The expected sign of this variable is negative; higher overlying tax burdens are likely to depress economic activity in the city.

Measures of Public Services. Public services are an important component of any study of the effects of state or local taxes. Since public services are valued and taxes are used to pay for them, failure to control for services could lead to incorrect estimates of the effects of taxes alone. In principle, we need to control for all services available to city firms and households regardless of whether the services are provided by the city government itself or by some overlying government such as a state or county government or an independent school district.

Public expenditures typically serve as the standard measure of public services in studies of tax capitalization (e.g. Oates, 1969), but, as shown by Rosen and Fullerton (1977), output measures such as educational test scores are far superior. Hence, we have constructed three public service measures that are intended to measure public sector outputs rather than simply public inputs. The first is the number of crimes in the city expressed as a fraction of the city's total private sector employment (CRIME). Vocal public concern about crime makes it plausible that the decision to invest in a particular city might be influenced by the perceived risk of being assaulted or robbed. Higher crime rates per worker in the city are predicted to lead to lower property values.[8] The second and third variables (FIRESER and MISCER) are proxies for fire protection and miscellaneous services (consisting of local schools, sewers, sanitation, and health and hospitals) constructed from per capita state and local expenditure data by state deflated by the estimated costs of providing the respective service or sets of services in each city. The cost indexes are designed to measure the effects of city-specific environmental and demographic factors on the costs of providing a given package of public services and are described in more detail below. To the extent that the indexes correctly measure the costs per unit of final output, deflating expenditures by them should lead to reasonable proxies for the level of services actually available to city residents. We expect both variables to enter the base equation with positive signs since higher service levels should increase the size of a city's property tax base, ceteris paribus.

Lagged Base and Year Dummies. The final three variables are two-year dummies (YR82, YR77) and the dependent variable lagged one (five-year) period (PBASE-1). The year dummies are needed in the pooled regression to control for cyclical trends in the aggregate economy and for secular trends such as the fall in transportation costs that tend to decentralize business activity. The lagged dependent variable accounts for the fact that land rents and the intensity of economic activity that determine city property values may not adjust immediately to changing conditions over time.

More formally, if $PBASE_t^*$ is the long-run equilibrium tax base per capita in period t and $PBASE_t$ and $PBASE_{t-1}$ are the actual bases per capita in periods t and t − 1, then in multiplicative form

$$PBASE_t/PBASE_{t-1} \quad (5)$$
$$= (PBASE_t^*/PBASE_{t-1})^\lambda,$$

where λ is the proportional adjustment occurring in one (five-year) period. Taking natural logarithms yields:

$$\ln PBASE_t = \lambda \ln PBASE_t^*$$
$$+ (1 - \lambda) \ln PBASE_{t-1}. \quad (6)$$

Hence, the model now includes all the determinants of PBASE* described above plus the lagged base, $PBASE_{t-1}$. Recalling the formulation of equation (2), this yields the complete model

$$\ln PBASE = \lambda[a/(1 + b) + b/(1 + b)$$
$$\cdot \ln PTAX + c_1/(1 + b) \ln SMPOP$$
$$+ c_2/(1 + b) \ln LAND + c_3/(1 + b)$$
$$\cdot KEYCC + c_4/(1 + b) \ln PCY$$
$$+ c_5/(1 + b) TRINC + c_6/(1 + b)$$
$$\cdot TRSAL + c_7/(1 + b) \ln OVTAX$$
$$+ c_8/(1 + b) \ln CRIME$$
$$+ c_9/(1 + b) \ln FIRESER + c_{10}/(1 + b)$$
$$\cdot \ln MISCSER + c_{11}/(1 + b) YR82$$
$$+ c_{12}/(1 + b) YR77]$$
$$+ (1 - \lambda) \ln PBASE_{t-1} + e. \quad (7)$$

Determinants of Property Tax Revenues

The key to identifying the crucial coefficient of the endogenous variable PTAX in equation 7 is that there be good identifying variables, that is, variables that would clearly belong in a revenue equation but not in the base equation. One distinguishing characteristic of this study is the availability of such variables. These variables are derived from the following identity, which reflects the balanced budget requirement that local revenues equal local expenditures:

$$PTAX = \left(\sum_{i=1}^{I} E_i - OR\right) \quad (8)$$
$$\cdot (PTAX/TTAX)$$

where PTAX is property tax revenues, $\sum_{i=1}^{I} E_i$ is all city operating expenditures summed over I individual spending categories, OR is nontax exogenous revenues such as lump sum intergovernmental aid, and TTAX is total revenues from all local tax sources. To model this relationship, we specify first the demand for public services and hence total revenue requirements and second how cities choose among tax sources.

Demand for Local Public Expenditures. The literature on local public expenditures is well developed and needs only brief review here.[9] The typical starting point is that the quantity of public services demanded is a function of resident income, per unit costs, and tax prices. Desired expenditure on the ith expenditure category (E_i) is the product of costs and quantity demanded. Hence,

$$E_i = C_i Q_i = f(Y, C_i, TS), \qquad (9)$$

where Y is the income of the decisive voter, C_i is per unit cost of the ith expenditure category, and TS is the decisive voter's share of the local tax burden.

Appropriately measured cost variables not only would reflect the costs of inputs, but, following the logic of Bradford, Malt and Oates (1969), would also incorporate the amount of intermediate goods such as police patrols that are needed to produce a given level of output such as protection from crime. The idea here is that environmental conditions in the city that are outside of the control of city officials, such as city density and the incidence of poverty, may affect the costs to the city of providing a given level of the output, such as police protection, ultimately valued by city residents. To reflect such cost variations, we have included three cost indices for miscellaneous public services (MCOST), police protection services (PCOST), and fire protection services (FCOST). The cost indices are derived from a regression model that estimates the average impact on city expenditures of each cost factor, controlling for other determinants of city spending such as resident income and preferences.[10]

Given the purpose of this study, we need not be precise about the identity of the decisive voter. The goal is simply to use the essentials of a basic expenditure model to determine which variables belong in the tax revenue equation and can serve to identify the coefficient of the property tax variable in the base equation. In the estimated equations, per capita income (PCY) serves as a reasonable proxy for the relevant income measure and is expected to have a positive effect on taxes. We control for the decisive voter's tax share with a measure of property tax exporting (the greater the exporting, the lower the burden on city residents), which is also expected to influence the choice among revenue sources, described in the next subsection of the paper.[11]

As specified so far, desired expenditures are not explicitly dependent on the size of the property tax base. This primarily reflects the simplicity of the decisive voter model, particularly in its median voter form, rather than economic reality. In more realistic models, the tax base or its components might well influence demand. The value of residential property, for example, might better reflect residents' permanent income and, consequently, their willingness to pay for public services than does current income. Or higher-valued property (whether residential or business) may require greater services in the form of protection from crime. Hence, using the simple model presented in equation 9 to justify excluding the size of the property tax base as an explanatory variable would be a mistake. Moreover, as discussed below, the revenue mix component of the model also implies that the property tax base is a determinant of property tax revenue.

The analysis to this point argues for including in the revenue equation standard determinants of the demand for spending on individual public services: resident income, a tax exporting measure, service-specific measures of costs, and the property tax base. One additional variable related to expenditures dominates all the others in terms of its relevance to this study, namely a measure of the services for which each city government in the sample is responsible. Given the cross-sectional nature of the data set, variation in service responsibilities is likely to be a primary determinant of the variation in total expenditure. Stated differently, the number of expenditure categories over which the summation applies in equation 8 varies substantially among cities.

The variable measuring the total service responsibilities assigned to each city (TSRI) indicates the per capita spending net of user charges that would be required in each city to achieve national average per capita state-local spending on each of 17 designated services, given the particular allocation of spending responsibilities in each city's state. Constructed from statewide rather than city-specific expenditure data, the measure avoids the potential problem of attributing high service responsibilities to cities which choose to provide high service levels. The measure varies substantially across cities. The most obvious variation relates to services such as elementary and secondary education and municipal hospitals for which a city has either complete spending responsibility or none. Some cities are also responsible for services provided by counties in other states. Variation across states in the role of state government also accounts for a substantial portion of the variation in service responsibilities across states; the greater the state role in welfare, health, and corrections, the lower, in general, is the city role.[12]

Choice among Revenue Sources. Subtracting nontax exogenous revenues (OR in equation 8) from total desired expenditures yields the amount of revenue that must be raised from local tax sources. Nontax revenue is primarily intergovernmental aid, but in principle, only the aid that is truly exogenous. As measured, however, some of the per capita federal aid (FAID) and per capita state aid (STAID) may be matching aid.

How the remaining revenue requirements are allocated among local tax sources has received much less attention from economists than has the expenditure decision.[13] Consistent with the decisive voter approach, one might hypothesize the following model of the city decision regarding how much to rely on local property taxes:

$$PTAX/TTAX = f(PBASE, AV, ER) \quad (10)$$

where PBASE, as before is the per capita property tax base, AV is a vector of dummy variables indicating the legal availability of alternative local taxes, and ER is a vector of export ratios for alternative taxes.[14]

The larger is the property tax base per person, the easier it should be for the city to raise revenue through the property tax. A larger tax base allows the city to raise a given amount of revenue with a lower tax rate and thereby to avoid the potentially distorting effects and heavy tax burdens of high tax rates.

In most cases, authorization of alternative revenue options is a state, rather than a city, decision. Yet, authorization to use nonproperty taxes plays a key role in the city tax decision given the stringent restrictions often placed on city revenue-raising authority. As already noted, only 18 of the 86 sample cities are currently allowed to use some form of local income or payroll tax, and 47 cities a general sales tax. A higher proportion of cities are permitted to impose some form of selective sales tax. Availability of alternative tax sources is likely to decrease a city's reliance on the local property tax. Availability is indicated with dummy variables: AVINC refers to local income, earnings, or payroll taxes; AVGSAL refers to the general sales tax; AVSSAL refers to selective sales taxes.

Not all taxing instruments impose equal burdens on resident voters. A portion of the burden of a local sales tax, for example, might be shifted onto nonresident tourists and commuters in the form of higher prices. Or a payroll tax may fall partially on nonresident commuters. Similarly, part of the property tax burden may ultimately be borne by nonresidents in the form of lower profits, higher prices, or lower wages. The export ratios (ER), defined as the proportion of the tax burden associated with each of the major local taxes that can be shifted to nonresidents, are included in the equation to account for this burden shifting. The hypothesis is that local voters choose taxes in such a way as to minimize burdens on themselves. Hence, a higher export ratio for the property tax (ERPROP) is expected to lead to greater reliance on property taxes, but higher export ratios for sales (ERSAL) or income taxes (ERINC) are expected to reduce city reliance on property taxes.

The calculation of each export ratio relies first on assumptions about which groups—consumers, workers, or owners of property—bear the burden of each tax and second on estimates of the proportion of each group that lives outside the city. The incidence assumptions are straightforward for the income and sales taxes; local income taxes are assumed to be borne fully by workers in the form of lower wages and local sales taxes by consumers in the form of higher prices. The incidence assumptions used for the property tax are much more complex and are spelled out elsewhere.[15] Calculated export ratios for all three taxes vary substantially across cities because of differences in how cities define their tax bases, the diversity of city roles in metropolitan areas, and variations in the mix of shoppers, job-holders, or property types across cities.

In summary, the property tax revenue equation incorporates the determinants of total revenue requirements, including resident income, service-specific cost indices, the property tax base, and a measure of city government service responsibilities, as well as the determinants of revenue mix, such as exogenous intergovernmental aid and the availability and exportability of nonproperty tax sources:

PTAX = f(PCY, MCOST, PCOST,

FCOST, PBASE, TSRI, FAID, STAID,

AVINC, AVGSAL, AVSSAL, ERINC,

ERSAL, ERPROP, YR82, YR77). (11)

As in the base equation, the variables are expressed in logarithmic form for estimation.[16]

III. Estimation and Results

Careful specification of the revenue equation provides a rich set of potential instruments for our 2SLS estimation of the tax base equation. In particular, the 12 variables that appear as control variables in the tax revenue, but not in the base equation, are logical candidates for instruments than can serve to identify the coefficient of the endogenous revenue variable in the base equation. One must be careful, however, to assure that each of the proposed instruments is truly exogenous in the two-fold sense that 1) it does not belong in the equation as an explanatary variable and 2) conditional on 1) it is uncorrelated with the error term.

Following Lugar and Stahl's (1986) exposition of Hausman (1978), we perform a set of simple t-tests to determine whether each of the variables excluded from the base equation is truly exogenous in the sense just stated. For example, consider a variable such as the index of service responsibilities. Based on our conceptual framework, this variable belongs in the revenue equation but not in the tax base equation. The division of service responsibilities among levels of government should have no effect on city property values, controlling for public service levels, aside from its effect through property tax liabilities. By adding it to the base equation and testing the hypothesis that its coefficient is zero, we are testing the joint null hypothesis required for exogeneity. Through a process of trial and error, we obtain a set of instrumental variables whose members all pass the exogeneity test.

These exogeneity tests lead us to reject as instruments two of the excluded variables: the export ratio for property tax burdens (ERPROP) and the cost index for police services (PCOST). Failure to pass the exogeneity test, however, need not mean that the variables belong in the base equation as explanatory variables; conditional on a true model that excludes them, the variables may simply be correlated with the error term. This latter interpretation applies to both variables. Variation in neither variable can be said to cause variation in the tax base. Instead, the causation probably goes in the other direction; cities with larger per capita tax bases simply tend to have greater potential to export property tax burdens and higher costs of providing police services than those with smaller tax bases.[17]

An additional econometric problem could arise from the presence in the base equation of the lagged dependent variable. As is well known, the coefficient of the lagged variable will be inconsistently estimated if the equation error in time t is correlated with the error in time t − 1. Fortunately, however, inconsistency is not a problem here; using a Hausman test of the form elaborated by Lugar and Stahl (1986), we reject the null hypothesis that the lagged base is correlated with the error term.[18]

Table 3 presents the coefficients estimated using two-stage least squares with data for 1972, 1977, and 1982 for two equations: the partial adjustment equation that corresponds to equation 7 and, for comparison, an equation that excludes the lagged dependent variable. Columns 2 and 4 represent the structural coefficients of the model derived from the estimated parameters of each equation. These can be interpreted as the long-run responses of the logarithm of the tax base to each variable. The following discussion focuses primarily on the partial adjustment model, which we prefer because it allows for the dynamics of property market adjustments over time.

Overall, the equations perform well. The coefficient of primary interest, that of the property tax variable, is −0.080 and significantly different from zero. Ignoring for a moment the lagged adjustment term and recalling from equation 2 that this estimated coefficient equals $(b/(1 + b))$, we estimate the short-run elasticity of a city's per capita property tax base with respect to its property tax rate to be approximately −0.075, where the short run is a period of 5 years.

The long-run response can be calculated by combining this estimate with our estimate of λ, the partial adjustment parameter. The estimated coefficient on the lagged base variable, 0.54, implies that λ is 0.46 and that slightly less than half of the adjustment to long-run equilibrium occurs during a five-year period. This adjustment speed means that our best estimate of the long-run elasticity of the tax base to the property tax rate is −0.15 (equals −0.075/0.46). Thus, if the property tax rate in one city were twice that of another city and this difference persisted over time, we predict that per capita property values would be 15 percent lower in the higher tax city.

A more direct estimate of the long-run response emerges from the equation without the lagged dependent variable. The coefficient of −.14 implies that a one percent difference in a city's property tax rate leads to a .12 percent difference in the size of its base. The long-run equilibrium assumption implicit in this equation makes this somewhat-smaller estimate less appealing than the estimate from the partial adjustment model.

The three additional tax variables provide some interesting new insights about the effects of alternative revenue sources on the size of a city's property tax base. City income taxes and non-city taxes both reduce the size of a city's property tax base, but, somewhat surprisingly, city sales taxes do not. This finding about sales taxes may not surprise business owners, many of whom seem to prefer sales taxes over other state and local taxes on the grounds that they can shift the tax burden to consumers in the form of higher prices. To economists, however, the finding is still somewhat surprising; by discouraging consumption of taxed items, the higher prices should reduce the city's level of economic activity.

Once it has been multiplied by our estimate of $((1 + b)/\lambda)$, the coefficient of the overlying tax burden variable (LOVTAX) can be interpreted directly as a long-run elasticity. In contrast, the coefficient of the income tax rate variable (TRINC), which is not in logarithm form, must be multiplied by its mean value in addition to $((1 + b)/\lambda)$ to convert it to an elasticity. These calculations produce the following elasticities: −0.10 for overlying taxes and −.065 for income taxes. These magnitudes are comparable to, but, not surprisingly, smaller than the property tax rate elasticity of −.15. The policy significance of the relative sizes of these magnitudes is discussed in the concluding section.

In contrast to the tax variables, the performance of the service variables is somewhat disappointing. The measures of crime and miscellaneous services enter the preferred equation with the predicted signs, but with relatively large standard

Table 3
TAX BASE EQUATION
Dependent Variable: LPBASE

Independent Variables	Partial Adjustment (Equation 7)		Full Adjustment (No lagged dependent variable)	
	Estimated Coefficients (1)	Structural Parameters (2)	Estimated Coefficients (3)	Structural Parameters (4)
LPTAX	-.081* (.032)	-.15	-.14* (.040)	-.12
LPCY	.95* (.16)	1.8	1.5* (.18)	1.3
LSMPOP	.061* (.033)	.11	.17* (.040)	.15
LLAND	-.026 (.022)	-.048	-.053* (.026)	-.046
KEYCC	.015 (.047)	.028	.12* (.057)	.10
TRINC	-8.3* (2.7)	-15	-16* (3.3)	-14
TRSAL	.61 (2.4)	1.1	1.8 (2.8)	1.5
LOVTAX	-.054 (.034)	-.10	-.098* (.043)	-.086
LCRIME	-.041 (.046)	-.076	-.10 (.070)	-.088
LFIRESER	-.0024 (.046)	-.0045	.061 (.058)	.054
LMISCSER	.097 (.097)	.18	-.11 (.12)	-.10
YR82	.064 (.043)	.12	.21* (.051)	.18
YR77	.025 (.041)	.046	.11* (.049)	.099
LPBASE-1	.54* (.056)	–	–	–
Constant	-7.0* (1.4)	–	-9.5* (1.6)	–

Table 3 - continued

Independent Variables	Partial Adjustment (Equation 7)		Full Adjustment (No lagged dependent variable)	
	Estimated Coefficients (1)	Structural Parameters (2)	Estimated Coefficients (3)	Structural Parameters (4)
Adjusted R^2	.67		.48	
Standard Error	.22		.29	
Sample Size	202		225	

* Coefficient significantly different from zero at 5% level, one-tailed test.

Notes: Pooled time series and cross-section using data for 1972, 1977, and 1982.
Estimated with two-stage least squares; LPTAX treated as endogenous.
LPBASE-1 is LPBASE lagged one period (five years); missing data for LPBASE in 1967 account for the difference in sample size between the two equations.
Instruments: LTSRI, LMCOST, LFCOST, AVINC, AVGSAL, AVSSAL, ERINC, ERSAL, LFAID, LSTAID, and exogenous explanatory variables in the equation.
Asymptotic standard errors in parentheses below coefficients.

errors. This provides at best weak support for the conclusion that higher crime rates reduce property values and that higher miscellaneous services, such as education and sanitation, increase property values in the city. Our proxy for fire protection services enters with an unexpected negative sign but its coefficient is virtually zero.

The variables derived from the urban monocentric model all have the expected signs in both equations. As predicted, higher metropolitan population, higher income of city residents, and status as a dominant central city all produce higher per capita property values in the central city while larger land area decreases per capita values. However, the presence in the preferred equation of the city's tax base in an earlier year makes it difficult to obtain precise estimates for KEYCC and LLAND. This follows because a city's status as a dominant central city within a multi-city SMSA typically does not change over time. In addition, its land area does not change much except in cities engaged in extensive annexation. Omitting the lagged base term increases the independent variation in these two variables and yields more precise estimates of their effects.

We interpret the positive sign of metropolitan population and the negative sign on city land area to mean that the impacts of these variables on rent and business density gradients are greater than on population gradients. For example, the positive coefficient of the metropolitan population variable suggests not only that the market value of property in the central city per unit of land is higher in larger metropolitan areas, but also that the higher value per unit of land is not offset by a sufficiently higher population density in the central city to produce a lower value of property per city resident.[19]

IV. Interpretation: The Effects of Taxes on City Property Tax Bases

Our best estimate of the long-run elasticity of a city's property tax base with respect to its tax rate is −0.15. This estimated response appears to be well identified in a statistical sense thanks to the nature of the data base and the attention devoted to the specification of the revenue equation as well as to the base equation.

This −0.15 would be easy to interpret if the implicit experiment underlying our approach were unambiguous. The estimating equation, however, focuses on comparisons among large central cities, setting aside intrametropolitan differences in tax rates and service levels.[20] If one were willing to assume that city and suburban tax rates and service levels move together, the coefficient estimate would imply that a 10 percent increase in a central city's property tax rate, accompanied by a proportionate change in suburban tax rates, would decrease the central city's tax base by 1.5 percent. Although the level of tax rates and services in central cities typically differ significantly from those of other cities within the metropolitan area, the assumption that central city and suburban tax rates and service levels move together over time is plausible because cities within a metropolitan area are subject to similar state fiscal institutions and economic pressures. For example, a reduction in state aid for local governments or a turndown in the state economy are likely to put upward pressure on local tax rates both in central cities and in their suburbs.

In reality, however, central city and suburban tax rates exhibit some independent variation. This observation implies that the −0.15 elasticity indicates the average long-run effect of a change in the central city tax rate plus the effects of corresponding changes in suburban tax rates and service levels that occurred during the sample period. Provided suburban tax and service levels continue to move in the same way as they have done in the past relative to changes in the central city tax rate, the reported elasticity accurately predicts the long-run effects of a change in central city tax rates.

The reported elasticity could, however, understate the effects of future increases in central city tax rates. The elasticity was estimated for a period of time characterized by rapid increases in federal aid to cities, with more going to large central cities than to their wealthier suburbs. With the recent dramatic decline in direct federal aid to cities at the same time that costly-to-serve households such as the poor tend to be increasingly concentrated in central cities, such cities may need to increase local tax rates more relative to their suburbs than they have in the past (Ladd and Yinger (1989)). If this outcome occurs, city tax bases may decline more than predicted in this study because investors would find cities even less attractive than in the past relative to their surrounding areas.

How reasonable is the preferred estimate? In the absence of comparable studies, one approach is to evaluate it with reference to the theory of capitalization. Consider, for example, what would happen if property tax rates were fully capitalized into property values. By way of illustration, consider a parcel of property worth $100,000 and subject to a 0.8 percent tax rate, the average city's rate in the sample. Then consider the change in value predicted to occur with a 10 percent increase in the tax rate, to 0.88 percent. Assuming the resulting $80 tax increase were expected to continue indefinitely, full capitalization would lead to a 1.5 percent reduction in the value of the property (as our equation predicts) provided the relevant discount rate were 5.3 percent (since $80/0.053 = $1500 = 1.5 percent of $100,000). Thus, at a discount rate of 5.3 percent, the estimated long-run elasticity of −0.15 would be fully consistent with 100 percent capitalization. For higher discount rates, the estimated elasticity indicates a larger impact than would be implied by capitalization alone and for lower rates, it indicates a smaller impact.

Even if one accepted 5.3 percent as the correct discount rate, one should not interpret our results as evidence that property taxes are fully capitalized into values. In contrast to previous studies that explicitly measure capitalization (e.g. Oates, 1969), we purposely do not control for the amount of capital in the city. Hence the estimated response of property values represents the combined effects of some capitalization (price change) and some physical disinvestment in the city (change in the quantity of capital). That is, part of the reduction in the base probably represents the decision of some potential residents (households and firms) not to move into the city, the decision of some firms to let their city property depreciate as they invest elsewhere, and the decision of some city residents to disinvest in their residential structures by reducing maintenance. This decrease in investment occurs simultaneously with a fall in the price of city land and stops once the after-tax rate of return to investment is again equalized across jurisdictions.

As noted earlier, this study provides new evidence that taxes other than city property taxes also affect the size of a city's property tax base. The one exception is local sales taxes which appear to have virtually no effect on the property tax base. Table 4 compares the effects of the various taxes, using the coefficients from the partial adjustment equation. The entries in the first column show the impact on the logarithm of the property tax base of a 10 percent increase in a particular tax rate or, equivalently for nonproperty taxes, in tax revenues. As changes in logarithms, the entries (multiplied by 100) can be interpreted as percentage changes in the base. Thus, a 10 percent increase in the property tax rate is predicted to reduce the base by 1.5 percent, while a 10 percent increase in the local income tax rate is predicted to reduce the base by only 0.7 percent. The estimated impact of a 10 percent increase in overlying taxes is a 1.0 per-

Table 4
Impacts on the Property Tax Base
(By Type of Tax)

	10 Percent Increase in Tax Rate or Tax Revenues	$10 Per Capita[a] Increase in Taxes
Property Tax	-.015	-.014 or -.020[b]
City Income Tax	-.0065	-.025
City Sales Tax	0	0
Taxes Imposed by Overlying Governments	-.010	-.0026

Notes: Entries are predicted impacts on the natural logarithm of the per capita property tax base. When multiplied by 100 they can be interpreted as percentage changes in the tax base. Calculated from estimated coefficients from the partial adjustment equation shown in Table 3.

[a] 1972 dollars.
[b] The first entry was evaluated at the average tax base and tax rate in the sample. The second entry was evaluated for average tax revenues.

cent decline in the base, halfway between the impacts of local income and property taxes. These findings have two clear implications. First, a 10 percent increase in a city's property tax rate will produce only an 8.5 percent increase in property tax revenues on average in the long run. Second, increases in city income tax rates or in taxes levied by overlying jurisdictions such as state and county governments will reduce the property tax revenues collected with a given property tax rate.

The second column of Table 4 focuses attention on equal-yield revenue changes by showing the impact on the (logarithm of the) property tax base of a $10 increase in per capita tax revenues from each source. The two entries for the property tax reflect evaluation at different averages. The 1.4 percent decline was evaluated at the average property tax rate and tax base in the sample, while the 2.0 percent decline was evaluated at the average per capita tax revenues in the sample. Surprisingly, the calculations indicate that a $10 increase in local income taxes reduces the size of the property tax base on average by more than does a comparable per capita increase in property taxes. This finding is easily reconcilable with the apparently contradictory results in column 1: a $10 per capita increase in revenue from income taxes requires a much larger absolute and percentage increase in income tax rates than a $10 increase in property tax revenues does in property tax rates.

These results can be used to determine the net effect on the property tax base of substituting revenues from one tax for another. Assuming constant total tax revenue and after allowing time for all adjustments, the larger response for income taxes means that shifting away from property taxes toward income taxes reduces the size of the property tax base. Shifting away from property taxes in favor of local sales taxes, in contrast, increases the size of the local property tax base.

Alternatively if local officials choose to reduce property taxes by inducing higher levels of government to take over some of the city's service responsibilities and to finance them by higher noncity taxes, our estimates suggest that the city's property tax base will increase. Reducing property taxes by $10 per capita would increase the tax base by 1.4 to 2.0 percent, an increase that more than offsets the much smaller decrease of 0.3 percent associated with the $10 increase in the overlying tax burden on city residents and firms.[21]

V. Conclusion

Economic theory predicts unambiguously that, controlling for service levels, an increase in local property tax burdens reduces the size of the local property tax base. This outcome occurs through either or both of two mechanisms: 1) the tax reduces the level of economic activity or 2) it is capitalized into lower land prices. Despite this clear prediction, economists know little about the magnitude of the impact. This situation reflects the fact that previous researchers have tended to focus either on the location and investment decisions of firms and households or alternatively, controlling for the amount of capital in the city, on the extent to which taxes are capitalized into property or land values, but never on both mechanisms simultaneously.

Theoretical predictions about the effects of local income taxes on property values are somewhat more ambiguous because a higher tax on labor income could induce firms to substitute away from labor in favor of land and capital. In principle, this substitution effect could offset the output effect, but the standard presumption is that, like higher property taxes, higher local income taxes reduce the size of the local property tax base. This study contributes to our understanding of these behavioral responses by specifying and estimating a simultaneous model that permits us to determine the total impact on the size of the local tax base of various forms of local taxes, where the total impact includes both the investment and price effects of tax changes.

We conclude that taxes affect local property values more than is typically found in previous studies. In particular, we find that a 10 percent increase in a city's property tax rate decreases the city's tax base by about 0.75 percent during a five-year period and by 1.5 percent in the long run. In addition, local income taxes and taxes levied by overlying jurisdictions (such as county and state governments) also have negative impacts on the city's property tax base. In contrast, local sales taxes appear to have virtually no impact. One striking finding is that for a given amount of revenue, local income taxes have more deleterious effects than do local property taxes on the size of the local property tax base. Thus, not only property taxes but also other forms of local taxes have adverse effects on the local property tax base. These effects are important because lower property tax bases require higher local property tax rates to finance a given package of public services.

ENDNOTES

***The authors thank Ilhong Cho for research assistance and John Yinger, Lynn Browne, and anonymous referees for advice and comments. They are also grateful for helpful suggestions from the participants at the NBER Conference on State and Local Government Finance (Cambridge, MA, December 12–13, 1986) at which an earlier version of this paper was presented. The research reported here is part of the NBER's research project in State and Local Finance. Any opinions expressed are those of the authors and not those of the National Bureau of Economic Research.

[1] The Census of Governments reports assessed values of locally-assessed taxable and exempt real and personal property and state-assessed property, as well as the percentage distribution of real property values among residential (total and single-family housing), acreage, vacant platted, commercial and industrial and other uses. These value data were combined with assessment/sales ratios (reported by the Census of Governments for all real property, single-family residential property, and in some cases, vacant property), information on assessment practices for personal and state-assessed property from the Census of Governments, and economic data from other sources to estimate the market value of property in eight classes for each city. These estimates are described in more detail in the appendix to Bradbury and Ladd (1985). Because personal property is partially or completely exempt from property taxation in many states, the reported "exempt" values for personalty were generally incomplete. Personal property values were imputed for most cities based on their commercial and industrial real property values and the relationship between personal property values and commercial and industrial real property values in those cities fully taxing personal property.

[2] This means that the equation modeling tax revenues (discussed below) is less appropriate for Boston and the California cities in 1982 than for other cities. But deleting those observations does not affect the coefficient estimates.

[3] See Bradbury, Downs, and Small (1982) for an attempt to model the simultaneous determination of city population, employment, and per capita income.

[4] More precisely, we have

ln (B/LAND) = $c_0' + c_1'$ ln SMPOP

  + c_2' ln LAND + e' and

ln (POP/LAND) = $d_0 + d_1$ ln SMPOP

  + d_2 ln LAND + u,

so that

ln (B/POP) = $(c_0' - d_0) + (c_1' - d_1)$ ln SMPOP

  + $(c_2' - d_2)$ ln LAND + (e' - u).

Hence, c_1 should be interpreted as $c_1' - d_1$ and c_2 as $c_2' - d_2$.

[5] This prediction should not be confused with the more ambiguous effects of income that typically emerge from an urban model. According to that model, household income of the residents of a metropolitan area exerts two opposing forces on the slope of the price gradient. On the one hand, higher income increases the demand for space, which tends to flatten the gradient. On the other, higher income increases the value of travel time and thereby raises the cost of transportation which leads to steeper gradients. With the relevant variable specified as the per capita income of city residents alone, the effects of income on city vs. suburban location are already accounted for and the issue becomes solely one of the demand for housing services.

[6] Statutory rates for cities imposing a sales tax were pieced together from a variety of sources. The four main sources are the Commerce Clearing House, *State Tax Guide*; Due and Mikesell, (1983); Due (1971) and Advisory Commission on Intergovernmental Relations, *Significant Features of Fiscal Federalism*, various years.

[7] The estimated overlying tax burden for all other California cities in the sample exceeds that for San Francisco, because they all have overlying counties. See Ladd and Yinger (1989), ch. 7, for a complete discussion of the complexities of calculating measures of overlying tax burdens in a slightly different context.

[8] Previous studies have shown that higher crime rates reduce housing values. See, for example, Rizzo (1979) and Gray and Joelson (1979). We have normalized the number of crimes (both property and violent crimes as reported in The Uniform Crime Reports) by employees rather than by city population because crimes rates per resident appear to be strongly correlated with the amount of a city's nonresidential activity, especially commercial activity. Hence, normalizing by resident population rather than by employees would lead to a severe reverse causation problem; higher tax bases per capita would be associated with higher crime rates per capita.

[9] The literature on local public goods contains two approaches to the modeling of the local decision to tax and spend. First and most common is the positive, predictive theory of the decision-making process that starts with the decisive voter's demand for local public goods. According to this approach, local public goods are viewed as providing consumption benefits to consumer-voters in the same manner as private goods. See, for example, Bergstrom and Goodman (1973), and Borcherding and Deacon (1972). The alternative approach emphasizes the investment aspect of public goods provided by local governments. According to this view, voters choose an expenditure and tax package to maximize the value of their property independent of their demand for public goods. See, for example, Sonstelie and Portney (1978), Brueckner (1979), and Brueckner (1982). Implicit here is the view that rational asset-owning voters *should* behave this way since consumption interests "can be satisfied through migration, if necessary" (Sonstelie and Portney, p. 271). Two considerations lead us to use the standard demand approach. First, we question the applicability of the assumptions of the investment approach to heterogeneous voters in the large central cities of our sample; to satisfy their preferences for public services, many residents of central cities would face high costs of moving to other jurisdictions. Furthermore, many of the voters in central cities are not property owners. Second, the demand approach forms the basis for many previous empirical studies of local public spending that yield reasonable results. We know of few studies that use the investment approach as the basis for predicting the behavior of local voters (an exception is Brueckner (1982)). We emphasize, however, that this paper does not explicitly test one approach over the other.

[10] For a complete description of the basic methodology, see Ladd and Yinger (1989). A similar methodology based on Massachusetts communities is described in Bradbury et al. (1984).

[11] Use of the property tax export rate for the decisive voter's tax share implicitly assumes that the property tax is the marginal tax. If income or sales taxes were instead the marginal tax, we would expect their export ratios to be positively associated with total spending and hence with property tax revenues. But in the choice among revenue sources, higher export ratios for nonproperty taxes should have a negative effect on property tax revenues, as discussed below. Export ratios for income and general sales taxes consistently obtain negative signs in the estimates of the property tax revenue equation (not reported) and those for the income tax differ significantly from zero. This implies either that the property tax is the marginal tax or that the negative effect of higher nonproperty tax exporting on revenue choice more than offsets its positive effect on total revenue raising where nonproperty taxes are used at the margin.

[12] For a complete derivation and discussion of this measure, see chapter 8 in Ladd and Yinger (forthcoming).

[13] One notable exception is Inman (1982).

[14] To the extent that city officials are concerned about deadweight loss, tax rates on alternative tax instruments also belong in the equation. The data allow us to reject this hypothesis: The tax base variables (TRINC and TRSAL) pass the exogeneity test described later and thus are appropriately excluded from the revenue equation.

[15] See appendix to Bradbury and Ladd (1985) for a full description of how the export ratios were calculated. As noted in the text, the analysis is most complicated for the property tax. In brief, the share of the property tax falling on land is assumed borne by landowners. Capital is assumed to be mobile across cities, so the portion of the tax with an initial incidence on capital is assumed to be borne partially by consumers in those markets where taxed producers dominate, and partially by labor and land, approximately in line with factor shares. The share of the tax that is exported then further depends on the fractions of consumers, landowners, and workers who live inside vs. outside the city.

[16] Estimates of the revenue equation are not reported in this paper. Coefficient estimates are available from the authors upon request.

[17] Consistent with our model, the Hausman tests show that the state and federal aid variables are appropriately excluded from the base equation. An alternative view that intergovernmental aid belongs in the base equation makes sense only if tax burdens are not included in the equation. The logic would be that, after controlling for service levels and their costs of provision, higher intergovernmental transfers lead to lower local tax burdens and that these lower tax burdens are capitalized into a higher valued tax base. In our model, the tax variables fully capture the indirect effects on the tax base of federal and state aid.

[18] The test works as follows: first, the residuals are calculated from an auxiliary regression of the lagged base on the set of exogenous variables in the base equation, not including the lagged base, plus other variables hypothesized to be exogenous. Second, one tests the null hypothesis that the coefficient of the residuals is zero when they are included as an explanatory variable in the base equation.

[19] That is, $(c_1' - d_1)$ and $(c_2' - d_2)$ from footnote 4 are positive.

[20] Given the number of communities in the typical metropolitan area, determining the relevant indicators of suburban tax rates and service levels is a complicated task. Furthermore, the data to implement any such measures are not readily available.

[21] Furthermore, if it typically costs the city more on a per capita basis to provide the shifted service than it costs other municipalities within the jurisdiction assuming the responsibility, overlying taxes may rise by less than $10 per capita; hence, the net increase in the property tax base may be slightly greater.

REFERENCES

Advisory Commission on Intergovernmental Relations (1981). "Regional Growth: Interstate Tax Competition," Report A-76. March 1981 (Washington, D.C.)

Bartik, Timothy J. (1985). "Business Location Decisions in the United States: Estimates of the Effects of Unionization, Taxes, and Other Characteristics of States," *Journal of Business and Economic Statistics*, 3.

Bartik, Timothy J. (1986). "Tax Effects on the Location of New Branch Plants in the United States," Working Paper 86-W19, Department of Economics and Business Administration, Vanderbilt University.

Bergstrom, T., and R. Goodman (1973). "Private Demands for Public Goods," *American Economic Review*, vol. 63, pp. 280-296.

Bloom, H. S., and H. F. Ladd (1982). "Property Tax Revaluation and Tax Levy Growth," *Journal of Urban Economics*, Winter.

Borcherding, T., and R. Deacon (1972). "The Demands for Services of Non-Federal Governments," *American Economic Review*, vol. 62, pp. 891-901.

Bradbury, Katharine L., Anthony Downs, and Kenneth A. Small (1982). *Urban Decline and the Future of American Cities.* Washington, D.C.: The Brookings Institution.

Bradbury, Katharine L., and Helen F. Ladd (1985). "Changes in the Revenue-Raising Capacity of U.S. Cities, 1970-1982," *New England Economic Review*, March/April.

Bradbury, Katharine L., Helen F. Ladd, Mark Perrault, Andrew Reschovsky, and John Yinger (1984). "State Aid to Offset Fiscal Disparities Across Communities," *National Tax Journal*, vol. 37, no. 2 (June).

Bradford, David F., R. A. Malt, and Wallace E. Oates (1969). "The Rising Cost of Local Public Services: Some Evidence and Reflections," *National Tax Journal*, vol. 22, no. 2 (June).

Brueckner, Jan K. (1982). "A Test for Allocative Efficiency in the Local Public Sector," *Journal of Public Economics*, 19, 311-331.

Brueckner, Jan K. (1979). "Property Values, Local Public Expenditures, and Economic Efficiency," *Journal of Public Economics*, 11, 223-245.

Carlton, Dennis (1979). "Why New Firms Locate Where They Do: An Econometric Model," in *Interregional Movements and Regional Growth*, edited by William Wheaton. Washington, D.C.: The Urban Institute.

Case, Karl, Leslie Papke, and Susan Koenigsberg (1983). *Taxes and Business Location*, final report submitted to New York State Legislature.

Due, John F. (1961). "Studies of State-Local Tax Differences on Location of Industry," *National Tax Journal*, 14.

Due, John F. (1971). *State and Local Sales Taxation.* Chicago: Public Administration Service.

Due, John F., and John Mikesell (1983). *Sales Taxation: State and Local Structure and Administration.* Baltimore: Johns Hopkins University Press.

Gray, Charles M. and Mitchell R. Joelson (1979). "Neighborhood Crime and The Demand for Central City Housing," in Charles M. Gray, *The Costs of Crime,* Sage Criminal Justice System Annuals; Vol. 12, pp. 47-61.

Hausman, J. A. (1978). "Specification Tests in Econometrics," *Econometrica*, 46 (6), 1251-1271.

Inman, Robert P. (1982). "The Local Decision to Tax," unpublished paper presented at the 1982 meetings of Taxation, Resources, and E onomic Development (TRED), Lincoln Institute of Land Policy Research, Cambridge, MA.

Kieschnick, Michael (1981). *Taxes and Growth: Business Incentives and Economic Development.* Council of State Planning Agencies, Washington, D.C.

Ladd, Helen F. and John Yinger (1989). *America's Ailing Cities: Fiscal Health and The Design of Urban Policy.* Baltimore: Johns Hopkins Press.

Lugar, Michael I., and Dale O. Stahl, II, (1986) "Specification Errors in Models of Aggregate Labor Supply," *The Review of Economics and Statistics,* LXVIII (2), pp. 274-283.

Oakland, William H. (1978). "Local Taxes and Intra-Urban Industrial Location: A Survey." In George Break (ed.), *Metropolitan Financing and Growth Management Policies.* Madison: University of Wisconsin Press.

Oates, Wallace E. (1969). "The Effects of Property Taxes and Local Public Spending on Property Values: An Empirical Study of Tax Capitalization and The Tiebout Hypothesis," *Journal of Political Economy,* 77, no. 6 (November/December); pp. 1004-08.

Papke, Leslie (1986). "Subnational Taxation and Capital Mobility: Estimates of Tax-Price Elasticities." MIT mimeo.

Rizzo, Mario J. (1979). "The Loss of Time to Victims: An Empirical Analysis," in the *Journal of Legal Studies,* Vol VIII (1), pp. 477-506.

Rosen, Harvey S. and David J. Fullerton (1977). "A Note on Local Tax Rates, Public Benefit Levels, and Property Values," *Journal of Political Economy,* 85, no. 21, pp. 433-440.

Schmenner, Roger W. (1982). *Making Business Location Decisions.* Englewood Cliffs, New Jersey: Prentice-Hall, Inc.

Sonstelie, Jon C. and Paul R. Portney (1978). "Profit Maximizing Communities and the Theory of Local Public Expenditure," *Journal of Urban Economics,* 5, 263-277.

Wasylenko, Michael (1981). "The Location of Firms: The Role of Taxes and Fiscal Incentives." In R. W. Bahl (ed.), *Urban Government Finance: Emerging Trends,* Vol. 20, Urban Affairs Annual Reviews, Sage.

White, Michelle J. (1986) "Property Taxes and Firm Location" in Harvey S. Rosen (ed.) *Studies in State and Local Public Finance.* Chicago: University of Chicago Press.

Spatially Targeted Economic Development Strategies: Do They Work?

Helen F. Ladd
Duke University

Throughout the 1980s and early 1990s, U.S. policymakers have shown interest in geographically targeted urban economic development strategies, specifically in the form of enterprise zones. Originating in England, these zones captured the imagination of U.S. Federal Government policymakers in the early 1980s as a potentially powerful strategy for promoting economic development in pockets of urban distress. The English model involved deep tax breaks and regulatory relief to small geographic areas within a city. In 1980 conservative Republican congressman Jack Kemp (who became Secretary of Housing and Urban Development under President Bush) teamed up with Robert Garcia, a liberal Democrat from the South Bronx, to propose a Federal enterprise zone program. Although never passed by Congress, this Federal proposal, plus others in subsequent years, apparently played a catalytic role in spurring the development of such zones in States throughout the country.[1] Despite the absence of a Federal program, 37 States and the District of Columbia had enacted enterprise zone programs by 1993. Congress finally passed a modified Federal program as part of the 1993 Budget Reconciliation Act.

As elaborated below, the conceptual underpinnings of enterprise zones changed significantly as the idea crossed the Atlantic. Moreover, in practice the programs have taken on different forms in different States. Given the new Federal legislation and the decade of experimentation at the State level, the time is now ripe for reviewing what is known about these spatially targeted urban economic development strategies.

The first section begins by placing enterprise—or, in the language of the new Federal legislation, empowerment—zones in the broader context of three policy approaches to meeting the challenge of urban distress: a people-oriented strategy, a place-based people strategy, and a pure place strategy. The second section examines the policy tools used to promote place strategies, and the third section looks closely at the lessons from specific programs and summarizes what is known about the cost-effectiveness of existing enterprise programs.

People and Place Strategies for Combatting Urban Distress

The focus here is on strategies to deal with pockets of distress or blight within an urban area.[2] A major contributor to the distress in many U.S. cities is the decline in manufacturing activity. This decline reflects economic forces outside the control of public officials, such as productivity improvements that reduce the demand for labor, and the movement of manufacturing firms from the central city to the suburbs (where land is cheaper) or to the southern United States or overseas (where unions are weaker and wages lower). Even if partially offset by the growth of service jobs in finance, insurance, and real estate, as has occurred in many urban areas, the loss of manufacturing jobs can have a big impact on the urban landscape and on certain geographically concentrated groups of urban workers who often lack the skills required for the new jobs. In addition, the outmigration of middle and upper income households, both white and black, in search of better housing, better schools, and decreased crime in the suburbs—combined, in many cases, with discriminatory policies that confine minorities to certain sectors of the city—contributes to the existence of distressed neighborhoods.

Three basic policy approaches can be identified for dealing with pockets of distress in urban areas. The first, a pure people-oriented strategy, focusses on helping people, with little or no attention to revitalizing the areas in which they live. The second, a place-based people strategy, uses a variety of place-specific strategies to increase the economic well-being of people living in a distressed area of the city. The third, a pure place strategy, focusses on improving the physical and economic vitality of a geographically defined area without explicit attention to the people who live there. As explained below, the English enterprise zone program is a pure place strategy, while the new U.S. Federal policy strives to be a place-based people strategy. The State programs have elements of both the place-based people and the pure place strategies.

Pure People-Oriented Strategy

A pure people-oriented economic development strategy would assist people regardless of where they live and would focus on increasing their human capital and mobility. This approach starts with the observation that poor people and those with low skills need assistance regardless of whether they live in distressed or relatively well-off places. Philosophically the approach is grounded in the free market economy—specifically the view that the market economy works most efficiently and effectively when both labor and capital are sufficiently mobile to take advantage of economic opportunities wherever they may be and when there are no artificial barriers to movement. Supporters of this view oppose place-based economic development strategies because they may encourage firms to locate in places not justified on economic grounds and because they reduce the incentive for residents of distressed areas to relocate in order to become more productive.

A pure people-oriented Federal economic development strategy would focus on moving people from welfare to work and on programs such as education assistance for children from disadvantaged households (for example, Chapter I of the Elementary and Secondary Education Act) and job training (for example, Job Training Partnership Act and Trade Adjustment Assistance programs). In addition, such a strategy might include more Federal Government assistance that would foster labor mobility. Following the Canadian model, the U.S. Government might offer a national computerized job search program or, following the Swedish model, might make assistance with housing and moving costs for displaced workers more generally available (Hanson, 1991, p. 19).

In the context of distressed urban areas, the observation that racial discrimination in the housing market has contributed to the growth of urban ghettoes provides an additional underpinning for a people-oriented strategy. Housing market discrimination that keeps blacks in the central city as jobs move to the suburbs leads to a "spatial mismatch" between jobs and residential locations (see Kain, 1992, for a thorough review of the current status of the spatial mismatch hypothesis). In a well-known and provocative 1969 paper, "Alternatives to the Gilded Ghetto," John Kain and Joseph Persky argued forcefully against place-based strategies designed to increase jobs in urban ghettoes or otherwise to promote economic development within the ghetto. Instead, Kain and Persky supported "dispersal" strategies designed to encourage and assist blacks to leave the ghetto for the suburbs, where they could obtain better and cheaper housing, live in safer neighborhoods, attend good public schools, and gain access to jobs. Such policies, they argued, would be more cost-effective not only in the short run but also in the long run. They argued that a dispersal strategy, by slowing or reversing the growth of massive central-city ghettoes, would alleviate the problems of unemployment, poverty, and crime associated with such ghettoes. Kain has recently acknowledged that the choice of the word "dispersal" was unfortunate, in that "many critics interpreted it as a call for the forced or involuntary dispersal of Afro-Americans from central-city ghettoes. [But] nothing could have been further from our minds" (Kain, 1992, p. 445). Instead, the goal was to reduce existing barriers in order to provide black households and workers with meaningful choices in jobs, housing, and education throughout the metropolitan area.

A narrower approach to the spatial mismatch problem focusses on making suburban jobs more accessible to ghetto residents (Hughes, 1991). Criticizing the dispersal approach on the grounds that the changes it requires, such as fair housing in the suburbs, are subject to enormous political obstacles, Hughes proposed a six-part mobility strategy incorporating job training, job information systems, restructured transportation systems, day care facilities, higher earned-income tax credits to supplement entry-level wages, and a place-based policy of reducing crime in urban ghettoes (see Hughes, 1991, and discussion in Kain, 1992, pp. 446–450). In fact, however, Hughes' mobility strategy is not inconsistent with a dispersal strategy, in that it would provide more opportunities for residents of inner-city areas to improve their economic well-being and, if they chose, to move out of the ghetto. It differs in that it focusses exclusively on access to jobs and, in Kain's view, pays too little attention to other ingredients of long-term economic success such as the good schools and good housing that are most often found in the suburbs.

Both the Kain and Persky and the Hughes approaches are primarily people-oriented strategies, and the difference between the two draws attention to the possible desirability of place-based strategies. Compared to the Kain and Persky dispersal approach, Hughes' approach emphasizes the distressed areas within cities. Implicit in his approach is the belief that one can change the culture of unemployment and welfare dependency in distressed inner-city neighborhoods by providing people with access to jobs, even if those jobs are in the suburbs. The major weaknesses of Hughes' approach are the difficulties of solving the transportation problem in a cost-effective manner,[3] the observation (discussed below) that the labor-market isolation of city residents in distressed neighborhoods entails more than just their spatial isolation from jobs, and the possibility that the community, per se, contributes to its residents' well-being.

Place-Based People Strategy

A more direct approach to dealing with pockets of urban distress in urban areas involves using place-specific assistance to help the residents—especially the disadvantaged residents—of distressed urban areas. Central to this approach is the view that the community plays an important role in its residents' well-being. Thus, in order to help people, one must build or revitalize communities. While the concept of "community" for upper income, well-educated working households need not be defined by a geographic area—instead, it might be defined by one's working or professional community—for low-income people, community is most appropriately defined in terms of a geographic area or neighborhood. Thus a place-based people strategy starts from the view that "in a very meaningful sense people cannot be separated from place, and that an antipoverty strategy needs to treat individuals in the context of their community" (Butler, 1991,

p. 35). The place-based people strategy aims to preserve and strengthen community institutions and ultimately to generate more jobs and a higher standard of living for residents.

Consistent with this view are recent works by O'Regan and Quigley (1991, 1993) and Ludwig (1993) that document the social isolation of many residents in distressed areas. To the extent that the isolation results in incomplete knowledge of the labor market and limited exposure to people in the labor market who may serve as the informal contacts needed for successful job searches, transportation strategies designed to improve access to suburban jobs may not be sufficient to improve the economic condition of inner-city residents. Instead, place-based strategies may be needed. By bringing jobs to distressed urban areas, proponents of enterprise zones hope to reduce the isolation of inner-city residents from the labor market. However, success in this endeavor requires not just that there be local jobs but that the jobs be given to local residents. Such an outcome is not assured. Few local residents will be hired if firms require skill levels not generally present in the local population or if they continue to fill jobs by relying on existing labor market networks from which ghetto residents are isolated.[4]

Proponents of a place-based people strategy agree that the targeted geographic area or zone should contain a mix of land uses, including residential, industrial, and commercial activity. Mixed-use neighborhoods are important to enable the area to adapt to changing economic conditions and to promote a flourishing street life that can reduce crime and other social problems which might inhibit local economic development (Butler, 1991, p. 35). A mix of land uses also provides linkages between various firms and people that can lead to multiplier effects within the communities. For example, a firm may buy some of its input from other local firms, and the increased income of resident workers may generate more consumption spending in the neighborhood (Rubin, 1993, p. 3).

In addition, proponents favor small firms over large ones (Butler, 1991, pp. 32–37). Small firms are viewed as more likely than large firms to hire local residents and unleash their latent entrepreneurial energy. Small firms are also preferred because of the greater likelihood that they can use existing buildings; large firms typically need to build their own customized facilities. Proponents of this small firm strategy buttress their arguments by referring to David Birch's conclusions that small firms are the most important generators of new jobs and are the only net producers of jobs in poor, urban neighborhoods (Birch, 1981, 1987). Although commonly cited, this picture of small firms is somewhat misleading. As elaborated by Brown, Hamilton, and Medoff (1990), small firms do not create as large a share of the jobs as claimed by Birch, and when their high failure rate is taken into account, small firms do not grow faster than large firms. Moreover, small firms offer lower wages, lower benefits, and less job security than large firms.[5]

Conceptually, the small firm strategy is a crucial component of a place-based people approach to local development. Without it, any place-based program is subject to the potentially serious criticism that it simply moves jobs from one location to another. Based on metropolitanwide data, Bartik (1991, 1993) claims that net gains to society can emerge even in the absence of an increase in the total number of jobs, provided the jobs are moved from areas where labor is in short supply to areas where it is in surplus. If Bartik is correct, even a program that simply moves jobs around may be justifiable on economic grounds. Generally, however, such a program faces the tougher political hurdle of needing to be justified on distributional grounds alone. The small firm strategy is appealing because it makes plausible the possibility that jobs will be generated which will increase the total output of the economy, that the new jobs may go to disadvantaged local residents, and that, because some of the residents will become owners of local firms, they will have a larger stake in the economic stability of the community.

Spatially Targeted Strategies

The new empowerment zones and enterprise communities proposed by President Clinton and passed by Congress in the 1993 Budget Reconciliation Act represent the clearest, most recent attempt by the United States to pursue a place-based people strategy. It is place based in the sense that the incentives and other benefits are targeted to geographically defined zones that are substantially larger than many of the zones in the State programs. The Act authorizes the Secretary of Housing and Urban Development to designate 6 urban and 3 rural empowerment zones and 65 urban and 30 rural enterprise communities. While the designation criteria and other details have yet to be resolved, the goals of the program are quite clear: to build communities and empower residents of distressed areas so that they may prosper. The tax incentives include a 20-percent tax credit covering the first $15,000 of wages and certain types of training that a business provides to each employee who lives and works in the zone, as well as tax and financial incentives for investment in the zone. In addition, the program creates a block grant that will direct money for social services to disadvantaged residents of the zone.[6]

Most of the 38 State enterprise zone programs can also be categorized as place-based people strategies, at least in part. In their statement of intent, 18 of the State programs list the goal of increasing health, safety, and welfare; 3, the goal of promoting community development; and 11, the goal of revitalizing neighborhoods. Many also cite job creation as a goal. Twenty-seven States either include as part of the eligibility criteria the hiring of zone residents or provide financial incentives for the selective hiring of zone residents or disadvantaged workers (Erickson and Friedman, 1991, pp. 160–163). However, since many of the State programs are also intended to revitalize economic areas regardless of who receives the jobs and other benefits, many can also be characterized, at least in part, as pure place strategies.

Pure Place Strategy

Urban distress within a narrowly defined geographic area need not refer to the distress of that area's residents. Instead, it may refer to blighted or vacant areas of cities in which few people live or to deteriorating downtown business districts that house few city residents. Pure place-based strategies involve either improvements to the physical landscape of the area or its economic revitalization, defined as new investment and new jobs within the area. With respect to the provision of jobs, the pure place strategy differs from the place-based people strategy in that it is intended to improve the economic well-being of people in a geographic area extending well beyond the boundaries of the targeted area rather than to help only the residents of the targeted area. Implicit in this strategy is the view that pockets of blight are detrimental to the economic vitality of the larger jurisdiction.

Externalities are sometimes used to justify geographically targeted government interventions of this type. Small investors acting alone may have little incentive to invest in a blighted area because of the risk that the area will remain blighted. This argument is especially valid for firms that plan to buy property in the area and for whom costs and revenues are directly related to the characteristics of the area, such as a high crime rate. However, if many investors simultaneously invested in the area, they would all benefit from one another's investments. Government intervention can alter the situation in one of two ways. One is to provide financial incentives to induce large companies to invest in the areas, especially companies large enough to internalize the externalities involved in investing in the blighted areas.[7] The other is to signal to many smaller investors that the area is about to grow. Convincing investors that others will simultaneously invest in an area mitigates the externalities problem.

The enterprise zone approach, as conceptualized and used in England, illustrates this pure place-based strategy.[8] The term "enterprise zone" was initially used in a speech by Sir Geoffrey Howe in 1978 to describe a new policy for dealing with small areas in the most derelict and depressed sections of British cities. The areas, about 1-mile square, were typically old industrial areas, often near ports, which became vacant and rundown as economic forces reduced the demand for the warehouses or other businesses that once formed the economic basis for the area. Most of the zones housed very few residents; indeed, residential areas were often explicitly excluded from the zones. A zone program, it was hoped, would produce a small urban industrial park that would yield economic benefits to the larger geographic area.

As discussed below, the governmental policy designed to achieve the goal was deep regulatory and tax relief. Deep tax breaks were required, it was believed, to induce large corporations to invest in the zone. Attracting the investment of large corporations was deemed essential, because only they would have the resources and incentive to redevelop the entire area.

The closest thing to a pure place approach in the U.S. urban context is the revitalization of downtown business districts. Because so few people typically live in the downtown or central business district (CBD), a CBD development strategy should not be viewed as one designed to help distressed residents in the district. Instead, it must be justified as a provider of additional jobs for residents throughout the city. Whether downtown revitalization in fact helps poor city residents is a controversial issue beyond the scope of this article.[9]

As already noted, to the extent that State enterprise zone programs aim to provide new jobs to people beyond the zone, they can be classified, at least in part, as pure place strategies. Thus they combine the elements of a pure place strategy with those of a place-based people strategy.

Policy Tools to Promote the Development of Places

To promote the economic development of places, enterprise zone programs typically rely primarily on the supply-side policy instruments of geographically targeted tax abatements and, in some cases, the relaxation or streamlining of regulation. Three key issues arise with respect to these policy tools: (1) what specific forms of tax reduction are most appropriate; (2) are supply-side policy instruments appropriate or sufficient for achieving the goals of place-based programs; and (3) can any place-based strategy improve the welfare of local residents?

Forms of Tax Reduction and Other Financial Incentives

The philosophy underlying the enterprise zone concept in England called for lower regulatory barriers and reduced taxes. The original idea in the United States was to promote local development in distressed areas primarily by reducing regulatory barriers. However, opposition from unions and environmentalists quickly shifted the emphasis to tax reduction.

In the United States, the State enterprise zone programs vary in the types of tax and financial incentives they offer to encourage firms to locate or expand in the zone. A recent study showed that most zones used tax incentives, with 51 percent offering sales or use tax credits; 51 percent, job creation and wage credits; 49 percent, employer income tax credits; 43 percent, selective hiring credits; and 37 percent, investment credits. In addition, 20 States either provided property tax credits or made them available at the option of local governments (Erickson and Friedman, 1991, p. 160).

In light of the small firm strategy discussed earlier, it is somewhat surprising to find that many of the enterprise zones include tax abatements that are not particularly useful for small firms. For example, a reduction in corporate tax rates does not help small firms that are sole proprietorships or partnerships, and property tax abatements may not help small firms that rent, rather than own, their property. Moreover, some tax preference provisions seem better designed to transfer benefits to established firms than to induce them to invest more dollars or hire more workers. However, the form of the tax break may help determine which types of firms choose to locate in the zone. For example, as documented below, the Indiana inventory tax credit provides a strong incentive for warehouses and similar businesses to move into the zone. Proponents of the small firm strategy most likely did not have warehouses in mind as the ideal type of business around which to build a vital community.

In addition, many analysts have observed that, given the goal of increasing local employment, subsidies to capital make less sense than subsidies to labor (see, for example, Gravelle, 1992). A capital subsidy is attractive to capital-intensive firms to move away from labor in favor of capital. Only by reducing production costs and inducing more production can such a subsidy generate jobs. In contrast, a subsidy to labor would be more attractive to labor-intensive firms and would encourage more use of labor relative to capital.

Leslie Papke (1993) builds on Gravelle's work to simulate the effects of enterprise zone tax incentives on zone wages and employment within the context of a standard neoclassical model. The key parameters in her model are, first, the determinants of the demand for labor, namely the elasticity of demand for the products produced in the zone and the ease with which labor and capital can be substituted in production and, second, the elasticity of the supply of labor to zone firms. If zone products tend to be manufactured goods, the demand for zone output is likely to be highly price elastic, as the goods are close substitutes for those produced outside the zone. However, given that much zone production is for local trade and service markets, the relevant elasticity may be quite low.[10] Papke uses a range of elasticities to cover these cases. In all her simulations, she assumes a unitary elasticity of substitution in production. With respect to the elasticity of the supply of labor, she uses a range of estimates, with the higher estimates reflecting possible behavior of disadvantaged or unskilled workers.

Papke's most important finding is that for low price elasticities of product demand, a subsidy to capital *reduces* zone wages. Thus the benefits of the subsidy accrue to the owners of capital or, in the context of a more complete model, to the owners of land in the form of higher land prices. Consistent with economic theory, regardless of the elasticity of demand, zone wages increase much less with a 10-percent capital subsidy than with a 10-percent labor subsidy. Thus, assuming that the goal of the development strategy is more jobs, the works of both Gravelle and Papke provide compelling evidence that labor subsidies should be an important part of the incentive package. Papke also shows that a labor subsidy targeted to zone residents increases zone wages by more than a general labor subsidy.

Many people acknowledge that small firms have difficulty obtaining access to financial capital. Consequently, many of the Federal proposals for enterprise zones during the

1980s included tax incentives to make capital available to small firms. For example, the House version of the bill vetoed by President Bush on other grounds included a 50-percent exclusion of capital gains to encourage people to invest in high-risk areas. Critics of this proposal argue that such a strategy would simply bring venture capitalists from outside the area to invest in small businesses (see the George Peterson interview in Noah and Wartzman, 1993). A preferred alternative, Peterson argues, is to assist community development banks, which are in a better position to foster indigenous businesses.

Supply-Side Tax Reductions Versus a More Active Governmental Strategy

The appropriate policy tools for pursuing the economic development of areas depends on one's policy goals, one's views about the existing obstacles to local economic development, and one's philosophy about the role of government. In England, policymakers argued that the blighted industrial areas remained blighted because of governmental obstacles to entrepreneurial activity. Hence, especially for those who were philosophically opposed to large government, the preferred policy tool was to eliminate taxes and regulatory burdens in the blighted areas in order to stimulate private market activity. In the United States, where a primary goal of enterprise zone programs is to improve the economic well-being of disadvantaged residents in distressed areas, some observers emphasize additional obstacles to economic development, such as small businesses' need for technical assistance, high crime rates, the limited skills of zone residents, and the lack of child care. To reduce these obstacles, a more activist governmental program is needed. This additional government involvement clearly conflicts with the basic philosophy underlying the British version of enterprise zones.

What is known about the effectiveness of supply-side incentives? Recent literature on the effects of taxes on the location and investment decisions of firms implies that, in principle, they could be effective in enticing firms to locate in the designated zones. However, various studies of specific U.S. enterprise zone programs cast serious doubt on the effectiveness of supply-side incentives as a mechanism for helping disadvantaged people in distressed urban areas.

Starting with John Due's 1961 survey of the literature on the effects of taxes, the conventional wisdom among economists held that taxes had little or no effect on the business and investment decisions of firms. A 1988 survey of the literature written before 1986 (Newman and Sullivan, 1988) came to a more agnostic conclusion. Based on a careful review of the methodological issues raised in the studies, Newman and Sullivan concluded that the impact of taxes on industrial location "should be treated as an open rather than a settled question" (p. 232). More recently, Bartik's review of 57 empirical studies, including 36 written after 1986, has generated a new conventional wisdom, namely that taxes have significant and policy-relevant impacts on the interstate and interregional investment and location decisions of firms (1991, chapter 2). Table 1 summarizes Bartik's results, showing that the estimated elasticities range from -0.25 for all studies to -0.51 for studies that include controls for both public service and fixed effects. The -0.25 estimate implies that a 10-percent tax reduction in all State and local taxes would generate a 2.5-percentage point increase in business activity in the long run.

These results understate the effect of taxes on the investment decisions among suburban communities within a metropolitan area. Compared with the interstate or interregional decisions summarized in Table 1, the choice among suburban communities within a metropolitan area provides more leeway for tax differences to dominate other differences among communities. However, intrametropolitan location studies that focus on the way

Spatially Targeted Strategies

that taxes affect the movement of firms between central cities and suburbs typically yield negligible effects (Bartik, 1992, p. 108). Only one of four studies (Luce and Summers, 1987) finds a statistically significant impact. These latter studies imply that cities, which need economic development the most, may be the least able to use business tax reductions to achieve it. At the same time, Bartik's more general conclusion that taxes do matter leaves open the possibility that taxes in small geographically defined zones could induce investments from other parts of the city to shift to those zones. Studies of the English enterprise zone program, summarized below, indicate that that is exactly what has happened. The first major study showed that 86 percent of the firms locating in the zones came from the same county.

Various empirical studies of U.S. enterprise zone programs shed light on the comparative importance of tax reductions or other considerations in generating economic activity in enterprise zones.[11] For example, a study of Connecticut's program, one of the earliest, was made after 2 1/2 years of operation. It provided a generally positive picture in terms of jobs created, businesses started, vacant buildings recycled, and investments made, but could not attribute the increased activity to the specific inducements offered. Instead the results were best explained by the "psychological stimulus created by the excitement of a new program" (Eisinger, 1988, p. 196).

The most surprising finding of the Connecticut study was that firms made little use of the tax incentives. For example, few firms in the zones took advantage of the property tax abatements or applied for job incentive grants or low-interest loans. In fact many firms were ineligible for some of the benefits, because fewer than 30 percent of their new hires were zone residents or because the firm leased rather than owned property. The authors of the study concluded that zone designation alone, rather than specific incentives, may have spurred the economic activity. This conclusion also emerged from a 1986 U.S. Department of Housing and Urban Development study of 10 enterprise zones in 9 states (Battle and Underhill, 1986, summarized in Eisinger, 1988, p. 198).

A more recent comparative analysis of four State-specific enterprise zone programs directly compares the effectiveness, or lack thereof, of supply-side incentives relative to an interventionist governmental strategy for promoting local economic development. Elling and Sheldon (1991) examined the effectiveness of supply-side incentives in 47 enterprise zones in Illinois, Indiana, Kentucky, and Ohio. All four States had well-established programs, and all restricted the zones to small, blighted areas: The median-sized zone was 13.4 square miles in Kentucky, 7.5 in Ohio, 5.0 in Illinois, and 3.0 in Indiana. Most of the zones provided local property tax relief, and some had reduced local sales and utility taxes. In addition, some zones provided additional financial benefits to firms through fee waivers and below market-rate financing. Contrary to the spirit of the English form of enterprise zones, few of the zones in this study provided regulatory relief. Elling and Sheldon described the three forms of incentives (direct tax savings, direct nontax savings, and deregulation) as classic enterprise zone program components, or supply-side incentives.

In addition, more than half the zones in Illinois and Indiana improved their infrastructure, and many zones in the four States provided technical assistance and other services. The amount of administrative staffing of the zones varied significantly across zones and across States. For example, the median number of hours per week devoted to administrative staffing varied from 5.5 hours in Ohio to 40 in Indiana. Finally, in some zones special public-private partnerships were set up. Elling and Sheldon characterized these strategies as interventionist.

In a regression model to explain zone success, Elling and Sheldon measured zone success by the number of firms applying for zone benefits each year. Although they justified their measure on the grounds that successful local economic development requires the birth and relocation of many small firms, the limitations of this measure should be noted. Unfortunately they used no additional measures, such as the value of investment per year or the number of jobs created or retained each year. Moreover, they measured some of the key explanatory variables, such as tax abatements, quite crudely by the number of abatements offered.

Nonetheless their results are suggestive. Focussing on all firms, they found that the interventionist components accounted for much more of the variation in success rates across zones than the supply-side components, which seemed not to work. Instead, the main contributors to overall zone success were the administrative resources devoted to the zone and the services, such as technical assistance, that the zone provides. Disaggregating the analysis to new firms, expanding firms, and relocating firms confirms the importance of staffing levels in each case and also indicates the role of program services for new firms. Only in the regression for firms expanding in the district does any supply-side component emerge as an important determinant. The provision of more nontax incentives in the form of waivers or below market-rate financing apparently contributed to the expansion of existing firms. Nonetheless, the bottom line of this study is that the tax and financial incentives appear to be a relatively ineffective part of the policy package. Additional research along these lines, with more careful attention to the specification of variables, would be desirable.[12]

Can Any Place-Based Strategy Improve the Welfare of Local Residents?

Even if a place-based strategy were successful in increasing the number of jobs and the amount of investment in the zone, the welfare of local residents might not be improved. One reason for this outcome, which has already been mentioned, is that the new jobs may not go to local residents. In addition, even if many of the jobs were to go to local residents, the process of capitalization could transfer some of the benefits to people outside the zone. For example, a place-specific development strategy could transfer benefits in the form of higher land prices or higher rents to nonresident landlords. As a result, with capitalization the benefits of higher wages to local residents would be offset, at least in part, by higher rents, with the impact of residential rents dependent on firms' demand for land.[13] On the other hand, residents who owned property in the zone at the time the tax incentives were introduced would benefit from the higher property values. Thus, while capitalization clearly affects the distribution of the benefits, its precise implication for improving the real income of disadvantaged local residents remains an empirical question.

Evaluation of Specific Enterprise Zone Programs

Determining the effectiveness of enterprise zones is complicated by the fact that both the goals and the characteristics vary across programs. In addition, two serious methodological issues arise: How can one distinguish the effects of the zone and its various incentives from what otherwise would have occurred in the zone, and how can one determine whether the jobs in the zone are new or simply have been moved from nearby locations? Several recent studies have grappled with these issues using various methodologies in the context of specific enterprise zone programs. The following sections summarize the studies.

The English Experience[14]

The English enterprise zone program offered firms three tax incentives: an exemption from the property tax, full expensing of capital expenditures on industrial and commercial buildings, and exemption from the development land tax. The program also reduced the burden of regulatory controls in various ways, such as by streamlining procedures and by relaxing certain reporting and planning requirements.[15] These incentives were designed to generate economic activity in the zone and create jobs. According to Rubin and Richards (1992), the goal was clearly to generate *new* activity, not simply to redistribute activity or jobs from one part of the region to another.

A 1984 government-funded study, the Tym Report, produced some pessimistic conclusions. First, employment grew at a slower pace in the zones (13 percent) than in comparable firms outside the zones (24 percent). Second, the majority of new jobs in the zones could not be attributed to either the enterprise zone designation or the specific incentives provided. Third, and perhaps most devastating, most of the new economic activity in the zones simply represented activity that had been relocated from nearby counties. Specifically, during the first 3 years of the program, 86 percent of the firms relocating to the zones came from the counties in which the zones were located.

More recent studies reinforce the criticism of the English enterprise zone program, confirming that most of the new economic activity in the zones simply relocated from nearby counties. In addition, several studies emphasize that, contrary to the original zone philosophy, the government invested large amounts of money to build infrastructure and buy land. Hence most of the positive impacts of zone designation probably have more to do with public spending than with incentives. The only incentive that appeared to have an impact was the property tax, and it proved most attractive to the larger firms, particularly those with higher capital-to-labor ratios and smaller job-generation potential per dollar of new investment.

Various authors have made estimates of the cost per job, with one study concluding that the cost per zone job between 1981 and 1986 for the original 11 zones was £45,000, or $67,000. This estimate counted as costs foregone tax revenues and public expenditures and assumed, based on the Tym Report, that only 25 percent of the jobs in the zones could be attributed to zone designation. A 1987 study covering all 24 zones reported a cost per job of only £23,000 per job, but recalculations by Rubin and Richards to make it comparable to other cost figures raised the figure to £50,000, or $75,000 per job. Both the original estimate and the new one subtract from the total of new jobs those attributable to relocation. The modified estimate, however, excludes from the job count those attributable to multiplier or spillover effects. Neither estimate corrects for the fact that many of the jobs would have been generated in the zone even in the absence of zone designation and thus represent underestimates of the costs of generating jobs in the zone. Given the 5-year time horizon of the study, the $75,000 translates into an annual cost per job of about $15,000. Adjusting for the fact that only 25 percent of the jobs should probably be attributed to zone designation, the annual cost per job generated rises to $60,000 per job.

Maryland

A 1987 study by the U.S. General Accounting Office provides one of the most pessimistic evaluations of a State's enterprise zone program. The Maryland program offers investment credits and also employment credits aimed at hiring both disadvantaged and nondisadvantaged workers. Over a 4-year period, employment by participating businesses in Maryland zones increased by a low of 8 percent (63 workers) in one zone and a high of

76 percent (555 workers) in another, but factors other than the program apparently accounted for most of these increases.

The study focussed on three Maryland zones: Hagerstown, Cumberland, and Salisbury. The program offers investment credits and also employment credits aimed at the hiring of disadvantaged and nondisadvantaged workers. Using monthly data from the State's unemployment insurance program, dealing with participating firms, the researchers used interrupted time series analysis to determine abrupt and gradual changes in employment following the implementation of the program at each site.

The analysis of employment effects in Hagerstown illustrates this approach. The Hagerstown enterprise zone (EZ) covers about 2,000 acres, which include the old central business district, several industrial areas, and a large industrial park. In 1982, at the time of EZ designation, about 3,300 workers were employed in businesses with at least 5 employees. The initial analyses of employment by the 64 participating firms showed that employment increased in August and October 1984, 8 and 10 months after the program was implemented. The question, then, was whether these employment jumps could be attributed to the program. In fact, two new employers accounted for the two employment jumps. Interviews with both employers indicated that the program was not the catalyst for the change. In one case, the employer was not aware of the program at the time of the hiring. In the other case, the firm indicated that it would have located in Hagerstown without the program. When data for these two employers are removed, the employment trends reveal no employment effect of the program. Comparable results are found for Cumberland and Salisbury.

The absence of employment effects implies that the program would not pass a cost-benefit test. In effect the program represents a transfer of resources from Maryland taxpayers to participating firms or to local landowners to the extent that the geographically targeted tax savings are translated into higher land prices.

Indiana

The Indiana program was established in 1983 to create and retain jobs in some of the State's most distressed urban communities. Zone size was limited to 3 square miles, and 14 zones had been created by 1990. Unlike most other States, the Indiana property tax includes business inventories as part of the local property tax base. In response to business criticism of this tax, the major tax incentive under the zone program is a generous 100-percent credit against the local inventory tax for all inventories in the zone. In addition, the EZ legislation provides an exemption of all incremental income from the corporate income tax, a tax credit for lenders of 5 percent of the interest income from loans to participating lenders, an income tax credit for hiring zone residents, and an income tax deduction for zone residents. Because of the generosity of the inventory credit, the revenue foregone by local governments accounts for about 85 percent of State and local program costs.

A recent program evaluation of Indiana enterprise zones (Indiana Department of Commerce, 1992) provides information on the costs of the program, number of new jobs, and number of new jobs for zone residents. The total costs in 1990 were $20.6 million, and 2,024 new jobs were reported. Of the new jobs, only 19 percent (385) were held by zone residents. Based on these official figures, the average cost per job in the Indiana program is $10,178, and the cost per new job for a zone resident is $53,506.

Recognizing that some of the Indiana programs may be more cost-effective than others and that not all new jobs in a zone should be attributed to the creation of the zone, Rubin and Wilder (1989) applied shift-share analysis to one of the more successful zones within the Indiana program, seeking additional insight into the potential cost-effectiveness of the Indiana zones program. The shift-share methodology addresses one of the two major methodological challenges associated with the evaluation of enterprise zones, namely isolating the changes that occur in the zone as a result of zone designation from those that would have occurred in any case. The basic approach is straightforward. The total growth in zone jobs is decomposed into that associated with overall growth in the regional economy, that associated with differential growth rates by economic sector, and a residual not attributable to either regional or sectoral growth. The unexplained residual, according to the authors, plausibly represents the effects of the zone.

For the 1983–86 period, the authors determined that 1,430 of the 1,878 new jobs in the Evansville zone could not be explained by either growth or industry-mix effects and, hence, plausibly represent the impact of zone policies.[16] It is noteworthy, however, that 1,005 of these jobs are in the transportation, communications, and utility sector, which includes warehousing and distribution; 605 of the jobs were accounted for by a single regional distribution center. Given that the largest tax break in the Indiana enterprise zone program is a full exemption from the local property tax on inventories, it is not surprising that the distribution center should choose to locate in the zone. Indeed, the corporate head of the firm explicitly stated that the enterprise zone was the primary reason for the firm locating in Evansville (Rubin and Wilder, 1989, p. 428).

Although they recognized that not all zones are as successful as Evansville, Rubin and Wilder used that site to argue that zones can be a cost-effective generator of jobs. The Evansville program, they argued, cost the city $4,117 over a 3-year period per job created, which translates into an annual cost of only $1,372. One criticism of this figure is that it understates the full cost of the program by excluding foregone revenues to the State. Assuming that the local revenues foregone represent 84 percent of the total costs (based on budgetary figures for all Indiana zones summarized in Papke, 1991), the annual cost should be increased to $1,633.

A much more serious criticism, however, implies that Rubin and Wilder grossly understated the cost per *net* new job, as distinct from new jobs in the zone. Given the large contribution of warehouse activity to the zone, it is highly likely that the warehouses would otherwise have located somewhere else in the region. Stated differently, the Rubin and Wilder methodology is reasonably well suited to isolating the effects of the zone on activity in the zone but has nothing to contribute to the methodological challenge of determining whether a net increase in jobs occurs. If all the warehouse jobs simply represent relocations, the cost per net new job would be much higher. For example, if one uses this logic to exclude all the new zone jobs in the transportation, communications, and utility sector as well as those in wholesale trade, Rubin and Wilder's figures imply only 282 jobs and a cost per net new job of $8,280. How many of these jobs accrued to zone residents is not clear. However, using the statewide average for all enterprise zones of 19 percent, the cost per new job per zone resident increases to $43,579.

Papke (1991, 1993) has undertaken the most thorough analysis of Indiana's enterprise zone program. Her 1991 study used three outcome measures of the effects of enterprise zones in Indiana: unemployment claims, capital investment, and inventories. Her interest in inventories simply reflects the peculiarities of Indiana property tax law and tax incentives under the zone program. According to Papke, 1,000 firms participated in EZs annually, with retailers most heavily represented. Over time the program experienced an increase in the proportion of manufacturing and wholesale distributors. Consistent with the philosophy of enterprise zones, many of the participating firms were small, with almost two-thirds of them having fewer than 20 employees. However, a majority of the jobs were provided by larger firms.

Controlling for zone-specific and time effects, Papke estimated the average effect of the enterprise zone on each of the three outcome measures. According to the simplest model, enterprise zones generated a 9.8-percent decline in machinery and equipment investment, an 8.3-percent increase in inventories, and a 25-percent decrease in unemployment claims, where unemployment claims include those from nearby offices as well as in the zones themselves. Models somewhat richer in the specification of the time variable and in the timing of the effects of the zone yield similar results. The findings for investment in inventories versus machinery and equipment were consistent with expectations: Those firms that will benefit most from the tax incentives, mainly the warehouses, will replace those that receive fewer benefits from zone investment.

The most hopeful finding was the reduction in unemployment claims. To the extent that this reduction translates into increased output that otherwise would not have been produced, it represents a benefit for society. A subsequent analysis (Papke, 1993, p. 37) using census data to compare changes in the well-being of zone residents with people in other areas of Indiana cities between 1980 and 1990, is less sanguine. Over the 10-year period, population loss was greater for the zones, and per capita income, which started at a lower level in 1980, fell in the zones while it increased in the control areas. Unemployment fell more in the zones than in the control groups, but the difference was small. On balance, the zones seem to have had little positive impact on the economic well-being of their residents.

New Jersey

Marilyn Rubin's 1990 article on New Jersey enterprise zones summarizes the results of a major survey-based study of that State's urban enterprise zone (UEZ) program. Two specific characteristics of the study are noteworthy. First, Rubin attempted to estimate indirect as well as direct effects of the program. Second, she attempted to isolate the effects that are attributable to the program. Somewhat surprisingly her overall evaluation of the program was based heavily on a narrow budgetary perspective.

The New Jersey UEZ program is based in 10 cities selected by the State from 18 proposals. The program provides eight major benefits to qualified UEZ businesses; two involve reduced regulation, three provide incentives to businesses to hire workers with specific characteristics, and three provide general investment incentives. The costs of the program are the administrative costs plus the foregone revenues associated with sales tax exemptions or rate reductions, corporate tax credits, and rebates on unemployment insurance taxes.

The direct results of the program are based on survey data collected during 1987 and 1988 from almost 500 participating firms. Because those firms that responded to the survey accounted for only 49 percent of all participating firms, responses had to be extrapolated to the nonresponding firms. Fortunately, the nonresponding firms were similar in size and type of industry to the responding firms. Based on the survey responses, adjusted to account for the nonrespondents, Rubin reported that participating firms provided more than 9,000 new jobs, $242 million in additional wages, $1,776 million in additional production, and $803 million in investment.

According to Rubin, these direct effects produce indirect ones through a multiplier effect on the State economy. Using a 127-sector input/output model, she estimated the impact of the direct effects on the outputs of other sectors in the economy. The first simulation determined the induced effects associated with the increase in disposable personal income of workers in UEZ businesses. The second simulation determined the induced impacts associated with the spending of workers hired as a result of the first round of induced effects. The total estimated effects are huge, both in absolute terms and relative to the direct effects. For example, the total number of jobs that emerged from this exercise was 42,700, or more than 4 times the number of new jobs in participating firms.

Two criticisms can be lodged against this methodology. First, the direct effects may not all be attributable to the EZ program. Indeed, only 32 percent of the businesses reported that UEZ benefits were the primary or only reason for their location or expansion decision. In light of this finding, Rubin redid the analysis basing it only on the firms whose behavior was affected by the program. This adjustment reduced the total number of jobs generated to 16,280. Even that estimate represents an overstatement, because some of the job increase in the relocating or expanding firms presumably responded to the booming New Jersey economy rather than to the UEZ program.

A second criticism, more serious yet not emphasized by Rubin, is that the case for adding indirect impacts is weak. Almost certainly, most of the second-round effects would be offset by reduced activity elsewhere in the State economy. The potential for offsetting reductions applies as well to the direct effects but is potentially less compelling for them, provided that jobs go to people who were otherwise unemployed or underemployed. This criticism implies that the study overestimates the true effects of the UEZ program.

To provide an overall evaluation of the program, Rubin concentrated initially on a narrow budgetary perspective. If the indirect effects are not counted, the additional taxes generated fall short of the costs of the program. However, when the indirect effects are included, additional revenue exceeds costs by 90 percent. Rubin preferred this latter result and concluded that the benefits of New Jersey's UEZ exceed the costs. However, a more careful consideration of the displacement issue could lead to a less favorable conclusion.

Interestingly, Rubin provided information on the economic effectiveness of the program almost as an afterthought. Her estimates suggest that the cost per job is $13,070 if only the direct effects are considered and $3,171 if both direct and indirect effects are included. Given the displacement issue, the higher figure is probably the more plausible. Even this figure, however, could substantially understate the true cost, given Rubin's inability to rule out the employment growth that would have occurred anyway under New Jersey's booming economy at that time.[17]

Cost-Effectiveness of the Enterprise Zone Programs

The experience to date with enterprise zones provides a reasonably clear indication that, as implemented in England and in the United States, the zones have not proved to be a cost-effective means of providing jobs. The cost-effectiveness estimates from the various studies are summarized in Table 2. As shown, the basic estimates range from a low of $1,633 for the Evansville program to a high of infinity for the Maryland program. However, as indicated in the right-hand column, various adjustments to these figures suggest that the true annual costs per new job fall into the $40,000 to $60,000 range. The $60,000 figure for the English program refers to the cost per net new job. Given the greater focus on zone residents in the U.S. programs, the preferred estimates for the State programs refer to the cost per job for a zone resident. Unfortunately, lack of data on the number of jobs for residents make it impossible to convert the New Jersey cost per job to the preferred measure of the cost per job for a zone resident. Nonetheless, the conclusion is clear: None of the programs generates jobs in a cost-effective manner.

Conclusion

Pure place strategies of the type represented by the English enterprise zone program are not an effective approach to pockets of urban distress. The main effect of the tax and regulatory relief provisions is simply to relocate firms to the zones from nearby locations. The combined place and place-based people strategies implicit in the State versions of the enterprise approach do not fare much better. Supply-side incentives alone appear to be a costly and not very effective means of generating net new jobs or improving the welfare of disadvantaged zone residents. The Clinton Administration appears to have understood these lessons from the State experience and, consequently, has included more community-building components in its new Federal empowerment zone program. However, whether or not the new program, with its larger zones and its greater emphasis on improving the local social environment, will fare any better remains to be seen. Unfortunately, the limited information available on the role of the social environment as an economic development tool does not encourage great optimism (see Lynn's article "Social Structures as Economic Growth Tools" on page 245 in this volume).

Author

Helen F. Ladd is a professor of public policy studies and economics at Duke University, where she also directs the master's program in public policy studies. The author thanks Ed Harris for research assistance and the Duke Arts and Sciences Council for financial support.

Notes

1. The U.S. Congress authorized an enterprise zone program in 1987. However, because it included no tax incentives, the Bush administration chose not to implement it.

2. Although enterprise zones are sometimes used in rural areas, this article focusses only on urban areas.

3. The two principal transportation problems are that disadvantaged city residents typically do not have access to a car and that standard public transportation systems poorly serve the reverse commuter, who often cannot walk from a suburban transit stop to a job. Proposed solutions such as publicly funded car pools, flexible jitney service along major suburban routes, and employer-provided transportation for inner-city workers are worth exploring but tend to be expensive or difficult to implement. See Bahl and Ihlanfeldt, 1993, for a discussion of these options.

4. In a recent study of the Red Hook area of Brooklyn, Philip Kasinitz concluded that "in a loose labor market it is easier and more efficient for employers to find new employees through informal referral systems, particularly when local residents are perceived as unreliable and prone to crime" (1993). He argues that a more promising approach to connecting ghetto residents with private-sector jobs than one that tries to bring jobs to ghettoes would be to create proxy networks that can "inform, socialize, and vouch for employees in much the same way social and ethnic networks now do."

5. In his 1981 article, Birch concluded that between 1969 and 1976 "small business" created 8 out of 10 new jobs. Brown, Medoff, and Hamilton point out that Birch overstated the case by defining business size in terms of the number of people working at a given location (such as a Sears outlet) rather than the total number working for the firm. Moreover, they point to the high failure rate of small firms and argue that one should focus on the growth of nontransitory jobs, to which small firms make a smaller contribution (Brown, Hamilton, and Medoff, 1990, pp. 2–3).

6. The Clinton administration has not restricted itself to spatially targeted strategies. While it supports and will implement the empowerment zone legislation, it is simultaneously developing a larger set of strategies that may or may not be limited to the designated zones. These strategies include working with the Small Business Administration to develop one-stop investment centers, making billions of dollars available for home ownership in distressed communities, and working with various cabinet secretaries to bundle programs that can be targeted to the cities. (Based on a speech by Paul Dimond at the Hudson Institute National Urban Enterprise Zones Conference, October 21–23, 1993, Indianapolis, Indiana.)

7. However, if a firm is large enough to internalize the externalities, the question arises as to why the firm would not invest there without government subsidy. British proponents of enterprise zones claimed that large firms were hindered by government regulation and high taxes.

8. The following discussion relies heavily on Butler, 1991.

9. A major problem is that often a large percentage of the jobs go to suburban rather than city residents. Ladd and Yinger (1991, p. 25) document that in 48 of 86 large cities in 1982, more than half of the payroll paid by private employers in the city accrued to nonresidents. In a recent study that compared changes in the economic well-being of residents in cities that revitalized their downtown areas between 1980 and 1990 with those that did not, Wolman, Ford, and Hill (forthcoming) concluded that, with the exception of Atlanta, Baltimore, and Boston, the revitalized cities performed no better with respect to change in the economic well-being of their residents than did other cities that were equally distressed in 1980.

10. Papke reports, for example, that in Indiana, 74 percent of total receipts of firms participating in the program are derived from firms inside the zone.

11. Also see discussion below on the English enterprise zones.

12. Wassmer (1992) provides a somewhat more optimistic view of the power of tax incentives or abatements to promote local economic development, albeit in the contest of communities, rather than small enterprise zones. Based on pooled time series cross-section data for communities in the Detroit metropolitan area and a 10-equation model, he concludes that tax abatements can increase a community's manufacturing and commercial property tax base, especially when the abatements are used to overcome adverse characteristics of an area that are not already capitalized into lower property values. Wassmer emphasizes, however, that the impact of such abatements on the real income of local residents is unclear, given that such abatements in his sample appeared to lead to higher local crime rates and decreases in the value of owner-occupied homes.

13. The concept of capitalization technically refers to the impact of a flow (in this case, a subsidy) on the price of an asset (in this case either land or land and buildings). Although impacts on rents are technically not an example of capitalization, they are usually included in the term. Ross (1993) has built a formal urban model to examine the impact of local economic development strategies on resident welfare. Based on his assumption that all the land is owned by absentee landlords, he concludes that the direction of the impact of local economic development on resident welfare is indeterminate, because the increased demand by firms for land in the zone generates higher prices for all property in the zone.

14. The following discussion relies heavily on Rubin and Richards, 1992.

15. The English program is now being phased out.

16. This inference can be criticized on two grounds. The first is based on the problem of regression to the mean. Because enterprise zones are likely to be established in areas with unusually high unemployment or at times when unemployment is at a peak, employment is likely to go up relative to other areas or over time, even in the absence of the program. Working in the other direction is the possibility that the regional growth trends may overstate the expected growth in distressed areas in the absence of the program. Given that the criticisms work in opposite directions, the direction of the bias cannot be determined.

17. In a recent empirical study based on municipal data, Boarnet and Bogart (1993) found no measurable effects of the New Jersey Urban Enterprise Zone program on jobs, wages, or property values. Hence not all researchers agree with Rubin that the program generated a significant number of new jobs.

Table 1

Summary of results from various types of recent studies of State and local taxes on the economic activity of a State or metropolitan area

Type of study	Percentage of studies with at least one negative and statistically significant tax effect	Mean elasticity of economic activity with respect to taxes (standard error of mean)	95-percent confidence interval for mean
All studies	70 percent [57 studies]	-.25 (.053) [48 studies]	-.14 to -.36
Studies with public service controls	80 [30 studies]	-.33 (0.85) [25 studies]	-.15 to -.51
Studies with fixed effect controls	92 [12 studies]	-.44 (.106) [11 studies]	-.20 to -.68
Studies with both public service and fixed effect controls	100 [7 studies]	-.51 (.134) [6 studies]	-.17 to -.85

Notes:

Figures in brackets are the number of studies used in the calculations. This table is derived from Bartik, 1991, Table 2.3. The elasticity numbers used are the long-run percentage effects on each study's measure of local business activity (employment, etc.) of a 1-percent increase in all State and local tax measures used in the study. The calculation of the mean elasticity includes all studies in which such elasticity can be calculated, including studies in which taxes had a positive effect. Studies with public service controls include as a control variable at least one measure of the level of public services for each State or metropolitan area. Studies control for fixed effects by differencing all variables from the previous year's value or the sample mean for that State or metropolitan area, or by including a set of dummy variables for each State or metropolitan area.

Reproduced from Bartik, 1992, Table 1.

Table 2

Cost-effectiveness of enterprise zone programs
(Annual cost per job or per job for zone resident)

Program or study	Basic estimate	Adjusted preferred estimate
England	$15,000 per job	$60,000 per job (assumes only one in four jobs attributable to the zone)
New Jersey (Rubin)	$13,070 per job[a]	>$13,070 per job[b] (no adjustment for growth of New Jersey economy)
Indiana Commerce Department	$10,170 per job $53,507 per job for zone residents	$53,506 per job for zone residents
Evansville (Rubin and Wilder)	$1,633 per job[c]	$43,579 per job for zone residents (subtracts warehouse jobs and assumes 19 percent of jobs accrue to zone residents)
Maryland	Infinite	Infinite (no new jobs)

Notes:
[a] Direct effects only for reasons given in the text.
[b] No reasonable way to estimate cost per job for zone resident.
[c] Adjusted upward to account for State share of costs.

Sources:
Papke, 1991; Rubin and Wilder, 1989; Rubin and Richards, 1992; Rubin, 1990; and U.S. General Accounting Office (GAO), 1988.

Bibliography

Alsop, Ronald. 1978. "Abatement Debate: Property-Tax Breaks for Firms Proliferate, But Need Is Disputed," *Wall Street Journal* (June 30), p. 1.

Anderson, James. 1990. "The 'New Right' Enterprise Zones and Urban Development Corporations," *International Journal of Urban and Regional Research*, 14(3) (September), pp. 468–489.

Bahl, Roy, and Keith Ihlanfeldt. 1993. "The Economic and Fiscal Transformation of American Cities: Policy Implications," paper prepared for the U.S. Department of Housing and Urban Development Conference on Regional Growth and Community Development.

Bartik, Timothy J. 1991. *Who Benefits From State and Local Economic Development Policies?*, Kalamazoo, Michigan: W.E. Upjohn Institute for Employment Research, pp. 17–62.

———. 1992. "The Effects of State and Local Taxes on Economic Development: A Review of Recent Research," *Economic Development Quarterly*, 6(1), pp. 102–111.

———. 1993. "Who Benefits From Local Job Growth: Migrants or the Original Residents?" *Regional Studies*, 27(4), pp. 297–311.

Battle, Virginia, and Jack Underhill. 1986. "Coming to Grips With the U.S. Enterprise Zone Experiment: A Summary of Ten Case Studies," *Enterprise Zone Notes*, Washington, D.C.: U.S. Department of Housing and Urban Development.

Baum, Donald N. 1987. "The Economic Effects of State and Local Business Incentives," *Land Economics*, 63(4) (November), pp. 348–360.

Beck, John H. 1983. "Tax Competition, Uniform Assessment, and the Benefit Principle," *Journal of Urban Economics*, 13 (March), pp. 127–146.

Birch, David L. 1981. "Who Creates Jobs?" *Public Interest*, 65 (Fall), pp. 3–14.

———. 1987. *Job Generation in America*, New York: Free Press.

Bird, Kevin D., and Mark S. Dennison. 1989. "Enterprise Zones: Implementing Economic Revitalization in Blighted Urban Areas," *Zoning and Planning Law Report*, 12(4), pp. 113–120.

Boarnet, Marlon G., and William T. Bogart. 1993. "Economic Development Policy and Municipal Growth: Evidence From the New Jersey Urban Enterprise Zone Program," unpublished manuscript, Department of Urban and Regional Planning, School of Social Ecology, University of California, Irvine.

Brown, Charles, James Hamilton, and James Medoff. 1990. *Employers: Large and Small*, Cambridge, Massachusetts: Harvard University Press.

Butler, Stuart M. 1981. *Enterprise Zones: Greening the Inner Cities*, New York, New York: Universe Books.

———. 1991. "The Conceptual Evolution of Enterprise Zones," in *Enterprise Zones*, Roy E. Green, ed., Newbury Park, California: Sage Publications, pp. 27–40.

Coffin, Donald A. 1982. "Property Tax Abatement and Economic Development in Indianapolis," *Growth and Change*, 13(1) (January), pp. 18–23.

Dandridge, Thomas C., and Paul Miesing. 1990. "Underlying Patterns in a Current Economic Development Model," *Policy Sciences*, 23, pp. 231–249.

Due, John F. 1961. "Studies of State-Local Tax Influences on the Location of Industry," *National Tax Journal*, 14 (June), pp. 163–173.

Eisinger, Peter K. 1988. *The Rise of the Entrepreneurial State: State and Local Economic Development Policy in the United States*, Madison, Wisconsin: University of Wisconsin Press, pp. 189+.

Elling, Richard C., and Ann Workman Sheldon. 1991. "Determinants of Enterprise Zone Success: A Four State Perspective," in *Enterprise Zones*, Roy E. Green, ed., Newbury Park, California: Sage Publications, pp. 136–154.

Erickson, Rodney A., and Susan W. Friedman. 1991. "Comparative Dimensions of State Enterprise Zone Policies," in *Enterprise Zones*, Roy E. Green, ed., Newbury Park, California: Sage Publications, pp. 155–176.

Funkhouser, Richard, and Edward Lorenz. 1987. "Fiscal and Employment Impacts of Enterprise Zones," *Atlantic Economic Journal*, 15(2) (July), pp. 62–76.

Gravelle, Jane G. 1992. "Enterprise Zones: The Design of Tax Subsidies," CRS Report for Congress (June 3).

Green, Roy, ed. 1991. *Enterprise Zones: New Directions on Economic Development*, Newbury Park, California: Sage Publications.

Green, Roy E., and U.S. General Accounting Office. 1991. "Overview of Enterprise Zone Experiments: Here and Abroad," Government "National Tax Association—Tax Institute of America," 83rd annual conference on taxation, November 11–14, 1990, San Francisco, California, and Columbus, Ohio: National Tax Association—Tax Institute of America.

Gunther, William D., and Charles G. Leathers. 1987. "British Enterprise Zones: A Critical Assessment," *The Review of Regional Studies*, 17(1) (Winter), pp. 1–12.

Hanson, Susan B. 1991. "Comparing Enterprise Zones to Other Economic Development Techniques," in *Enterprise Zones*, Roy E. Green, ed., Newbury Park, California: Sage Publications, pp. 7–26.

Hawkins, Benjamin M. 1984. "The Impact of the Enterprise Zone on Urban Areas," *Growth and Change*, (January), pp. 35–40.

Hughes, Mark A. 1991. "Emerging Settlement Patterns: Implications for Antipoverty Strategy," Princeton, New Jersey: Center of Domestic and Comparative Policy Studies, Woodrow Wilson School.

Indiana Department of Commerce. 1992. "Indiana Enterprise Zones: A Program Evaluation for 1989 & 1990," October.

Jacobs, Susan S., and Michael Wasylenko. 1983. "Government Policy to Stimulate Economic Development: Enterprise Zones," in *Financing State and Local Governments in the 1980s: Issues and Trends*, Norman Walzer and David L. Chicoine, eds., Cambridge, Massachusetts: Oelgeschalager, Gunn, and Hain Publishers, Inc., pp. 175–201.

Joint Committee on Taxation. 1983. *Description of Bills Relating to Enterprise Zones*, Washington, D.C.: Government Printing Office.

Joint Committee on Taxation. 1989. *Description of Enterprise Zone Proposals (H.R. 6 and Administration Proposals*, Washington, D.C.: Government Printing Office.

Joint Committee on Taxation. 1991. *Description and Analysis of Proposals Relating to Tax Incentives for Enterprise Zones (H.R. 11, H.R. 23, and Other Proposals)*, Washington, D.C.: Government Printing Office.

Joint Committee on Taxation. 1992. *Proposals and Issues Relating to Tax Incentives for Enterprise Zones*, Washington, D.C.: Government Printing Office.

Kain, John F. 1992. "The Spatial Mismatch Hypothesis: Three Decades Later," *Housing Policy Debate*, 3(2), pp. 371–460.

Kain, John F., and Joseph J. Persky. 1969. "Alternatives to the Gilded Ghetto," *The Public Interest*, (Winter), pp. 74–88.

Kasiwitz, Philip. 1993. "The Real Jobs Problem," *Wall Street Journal*, November 26.

Katz, Jeffery L. 1993. "Enterprise Zones Struggle to Make Their Mark," *Congressional Quarterly Weekly Report*, 51(29), pp. 1880–1884.

Ladd, Helen F., and John Yinger. 1991. *America's Ailing Cities: Fiscal Health and the Design of Urban Policy*, updated edition, Baltimore: Johns Hopkins University Press.

Levitan, Sar A., and Elizabeth I. Miller. 1992. *Enterprise Zones: A Promise Based on Rhetoric*, Washington, D.C.: Center for Social Policy Studies, George Washington University.

Luce, Thomas F., and Anita A. Summers. 1987. *Land Fiscal Issues in the Philadelphia Metropolitan Area*, Philadelphia: University of Philadelphia Press.

Ludwig, Jens. 1993. "Information and Inner City Educational Attainment," paper prepared for presentation at the 1993 APPAM Research Conference, Washington, D.C., October 28–30.

McDonald, John F. 1983. "An Economic Analysis of Local Inducements for Business," *Journal of Urban Economics*, 13 (May), pp. 322–336.

Morse, George W., and Michael G. Farmer. 1986. "Location and Investment Effects of a Tax Abatement Program," *National Tax Journal*, 39 (June), pp. 229–236.

Newman, Robert J., and Dennis H. Sullivan. 1988. "Economic Analysis of Business Tax Impacts on Industrial Location: What Do We Know and How Do We Know It?" *Journal of Urban Economics*, 23, pp. 215–34.

Noah, Timothy, and Rick Wartzman. 1993. "Hope or Hype?" *Wall Street Journal*, (February 19).

O hUallachain, Breanden, and Mark A. Satterthwaite. 1992. "Sectoral Growth Patterns at the Metropolitan Level: An Evaluation of Economic Development Incentives," *Journal of Urban Economics* (31) pp. 25–58.

O'Regan, Katherine M., and John M. Quigley. 1991. "Labor Market and Urban Youth," *Regional Science and Urban Economics*, 21(2), pp. 277–294.

———. 1993. "Family Networks and Youth Access to Jobs," *Journal of Urban Economics*, 34, pp. 230–248.

Papke, James A., and Leslie E. Papke. 1991. "State-Local Tax Concessions as Urban Redevelopment Tools: Incentives, Subsidies or Windfalls?" *NTA-TIA Proceedings of the Eighty-Third Annual Conference on Taxation*, pp. 215–225.

Papke, Leslie E. 1991. "Tax Policy and Urban Development: Evidence From an Enterprise Zone Program," working paper series, National Bureau of Economic Research, (3945). Also forthcoming in *Journal of Public Economics*.

Papke, Leslie E. 1993. "What Do We Know About Enterprise Zones," in *Tax Policy and the Economy*, J.M. Poterba, ed., vol. 7, National Bureau of Economic Research, MIT Press, pp. 37–72.

Pomp, Richard D. 1988. "The Role of State Tax Incentives in Attracting and Retaining Business," *Economic Development Review*, 6(2) (Spring), pp. 53–62.

Robinson, Kenneth L., and Richard J. Reeder. 1991. "State Enterprise Zones in Nonmetro Areas: Are They Working?" *Rural Development Perspectives*.

Ross, Steven L. 1993. "Economic Development Policy and Resident Welfare: An Urban Economic Perspective," Metropolitan Studies Occasional Paper no. 164, Syracuse University.

Rubin, Barry M. 1993. "Are Enterprise Zones Effective Tools for Urban Economic Development?" unpublished manuscript, School of Public and Environmental Affairs, Indiana University.

Rubin, Barry M., and Craig M. Richards. 1992. "A Transatlantic Comparison of Enterprise Zone Impacts: The British and American Experience," *Economic Development Quarterly*, 6(4) (November).

Rubin, Barry M., and Margaret G. Wilder. 1989. "Urban Enterprise Zones: Employment Impacts and Fiscal Incentives," *Journal of the American Planning Association*, (Autumn), pp. 418–431.

Rubin, Marilyn. 1990. "Urban Enterprise Zones: Do They Work? Evidence From New Jersey," *Public Budgeting and Finance*, 10(4) (Winter), pp. 3–17.

Severn, Alan K. 1992. "Building-Tax Abatements: An Approximation to Land Value Taxation," *American Journal of Economics and Sociology*, 51(2) (April), pp. 237–245.

Talbot, Jonathan. "Have Enterprise Zones Encouraged Enterprise? Some Empirical Evidence from Tyneside," *Regional Studies*, 22(6), pp. 507–514.

U.S. General Accounting Office. 1988. *Enterprise Zones. Lessons From the Maryland Experience: Report to Congressional Requestors*, Washington, D.C.: Government Printing Office.

Wassmer, Robert W. 1989. "Property Tax Abatements and Municipal Expenditures," Working Paper 89–10, ASSA annual meeting (December 28).

———. 1992. "Property Tax Abatement and the Simultaneous Determination of Local Fiscal Variables in a Metropolitan Area," *Land Economics*, 68(3), pp. 263–82.

Wolkoff, Michael J. 1985. "Chasing a Dream: The Use of Tax Abatements to Spur Urban Economic Development," *Urban Studies*, 22(4), pp. 305–15.

Wolman, Harold L., Coit Cook Ford III, and Edward Hill. Forthcoming. "Evaluating the Success of Urban Success Stories," *Urban Studies*.

PART IV

SCHOOL FINANCE

Statewide Taxation of Nonresidential Property for Education

HELEN F. LADD AND EDWARD W. HARRIS

The property tax is currently the principal source of local funding for school districts in New York State. As such, the property tax deserves primary attention in any policy discussion of local funding for schools. This policy brief focuses on the following policy question related to the property tax:

> Assuming the state chooses to continue relying heavily on the property tax to pay for schools, should it consider removing nonresidential property from the local property tax base for the purposes of education, taxing it at a statewide uniform rate, and returning the revenues to the local school districts in an equalizing manner?

This brief starts from the assumption that the state will continue to rely heavily on the property tax as a revenue source for education. Whether or not the state should continue to do so raises a broader set of issues that are beyond the scope of this paper.

The first section summarizes the conceptual arguments for statewide taxation of business property for education. The next two sections report our empirical analysis of this policy option for New York State. The final section summarizes the policy-relevant lessons that emerge from the analysis.

THE CASE FOR STATEWIDE TAXATION OF NONRESIDENTIAL PROPERTY[1]

The most compelling argument for substantial local funding, as opposed to full state funding, of local schools is that it strengthens the link between the spending or benefit side of the budget

---

1. This discussion draws heavily on Helen F. Ladd, "State-wide Taxation of Commercial and Industrial Property for Education," *National Tax Journal*, 24 (June 1976): 143-153.

Helen F. Ladd is a Visiting Fellow at the The Brookings Institution, Washington, DC, and Edward W. Harris is with the Analysis and Studies Division, Internal Revenue Service, Washington, DC.

and the tax or cost side. That is, with local funding, those who live in the geographic area receiving most of the public benefits also pay the costs and, through the local political process, make the decision about how much to spend. From this perspective, a local property tax on residential property receives high marks as a revenue source for K-12 education. The owners of the *residential* property benefit from additional education spending either directly by having children in the schools or, provided the typical buyer in the community values high-quality education services, indirectly through increases in the value of their home.

By this criterion of linking benefits and costs, the *nonresidential* component of the local property tax is less appropriate than the residential component as a revenue source for K-12 education. Firms clearly benefit from having an educated labor force. However, because firms typically draw on a labor pool for their employees that extends well beyond the school district in which they are located, the link between the education provided within a particular school district and the quality of the labor force available to a firm in that district need not be close. By this benefit logic, it may make sense to tax business property for the purposes of education at the regional or state level, rather than at the district level. Hence, the first argument for shifting to statewide taxation of business property for education purposes rests on a benefit rationale.

A second related argument for moving away from local taxation of business property toward state taxation emerges from the possibility that, under the current arrangement, school districts with large amounts of business property may overinvest in education relative to private goods. This outcome occurs because the price to local residents of expanding education is less than the full cost whenever a portion of the amount is paid by business firms. In effect, business firms subsidize the cost to local residents of providing more education and thereby induce them to overinvest. Taxing all business property at a statewide uniform tax rate for the purposes of K-12 education would eliminate this distorting price incentive.

A third argument is that local taxation of business property for education purposes may distort the location decisions of firms. Local taxes on firms for schools differ from local taxes on firms for nonschool public services, such as public safety and sanitation. While taxes for nonschool purposes may serve as a reasonable, albeit imperfect, proxy for the benefits received by firms or the costs they impose on the local community, and, hence, do not generate inappropriate location incentives, the same cannot be said for local school taxes. All other factors held constant, firms will have incentives to locate in areas where the education-related taxes are low, provided, of course, that they retain access to well-educated workers. Thus, statewide taxation of firms for education purposes would remove a major distorting influence on firm location decisions within the state and would allow firms to make location decisions on the basis of real resource costs rather than tax-related considerations.

A fourth potential argument for shifting to statewide taxation of business property for education is more speculative and requires empirical investigation. The argument is that taxing business property at a statewide uniform rate and channeling the money back to the districts for education purposes could generate a fairer pattern of education spending across the state than the current pattern. Whether or not that outcome will occur depends on a variety of issues, such as how nonresidential property is currently distributed among school districts, how decision makers in school districts respond to the changes in tax base and new aid, and the nature of the formula that would be used to distribute the revenue from business property back to the local school districts.

At one extreme, if the business property were disproportionately located in areas where the average income were low and the distribution formula did a poor job of targeting aid to low-income areas, one would predict that the policy change would widen the variation in education spending and increase the link between education spending and the income or wealth of local residents. Low-income or low-wealth districts would reduce their spending as they lost substantial amounts of their taxable capacity and were not compensated with offsetting inflows of new state aid, while high income or high wealth districts might be able to expand their spending on education.

At the other extreme, if the business property were disproportionately located in higher income areas and the distribution formula effectively targeted aid to low-income areas, the policy change could improve educational equity both in the sense of reducing the variation in spending and by weakening the positive link between resident income or wealth and spending.

The next section of this policy brief summarizes the effects of the policy change on per pupil spending in New York school districts. The simulation and discussion are designed to determine whether the policy change would improve or worsen the distribution of per pupil spending across school districts in the state.

IMPACTS OF THE POLICY CHANGE ON PER PUPIL SPENDING

The simulation analysis summarized in this section provides rough estimates of the effects of the policy change on the distribution of per pupil spending using data for 1990-91. Should state officials wish to pursue this policy option further, they would need to refine the analysis and use more recent data. At a minimum, we would recommend the following two refinements. First, the state should adjust the per pupil spending levels in each district for the differential costs of educating students that are outside the immediate control of local officials. These costs vary across districts in part because some types of children, such as those with special needs, those with limited proficiency in English, or those from disadvantaged households, are more expensive to educate than others. In addition, they vary because school districts in areas where the cost of living is high must pay higher salaries to attract teachers than school districts in areas where the cost of living is lower. Second, if data were available, it would be desirable to adjust the income or wealth measures used in any formula for distributing state aid by the local cost of living. In the absence of such an adjustment, the income of residents in downstate areas relative to upstate areas overstates the difference in real income between the two areas. According to one set of estimates, the cost of living in the New York City area is 213 percent of the U.S. average, that in Nassau-Suffolk is 148 percent of the U.S. average, while that in the Albany-Schenectady-Troy metropolitan area is only about 106 percent of the national average.[2] If these estimates are correct, they imply that the purchasing power of a given level of household income in the Albany area is equivalent to about twice the purchasing power of that same level of income in the New York City area.

Table 1 reports the current distribution of property tax revenues, and hence of effective tax bases, for schools by category of property for seven types of school districts. Of most impor-

---

2. Constructed by the American Chamber of Commerce Researchers Association, these cost-of-living estimates are for the third quarter of 1991 and refer to a mid-management standard of living. Exceptionally high housing costs account for the high New York City area figure. Other components vary across the three areas but by less than the composite index. For example, for grocery items alone, the indices are 145 for New York City, 122 for Nassau-Suffolk, and 108 for Albany-Schenectady-Troy. *See* U.S. Department of Commerce, Bureau of the Census, *Statistical Abstract of the United States, 1992* (Washington, D.C.: Government Printing Office, 1992), Table 745.

TABLE 1
DISTRIBUTION OF PROPERTY TAX REVENUE BY TYPE OF SCHOOL DISTRICT, 1991

	All Districts	Downstate Cities	Downstate Suburbs	New York City	Big 4 Cities	Upstate Cities	Upstate Suburbs	Rural
(Number of Districts)	*(683)*	*(7)*	*(162)*	*(1)*	*(4)*	*(50)*	*(243)*	*(216)*
Residential	61.8	59.4	70.1	22.9	45.8	56.3	63.4	55.7
Commercial	12.2	26.8	15.2	62.1	32.6	20.9	11.5	7.7
Industrial	4.1	3.2	6.0	2.2	6.0	5.6	3.9	2.4
Agricultural	5.0	0.0	0.3	0.0	0.0	1.3	5.1	9.5
Other	16.9	10.6	8.4	12.8	15.6	15.9	16.1	24.7
Total	100	100	100	100	100	100	100	100

Source: State Division of Equalization and Assessment, Report of Effective Full Value and Tax Levy by Property Class for the 1991 Assessment Rolls.

tance is the first row of the table which documents the wide variation across types of districts in the average share of the effective property tax base that is residential.³ As shown, the proportion of the tax base that is residential in the typical district is 62 percent, but the average ranges from 23 percent in New York City to 70 percent in the downstate suburbs.

In addition, New York City receives a huge 62 percent of its revenue from commercial property in contrast to the average of 33 percent from that source in the Big Four cities (Buffalo, Rochester, Syracuse, and Yonkers). Not surprisingly, the rural districts have the largest proportion of agricultural property. Because of the presence of large power plants in some rural areas, the rural districts also derive the largest average share of revenue from the "other" category which includes public service property. This variation in the average mix of tax bases across the seven groups hides even greater variation among individual districts. Consequently, the proposed policy of removing nonresidential property from the local tax base for education purposes will clearly affect some districts more than others.

Our simulation analysis proceeds in three steps. First, we use data on all school districts in the state to estimate a statistical model to explain the variation in per pupil spending across school districts in 1991. Second, we use the estimated equation to simulate how much each district would have been likely to spend if it had been restricted to taxing only its residential property. Because the new tax base in each district implies that every dollar of local taxes is paid by residents, this initial simulation generates less spending in each district than the district actually spent. Third, we predict the level of spending in each district in the presence of the full policy package, that is, taking account of both the restricted tax base and the additional aid financed through the state taxation of nonresidential property. Because the aid can be distributed among districts in many alternative ways, this step could generate many different sets of results. As elaborated below, we simplify by specifying a few illustrative distribution formulas.

The determinants of per pupil expenditure include local income and wealth variables (specifically, New York State adjusted gross income of residents per weighted pupil and residential property tax wealth per weighted pupil); intergovernmental aid variables (Federal aid and state aid per pupil); the residential share of the property tax base; and, as a control for the characteristics of

---

3. The category of residential property excludes apartment buildings with 5 or more units.

the students, the fraction of students eligible for subsidized lunches. As discussed in the appendix, two forms of the equation were estimated, a linear equation and a logarithmic equation. All results described in the text are based on the linear model. Two variables in this equation are particularly important for the simulations: the residential share of the property tax base and state aid.

Table 2 presents simulation results for the districts grouped by district type. The first row reports the starting point to which the simulation results should be compared, namely the variation in average per pupil spending in 1990-91. Average spending varies from $7,441 in the upstate cities to $12,204 in the downstate cities. Per pupil spending in New York City is $7,463, substantially below the spending in the other downstate districts. As we noted above, it would be desirable to adjust these spending figures by the differential costs of educating students, where such differentials are caused by factors largely outside the control of local school officials. Making such an adjustment would have the following effects: Adjusted spending in the upstate and rural districts would rise somewhat, adjusted spending in the downstate cities and suburbs would fall by a larger amount, and, because of its large percentage of disadvantaged students and above-average salary requirements, New York City's adjusted spending would fall dramatically.[4] Hence, the variation in adjusted spending between downstate and upstate districts would be less than that indicated in the table, and New York City would emerge as an extremely low-spending district.

The second row shows the effect on per pupil spending of removing the nonresidential portion of the local tax base. In all districts, this part of the policy package puts downward pressure on per pupil spending through the following mechanism. Before the simulated policy change, local residents in each district faced a tax price of education equal to the share of the tax base that is

---

4. Average estimated cost indexes relative to the state average of 100 for each type of district are: downstate cities, 129; downstate suburbs, 116; New York City, 148; the Big 4 cities, 122; upstate cities, 97; upstate suburbs, 94; and rural, 94. These cost differences were provided to us by William Duncombe of Syracuse University. They were derived from a cross section regression using data for all New York school districts of per pupil district expenditures on test scores as a measure of outcome, taste variables, and cost factors. The estimated coefficient of each cost factor indicates the average impact on costs of an increase in that factor. The cost factors included in the analysis are the percentage of the students at risk (children under 6, single moms, living in poverty), the percent of pupils with limited English proficiency, and an adjusted teacher salary index. Other forms of the equation, such as one that includes student enrollment as a cost factor would yield even greater cost differentials across types of districts.

TABLE 2
SIMULATED SPENDING PER PUPIL,
BY DISTRICT TYPE, 1990-91, DOLLARS PER PUPIL

	All Districts	Downstate Cities	Downstate Suburbs	New York City	Big 4 Cities	Upstate Cities	Upstate Suburbs	Rural
Actual Spending per Pupil	8,728	12,204	12,151	7,463	8,574	7,441	7,651	7,566
Predicted Spending:								
No Aid	7,464	10,854	11,177	4,902	6,77	5,988	6,434	6,094
Flat Grant per Pupil	9,167	12,557	12,870	6,605	8,474	7,691	8,137	7,796
Equalizied Grant per Pupil	9,723	11,331	11,743	6,492	8,559	8,084	8,769	9,655

The equalizing grant per pupil is distributed to districts in inverse proportion to district income per weighted pupil. Grants are given only to the 75 percent of the districts with the lowest per pupil income.

residential. For example, if 60 percent of the tax base were residential, residents would pay directly only 60 cents for each dollar of local taxes raised for education.[5] To simulate the initial impacts of the policy proposal, the tax price term is set at 1.00 in each district to reflect the fact that, with nonresidential property removed from the tax base, residents would pay the full cost of each additional dollar that they chose to spend on education. Thus, for example, as a result of restricting the local tax base to the residential component, the tax price of a dollar of education services for a resident in a typical district would rise from 62 cents to $1.00 which would provide a strong incentive for the district to reduce its spending on education. The coefficient of the residential share variable in the spending equation provides an estimate of the magnitude of the response. On average, the response elasticity is estimated to be −0.23. This elasticity means that if the price rises by 50 percent, say from 0.66 to 1.00, the desired level of spending would fall by almost 12 percent.

As shown by the estimates in row 2, the predicted impact is the greatest in New York City and the least in the downstate suburbs, a pattern that reflects the high proportion of nonresidential property in New York City and the relatively low proportion in the downstate suburbs. These predictions should be interpreted as long run responses. The removal of business property from the local tax base would create a dramatic revenue shortfall in many districts, but in the short run taxpayer voters might not be willing to cut spending immediately to the level they would ultimately prefer given their new higher tax prices. The simulation ignores the timing of the response, and predicts the full long run adjustment.

The results for New York City should be interpreted cautiously. The analysis assumes that the property tax is the marginal revenue source in the sense that it is the source of revenue for any additional spending on education. To the extent that other taxes such as the income or the sales tax represent the marginal tax, the estimate in the table may overstate the impacts of removing the nonresidential component of the tax base in New York City. Moreover, given that New York City is not an independent school district, the policymaking procedure is more complex than in other

---

5. This assertion assumes that landlords in small structures are able to shift fully the burden of the tax on residential rental property to renters so that renters in small structures as well as homeowners pay property taxes. In addition, it ignores the possibility that residents may bear part of the burden of the other 40 percent as a consequence of the ability of firms to shift the burden to them through higher prices of goods and services or lower wages for residents.

areas and may not be accurately modeled. These qualifications apply as well to other districts that rely on broad-based local taxes other than the property tax and to the other Big Four city school districts that are fiscally dependent.

The third and fourth rows show the effects of the full policy package for two of the many possible distributions of the revenue from a statewide tax on nonresidential property, taking account of the fact that the local districts are free to choose whether to spend the additional revenue or to use it to reduce local tax burdens. These simulations are simply illustrative. In all of our simulations, including eight others in the appendix, we assume no change in the distribution of existing state aid. In addition, we assume that the new aid is distributed by a formula which permits no special treatment of specific districts, such as New York City, or of categories of districts. Clearly the results would differ if special treatment were given, say, to New York City. According to the preferred estimate of the behavioral response to aid from the expenditure equation, an additional dollar of state aid leads on average to 78 cents in additional spending on education, with the rest allocated either to lower local school taxes or, in the case of fiscally dependent districts, possibly to higher spending on other publicly provided goods and services. In both policy simulations, the amount of revenue to be distributed is simply the total amount of revenue currently collected from nonresidential property for education purposes. In practice, this revenue would be generated by imposing a statewide uniform rate equal to the current average tax rate on all nonresidential property.[6]

In row 3, the revenue is distributed among school districts strictly on a per pupil basis; in row 4, it is distributed in a much more equalizing manner. In particular, in row 4, aid is given only to the poorest 75 percent of the districts and is distributed by formula among those districts inversely with respect to the income (as measured by New York State adjusted gross income of residents) per weighted pupil in the district. Comparing rows 3 and 4 shows that the distribution formula matters a lot, and that if narrowing disparities is a primary goal, that the more equalizing aid formula is preferred to the flat per pupil grant. With the targeted grant program, average per pupil spending would have a tendency to be reduced in the three district types that currently spend the most on education and to rise in the three types of dis-

---

6. This revenue amounted to $5.4 billion in 1991, which is about 26 percent of total spending on education in that year and about 60 percent of state aid for education.

tricts that begin with the lowest spending per pupil, other than in New York City where the spending is predicted to fall from its already low level. We note, however, that the large predicted increases in the rural districts would probably be smaller if the formula for distributing the new aid were designed to take into account the lower cost of living in those districts.

Table 3 summarizes more fully the distributional effects of the policy change across all districts in the state. Once again the first row represents the baseline to which the policy change should be compared. It shows that average spending across all districts was over $8,700 and that, leaving out the bottom and the top 10 percent of the districts, that it ranged from $6,516 to $12,357. An alternative measure of variation is given by the standard deviation, which measures the typical difference between spending in a district and average spending. The larger is the standard deviation relative to the average, the larger is the dispersion around the average. The final three columns report the correlation across districts between per pupil spending and income, wealth, and the fraction of children receiving subsidized lunches. The correlations show that in 1990, per pupil spending was highly and positively correlated with income and wealth and negatively correlated with the proportion of poor students. In other words, districts that had higher average income or residential wealth or that had smaller proportions of poor students typically spent more per pupil than did poorer districts.

The policy proposal improves the pattern of spending to the extent that it reduces the variation across districts and weakens the correlation between spending and wealth. *Rows 2, 3, and 4 illustrate that only if the revenue from the statewide taxation of nonresidential property is distributed in a highly equalizing manner will the policy proposal make the distribution of education spending more equitable.*

Row 2 shows that the first part of the proposal, namely restricting the local tax base to residential property, has undesirable effects on the pattern of spending: in addition to putting significant downward pressure on spending, it increases the variation across districts and makes spending somewhat more highly correlated with wealth or income. Distributing the state aid on the basis of a flat grant per pupil does little to improve the situation. Relative to the current distribution, it increases average spending, has little impact on the variation, and slightly worsens the correlations. Only when the revenue from the statewide taxation of nonresidential property is distributed in a highly equalizing

TABLE 3
SUMMARY OF EXPENDITURE PATTERNS
FOR VARIOUS POLICY SIMULATIONS, ALL DISTRICTS

	Average Expenditure per Pupil ($)	Measures of Variation		Correlation of per Pupil Expenditure		
		Standard Deviation ÷ Average (x 100)	10th to 90th Percentile ($)	Income*	Residential. Wealth[†]	Subsidized. Lunch[‡]
Actual Spending per Pupil	8,728	30.2	6,516-12,357	0.64	0.64	-0.36
Predicted Spending:						
No Aid	7,463	36.8	5,119-11,284	0.66	0.66	-0.41
Flat Grant per Pupil	9,167	29.9	6,821-12,987	0.66	0.66	-0.42
Equalizing Grant per Pupil	9,723	23.1	7,551-12,598	0.28	0.52	-0.05

* Income per weighted pupil.
† Residential property tax wealth per weighted pupil.
‡ Fraction of pupils eligible for free or reduced price lunch.

manner do the summary measures improve: in that case, the 10th-90th percentile range decreases somewhat, the standard deviation falls as a percent of the average, and the correlations all move toward 0. In other words, by these summary measures, the policy change makes the overall distribution of per pupil spending across districts somewhat more equitable.

WINNERS AND LOSERS

Table 4 clarifies which types of districts win and lose from the policy change. Panel A reports results with the flat per pupil grant and Panel B with the equalizing grant. As shown in the first row of both panels, the downstate cities, the downstate suburbs, and New York City are net losers under both policy proposals in that the net change in revenue, including both the new state aid and the loss in revenue from nonresidential property, is negative. In other words, for districts in the losing categories, the additional aid is not large enough to offset the loss of revenue to the typical district from the removal of nonresidential property from the local tax base for education, regardless of whether the aid is provided on a flat per pupil basis or in an equalizing manner. The winners under both versions are the Big Four cities, the upstate cities, the upstate suburbs, and the rural districts. Those districts on average receive enough new aid to more than offset the revenue loss from not taxing nonresidential property.

The next two rows incorporate the estimated behavioral responses to the policy change to show what is likely to happen to per pupil spending and to locally generated tax revenues. Bear in mind that the locally generated revenues would come exclusively from residential property. With the flat grant distribution formula, per pupil spending is predicted to rise in all district types except for New York City and the Big Four cities.[7] Only in the downstate cities and suburbs would local residential property tax burdens have to rise. In the upstate areas, the increase in spending is less than net increase in revenue which permits local property tax burdens to fall. Local tax burdens are also predicted to fall in New York City and in the Big Four cities, but at the cost of a decline in per pupil spending.

The differential effects are most striking when the aid is dis-

---

7. The rise in average spending in the downstate cities and downstate suburbs in the simulation with the flat per pupil grant is somewhat surprising in light of the large average declines in external revenue in those types of districts. It simply reflects the fact that the downward responsiveness of spending to the change in the tax price is low relative to the upward responsiveness of spending to the new state aid.

TABLE 4
Change in Educational Revenues and Spending by District Type, Dollars per Pupil

	Down-state Cities	Down-state Suburbs	New York City	Big 4 Cities	Upstate Cities	Upstate Suburbs	Rural
Panel A – Flat Grant							
Net Change in External Revenue per Pupil*	-1,255	-692	-705	155	732	770	745
Change in Spending per Pupil†	353	729	-858	-99	250	486	230
Change in Locally Raised Revenue‡	1,608	1,421	-153	-254	-482	-284	-515
Panel B – Equalizing Grant							
Net Change in External Revenue per Pupil*	-2,818	-2,141	-849	263	1,234	1,562	3,113
Change in Spending per Pupil†	-874	-408	-971	-14	643	908	2,089
Change in Locally Raised Revenue‡	1,944	1,733	-122	-277	-591	-654	-1,024

* Defined as the difference between revenue lost due to removal of nonresidential property from the tax base and new state aid financed by the statewide taxation of nonresidential property.
† As predicted by the linear form of the spending equation.
‡ Calculated as the change in spending per pupil minus the net change in external revenue per pupil.

tributed in an equalizing manner as shown in Panel B. The effects can be summarized as follows:

- *Downstate cities and suburbs* are net losers of external revenue. Per pupil spending goes down, and local residential property tax burdens rise. Note that these districts currently have the highest per pupil spending, so a reduction in such spending tends to equalize education spending throughout the state.[8]
- *New York City* loses external revenue, per pupil spending goes down, and local residential property tax burdens go down. The large predicted fall in per pupil spending ($971) is an undesirable outcome of the policy change given that

---
8. We believe that this basic conclusion would still hold even if the analysis fully incorporated differences in the cost of education across districts, but that analysis remains to be done.

New York City currently spends well below the average, despite the fact that it faces more severe educational challenges than most other New York districts.
- *The Big Four cities* are net gainers of external revenue which allows them to reduce local residential property taxes. However, they are also predicted to reduce slightly per pupil spending.
- *Upstate cities and suburbs* gain substantial amounts of external revenue, some of which they use to increase per pupil spending, and some of which they use to reduce residential tax burdens. Residents, including pupils, in such districts are clear winners from the policy change. The increase in per pupil spending in such districts helps to equalize spending throughout the state.
- *Rural areas* gain large amounts of external revenue. The model predicts that they will increase per pupil spending by over $2000 per pupil and that they will reduce local property taxes by over $1000 per pupil. Although the overall equity of the state's education system may be enhanced by the increased spending in the rural districts, the changes may be excessively large given the lower cost of living, and hence, cost of providing education, in such areas.

DISCUSSION AND CONCLUSION

The thrust of this policy brief is that New York state policymakers should take a closer look at the possibility of shifting to statewide taxation of nonresidential property for education. The change would improve local decision-making by strengthening the link between those who make local decisions about education spending and those who pay, and would reduce incentives for firms to choose among local districts based on education-related tax rate differentials. To mitigate the effects of the large revenue shifts, the state would presumably want to phase in the change. In addition, state policy makers should consider the following lessons that emerge from the simulations:

1. The way in which the revenue from the state tax on nonresidential property is distributed to the local school districts is a crucial component of the policy proposal. A highly equalizing distribution formula such as the one described in the text is required if the goal is to reduce spending differences across districts. However, even that one is limited in two ways. First, it does not account for the fact

that the purchasing power of income is greater in upstate districts than in downstate districts. Second, it inadequately accounts for differences in education costs that are outside the control of local officials, a limitation that works to the disadvantage of the large cities and downstate districts.

2. The policy proposal would lead to highly undesirable consequences for the school children in New York City unless specific policy actions were taken to reduce or eliminate those adverse effects. Refining the distribution formula to account for educational cost differences and cost-of-living differences would help, but probably would not solve the problem completely. Instead, state policymakers should consider moving New York City outside the aid formula and giving it special treatment.

3. The program would operate in a more equitable manner if the state were able to incorporate cost-of-living differences into the distribution formula. In the absence of an adjustment for cost-of-living differences, the rural areas of the state would be treated too generously.

4. To implement the program, state policymakers need to clarify the definition of residential property and, in particular, the treatment of large apartment buildings.

5. Finally, it would be worth simulating the effects of such a policy proposal at the regional level, rather than the state level. Provided the plan applied to all districts, voters in every district would still face a tax price of one dollar for each additional dollar of spending. Tax rates on nonresidential property could either be set at regional averages or at a statewide uniform rate. If the latter were the case, the plan would be similar to a statewide plan in terms of the benefits it would generate from reducing distortions in business location decisions. The difference would be that the revenue from the nonresidential property would be distributed only among the districts within the region from which it came. In this way, the state could avoid the major revenue shifts from downstate to upstate districts implicit in the statewide plan.

This policy proposal for New York state differs in some important ways from the recently enacted school finance reform in Michigan, but also bears some similarities worth highlighting.[9] The major changes in Michigan were the increase in the state share of funding for local schools from under 35 percent to almost 80 percent and the virtual elimination of local control over spending levels. In contrast, local control would remain a central feature of school finance under the proposal discussed in this policy brief. Contrary to popular impression, Michigan did not completely eliminate the property tax as a source of funding for schools. In fact, property taxes still contribute more than 30 percent of the total state and local revenue for schools. After the reform, the state levies a property tax on all property at a statewide uniform rate of 6 mills, and, in effect, requires a tax rate of 18 mills on nonresidential property at the local level. Hence, from the benefit perspective which serves as a major rationale for our proposal for New York, in the aggregate, Michigan may have moved in the wrong direction in that it increased the tax burden on nonresidential property relative to that on residential property.

Despite the differences, two similarities are worth noting. First, Michigan now has the equivalent of a statewide uniform rate on nonresidential property, as is being proposed here for New York. Second, in the 37 high-spending local districts which have retained some discretion over spending levels, any additional spending over the foundation level will be financed out of local homestead property alone. Thus, the tax price to local residents of raising an additional dollar of revenue will be one dollar in those districts, as it would be with this proposal for New York. In summary, the proposal for statewide taxation of nonresidential property at a uniform rate in New York draws on two of the ideas implicit in the Michigan reform. However, the proposal for New York avoids the dramatic reduction in local control implicit in the Michigan program.

---

9. This discussion of Michigan draws on descriptions of the reform in C. Philip Kearney, "Reducing Local School Property Taxes: Recent Experiences in Michigan," A Policy Brief for the New York State Education Department, December, 1994, and Paul N. Courant, Edward M. Gramlich, and Susanna Loeb, "A Report on School Finance and Educational Reform in Michigan," Proceedings of a Federal Reserve Bank of Chicago Conference on Midwest Approaches to School Reform, forthcoming.

APPENDIX

This appendix includes two tables. Appendix Table 1 reports the regression equations which provide the basis for the spending simulations. The first equation is in linear form and is the basis of the simulations reported in the text. The second equation is in logarithmic form. Neither equation suits our needs perfectly. The first equation provides the most reasonable, and easy to interpret, estimate of the effect of state aid on local spending, but imposes a linear specification of the price variable, the percent of the tax base that is residential. The logarithmic specification is preferred because it imposes a constant elasticity on the tax price term, but it less appropriate because it imposes a constant elasticity on the aid variables as well.

In both regressions, all the variables are weighted by district enrollment, a procedure that improves the precision of the estimates. New York City has been excluded from the regressions to avoid the concern that because of its large student enrollment, it would drive the results. In fact, including New York City in the regressions does not markedly change the estimated coefficients.

Appendix Table 2 provides a richer set of simulation results than those reported in the text. Simulations are reported for both forms of the equation and for a variety of distribution formulas as described at the bottom of the table.

APPENDIX TABLE 1
REGRESSION EQUATIONS USED IN POLICY SIMULATIONS

	Dependent Variable: Expenditure per Pupil	
	Linear Model	Logarithmic Model
Residential Property Value per Weighted Pupil	0.007 (10.3)	0.48 (26.1)
Percent of Taxable Property Values that is Residential	-3,323 (7.0)	-0.45 (22.0)
Income per Weighted Pupil (NYS AGI)	0.034 (17.9)	0.15 (7.9)
% of Students Receiving Subsidized Lunches	-4,061 (7.4)	-0.04 (6.9)
State Revenue per Pupil	0.78 (11.5)	0.56 (24.0)
Federal Revenue per Pupil	2.5 (4.2)	0.05 (5.5)
Intercept	4,960 (13.0)	-3.12 (8.9)
R^2	0.59	0.77

Absolute values of t-statistics are in parentheses below the coefficient. Both of these equations are estimated using weighted least squares (weighted by the number of pupils) with New York City excluded.

APPENDIX TABLE 2
SIMULATION RESULTS USING DIFFERENT MODELS SPECIFICATIONS AND STATE AID FORMULAS, DOLLARS PER PUPIL

	Down-state Cities	Down-state Suburbs	New York City	York Cities	Big 4 Cities	Upstate Suburbs	Upstate Rural
Current Expenditures	12,204	12,151	7,463	8,574	7,441	7,651	7,566
Sim0	10,854	11,177	4,902	6,772	5,988	6,434	6,094
LSim0	9,551	10,265	3,828	6,009	5,663	6,169	5,728
Sim1	12,557	12,880	6,605	8,474	7,691	8,137	7,796
LSim1	13,231	15,198	5,121	7,648	7,229	8,153	7,299
Sim2	11,577	11,749	7,342	8,625	7,650	7,798	7,880
LSim2	10,825	11,604	5,607	7,487	7,119	7,536	7,143
Sim3	11,728	12,333	6,310	6,603	7,967	8,658	9,254
LSim3	11,114	13,226	4,917	7,523	7,387	8,416	8,290
Sim4	11,265	11,443	7,453	8,537	7,725	7,811	7,919
LSim4	9,949	10,601	5,677	7,302	7,180	7,468	7,110
Sim5	11,331	11,743	6,492	8,559	8,084	8,759	9,655
LSim5	10,009	11,118	5,044	7,313	7,403	8,328	8,565

Model Definitions for Table A-2

L Before the model name means that the simulation model used a logarithmic, rather than linear, regression equation.

Sim0 Removes nonresidential property with no accompanying state aid.

Sim1 Distributes state aid as a flat per pupil grant to all districts.

Sim2 Distributes state aid to all districts as a per pupil grant, inversely proportional to the per pupil residential value of district property.

Sim3 Distributes state aid to all districts as a per pupil grant inversely proportional to district income per pupil.

Sim4 Distributes state aid to the 75 percent of districts with the lowest residential wealth as a grant inversely proportional to per pupil residential wealth.

Sim5 Distributes state aid to the 75 percent of districts with the lowest income as a grant inversely proportional to income per pupil.

[21]
How School Districts Respond to Fiscal Constraint

Helen F. Ladd
Sanford Institute of Public Policy
Duke University

Introduction

Throughout the 1980s and early 1990s, many school districts were less fiscally constrained than they are likely to be in the future. Many state governments responded to the 1983 report, *A Nation at Risk*, by providing substantial additional resources to local schools to improve education. In addition, the 1980s expansion of the economy made it possible for districts to raise additional funds from local sources, and declines in student enrollment meant that per pupil spending could rise even in districts where spending was not increased. The situation in the early 1990s and the outlook for the future are less sanguine. Projections of increasing enrollment, less rapid growth in the economy, and increasing competition for funds at the state and local level mean that school districts are likely to experience significantly more fiscal pressure in the future than they have in the recent past.

Given the outlook for more fiscal constraint, it would be useful to know something about how districts typically respond to fiscal constraint. Hence the purpose of this paper is to determine how districts have responded to fiscal constraint in the past as a way of gaining insight into how they might respond in the future.

This question can be addressed in various ways. One approach is to use a panel data set for districts in a specific state to look at how school districts have responded over time to various pressures such as increasing enrollments, the growth in students requiring special education, or cutbacks in aid. A recent paper by Hamilton Lankford and James Wyckoff (1996) provides an excellent example of this approach. Using a rich data set for 693 districts in New York state covering the period 1960 to 1993, they found that a substantial fraction of the increase in education spending was allocated to special education. In addition, they discovered that districts adjusted their administrative spending asymmetrically in response to changes in resources: districts increased administrative spending more in response to an increase in resources than they decreased administrative spending in response to a reduction in resources. Moreover, because Lankford and Wyckoff were in effect modeling changes in budget allocations, they were able to use their estimated parameters to project how New York school districts were likely to respond to future changes in fiscal pressures. As is evident from their study, the use of a panel data set is clearly essential for examining the short run dynamic responses of districts to fiscal pressure.[1]

A second approach is illustrated in a recent paper by David Figlio (1996). He used data from the Schools and Staffing Survey (SASS) to examine how local tax limitation measures affected school inputs and some school outputs. Because property taxes account for almost all the tax revenue of local school districts, statewide constitutional amendments or statutory requirements that limit the local property tax can directly affect the ability of local school districts to raise money for education. Exploiting the fact that not all states have such limitation measures, Figlio found that such limitations were associated with larger classes, shorter instructional periods, lower starting salaries for teachers, and lower lifetime discounted teacher salaries. Figlio's use of the SASS data represents an innovative approach for examining the impact of tax limitations. It also represents a creative way to examine how districts respond to fiscal constraint, an approach that is marred only by the observation that until one does the analysis, one cannot be sure that the limitations are binding and that, therefore, the districts are constrained.

In the same spirit, Dye and McGuire (1996) examined the effects of property tax limits on school districts in the Chicago metropolitan area. Building on the observation that not all school districts in the relevant counties were subject to property tax limits, Dye and McGuire found that property tax limits reduced the growth in total education spending by about 3 percent and spending per pupil by about 2.5 percent. Interestingly, however, they found no statistically significant evidence of any reduced growth in instructional spending. Thus, in the face of binding tax limits school districts appear to have tried to preserve the growth of instructional spending.

In this paper, I develop a third approach, one with its own strengths and weaknesses. One of my initial goals was to develop a methodology that could be used for a large number of states using the Common Core of Data (CCD) generated by the National Center for Education Statistics (NCES). Because the CCD information on finances is available only for the fiscal years 1990, 1991, and 1992, it does not represent a long enough panel to examine the short run dynamics of school district responses over time. Instead, the data are better suited for cross sectional analysis. Hence, my research strategy is to use cross sectional data at one point in time first to develop a measure of the fiscal condition of each district and second to examine the choices made by school districts that face differing degrees of fiscal pressure. This strategy sheds no light on how districts are likely to respond in a short run, dynamic sense to changes in their fiscal constraints. Any predictions from this analysis about responses to **changes** in constraints must be made with caution. At best, the cross sectional results reported below apply to the effects of changes in fiscal constraints that are in place for a period of time long enough for districts to fully adjust.

In section I, I explain and present my preferred measure of a district's fiscal condition and in section II show how I implemented it for Texas. Unfortunately, the measure cannot be estimated based on the CCD data alone.

---

[1] In the same vein, other researchers have examined the dynamic responses to fiscal constraints in specific districts. For example, see Hess (1991) for an examination of staff cuts during the fiscal crisis of the Chicago School System in the early 1980s. Hess reports that in response to the fiscal crisis, employees with student contact (such as classroom teachers and aides) were cut 18 percent, administrative and technical personnel were cut 14 percent, and support staff (including clerical and maintenance personnel) were cut 17 percent (p. 24, table 1.3). Interestingly, the relatively large cut in personnel with student contact occurred not in the subcategories of teachers and educational support staff but rather in the category of teacher aides.

Hence, I had to turn to state-specific data. In section III, I examine the choices made by Texas school districts in response to their differing fiscal conditions. These choices are of three types: those relating to the allocation of the budget among spending categories, the pattern of staffing, and the quality of the educational environment as measured, for example, by the ratio of pupils to teachers. Data about these choices come both from state-specific sources and from the CCD. In section IV, I look at comparable choices made by the New York Districts based on the CCD data alone.

Measuring a District's Fiscal Condition

By the fiscal condition of a school district, I am referring to the gap between a district's capacity to raise revenue for education and its expenditure need, where both capacity and need reflect factors outside the immediate control of local school officials (see Ladd and Yinger, 1991 for the development of this approach and its application to major U.S. cities). The idea is to develop a measure that is independent of the district's specific spending and taxing decisions but that accurately reflects the fiscal constraints it faces in making those decisions. In contrast to simpler measures of fiscal condition that typically focus exclusively on a district's capacity to raise revenue, this measure also incorporates the fact that some districts must spend more money per student than others to attain a given level of educational services.

As I described in an earlier article, (Ladd 1994), a jurisdiction's revenue-raising capacity and its expenditure need can each be measured in two ways. The primary component of a jurisdiction's revenue-raising capacity is the amount of revenue it could reasonably be expected to generate from local taxes. The simplest approach to measuring that capacity is as a weighted average of the jurisdiction's tax bases, where the weights are state-wide average tax rates for each base. Because school districts rely almost exclusively on property taxes, this approach would focus only on the base of the property tax and would calculate how much revenue the district would generate per pupil if it taxed that base at an average rate. Implicit in this approach is the value judgement that the appropriate way to achieve comparability across districts is to ask how much revenue they each would generate if they had a similar tax rate.

A second, and conceptually more satisfying, approach would start with the income of the district's residents and ask how much revenue the district could generate if it imposed an average tax burden on its residents (defined as taxes collected from residents as a proportion of their income), taking into account that the taxes from residents would be augmented by tax revenue from nonresidents. Nonresidents bear part of the burden of the property tax either because they own property in the district or because the burden of part of the tax is shifted to them in the form of higher prices, lower wages, or lower returns to capital. In contrast to the first approach, this second approach achieves comparability across districts by treating all districts as if they were willing to impose the same tax burden on district residents.

Although the second approach is conceptually more appealing than the first approach, it is difficult to implement. Not only does it require information on the composition of the tax base in each district, but it also requires that estimates be made about how much of the tax burden on each type of property is shifted to nonresidents. Therefore, in this study, I rely exclusively on the tax base approach. Fortunately, the two measures are often highly correlated. For Minnesota cities, for example, Ladd, Reschovsky, and Yinger (1991) found that the correlation was 0.92. However, for New York the correlation is only 0.7 (Duncombe and Yinger, 1995). Nonetheless, practicality argues in favor of the tax base approach. Because even the more limited data requirements for this approach are not met in the CCD given that the data base includes no information on the size of the property tax base, I must rely on state-generated data for at least part of the information needed to implement this measure of capacity. Note, in addition, that revenue-raising capacity has a second component, namely, revenue in the form of federal or state aid. Hence, the amount of intergovernmental aid received by a district must be added to the measure of own-source capacity to get a complete picture of a district's capacity to generate revenue.

With respect to expenditure need, the task is to determine how much it would cost per pupil for a district to provide an average level of services to its students, given that the costs of educational inputs vary across districts and some types of students are more costly to educate than others. Two approaches are available. With either approach, the goal is to measure differences in costs that reflect only those factors outside the control of local school officials. For example, consider a district that pays above-average salaries to its teachers. Whether these high salaries translate into above-average costs as defined here, and consequently into high need, depends on the reason the salaries are high. If they reflect the district's decision to recruit high quality teachers or its inability to bargain effectively with the teacher's union, then the high salaries are under the district's control and not part of the constraints it faces. However, to the extent that the high salaries reflect an above-average local cost of living which forces the district to pay more simply to attract teachers, then the high salaries are outside the control of school officials and are appropriately included.

One approach to measuring educational costs by district would be to combine measures of appropriately-measured differences in the costs of teachers and other inputs with estimates of the differential costs associated with educating different types of students, such as those with learning disabilities or those with limited proficiency in English. Note that both parts are needed. A resource cost index alone of the type developed for teachers, for example, by Jay Chambers would not be sufficient.[2] Even if Chambers' measure were extended to include the cost of inputs other than teachers, it would be necessary to supplement it. The cost index for teachers indicates the differential costs of hiring a teacher, but does not incorporate the fact that more teachers may be needed to educate certain groups of children. Thus, at a minimum the resource cost index would need to be supplemented with a measure of the differential costs of educating different groups of students. However, this approach is problematic because of the ad hoc nature of most of these cost estimates.[3]

A second approach to measuring interdistrict variation in the costs of providing an average level of education services is to estimate them from an equation explaining the variation in per pupil spending across districts. Provided that the equation controls for the other major determinants of spending differences, such as those associated with wealth differences across districts, the coefficients of "cost factors" can be used to develop a cost index for each district. This second strategy is the one I pursue in this study. For Texas, I have implemented the strategy with data generated by the Texas Education Agency. For New York, I relied on cost estimates produced by Duncombe and Yinger (1995).

---

[2] The teacher cost index developed by Jay Chambers uses a hedonic wage model to determine what each district would have to pay for teachers with similar characteristics given the factors outside the district's control (Chambers and Fowler, 1995). These factors include the tightness in the labor market for teachers, the local cost of living, and the amenities (or disamenities) of the local region.

[3] See, for example, the discussion of adjusting for student needs in NCES (1995). The ad hoc nature of the student-need adjustments used in New York state's school aid formula is documented in a recent study of cost differentials in New York (Duncombe, Ruggiero, and Yinger, 1996).

Fiscal Condition of Texas School Districts

Table 1 provides the spending equation from which the cost indexes and expenditure need estimates were calculated for Texas school districts. Most of the data used to estimate the equation came from the Texas Academic Excellence Indicator System (AEIS), not from the CCD. The equation is based on 993 districts, all of which go through the 12th grade. Following Ladd and Yinger (1991), the equation models district spending per pupil as a function of demand and preference variables, and a set of cost factors. Although the effects of the cost factors are of most interest, other variables representing the local demand for education services must be included in the equation as control variables. The first seven variables in table 1 are included for that reason. They are: the market value of property per pupil, the percentage of the tax base that is residential, the average number of pupils per household, personal income in the district per pupil, federal and state aid per pupil, and transportation costs per pupil. The residential share of the tax base represents a "tax price" variable, in that the higher is the share, the higher is the share paid directly by residents. Because a higher price typically leads to lower demand, the sign is expected to be negative. All of the variables come in with the expected signs and, with the exception of the percentage of the tax base that is residential, all are statistically significant at standard levels.

Of more direct interest are the eight cost factors, all of which represent characteristics of the district that may affect the per pupil costs of educating students. These variables include the percentages of students who are in special

Table 1.—Expenditure equation used to estimate the cost index for Texas school districts (Dependent variable: log per pupil spending)

	Coefficient	t-statistic
Cost variables		
Property tax base per pupil (log)	0.162	12.50
Income per pupil (log)	0.079	4.09
Residential percent of tax base (log)	-0.011	-1.50
Students per household (log)	0.172	8.70
Federal revenue per pupil (log)	0.081	9.28
State revenue per pupil (log)	0.033	3.72
Transportation costs per pupil (log)	0.018	3.58
Cost factors		
Special education students as a percent of all students	0.003	3.12
Limited English speaking students as a percent of all students	0.002	4.13
Economically disadvantaged students as a percent of all students	0.002	5.77
Secondary students as a percent of all students	0.004	7.91
Student enrollment (log)	-0.335	-15.95
Student enrollment squared (log)	0.018	13.66
Cost of living (log)*	0.194	1.26
Rural - 1 if district is rural, 0 otherwise	-0.002	-0.21
Constant	5.283	7.13
Number of observations	993	
Adjusted R^2	0.77	

* Based on 1991 study by McMahon and Chang, as reported in NCES, 1995, *Disparities in Public School District Spending, 1989–90*. 95-300, Washington, DC.

SOURCE: Except as noted, the data are from the Texas Academic Excellence Indicator System.

education programs, have limited English proficiency, are economically disadvantaged, and are in secondary school; the logarithm of student enrollment and its square; a cost-of-living index; and an indicator variable that reflects whether or not the district is in a rural area. Higher percentages of each of the specified categories of students are likely to raise the per pupil cost of education and, as indicated by the positive coefficients, do so in all cases. The negative coefficient on the student enrollment variable and the positive coefficient on the squared term indicate the presence of economies of scale up to an enrollment of about 11,000 students beyond which costs per student begin to rise.

The cost-of-living index serves as a proxy for the costs of educational inputs; in areas with a higher cost of living, school districts have to pay more to attract teachers and to purchase supplies. This index distinguishes between costs only in the major metropolitan areas and the nonmetropolitan areas.[4] In contrast to many other states, the variation across Texas school districts is not very great, which probably accounts for the variable's statistical insignificance. Although the rural indicator variable is not significant, it has been included for completeness given that many people believe that rural areas face special educational challenges.

From this spending equation, a cost index was constructed for each district using the following procedure. The per pupil expenditure of each district was simulated based on the assumption that the district had average values of all the control variables, but its actual values for all the cost factors. Hence, the variation across districts in the simulated expenditure represents variation only in the cost factors, that is, in characteristics of each district that are outside the immediate control of school officials and that are likely to affect how much it has to spend to provide a given quality of education. Dividing a district's simulated spending by average per pupil spending generates an index of costs for each district in which the district with average costs has a cost index equal to 1. An index above 1 indicates that a district must spend more than the typical district to purchase a given level of educational outcomes. An index below 1 indicates that the district has an advantage relative to other districts in that the cost of providing a given package of education services to its students is below the state average. A district's expenditure need is then calculated as state-wide average per pupil spending adjusted by the district's cost index.

The fiscal condition of each district is defined as:

$$FC_i = (RRC_i - EN_i)/RRC_i$$

where RRC_i is the district's capacity to raise revenue (including local taxes and intergovernmental aid) and EN_i is the district's expenditure need, both of which are measured per pupil. Fiscal condition greater than zero implies that the district has sufficient revenue-raising potential to meet its expenditure need, where both are measured relative not to an absolute standard but rather relative to other districts within the state. A negative value indicates that the district has a large expenditure need relative to its capacity to raise revenue and, hence, is in relatively poor fiscal

---

[4] The cost-of-living indexes were produced by McMahon and Chang (1991) and reported in NCES (1995), Appendix D. In place of the cost-of-living index. I could have used Chamber's cost index for teachers (see footnote 2). The cost-of-living index has two small advantages over Chamber's teacher-cost-index. First. it is relevant for the costs of all inputs, not just teachers, and second, as Chambers acknowledges, the teacher-cost-index may be slightly biased given that the hedonic wage equation from which it is derived does not fully control for teacher quality. One potential disadvantage of the cost-of-living index, namely that it does not account for the effect on salaries of variation across districts in the characteristics of students, does not apply in this case since student characteristics are also included in the spending equation reported in table 1. This means that the cost-of-living index—or the Chambers teacher-cost-index if that were used—picks up the effects on spending only of the differing costs of inputs and that the variables that characterize the students, such as the percent with limited proficiency in English, pick up the effect of such students both on the salaries of teachers and on the quantity of such teachers who are hired.

condition. The more negative is the index the greater is the fiscal pressure faced by the district. The index has a straightforward interpretation. For example, a negative index value of -0.20 indicates that the district would need a boost in its per pupil revenues of 20 percent to meet its expenditure need. Conversely, a positive index value of +0.20 indicates the district could raise 20 percent more revenue at the average tax rate than it would need to meet its expenditure need, and hence has the option of setting a lower tax rate or of providing an above-average quality of education.

The index of fiscal condition ranges from -0.31 to +0.93 across the 993 Texas districts, with a mean of 0.07 and a standard deviation of 0.15.[5] To reiterate, the fiscal condition measure should be interpreted strictly in state-specific terms: capacity to provide what is deemed an average quality of education in Texas could be deemed inadequate for a district in another state in which average spending, and presumably, the quality of education were higher.

Moreover, what matters for the subsequent analysis is not so much the specific value of a district's fiscal condition as the condition of one district relative to another.

Table 2 presents descriptive information by districts grouped into quintiles by fiscal condition. As shown in the first column, the average index of fiscal condition ranges from -.08 to 0.31 across the five categories. The revenue shares and spending measures are calculated from both state-specific AEIS data and data from the CCD. As can be seen, the two data sources provide comparable information. The table indicates that the districts in the strongest fiscal condition receive a substantially larger share of their revenue from local taxes than do districts in poorer fiscal condition and that their share of revenue from the state government is correspondingly lower. Despite the fact that, by construction, additional intergovernmental aid adds to a district's capacity to raise revenue, it is the capacity to raise revenue from local sources that distin-

Table 2.—Sources of revenue and spending levels by categories of fiscal condition (Texas school districts)

Categories of fiscal condition (observations)	Average fiscal condition	Average share of revenue[1]			Average spending per pupil[1] (in dollars)	
		Local	State	Federal	Unadjusted[2]	Adjusted[3]
I - Poorest	-0.082	0.417	0.519	0.064	$4,252	$4,324
(198)		0.416	0.512	0.072	4,283	4,338
II - Poor	-0.002	0.412	0.517	0.071	4,367	4,544
(199)		0.407	0.517	0.076	4,327	4,493
III - Average	0.049	0.359	0.568	0.074	4,652	4,705
(199)		0.356	0.563	0.081	4,537	4,588
IV - Good	0.100	0.412	0.512	0.076	4,970	4,953
(199)		0.413	0.506	0.081	4,695	4,685
V - Best	0.309	0.602	0.333	0.065	6,221	5,806
(198)		0.594	0.339	0.066	5,942	5,562

[1] First entry in each cell is based on Academic Excellence Indicator System (AEIS) data. Second entry is based on Common Core of Data (CCD) data.
[2] Current spending per pupil not adjusted for estimated cost differences.
[3] Current spending per pupil deflated by estimated cost differences.
SOURCE: Based on data from the CCD and the Texas AEIS.

[5] Note that I could easily have normalized the index to have a mean of zero, but saw no compelling reason to do so. The fact that the mean is not zero simply reflects that some districts have disproportionately large tax bases.

guishes the districts with the strongest fiscal condition from those facing more fiscal pressure. The final two columns report average spending per pupil, adjusted and unadjusted for cost differences. Based on the CCD data (the second entries in each cell), average unadjusted spending varies from about $4280 per pupil to $5940 per pupil. After adjusting for the costs, using the cost index described earlier, per pupil spending ranges from $4320 to about $5560. This smaller range reflects the fact that the costs in Texas of providing a given quality of education services tend to be higher in the districts in good fiscal condition than in those in poor fiscal condition.

To summarize, as measured here, a district's fiscal condition is intended to represent the fiscal constraint under which the district operates, relative to that in other districts. On average, stronger fiscal condition is associated with higher cost-adjusted per pupil spending on education and presumably, to better educational outcomes.

Effects of Fiscal Constraint on Decisions of Texas School Districts

Armed with this measure of fiscal condition, we are now in a position to look at how fiscal condition affects the school district budget allocation and staffing decisions in Texas, using both AEIS data and the CCD. The locally generated AEIS data set is useful for its richness. The CCD data are advantageous in that results based on that nationally produced data set can be directly compared across states.

The analysis is designed to shed light on how school districts have adjusted to differences in their fiscal condition associated with any one of a variety of causes outside the control of local school officials, such as differences in the amount of intergovernmental aid they receive, differences in the value of their property tax wealth, and differences in the proportions of high-cost students they serve. This research strategy is not designed to look in detail at fiscal responses to each component separately. Instead, it captures all their effects in a single variable, fiscal condition.

My empirical strategy is straightforward. The idea is to see how budget shares or staffing patterns are affected by a district's fiscal condition, controlling for other obvious determinants of such patterns. Thus, the dependent variable in most of the equations is a variable such as the proportion of the operating budget allocated to instruction, or the share of the staff working in administration. The main explanatory variable is the district's fiscal condition, which is included in both its linear and squared form to allow its effects to be nonlinear. All equations also include four other control variables: student enrollment (and its square), personal income per pupil, and the fraction of students from economically disadvantaged households. These variables are included to control for the fact that budget and staffing decisions are likely to be influenced by the number of students in the district, the preferences of the district's taxpayers (as proxied by personal income), and the need for special programs as proxied by students from economically disadvantaged households. For example, to the extent that there are economies of scale in administrative expenditures, we would expect the share of spending on administration to be smaller in large school districts than in small districts. While the specific choice of control variables is somewhat arbitrary, it is important that a reasonable set be included so as to isolate the independent effects of fiscal condition.

Reported in the tables are three summary measures of how fiscal condition affects budget and staffing patterns. (Full equations are available from the author.) The first is the marginal effect of fiscal condition, calculated at the mean value of fiscal condition. The other two measures indicate the differences in the budget or staffing shares associated with differences from the mean of one standard deviation in either direction. The more nonlinear is the estimated equation, the more these final two measures of impact differ. The entries in the final column are of most interest in that they indicate the impact on budget shares of fiscal constraint, where a fiscally constrained district is defined to be one that has a fiscal condition index that is one standard deviation below the average.

Given that most of the dependent variables are expressed as proportions or shares of the total, one must be careful in interpreting the results. First, consider a finding that fiscal condition has no measurable impact on, for example, the share of spending allocated to administration at the school level. This finding does not imply that a district in poor fiscal condition would spend the same **amount** on school administration as a district in strong fiscal condition. In fact, because weaker fiscal condition is associated with lower per pupil spending on education (as can be seen, for example, by the average spending patterns in table 2), the finding that fiscal condition exerts no impact on the **share** of spending devoted to administration simply means that administrative spending would vary across districts in line with the variation in per pupil spending.

Consider first the signs of the estimated marginal impacts on the shares. They indicate the direction of the nonproportional differences in the various spending and staffing categories associated with differences in a district's fiscal condition. As such, they indicate which categories of spending districts are likely to protect or disproportionately cut as part of their equilibrium response to a long-run deterioration in their fiscal condition. The signs in the following tables should be interpreted as follows. A **positive** marginal impact of fiscal condition implies that spending or staffing on the specified category is disproportionately higher in districts in stronger fiscal condition than in others. A **negative** marginal impact implies that spending or staffing on that category is disproportionately lower in districts in strong fiscal condition. As I noted earlier, the final column is of most interest. A positive entry in this column indicates that a constrained district spends a larger share on the indicated category. A negative entry indicates that it spends a smaller share.

It is worth emphasizing once again that the estimated impacts come from a cross sectional model and at best, reflect long run responses to changes in fiscal condition that are anticipated to continue for a long period of time. In the short run, the existence of long-term contracts and various types of political pressures may make school districts respond differently in the short run than in the long run to changes in their fiscal condition, especially if they expect the change to be temporary. In the short run, districts may not have much choice in how to respond to a deterioration in their fiscal condition; the question in the short run may well be not what would they like to cut, but what **can** they cut? The long run equilibrium nature of the estimates reported here mean that such short run considerations are not directly relevant.

Impacts on Budget Allocations

Table 3 reports results for a variety of budget categories. Looking first at the categories defined by the AEIS, and focusing on the results in the final column of the table, we find that fiscally constrained districts devote about 1.6 percent more of their operating budgets to instruction than do districts with average fiscal condition. This larger share comes at the expense of the shares devoted to instructional administration (down 4.8 percent), central administration (down 6.1 percent), and plant services (down 2.7 percent). The shares devoted to student support services, campus administration, and "other" do not vary systematically with a district's fiscal condition.

These estimates imply first that fiscally constrained districts try to protect instructional spending. However, they are not able to do so very effectively in that the small 1.6 percent increase in the share devoted to instruction applies to a significantly lower overall operating

Table 3.—Estimated impact of fiscal condition on budget categories, Texas school districts[1]

Budget category (mean value)	Marginal effect of fiscal condition[2]	Impact of 1 standard deviation difference	
		Positive (%)	Negative (%)
As a proportion of operating budget (AEIS)			
Instruction (0.579)	-0.055	-1.4	1.6
Instructional administration (0.011)	0.004	5.6	-4.8
Student support services (0.044)	not significant	—	—
Campus administration (0.054)	not significant	—	—
Central administration (0.080)	0.031	5.5	-6.1
Plant services (0.106)	0.017	1.9	-2.7
Other (0.126)	not significant	—	—
As a proportion of total budget (AEIS)			
Operating (0.894)	-0.037	-0.7	0.6
Capital outlay (0.056)	0.052	13.9	-14.5
As a proportion of current expenditures (CCD)			
Instruction (0.592)	-0.059	-1.4	1.5
Support services (0.328)	0.068	3.0	-3.2
Central administration (0.080)	0.020	3.6	-4.0
Non-instruction (0.080)	-0.009	-1.6	1.8
As a proportion of total expenditure (CCD)[3]			
Capital outlay (0.078)	not significant	—	—

— Not applicable because of insignificant coefficient.

[1] The Academic Excellence Indicator System (AEIS) equations are based on data from FY 1994 and the Common Core of Data (CCD) data from FY 1992. See appendix for further explanation.

[2] Based on coefficients of fiscal condition and fiscal condition squared in a regression equation that also includes student enrollment, student enrollment squared, personal income per pupil, percent of students who are economically disadvantaged and a constant. The full equations are available from the author. The estimated impacts were calculated at the mean value of fiscal condition, 0.07.

[3] Capital outlays and total expenditures were both averaged over fiscal years 1990 to 1992. The figures were all deflated by the Gross National Product (GNP) deflator for structures as reported in the *1996 Economic Report to the President*.

SOURCE: Texas AEIS and CCD.

budget. Specifically, a one standard deviation decline in fiscal condition is associated with about a 13 percent decline in the operating budget.[6] Despite its somewhat larger share, per pupil spending on instruction is about 11 percent less in the fiscally constrained district than in the average district.

Constrained districts also spend less per pupil on central administration and instructional administration. In these cases the two effects move in the same direction: constrained districts have smaller operating budgets and on average devote smaller proportions of these budget to these administrative categories. Some observers might be tempted to conclude from these estimates that fiscal pressure is a reasonable way to induce districts to reduce their spending on administration. However, that conclusion would be simplistic and inappropriate. Even if cuts in administration, especially central administration, were deemed desirable, inducing reductions through cutbacks in the resources available to school dis-

---

[6] This estimate comes from an equation in which the operating spending (in logarithmic form and based on the AEIS) is regressed on fiscal condition, fiscal condition squared, and the four control variables. The equation implies that a difference in fiscal condition of 0.15 (equal to one standard deviation) is associated with a 0.13 difference in operating spending per pupil.

tricts would carry a large cost in the form of reduced instructional spending, and, as noted below, larger class sizes. Moreover, it could be the case that the long run equilibrium results reported here overstate the short run changes that are likely to occur in response to a deterioration in fiscal condition. As noted in the introduction, Lankford and Wyckoff (1996) find that in the short run, school districts decrease central administrative expenditures less in response to a deterioration in fiscal pressure than they increase such spending in response to an improvement in their fiscal situation.

The finding that fiscal constraint is associated with a lower share for plant services, that is for maintenance, is consistent with the finding in the next part of the table for capital outlays. Like maintenance, capital outlays (expressed as a proportion of the total budget) are positively related to a district's fiscal condition. The estimate implies that the share of spending that a fiscally constrained district devotes to capital spending would be about 14.5 percent below that in the district with average fiscal condition. Thus, poor fiscal condition imposes a double whammy in that overall spending is lower and a smaller share of that spending is devoted to building and maintaining school facilities than is true for better off districts. Thus, a district that is fiscally constrained over a long period of time is likely to end up with significantly worse educational facilities than other districts.[7]

A similar picture emerges from the CCD spending categories reported at the bottom of table 3. Again, better fiscal condition is associated with a decline in the share of the total expenditure allocated to instruction, and an increase in the share for support services. Support services in the CCD is a broad category that includes student support services such as guidance and health; instructional support and librarians; central administration; school administration; business, operation and plant maintenance; student transportation services; and central expenditure such as information services and data processing. The only subcategory for which data were available and which yielded a statistically significant impact is central administration.[8]

The results for this subcategory are comparable but somewhat smaller than those based on the CCD data : fiscal constraint leads to a 4 percent reduction in the share which contrasts with a 6.1 percent reduction according to the AEIS data. The share devoted to non-instructional spending, which includes food services and other auxiliary enterprise operations such as bookstores, is slightly negatively related to fiscal condition. Hence, fiscally constrained districts devote slightly larger shares of their budgets to this category than do other districts.

The final section of table 3 reports the insignificant relationship between fiscal condition and capital outlay based on the CCD data. This finding is surprising and contrasts quite sharply with the large impact that emerged from the AEIS data. I explored two measures of capital outlay. The first is simply capital outlay in 1992 as a share of total expenditures in 1992. Because capital spending can be lumpy, the second measure is calculated as the average capital outlay relative to spending over a three year period. The table reports the latter measure. However, for neither measure did a statistically significant impact emerge.[9]

Impacts on Staffing Patterns

As reported in table 4, the findings for staffing patterns tell a similar story. As shown

---

[7] This finding about capital outlays is fully consistent with the findings reported by the NCES in their study of disparities in education spending (NCES, 1995).

[8] The general subcategory called "other" was not available for Texas school districts. This category includes, among other things, spending on maintenance.

[9] I have not been able to determine the cause of the different results for the AEIS and the CCD data. The two series are not very highly correlated which by itself is not too surprising given that the AEIS is for the 1993–94 fiscal year and the latest single year for the CCD is 1991–92. Because fiscal condition best reflects the more recent period, the AEIS estimates are preferred.

Table 4.—Estimated impact of fiscal condition on staffing patterns, Texas school districts[1]

Staff category (mean value)	Marginal effect of fiscal condition[2]	Impact of 1 standard deviation difference	
		Positive (%)	Negative (%)
As a proportion of professional staff (AEIS)			
Teachers (0.857)	-0.027	-0.5	0.5
Professional support (0.067)	not significant	—	—
Campus administration (0.045)	not significant	—	—
Central administration (0.031)	0.017	7.7	-8.7
As a proportion of total staff (AEIS)			
Professional (0.630)	-0.044	-1.0	1.1
Educational aides (0.103)	-0.005	-0.6	0.9
Auxiliary staff (0.266)	0.056	2.6	-2.8
As a proportion of total staff (CCD)			
Teachers (0.729)	not significant	—	—
Aides (0.142)	not significant	—	—
Special[3] (0.033)	not significant	—	—
School administration[4] (0.045)	0.011	3.6	-3.8
District administration[5] (0.026)	0.008	4.2	-5.0

— Not applicable because of insignificant coefficient.

[1] The Academic Excellence Indicator System (AEIS) equations are based on data from FY 1994 and the Common Core of Data (CCD) data are from FY 1993. See appendix for further explanation.

[2] Based on coefficients of fiscal condition and fiscal condition squared in a regression equation that also includes student enrollment, student enrollment squared, personal income per pupil, percent of students who are economically disadvantaged, and a constant. See appendix for sample size. The estimated impacts were calculated at the mean value of fiscal condition, 0.07

[3] Includes instructional coordinators, guidance counselors, and library/media specialists.

[4] Includes school administration, support staff, and student support staff.

[5] Includes local education agency (LEA) administration and support staff.

SOURCE: Texas AEIS and CCD.

in the final column, teachers account for a slightly larger proportion of the professional staff in fiscally constrained districts than in the typical district while central administration accounts for a smaller share. Because teachers account for so much more of the professional staff, the positive percentage impact on the share for teachers is tiny compared to the 8.7 percent reduction in the share of central administration. Once again, however, one must be careful in drawing policy implications: While fiscal constraint reduces the share of central administration, it does so at the cost of reducing the number of teachers. The middle panel indicates that fiscally constrained districts have slightly higher proportions of their total staffs in teaching positions and smaller proportions in nonteaching positions.

The CCD data yields a relatively comparable picture. The primary difference is that fiscal constraint appears to have no observable impact on the share of the professional staff employed as teachers, aides, or for special purposes. However, comparable to previous findings, fiscal constraint is associated with smaller shares of school administrative staff and district administrative staff. Hence, fiscally constrained districts have disproportionately fewer support staff to address the range of problems such districts face. They are clearly caught between a rock and a hard place. The only way to maintain the share of administrators would be to reduce the number of teachers, teacher aides, and related personnel.

School Quality

Studies of school quality typically focus on three measurable school inputs: pupil teacher ratios (which are positively correlated with, but are not the same thing as, class size[10]), the experience of teachers, and the post graduate education of teachers. The extent to which these measurable school inputs affect student performance as measured by test scores remains in doubt. In a recent paper based on Alabama data, Ferguson and Ladd (1996) find evidence that smaller class sizes, and a greater proportion of teachers with post graduate degrees positively affect student performance. In contrast we find no evidence that years of experience matter. Here, I look at how fiscal condition affects school districts' decisions about the three types of school inputs.

As shown in the top section of table 5, fiscal condition directly affects pupil teacher ratios. More specifically, better fiscal condition is associated with lower pupil teacher ratios. The estimated marginal impacts imply that fiscally constrained districts are likely to have pupil-teacher ratios, and hence class sizes, that are 6-8 percent higher than typical districts. The findings in Ferguson and Ladd (1996) imply that this difference would translate into weaker student performance.

Table 5 also shows the impact of fiscal condition on the distribution of teachers in terms of teacher experience. Stronger fiscal condition is associated with smaller proportions of beginning teachers and those with 6 to 10 years of experience and larger proportions of teachers with more than 10 years of experience. For fiscally constrained districts (as shown in the final column), the shares of beginning teachers exceed those of the average district by 9 percent and their share of experienced teachers falls short of the typical district by 5.8 percent. Although the empirical linkage between fiscal condition and teacher experience is quite clear, the implications for student learning are less clear. Ferguson and Ladd's estimates suggest that these differences might have little effect on student learning. Finally, the bottom row of the table summarizes the effects of fiscal condition on several measures of the distribution of teachers by their educational background. For none of the included variables (such as proportion of teachers with a master's degree) did a statistically significant coefficient emerge.

The clearest story to emerge from table 5 is that fiscal constraint hurts students by making it necessary for schools to have larger classes.

New York School Districts

In contrast to Texas, New York school districts spend a lot more money on elementary and secondary education and exhibit greater variation across districts. These differences make New York an interesting state for exploring the generalizability of the Texas findings about how school districts respond to fiscal constraints. Unfortunately, I do not have access to the detailed data by district for New York that I had for Texas and must rely more heavily on the CCD data.

However, missing from the CCD data are some of the key variables needed to estimate a district's revenue-raising capacity and its expenditure need. With respect to revenue-raising capacity, the main missing variable is the

---

[10] Pupil-teacher ratios typically understate average class size since not all teachers spend all of their time in class. Moreover, the concept of an average class size may be misleading to the extent that it includes both very small classes for students with special needs and potentially much larger classes for regular students. Ideally, it would be preferable to measure class size from information on teacher files that indicates the class sizes for the regular classes that they teach. See, for example, Ferguson and Ladd, 1996.

Table 5.—Estimated impact of fiscal condition on measures of school quality, Texas school districts[1]

Staff category (mean value)	Marginal effect of fiscal condition[2]	Impact of 1 standard deviation difference	
		Positive (%)	Negative (%)
Pupils per teacher			
AEIS (13.61)	-6.89	-7.4	7.8
CCD (13.87)	-5.62	-5.9	6.3
Experience of teachers			
As a proportion of all teachers (AEIS)			
Beginning (0.066)	-0.039	-8.4	9.0
1–5 years (0.266)	not significant	—	—
6–10 years (0.197)	-0.067	-5.1	5.3
11–20 years (0.309)	0.087	3.9	-4.5
> 20 years (0.162)	0.061	5.4	-5.8
Post-graduate education of teachers	not significant	—	—

— Not applicable because of insignificant coefficient.
[1] The Academic Excellence Indicator System (AEIS) equations are based on data from FY 1994 and the Common Core of Data (CCD) data are from FY 1992. See appendix for further explanation.
[2] Based on coefficients of fiscal condition and fiscal condition squared in a regression equation that also includes student enrollment, student enrollment squared, personal income per pupil, percent of students who are economically disadvantaged, and a constant. The full equations are available from the author. The estimated impacts were calculated at the mean value of fiscal condition, 0.07.
SOURCE: Texas AEIS and CCD.

value of the district's property tax base. With respect to expenditure need, a crude estimate of a district's cost index could be estimated from CCD data, but state-generated data allows for a more complete estimate. Given these limitations of the CCD data, I chose to use cost indexes recently estimated for New York by Duncombe and Yinger (1995) with Ruggiero (1996) and also their data on property tax valuations. With these two additions, I then used the CCD data to estimate the fiscal condition of 632 New York school districts.

Duncombe and Yinger's cost index is similar in spirit to the one discussed in section I for the Texas districts in that the goal was to determine the average impacts on costs of a variety of cost factors. However, Duncombe and Yinger have refined the approach in two significant ways. First, because they had access to data on educational outcomes, they were able to replace the demand variables in the spending equation, such as income and the tax price variable, with what the districts actually chose, as measured by three educational outcome variables (percent of students with high test scores, the percent receiving the Regents diploma, and the percent who do not drop out). This substitution is appropriate provided that the authors recognize, as they did, that the outcome measures are simultaneously determined with public spending and therefore require the use of statistical techniques to account for simultaneity. Second, they included an efficiency index intended to control for differences in the efficiency with which districts provide education.[11] The cost factors used to construct the cost index include an estimate of teacher salaries (standardized for a given level of education and experience

---

[11] Their measure of inefficiency is based on a technique called data envelopment analysis, or DEA. This nonparametric programming technique compares the spending of each district with the spending of other districts that deliver the same quality of public services. See Duncombe and Yinger, 1995, p. 10 and Duncombe, Ruggiero, and Yinger (1996). Both the outcome variables and the efficiency variable were estimated as endogenous variables in the spending equation.

so as to minimize the potential for this to be a variable chosen by the district), student enrollment (and its square), and the percentages of children in poverty, of households that are headed by females, of students who are severely handicapped, of students who have limited English proficiency, and of students who are in high school.

Based on the same measure of fiscal condition as described earlier, the resulting measure of fiscal condition for 632 New York districts has an average value of -0.017, a standard deviation of 0.23, and ranges from -1.33 to +0.82. Thus, as measured both by the standard deviation and the range, the variation in fiscal condition across the New York districts exceeds that for the Texas districts.

Table 6 essentially replicates for New York the summary data presented in table 2 for Texas school districts. Notice the much larger variation across the district groupings in the share of revenue from local taxes and correspondingly from the state government. The average share of revenue from local taxes in the districts with the best fiscal condition is about twice that in the districts with the poorest fiscal condition. Also the share of revenue from the federal government is smaller in all five categories than it was in Texas, which largely reflects the much greater spending by New York districts. This spending is shown in the final two columns. Before it is adjusted for differences in costs, (see the first of the two spending figures), average per pupil spending varies from $6,722 to $10,491. That the lowest average spending emerges for the second rather than the first group of districts reflects the fact that many of the districts in the poorest fiscal condition face high costs. This explanation is confirmed by the next column, which represents per pupil spending adjusted by the cost index provided by Duncombe and Yinger, which is also the one used to construct the measure of fiscal condition. Note that once this adjustment for costs is made, the districts in the worst fiscal condition are seen to spend the least per student.

Impact of Fiscal Condition on Budget Categories

Table 7 reports the estimated impacts of fiscal condition on the budget categories for New York school districts. The marginal impacts reported in the first column are directly comparable to those reported for Texas districts in the bottom panel of table 3 and exhibit similar patterns. In particular, better fiscal condition is associated with a smaller budget share for instruction and a larger share for support services, which includes administrative expenditures and maintenance. The marginal impacts are generally smaller for New York but the implications are essentially the same: New York districts that are fiscally constrained devote smaller shares of their budgets to support services in return for an increase the share for instruction. Because instructional spending accounts for such a large share of current expenditure, the percentage reductions in shares for support services exceed the gain in shares for instructional spending.

Also, like the results for capital outlays based on the AEIS data for Texas (but, curiously, not the CCD data) differences in fiscal condition across New York school districts lead to the greatest variation in capital outlays. According to the table, fiscally constrained districts devote to capital outlays a share of the total budget that is about 10.4 percent lower than that in the typical district.

Impact on Staffing Patterns

Table 8 reports the impacts fiscal condition on district staffing decisions. The pattern with respect to teachers is as expected: better fiscal condition leads to a smaller share of teachers and poorer fiscal condition to a greater share of teachers. Virtually no effect emerges for teacher aides, although the squared term enters with a positive and statistically significant coefficient.

Table 6.—Sources of revenue and spending levels, by categories of fiscal condition, New York school districts

Categories of fiscal condition (observations)	Average fiscal condition	Average share of revenue			Average spending per pupil (in dollars)	
		Local	State	Federal	Unadjusted[1]	Adjusted[2]
I - Poorest (126)	-0.303	0.375	0.583	0.042	$7,042	$6,042
II - Poor (127)	-0.111	0.388	0.578	0.035	6,722	6,825
III - Average (126)	-0.028	0.438	0.534	0.028	7,064	7,612
IV - Good (127)	0.053	0.519	0.453	0.028	7,749	8,382
V - Best (126)	0.305	0.735	0.248	0.017	10,491	10,733

[1] Current spending per pupil not adjusted for estimated cost differences.
[2] Current spending per pupil adjusted by cost index from Duncombe and Yinger.
SOURCE: Common Core of Data (CCD) and data provided by William Duncombe and John Yinger.

Table 7.—Estimated impact of fiscal condition on budget categories, New York school districts[1]

Budget category (mean value)	Marginal effect of fiscal condition[2]	Impact of 1 standard deviation difference	
		Positive (%)	Negative (%)
As a proportion of current expenditure			
Instruction (0.639)	-0.025	-0.9	0.9
Support services (0.335)	0.026	1.8	-1.8
Central Administration (0.028)	0.008	6.8	-6.4
Instructional Staff (0.030)	0.006	4.0	-4.7
Other, including maintenance (0.196)	0.022	2.6	-2.6
Non-instruction (0.026)	-0.001	-0.8	1.1
As a proportion of total expenditure[3]			
Capital outlay (0.082)	0.036	10.4	-10.4

[1] The equations are based on budget data from FY 1991. See appendix for further explanation.
[2] Basic measure of fiscal condition is the measure described in text as the gap between a district's revenue-raising capacity and its expenditure need as a proportion of its revenue-raising capacity. The entries in this column are calculated from the coefficients on the fiscal condition variable and fiscal condition squared in a regression equation that also includes student enrollment, student enrollment squared, personal income per pupil, percent of children living in poverty, and a constant term. The estimated impacts were calculated at the mean value of fiscal condition, -0.017.
[3] Capital outlays and total expenditures were both averaged over fiscal years 1990 to 1992. The figures were all deflated by the Gross National Product (GNP) deflator for structures as reported in the *1996 Economic Report to the President*.
SOURCE: Common Core of Data (CCD).

Somewhat perplexing are the results for the shares of the staff devoted to school administration and central administration. Previous findings for both Texas and New York would have led one to predict that stronger fiscal condition would be associated with greater staffing shares devoted to both categories of administration and that fiscal constraint would be associated with lower shares. Yet, the patterns are just the reverse: compared to the typical district, fiscally constrained districts appear to have larger shares of their staffs in administrative positions.

The puzzle is most obvious for central administration. According to table 7, stronger fiscal condition is associated with a greater share of spending on central administration.

But table 8 implies the apparently contradictory conclusion that stronger fiscal condition is associated with a smaller share of staff in central administration. The most obvious explanation has to do with the likely pattern across districts of salary levels for administrative staff. It could well be that the fiscally constrained districts choose to keep former teachers employed by moving them into administration at relatively low salaries while the districts with stronger fiscal condition employ fewer administrators but at higher salaries.

Impact on Pupil Teacher Ratios

Finally, table 9 reports the impacts of the two measures of fiscal condition on the pupil-teacher ratio. As was true for Texas school districts, better fiscal condition is associated with fewer pupils per teacher. The implication for districts with poor fiscal condition are clear: such districts are likely to have larger classes than districts with average fiscal condition. Ferguson and Ladd's study (1996) suggests that if the resulting class sizes were in the mid to high 20s for the elementary grades, student test scores are likely to be lower than they would be with smaller classes.

Generalizability

The picture that emerges from the analysis of New York school districts is very similar to that which emerges for Texas school districts. Poorer fiscal condition is associated with a greater **share** of spending on instruction and a larger **share** of the staff in teaching. Nonetheless, their limited overall spending means that districts in poor fiscal condition are likely to spend less per pupil on instruction and to employ fewer teachers relative to the number of their students. The effect is larger pupil-teacher ratios and larger class sizes. That the New York findings generally confirm those for Texas suggests that the patterns reported for Texas are not idiosyncratic and that the story summarized here is apparently generalizable across states.

Table 8.—Estimated impact of fiscal condition on staffing patterns, New York school districts[1]

Staff category (mean value)	Marginal effect of fiscal condition[2]	Impact of 1 standard deviation difference	
		Positive (%)	Negative (%)
As a proportion of total staff			
Teachers (0.517)	-0.028	-1.2	1.4
Aides (0.069)	0.000	-0.2	0.1
Special[3] (0.023)	not significant	—	—
School administration[4] (0.101)	-0.019	-4.4	4.5
Central administration[5] (0.075)	-0.010	-3.2	3.2

— Not applicable because of insignificant coefficient.
[1] The equations are based on staffing data from FY 1993. See appendix for further explanation.
[2] Basic measure of fiscal condition is the measure described in text as the gap between a district's revenue-raising capacity and its expenditure need as a proportion of its revenue-raising capacity. The entries in this column are calculated from the coefficients on the fiscal condition variable and fiscal condition squared in a regression equation that also includes student enrollment, student enrollment squared, personal income per pupil, percent of children living in poverty, and a constant term. The estimated impacts were calculated at the mean value of fiscal condition, -0.017.
[3] Includes instructional coordinators, guidance counselors, and library/media specialists.
[4] Includes school administrators, support staff, and student support staff.
[5] Includes local education agency (LEA) administration and support staff.
SOURCE: Common Core of Data (CCD).

Table 9.—Estimated impact of fiscal condition on measures of school quality, New York school districts[1]

Measure (mean value)	Marginal effect of fiscal condition[2]	Impact of 1 standard deviation difference	
		Positive (%)	Negative (%)
Pupils per teacher			
Common Core of Data (CCD) (13.8)	-2.70	-4.6	4.6

[1] The equations are based on budget data from FY 1991. See appendix for details.

[2] Basic measure of fiscal condition is the measure described in text as the gap between a district's revenue-raising capacity and its expenditure need as a proportion of its revenue-raising capacity. The entries in this column are calculated from the coefficients on the fiscal condition variable and fiscal condition squared in a regression equation that also includes student enrollment, student enrollment squared, personal income per pupil, percent of children living in poverty, and a constant term. The estimated impacts were calculated at the mean value of fiscal condition, -0.017.

SOURCE: Common Core of Data (CCD).

Conclusion

This investigation shows that districts respond to fiscal constraints by trying to protect the level of instructional spending. Evidence for this emerges from the finding that the share of the budget allocated to instructional spending is slightly higher in fiscally constrained districts than in districts in average fiscal condition. However, despite these efforts, districts experiencing serious fiscal constraint are still likely to spend less on instructional spending than their better-off counterparts: a larger share of a smaller total pie still leads to lower spending on instruction. The primary consequences are a higher pupil-teacher ratio and the use of less experienced teachers. These results are consistent with those that emerge from David Figlio's 1995 study of the effects of property tax limitation measures in which he finds that tax limitations are associated with larger classes, shorter instructional periods, and lower teacher salaries.

A second finding is that central administration spending and staffing appear to be a luxury. That is, stronger fiscal condition is associated with a larger share of spending on central administration and conversely, poorer fiscal condition is associated with lower spending on administration—both because of lower overall spending and because the share of that spending devoted to central administration would be lower. This finding, it should be noted, runs counter to that of Figlio who finds no evidence that districts subject to property tax limitations reduced their spending on administration. In light of the finding reported here, some people might be tempted to argue for increasing fiscal stringency as a way to reduce administrative spending. However, this study shows that there could be significant costs associated with that strategy. Even if districts tried to become leaner and meaner, the evidence reported here suggests that muscle, in the form of instructional spending, would also be cut.

A third finding is that the category of capital outlays emerges as the most responsive to a district's fiscal condition. According to the best estimate for Texas (based on the AEIS data), capital spending in a district with fiscal condition one standard deviation below the average is likely to account for about 15 percent less as a share of total spending than in a district with average spending. When combined with the fact that the total budget in such a district is also likely to be lower by about 13 percent, this 15 percent decline in the share translates into about a 26 percent shortfall in capital spending relative to that in a district in average fiscal condition.[12] New York districts also appear to respond to fiscal constraint by spending a smaller proportion on capital spending. While the magnitude of the response is a bit smaller than in the Texas districts, the overall conclusion is the same and fully consistent with, it should be noted, to the findings of a recent NCES study of variation in spending patterns across districts. Such a finding is not at all surprising given that politicians facing fiscal constraints have strong incentives to try cut the least visible spending categories. Yet the consequences are potentially severe. Annual shortfalls in capital spending and maintenance in response to an extended period of fiscal constraint are likely to leave some districts with serious deficiencies in their capital plants.

---

[12] This estimate was calculated as follows, where C is capital outlays, s is the budget share, and B is the total budget for a typical district. For a fiscally constrained district, the capital share is (0.85)s and the total budget is (0.87)B. Capital spending in that district is (0.85)(0.87) =0.74 times the capital spending in the typical district, therefore, capital spending is lower by 26 percent.

Appendix

The full equations underlying the results reported in the text tables are available from the author. As noted in the text, the dependent variable in most of the equations is a variable such as the proportion of the operating budget allocated to instruction, or the share of the staff working in administration. The explanatory variables are the district's fiscal condition (included in both linear and squared form), and the following control variables: student enrollment (and its square), personal income per pupil, and the fraction of students from economically disadvantaged households.

Texas

The Texas equations are all based on 1993 school districts. This set of districts represents those that remained after the Academic Excellence Indicator System (AEIS) and Common Core of Data (CCD) data sets were merged and observations not common to both were dropped. In addition, six observations were dropped because total property value was zero, six were dropped because the district reported no residential property, and six were dropped because the district reported no federal revenue. Finally, 14 outliers were dropped.

All AEIS information is based on fiscal year 1994, the staffing data are from the CCD fiscal year 1993, and all other CCD data are for fiscal year 1992.

New York

The New York equations are based on 632 observations which represents the set for which all data, including the cost index from Duncombe and Yinger, were available. The budget share equations are based on CCD data for fiscal year 1990–91. The staffing equations for fiscal year 1991–92. The cost index for New York is based on 1991 data.

References

Chambers, J.G. and W.J. Fowler, Jr. 1995. *Public School Teacher Cost Differences Across the United States*. NCES 95-758, Washington, DC: U.S. Department of Education, National Center for Education Statistics.

Duncombe, William, John Ruggiero, and John M. Yinger. 1996. "Alternative Approaches to Measuring the Cost of Education," in *Holding Schools Accountable: Performance Based Reform in Education,* Helen F. Ladd, editor. Washington, DC: The Brookings Institution.

Duncombe, William and John Yinger. November, 1995. "School Finance Reform: Aid Formulas and Equity Objectives." Processed, Maxwell School, University of Syracuse.

Dye, Richard F. and Therese McGuire. 1995. "The Effect of Property Tax Limitation Measures on Local Government Fiscal Behavior." Processed, Institute of Government and Public Affairs, University of Illinois.

Ferguson, Ronald and Helen F. Ladd. 1996. "How and Why Money Matters: An Analysis of Alabama Schools," in *Holding Schools Accountable: Performance-Based Reform in Education,* Helen F. Ladd, editor. Washington, DC: The Brookings Institution.

Figlio, David N. July, 1995. "Did the "Tax Revolt" Reduce School Performance?" Processed, University of Oregon.

Hess, G. Alfred, Jr. 1991. *School Restructuring, Chicago Style.* Corwin Press, Inc.

Ladd, Helen F. 1994. "Measuring Disparities in the Fiscal Condition of Local Governments," in *The Challenge of Fiscal Equalization,* John Anderson, editor. Praeger Press. pp. 21–55.

Ladd, Helen F., Andrew Reschovsky, and John Yinger. 1991. *Measuring the Fiscal Condition of Cities in Minnesota.* Final report submitted to the Legislative Commission on Planning and Fiscal Policy, Minnesota, April 1991

Ladd, Helen F. and John Yinger. 1991. *America's Ailing Cities: Fiscal Health and the Design of Urban Policy, Updated Edition.* Johns Hopkins University Press.

Lankford, Hamilton and James Wyckoff. 1996. "The Allocation of Resources to Special Education and Regular Education," in *Holding Schools Accountable: Performance-Based Reform in Education,* Helen F. Ladd, editor.

McMahan, W. W. and Chang, S. April, 1991. *Geographical Cost of Living Differences: Interstate and Intrastate, Update 1991.* MacArthur/Spencer Series Number 20. Normal, Illinois: Center for the Study of Educational Finance, Illinois State University.

U.S. Department of Education, National Center for Education Statistics. February, 1995. *Disparities in Public School District Spending, 1989–90.* NCES 95-300. Washington, DC.

[22]

How and Why Money Matters: An Analysis of Alabama Schools

Ronald F. Ferguson and Helen F. Ladd

Oᴠᴇʀ ᴛʜᴇ ʟᴀsᴛ ᴛʜɪʀᴛʏ ʏᴇᴀʀs, many researchers have investigated the empirical relationship between measurable inputs into schooling and outcomes as measured by student performance. Yet the correct reading of the evidence is not clear. In a series of influential survey articles covering most of the published empirical literature, Eric Hanushek argued that the public inputs into schooling—namely, teacher-pupil ratios, attributes of teachers such as advanced education and years of experience, and expenditures on administration and facilities—exert no consistent effect on student performance on standardized tests.[1] In a reanalysis of essentially the same literature, Larry Hedges, Richard Laine, and Rob Greenwald come to the opposite conclusion: that school inputs not only affect student outcomes, but also that the effects are large enough to be relevant for policy.[2]

To some people, the entire debate about whether school resources affect educational outcomes is frivolous, either because the answer is obvious or because even if systematic relationships are not found, the policy implications are not clear.[3] To others, the empirical studies are not very meaningful because they focus on too narrow a range of educational outcomes (like test scores) and include the wrong explanatory variables.[4] This paper starts from a different observation: none of the literature surveys just mentioned makes an attempt to distinguish the more methodologically sound studies from those with significant weaknesses. For reasons that we spell out be-

---

The authors would like to thank Anthony Shen for able research assistance. In addition, they are grateful for the thoughtful comments of William Clune, Ronald Ehrenberg, Eric Hanushek, Richard Murnane, and other participants in the Brookings conference.

1. Hanushek (1986, 1989, 1996).
2. Hedges, Laine, and Greenwald (1994).
3. See Murnane (1991).
4. See, for example, Smith, Scoll, and Link (1995).

low, we believe that an additional attempt to quantify the relationship between certain school inputs, such as class size, and outcomes, such as student performance on standardized tests, can be a worthwhile and important endeavor.

This paper reports the results of such an attempt to measure the systematic effects of school inputs on student test scores. The study is based on both district-level and student-level data from Alabama. The district-level analysis allows us to compare results from Alabama with those from Ferguson's widely cited study of Texas school districts that finds systematic relationships between school inputs and student outcomes.[5] The analysis at the student level allows us to compare the district results with those from a more disaggregated analysis that is more methodologically sound. This chapter provides new evidence that schools' inputs affect educational outcomes and that the effects are large enough to be relevant for deliberations about educational spending.

Methodological Considerations

When economists investigate the relationship between educational inputs and outputs, they use a production function approach. In the education context, this usually means a function in which the output is a measure of student achievement, like test scores, and the inputs include measures of purchased school inputs (like the ratio of teachers to pupils) and other inputs like student, family, and community background characteristics. The production function approach immediately raises a number of questions. We will begin by defending the use of test scores as a reasonable measure of educational output. Then, we address three further methodological considerations: specification, aggregation, and measurement of the key school inputs. We believe that empirical work done with attention to these methodological issues, like the work we present, is worthy of greater attention than other studies, because it is more likely to generate accurate results.

Using Test Scores to Measure Educational Outcomes

There is a long tradition of using test scores to measure educational outcomes—and an equally long tradition of researchers and educators who

---

5. Ferguson (1991a, b).

are skeptical of the practice. In the tradition of human capital models, education is an investment that yields returns primarily in the form of higher income. Hence, to many economists, the more interesting and relevant outcomes are subsequent returns in the labor market. In one well-known study, David Card and Alan Krueger claim that variations in school inputs across states in the 1920s and 1930s influenced the earnings of men in the 1960s and 1970s.[6]

Such work is thought-provoking and worthwhile, but it inadvertently points out a major advantage of using test scores rather than labor market returns to measure student outcomes: Test scores are available at the time the education is provided, while earnings and labor market histories are not available for years or decades.[7] Fortunately, test scores are also a proxy, albeit imperfect, for future success. They are clearly a good indicator of the probability of additional schooling, which has been shown to affect future income. In addition, test scores are among the variables that predict later earnings of those students who do not continue beyond high school. For example, Richard Murnane, John Willett, and Frank Levy show that cognitive ability in math, as measured by math test scores, is a determinant of the wages of 24-year-old men whose education ended with high school. Also of interest is their finding that the effect of cognitive ability on labor market returns has been increasing over time, making test scores a better predictor of future performance now than in the past.[8]

Economists emphasize the effects of education on labor market outcomes. However, to many others, cognitive ability is an end in itself. From this perspective, test scores serve as reasonable measures of the outcomes of education if the tests adequately measure what society wants children to know and be able to do. Standardized tests are clearly imperfect measures of these cognitive skills, especially with respect to higher-order thinking skills. Many states have begun to experiment with alternative forms of assessment. Nonetheless, standardized tests remain the best available measures of output that are valid for comparisons over time and across schools.

---

6. Card and Krueger (1992).

7. In fact, some skeptics make the case that the linkages between educational inputs and labor market returns implied in the Card and Krueger study are so long and tenuous as to be implausible. See, for example, the conclusions of Speakman and Welch (1995).

8. Murnane, Willett, and Levy (1995). Also see evidence on test scores as predictors of racial differences in earnings in Ferguson (1995).

Specification

The production function approach to education, as already mentioned, generally models student learning as a joint product of measured school inputs, student characteristics, and family and community background variables, and a variety of influences that are hard to measure, such as student motivation.

But notice that this specification implies that the input variables all come from the same time period as the measure of outcomes. This assumption raises questions. After all, learning is a cumulative process. Achievement during a given school year will depend not only on the current-year schooling and background variables but also on values of those variables from prior years. Only if the current-year schooling and background variables can reasonably represent values from prior years would the problem of omitting variables from earlier years not be a major concern. For example, if differences across districts in the level of school inputs and background variables had remained relatively stable over time and the pattern of schooling inputs across grades were similar across districts, then district averages of school inputs and background characteristics would capture the effects of both present and prior variables. This condition might be plausible for a model explaining differences in average student achievement across school districts. In fact, if values of school inputs and background characteristics have changed little over time, it could be problematic or even inappropriate to include values for prior years in a production function approach; including separate variables that are very similar over time can create a problem of multicollinearity.

However, when the values of school inputs and background characteristics have changed over time, then an alternative solution is needed. There are several possibilities. One is to argue that a student's learning is determined not only by this year's school inputs and background characteristics, but by all past values of school inputs and background characteristics as well.[9] An alternate possibility is to ask how this year's combination of school inputs and background characteristics affected not the level of a student's achievement, but the gain that the student has made during the last year; this formulation uses only current variables for inputs to education, but looks at change in output.[10] However, these formulations have

---

9. See, for example, Hanushek and Taylor (1990).

10. Actually, these two formulations can be identical, provided that achievement in year $T - 1$ is determined by a model similar in structure to achievement in year T. To see why, consider the following model of the learning of the ith student in year T: $A_{iT} = \alpha_T S_{iT} + \beta_T F_{iT} + \sum_{t=1}^{T-1} \alpha_t S_{it} + \sum_{t=1}^{T-1} \beta_t F_{it} + \epsilon_{iT}$. According to this model, achievement in year T depends not only on the student's schooling experience measured

their difficulties as well. Complete information for all past years is difficult to accumulate and time-consuming to estimate, and, as mentioned before, problems of multicollinearity can easily arise. Using the gain in achievement from one year to the next implies the generally unrealistic assumption that achievement in the current and previous periods are commensurate, so that the difference between them represents learning from one period to the next. It also assumes that past learning does not decay naturally, for example, during the summer vacation.

A closely related specification deals with many of these problems. The achievement of student i at time T appears on the left-hand side of the equation as the dependent variable A. Present achievement then depends on the level of achievement in the previous time period, a vector of school input variables summarized in S, a vector of background characteristic variables summarized in B, and a constant, δ. The task of the researcher is then to estimate the parameters in the regression equation:

$$A_{iT} = \delta + \gamma A_{i,T-1} + \alpha_T S_{iT} + \beta_T B_{iT} + \mu_{iT}.$$

Notice that because of the coefficient before last year's achievement level, there is no longer any need to assume that last year's achievement has not decayed or is immediately comparable to this year's achievement. However, the level of past achievement captures the effect of past inputs into education.

Some authors assert that this value-added formulation also solves the potential bias problem caused by the omission of other unmeasured characteristics, such as student motivation or ability, that might otherwise be correlated with included variables, because the past achievement variable will also capture these effects. However, it does so only under the unrealistic assumption that the omitted variables affect the level of achievement and not its rate of growth.[11] In the more realistic situation in which motivation or ability affects the rate of learning as well as the level of learning, researchers using the value-added form of the equation continue to face the challenge of including a sufficient set of student background variables

---

by S and background characteristics B in year T but also on past history of schooling and family characteristics, as well as on unmeasured factors such as motivation and ability included in the error term, ϵ_{iT}. Now, subtract prior-period achievement from current period achievement, which yields $A_{iT} - A_{i,T-1} = \alpha_T S_{iT} + \beta_T B_{iT} + \mu_{iT}$, where μ_{iT} is the difference between the error term in period T and that in period $T-1$.

11. For example, in the special case in which the unmeasured variable for each student has a constant effect on achievement in each year, the variable cancels out in the change form of the equation. This is the special case used by Hanushek and Taylor (1990).

to minimize the problem of bias from the omitted variables, like motivation or ability, that may be correlated with included regressors.

The analysis of this chapter uses this value-added specification for the equations that treat students as the units of observation. Our school input variables are all measured for a specific grade in a specific year within a school. Because we have data on test scores for individual students and can match a student's test scores to prior-year test scores, our achievement equations include the prior-period test scores of the identical students whose achievement we are trying to explain. Moreover, we can restrict the sample of students to those who were enrolled in that grade in that school throughout the year. Given our goal of determining the effect of school inputs on student achievement, it would be inappropriate to include in the sample students who entered or left the school in the middle of the year. We include a variety of family and school background variables: some are from administrative data at the school level and others are from the census at the level of the zip code area or the school district.

For our district-level analysis, we again focus on the learning of a specific group of students over a well-defined period of time, from the fourth to the ninth grade. However, we are forced to rely on a proxy for prior-period achievement: the test scores of current third and fourth graders, rather than the third and fourth grade scores of current ninth graders five years earlier. Although this synthetic cohort procedure would be unacceptable at the school level, because it would not account for the mobility of students, it is more acceptable at the district level, since it can be regarded as an adjustment for the pre-existing level of learning in the district (see note 31). The analysis below that uses districts as the units of analysis is less precisely specified than the analysis that uses individual students and schools, but it is, nevertheless, in the spirit of a value-added approach.

Aggregation

Various researchers have noted that the quality of a student's school experience varies greatly not only across districts, but also across schools within districts and, what is even more important, among classrooms in specific schools. This observation has led some people to argue that school input variables should be specified at the classroom level, provided that other variables can be appropriately measured.[12] Working in the other direction, however, is the possibility of excessive variation or noise in the

---

12. See Monk (1992).

explanatory variables when disaggregated analysis is used. That noise can be reduced by aggregating the school input variables to a higher level such as the school, the district, or the state. For this reason, the literature on education production functions yields mixed advice on the appropriate degree of aggregation of the school input variables.

Eric Hanushek, Steven Rivkin, and Lori Taylor have recently explored the aggregation issue in the presence of omitted-variable bias.[13] They point out that in studies that use aggregated school data, relevant family or community control variables are left out of the equation. For example, if the study is based on a national survey of youth, community variables are often unavailable since they would require that the location or name of the school be identified. The direction of the bias cannot be unambiguously predicted. However, based on data from the survey High School and Beyond, they conclude that the coefficients of the school input variables that are aggregated to the state or district level are biased upward. Based on this argument, they discount the production function studies that use district- or state-level school variables. Given that a higher proportion of such studies exhibit positive and statistically significant coefficients than is true for the more disaggregated studies, Hanushek, Rivkin, and Taylor conclude that their analysis supports Hanushek's earlier conclusion that school inputs exert no systematic effects on student test scores. These authors are correct that the use of relatively disaggregated school input variables should be preferred to the use of more aggregated variables whenever key control variables are omitted.

However, their criticism falls short of a general indictment. Our empirical work in this chapter is designed to shed light on the aggregation issue through our estimation of equations based on both aggregated and disaggregated data. Our finding that measured school inputs have effects on achievement in both the student- and the district-level analysis counters the conclusion that positive findings emerge only in misspecified models.

Measurement of School Input Variables

Much of the literature concerns the effects of three key measures of schooling inputs: class size, teachers' experience, and teachers' postcollege education. Some studies, however, also examine the role of teacher quality as measured by teacher test scores. Several studies have documented that

---

13. Hanushek, Rivkin, and Taylor (1995).

teachers with higher test scores tend to increase the learning of their students more than teachers with lower scores.[14] Moreover, Ferguson has shown that, other things being equal, school districts have to pay more to attract and retain teachers with higher test scores.[15] Hence we believe it is important to include measures of teachers' skills, and we do so in the equations reported below.

Instead of using a direct measure of class size, most researchers use a proxy: pupils per teacher, or its inverse, teachers per pupil. Pupils per teacher is an imperfect proxy for class size for at least two reasons. First, it understates the true average class size by 20 to 25 percent, because not all teachers are in the classroom all the time. Some have administrative duties, and many have some time away from the classroom during the day. A second problem is that the pupil-teacher ratio typically represents an average across all teachers and students in a school or district. Because some teachers may be teaching special education students in small classes while others are teaching regular students in much larger classes, the average could represent a highly misleading picture of the class size for the typical student who is subject to the standardized tests.[16] Moreover, these factors vary across both schools and districts, which creates a measurement problem and may produce estimates of the effect of class size that are biased toward zero. Clearly, a direct measure of class size is preferable to the use of pupils per teacher, especially when the units of analysis are at a disaggregated level such as a grade within the school, and we use such a measure in this chapter.

Disaggregated Student-Level Analysis

The disaggregated analysis reported in this section is consistent with the criteria set out above for a methodologically sound investigation of the links between school inputs and student outcomes, and thus provides an excellent test of whether school resources matter. We focus on a single cohort of students, those in the fourth grade in Alabama in 1990-91, which consists of 29,544 students in 690 schools.

---

14. Ferguson (1991a, b); Ehrenberg and Brewer (1995).
15. Ferguson (1991a).
16. Typically, special education students are not tested. Only those who are mainstreamed into the regular class take the standardized tests. Hence the appropriate measure of class size is the one that is experienced by the students who are not in special education programs.

Model and Data

The particular version of the value-added model that we use appears as follows:

$$TS_{ij} = \alpha + \beta S_j + \gamma X_{ij}(1 + \lambda Z_j) + \delta Z_j + \mu_j + \epsilon_{ij}.$$

The dependent variable *TS* refers to a student's test score in reading or in math, where the students are indexed with a subscript *i* and the districts are indexed with a subscript *j*. The students included in the sample are those for whom we have fourth grade scores in reading and math on the Stanford Achievement Test (SAT) and third grade scores in the same subjects on the Basic Competency Test (BCT). All student test score data have been standardized across all students in the state who took the particular test to have a mean of zero and a standard deviation of one. Because the students are not identified by name or number in the test score data sets, we matched students by their birthday, gender, grade, and school. In other words, test score data for a fourth grade student were matched to test score data for a third grade student if that student was in the same school and had the same birth date and sex.[17] Although this process may generate some errors, the errors are likely to be small and to exert no obvious bias.

S is a vector of four school input variables, measured for the fourth grade: three teacher variables and class size. All four variables were calculated from teacher files that include teacher responses to a series of questions about their teaching responsibilities, including the size of the classes they teach. We included regular fourth grade teachers; we excluded teachers who taught special education or who were not teaching in the regular classroom. In the absence of data on a student's specific teachers, we assigned to each student in the sample the average characteristics of the fourth grade teachers in the student's school and the average fourth grade class size in the school.

The three variables that measure the characteristics of teachers are the percentage of teachers with more than five years of experience, the percentage of teachers with a master's degree, and average teachers' test scores. The five-year experience horizon reflects the conventional wisdom that new teachers face a learning curve that flattens out after about five years, although experimentation with other cutoffs yields comparable results. Data for teachers' test scores come from the ACT exams that teachers took

---

17. If a double match occurred, we dropped both students from the sample to minimize the chances of including students who were incorrectly matched.

in the process of applying to college.[18] The teachers' test scores have been standardized to have a mean of zero and a standard deviation of one across all teachers of fourth graders for whom we have ACT test scores. Unfortunately, data are available for only one quarter of all the fourth grade teachers and for all the fourth grade teachers in each school in only 35 of the 690 schools in the sample.[19] Where test scores for some, but not all, fourth grade teachers in a school were available, we simply averaged the scores for fourth grade teachers that were available for that school. When no test scores were available at the school level, we substituted the mean of the fourth-grade teacher test scores at the district level. This procedure generated three different variables for teachers' scores, each representing a different degree of completeness in the sample of scores. Of course, the estimates for the variable representing the 35 schools with full data on scores should yield the best estimates of the effect of teacher quality.

X is a vector of student-specific variables, including third-year test scores, and age, race and gender. The age of the student is included to control for whether a student has been held back. Z is a vector of school or district characteristics, while Z' is a subset of the school or district characteristics that are interacted with some of the student-specific variables. In the absence of student-specific data on family income and educational background of the students' parents, the model includes family background measures reported at the zip code level based on 1990 census data or reported at the school level based on administrative records. On average, there are about three schools per zip code area. The parental education variables include the percentages of adults with sixteen or more years of schooling, with twelve to fifteen years, nine to eleven years, and with less than nine years.[20] Family income is proxied by the log of per capita income

---

18. Access to these data was arranged by state officials during the summer of 1992 to facilitate Ferguson's participation in a court challenge to the constitutionality of Alabama's system of public schooling. Given the importance of teachers' test scores and other schooling inputs in predicting student performance in Texas (Ferguson 1991a, b), the purpose of the analysis was to discover for the plaintiffs whether the importance of resources in prior results for Texas applied to schools in Alabama as well.

19. The sample of 690 schools includes 69 for which we had to fill in some missing data for some of the control variables. Data were sometimes missing on parental education at the zip code level and, in a few cases, for the percentage of students on free or reduced-price lunch. To fill in the missing parental education data, we used districtwide values from the census. For the free and reduced-price lunch variables, we used other socioeconomic variables in the model to predict the missing values. Note that any school that teaches fourth grade but not third grade is excluded because we had to match students by school. Had students been identified by number on the files, these schools could have been included.

20. The first three of the parental education variables are available from the census at the zip code level. The last one, the percentage of adults with less than a high school

at the zip code level and the percentage of students in the school who are approved for either free or reduced-price lunch.[21] The model also includes one other school-level variable—the percentage of students in the school's fourth grade who were not at that same school in the third grade—as a measure of the mobility of students into the school, and four other district characteristics: district enrollment, the percentage of students in public schools, the percentage of the district that is urban, and a variable to indicate whether the district is a city district in contrast to a county district.

Finally, α, β, γ, and δ are scalars to be estimated in the equation. ϵ is a student-specific error term, and μ is a school-specific error term. Both μ and ϵ are assumed to be independent of the included explanatory variables and to be uncorrelated across units of observation.

Because students are grouped within schools, we estimated the equation as a hierarchical linear model rather than as a standard regression model. The advantage of a hierarchical linear model is that it explicitly embeds the student-level model within a school- or district-level model, and thus allows us to account for grouping of students by schools.[22] (See the appendix for the full model and description of all the variables.)

Results for Control Variables

This equation explains from 54 to 62 percent of the variation in test scores among students and from 59 to 80 percent of the variation among schools. The four school input variables are clearly the focus of our analysis. But before discussing them, we briefly summarize the effects of some of the other variables. A complete summary of regression results appears in the appendix.

At the student level, the model includes prior-year test score variables; indicator variables for being African American, other nonwhite, or male; and an age variable, with the latter four interacted with some school-level variables. Prior-year reading and math scores are each entered as two variables to allow for the possibility that students who performed well on the third grade test may have gained at a different rate compared with those who performed poorly. In each case, the third grade test score variable

---

education, is available only at the district level.

21. Because the state does not collect school-level information on the number of students approved for free or reduced-price lunches, we worked with the Alabama Department of Education to collect this information directly from every district in the state.

22. See Bryk and Raudenbush (1992).

is split at its mean of zero, with above-average test scores generating an additional coefficient to be added to the coefficient on the basic variable. Third grade reading scores emerge as an important predictor of both reading and math scores in the fourth grade. Third grade math scores are also a significant predictor but, not surprisingly, math skill seems to be less important for reading than reading is for math. In addition, the positive coefficients on the third grade test scores for students scoring above average indicate that students who scored well in the third grade appear to retain more and to gain more during the fourth grade than their fellow students.

African American students typically perform less well than white students even after controlling for the other variables in the equation, a pattern that Ferguson has shown becomes even more pronounced in later grades.[23] In interviews, teachers and other community-based professionals who work with African American youth suggest that attitudes and behaviors that interfere with academic performance operate most strongly in urban environments and tend to become more prevalent (especially for boys) when children reach the ages of 9 or 10—around the fourth grade. At this age, they argue, community-based interventions can make a tremendous difference.[24]

If various attitudes and behaviors cause the academic performance of African American boys to drift downward beginning in the middle elementary years, and if the same behaviors are more prevalent in urban than in rural environments, then one would expect to observe some interaction effects between race and gender and between race and urban residence. We find such effects. The estimated coefficient on the interaction of race and urban residence indicates that differences in test scores between African Americans and whites are larger in districts that are more urban. Further, while males on average do less well on fourth grade tests than do females of the same racial group, male fourth graders in schools where high percentages of the students are African American do even less well relative to their female counterparts than males in schools with fewer African Americans. Although these interaction effects are not very large, they are statistically significant and they probably foreshadow trends that continue beyond the fourth grade.

As noted earlier, all of the variables that represent socioeconomic indexes are measured at the group level. Among the parental education variables, only the presence of a large proportion of college-educated adults

23. Ferguson (1991b).
24. Ferguson (1994).

appears to exert a consistent and positive effect on student test scores. The percentages of students receiving free or reduced-price lunches enter negatively, as expected, but with more consistency and precision for the free-lunch than the reduced-price lunch category. Per capita income adds no explanatory power. In the math equation, the negative coefficient on the fraction of students who were new to the school in the fourth grade indicates that the demands of accommodating new students have adverse effects on the learning of students continuing from the previous year. The district-level variables contribute little with the exception of district enrollment; this coefficient implies that students in large districts perform better, all else being equal, than their peers in smaller districts.

Effects of School Inputs

The estimates here show that measurable school inputs—specifically teacher quality, percentage of teachers with master's degrees, and class size—do affect student test scores.

The first measure of teachers' test scores (and the only one based on complete data) enters with a positive and statistically significant coefficient in the reading equation.[25] The coefficient in the math equation is positive but smaller relative to its standard error.[26] Measurement error in the other two test score variables suggests their coefficients are downward biased and can be largely discounted.

How large is the effect of teacher quality, as measured by test scores? The 0.10 coefficient for reading implies that a difference of one standard deviation in the distribution of teacher test scores would generate a difference of 0.10 standard deviations in the distribution of student test scores. To put this figure in perspective, consider two schools, one serving pre-

---

25. We experimented with two additional indicator variables that are not reported here. One variable equaled one for observations that used the school-level measure for teachers' scores and was zero otherwise. The second equaled one for observations that used the district-level measure and zero otherwise. The omitted base category was for the thirty-five schools that had test scores for all fourth grade teachers. These indicator variables had very small coefficients with t-statistics well below one. Other coefficients were essentially unchanged.

26. The lack of precision is not surprising, given the limited number of schools for which complete data are available. Recall that the coefficient is estimated based on a sample of only thirty-five schools.

dominantly African American students with low-quality teachers and one serving predominantly white students with higher-quality teachers. Our results imply that an increase of one standard deviation in the quality of the first school's teachers could offset about half of the average negative effect on reading scores estimated for an African American student relative to a white student in a school district that is 50 percent urban.[27] For the combined math and reading results, the coefficients suggest that the increase in teacher test scores would offset about two-thirds of the average difference between being African American and being white in a 50 percent urban district.

Alternatively, the effect of teacher test scores can be compared with the estimated effects of the socioeconomic characteristics of the community. For example, the estimated coefficients imply that it would take an increase of 25 percentage points in the percentage of college-educated adults (which is equivalent to slightly less than a two–standard deviation change) to achieve the same gain in reading test scores that could be obtained by substituting teachers with test scores one standard deviation higher than those of the school's current teachers.[28]

Although the fraction of teachers with master's degrees appears to have little or no effect on reading scores, it exerts a small positive effect on student math scores: a one–standard deviation increase in the fraction of teachers with a master's degree (0.33 points) would increase student test scores by 0.026 standard deviations, about one-quarter the effect of a standard deviation increase in teacher test scores. In contrast, the teacher experience variable, teachers with five or more years of experience, apparently exerts no significant effect in either subject.[29]

---

27. Calculated from the reading equation as $-0.156 + 50 \times -0.001$.

28. The effect of the socioeconomic status of the community should be distinguished from that of the student's family. We predict that if data had been available on the education level of the student's parents, larger estimated effects of adult education would have emerged. The results for the community-level education variable correspond to the following thought experiment: they measure the effects of taking a child (and her family) out of a poor environment, for example, an urban housing project, and putting that child down in a school in an upper-class neighborhood where a much larger proportion of the adults have a college education, while holding all else constant, including school input measures.

29. Although this latter finding may well represent the true relationship, a cleaner test of the relationship between teacher experience and student learning requires more complete data on teacher test scores. Within our sample, teacher test scores are negatively associated with experience, presumably because many teachers with high scores do not remain in the profession. Because old teachers are underrepresented in the data on ACT scores, the experience variable may be picking up some teacher quality effects as well as experience, which would bias the coefficient downward.

Figure 8-1. *Effect of Lower Class Size on Reading and Math Test Scores for Fourth Graders*[a]

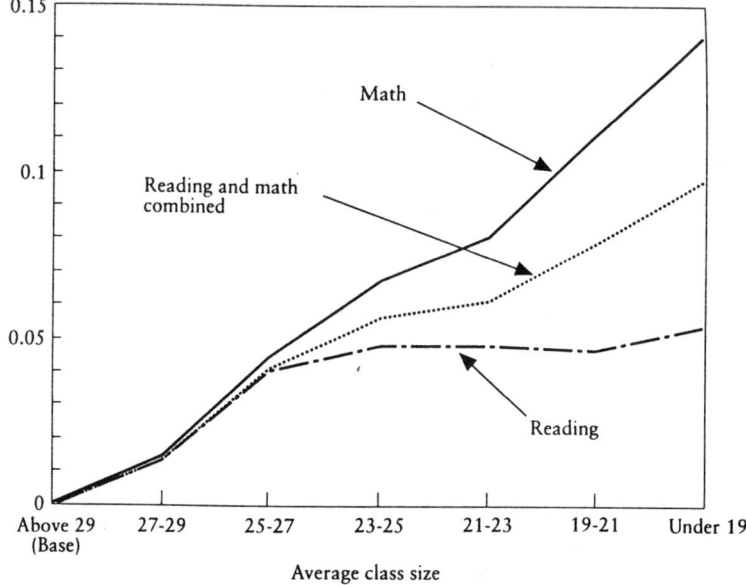

a. The endpoints of the graph correspond to the estimated coefficients for the largest and the smallest class sizes (reported in table 8A-1). The intermediate points are averages of the coefficients of the specified class size and the next larger and next smaller size.

Class size is specified as a series of variables, which allows us to examine the pattern of effects as class sizes are reduced over the relevant range. Each estimated coefficient represents the difference in student test scores relative to the base class size of over twenty-nine students. Although the pattern in the coefficients is not completely monotonic, the general trajectories are clear and are shown graphically in figure 8-1. For math, class sizes of under nineteen generate student test scores that exceed those for the base by 0.14 standard deviations. For reading, the estimated effects are somewhat smaller, about 0.05 standard deviations, and for the combined scores, about 0.10 standard deviations. For reading, the gains level off at a class size in the mid-twenties. But for math and for the combined scores, gains in test scores occur throughout the relevant range of reductions in class size. More learning apparently occurs in smaller fourth grade classes than in larger classes, especially in math. Further investigation of the math gains indicates that the gains from smaller classes are greater for girls than for boys; a class size of less than nineteen increases girls' math scores by 0.17 standard deviations relative to the base case, while a similar class size increases boys' scores by only 0.10 standard deviations.[30]

This student-level analysis supports the view that various measurable school inputs affect student learning. In particular, teacher quality—as measured by test scores and the proportion of teachers with master's degrees—and class size appear to affect learning. In contrast, we have no evidence that more teacher experience, all else held constant, generates gains in student learning. These measurable effects at the micro level for fourth graders are supported by similar findings from analysis at the district level for eighth and ninth graders.

District-Level Analysis

Compared with the student-level analysis, the district-level models we present here are potentially subject to more methodological criticism. Nonetheless, we believe they contain some useful information. Our analysis of student test scores for 127 public school districts in Alabama indicates once again that students learn more when their teachers are more skilled as measured by their own test scores, when a larger proportion of teachers have master's degrees, and when class sizes are smaller. Once again, teacher experience has no measurable effect. These effects emerge for both reading and math. For economy of exposition, we report here only the results for math, which tend to be a bit stronger than those for reading. The consistency of results between the student-level and the district-level findings suggests that the assumptions underlying the district-level analysis are plausible.

The Model and Data

At the district level, we estimate gains in learning between the fourth and the ninth grades as a function of, among other things, the school inputs

---

30. For girls, the relevant coefficients (and t-statistics) on the six class-size variables, in descending order, are 0.007 (0.16), 0.057 (1.40), 0.034 (0.82), 0.063 (1.38), 0.107 (2.13), 0.169 (3.05). For boys, they are 0.024 (0.58), 0.074 (1.78), 0.057 (1.37), 0.105 (2.28), 0.103 (2.00), and 0.105 (1.86). These results emerge from models not reported here that are estimated separately for girls and boys. Coefficients for the other school inputs, such as teacher test scores and master's degrees, are virtually identical for girls and boys.

available to students at the intervening grade levels. The choice of grades was dictated largely by the availability of test data. The state administers the Stanford Achievement Test in grades 4 and 8 and the Basic Competency Test in grades 3, 6, and 9. We define the dependent variable as the average composite of math scores from the SAT for the eighth grade and from the BCT for the ninth grade for the 1989–90 school year. The SAT, BCT, and composite scores have all been standardized to have a mean of zero and a standard deviation of one across districts.

Because we have data at the district level for only one year, 1989–90, we are unable to implement a true value-added model. Instead, we include as explanatory variables reading and math scores based on the average of the third grade BCT and the fourth grade SAT during the 1989–90 school year. One can view these as the scores of the younger brothers and sisters of the current eighth and ninth grade students and, therefore, as proxies for the scores that the current eighth and ninth graders would have earned when they were in the third and fourth grades.[31]

Like the disaggregated analysis, the equations include four school input variables: three teacher variables and class size. Except for the teacher test score variable, the input measures are based only on regular classes and regular teachers in grades 4 through 9. For example, class sizes are based on the responses of teachers who taught in one of those grades rather than on those of all teachers in the district. Because of the large amount of missing data on teacher test scores, the average teacher test score variable is based on all teachers teaching regular classes in the district rather than just those in grades 4 through 9.[32] Like the scores for the students, the test scores

31. This approach is reasonable if the following assumptions are met. First, the position of each district relative to all the other districts in terms of the distribution of families by socioeconomic status remains relatively constant over the five-year period. From this assumption, it follows that the backgrounds of the students in each district in the third (or fourth) grade in 1984–85 would be similar to the backgrounds of third (or fourth) grade students in the district in 1989–90. Second, the position of each district relative to all other districts in terms of the school resources available in each grade remains relatively constant over the same period, which implies that the third and fourth grade students in 1984–85 would have been exposed to the same school effects in the earlier grades as third and fourth grade students in 1989–90. Third, the exposure to learning during grades 4 through 9 in each of the following years can be measured by the resources available in each grade in 1989–90. Although these assumptions are quite strong, we believe that they hold in an approximate way for data at the district level. They would clearly be much less acceptable at the school level.

32. Moreover, the district average was calculated as a weighted average of the actual average for young teachers and an estimate for more experienced teachers. We used this procedure because teacher ACT scores were available for about 60 percent of the relevant teachers who had less than five years of experience but for only a much smaller proportion of more experienced teachers. For the young teachers, we used the actual average ACT

for teachers have been standardized across districts to have a mean of zero and a standard deviation of one.

In addition to the school input variables, the equation includes parental education variables, per capita income, and a family poverty variable (the percentage of families with children ages 5 to 18 living in poverty) to control for the socioeconomic backgrounds of the students. All of these data come from the 1990 Census of Population. Conveniently, school districts in Alabama have boundaries that correspond to either cities or counties, so that data from the census cover the appropriate geographic areas. The equation also includes two enrollment variables—total enrollment and percentage of students who are nonwhite, with the latter also interacted with the percentage of the district that is urban—and three other district characteristics: the percentage of students in public schools, the percentage of the district that is urban, and a variable to indicate if the district is a city district.

The regressions are based on data for the 127 of the 131 districts for which complete data are available. Each observation is weighted by the square root of the district's enrollment, the standard correction for heteroskedasticity when observations are averages of groups that differ in size.

Results

The coefficients for various multivariate regression models were estimated using weighted least squares. The complete results are reported in the appendix. But the clear conclusion emerges that measurable school inputs affect educational outcomes. Only teacher experience has no estimated effect. A difference of one standard deviation in teacher test scores increases student test scores by about 0.25 standard deviations. Given that the analysis covers five years of schooling, the magnitude of this effect is proportionate to the smaller (and less precisely estimated) figure of 0.055 for math from the student-level analysis, which applies to a single year.

The fraction of teachers with master's degrees exerts a positive effect on student learning. A difference of 8 percentage points in the proportion of

---

scores within each district. For the more experienced teachers, we regressed their average test scores by district on the average scores for the younger teachers and the average experience of the older teachers for whom we had test scores, and used the regression to predict the average test scores of all the older teachers within each district. We then calculated the district average as the weighted average of the average ACT scores for young teachers within the district and the estimated average for old teachers, weighted by the district-specific shares of young and old teachers.

such teachers (equivalent to one standard deviation in the distribution across districts) is associated with a difference of 0.11 standard deviations in student test scores (0.08 times 1.43). These effects are smaller than those for teacher test scores, but not trivial.

Within the range of average class sizes in the sample, smaller class sizes typically generate higher test scores. When class size is measured as a simple average across the district, a reduction of three in average class size (say from twenty-seven to twenty-four) would increase student test scores by 0.26 (three times the coefficient), a magnitude only slightly smaller than the effect of an increase of one standard deviation in teacher test scores. These results are robust to different specifications. For example, when we estimated these equations *without* using the third and fourth grade test scores as a control, it remained true that the school input variables were significant and of the expected direction. To check for nonlinearities in the relationship and the possibility of a threshold class size below which no further gains would be obtained, we entered class size as a series of variables. We found that reducing class size from an average of twenty-six to twenty-five or twenty-four is associated with increasingly higher math test scores. There are few observations below that number, which makes the results unstable, but it is fair to say that we find no evidence that eighth and ninth grade test scores are higher as students are exposed to class sizes below twenty-three. Specific results for these alternate regressions are also presented in the appendix.

With respect to the control variables, we note that neither per capita income nor the poverty rate among families with children enters with a statistically significant coefficient. This lack of effect emerges despite the fact that the simple correlation between the log of per capita income and test scores for math is large and positive ($r = 0.59$) and that between the poverty rate and test scores for math is large and negative ($r = -0.57$). Presumably, any effects of income operate through the correlation of income with other variables in the equations, such as the fraction of adults with a college education, the fraction of the population that is urban, or the fraction of students who are African American. Using the percentage of students on free and reduced-price lunch does not change any of the results.

The relative importance of the estimated effects is shown in table 8-1. The table shows the contributions of each type of variable to the predicted difference between districts that score in the top quartile and those that score in the bottom quartile of the distribution of district-average math scores. The actual difference between the high- and the low-scoring dis-

Table 8-1. *Components of the Predicted Difference in Eighth and Ninth Grade Math Scores*

Component	Contribution to predicted difference (percent)
School inputs	
Teachers' ACT scores	15.1
Teachers with master's degrees	6.1
Teachers with 5 or more years' experience	2.8
Average class size	7.5
Other determinants	
Adults with 16 or more years of schooling	17.0
Poverty rate	2.1
Percent nonwhite	3.3
Interaction of percent nonwhite with percent urban	7.1
District enrollment characteristics (enrollment, city versus county, percent public schools, percent urban)	8.2
Third and fourth grade reading and math scores	30.9

Source: Based on coefficients in column 2 of table 8A-2 and mean values of explanatory variables for districts in the top and bottom 25 percent of the distribution of district-average math scores for eighth and ninth grades.

tricts in the math scores for eighth and ninth graders is 2.77 standard deviations. The predicted difference is 1.57 standard deviations. Hence the prediction captures more than half of the actual difference. The school input variables combine to account for 31 percent, with teachers' scores accounting for half of this contribution. Race, parental education, and variables that control for characteristics of the district account for an additional 38 percent of the predicted difference. The third and fourth grade scores contribute 31 percent of the total predicted difference in eighth and ninth grade scores.

The contributions of the school input variables reflect input levels that vary between the low- and high-scoring districts. Expressed in standard deviations of each input variable, the differences between the high- and the low-scoring districts are 1.22 for teachers' ACT scores, 1.53 for the share of teachers with master's degrees, 0.55 for the share of teachers with over five years' experience, and 0.76 (1.74 students per class) for average class size. The analysis implies that a narrowing of these differences in school inputs would lead to smaller differences in student test scores between low- and high-scoring districts. Because the three schooling inputs that exert some explanatory power—teachers' test scores, teachers' education, and class size—all cost money, our finding that they affect student test scores means that money matters as well. We now address the importance of money more directly.

Instructional Spending

One additional benefit of carrying out the district-level analysis is that it allows us to generate estimates of how changes in instructional spending could affect students' test scores. The obvious approach here is simply to use the same basic specification and the same dependent variables, but to replace the school input measures with the level of per pupil spending. However, this approach will not work well, because spending cannot be treated as an exogenous variable. In Alabama, there is compensatory spending in districts where student performance on standardized tests is the poorest. Thus, not only does spending affect performance, but student performance affects spending. As a result, no systematic relationship emerges between student test scores and actual instructional spending.

The reverse causality is confirmed by formal tests for endogeneity. Specifically, a Durbin-Wu-Hausman test for endogeneity (not shown here) clearly rejects the null hypothesis that spending is exogenous. In contrast, the same test implies that teachers' test scores are exogenous to student performance. Results for class size, teachers' experience and master's degrees are more mixed, but our judgment is that these variables should also be treated as exogenous to student performance for the present analysis.[33] Spending is the only measure of schooling resources for which the null hypothesis of exogeneity is clearly and persuasively rejected.[34]

To find the effect of spending on student performance, we use an instrumental variable approach that provides estimates of instructional spending

---

33. When an instrumental variables estimate for class size is used along with the unadjusted numbers for the other variables, the estimated effects of class size are even larger than those reported here. Similarly, when instrumental variables estimates for teacher experience or master's degrees are used, the measured effects are stronger for some, though not all, specifications. When instrumented estimates for class size, experience and master's degrees are entered together, an F-test for joint significance shows statistical significance but collinearity among the three that makes their separate effects difficult to distinguish.

34. The endogeneity of spending can be reconciled with the exogeneity of class size as follows. A close look at the districts that rank in the bottom 10 percent of the test score distribution shows that such districts actually spend 12 percent more per student for instruction and 17 percent more per student for noninstructional inputs than would be predicted by the exogenous explanatory variables reported in table 8-2. While these eleven districts clearly spend more money than the equation would otherwise predict, they do not have smaller class sizes than predicted. Thus the additional spending is apparently not being allocated to smaller class sizes for the typical student.

Table 8-2. *Determinants of Instructional and Noninstructional Spending per Pupil*[a]

Dependent variable	Ln (instructional spending per pupil)	Ln (noninstructional spending per pupil)
Ln (property value per student)	0.079	0.111
	(3.68)	(3.59)
Ln (per capita income)	0.192	0.035
	(5.16)	(0.65)
Enrollment in the district	−0.005	−0.012
	(4.55)	(7.25)
Number of schools in the district	0.003	0.007
	(3.35)	(6.59)
Constant	4.683	5.743
	(16.08)	(13.68)
Adjusted R^2	0.453	0.401
N	129	129

a. Estimated using weighted least squares. Numbers in parentheses are absolute values of *t*-statistics. Dependent variable is natural logarithm of instructional or noninstructional spending per pupil, by district.

that are purged of the reverse causation from poor student performance to more spending. Our predictors for (the natural logarithm of) instructional spending per pupil, and also for comparison, noninstructional spending, are shown in table 8-2. Property value and per capita income represent demand variables: the greater the local wealth, the greater is likely to be the local financial support for education. The other two variables represent cost variables. Larger enrollment will lead to lower costs per student if there are economies of scale. Controlling for enrollment, more schools may mean higher costs because of the fixed costs of running each school. These variables enter with the predicted signs and are statistically significant. The only anomaly is the income variable in the noninstructional spending equation, which might possibly be explained by high noninstructional costs associated with the administration of special education programs. The high correlation between instructional and noninstructional spending and the stronger conceptual link between instructional spending and student performance led us to include only instructional spending in the equation that predicts students' test scores.

The new equation for test scores uses the same basic specification and the same dependent variables as before, but replaces the school input measures with the *estimated* measure of spending. We tried two different ways of specifying the spending variable: log-linear form and a form that allows the effect of spending to vary depending on whether spending is below or above the median.[35] Complete results from the estimation are available in the appendix.[36] We conclude that, all else held constant, districts with lower estimated spending have lower test scores.

Consider the estimated effect of a 10 percent difference in instructional spending, which would represent about one and one-half standard deviations in the distribution of predicted instructional spending across Alabama districts. With the linear specification of the spending variable, this difference in spending would correspond to a difference of 0.356 standard deviations in average scores across districts. The nonlinear specification indicates that the effect of increased spending is concentrated among the districts whose spending levels are below the median: for these districts, the jump would be 0.881 standard deviations. This large effect approximates the difference between the tenth percentile and the median of student test scores. When spending is above the median, the estimated effect of higher spending is small and not statistically different from zero. This general pattern holds true whether or not third and fourth grade scores are included in the regression.

The implicit consequences for individual students are not trivial. The student-level data used above for the third and fourth grades show that the standard deviation of BCT scores in the student-level data is about twice the standard deviation of the district-average score. For the SAT, the student-level standard deviation is three times the district-average deviation. If the same proportions hold for eighth and ninth graders, a 10 percent difference in spending for districts that are below the median in spending

---

35. If instructional spending is above its median value, the marginal effect of spending is the sum of the estimates from the first and second row of the table. To implement this specification, the supplementary variable to which the second coefficient for instructional spending applies equals zero when the log of instructional spending is below its median value. Above the median spending level, it equals the log of instructional spending minus its median value. Hence the variable to which the second coefficient applies "turns on" at the median value of instructional spending. Alternative specifications that allowed for changes in slope at the first and third quartiles of instructional spending showed no statistically significant changes in slope at these points.

36. Because the coefficients of per capita income were small and insignificant in table 8A-2, we treated it as an exogenous instrument for the purposes of modeling instructional spending and excluded it from the equations explaining test scores reported in table 8A-3. Its negative correlation with student test scores, all else held constant, means that its inclusion in the table 8A-3 equations strengthens the conclusion that instructional spending affects test scores. When per capita income is included in the equations of table 8A-3, its coefficient is always negative with t-values that range from -1.0 to -1.92. All of the coefficients on instructional spending become larger by about 20 percent.

corresponds to roughly one-third to one-half of a standard deviation of change among individual students in the statewide distribution.

The predicted effects of spending in Alabama, especially for districts below the median in terms of per pupil spending, are remarkably large. Because most other states spend more than Alabama, we would not expect to find such large spending effects in other states. But Alabama has been among the states spending the least for education for decades, and districts at the bottom of the Alabama distribution of spending are surely among the most weakly staffed and poorly equipped in the country. For such districts, our results suggest that sustained additional funding can make a substantial difference. Current spending patterns suggest that the state is now addressing some of the historical inequalities in spending.

Conclusions

Our analysis of the determinants of student test scores in Alabama provides strong support for the hypothesis that measurable school inputs affect student learning. Moreover, the results for the district-level analysis confirm and reinforce Ferguson's 1991 results for school districts in Texas. Given our attention to good data, a large sample, and a sound specification, we believe that these results are credible and deserve attention.

Three of the four school input variables we consider—teacher test scores, teacher education, and class size—appear to affect student learning. The skills of teachers as measured by their test scores exert consistently strong and positive effects on student learning despite the fact that the data are limited and test scores are an imperfect measure of teachers' skill, which suggests that teacher skills are extremely important. The primary unresolved issue is the level of the class size threshold below which further reductions would lead to no additional systematic gains in student learning. If a threshold exists, we are confident that it is no higher than the mid-twenties—in the range of twenty-three to twenty-five.

Finally, the finding that measurable and costly school inputs affect learning means that money matters. Our direct analysis of the effects of instructional spending based on an instrumental variables approach reinforces this conclusion, especially for low-spending districts. Of course, we are not suggesting that additional spending will always or immediately increase student learning or that it is a prerequisite for learning gains. In some schools, significant gains may come not through additional funding, but rather through school restructuring.[37] Indeed, significant restructuring may well be a more productive alternative for schools that already have relatively high quality teachers or small class sizes but still perform poorly. However, restructuring and higher spending are not mutually exclusive; there will be times to focus on one, or the other, or on a combination of the two.

Some other suggestive findings emerge from our analysis. For example, we find that introducing new students into schools at the fourth grade reduces the performance of students in those schools who are continuing from the third grade. If this finding is borne out in other studies, it would suggest that housing and education policies designed to reduce the frequency with which students change schools may improve test scores even for the students who would not have been among the movers.

In addition, this study hints that it may be beneficial to devote resources to activities that strengthen the academic commitment of students who are prone to disengage from classroom learning. Even after controlling for measured school and community inputs, African American children—and especially boys in urban areas—have smaller test score gains between the third and fourth grades than whites. These findings may reflect systematic social forces that operate inside and outside of the classroom to reduce the academic commitment of a disproportionate share of African American children. Hence, in addition to delivering adequate and equitable levels of the educational inputs upon which this chapter focuses, it may also be necessary to allocate resources to identify, to understand, and to confront destructive social forces that operate in and around local school communities.

Appendix

The hierarchical linear model takes the following form where all variables other than the dependent variable Y are defined in table 8A-1. Y is the math, reading, or composite test score for the ith student in the jth school. As can be seen, we implemented the model as a random-intercept model, which limits the error terms to two types, one that appears in the level 1 model (R) and one ($U0$) that appears in the equation for $B0$ at the second level. Other coefficients in the second level are estimated as fixed effects, or in other words, without error terms.

37. As examples of restructuring, see chapter 9 in this volume.

Level-1 model:

$$Y = B0 + B1 \times (ZR90) + B2 \times (ZM90) + B3 \times (ZR90H)$$
$$+ B4 \times (ZM90H) + B5 \times (BLACK) + B6 \times (OTHER)$$
$$+ B7 \times (AGE91) + B8 \times (MALE) + R.$$

Level-2 model:

$$B0 = G00 + G01 \times (ZREALACT) + G02 \times (ZREALSCH)$$
$$+ G03 \times (ZREALDIS) + G04 \times (CS2728)$$
$$+ G05 \times (CS2526) + G06 \times (CS2324) + G07 \times (CS2122)$$
$$+ G08 \times (CS1920) + G09 \times (CSLT19)$$
$$+ G010 \times (P5PLUS4) + G011 \times (MASTER4)$$
$$+ G012 \times (LTHS) + G013 \times (PCTHSGZ)$$
$$+ G014 \times (PCOLGRZ) + G015 \times (PLUNCHF)$$
$$+ G016 \times (PLUNCHR) + G017 \times (PCTPUBS)$$
$$+ G018 \times (PCTURB) + G019 \times (CAME)$$
$$+ G020 \times (CITYDIST) + G021 \times (ENRL) + U0.$$

$B1 = G10$

$B2 = G20$

$B3 = G30$

$B4 = G40$

$B5 = G50 + G51 \times (PCTURB)$

$B6 = G60 + G61 \times (PCTURB)$

$B7 = G70 + G71 \times (PCTURB) + G72 \times (SBLACK)$
$\quad + G73 \times (SOTHER)$

$B8 = G80 + G81 \times (PCTURB) + G82 \times (SBLACK)$
$\quad + G83 \times (SOTHER).$

Table 8A-1. *Determinants of Reading and Math Test Scores for Fourth Graders in Alabama Schools*[a]

Variable	Reading	Math	Reading and math combined
School input variables			
Teacher ACT score (average for schools with scores for all teachers)	0.103** (2.01)	0.055 (0.85)	0.079 (1.52)
Teacher ACT score (average for schools with scores for some teachers)	0.011 (0.96)	0.003 (0.19)	0.007 (0.56)
Teacher ACT score (district average for schools with scores for no teachers)	−0.011 (0.37)	0.004 (0.11)	−0.003 (0.09)
Teachers with master's degrees (proportion)	0.016 (0.52)	0.080** (2.05)	0.048 (1.54)
Teachers with 5 or more years' experience (proportion)	−0.016 (0.40)	−0.044 (0.87)	−0.030 (0.73)
Class size			
29 and over	Base	Base	Base
27 to 28	0.013 (0.44)	0.014 (0.34)	0.013 (0.42)
25 to 26	0.055* (1.83)	0.069* (1.74)	0.062** (1.98)
23 to 24	0.048 (1.62)	0.048 (1.24)	0.048 (1.56)
21 to 22	0.030 (0.90)	0.085** (1.96)	0.057* (1.67)**
19 to 20	0.055 (1.50)	0.107** (2.23)	0.079** (2.10)
Under 19	0.053 (1.31)	0.140** (2.71)	0.097** (2.35)
Student-level control variables			
Third grade reading score	0.213** (27.07)	0.084** (10.84)	0.149** (22.36)
Third grade reading score if greater than 0 (add coefficient to previous coefficient)	1.201** (59.84)	0.791** (40.09)	0.997** (58.86)
Third grade math score	−0.008 (0.95)	0.187** (22.90)	0.090** (12.80)
Third grade math score if greater than 0 (add coefficient to previous coefficient)	0.499* (28.73)	0.825** (48.26)	0.663** (45.18)
African American, 0-1 variable	−0.156** (7.35)	0.016 (0.77)	−0.070** (3.84)

Table 8A-1 *(continued)*

Variable	Reading	Math	Reading and math combined
African American, interacted with percent of district that is urban	−0.001** (3.06)	−0.001** (2.79)	−0.001** (3.39)
Nonwhite, non-African American, 0-1 variable	0.052 (1.18)	0.064 (1.46)	0.058 (1.55)
Nonwhite, non-African American, interacted with percent of district that is urban	−0.002** (2.91)	0.001 (1.44)	−0.000 (0.88)
Age of student (years)	−0.171** (13.85)	−0.148** (12.15)	−0.159** (15.28)
Age of student, interacted with percent of district that is urban	0.000 (0.20)	0.000 (0.54)	−0.000 (0.20)
Age of student, interacted with fraction of African American students in fourth grade in the school	0.011** (1.98)	0.018** (2.73)	0.015** (2.86)
Age of student, interacted with fraction of nonwhite and non-African American students in fourth grade in the school	−0.002 (0.17)	−0.006 (0.39)	−0.004 (0.30)
Male student, 0-1 variable	−0.015 (1.01)	−0.052** (3.54)	−0.033** (2.66)
Male student, interacted with percent of district that is urban	−0.000 (0.66)	0.001** (2.66)	0.000 (1.17)
Male student, interacted with fraction African American in grade in school	−0.007 (0.29)	−0.050** (2.22)	−0.028 (1.47)
Male student, interacted with fraction nonwhite and non-African American in grade in school	−0.101 (0.94)	−0.109 (1.04)	−0.103 (1.14)
Group variables[b]			
Adults with 16 or more years of school (percent) (Z)	0.004** (3.58)	0.004** (2.63)	0.004** (3.33)
Adults with 12–15 years of schooling (percent) (Z)	−0.002 (0.98)	−0.001 (0.25)	−0.001 (0.64)
Adults with 9–11 years of schooling (percent) (Z)	Base	Base	Base

Table 8A-1 *(continued)*

Variable	Reading	Math	Reading and math combined
Adults with less than 9 years of schooling (percent) (D)	0.003 (0.75)	0.014** (3.00)	0.008** (2.25)
Per capita income (logarithm) (Z)	−0.017 (0.24)	0.009 (0.10)	0.001 (0.01)
Students receiving free lunch (percent) (S)	−0.003** (4.68)	−0.003** (3.09)	−0.003** (4.34)
Students receiving reduced-price lunch (percent) (S)	−0.003 (1.04)	−0.001 (0.26)	−0.002 (0.65)
New students as percent of fourth grade students (G)	−0.201 (1.46)	−0.487** (2.74)	−0.347** (2.46)
Public school students as percent of all students (D)	0.001 (0.18)	−0.000 (0.03)	0.000 (0.09)
Urban population as percent of district population (D)	0.000 (0.10)	0.001 (0.43)	0.000 (0.33)
City district (not county), 0-1 variable, (D)	0.004 (0.08)	0.031 (0.54)	0.015 (0.33)
District enrollment (D)	0.001* (1.73)	0.003** (3.39)	0.002** (2.92)
Intercept	1.42** (2.09)	0.715 (0.81)	1.02 (1.47)
Number of observations (students)	29,544	29,544	29,544
Number of schools	690	690	690
Variance components			
Student level			
Unconditional variance	0.8301	0.8313	0.7179
Conditional variance	0.3798	0.3660	0.2697
Proportion explained (percent)	54	56	62
School level			
Unconditional variance	0.1877	0.1890	0.1738
Conditional variance	0.0404	0.0774	0.0474
Proportion explained (percent)	79	59	73

*Significant at the .1 level.
**Significant at the .05 level.
a. Based on a random-intercept hierarchical linear model. Dependent variable is fourth grade Stanford Achievement Test Scores. Numbers in parentheses are absolute values of t-statistics.
b. Z = zip code; D = district; S = school; G = grade.

Table 8A-2. *Determinants of Eighth and Ninth Grade Math Scores in 127 Alabama Districts*[a]

Variable	Linear class size		Nonlinear class size	
	Without scores for grades 3 and 4	With scores for grades 3 and 4	Without scores for grades 3 and 4	With scores for grades 3 and 4
Teacher ACT score	0.251** (3.38)	0.223** (3.19)	0.278** (3.60)	0.248** (3.47)
Teachers with master's degrees (percent)	2.442** (2.96)	1.430* (1.81)	2.326** (2.71)	1.172 (1.44)
Teachers with 5 or more years' experience (percent)	0.754 (0.77)	0.859 (0.96)	1.13 (1.13)	1.236 (1.34)
Class size, average	−0.086** (2.98)	−0.078** (2.94)	...	...
Class size				
Over 26	...	...	Base	Base
25–25.9	...	...	0.355** (1.95)	0.349** (2.11)
24–24.9	...	...	0.383** (2.06)	0.444** (2.63)
Under 24	...	...	0.460** (2.76)	0.489** (3.24)
Adults with 16 or more years of schooling (percent)	0.064** (2.58)	0.032 (1.32)	0.064** (2.55)	0.31 (1.24)
Adults with 12–15 years of schooling (percent)	0.022 (0.76)	0.006 (0.22)	0.019 (0.65)	0.002 (0.81)
Adults with 9–11 years of schooling (percent)	Base	Base	Base	Base
Adults with less than 9 years of schooling (percent)	0.055 (1.05)	0.029 (0.61)	0.052 (0.98)	0.002 (0.08)
Per capita income (natural logarithm)	−0.281 (0.303)	−0.484 (0.56)	−0.317 (0.33)	−0.530 (0.60)
Poverty rate for families with children aged 5–18	−0.009 (0.51)	−0.004 (0.21)	−0.007 (0.37)	−0.002 (0.09)
Nonwhite students (percent)	−0.007 (1.15)	−0.002 (0.28)	−0.007 (0.37)	−0.001 (0.20)
Enrollment, total (in thousands)	0.022** (3.87)	0.018** (3.38)	0.021** (3.72)	0.018** (3.45)
Public school students as percent of all students	0.003 (0.13)	−0.015 (0.67)	0.001 (0.04)	−0.018 (0.79)
Urban population (percent)	−0.007* (1.72)	−0.005 (1.30)	−0.008* (1.93)	−0.005 (1.39)

Table 8A-2 *(continued)*

Variable	Linear class size		Nonlinear class size	
	Without scores for grades 3 and 4	With scores for grades 3 and 4	Without scores for grades 3 and 4	With scores for grades 3 and 4
Interaction between percent nonwhite students and percent urban	−0.0002** (2.59)	−0.0001* (1.77)	−0.0001** (2.57)	−0.0001* (1.88)
City district (0-1 variable)	1.48** (5.36)	1.03 (3.78)	1.55** (5.34)	1.06** (3.79)
Reading scores, grades 3 and 4	. . .	0.319* (1.72)	. . .	0.330* (1.77)
Math scores, grades 3 and 4	. . .	0.187 (1.58)	. . .	0.209* (1.76)
Constant	0.164 (0.02)	5.257 (0.54)	−1.809 (0.17)	3.76 (0.38)
Adjusted R^2	0.71	0.75	0.70	0.75

*Significant at the .1 level.
**Significant at the .05 level.
a. Estimated using weighted least squares. Numbers in parentheses are absolute values of *t*-statistics.

Table 8A-3. *Effect of Instructional Spending on Eighth and Ninth Grade Math Scores in 127 Alabama Districts*[a]

Variable	Without scores for grades 3 and 4		With scores for grades 3 and 4	
	Linear spending	Nonlinear spending	Linear spending	Nonlinear spending
Ln (predicted instructional spending per student)	4.07** (2.79)	10.36** (3.37)	3.56** (2.72)	8.81** (3.19)
Ln (spending above median)[b]	...	−11.00** (2.31)	...	−9.19** (2.15)
Adults with 16 or more years of schooling (percent)	0.042* (1.62)	0.053** (2.14)	0.011 (0.48)	0.021 (0.87)
Adults with 12–15 years of schooling (percent)	0.016 (0.54)	−0.002 (0.05)	0.005 (0.18)	−0.010 (0.37)
Adults with 9–11 years of schooling (percent)	Base	Base	Base	Base
Adults with less than 9 years of schooling (percent)	0.045 (0.83)	0.027 (0.50)	0.027 (0.55)	0.011 (0.23)
Poverty rate for families with children aged 5–18	0.007 (0.39)	0.016 (0.89)	0.010 (0.64)	0.018 (1.10)
Nonwhite students (percent)	−0.013** (2.17)	−0.013** (2.14)	−0.005 (0.91)	−0.005 (0.85)
Enrollment, total (in thousands)	0.010** (1.99)	−0.013** (2.14)	0.008* (1.77)	0.013** (2.55)
Public school students as percent of all students	0.032 (1.37)	0.022 (0.93)	0.009 (0.42)	0.0007 (0.031)
Urban population (percent)	0.004 (0.88)	0.0007 (0.16)	0.004 (1.10)	0.0015 (0.40)
Interaction between percent nonwhite students and percent urban	−0.0001** (2.54)	−0.0002** (3.18)	−0.0001** (1.80)	−0.0001** (2.41)
City district (0-1 variable)	0.845** (2.80)	1.15** (3.54)	0.419 (1.50)	0.682** (2.26)
Reading scores, grades 3 and 4	...	...	0.193 (1.01)	0.210 (1.12)
Math scores, grades 3 and 4	...	...	0.339** (2.84)	0.317** (2.69)
Constant	−35.02** (2.99)	−79.22** (3.55)	−28.20** (2.66)	−65.13** (3.24)
Adjusted R^2	0.65	0.67	0.73	0.73

**Significant at the .05 level.
a. Weighted least squares. Numbers in parentheses are absolute values of *t*-statistics.
b. Add coefficient to previous coefficient if spending is above its median.

References

Bryk, Anthony S., and Stephen W. Raudenbush. 1992. *Hierarchical Linear Models: Applications and Data Analysis Methods.* Sage Publications.

Card, David, and Alan B. Krueger. 1992. "Does School Quality Matter? Returns to Education and the Characteristics of Public Schools in the United States." *Journal of Political Economy* 100 (February): 1–40.

Ehrenberg, Ronald G., and Dominic J. Brewer. 1995. "Did Teachers' Race and Verbal Ability Matter in the 1960s? *Coleman* Revisited." *Economics of Education Review* 14 (June): 291–99.

Ferguson, Ronald F. 1991a. "Paying for Public Education: New Evidence on How and Why Money Matters." *Harvard Journal on Legislation* 28 (Summer): 465–97.

———. 1991b. "Racial Patterns in How School and Teacher Quality Affect Achievement and Earnings." *Challenge: A Journal of Research on Black Men* 2 (May): 1–35.

———. 1994. "How Professionals in Community-Based Programs Perceive and Respond to the Needs of Black Male Youth." In *Nurturing Young Black Males,* edited by Ronald B. Miney, 59–98. Washington: Urban Institute Press.

———. 1995. "Shifting Challenges: Fifty Years of Economic Change toward Black-White Earnings Equality." *Daedalus* 124 (Winter): 37–76.

Hanushek, Eric A. 1986. "The Economics of Schooling: Production and Efficiency in Public Schools." *Journal of Economic Literature* 24 (September): 1141–77.

———. 1989. "The Impact of Differential Expenditures on School Performance." *Educational Researcher* 18 (May): 45–51.

———. 1996. "School Resources and Student Performance." In *Does Money Matter? The Link between Schools, Student Achievement, and Adult Success,* edited by Gary Burtless. Brookings.

Hanushek, Eric A., and Lori L. Taylor. 1990. "Alternative Assessments of the Performance of Schools: Measurement of State Variations in Achievement." *Journal of Human Resources* 25 (Spring): 179–201.

Hanushek, Eric A., Steven G. Rivkin, and Lori L. Taylor. 1995. "Aggregation Bias and the Estimated Effects of School Resources," Working Paper 397. University of Rochester, Center for Economic Research.

Hedges, Larry V., Richard D. Laine, and Rob Greenwald. 1994. "Does Money Matter? A Meta-Analysis of Studies of the Effects of Differential School Inputs on Student Outcomes," *Educational Researcher* 23 (April): 5–14.

Monk, David H. 1992. "Education Productivity Research: An Update and Assessment of Its Role in Education Finance Reform." *Educational Evaluation and Policy Analysis* 14 (Winter): 307–32.

Murnane, Richard J. 1991. "Interpreting the Evidence on 'Does Money Matter.'" *Harvard Journal on Legislation* 28 (Summer): 457–64.

Murnane, Richard J., John Willett, and Frank Levy. 1995. "The Growing Importance of Cognitive Skills in Wage Determination." *Review of Economics and Statistics* 77 (May): 251–66.

Smith, Marshall S., Brett W. Scoll, and Jeffrey Link. 1995. "Research-based Reforms: The Clinton Agenda." U.S. Department of Education.

Speakman, Robert, and Finis Welch. 1995. "Does School Quality Matter? A Reassessment." Texas A&M University, Department of Economics.

Name index

Aaron, H. 292
Alm, J. 140
Altshuler, A. 346, 348
Anderson, A. 19
Auerbach, A.J. 139

Bartik, T.J. 350, 374, 378–9, 390
Battle, V. 379
Baumol, W.J. 224
Benker, K. 292
Bergstrom, T.C. 6, 182, 335
Besley, T. 147
Birch, D.L. 374, 387
Bird, R. 294
Bittker, B.I. 294
Black, D. 4
Bloom, H.S. 181, 183–4
Boarnet, M.G. 389
Bogart, W.T. 389
Borcherding, T.E. 182, 335
Bowden, R.J. 96
Bradbury, K.L. 39, 42, 52, 61, 64, 66, 85–7, 305, 307, 350, 369
Bradford, D.F. 18, 20, 72, 86, 225, 291, 303, 329, 359
Brazer, H. 19
Brennan, G. 182
Brooks, N. 294
Brown, C. 374, 387
Bruce, N. 292
Buchanan, J. 182, 235
Bush, G. 378, 387
Butler, S.M. 373–4

Card, D. 442
Carlton, D. 350
Case, A.C. 147, 165–6, 171, 176–7
Case, K. 350
Chambers, J.G. 19, 422
Chang, S. 424
Chernick, H. 140, 163, 179
Chinitz, B. 327
Citrin, J. 257, 283
Clinton, B. 375, 386–7
Clotfelter, C. 296
Cohen, C.E. 52, 60
Courant, P.N. 209, 257, 283, 415
Craig, S.G. 118, 130
Cuciti, P. 34, 118

Deacon, R.T. 182, 335
Dimond, P. 387
Dixit, A.K. 139
Doolittle, F.C. 118
Downes, T.A. 43, 68, 320
Downing, P.B. 306, 330
Downs, A. 350
Due, J. 378
Duncombe, W. 405, 421–2, 432–4
Dye, R.F. 420

Eisinger, P.K. 379
Elling, R.C. 379–80
Erickson, R.A. 375, 377

Fastrup, J.C. 68
Feenberg, D.R. 199, 209, 212
Feldstein, M.S. 76, 81–2, 296

Ferguson, R.F. 40, 42–3, 431, 435, 447, 449
Figlio, D. 420, 436
Filimon, R. 209
Fisher, R.C. 209, 216
Ford, C.C. 388
Frank, J.E. 347
Friedman, S.W. 375, 377
Fullerton, D.J. 357

Garcia, R. 371
Gold, S. 74, 117, 203
Goodman, R.P. 6, 182, 335
Gramlich, E.M. 257, 415
Gravelle, J.G. 377
Gray, C.M. 368
Green, R.K. 51–2, 58, 64
Greenwald, R. 440
Gustely, R.D. 306, 330

Hamilton, J. 374, 387
Hanson, S.B. 372–3
Hanushek, E.A. 440, 444, 446
Harmon, O.R. 138, 143, 156
Harris, J.E. 295
Hausman, J.A. 96, 361
Hedges, L.V. 440
Hess, G.A. 420
Hettich, W. 140, 163, 294
Hicks, S.A. 295
Hill, E. 388

Hines, J.R. 165
Hirschman, A.D. 164
Howe, G. 376
Hughes, M.A. 373

Inman, R.P. 20, 21, 118, 130, 163

Jacobson, J. 214
Joelson, M.R. 368
Johnson, L. 117
Joulfaian, D. 193

Kain, J.F. 330, 372
Kasnitz, P. 387
Kearney, C.P. 415
Kemp, J. 371
Kesselman, J.R. 294
Kieschnik, M. 350
King, R.F. 294
Kleine, R.J. 138
Koenigsberg, S. 350
Krueger, A.B. 442

Ladd, H.F. 38, 40, 42–3, 46, 51–2, 57, 63–4, 68–9, 81, 85–7, 91, 97–8, 117, 130, 138, 181, 183–4, 305, 307–8, 317, 320, 328–30, 339, 365, 369, 388, 421, 423, 431, 435
Laine, R.D. 440
Lankford, H. 419, 429
Levy, F. 442
Loeb, S. 415
Lovell, M.C. 235
Luce, T.F. 379
Ludwig, J. 374
Lugar, M.I. 361

Mackay, R. 182
Mallick, R. 138, 143, 156
Malt, R.A. 18, 20, 72, 86, 225, 359
Marks, L.R. 52, 60, 65, 67
McCallin, N.J. 140
McDaniel, P.R. 291, 294, 296
McGuire, T. 420
McMahan, W.W. 424
Medoff, J. 374, 387
Metcalf, G.E. 214
Mieszkowski, P. 164
Murname, R.J. 442

Nathan, R.P. 118
Neubig, T. 291, 293
Newman, R.J. 378
Nixon, R. 117
Noah, T. 378

O'Regan, K.M. 374
Oakland, W.H. 37, 42, 80–83
Oates, W.E. 18, 20, 72, 86, 164, 199, 209, 225, 305, 325, 359, 365
Okun, A. 199
Orr, L.L. 114

Papke, L. 350, 377, 383–4, 391
Pauly, M.V. 108-10
Perrault, M. 52
Persky, J.J. 372–3
Peterson, G.E. 6, 118, 308, 378
Phares, D. 157
Plotnick, L. 105
Poddar, S. 294
Pogue, T.F. 43, 68, 320
Pomp, R.D. 291
Portney, P.R. 369

Quigley, J.M. 374

Rafuse, R.W. 52–3, 58–60, 65, 67
Reagan, R. 101
Reschovsky, A. 51–2, 57–8, 63–4, 66, 69, 77, 81–2, 421
Richards, C.M. 381, 391
Riddle, B. 69
Ring, R.J. 159
Rivkin, S.G. 446
Rizzo, M.J. 368
Romer, T. 182
Rosen, H.S. 165, 199, 209, 212, 357
Rosenthal, H. 182
Ross, S.L. 388
Rubin, B.M. 374, 381–3, 391
Rubin, M. 384–5
Rubinfeld, D.L. 257
Ruggiero, J. 432

Schick, A. 292
Schmenner, R.W. 350
Schussheim, M.J. 330
Schwab, R.M. 164
Schwartz, A. 66
Shannon, J. 138
Sheldon, A.W. 379–80
Skidmore, F. 105
Small, K.A. 350
Snyder, T. 310, 347
Sontelie, J.C. 369
Southwick, L. 110
Stahl, D.O. 361
Stegman, M. 310, 347
Steuerle, C.E. 296
Stubblebine, W.C. 235

Sullivan, D.H. 378
Summers, A.A. 379
Surrey, S.S. 290–91, 293–6

Taylor, L.L. 444, 446
Toder, E. 8
Tullock, G. 235
Turkington, D.A. 96

Underhill, J. 379

Wagner, R.E. 209
Wartzman, R. 378
Wassner, R.W. 388
Wasylenko, M. 52, 69, 305
Weaver, C. 182
Weist, D. 138, 179
Wendling, W. 19

Wheaton, W.L. 330
White, F.C. 138, 156
Wildasin, D.E. 164
Wilder, M.G. 383, 391
Willett, J. 442
Wilson, J.D. 164
Windsor, D. 307
Winer, S.L. 140, 163, 294
Wolman, H.L. 388
Wyckoff, P.G. 834
Wyckoff, J. 419, 429

Yinger, J. 38, 46, 51–2, 57, 63–4, 68–9, 81, 85–7, 91, 97–8, 117, 130, 305, 307, 330, 365, 388, 421–3, 432–4

Zodrow, G. 164